Problems and Perspectives

Problems and Perspectives

Studies in the Modern French Language

Wendy Ayres-Bennett and Janice Carruthers
with Rosalind Temple

An imprint of **Pearson Education**

Harlow, England · London · New York · Reading, Massachusetts · San Francisco · Toronto · Don Mills, Ontario · Sydney
Tokyo · Singapore · Hong Kong · Seoul · Taipei · Cape Town · Madrid · Mexico City · Amsterdam · Munich · Paris · Milan

Pearson Education Limited
Edinburgh Gate
Harlow
Essex CM20 2JE
England

and Associated Companies throughout the world

Visit us on the World Wide Web at:
www.pearsoneduc.com

First published 2001

© Pearson Education Limited 2001

ISBN 0-582-29345-6 CSD
ISBN 0-582-29346-4 PPR

British Library Cataloguing-in-Publication Data

A catalogue record for this book is available from the British Library

Library of Congress Cataloging-in-Publication Data

Ayres-Bennett, Wendy.
    Problems and perspectives : studies in the modern French language / Wendy Ayres-Bennett and Janice Carruthers with Rosalind Temple.
    p.   cm. — (Longman linguistics library)
    Includes bibiliographical references and index.
    ISBN 0-582-29345-6 (csd) — ISBN 0-582-29346-4 (ppr)
    1. French language — Phonology. 2. French language — Morphology. 3. French language — Syntanx. I. Title: Studies in the modern French language. II. Carruthers, Janice, 1964– III. Temple, R.A.M. (Rosalind A.M.) IV. Title. V. Series.
PC2131.A97 2000
440—dc21   00-061374

Set by 35 in 10/12pt Janson Text
Produced by Pearson Education Asia Pte Ltd.
Transferred to digital print on demand, 2006
Printed and bound by CPI Antony Rowe, Eastbourne

LONGMAN LINGUISTICS LIBRARY

General Editors:

The Late R.H. ROBINS
University of London

GEOFFREY HORROCKS
University of Cambridge

DAVID DENISON
University of Manchester

Introduction to Text Linguistics
ROBERT DE BEAUGRANDE and
WOLFGANG DRESSLER

Psycholinguistics
Language, Mind and World
Second edition
DANNY D. STEINBERG

Principles of Pragmatics
GEOFFREY N. LEECH

The English Verb
Second edition
F.R. PALMER

Pidgin and Creole Languages
SUZANNE ROMAINE

General Linguistics
An Introductory Survey
Fourth edition
R.H. ROBINS

Generative and Non-linear Phonology
JACQUES DURAND

Modality and the English Modals
Second edition
F.R. PALMER

Dialects of English
Studies in Grammatical Variation
PETER TRUDGILL and
J.K. CHAMBERS (eds)

An Introduction to Bilingualism
CHARLOTTE HOFFMANN

Linguistic Theory
The Discourse of Fundamental Works
ROBERT DE BEAUGRANDE

A History of American English
J.L. DILLARD

Aspect in the English Verb
Process and Result in Language
YISHAI TOBIN

The Meaning of Syntax
A Study in the Adjectives of English
CONNOR FERRIS

Latin American Spanish
JOHN LIPSKI

A Linguistic History of Italian
MARTIN MAIDEN

The History of Linguistics
All edited by GIULIO LEPSCHY

Volume III:
Renaissance and Early Modern
Linguistics

Volume IV:
Nineteenth Century Linguistics
ANNA MORPURGO DAVIES

To come:
Volume V:
The Twentieth Century

Modern Arabic
Structures, Functions and Varieties
CLIVE HOLES

Frontiers of Phonology
Atoms, Structures and Derivations
JACQUES DURAND and
FRANCIS KATAMBA (eds)

An Introduction to the Celtic
Languages
PAUL RUSSELL

Causatives and Causation
A Universal-typological perspective
JAE JUNG SONG

A Short History of Linguistics
Fourth edition
R.H. ROBINS

Grammar and Grammarians in the
Early Middle Ages
VIVIEN LAW

Greek
A History of the Language and its
Speakers
GEOFFREY HORROCKS

The New Comparative Syntax
LILIANE HAEGEMAN (ed.)

The Structure and History of
Japanese
LONE TAKEUCHI

The Acquisition of Syntax
Studies in Comparative Developmental
Linguistics
MARC-ARIEL FRIEDEMANN and
LUIGI RIZZI (eds)

Experimental Phonetics
KATRINA HAYWARD

Explaining Language Change:
An Evolutionary Approach
WILLIAM CROFT

Linguistic Typology:
Morphology and Syntax
JAE JUNG SONG

Problems and Perspectives:
Studies in the Modern French Language
WENDY AYRES-BENNETT and JANICE
CARRUTHERS with ROSALIND TEMPLE

Contents

Preface   xvi
Publisher's Acknowledgements   xviii

Part I: Preliminaries   1

Section 1   French: standards and variation   3

1.1   What is 'French'?   3
1.2   Parameters of variation   4
    1.2.1   Written and spoken French   4
    1.2.2   Register   4
    1.2.3   Field, domain or discourse type   5
    1.2.4   Geographical variation   6
    1.2.5   Age, sex and socio-economic status (SES)   6

Section 2   Introduction to the description of French:
           definitions and metalanguage   8

2.1   The Sounds of French   8
    2.1.1   Syllable structure   8
    2.1.2   Rhythmic groups   9
    2.1.3   Consonants   10
    2.1.4   Vowels   11
    2.1.5   Semivowels   13
2.2   Morphology   13
2.3   Syntax   16
    2.3.1   Syntax and the verb system   17

	2.3.2	Word order	19
	2.3.3	Subordination and coordination	20
	2.3.4	Textual cohesion	22
2.4	Lexis		22
	2.4.1	Derivational processes	23
	2.4.2	Composition	23
	2.4.3	Abbreviation	24
	2.4.4	Semantic change	24
	2.4.5	Borrowing	25

Section 3   Approaches and schools   27

3.1	A multiplicity of approaches . . .		27
3.2	Structuralism		28
	3.2.1	Phonology	28
	3.2.2	Morphology	30
	3.2.3	Syntax	32
3.3	Generative grammar		33
	3.3.1	Introduction	33
	3.3.2	Generative syntax and its place in the grammar	34
	3.3.3	Generative phonology	39
	3.3.4	Autosegmental phonology	41
	3.3.5	Morphology in generative grammar	42
3.4	Other approaches to the analysis of French		45
	3.4.1	Typological models of change	45
	3.4.2	Language in use	46
3.5	Variationist approaches		48
3.6	National French approaches		50
	3.6.1	Guillaume and the Guillaumeans	50
	3.6.2	*L'Approche pronominale*	51

Section 4   Choice of topics and approaches   53

Part II: Issues   57

Chapter 1   Word-final consonants   59

1.1	Introduction	59
1.2	The problem in detail	60
1.3	Orthographically based accounts of liaison	62

1.4   Theoretical accounts of word-final consonants 63
    1.4.1   The phonemic perspective 63
    1.4.2   Generative phonology 63
        1.4.2.1   Abstract generative phonology 63
        1.4.2.2   Concrete generative phonology 66
    1.4.3   Non-linear phonology 68
1.5   Liaison and syntax 72
1.6   Variationist analyses of liaison 72

Chapter 2   Nasal vowels 77

2.1   Introduction 77
2.2   The history of nasal vowels 78
    2.2.1   Textual evidence 78
    2.2.2   Phonetic explanations 80
2.3   Structuralist accounts: the phonemic status
      of nasal vowels 80
2.4   Generative and post-generative accounts of the nasal vowels 82
    2.4.1   Nasal vowels in abstract generative phonology 83
        2.4.1.1   Alternating forms 83
        2.4.1.2   Non-alternating forms 86
    2.4.2   Nasal vowels in concrete generative phonology 87
        2.4.2.1   Non-alternating forms 87
        2.4.2.2   Alternating forms 88
    2.4.3   A non-linear proposal 90
2.5   Nasal vowels and liaison 92
2.6   Nasal vowels in southern French 94

Chapter 3   Schwa: a maverick vowel 98

3.1   Introduction: 'Qu'est-ce que le "e muet"?'
      (Martinet (1974a)) 98
3.2   Terminology 99
3.3   The phonetic identity of schwa 99
3.4   The variable phonological behaviour of schwa 100
    3.4.1   The data 100
    3.4.2   Descriptive accounts 101
3.5   The phonemic identity of schwa 103
3.6   Schwa ~ zero alternation: epenthesis versus deletion 105
    3.6.1   Schwa ~ zero alternation as deletion 105
    3.6.2   Schwa ~ zero alternation as epenthesis 106
    3.6.3   The special case of word-final schwa 108
3.7   Non-linear accounts of schwa ~ zero alternation 109

3.8   Changing patterns of schwa ~ zero alternation   111
   3.8.1   Word-initial schwa: stabilization in progress?   112
   3.8.2   Change in non-initial schwa   114

Chapter 4   Verb morphology: conjugation classes and the
               definiton of regularity   118

4.1   Introduction   118
4.2   Preliminaries: segmentation   118
   4.2.1   Problems of segmentation   119
   4.2.2   Stem and ending versus stem, infix and ending   120
4.3   Classification into verb conjugation classes: desiderata   123
4.4   Traditional classifications   124
4.5   Stem-based models   126
4.6   'Two-class' models   131
4.7   Defining irregularity   135
4.8   Variation and change   138

Chapter 5   Aspect in French   143

5.1   Introduction: tense versus aspect   143
5.2   Aspectual categories and distinctions   145
5.3   Lexical versus grammatical aspect   146
5.4   Approaches to aspect in French   148
   5.4.1   Introduction   148
   5.4.2   Brunot (1922)   148
   5.4.3   Guillaume (1929, 1964)   151
   5.4.4   Imbs (1960)   153
   5.4.5   Reid (1970)   154
   5.4.6   Martin (1971)   155
   5.4.7   Wilmet (1991, 1995, 1997)   157
   5.4.8   General issues   158
5.5   Applications of the notion of aspect   159
   5.5.1   Introduction   159
   5.5.2   Diachronic phenomena   160
   5.5.3   Aspectual concepts   160
   5.5.4   Aspect and discourse-pragmatics   160

Chapter 6   Past tenses: complex and changing relationships   164

6.1   Introduction   164
6.2   The *passé simple/passé composé* relationship:
      a complex history   168
   6.2.1   The development of the compound tenses   168

	6.2.2	'Functional multiplicity' in the Old French period	169
	6.2.3	Developments in Middle French, and Early Modern analyses	172
6.3	The *passé composé/passé simple* in Modern French: changing relationships		175
	6.3.1	Introduction	175
	6.3.2	Two 'textual' models	175
	6.3.3	*Passé simple/passé composé* alternation	176
	6.3.4	The PS as story marker?	178
	6.3.5	The PC: a semantic hybrid?	179
6.4	The Imperfect		181
	6.4.1	Diachronic perspectives	181
	6.4.2	Developments in Modern French	182
		6.4.2.1 Analysis of the imperfect	182
		6.4.2.2 Discourse-pragmatic developments	183
6.5	Past in the past: *plus-que-parfait, passé antérieur* and *passé surcomposé*		185
	6.5.1	Diachronic perspectives	185
	6.5.2	Developments in Modern French	186
		6.5.2.1 The pluperfect	186
		6.5.2.2 The past anterior	188
		6.5.2.3 The *passé surcomposé*	188

Chapter 7	Mood and modality: the French subjunctive		192
7.1	Introduction		192
7.2	Explaining the use of the subjunctive		193
	7.2.1	The French subjunctive: several 'values' or a unified account?	194
	7.2.2	Formal or mechanical approaches	197
	7.2.3	Other approaches	199
7.3	Problematic cases		202
	7.3.1	Noun clauses	202
	7.3.2	Adjectival clauses	204
7.4	The vitality of the subjunctive		206
	7.4.1	The history of the subjunctive	206
	7.4.2	The vitality of the subjunctive in Modern French	209
	7.4.3	The vitality of the subjunctive and variation	210
		7.4.3.1 Written and spoken French	210
		7.4.3.2 SES and register	211
		7.4.3.3 Geographic variation	212
	7.4.4	The imperfect subjunctive	212
	7.4.5	Alternative markers of modality	216

Chapter 8   Pronominal verbs   221

8.1   Introduction   221
8.2   Pronominal verbs and voice   221
      8.2.1   How many voices for French?   221
      8.2.2   Guillaume   223
      8.2.3   Generative approaches to voice   224
8.3   The classification of pronominal verbs   225
      8.3.1   Fourfold schemes   226
              8.3.1.1   Dangeau's tradition   226
              8.3.1.2   Subcategorizing the *pronominaux subjectifs*   227
      8.3.2   Problems with differentiating the categories   229
      8.3.3   Alternative classifications   231
      8.3.4   Unified explanations   231
8.4   The pronominal passive   237
      8.4.1   Constraints on the usage of the pronominal passive   237
      8.4.2   Limits on the usage of the 'true' passive   240
              8.4.2.1   Syntactic constraints   240
              8.4.2.2   Lexical constraints   241
              8.4.2.3   Semantic constraints   241
              8.4.2.4   Aspectual questions   241
      8.4.3   Reasons for selecting the 'true' passive   242
      8.4.4   Other alternatives to the passive   244

Chapter 9   Declarative word order: French as an SVO language   248

9.1   Introduction   248
9.2   Historical analyses   249
      9.2.1   The data   249
      9.2.2   Traditional analyses   250
      9.2.3   Typological approaches   251
      9.2.4   Marchello-Nizia (1995): the role of the object   253
      9.2.5   Examples   254
9.3   Modern French as an SVO language   255
      9.3.1   The data: statistics and corpora   255
      9.3.2   A fixed exception   256
      9.3.3   Detachment   257
              9.3.3.1   The data   257
              9.3.3.2   Problematic issues   259
              9.3.3.3   Discourse function   260
              9.3.3.4   Stylistic factors   262
              9.3.3.5   Sociolinguistic factors   262
              9.3.3.6   Theoretical implications and further
                        questions   262

9.3.4   Inversion   264
9.3.5   Cleft constructions   267
9.3.6   Binary constructions   268
9.3.7   Other constructions   269
9.4   Conclusions   270

Chapter 10   Relations between clauses: subordination, coordination,
             parataxis   273

10.1   Introduction   273
10.2   Relations within the sentence: questions of definition   273
       10.2.1   Introduction   273
       10.2.2   Defining subordination   275
       10.2.3   Subordinating and coordinating conjunctions,
                and coordinating adverbs   279
10.3   Spoken French: a case study of the *relative du français*
       populaire   282
10.4   Relations within discourse: parataxis, coordination
       and subordination as degrees of progression in
       lingustic sophistication?   287
       10.4.1   Language acquisition   287
       10.4.2   Social groups   289
       10.4.3   Medium/discourse type   291

Chapter 11   Negation   297

11.1   Introduction   297
       11.1.1   The nature of the component elements   298
11.2   Scope   301
       11.2.1   Scope and context   301
       11.2.2   Negative raising?   302
11.3   *Ne . . . que* and expletive *ne*   305
       11.3.1   *Ne . . . que*   305
       11.3.2   Expletive *ne*   309
                11.3.2.1   Usage of expletive *ne*   309
                11.3.2.2   The value and currency of expletive *ne* 310
                11.3.2.3   *Ne* alone to mark negation   312
11.4   The loss of *ne* and the marking of negation by *pas* alone   312
       11.4.1   The historical background   312
       11.4.2   Factors influencing the use or non-use of *ne* in
                contemporary French   313
                11.4.2.1   Syntactic factors   313
                11.4.2.2   Phonetic factors   314

		11.4.2.3	Semantic factors	315
		11.4.2.4	Frequently used expressions	315
		11.4.2.5	Stylistic factors	316
		11.4.2.6	Demographic factors: region, SES, and age	316
	11.4.3	Other examples of the rise of *pas*		318

Chapter 12   Neologisms: internal versus external factors   323

12.1	Introduction		323
12.2	Definitional questions and statistics		324
	12.2.1	What is a borrowing?	324
	12.2.2	Types of borrowing	325
	12.2.3	Statistical considerations	326
12.3	The linguistic integration of borrowings		327
	12.3.1	Phonological integration	327
		12.3.1.1 The issues	327
		12.3.1.2 The implications	328
	12.3.2	Morpho-syntactic integration	330
	12.3.3	Semantic integration	333
12.4	'Hybrids' and pseudo-anglicisms		335
12.5	The status of Latin (and Greek) material		337
12.6	Attitudes towards borrowing		339

Chapter 13   'Internal' processes of word creation in French   343

13.1	Introduction		343
13.2	Definitional issues		343
	13.2.1	Neologisms	344
	13.2.2	Suffixes and prefixes	344
	13.2.3	Prefixes and compounds – problematic distinctions	344
	13.2.4	Identifying compounds	345
	13.2.5	*Recomposés*	346
	13.2.6	Compounds versus free combinations	347
	13.2.7	Compounds and phrases	350
13.3	Productivity		351
	13.3.1	Variation	351
	13.3.2	Language change	352
	13.3.3	Linguistic constraints	353
13.4	Neologisms and linguistic theory		354

13.5   The impact of internal lexical creation on French   358
       13.5.1   Semantic complexities   359
       13.5.2   Morphosyntactic complexities: compounds
                and abbreviations   360
       13.5.3   Phonological complexities   361

       References   364
       Index of Concepts   391
       Index of Names   402

Preface

If books on variation in French, and notably regional and sociolinguistic variation, have continued to multiply, works in English focusing on structural aspects of the language have been in rather shorter supply. Moreover, those that exist often adopt a descriptive 'factual' approach, or are focused on specific areas of structure or theory. The aim of this book is rather to concentrate on a number of interesting or problematic areas in the phonology, morphology, syntax and lexis of French, and to encourage the reader to think critically about different ways of approaching, describing and explaining these issues or data.

The book is divided into two parts. The first and shorter part, in four sections, is intended to be preliminary to, and to contextualize, the discussion of the more specialized topics of the second part. Its purpose is to define the object of study, to explain terminology and to give a broad outline of the different levels of language. In addition, there is a survey of some of the main approaches we have used to describe and analyse the French language, whether they reflect a specifically French tradition or have wider international currency. Finally, we outline the methodology chosen for the book and offer reasons for the selection of topics covered. Since this part is introductory in intention and scope, it may be passed over by the more advanced reader.

The second, substantial part presents problematic and controversial areas in the description and analysis of the contemporary language. The chapters do not follow one rigid template, but are rather tailored to the demands of the particular data. In some chapters the focus is on one major question raised by the data, in others several problematic areas are covered. Elsewhere the spotlight is less on questions of description, and more on the strengths and weaknesses of different approaches to the analysis of a given topic. In each case, the aim has been to be guided by the issues, but always to problematize, to evaluate different approaches and explanations, and to suggest criteria for approaching the French language critically, without necessarily offering 'solutions'.

This book is also intended to differ from certain others on the market in attempting to integrate historical and sociolinguistic issues where appropriate within the individual chapters. We have rejected the approach whereby history – and this in general means external history – is tagged on in a separate section divorced from the structural analysis elsewhere. The discussion of variation has frequently been treated in the same way. Yet a factor in evaluating different accounts of, say, schwa, might be how well they account for regional variation; equally, accounts of negation which argue that the loss of *ne* from speech is a recent innovation may need to be tested against diachronic evidence.

All too often students, even quite advanced students, cling to the belief that linguistics is somehow about 'facts'; we hope to show that the analysis of French is a much more challenging and demanding, but at the same time a much more rewarding, pursuit.

We are immensely indebted to Rosalind Temple, who has not only contributed all the material on the phonetics and phonology of French and written a number of sections of Part I, but who has also been closely involved with all stages of the project, from planning to proofreading. Grateful thanks are also due to all those who have taken the trouble to read the book in typescript and to comment on it, especially John Green, Sophie Marnette and Henriette Walter. We would also like to thank the editors of the series, and our long-suffering partners whose practical and moral support has been invaluable.

Wendy Ayres-Bennett   Janice Carruthers

Publisher's Acknowledgements

We are grateful to the following for permission to reproduce copyright material:

Table 1 from Müller, B. (1985) *Le Français d'aujourd'hui* and Figure 11.1 from Tesnière, L. (1959) *Eléments de syntaxe structurale*, reprinted by permission of Klincksieck Editions; Tables 4.1 and 4.2 from Price, G. (1971) *The French Language: Present and Past*, reprinted by permission of Arnold; Tables 4.3 and 4.4 from Pinchon, J. and Coute, B. (1981) *Le Système verbal du français: description et applications pédagogiques* (pub Nathan), Table 4.6 from Gardes-Tamine, J. (1988) *La Grammaire*, Vol. 1 (pub Colin), Table 5.1 from Brunot, F. (1922) *La Pensée et la langue: méthode, principes et plan d'une théorie nouvelle du langage appliquée au français* (pub Masson) and Table 11.3 from Pohl, J. (1972) '*Ne* et les enfants' from *L'Homme et le signifiant* (pub Nathan), reprinted by permission of Activités Internationales, Paris; Table 4.5 from Pinchon, J. (1986) *Morphosyntaxe du français: étude de cas* (pub Hachette) and Figure 5.1 from Wilmet, M. (1997) *Grammaire critique du français* (pub Duculot-Hachette), reprinted by permission of Hachette Groupe Livre; Table 3 from Walter, H. and Walter, G. (1991) *Dictionnaire des mots d'origine étrangère*, © Larousse, 1991, reprinted by permission of Larousse; Table 9.1 from Harris, M. B. (1978) *The Evolution of French Syntax: A Comparative Approach* (pub Longman) and Figure 5 from Horrocks, G. (1987) *Generative Grammar* (pub Longman) reprinted by permission of Pearson Education Ltd; Tables 9.2 and 9.3 from Ashby, W. J. (1988) 'The Syntax, Pragmatics, and Sociolinguistics of Left- and Right-Dislocations in French' *Lingua* 75 and Table 11.4 from Ashby, W. J. (1976) 'The Loss of the Negative Morpheme, *ne*, in Parisian French' *Lingua* 39, reprinted with permission of Elsevier Science; Table 10.1 from Hobaek-Haff, M. (1987) *Coordonnants et éléments coordonnés*, reprinted by permission of Didier-Solum; Table 11.1 from Ashby, W. J. (1991) 'When Does Variation Indicate Linguistic Change in Progress?' *Journal of French Language Studies* 1, reprinted by permission of Cambridge

University Press; Table 12.1 from Délégation générale à la langue française (1994) *Dictionnaire des termes officiels de la langue française*, reprinted by permission of Direction des Journaux Officiels, République Française; Figure 8.1 from Melis, L. (1990) *La Voie pronominale: la systématique des tours pronominaux en français moderne* and Figures 13.1 and 13.2 from Corbin, D. (1991) 'La Morphologie lexicale: bilan et perspectives' *Travaux de linguistique* 23, reprinted by permission of Duculot SA; Figure 10.1 from Carruthers, J. (1996) 'The *passé surcomposé général*: On the Relationship between a Rare Tense and Discourse Organization' *Romance Philology* 50 (2), reprinted by permission of University of California Press; Figure 12.1 from Poplack, S., Sankoff, D. and Miller, C. (1988) 'The Social Correlates and Linguistic Processes of Lexical Borrowing and Assimilation' *Linguistics* 26 (1), reprinted by permission of Mouton de Gruyter; Figure 13.3 from Corbin, D. (1991) 'La Formation des mots: structures et interprétations' *Lexique* 10, reprinted by permission of Presses Universitaires de Lille.

While every effort has been made to trace the owners of copyright material, in a few cases this has proved impossible and we take this opportunity to offer our apologies to any copyright holders whose rights we have unwittingly infringed.

Part

I

Preliminaries

Section 1

French: standards and variation

1.1 What is 'French'?

French is characterized by an abundance of different varieties both within France and beyond. Clearly there is a need for a single, nationally accepted language which people of different status and region may use to communicate with each other and which may be employed in fields such as education and the law. Standard languages are generally associated with authority and power, and possess a high degree of prestige. Gradually during the history of France, speakers have come to adopt the prestige variety for a number of political, social and geographical reasons. Notably since the seventeenth century there has been considerable emphasis on standardizing French and on providing a norm for 'good' French and an idea of what constitutes correct and incorrect usage. The Revolution, the advent of free and compulsory education in the late nineteenth century, enhanced mobility, communication and the birth of the mass media have all contributed to the strength of the standard. Today it is the (predominantly written) usage of the educated Parisian which is generally taken as the standard and other varieties have been, and still sometimes are, considered inferior to this variety. This is the variety promoted by the French government, used in education and the media, and codified in grammars and dictionaries.

There is plenty of evidence for standard forms of the written language, and thus by extension what might be considered the standard point of reference for the syntax of the spoken language, against which we can compare any variable usage. However, it is perhaps more difficult to identify a norm for the phonology. Various attempts have been made to identify such a standard system; for example, Martinet and Walter's study of Parisian speakers was carried out on the premise that a new, hybrid phonological system would arise from the contact between speakers of different varieties of French who had come to Paris in the great rural exodus (Martinet and Walter 1973; Walter 1977). However, most linguists take as their starting point an idealized system representing all the possible contrasts that could be made by an educated speaker speaking slowly and carefully, and we have followed the same practice in the systems set out in Section 2.1 below.

1.2   Parameters of variation

A speaker's choice of language in any given situation will be influenced in no small way by a combination of interactional features – that is, features which differ according to the content of the speech or writing, the situation and medium, the addressee – and factors which are determined by the speaker's identity – his or her sex, age, socio-economic status, and regional origin. Each individual speaker is, of course, affected by a unique combination of these factors, so that it is to some degree true to say that each speaker uses his or her individual language or idiolect.

1.2.1   Written and spoken French

In Part II we shall make frequent reference to differences in usage according to the medium selected, that is, between written and spoken French. Whether we consider French morphology, syntax or lexis, it is not difficult to find differences between the oral code and the written code. For example, the categories of gender, person and number are morphologically marked much more regularly and explicitly in written French. Many of the different verb endings marked by distinctive orthographic forms in writing are homophonous in speech. Consider the form [truve]: this is represented in writing by the forms *trouver, trouvez, trouvez!, trouvé, trouvés, trouvée, trouvées.* The syntax of spoken French is often thought to be characterized, for instance, by parataxis or the simple juxtaposition of clauses, a more frequent usage of presentatives such as *voilà, il y a,* and the marking of negation by *pas* alone.

So far the choice of medium has been presented as a simple dichotomy; much of the treatment of the differences between written and spoken forms focuses in practice on the differences between casual conversation and careful written language. Within each medium there is, however, considerable variation or difference of register, ranging within the oral code from a formal lecture or poetry recitation to very informal speech, and in the written code from a carefully crafted essay to an informal e-mail message or 'post-it' note.

1.2.2   Register

Register relates to the degree of formality or informality of usage. For instance, a speaker's language may be varied according to how well the speaker knows the addressee and how close s/he feels to him or her in terms of age, sex, and socio-economic status, and according to the nature of the communicative situation. The closer the social group, the less formal usage will tend to be.

There is a wide range of different schemes available which attempt to describe register variation in French. One such is that proposed by Müller (1985:226):

Table 1 Müller's scheme for the analysis of register variation

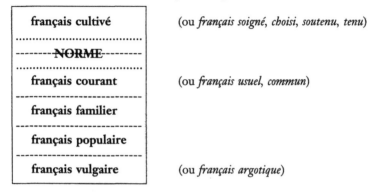

français cultivé	(ou *français soigné, choisi, soutenu, tenu*)
~~NORME~~	
français courant	(ou *français usuel, commun*)
français familier	
français populaire	
français vulgaire	(ou *français argotique*)

Note how in this scheme the norm is seen as partaking of both *français cultivé* and *français courant*, and that there are more registers below the norm than above it. There is considerable vagueness surrounding the definitions of each of these registers, and notably of the informal varieties of French. Some schemes differentiate, for example, between *français populaire*, *français branché* and *argot*, but these registers all share the primary property of being colloquial (i.e. informal). All areas of language show variation across different registers. To take the example of lexis, low-register French is noted for its innovation in the creation of new words and for phenomena such as *verlan* (see **13**.3.1).[1] In general in Part II references to differences of register will be made in terms of more or less formal usage.

1.2.3   Field, domain or discourse type

Variation may occur according to the topic or field under discussion. Obvious examples are the language of lawyers or of science and technology. For instance, scientific writing tends to favour structures which imply impersonality and objectivity such as the passive, impersonal constructions and the pronoun *on*. Similarly, journalistic French – whether oral or written – favours certain patterns of structuring information in particular contexts; a journalist's choice of syntactic structure (e.g. active vs passive, use of subordinate clauses) may thus be determined by the particular way in which s/he chooses to present an event to the reader or listener (we shall return to this in Chapter 10). In technical vocabulary (e.g. scientific, technological, economic, medical, musical, or sporting vocabulary) new words or neologisms are particularly frequent. The reasons for this are obvious: as new objects are invented and new concepts coined in a whole range of disciplines, new vocabulary is needed.

1.2.4   Geographical variation

Perhaps the most obvious cause of variation in French is the geographical origin of the speaker. Various regions of France still retain to some extent the historical dialects of northern France such as *picard* and *normand* despite the fact that there has been a marked decline in their vitality over the last century. A number of regional languages are also spoken in France, some of Romance origin (Catalan, Corsican, Occitan varieties), others non-Romance (Alsatian, Basque, Breton, Flemish) and these may leave their impression on the French spoken in the relevant geographical area. More important today are the various *français régionaux*, or regional varieties of French, which may perhaps be thought of as the substrate 'colouring' left by the dialect or the regional language on the French of a region when standardized French was imposed. Regional varieties generally permit inter-comprehension between speakers of different regions. They are characterized primarily by differences of accent and by local lexical items and meanings; morphological and syntactic differences are much less marked (although note, for example, regional usages of the so-called *formes surcomposées*; see **6.5.2.3**).

The boundaries around the French-speaking area do not coincide with political boundaries, but rather extend northwards and eastwards into southern Belgium, parts of Switzerland, Luxembourg, Monaco, and the Val d'Aosta in Italy. Beyond Europe varieties of French are spoken on all continents of the world, although the influence of French, for example, in Asia has greatly diminished. Estimates of the number of French speakers worldwide vary enormously, not least since the definition of a 'French speaker' is not straightforward. While in some places French both has official language status and is spoken by the majority of the people (for example in Quebec), elsewhere it may be an official language but only spoken by an elite (for instance in a number of sub-Saharan African nations), or be quite widely used without having any official status (such as in Morocco or Algeria). In a number of places – notably in the Caribbean and the Indian Ocean – French exists alongside French-lexicon creoles, themselves developed from earlier pidgins (see Battye and Hintze 1992:320–6).

1.2.5   Age, sex and socio-economic status (SES)

Factors in the speaker's sociolinguistic make-up can have a major effect on language use. For example, the language of a young child will obviously tend to be more limited in structure and lexis than that of an adult, reflecting the fact that the child is still in the process of acquiring the language. Once the language has been acquired, usage can still vary according to the age of the speaker. The speech of young people, notably those in their teens and twenties, is often characterized by its innovative nature, especially in the lexis, as shown by Henriette Walter's study (1984) of neologisms among young Parisians. Phonology and syntax can also show variable usage across age groups: younger Canadian French speakers, for example, were found to be more likely than older speakers to use the periphrastic future (i.e. the *aller faire* construction) rather than the simple forms (*ferai*, etc.) (Poplack and Turpin 1999).

The sex of a speaker can also affect his or her speech in ways beyond the obvious physiologically conditioned differences such as voice pitch. Socio-linguistic research has looked at questions of linguistic identity and at whether it is appropriate to view female speakers as more conservative and more inclined to employ 'standard' forms than males (see, for instance, Singy 1998).[2] As regards more specific linguistic phenomena, recent studies have shown, for example, that men tend to pronounce third person pronouns as [i] and [ɛ] rather than [il] or [ɛl] more frequently than do women (e.g. Ashby 1991; Poplack and Walker 1986).

Whereas age and sex are easily identifiable characteristics of speakers, their socio-economic status (SES) is less easy to define (see Section 3.5 below for a brief further discussion of this), but it is clear that, however measured, it can have a strong influence on speech patterns, with speakers who have a higher SES tending to adopt more standard forms. Thus, Ashby (1992) reports that speakers of 'higher social class backgrounds', defined in terms of education and employment, use *on* rather than *tu* or *vous* for indefinite reference significantly more than those of lower SES.

It is important to remember that speakers belong simultaneously to a particular age group and sex and have different socio-economic identities, and that the influences of these factors therefore interact, sometimes in quite complex ways. For example, according to Ashby's (1991) data, younger speakers always reduce the third person pronouns to [i] and [ɛ] more often than older speakers of the same sex and SES, and there is a general tendency for males to do this more than females; yet in the case of older speakers of the lowest class, it is the females who more frequently use the reduced form.

Section 2

Introduction to the description of French: definitions and metalanguage

For simplicity of exposition, we have assumed in this section that it is possible to view each level of linguistic analysis in isolation, starting first with the sounds of French, then examining in turn the morphology, syntax and lexis of the language. As will be clear from Section 3 below, this is not an assumption shared by all schools of linguistics, nor is it unproblematic. To take the case of morphology, cogent reasons have been advanced for considering it not as an autonomous level of analysis, but as interacting with the phonology (for example in the case of vocalic alternation in adjectival stems) or the syntax (for example in the case of adjectival agreement) of French. Furthermore, the formation of new words by the addition of prefixes and suffixes may be seen as a morphological question (see Section 2.2), or considered within the domain of lexical studies (see Section 2.4).

2.1 The Sounds of French

In this section we shall present a brief descriptive overview of the sound system of French, with indications of where more detailed information can be found.[3] Useful overviews can be found in Price (1991) and Valdman (1993).

2.1.1 Syllable structure

Phonetically, **syllables** consist of a **nucleus**, which in French is always a **vowel (V)**, plus an optional **onset** consisting of one or more **consonants (C)**, and an optional **coda** also consisting of one or more consonants. The nucleus and the coda (if present) together constitute the **rime** of the syllable. This hierarchical structure is illustrated in Figure 1 for the word *table*, where σ represents 'syllable'.

Figure 1 Syllable structure of *table*

When this type of representation is used, onsets or codas with more than one consonant are referred to as **branching**, as is the case in the coda here. The favoured syllable structure of French is CV, that is, an **open** syllable with an onset but no coda.[4] Indeed, the tendency toward this syllable structure is so strong that when a word with no onset in the first syllable (i.e. a word beginning with a vowel) immediately follows one with a coda in the last syllable (i.e. one ending in a consonant), the coda consonant 'transfers' to become the onset of the following syllable. Thus, [sɛt] in *cette fenêtre* forms a **closed** syllable with both onset and coda, but in [sɛ.ta.mi] *cette amie* (where '.' indicates division into syllables), the first consonant and the vowel form an open syllable, and the final consonant forms the onset of a syllable [ta] whose nucleus is the first vowel of *amie*.[5] This phenomenon is known as *enchaînement*.

2.1.2 Rhythmic groups

Partly because of *enchaînement*, words are often held to have no phonetic identity in French, in contrast to English, where *enchaînement* does not occur, and where polysyllabic words have at least one stressed syllable. When French polysyllabic words are pronounced in isolation, the final syllable is stressed, but when they occur in running speech it is only the final syllable of the **rhythmic group** which is stressed. This syllable is conventionally known as the **tonic** syllable, and the one preceding it as the **pretonic** syllable. The rhythmic group can consist of varying numbers of syllables, as shown in (1) (taken from Valdman 1993:28–9), where the first group has five syllables, the second four and the third six:

(1) Mon ami Marcel I est étudiant I à l'école des Beaux-Arts.

The words within a rhythmic group are always closely linked syntactically and semantically, although groups can vary in length according to speech rate and style. Rhythmic groups are the basic prosodic units of French, and many phonological processes are governed by them; for example, *enchaînement* and *liaison* (see Chapter 1) only occur within and not across rhythmic groups.

Table 2 The consonants of French

Place \ Manner	Bilabial	Labio-dental	Dental	Alveolar	Post-alveolar	Palatal	Velar	Uvular
Stop	p b		t d				k ɡ	
Nasal	m		n			ɲ	(ŋ)	
Trill				(r)				(ʀ)
Fricative		f v		s z	ʃ ʒ			ʁ
Lateral approximant				l				

2.1.3 Consonants

Table 2 presents the consonants of standard French[6], classified according to their place and manner of articulation, following the presentation conventions and using the symbols of the International Phonetic Alphabet (IPA) as revised to 1993.[7] Where two consonants appear in the same cell, the left-hand one is voiceless and the right-hand one voiced.

Stops and fricatives are frequently classified together as **obstruents,** and since there are similarities between the behaviour of these two classes in French, we have followed the same practice. There are three pairs of **stop** consonants: bilabial (/p,b/), dental (/t,d/) and velar (/k,ɡ/); and three pairs of **fricatives**: labiodental (/f,v/), alveolar (/s,z/) and post-alveolar (or pre-palatal[8]) (/ʃ,ʒ/). In each case, the first member of the pair is voiceless, and the second voiced.

The obstruents furthermore all have regular variants which vary in their voicing: they undergo 'anticipatory' or 'regressive' voicing assimilation when they come into contact with a following obstruent which has different voicing. That is, when a voiceless obstruent, such as the /p/ at the end of *coupe,* is immediately followed by a voiced obstruent, such as the /d/ at the beginning of *du,* the /p/ is pronounced with voicing in anticipation of the voicing in the following [d] (hence the term 'anticipatory' assimilation). Thus *la Coupe du monde* is pronounced [lakup̬dymɔ̃d] (compare *la Coupe française* [lakupfʁɑ̃sez], with no voicing of /p/). Likewise, when a voiced obstruent such as the /d/ of *de* comes into contact with an immediately following voiceless obstruent such as the /s/ of *suite,* it is devoiced in anticipation of the voiceless sound, as in *tout de suite* [tud̥sɥit] (compare *un coup de barre* [œ̃kudbaʁ], with no devoicing of /d/). The convention of indicating the difference between the two variants with diacritics rather than writing voiced /p/ as [b] and devoiced /d/ as [t] is used at least in part to reflect the fact that these variants are not always pronounced in a manner identical to, say, the [b] of *tube* or the [t] of *flûte*. The other voiced and voiceless obstruents also have devoiced or voiced variants respectively.

Table 2 above shows that **nasal** consonants occur at four different places of articulation in French: bilabial (/m/), dental (/n/), palatal (/ɲ/) and velar (/ŋ/). None of the nasals has regular variant pronunciations in the same way as the obstruents do. As indicated by the bracketing of /ŋ/ in Table 2, there is some debate as to whether the velar nasal properly belongs to the consonant system of French, but it is included here because at least some (and we would argue, most) French people produce a consonant which is phonetically a velar nasal at the ends of words such as *parking* and *camping* (see Chapter 12). What is not indicated by Table 2 is that the status of /ɲ/ has also been questioned by some phonologists. The pronunciation of this sound varies, and probably always has done to some extent: sometimes it is articulated as a palatal nasal [ɲ], but sometimes the articulation is more like a sequence consisting of a dental nasal [n] followed by a glide [j].

The remaining two consonants are classified together as **liquids**, although they are actually quite dissimilar in their articulation: [l] is a lateral **approximant**, formed with the tongue tip raised to the alveolar ridge and a frictionless airstream escaping over one or both sides of the tongue, whereas [ʁ], the most common pronunciation of /r/, is a uvular fricative (or sometimes approximant), formed by the back of the tongue being raised and retracted towards the uvula and velum. The other variants of /r/ are the apical and uvular trills [r] and [ʀ], of which the former was the normal pronunciation until about the seventeenth century but now persists only in certain regional varieties. Like the voiced obstruents, the liquids have devoiced variants, but whereas the obstruents are influenced by following obstruents, the liquids are devoiced under the influence of preceding voiceless stops which belong to the same syllable, as for example in *place* [pl̥as] (compare *bleu* [blø], where no devoicing occurs) or *trois* [tʁ̥wa] (compare *droit* [dʁwa]).

The most problematic issue as regards the consonants of French concerns not their phonetic identity, but how to account for their behaviour when they occur at the ends of words, a question to which we shall return in Chapter 1.

2.1.4   Vowels

Figure 2 shows the maximal system of vowels in French (that is, the system employed by speakers who make the largest number of contrasts between vowels), set out schematically (again following IPA conventions), with **front** vowels on the left and **back** vowels on the right, and with **close** or **high** vowels towards the top of the figure and **open** or **low** vowels towards

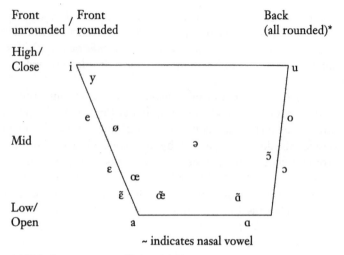

| Front unrounded | / | Front rounded | | Back (all rounded)* |

Figure 2   The maximal vowel system of modern French

the bottom. The front vowels outside the quadrilateral are all pronounced with **spread** or **unrounded** lips, whereas those within the quadrilateral are pronounced with **rounded** lips. All the back vowels are pronounced with rounded lips. In all cases, the degree of lip-rounding or lip-spreading is greater in close than in open vowels, and vowels such as /ɑ/ and /ɑ̃/ cannot truly be said to be rounded. There are sixteen **oral** vowels and four **nasal** vowels in this system, the latter being indicated with a superscript '~' over the vowel symbol. The particular problems posed by the nasal vowels will be the subject of discussion in Chapter 2. [ə] is canonically a central vowel, although as will be discussed in Chapter 3, the quality of the vowel conventionally represented by this symbol in French is highly variable.

The vowels of French do not have contextual variants in quite the same way as we have seen with variants of the consonants: regular variability in vowel quality is determined more by the type of syllable in which a vowel occurs than by the precise place, manner or voicing characteristics of a preceding or following segment. Thus, for example, vowel quality can be affected by syllable structure as well as, to a certain extent, by following consonants, and sometimes the choice between [e] and [ɛ], between [ø] and [œ], and between [o] and [ɔ] is determined by the context. For instance, although both [e] and [ɛ] occur in final open syllables (compare *chanté* [ʃɑ̃te], and *chantait* [ʃɑ̃tɛ]), only [ɛ] occurs in final closed syllables. In contrast, whereas only [ø], and never [œ], occurs in final open syllables, both [ø] and [œ] occur in final closed syllables, the choice in the latter case depending on the following consonant (e.g. only [œ] occurs before [ʁ] (cf. *peur* [pœʁ]), whereas only [ø] occurs before [t] (*meute* [møt])).

2.1.5   Semivowels

There are three **semivowels**, or **glides**[9], in French, /j/, /ɥ/ and /w/, whose articulation corresponds roughly to the three high vowels /i/, /y/ and /u/ respectively. Figure 3 represents schematically glide movement from the corresponding high-vowel positions to the position of various following vowels in the words *lion*, *Suède* and *roi*. Glides have the vowel-like articulatory property of offering no obstruction to airflow, but they have the distributional properties of consonants, in that they can occur only in the onset or coda of a syllable, and never as a syllable nucleus. There are restrictions on the distribution of the French semivowels: whereas /j/ can occur in onsets and codas (*hier* /jɛr/[10], *pied* /pje/, *fille* /fij/); /ɥ/ and /w/ can only occur in onsets (*huit* /ɥit/, *Suisse* /sɥis/, *oiseau* /wazo/, *pointu* /pwɛ̃ty/). For this and other reasons their status is a matter of some debate.

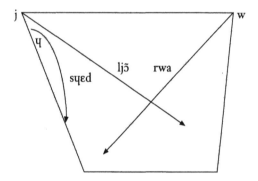

Figure 3   The semivowels of modern French

2.2   **Morphology**

Morphology is concerned with the forms of words or with their internal structure. Traditionally a distinction is made between **inflectional morphology**, which deals with the **affixes** which convey grammatical information, such as verb inflections or markers of number and gender on nouns and adjectives, and **derivational morphology**, which is concerned with the processes of word formation such as derivation and composition (see Section 2.4). Many of the key terms of morphology are used differently in different accounts[11]; the term 'morpheme' has, as Matthews notes (1991:120), a particularly complex history. Whilst strictly speaking in structuralist accounts a distinction is made between **morphs** (units which are the segments of a word form, see below) and **morphemes** (the abstract units parallel to the phoneme in phonology, see Section 3.2.2), many accounts now use the term morpheme to cover both senses. In this section we will retain the distinction for ease of exposition, while recognizing that it is not universally adopted.

The concept of the 'word' is notoriously difficult to define for French. Orthographic criteria – crudely speaking a word has a space on either side – are challenged by cases of elision such as *l'ami* where common sense tells us that it is comprised of two words comparable to *le copain*, but it is written as one unit. Phonological considerations are also problematic given the fact that French has group rather than word stress. The working definition commonly used of the word as 'a minimum free form' or as the smallest autonomous unit is equally undermined by articles and prepositions since it is difficult to think of these as being able to 'stand on their own'. A further difficulty arises from the fact that there are two common uses of the term 'word', the one to refer, for example, to each of the different forms of a verb such as *donne, donnons, donnerai*, etc., and the other to refer to what we might think of as the dictionary word DONNER (the convention is to use small capitals for this), the abstract unit realized in specific contexts by the appropriate word form. To avoid confusion the term **lexeme** is frequently used for the second sense, and the full set of words realizing a particular lexeme constitutes its **paradigm**.

Words may often be segmented into units known as morphs. For example, *fleur-ir* and *chou-fleur* can each be segmented into two morphs, while *fleur* is composed of one morph. Morphs are said to be **free** if they can stand on their own as words (e.g. *fleur*) and **bound** if they always have to appear with another morph (e.g. *-ir*). The term **root** is used to refer to that part of the word form which remains when all the inflectional and derivational affixes have been removed (e.g. *vol-* in *voleur*) and which cannot be further analysed into smaller constituents. The term **stem** is used to refer to the form to which inflexional affixes are added, but which may itself already include derivational affixes; for instance, *retrouv-* is the stem of the verb *retrouver*, but its root is *trouv-*.

Historically, phonetically different verb stems were often created by regular sound change operating according to whether the stem was stressed or not; many of these alternating stems were, however, subsequently levelled by means of analogy. A distinction is frequently made between the **weak** stem where historically the stress fell on the ending (typically used for the first and second persons plural of the present indicative, the imperfect and the present participle) and the **strong** stem, where it was the stem that was stressed (e.g. in the first three persons present indicative). For many the weak stem is viewed as the basic stem and the strong one as a variant. Generally *-er* verbs do not have phonetically different strong and weak stems, although there are verbs like *acheter* and *jeter* which do ([aʃɛt]/[aʃtɔ̃]; [ʒɛt]/[ʒətɔ̃]).

So far the identification of morphs has been presented as being relatively simple, but this is not always true. Take the case of *au* (phonetically [o]); this may be considered a complex form comparable to *à la*, yet it is impossible to segment the word into two concatenated units, *à* and *le*; such unsegmentable forms are known as **portmanteau** morphs. Rather than there being a simple one-to-one relationship between form and meaning (as is required in classic morpheme theory, see Section 3.2.2 below), here the morph carries more than one meaning. Conversely, a single meaning may be conveyed by two or more morphs which are separated by other elements. Thus *ne* and *pas* together convey verb negation, but are typically separated by a finite verb form; these are known as **discontinuous** morphs. There are also cases of accidental homophony where a single form may convey different meanings; for example, while the suffix *-ier* in *sucrier* indicates a container (cf. *beurrier*, *panier*), in the case of *saucier* the sense is not 'sauce-boat' but the occupation of 'sauce chef' (cf. *pompier*, *plombier*).

Whilst morphologists aim always to look for regularities, there are cases where this is difficult. Whereas there is a regular patterning of the stem in the case of *donn-e/donn-er-ai/donn-ais* and *rend-s/rend-r-ai/rend-ais*, this is not the case with *vais/ir-ai/all-ais*. Forms which are not regularly related are known as **suppletive** forms. As we shall see in Chapter 4, the boundary between regularity and suppletion is not clear-cut, and different analyses draw it in different places.

A striking feature of French morphology is that there are significant differences between the morphological systems of written and spoken French. It is easy to think of numerous asymmetries between the verb morphology of the two media, since the system of spoken French is much reduced compared to that of written French. Curat's tables (1991:38–40) show, for instance, that if one counts only those (word) forms which are on the one hand graphically distinctive and on the other hand phonetically different from one another, the verb *avoir* has 44 different written forms compared with just 23 phonetic ones, *être* has 41 written but only 25 phonetic forms, while a regular *-er* verb has 42 different graphic forms, but only 19 different spoken ones.[12] The difference is easily visible from a glance at the forms of the present indicative of *chanter*; the written language displays five different forms compared with only three in the spoken language:

(2) *(je) chante*   [ʃɑ̃t]
     (tu) chantes   [ʃɑ̃t]
     (il/elle) chante   [ʃɑ̃t]
     (nous) chantons   [ʃɑ̃tɔ̃]
     (vous) chantez   [ʃɑ̃te]
     (ils/elles) chantent [ʃɑ̃t]

Given that *on* is sometimes used as an alternative for *nous*, then there is a further loss of a distinctive form in spoken French.[13] Similarly, in the imperfect tense, [ɛ] may be represented orthographically by *-ais, -ait, -aient*. Problems posed by the frequent 'mismatches' between oral and written forms of French, particularly in verbal inflections, will be discussed in Chapter 4.

2.3   Syntax

Syntax is concerned with the organization of words into larger structures such as clauses and sentences. **Noun phrases (NPs)** such as *mon frère* and *la Tour Eiffel* in (3) below are key constituents of many sentences:

(3)   **Mon frère** (NP) a vu **la Tour Eiffel** (NP).

With the exception of fixed phrases (e.g. *avoir chaud*) and proper names, the noun in French does not normally appear alone in the noun phrase, but is always accompanied by a **determiner** such as an article (e.g. *le, la, un, une*), a demonstrative (e.g. *ce, cette, ces*), a possessive (e.g. *mon, ton, leur*), a quantifier (e.g. *quelques, plusieurs, cinq, onze*) or an interrogative (e.g. *quel, combien*). French also has a wide range of **pronouns** including subject pronouns (e.g. *je, tu, ils*), direct object pronouns (e.g. *me, te, eux*), indirect object pronouns (e.g. *me, te, leur*), stressed pronouns (e.g. *moi, toi, lui*), demonstratives (e.g. *celui, celle*), interrogatives (e.g. *qui, que, lequel*) and relatives (e.g. *lequel, dont*). Subject and object pronouns which are unstressed and which must be attached to the verb are known as **clitic pronouns**:

(4)   **Je les** ai vus.

We shall return to the question of the order of these constituents in Section 2.3.2. **Adjective phrases** may be composed of an adjective alone, or an adjective alongside a modifier such as *très, trop, peu* etc. (e.g. *trop petit*); an adjective phrase can form part of a noun phrase (e.g. *une grande table, un bateau rouge*).

The grammatical unit around which any sentence is structured is the verb; the verb and any other verbal constituents such as auxiliaries together form the **verb phrase (VP)**, which has the same syntactic function as a single verb. The **predicate** is also an important feature of sentence structure; it concerns 'all obligatory constituents other than the subject' (Crystal 1992:311). For example in (3), the predicate consists of the elements: *a vu la Tour Eiffel*. Since there is particular emphasis in Part II on the French verb system, some of the principal concepts used in the analysis of French verbs will be introduced and discussed in the following section.

2.3.1   Syntax and the verb system

First, it is important to distinguish between the concepts of **tense** and **time**. Time is usually considered in terms of very broad categories such as past, present and future; tense is normally defined as 'grammaticalized expression of location in time' (Comrie 1985:9). In this sense, tense is said to be **deictic**[14], in that it relates to a reference point, whether this is the moment of speech or a point in time established in a text. For example, in (5) a speaker uses the *passé composé* for an event which relates to the speaker's present (indicated by the combination of *je* and *aujourd'hui*):

(5)   J'ai soutenu ma thèse aujourd'hui.

In (6) the reference point is in the past (at the time when the subject's wife died), and the event marked by the pluperfect takes place prior to the reference point:

(6)   Il avait déjà décidé de quitter le pays avant la mort de sa femme.

A number of tenses, although perhaps having one or more principal temporal functions, may be used to mark a variety of times. Past tenses, for example, can mark future time:

(7)   J'ai fini dans un instant.

The present tense can mark past time, as is the case with the *présent historique* (see 5.5.4). Indeed, various effects can be created by the unexpected or non-standard use of tenses, some of which will be discussed in Chapters 5 and 6.

One of the most widely used models of tense is that of Reichenbach (1947), a model which has been developed and refined by a number of scholars and on which we shall draw in Part II. Reichenbach employs three key concepts to account for tense usage along a notional time line: S refers to the speaker's 'here and now'; R refers to the temporal reference point, and E relates to the point where the event occurs. So, for example, in (5), which is a case of **absolute time** since the reference point is the 'here and now' of the speaker, S and R coincide and E is prior to S and R:

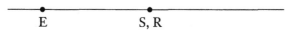

E   S, R

In (6), S is outside the text, R is the reference point within the text, that is, the point in past time which corresponds to *la mort de sa femme*, and E is the point prior to R where the event *décider* occurs:

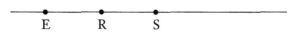

E   R   S

Cases such as (6), where events are expressed relative to a point which differs from the speaker's present, constitute examples of **relative time**. A further verbal category associated with the expression of time is that of **aspect**, a concept concerned with an internal subjective perspective on time and frequently connected with notions of completion. Aspect is, however, an extremely problematic category, one to which we shall devote a whole chapter (Chapter 5) in Part II.

A distinction is commonly made between **mood** and **modality**. The term **mood** is used to refer to a 'formally grammaticalized category of the verb which has a **modal** function. Moods are expressed inflectionally, generally in distinct sets of verbal paradigms' (Bybee and Fleischman 1995:2); thus in French there are specific forms for the subjunctive mood. **Modality**, on the other hand, 'is the semantic domain pertaining to elements of meaning that the languages express'. It embraces a wide range of semantic nuances (e.g. jussive, desiderative, intentive, hypothetical, potential, obligative, dubitative, hortatory, exclamative), 'whose common denominator is the addition of a supplement or overlay of meaning to the most neutral semantic value of the proposition of an utterance, namely factual and declarative' (*ibid.*). Linguists have been much preoccupied with the question of the extent to which the subjunctive mood in French marks modality (see Chapter 7).

Voice (or diathesis) was traditionally viewed as a category of the verb used to characterize the Classical languages: it indicates the way the subject of the verb participates in the verbal process, that is, it involves the selection of the grammatical subject. According to this traditional definition, **active** voice indicates that the subject carries out the action, or that the logical subject of the action is made the grammatical subject as in (8):[15]

(8)   Le chat a tué la souris.

By contrast the **passive** voice involves the promotion of the direct object of the active sentence (or the logical object) to the grammatical subject position; the subject may then optionally appear in an agent phrase as in (9):[16]

(9)   La souris a été tuée (par le chat).

A third category, **middle** voice, was used notably for the description of Greek verbs which normally express reflexive or reciprocal action, that is, where the action performed by the subject is also seen as affecting that subject. The threefold distinction into active, passive, and middle voice, if not perfect for Latin is, however, even more difficult to apply to a modern language such as French. Consequently linguists have reviewed the number and nature of the categories of voice in French, and questioned whether, for example, the term passive should be used to refer simply to a form of the verb, or to a syntactic construction or sentence type, indicating certain relationships between the subject, object and verb. We will return to these issues in Chapter 8.

A particularly interesting class of verbs in French is that of the **pronominal verbs**. Pronominal verbs are characterized by two defining features: the presence of a 'reflexive' pronoun, and the use of *être* in compound tenses. The traditional label of 'reflexive verbs' is avoided here since the reflexive usage is only one of the functions of these forms. Indeed, in some examples, pronominal constructions may be broadly equivalent to a passive, as is the case with (10):

(10)   Ce produit se vend bien cette année.

The classification of pronominal verbs in French is highly problematic (see Chapter 8).

2.3.2   Word order

Word order plays a crucial syntactic role in French. For example, any speaker of Modern French will have no difficulty in recognizing (11) as unproblematic and both (12) and (13) as impossible:

(11)   Mon frère a vu la Tour Eiffel[17]

(12)   *Mon frère la Tour Eiffel a vu[18]

(13)   *A vu mon frère la Tour Eiffel.

In (11), *mon frère* is identified from its position in the clause as the **subject** (S) and *la Tour Eiffel* as the **direct object** (O) of the verb (V) *voir*. In (12), the ungrammaticality of the sentence stems from the fact that the order SOV is not possible in French where O is a lexical noun, while in (13) we find a different ungrammatical order, that is, VSO. In these very simple examples of **declarative** structures, subject and direct object are identified by their position in relation to the verb; the subject precedes the verb, the object follows it. In (11) the object is a direct object, but it is also possible to have other types of **complement** (C) (that is, elements which 'complete' the meaning specified by the verb), such as **indirect objects** (14), or **adverbs/adverbial expressions** (15):

(14)   Le président a parlé à mon frère

(15)   Le président a parlé lentement.

In Modern French, therefore, it is primarily word order which determines the assignment of subject and object status to different constituents in the simple declarative sentence. Given this standard word order in declaratives, French is described as an SVO or an SVC language. Note also that the subject is often the **topic** of the sentence, that is 'the thing which the proposition expressed by the sentence is about' (Lambrecht 1994:118). We shall return in Chapter 9 to the relationship between the grammatical subject and the topic of the sentence.

Although many structures (e.g. OVS, SO_NV (where $_N$ = noun) (as in 12) and VSO (as in 13)) which do not conform to the SVC pattern are unacceptable in French declaratives, a number of non-SVC structures are entirely unproblematic. Indeed, in the case of object pronouns (O_P), SO_PV is the compulsory order:

(16)   Je la vois (SO_PV).

Other non-SVC orders are also found, for example:

(17)   CVS: Ainsi vivait-elle en paix

(18)   VCS: Paieront une amende les automobilistes qui . . . (VO_NS; see Marchello-Nizia 1995:113)

(19)   CSV: (i)   Difficile elle l'est (CSC_PV)
             (ii)   Les Anglais je les déteste (O_NSO_PV)
             (iii) Le chocolat j'aime (O_NSV).

And while SVO is the standard word order for declarative sentences, this is not the case for certain types of **interrogative**:

(20)   Voulez-vous quitter le restaurant? (VSO)

In Chapter 9 we will discuss the description of French as an 'SVO language'.

2.3.3   Subordination and coordination

Most of the sentences encountered thus far have been simple sentences, containing a subject, verb and object or complement. Complex sentences have more than one clause, usually a main clause (*il regardait la télévision* in (21) below) and one or more subordinate clauses (*quand je suis rentrée du travail*):

(21)   Il regardait la télévision quand je suis rentrée du travail.

Subordinate clauses are usually introduced by a subordinating conjunction (*quand* in (21)). Alternatively, clauses may be joined by coordinators such as *et, mais, où.* According to traditional accounts, the notion of **dependence** is central to the difference between **subordination** and **coordination**. Thus Dubois and Lagane's *Nouvelle Grammaire du français* defines subordination as 'un lien de dépendance, qui unit des propositions de fonction différente au sein de la phrase' (1989:177), and coordination as follows: 'une phrase, ou proposition, est coordonnée à une autre quand elle a la même fonction que cette autre phrase et qu'elle lui est rattachée par une conjonction de coordination ou un adverbe de coordination, qui indiquent le type de rapport qui existe entre elles' (1989:178). Whereas coordination implies a relation between equals, subordination implies a hierarchical relation, where the subordinating conjunction often specifies the nature of the relation between the main and subordinate clauses (a temporal relation in the case of example (21)).

Traditionally, subordinating conjunctions are divided into three broad categories: relative clauses, completives and circumstantials (the last subdividing into various sub-categories). **Relatives** usually involve an antecedent followed by a relative pronoun (e.g. *qui, que, quoi, dont, où, lequel, quiconque*) and a clause containing a verb. For example:

(22)   La femme qui est responsable du magasin

(23)   Le projet que j'ai entrepris.

Completives are usually introduced by verbal antecedents followed by *que*:

(24)   J'ai appris que vous étiez en vacances.

Various types of **infinitive clauses** are also found following verbal antecedents:

(25)   Je voudrais partir

(26)   Il le fait travailler.

Circumstantials encompass a number of different types of subordinate clause, such as those expressing temporal relations (e.g. introduced by *avant que, aussitôt que, quand*); purpose (e.g. *pour que, afin que*); cause (e.g. *parce que, du fait que*); consequence (e.g. *de sorte que, de manière que*); concession (e.g. *bien que, quoique*); condition (e.g. *si, pourvu que, à condition que*), and comparison (e.g. *de même que, ainsi que*).

Typical coordinators include **conjunctions** which might express addition (e.g. *et*); opposition (e.g. *mais*); cause (e.g. *car*) or disjunction (e.g. *ou, ni*), and adverbs or adverbial expressions indicating, for example, addition (e.g. *puis*); opposition (e.g. *cependant, toutefois, par contre, pourtant*); cause (e.g. *en effet*) or consequence (e.g. *donc, par conséquent*).

2.3.4   Textual cohesion

In its broadest sense, textual cohesion is the area of syntax which concerns what Halliday and Hasan (1976:4) term 'relations of meaning that exist within the text, and that define it as a text'. As the term 'textual' suggests, cohesion operates at a level beyond the sentence. A wide variety of different linguistic elements can be involved in textual cohesion including pronouns (such as those functioning anaphorically to refer to people or concepts or objects already mentioned within the text), possessives, demonstratives, spatial or temporal deictics, as well as other elements involved in substitution, ellipsis or anaphora.[19] A key role in textual cohesion is also played by phenomena which link clauses within the text, such as subordination (notably circumstantials), coordination and **parataxis** (the simple juxtaposition of clauses with no explicit syntactic link between them). In (27)–(29), broadly the same set of semantic relations between the two clauses is conveyed using different cohesive elements, that is parataxis in (27), coordination in (28) and a subordinating conjunction (**hypotaxis**) in (29):

(27)   Il pleut je ne sors pas

(28)   Il pleut et je n'ai pas envie de sortir

(29)   Je ne sors pas quand il pleut.

We shall return to some of the more problematic questions in the analysis of textual cohesion in Chapter 10.

2.4   **Lexis**

One of the most fundamental differences between the vocabulary of a language and its grammar or sound system is the relative instability of the lexis. Whereas grammatical and phonological change tend to be slow gradual processes, lexical change is rapid in comparison. Evidence from surveys suggests that over a period of ten to fifteen years, approximately 20% of French vocabulary is replaced.[20] In this section we will give an introductory account of the main processes exploited by French in the creation of new words. In Chapter 13 we will re-examine the classification and definitions used here and explore questions of productivity, linguistic theory and the integration of new words or **neologisms** into French.

2.4.1   Derivational processes

New words are rarely created from nowhere. Most (70–80% according to Posner (1997:166)) are formed by what are often termed 'internal processes' using combinations of elements which already exist in the French language. The most productive of these is **derivation**, that is, the use of **affixes**. In essence, **suffixes** and **prefixes** are added to the stem (see Section 2.2 above) to form new words. These are processes which have been continuously exploited by French: suffixation in particular was highly productive in Latin, where a wide range of nominal, verbal and adjectival suffixes could be added to form new words, while prepositions such as *de* and *ad* were used frequently as verbal prefixes (e.g. Latin *ad-mittere* > French *admettre*).

Suffixes are most frequently found attached to nouns, adjectives or verbs and can in turn form nouns and adjectives (the number of suffixes here is very high) as well as verbs and adverbs (see Wise 1997:107–9). Unlike prefixes, they usually change the grammatical class of the word (e.g. from a verb to an adjective *porter* > *portable*, or from a verb to a noun, e.g. *humilier* > *humiliation*) but this is not always the case. Suffixes which do not change the word class tend to be less productive, but semantically relatively transparent, often adding nuances or making fine distinctions between different lexical items: e.g. *jaune* > *jaunâtre*, *pleuvoir* > *pleuvoter*, *pleuviner*, *pleuvasser* (see Wise 1997:109).

Prefixes are, for a number of reasons, more difficult to identify, quantify and categorize than suffixes, and we will return to this in Chapter 13. They can be applied to various parts of speech, though they are particularly common with verbs and adjectives (e.g. *monter* > *remonter*, *possible* > *impossible*; see table 2 in Wise 1997:110). In general, and unlike suffixes, prefixes do not change the grammatical class of the word. Prefixes and suffixes may combine to form **parasynthetic** formations such as *réutilisation*, *incroyablement* etc.

Non-affixal derivation refers to cases where a word can change class without the addition of an affix. This encompasses a number of different phenomena, including cases where an adjective may be used to form a noun (abstract or otherwise) which has the properties of the adjective (e.g. *les pauvres*), or vice versa (e.g. *une enquête bidon*). A verb may be used to form a noun (e.g. *le savoir*, *le pouvoir*) and present and past participles can be used as adjectives (e.g. *ennuyant*, *perdu*), the endings *-é* and *-ant* often serving as adjectival suffixes. There are also cases of ellipsis, where an element has been removed, causing a lexical item to change grammatical class (e.g. *un homme marginal* > *un marginal*).

2.4.2   Composition

A second process in the creation of new words is **composition** or **compounding** which Wise (1997:120) describes as 'an increasingly important process in French'. The majority of compounds are nouns and they demonstrate a number of different patterns, allowing considerable flexibility in the permutations and combinations possible. In broad terms, compounds consist of two or more identifiable and autonomous elements which are used together in such a way that they form a single lexical item (e.g. *porte-monnaie, télécarte, sans-travail, pause-café, auto-école, laissez-passer, hôtel de ville*). As these examples illustrate, there are a number of different possible grammatical relations between the elements in compounds, including amongst others a verb in combination with an object (e.g. *tire-bouchon*), two verbs in combination (e.g. *laissez-passer*), a preposition with a noun or an adjective (e.g. *sous-développé*), an adverb with an adjective (e.g. *mal-nourri*), two co-ordinated nouns demonstrating various types of semantic relation (e.g. *film-événement*), and two elements where one is in a relation of subordination to the other (e.g. *pause-café, presse-bouton*).

Compounds known as *recomposés* contain learned elements from Latin and Greek sources such as *micro, hyper, extra* (e.g. *micro-ondes, hyper-résistant, extra-terrestre*). Note that, unlike the compounds cited thus far, one or more of the elements in *recomposés* cannot function autonomously. A number of complex definitional issues arise with the process of composition which we shall discuss in Chapter 13. The **lexicalization of phrases** is a further source of neologisms (e.g. *le qu'en-dira-t-on, le va-et-vient*), one where definitional issues also arise and to which we shall return in Chapter 13.

2.4.3   Abbreviation

The term **abbreviation** covers a wide range of phenomena in French, and a number of these constitute productive sources of neologisms. In particular, **apocope** (truncation involving the suppression of one or more phonemes in final position) and **aphoeresis** (truncation involving the suppression of one or more phonemes in initial position) are widely used, the new abbreviated forms usually containing one or two syllables.[21] Apocope is the more productive of the two processes, some truncated forms ending in a consonant (e.g. *exam, agrég, prof, impec*), others in a vowel which is often an *-o* (e.g. *apéro, diapo, hebdo*). Most abbreviations are nouns, although some adjectives may be truncated (e.g. *impec*). **Acronyms** and *sigles* are a relatively productive source of neologisms, one which has been particularly widely used in recent years, especially in the media. The two terms are sometimes distinguished in French (only the term acronym tends to be used in English), acronyms referring to the combination of the beginning (usually the first syllable) of each word (e.g. *Boul' Mich'*), and *sigles* to the combination of initial letters to form a word (e.g. *SMIC, ENA, CAPES* etc.).[22]

2.4.4   Semantic change

Finally, one of the most economical ways to create a 'new' word is to give a new meaning to an existing form. Amongst the most productive of these processes are figurative ones such as **metaphor** (where the new usage is coined as an image, e.g. *banque de sang*) and **metonymy** (where there is a 'real' connection between the new usage and the former one such as a part/whole relationship (**synecdoche**; e.g. *chaussure de tennis > tennis*)). A minority of figurative creations are born of necessity in order to refer to new concepts or objects (e.g. *la bretelle d'autoroute*); the majority are entirely stylistic in motivation, often coined by writers or journalists to create a particular effect in a given context. Some metaphors are considered 'dead' in that they are no longer used (e.g. *moissonner* for *tuer* in seventeenth-century usage), while others are fully lexicalized and can be used productively in a variety of contexts (e.g. parts of the body such as *pied, dos, tête*).

2.4.5   Borrowing

In addition to the 'internal' processes we have just outlined, a minority of words enter French through the process of linguistic **borrowing**. Throughout its history, French has always borrowed words from other languages, from the earliest periods in the history of the language, when words of Celtic origin were adopted into the Vulgar Latin spoken in Gaul and subsequently into French, to the present day, where the current stock of words has been, and continues to be, enriched by many different languages.

The most obvious motivation for borrowing is the need to describe a new object or concept: at the same time as an object or concept is adopted from another culture the term is also borrowed by the host language (e.g. *leitmotiv/f, shinto, tapas*). Elsewhere, the borrowing may offer a refinement on the existing French term (e.g. *poster* vs *affiche, panneau*). In other cases, the primary motivation is stylistic. This is usually a question of fashion or prestige: the Anglo-American *walkman* may be perceived to be more fashionable than the French *baladeur*. It is also possible, albeit rarer, for the motivation to be linguistic, in that the foreign term may be more concise or precise in orthographic terms (e.g. *on-off* vs *marche-arrêt*), or in syntactic terms (compounds such as *chewing-gum, skate-board* are more concise than their French equivalents *gomme à mâcher, planche à roulettes*).

The most basic precondition for linguistic borrowing is contact between two languages, although the nature and strength of the contact may vary. One of the most intense forms of contact arises with diglossia, where the two languages are in daily contact and where many speakers are bilingual, as is the case, for example, in parts of Canada. The following chart from Walter and Walter (1991:19) presents, in broad terms, a chronology which sets linguistic borrowing into French in the context of both the evolution of the French language (*langue emprunteuse*) and the historical background:

Table 3 Linguistic borrowing in the history of French (Walter and Walter 1991:19)

Chronologie des emprunts			
	Époque	*Langue emprunteuse*	*Langue d'origine et exemple d'emprunt*
Avant le latin	avant la conquête romaine		LIGURE (avalanche) IBÈRE (calanque) GAULOIS (alouette)
Le latin	à partir du IIe s. av. J.-C.	LATIN POPULAIRE	LATIN D'ÉGLISE (sacrement)
Apports germaniques anciens	IIIe-Ve s. IXe-Xe s.	puis GALLO-ROMAN	FRANCIQUE (guerre) GOTIQUE (fredaine) LONGOBARD (toque) ALÉMANIQUE (cible) SCANDINAVE (turbot) FRISON (savon)
Le temps des foires	Moyen Âge	ANCIEN puis MOYEN FRANÇAIS	LANGUES RÉGIONALES (abeille) ARABE (algèbre) NÉERLANDAIS (bouquin)
Le temps des conquêtes	XVIe s.	FRANÇAIS	ITALIEN (ombrelle) ESPAGNOL (camarade) PORTUGAIS (autodafé)
Échanges européens	XVIIIe s.	FRANÇAIS	ITALIEN (sonate) ANGLAIS (pétition) ALLEMAND (cobalt) LANGUES SLAVES (icône) LANGUES SCANDINAVES (renne)
Les Temps modernes	XIXe-XXe s.	FRANÇAIS	ANGLAIS (rail, transistor) LANGUES D'AFRIQUE (banane) LANGUES D'EXTRÊME-ORIENT (sari) LANGUES D'INDONÉSIE (rotin)

The history of borrowing reveals certain peaks since early Old French; note, for example, during the Renaissance, the intensity of borrowing from Italian, when intellectual, cultural and political exchange was at its peak (e.g. *académie, alarme, balustrade, campagne, cavalier, douche, intrigue, pantalon, parasol, riposte, soldat*). More recently, the majority of borrowings have come from Anglo-American sources, particularly in fields such as science, technology, commerce, show-business, and popular culture. A number of problematic issues arise from the process of borrowing, including the definition of the term 'borrowing', the interaction of internal and external processes of word creation and the integration of borrowings into French; we shall return in Chapter 12 to these issues.

Section 3

Approaches and schools

3.1 A multiplicity of approaches...

Since one of the aims of Part II is to compare and contrast different approaches to a number of interesting issues regarding the structure of French, we have not espoused or promoted one 'school' of linguistics, but favoured instead a rather more eclectic approach, evaluating the strengths and weaknesses of different theories as they relate to different problematic issues. It seems, nevertheless, appropriate to provide here a brief introduction to some of the main theories to which we will be referring. We stress that there is no attempt to be exhaustive either in coverage or in exposition of the approach. While some of the theories we will be considering have tended to be restricted to French scholars and to analysis of the French language, others are ones which were first elaborated to account for other languages, notably English. There are, moreover, differences according to the domain of linguistics being studied. If, in the field of phonology, certain paradigms tend to predominate, there is a greater diversity of approaches towards French syntax and (albeit to a lesser extent) morphology. On the other hand, theoretical approaches to the lexis have typically been less numerous than purely descriptive accounts. In the domain of syntactic analysis the French have tended to work somewhat in isolation from scholars elsewhere. Both the Guillaumean model and the *Approche pronominale* have been predominantly espoused by French scholars working on French and these theories have been much less used outside France. Nonetheless, the French have embraced some of the dominant syntactic theories which have international currency, notably structuralism and generative theories. In virtually all cases, however, the theories have undergone some degree of modification as they have been applied to the analysis of French.

3.2   Structuralism

The Swiss linguist, Ferdinand de Saussure (1857–1913), is often termed 'the father of modern linguistics', not least for his key role in the elaboration of European **Structuralism**. In the *Cours de linguistique générale* (1916), reconstructed posthumously from lecture notes by two of his students, Saussure articulates his theory of language around a number of key dichotomies. First, a distinction is made between **diachronic** (historical) and **synchronic** (non-historical or descriptive) approaches to language. Second, *langue*, the social system of language, is differentiated from *parole*, the individual's use of language in a given context. Third, Saussure distinguishes two elements of the linguistic **sign**, the *signifiant*, the concrete sound image or form that signifies, and the *signifié*, the concept or thing signified. Fourth, he considers two different types of relationship which may obtain between linguistic signs, **syntagmatic** (or horizontal) relationships between elements in a linear sequence, and **paradigmatic** (or associative, i.e. vertical) relationships, those elements which can substitute for each other in a given context. Language is thus conceived of as a system of signs in which all the elements fit together; the 'value' of the elements is defined negatively by contrast with the other elements in the same system.

Structuralism developed in different ways in Europe and America. Much of the work on French phonology has been carried out within the European tradition (see Section 3.2.1); in the case of morphology and syntax the contribution of American structuralists such as Harris and Bloomfield has been important (Sections 3.2.2, 3.2.3).

3.2.1   Phonology

Perhaps the best known French phonologist of the twentieth century has been André Martinet, whose theoretical approach has been termed 'le réalisme fonctionnaliste' (Léon, Schogt and Burstynsky 1977:90). For European **Functionalists**, following in the tradition of Saussure, the most important patterns to be identified in the phonology of a language are the contrasts between distinctive sound units, termed **phonemes** in Martinet's case. For example, the vowels of *cri* and *cru* (/i/ and /y/) suffice to identify the two words as different, which indicates that the difference between the vowels is significant and that they are therefore linguistically significant units, 'phonemes', in their own right. The hypothesis is confirmed by similar **minimal pairs** such as *lis* (/li/) versus *lu* (/ly/), and a picture of the overall system can be built up by further pair-wise comparisons. Phonetic details such as the precise degree of frontness or backness of either vowel are irrelevant, so long as the vowels are sufficiently different to signal the contrast between the words.

To take a consonantal example given by Martinet (1968:29) himself, 'toute orale bilabiale d'un énoncé ne peut être que /p/ ou /b/ et jamais quelque chose d'intermédiaire entre /p/ et /b/; *bière* avec un *b* à moitié dévoisé n'indique pas une substance intermédiaire entre la bière et la pierre'; in other words, although it is not unheard of to encounter a partially devoiced [b̥] at the beginning of a word such as *bière* (see Temple 1998), this fact is irrelevant to the phonologist so long as the sound is sufficiently different from /p/ for the word still to be distinguishable from *pierre*. Moreover, the fact that the second pair of words we have cited, *lis* versus *lu*, involves different inflected forms of the same lexical item is also irrelevant to the phonology – the important point is that we can tell the difference between them; the semantic and functional relationship between them is the domain of grammar and not of phonology.

When the distinction between two phonemes ceases to function, either because only one can occur in a given context, as was the case with some of the vowels described in Section 2.1.4 above, or because most speakers have ceased to differentiate between them consistently, as is the case with /a/ versus /ɑ/, it is said to have been **neutralized**[23], that is it ceases to function to signal linguistic differences between higher order units (morphemes or words).[24] Neutralization effectively reduces the number of phonemes that can function to signify meaningful differences in certain positions and it is conventional to express the resultant system in terms of **archiphonemes**, which are represented with capital letters. Thus, (archi-)phonemic transcriptions of *peur* and *meute* (cf. Section 2.1.4 above) would be /pŒr/ and /mŒt/, to indicate that although the vowels are phonetically different ([pœʁ] and [møt]) there is no phonemic contrast in these contexts.

The concept of the phoneme and the terminology used to discuss it vary somewhat within the structuralist tradition. The most common use of the concept does have a place for phonetic variability, in the form of **allophones**. Allophones are what we have hitherto been calling 'variants' (the term favoured by Martinet) in order to present the sounds of French in a theory-neutral way. They are phonetic realizations of phonemes, the alternation among which is normally wholly determined by the phonological context. For example, as we have seen in Section 2.1.3, in French the lateral /l/ can be said to have two allophones, [l] and [l̥], the occurrence of which is regular and predictable. Allophones of a phoneme never contrast meaningfully with each other, and are in complementary distribution, that is, they occur in mutually exclusive phonological contexts: [l̥] never occurs where [l] occurs (*bleu* is never pronounced *[bl̥ø]), and vice versa (*peuple* is never pronounced *[pøpl]).[25] Conversely, [i] and [y] in *lis* versus *lu* cannot be considered as allophones of the same phoneme, even though the meaning of the root of the verb is the same, because they are not in complementary distribution (they both occur here after /l/ and before a potential pause), and they are contrastive in that the choice between them signals the difference between the two words *lis* (1st person singular of *lire*) and *lu* (past participle of *lire*).

3.2.2 Morphology

In American structuralist accounts of morphology, known as Item-and-Arrangement grammar, the morpheme is viewed as the basic unit of grammatical analysis, parallel to the phoneme in phonology. Morphemes have been variously defined as 'the smallest meaningful unit of analysis' or as 'the smallest individually meaningful element in the utterances of a language' (Hockett 1958:123). In Hockett's account then, the morph (e.g. /flœr/) is comprised of phonemes, and realizes the morpheme {'fleur'} (morphemes are usually enclosed within brace brackets) which has the meaning 'fleur' or 'flower'. While the relationship between the morph and the morpheme is simple in this case, the plural morpheme for nouns in French may be realized by different morphs: /o/ as in *chevaux*, /i/ as in *soprani*, or most commonly by nothing, as in *maisons*. Similarly, the stem of the verb {'want'} may be realized as /vul-/, /vø-/, /vud-/, /vœl-/. These different realizations of a given morpheme are dealt with in morphology using a construct analogous to the allophone, that is, the **allomorph**. Allomorphs may be phonologically conditioned; for example, the morpheme for {'fruit tree'} is typically realized by the allomorph *-ier* /je/ (*cerisier, pommier*), but is realized as *-er* /e/ if the stem ends in /ʃ/ or /ʒ/ (*pêcher, oranger*). They may also be grammatically conditioned; for example, the first person plural morpheme is typically realized as *-ons* /ɔ̃/, but as *-mes* /m/ in the *passé simple* (e.g. *nous allâmes*).

It is important to note that, while in the American tradition the morpheme is viewed as the smallest unit which has a meaning, in the European structuralist tradition, the minimal unit, termed *monème* by Martinet (1960:20), is seen as being comprised of a form (*signifiant*, e.g. /flœr/) and a meaning or value (*signifié*, e.g. 'fleur'). Martinet maintains that in a word like *travaillons* there are two *monèmes*, one which is lexical (*lexème*), /travaj/ and the other which is grammatical (*morphème*), /ɔ̃/.

In the Item-and-Arrangement model, morphemes are broadly identified by the processes of **segmentation** and **commutation** (what can be substituted for a given form). To take the example of *plongeur*, the root /plɔ̃ʒ/ which realizes the morpheme {'dive'} may be identified on the basis of comparison with *plong-eon, plong-eoir, plong-er*, etc. and the derivational suffix /œr/ is identified by comparison with *chant-eur, vol-eur, institut-eur*, etc. However, the segmentation of French words is not straightforward because of the existence, inter alia, of discontinuous and portmanteau morphs (see Section 2.2).[26] There are also difficulties with trying to associate a single meaning to morphemes. To take the best-known example, what is the meaning of the morpheme {'cran'} of cranberry which occurs only in this single word (such cases are consequently termed 'cranberry morphemes')? Finally in structuralist accounts a 'zero morph' is sometimes required to deal with cases where a morpheme appears to have no surface realization, as in those cases where nouns are created from verbs by the simple addition of a determiner (*devoir → le devoir; savoir → le savoir*); many scholars are concerned about this postulation of an underlying morpheme where there is no surface evidence for it.

The analysis of variation in the stem of verbs is not always as straight-forward as that of the case of *vouloir* discussed above. As we have seen, in general, morphemes are considered to be abstract units, and the various stems can therefore be deemed to be allomorphs of the morphemes, as illus-trated above. This, however, raises the question of the degree of abstraction permitted in the analysis. Whilst the allomorphs of *vouloir* are phonologically related to a degree, the various stems of the verb *aller* (*all-*, *va-*, *i-*) are not. Such cases are usually considered in American structuralist accounts to be examples of suppletion. We shall return to how such forms should be treated in Chapter 4.

As well as considering phonologically governed and grammatically governed alternations separately, structuralist accounts also consider morphology and syntax to be separate levels of analysis. For instance, verb morphology is concerned with verb forms and paradigms, whereas verb syntax deals with the usage of these forms. To take a different example, separate consideration may be given to the various ways in which nominal gender is expressed in French, whether by suffixation (*le prince/la princesse*; *l'instituteur/l'institutrice*) or by other means (by the determiner alone (*un/une enfant*)), lexically (*le roi/la reine*), or by adding a specifier of some kind (*un professeur/une femme pro-fesseur*), without taking account of the syntactic role of gender in agreement in French. Other schools favour a morphosyntactic approach on the grounds that it is artificial to make such a separation of levels, since inflectional morphology contributes to syntactic rules. Such an account would consider the marking of gender in conjunction with questions of agreement.

In an important paper, Hockett (1954) contrasts the Item-and-Arrangement model of American structuralism in which word formation is viewed as a concatenation of morphemes which are linearly arranged (and which there-fore has difficulty handling certain types of alternations) with the Item-and-Process model. This model assigns each morpheme an underlying form to which processes are applied. Such an approach finds resonances in early generative grammar in which basic abstract forms are related to their surface structure by rules (see below). In the Item-and-Process model the processes not only include addition of an affix, but also internal changes, or the sub-traction of an affix.

Hockett also refers briefly to a third model, the Word-and-Paradigm model, which recognizes the difficulties of segmentation alluded to above. For instance, a meaning may be represented by more than one segment, or one segment may 'realize' more than one 'value'. Take the example of *chanterions*: if we segment it as *chante-r-i-ons*, what is the value of /r/(*r*) or /j/(*i*)? We might consider the /r/ to be a future marker and /j/ an imperfect marker (not, however, used for all persons of the verb), but in the case of *chanterions* it is the combination of the two infixes which signals the condi-tional form. Is it therefore appropriate to segment *-ri-* or should it remain as one unit? To avoid such difficulties, the Word-and-Paradigm model argues instead that the word, rather than the morpheme, is the basic unit of morphological analysis, since certain generalizations can only be made at the level of the word. Each inflectional form is given a morphosyntactic description (e.g. 'present conditional form') and the grammar then makes available the paradigms that specify the forms required which correspond to the category. We shall see that in more recent morphological theory a version of this model has been revived especially for the analysis of inflection (see **4.8**).

3.2.3   Syntax

Both Tesnière's **dependency grammar** and **constituency grammars** of the type favoured by American **distributionalists** are broadly structuralist in character, although they differ in a number of important respects. In dependency grammar the main aim is the description of the dependency relations between the elements of a sentence. It is argued that when there is a syntactic connection between two elements, one is the governing element and the other the dependent element (which cannot therefore occur without the governing element). In constituency grammar, on the other hand, sentences are broken down into a hierarchically defined series of constituents (or a series of immediate constituents) which may be expressed in tree diagrams.

Tesnière's (1893–1954) dependency grammar attempts to explain grammatical relationships by setting up 'dependencies' or **valencies** between the elements of a construction. Using examples from a wide range of languages and with a pedagogical motivation, Tesnière's posthumous *Eléments de syntaxe structurale* (1959) provides a new approach to syntactic analysis in its rejection of the basic subject/predicate distinction. Rather, sentences are structured around a *nœud central*, usually the verb, and its dependent constituents or *actants*. Tesnière makes a clear distinction between different levels of his analysis. First, the *plan de la pensée* (or content) is distinguished from the *plan de la langue* (form). This latter is in turn divided into the 'forme extérieure' or sounds, and the 'forme intérieure'. The 'forme intérieure' of language may be considered in terms of its structural order (this is the domain of *syntaxe dynamique*) or its linear order (*syntaxe statique*). Whilst the latter deals primarily with grammatical categories, the former aims to explain function, and in particular three types of phenomena. First, *la connexion*, the use of hierarchies represented in stemmata to show the structure of the simple sentence; for example:

(30)

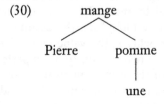

Second, *la jonction* (coordination in traditional accounts), allowing horizontal relationships between *nœuds*. Third, *la translation*, which permits the speaker to 'transférer un mot plein d'une **catégorie** grammaticale dans une autre catégorie grammaticale' (Tesnière 1959:364); this accounts not only for subordination, but also, for example, for nominal complements and agent constructions. In a phrase like *le livre de Pierre, de Pierre* is 'transposed' into an adjective (that is, it behaves syntactically like an adjective). While there are clearly some parallels with the transformations proposed by generative grammarians, Tesnière's *translations* are at once narrower and broader in their scope and there is nothing in his model comparable to Chomsky's 'deep structure' (see below).

In America, Structuralism developed in a different direction with the work of Leonard Bloomfield and others. American Distributionalism adopted the tests of commutation and segmentation to establish a taxonomy of units, but elaborated a method especially suited to the description of a corpus of a language not previously subjected to linguistic analysis. Linguists of this school favour an analysis into immediate constituents. In this model a hierarchy of elements is implied as in Tesnière's stemmata, but the traditional subject/predicate distinction is retained. The notion of a **transformation** was first introduced into the framework of distributionalism by Zellig Harris from the 1950s on (see, for example, Harris 1957); this depended on the notion of equivalence between structures (see Section 3.3.2 below). A number of French linguists have broadly adopted these principles, notably Jean Dubois and Maurice Gross. If the first volume of Dubois's *Grammaire structurale du français* (1965) uses immediate constituent analysis of the type associated with Distributionalism, the second volume, devoted to the French verb, introduces a number of transformations similar in conception to Harris's.

3.3 Generative grammar

3.3.1 Introduction

While Chomsky's syntactic theory built on aspects of the work of Harris, the originality of certain key elements of it has encouraged some to speak of a Chomskyan revolution in linguistics. Models of generative grammar have constantly evolved since Chomsky published *Syntactic Structures* in 1957. To trace the detail of this long evolution would be too complex, and indeed unnecessary, for our purposes. Rather we shall focus on those models and features which are important to the discussion in Part II, and no reference will be made, for example, to recent developments in the shape of Minimalist or Optimality theories. We shall begin by outlining the so-called 'standard' theory as articulated in *Aspects of the Theory of Syntax* (1965), and then consider some of the major changes associated with X-bar theory and Government-Binding Theory or Principles and Parameters. For further details of this evolution and of the models, see Horrocks (1987) and Ouhalla (1994), on which this account is largely based.

3.3.2   Generative syntax and its place in the grammar

In Chomsky's standard theory, syntax is at the heart of the grammar and it is viewed as autonomous. Chomsky's aim is to account for all, and only, the well-formed sentences of a language. A distinction is made between **competence** – a person's knowledge of a language – and **performance** – actual usage in a given situation and not a priority for generative linguistics. The object of study is not therefore a corpus; rather, grammaticality is judged by native-speaker intuition. Generative grammar focuses on the creativity of linguistic usage, the fact that out of a finite set of elements speakers are able to create an infinite number of new, well-formed sentences. In standard theory it is proposed to account for this creativity by elaborating **phrase-structure rules (PS rules)** which are a device for representing the distribution of phrases within sentences. The rules are context-free, rewrite rules of the type exemplified in (31a); they are used to generate a structural description of sentences – termed initial phrase markers – which may be represented as either a tree diagram as in (31b) or as a set of labelled bracketings as in (31c):[27]

(31a)   S   →   NP VP
        NP   →   (Det) (AdjP) N
        VP   →   V AdjP
        AdjP →   (Deg) Adj

where S = Sentence; NP = Noun Phrase; VP = Verb Phrase; V = Verb; N = Noun; Det = Determiner; AdjP = Adjective Phrase; Adj = Adjective; Deg = Degree

(31b)

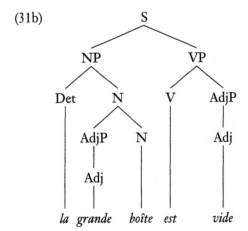

(31c) $[[[la_{Det}][[grande_{Adj}][boîte_N]_N]_{NP}][[est_V][vide_{AdjP}]_{VP}]_S]$.

The rules in (31a) will generate not only the sentence represented in (31b/c), but also a large number of other sentences, such as *Ces chats sont malins*, *Mon chien semble très farouche*, or *Les très vieux bâtiments restent solides*, since the elements in parentheses are optional.

These initial phrase markers are then modified by syntactic transformations – whether compulsory or optional – which have the power to delete, add or move material. The first of these transformations is the lexical insertion transformation which inserts the lexical items under the syntactically appropriate nodes in the phrase marker. For this to be possible, words are listed in the lexicon not only with their grammatical class (N, V, Adj, Prep, etc.) but also with subcategorization features (which show, for example, that transitive verbs are followed by a direct object), and selection restrictions (showing, for instance, that a given verb must generally have a subject which is human). A classic example of a transformation is the passive transformation which derives a passive sentence from the basic active form, as in:[28]

(32)   Jean aime Marie
         Structural description NP_1 V NP_2
                                   1   2   3
                                                              $\Rightarrow$

                                   Marie est aimée par   Jean
         Structural change NP_2 V   (par) NP_1
                                   3   2   (par) 1

As (32) illustrates, transformations have two parts, a structural description and a structural change, and are largely construction specific. Once all the transformations have applied the result is the syntactic surface structure. An important distinction is thus made between **deep structure**, the abstract underlying level generated by the base component comprised of the PS rules and the lexicon, and the **surface structure**. Chomsky's motivation for this distinction is based on pairs of sentences such as 'John is easy to please' and 'John is eager to please'. Whilst on the surface these sentences appear to have the same structure, at a deeper, underlying level they can be shown to have different structures, since, for example, although 'John' is the grammatical subject in both sentences, this NP is interpreted as the object of 'please' in the first example (cf. 'It is easy to please John'), but as the subject of the sentence in the second example (cf. *'It is eager to please John'). These differences can be captured by giving the sentences different underlying (deep structure) interpretations, with 'John' as the underlying object of 'please' in the first sentence, but not in the second.

In *Aspects* meaning and pronunciation are interpreted by two interpretative components, the semantic component and the phonological component (see Section 3.3.3).[29] Morphology is not recognized as an autonomous level of grammar in this model (see Section 3.3.4). The standard model of generative grammar can therefore be schematized as follows:

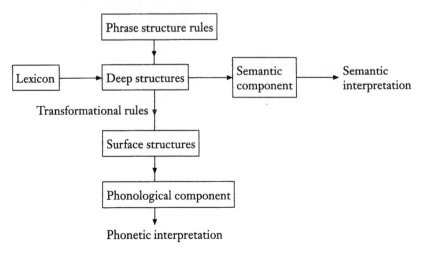

Figure 4   The 'standard' model of generative grammar

Perhaps the best-known exponent of standard generative grammar as applied to French syntax is the Belgian scholar, Nicolas Ruwet, and notably his *Théorie syntaxique et syntaxe du français*, published in 1972; another important generative account of French syntax is Kayne (1975).

A number of difficulties were associated with the standard model which have led to important developments within the generative school from so-called Extended Standard theory through to Principles and Parameters. Only a few key features can be mentioned here. Perhaps the most significant is the increasing tendency to try and derive general, and possibly innate, principles from the existing rules and to attribute these to Universal Grammar. First, it was noted that there was duplication in standard theory between the PS rules and the subcategorization properties of lexical items as specified in the lexicon. To avoid this duplication the specific PS rules were abandoned in favour of a general Principle, the Projection Principle, which requires lexical properties to be 'projected' from the lexicon to all levels of syntactic representation (i.e. the subcategorization properties of lexical items are accurately reflected in the structural representation). A central pillar of X-bar theory is the recognition that most, or perhaps all, phrasal constituents have **heads** on which other elements of the constituent are dependent. A lexical head, X (where X can stand for V, N, ADJ, P, ADV) and its complement form a constituent X', and in turn any specifier of this forms with it a higher level constituent, X". X" or XP is referred to as the maximal projection of the category X, the head. For example, (33a/b) formalizes the position of *professeur* within the NP, *Le professeur de maths*:[30]

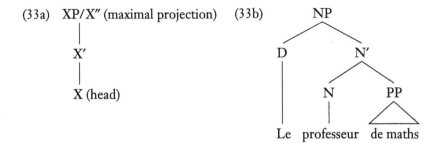

(33a) XP/X″ (maximal projection)   (33b)

The principles of X-bar theory do not therefore make reference to specific categories (such as V, N, ADJ), but express generalizations across categories.

Second, it was felt that the ever-increasing number of construction-specific transformations were becoming more and more disparate; gradually these were reduced to a single general Principle, Move-Alpha (Move-α or 'Move anything anywhere'), linking D-structures to S-structures (what were previously called deep and surface structures). Move-Alpha moves constituents freely subject to universal principles (see below), and to language-specific specifications as to which constituents may move. It was also noted that, contrary to the implications of the standard model, in which the semantic interpretation was derived from the deep structure, transformations did change meaning and that surface structure indeed played a role in semantic interpretation. Instead it was argued that while transformations do not change the semantic roles of the participants, other elements of meaning can alter. Semantic interpretation (or Logical Form) came to be derived from surface structure. If elements were moved by a transformation, their original place in deep structure was indicated by a 'trace', so that this information was available for the semantic interpretation.

Third, whilst early generative grammar concentrated very much on the analysis of English data, gradually a range of languages came to be considered. Language variation came to be accounted for in terms of parameters – a restricted set of options or values associated with a given principle or category. For example, many Romance languages (Italian, Spanish, etc.) allow pronominal subjects to 'drop', as in Italian, *Voglio questo* versus French *Je veux ceci*/English *I want this*. If it is a principle that all sentences have subjects, then there must be a parameter which, when set one way, requires subjects to be present in the surface structure, resulting in the French and English pattern, or when set the other way, allows the pronoun to drop as in Italian and Spanish. Moreover, a number of other properties (e.g. free inversion in simple sentences (Italian *telefona Gianni* vs French **téléphone Jean*) are said to be derivable from the pro-drop parameter. This parameter is particularly interesting in the case of French because the setting of the parameter has apparently changed over its history, since in Old French pronominal subjects were not obligatory.

A fourth major development was the adoption of a modular structure for the grammar whereby different subtheories deal with different aspects of the language. Each module is self-contained and consists of a set of principles which construct the relevant aspects of representation and each is subject to parametric variation. The core grammar of a language is then derived automatically from the interaction of the subtheories of Universal Grammar with their parameters appropriately set. The details of these subtheories are not important for our purposes; suffice it to note that they include (i) X-bar theory, which, as we have seen, provides the principle for the projection of lexical categories and imposes conditions on the hierarchical organization of categories; (ii) θ-theory, which deals with the assignment of 'thematic' roles such as agent, patient, beneficiary to sentence constituents; (iii) Case theory, which deals with principles of case assignment to nominal constituents: Chomsky argues that all NPs with lexical content are assigned abstract case under government; (iv) Binding theory, which is concerned primarily with the conditions under which NPs are interpreted as coreferential with other NPs; (v) Bounding theory, which constrains the movement of constituents, etc. The modular structures of Government-Binding theory are summarized in Figure 5:

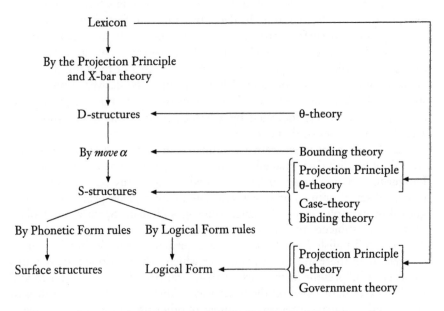

Figure 5   The essentials of Government-Binding theory (after Horrocks 1987:287)

While reference is made at times in Part II to articles written within the framework of Government-Binding or Principles and Parameters, we

have avoided wherever possible using the conventions of post-1980 generative syntactic theories so as to allow us to focus on the problematic
issues rather than the notations and conventions of particular generative
theorists.

3.3.3   Generative phonology

Generative phonology became one of the dominant paradigms in the analysis of the French sound system. As in structuralist approaches, contrasts
are important for generative phonology, but the contrastive units are characterized not as phonemes, but as collections of distinctive features. Distinctive
features, a construct first outlined in detail by the European Functionalist
Roman Jakobson (e.g. Jakobson, Fant and Halle 1952) and subsequently
developed in the foundational generative phonological work, *The Sound Pattern of English* (Chomsky and Halle 1968), are subphonemic units which can
serve to distinguish linguistic units from each other.

In the case of *pierre* versus *bière*, the sounds represented by the letters *p*
and *b* (in structuralist terms, the phonemes /p/ and /b/) share the same
feature values with the single exception of the feature 'voice': whereas the
sound represented by *p* has the value [−voice], the value for the sound represented by *b* is [+voice]; since the difference between the two is sufficient to
cue the difference between the two words, the feature is said to be distinctive, that is, able to cue a linguistically significant difference.

One important advantage of distinctive features is that they enable generalizations which hold across groups of sounds to be captured notationally.
Thus the three major classes of sounds we examined in 2.1 above are classified
by the combination of feature values for the features [+/−consonantal] and
[+/−syllabic], as illustrated in Table 4. Within each major class, subclasses
(and sub-subclasses) are identified similarly, so the obstruents can be identified as a class by the feature [−sonorant], the front vowels by the feature
[+front] and so on. This means that rather than expressing rules such as
regressive voicing assimilation in words ('all voiced obstruents are devoiced
when immediately followed by a voiceless obstruent'), or by listing the

Table 4   Feature values for the major classes of speech sounds

Feature	Class of sounds		
	Consonants	Vowels	Semivowels
Consonantal	+	−	−
Syllabic	−	+	−

phonemes involved ('/b, d, g, v, z, ʒ/ are pronounced [ḅ, ḍ, g̊, v̱, ẕ, ʒ̊] when immediately followed by /p, t, k, f, s, ʃ/'), it is possible to refer to the two sets of phonemes by the features [–sonorant] and [+/–voice], which when used in phonological rules are conventionally taken to mean 'all feature matrices[31] with the feature [–sonorant]' and so on.

The conventions for writing rules referring to features have been further abbreviated, so that they take the form in (34), where '→' means 'takes the following feature value', '/' means 'in the following context' and '___' represents the place where the matrix in question occurs (immediately before a matrix containing the features [–sonorant] and [–voice]); where two features occur within the same set of elongated square brackets, both must occur in the same matrix for the rule to apply.

(34)

$$[\text{–son}] \rightarrow [\text{–voice}] /\_\_ \begin{bmatrix} \text{–son} \\ \text{–voice} \end{bmatrix}$$

Despite these advantages, there was, in terms of the segments strung together, still much in common between the generative systems of bundles of distinctive features and systems of phonemes, as reflected in the use by generative phonologists of phonemic notation as abbreviations. The two levels of phonological representation in generative phonology, the systematic phonemic level and the systematic phonetic level, related to each other by rules of the kind exemplified in (34), were an extension of the levels of phonemic (contrastive) representation and allophonic representation (selection of phonetic variants according to the surrounding phonological context). (34) exemplifies rules which account for some of the phonotactic effects that obtain when morphemes or words are strung together in sentences, and which function in much the same way as allophonic rules.

However, the fundamental difference between structuralist and generative approaches went beyond this. Generative phonologists are concerned not exclusively with the number of contrastive units that make up a phonological system in a given language, capable of distinguishing all the words from each other and how they behave when strung together, but also with elaborating a system which will allow the expression of the relationships between semantically related forms which differ phonetically, such as the different forms of the prefix *in-*. Whereas in a structuralist account /in/, /ir/, /il/, /im/ and /ɛ̃/ would be listed as allomorphs of the morpheme {in-}, in early generative phonology (i.e. that which directly followed Chomsky and Halle (1968)) there is just one underlying systematic phonemic representation, |iN|, and the phonetic differences are generated by phonological (as opposed to morphological) rules producing the different representations [in], [iʁ], [il], [im] and [ɛ̃] at the systematic phonetic level.

As we shall see in Chapters 1–3 of Part II, this incorporation of morphology into the phonological component of the grammar, whilst simplifying the overall structure of the grammar, introduces further complications into the phonology, such as how to provide a coherent analysis which will derive such phonetically different elements as the root vowels of *prendre, prenons* and *prennent* (/ɑ̃/, /ə/ and /ɛ/ respectively) from a single underlying phonological representation. In generative phonology, one major evaluation measure of any proposal is the degree of complexity of the analysis: an important aim is to keep both the numbers of rules and the numbers of underlying representations to a minimum. Frequently, these twin ideals are in conflict with each other: an increase in the number of underlying representations may allow a corresponding decrease in the number of rules required in the phonology. The question of how 'economical' a particular proposal is will be raised on a number of occasions in Chapters 1–3.

3.3.4   Autosegmental phonology

There have been many developments out of the so-called 'classical' generative approach to phonology, all of which have tried to break down the strictly segmental sequences of units, be they phonemes or matrices of features. For this reason, they are collectively known as 'non-linear' phonologies. In this section we shall introduce some aspects of just one of these approaches which has been found to be particularly useful in analysing the phenomenon of *liaison*, which we shall be looking at in Chapter 1.

Autosegmental phonology arranges features and other phonological units on tiers which are linked by **association lines**. Whereas matrices of features in the classical generative model come as irreducible wholes, the units of autosegmental phonology exist independently of units on other tiers and are therefore known as **autosegments** (since they are autonomous). Speech sounds nevertheless occur in linear sequences, and so the autosegments need to be anchored in that sequence, and this is done by associating them with a **skeletal tier**. The skeletal tier consists either of a series of identical slots conventionally represented by 'X's, or of a series of consonant and vowel slots conventionally represented by 'C's and 'V's. These slots are then linked to the so-called **melodic tier**, which contains autosegments conventionally represented by IPA symbols for segments, to which the different tiers containing the different features are associated as necessary. Most of these tiers are usually left out of diagrams used to illustrate phonological points, to avoid the excessive complexity that their inclusion would entail. A simplified version of the first model is given in Figure 6 for the word

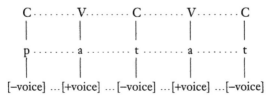

Figure 6   Partial autosegmental representation of the word *patate*

patate, which shows the feature [+/−voice] on its tier, but omits all other feature tiers. The solid lines are association lines, and the dotted lines represent the tiers on which the autosegments 'sit'.

Another innovation of autosegmental (and other non-linear) phonology is the integration into the representation of structures larger than segments, that is syllables and other prosodic units. This allows prosodic information to be incorporated into accounts of the behaviour of phonological units, as we shall see in Chapters 1–3 below.

Below the skeletal tier, the phonological units represented in Figure 6 are figuratively represented in a very different way from phonemes or feature matrices, but they still look segmental – that is, like phonemes and feature matrices, they still appear like series of self-contained wholes. One major innovation of this approach begins to emerge when the influences of adjacent sounds are examined. We shall again take voicing assimilation as our example. To recapitulate, both the structuralist and the classical generative accounts of regressive assimilation state that in a sequence of two obstruent consonants with different voicing, the second influences the first such that the voicing of the first changes. A representation of an autosegmental account is given in Figure 7, taking just the consonants involved from the sequence in

Figure 7   Regressive assimilation of voicing by feature spreading

tout de suite which we discussed earlier. The dotted association line between the feature [−voice] and /d/ on the melodic tier indicates the **spreading** of that feature to the preceding consonant. The double bar across the association line between /d/ and [+voice] indicates that the feature has been **delinked** and is no longer associated (in the technical sense) with the /d/. The advantage of the generative account over the structuralist one is the simplicity of the generalization that can be made with rules employing features.[32] The further advantage of autosegmental phonology is that the process of spreading is explicit in the representation. In Part II Chapter 1 we shall see the application of this to the problem of accounting for word-final consonants.

3.3.5   Morphology in generative grammar

As we have seen, in early generative theory syntax was central to the model and there were two interpretative components, the semantic component and the phonological component; by contrast there was no autonomous morphological component. As stated above (3.3.3), wherever possible the aim was to deal with morphological alternation (or allomorphy) in the phonology;

thus according to Schane (1968) related forms are said to have a single underlying representation and the particular morphemic variant is derived from
the underlying representation by means of a set of ordered phonological
rules. In order to try to account for as much allomorphy as possible in the
phonological component, the phonological representations are sometimes
far removed from the systematic phonetic representations. In the case of more
or less irregular or unproductive forms recourse is made to readjustment rules,
which apply to the surface syntactic structure. These rules can alter the
phonological shape of the item as specified in the lexicon before it enters the
phonological component, or mark it with a 'diacritic' to specify that it should
undergo some 'minor rule'. However, in early generative models there were
no clear-cut criteria for distinguishing which alternants should be handled
phonologically, which by readjustment rules, and which should simply be considered suppletive alternants outside the scope of generative phonology (our
example *vais/irai/allais*). Thus in his introduction Schane simply claims that the
alternants *doivent–devons* are more closely related than, for example, *fleur–
floral*, which are in turn are more closely related than *frêle–fragile*; he admits
that 'there exists no fixed set of principles for determining unequivocally
whether or not two or more forms are morphologically related' (1968:xviii–
xix). In practice the criteria used are (i) whether the forms can enter into a
paradigmatic relationship (i.e. inflectional morphology); (ii) for other alternants (derivation and doublets of the kind *frêle–fragile*), an appeal to the overall
complexity of the description. For example, he argues that it is not economical to give rules for the alternants, *mère/maternel; père/paternel; frère/fraternel*,
since these are the only three pairs in French to exhibit this opposition.

Aside from this treatment of allomorphy in the phonological component,
much of derivational morphology, including compounding, was dealt with by
the transformational component of the syntax. We can see the influence of
early generative work on derivation in Guilbert's *La Créativité lexicale* (1975),
where word formation is explained in terms of transformations. Thus, for
example, from the underlying structure *le verre est fragile* we can derive, by a
process of nominalization, the noun *la **fragilité** du verre* (1975:132). Similarly,
relativization is involved in the creation of adjectives; *la propagande est contre
la pollution* and *cette propagande envahit la télévision* are transformed into *la
propagande qui est contre la pollution envahit la télévision* which in turn generates
*la propagande **anti-pollution** envahit la télévision* (1975:134–45). In the case of
composition, a verbal predicate, usually *être*, is present in the underlying structure, such that, for instance, *il déteste la publicité* generates *il est N qui déteste
la publicité* by relativization, and subsequently, by a process of substitution
for the predicate by two morphemes (*publi-* and *-phobe*), the word *publiphobe*
is created (1975:222). Variation in the phonological form of morphemes is
dealt with by the phonology after the operation of the syntactic processes.

Models subsequent to Schane (1968), beginning with Chomsky (1970)
and developed by Halle (1973) and Aronoff (1976) adopted what was termed

a lexicalist approach, reintroducing an autonomous morphological component into derivational morphology. There are two central claims of the lexicalist view: the rules of derivation and compounding are transferred entirely to the lexicon, and there are specific Word Formation Rules (WFRs) to account for morphological facts. The Word Formation Rules (WFRs) posited by these models are different from syntactic rules and operate in the lexicon, both to combine morphemes and, to some extent at least, to deal with variability in their forms.

Where these models differ from each other is in how they conceive of the base forms on which WFRs operate. For Halle lexical entries are separate morphemes, which are 'put together' by WFRs. The WFRs may 'overgenerate' in the sense that they may produce words which are potentially possible, though actually non-existent; these are then blocked by the 'filter' to leave only the actual words of the language. Aronoff, however, assumes that morphological processes are not morpheme-, but word-based: the basic units in the lexicon are words, although derivational suffixes are stored separately in the WFR component, each with its own WFR. Because of this, Aronoff's model requires extra rules, known as Truncation Rules, to separate roots from suffixes before the addition of the required suffix by the WFRs. Thus *distribution* might be derived from *distribuer* by the application of a Truncation Rule to remove the suffix *-er*, followed by the application of a WFR to add the nominal suffix *-tion*. Aronoff also posits Rules of Allomorphy to relate forms like *fleur* and *floral*, which cannot easily be dealt with in the phonological component of the grammar. The reason that the vowel alternation is dealt with in the morphology rather than the phonology in this case is that there is no more general phonological rule in French whereby stressed /œ/ alternates with /o/.

Further modification of the treatment of derivational morphology came in the work of scholars such as Williams (1981), Selkirk (1982) and Di Sciullo and Williams (1987). They too argue that there is a separate morphological component. However, this is seen as being able to handle both derivational and inflectional morphology, thereby breaking down this traditional distinction. In addition, they maintain that word structure has the same general properties as syntactic structure (notably as regards the notion of 'head'), and, moreover, that it is generated by the same sort of rule system. As a result, the grammar may contain rules such as 'N → N + affix' (cf. Spencer 1991:182–202).

If Aronoff (1976) explicitly only deals with derivational morphology, believing all other aspects to be syntactic, more recent theories, growing out of the Word-and-Paradigm model (see Section 3.2.2) have returned to inflectional morphology. Exponents of this approach such as Anderson (1992), building on the work of Matthews (1972) and others, likewise take the word rather than the morpheme as the basis of morphemic analysis. The word's inflectional markings, whether affixal or nonconcatenative[33], are said to be determined by a set of inflectional rules. Anderson proposes to incorporate paradigms into generative grammar by generating them by a specifically constructed set of morpholexical rules. In this model the starting point is the relatively abstract aspects of how words function syntactically, that it, syntactic categories such as Case or Tense, and then consideration is given to how these categories are expressed inflectionally. In other words the approach considers how a cluster of morphosyntactic properties which a given word-form expresses are structured internally or 'spelled out' inflectionally.

It is interesting to note that while the lexicalist approach to derivational morphology has motivated important work on French, notably by Corbin (see Chapter 13), the Word-and-Paradigm approach to inflectional morphology has not yet generated a major monograph on its application to French, despite the various obvious problems of segmentation and of establishing a one-to-one correspondence between morphs and meanings in the case of French (see Sections 2.2 and 3.2.2 above).

3.4   Other approaches to the analysis of French

In Sections 3.2 and 3.3 we have focused on two schools of major importance and their influence on linguistic theory. Both adopt a formal and synchronic approach to the language. We now examine briefly several approaches to syntax which either adopt an historical perspective or favour a discourse-pragmatic viewpoint, and on which we draw at various points in Part II.

3.4.1   Typological models of change[34]

Typological approaches hold that languages can be divided into different types according to the patterning of certain features in the language. The features in question may be phonological, morphological or syntactic, although much of the published research on typological change concerns syntax. The concept of language universals as developed by Greenberg in the 1960s is of key importance to language typologies. Greenberg (1966) argues that it is possible to establish a series of implicational universals across a wide range of languages which predict that if a language has a certain feature (e.g. SOV word order), then it is likely also to have certain other features (e.g. a suffixed case system). Linguists such as Lehmann (1973) and Vennemann (1974, 1975) have further argued that the changes undergone by a language, taken together, will tend to move a language from one type to another, hence the notions of syntactic drift and typological shift. A change within a language which breaks with the features normally found in that particular type (e.g. SVO languages) will, it is argued, provoke a chain of other linguistic changes such that the language reestablishes a balance which is consistent with a particular language type. The evolution from Latin to French is viewed within a typological framework (for example, by Harris 1978) as a drift from an SOV language (Latin), to an SVO language (Modern French). Harris argues that language change from Latin to French across a wide range of linguistic features (e.g. word order, the case system, the development of auxiliary verbs, negatives) can be shown to demonstrate this syntactic drift.

Typological approaches raise a number of difficult questions, such as why, in an apparently typologically consistent language, one particular linguistic change can trigger a whole series of further changes, such that ultimately, the language changes type. Furthermore, accounting for inconsistencies within languages can be problematic, as can explaining why the pace of language change in particular cases is not always consistent with predicted patterns. A number of these issues will be discussed in Chapters 9 and 11. With specific reference to French, we shall also explore Harris's claim that modern popular French represents a new stage in the evolution of French towards a verb-initial language.

3.4.2   Language in use

A number of approaches favour considering language in use rather than as an abstract entity, many of which can be grouped together under the broad heading of 'discourse analysis'. In France, theories of *énonciation* have been highly influential in this domain. In essence, the ***courant énonciatif*** holds that language is centred in a context of communication; each utterance is viewed not just in terms of its syntactic or semantic properties, but with regard to the relationships which hold between, for example, the ***énonciateur*** and other elements in the discourse context such as other protagonists, or the specific circumstances of the discourse, as well as previous and subsequent utterances etc. One area which has been particularly important for theories of *énonciation* is that of deixis; much work has therefore been done on categories such as tense, aspect and modality (that is, categories which concern spatio-temporal relations and perspectives), and on the structure of discourse. Benveniste (1966:237–50), who made an important contribution to early theories of *énonciation*, posits two *registres énonciatifs*: *l'histoire* which favours the *passé simple* and is exclusively written (the 'présentation des faits survenus à un certain moment du temps, sans aucune intervention du locuteur dans le récit [. . .] Personne ne parle ici; les événements semblent se raconter eux-mêmes'), and *le discours* in which the principal tense is the *passé composé* ('toute énonciation supposant un locuteur et un auditeur, et chez le premier l'intention d'influencer l'autre en quelque manière'). Benveniste's binary analysis of levels of *énonciation* has been highly influential in the last fifty years or so, but has been challenged widely by evidence from a variety of sources, notably by researchers working within a discourse-pragmatic perspective (see Chapter 6).

Following on from Benveniste's work, Culioli (1991, 1999) also devotes considerable attention to deixis and *catégories énonciatives* such as person, tense and mood. Much of his work explores broad theoretical and epistemological issues, but again the emphasis is very much on language in use (see Fuchs and Le Goffic 1992, Chiss, Filliolet and Maingueneau 1993, Williams 1999). One of the primary exponents of a theory of *énonciation* and **polyphony** is Oswald Ducrot (Ducrot and others 1980, Ducrot 1984). Ducrot's work, along with that of Anscombre (Anscombre and Ducrot 1983), focuses not only on linguistic elements concerned with the expression of the self such as deictic categories, but also on the fact that each message may have more than one source, and may therefore represent several points of view. These qualities are grammaticalized in language, for example in the system of modalities. Once again, the pragmatic aspects of utterances are viewed as integral to their meaning, and there is particular emphasis on strategies of **argumentation** used by the speaker in discourse; for instance, the meaning of elements such as *mais* cannot be analysed, according to Ducrot, without reference to the parties of the dialogue, their mutual beliefs and expectations. The expression of subjectivity and traces of the subject in *énonciation* are also of central importance to Kerbrat-Orecchioni (1980).

A number of other types of approaches concerned with language in use could be grouped together as broadly **pragmatic** or **discourse-pragmatic**. In very general terms, what these approaches have in common is the view that that language use is not determined just by the propositional information, but also by pragmatic factors which are linked to the discourse context. One of the best-known exponents of such an approach in English is Halliday (e.g. 1985a, 1985b), whose work also explores many areas of textual cohesion (see Section 2.3.4 above). With particular reference to French, Fleischman, Waugh and Monville-Burston have published extensively on the discourse-pragmatic effects of tense and aspect (see Part II Chapters 5 and 6), the assumption behind their approach being that 'whatever intrinsic meaning grammatical categories may have, pragmatic factors and discourse context play a crucial role in the interpretation of their meaning' (Fleischman and Waugh 1991:1; see also Waugh and Monville-Burston 1986, Fleischman 1990).

Much recent illuminating work has been done by Lambrecht on information structuring in French clauses (e.g. 1994), and by Roulet (e.g. 1995) on *organisation informationnelle*. Lambrecht (1994) for example, on whom we shall draw in Chapter 9, explores the pragmatic phenomena of **topic** and **focus** and their syntactic expression in French discourse, the topic being defined as 'the thing which the proposition expressed by the sentence is about' (1994:118) and the focus (following Jackendoff (1972)) as 'the information in the sentence that is assumed by the speaker not to be shared by him and the hearer' (Jackendoff (1972:230) quoted in Lambrecht (1994:207)).

3.5   Variationist approaches

In Sections 3.2, 3.3 and 3.4 we have tended to look at different theories in relation to a particular level of language, whether phonological, morphological, syntactic or lexical, although clearly some schools such as structuralism have important contributions to make to all these domains. In this section we will outline briefly variationist or quantitative approaches which have been applied to all levels of linguistic analysis. The pioneering work in this area was done by William Labov on American English in the 1960s and 1970s, and while research in this paradigm has been less prolific with regard to French there is nevertheless a substantial body of important work, particularly, though not exclusively, on Canadian French.

Variationists have two major concerns: first, to account for observed patterns of linguistic variability and their implications for the way languages function as variable systems rather than relegating variation to the level of *parole* (see Section 3.2) or performance (Section 3.3.2) outside the system; and second, to gain insights into the mechanisms of linguistic change.[35] The linguistic phenomena under investigation can be phonological, syntactic, lexical or discourse phenomena, as seen in Section 1.2.5 above. Linguists working in this paradigm analyse variation in terms of alternation between **variants** of a given **variable**, for example, [il] versus [i] as variants of the variable *il* (see Section 1.2.5), or the occurrence versus non-occurrence of negative *ne* (see Chapter 11). In analysing patterns of variability, they typically look for statistically significant correlations between on the one hand the occurrence of the variants, and on the other hand social and linguistic factors such as the age, sex, SES and regional origin of the speaker, or the phonological or syntactic context in which the variable occurs. Originally, the aim was to model how the variation functioned for speakers by means of **variable rules**, which incorporated a probabilistic element to reflect the fact that what had been hitherto modelled as 'free variation' was not a matter of random choice between variants on the part of the speaker, but of choice which was constrained by complex interactions of social, stylistic and linguistic factors. More recently, the term 'variable rule' has come to apply to the statistical tools used for analysing these complex interactions of factors rather than a model of how the language functions per se (Sankoff 1982, 1988).

A number of different projects have been undertaken on French, some of which are morphosyntactic (e.g. Ashby's (1982) work on detachment and negatives (see Chapter 11) and Coveney's (1996) work on interrogatives and negatives), some lexical (e.g. Poplack, Sankoff and Miller (1988) on borrowings), and others phonetic/phonological (e.g. Pooley (1994) on word-final consonant devoicing and Hansen (1994) on schwa). Such projects have used a variety of fieldwork techniques and methods of analysis, including the Labovian sociolinguistic interview (see e.g. Poplack, Sankoff and Miller (1988),

Sankoff and Thibault (1980)), the directed interview (e.g. Coveney (1996)), and participant observation (e.g. Pooley (1994)). There is a considerable literature on sociolinguistic methodology, much of which discusses problematic issues such as gaining access to the vernacular and thus finding the best fieldwork technique, classing speakers for socio-economic status and analysing data (in particular the analysis of syntactic variables).[36]

The patterning of linguistic variables across social groupings, however the latter are defined, interacts in complex ways with register. In fact, explanations of traditional classifications of register in French, such as that given in Section 1.2.2 above, frequently make reference to different speaker groups, as is implicit in labels such as *français populaire*. We shall draw on the findings of a number of sociolinguistic surveys in Part II.

Variationists examine how linguistic change occurs in different ways. One is to compare corpora over time, which is an extension of traditional historical methods, but using data collected by methods such as those outlined above. This can obviously only be done in very long-term studies, or in studies which compare findings based on contemporary data to analyses of corpora collected some time previously, as Hansen (1994) did, for example, in her study of schwa (see Chapter 3). Alternatively, change can be studied in **apparent time**, that is, by examining the patterning of variation across age groups (**age-grading**) to see if there is any indication of **change in progress**, on the assumption that some of the innovative patterns characterizing the speech of younger age groups at a given point in time will be retained in their speech as they get older and thus spread across the speech community over time. The concept of change in progress is examined with reference to /l/ deletion in clitics and to *ne* deletion (see Chapter 11) by Ashby (1991), who concludes that the age-graded patterns in his data are consistent with their reflecting changes which will progress over **real time**. However, as he points out, a degree of caution needs to be exercized in interpreting these sorts of findings, which must always eventually be tested in real time, since it could be the case that certain patterns will not be retained by younger speakers as they get older.[37]

Change is also observable as it progresses across the linguistic system, a phenomenon of which linguists were already aware before the advent of Labovian sociolinguistics. Gilliéron is famously said to have stated that, 'chaque mot a son histoire' (Malkiel 1967:138), by which he was partly referring to the fact that phonetic changes do not necessarily occur regularly and without exception, as claimed by the nineteenth-century Neogrammarians, but rather progress, as it were, from word to word. This progression is known as the **lexical diffusion** of a sound change, and it appears to be playing a role in changes affecting the behaviour of schwa in French, as we shall see in Part II, Chapter 3. The rate and route of diffusion of a sound change through the lexicon can be affected by a number of factors, including the frequency of occurrence of the lexical items concerned.

3.6   National French approaches

In the course of our overview of approaches and schools we have mentioned a number of French scholars whose work falls within the broad headings of structuralist, generative, typological, pragmatic, or variationist approaches. In this final section, we will focus on two French schools on which we will draw in Part II and which are independent of any of the traditions so far discussed. Moreover, while both are well-known and well-represented within France, neither could be said to have international currency.

3.6.1   Guillaume and the Guillaumeans

Whilst Gustave Guillaume's (1883–1960) work falls very broadly within the structuralist tradition, it is concerned above all with the semantic content of grammatical classes. Perhaps its most striking feature is its complexity: the abstractness of Guillaume's thought, the heavy dependence on intuition and the difficulty of his terminology combine to make it relatively inaccessible to the uninitiated, a fact which perhaps explains why Guillaumean linguistics has had limited influence outside France and Belgium.

Guillaume's theory is a 'psycho-systematic' or 'psycho-mechanical' one: he starts by considering how man uses language to try to master the universe and thus is preoccupied with the operations of thought. For Guillaume, thought is not static, but in a state of flux; for this thought to be expressed in language it must be delimited, which is achieved by what Guillaume terms *coupes*. Meaning is defined in kinetic terms: for instance, the movement from the universal to the particular is used to help explain French determiners. The different movements of thought combine to form a system (*la langue*); the passage is made to *discours* by a second series of *coupes* which stop the movement of thought at a given point: whether this *coupe* is made at an earlier or later stage determines the value of the sign. To take the example of the indefinite article *un*, if the *coupe* is made relatively early in the movement of thought then *un* will have a generalizing value, whereas a later 'cut' will give a particularizing reading. In this sense, the model is chronogenetic, since a spatio-temporal model is employed. This allows Guillaume to differentiate, for example, different verb forms. An early intervention gives quasi-nominal forms such as the infinitive or participles (*temps in posse*), a later interruption gives the subjunctive (*temps in fieri*), whilst a cut at the furthest extreme gives the tenses of the indicative (*temps in esse*). We shall return to this in some detail in Chapter 5.

A number of linguists in France and Belgium have adopted a Guillaumean approach, particularly those interested in the semantics of grammatical categories. Of note here is the work of Martin (1971, 1983) on aspect and on negatives, of Wilmet (1991, 1995) on aspect, and of Stéfanini (1962) on pronominal verbs.

3.6.2   L'Approche pronominale

The *Approche pronominale* has been developed by the linguists connected with the *Groupe Aixois de Recherche en Syntaxe* (GARS), the key work being Blanche-Benveniste and others (1984). It is an approach to syntax which has been applied primarily to the GARS corpus of spoken French. It rejects the traditional notion of the sentence as the basic syntactic unit, a notion which is seen as inappropriate in the case of the spoken language, where high levels of truncation, repetition, circularity etc. are evident. Rather, in identifying the syntactic function of the various elements in the verb phrase, the *Approche pronominale* looks to **proportionality** with a pronoun. Thus in the following example the noun phrase *à mon père* has proportionality with the pronoun *lui*:

(35)   J'ai voulu la demander à mon père (Blanche-Benveniste and others 1990:41).

The elements governed by the verb (*à mon père*) would thus be referred to as being of the '*type lui*'. In other cases, the proportionality may be '*type en*', '*type ça*' etc. depending on the pronoun concerned. For instance, the elements governed by the verb in the following example (*à Paris*) would have proportionality with the pronoun *y*:

(36)   Il travaille à Paris (il y travaille).

The types of pronouns (or 'proforms') involved include clitics, direct and indirect object pronouns, *y*, *en*, forms such as *là, ainsi, cela, ça, quoi, où, quelque chose, personne, nulle part*, some of which (e.g. *ainsi*) do not fall traditionally into the class of pronouns (for a full list, see Blanche-Benveniste and others 1990:42). In practice, the governed slot in the phrase, of whichever pronominal type, can be filled by a variety of lexical elements. Blanche-Benveniste and others (1990:43) cite the following four possibilities for the '*type ainsi*':

(37)   **Comment** elle faisait son pot-au-feu
       Comme ma femme elle le faisait
       Elle a toujours fait le pot-au-feu **comme on le fait**
       Elle a toujours fait le pot-au-feu **naturel**.

In other words, all four examples would be possible cases of proportionality with the pronoun *ainsi*. Moreover, although the elements governed by the verb have proportionality with only one pronominal type, the slot in the sentence which corresponds to the pronoun may be filled several times in a given context by different lexical items. In the following example, a *type ça* slot is filled twice by two different lexical items, which can be represented in a paradigmatic list:

(38)   Je lui apprenais $\begin{Bmatrix} \text{à lire} \\ \text{à écrire} \end{Bmatrix}$

Note that elements appearing in the pronominal slots are normally said to be **governed** by the verb; those which are not only governed by the verb but also form part of the basic syntax of the verb in question are further said to form part of its **valency**.[38] For example, in (39) (adapted from Blanche-Benveniste and others 1990:44), both the subject (*ils*) and the complement (*à cette démarche*; *type y*) are part of the valency of the verb *répondre* which takes a subject and an indirect object:

(39)   Ils ont fini par répondre avec beaucoup d'humour à cette démarche.

On the other hand, the adverbial expression *avec beaucoup d'humour* (*type ainsi*), while part of the verb phrase in this particular example, is not part of the verb's valency, since it is an 'optional extra' and not part of the basic syntactic properties of *répondre*.

The *Approche pronominale* has the advantage of making a clear syntactic distinction between constructions which look alike but which are syntactically different (Blanche-Benveniste and others 1990:41), for example:

(40)   Je parle à son frère (*type lui*)

(41)   Je pense à son frère (*type y, à lui*).

On the other hand, constructions which are syntactically similar but where selection restrictions mean that one is acceptable and the other is not, are classified correctly in the same syntactic category (1990:41), for instance:

(42)   On va jeter cette eau

(43)   *On va jeter cette montagne.

We shall see in Chapter 9 that the *Approche pronominale* is able to shed light on the analysis of certain types of syntactic construction, such as left and right dislocation (where both the pronoun and the corresponding noun are usually present), and on the definition of subordination (Chapter 10), where notions of governance and dependency are crucial and where the pronominal proportionality plays a key role in determining the nature of the relations between a verb and potentially dependent elements.

Section 4

Choice of topics and approaches

The choice of issues and approaches covered in Part II is necessarily selective and, to some extent, personal. Three major considerations have, however, guided our choice and presentation of topics.

First, the aim has always been to examine problematic issues and to evaluate different approaches rather than to offer a descriptive account of the structures of French. For example, in Chapter 6 the focus is on the difficulties of analysing the complex relationship between the use of the *passé simple* and *passé composé*. Similarly, in the field of lexis, we have avoided simple elaboration of the processes of creating new words; rather, we have concentrated on problematic issues, such as the definition of, and interaction between, 'internal' and 'external' resources (see Chapter 12) as well as questions raised by the application of 'internal' creative processes in Modern French (see Chapter 13).

Second, we have selected topics which enable us to examine wider issues – such as the question of abstractness in phonology (e.g. Chapter 3) or the definition and classification of categories (see Chapters 4, 8, 10) – or to contrast different approaches. For instance, Chapter 5 on Aspect raises the important question as to whether it is possible, or indeed desirable, to describe French as an idealized system, or whether it is preferable to adopt a discourse-pragmatic approach, where the emphasis is on language in use. A number of chapters can then be viewed as case studies, which raise major issues which recur in the analysis of French, such as what the relationship is between variation and change (Chapter 3), or between written and spoken French (Chapter 4); how the non-standard is to be accounted for in a linguistic description (Chapter 10), or the extent to which a unified description of a linguistic category can be offered (Chapters 7 and 8). Wherever possible we have tried to examine the validity of generalizations commonly made about the French language. An obvious case is the claim that French favours the word order pattern Subject–Verb–Object, a claim which is investigated in Chapter 9.

Third, in reviewing the literature available on the contemporary French language, particularly that in English, it became clear that less material of the type we envisaged was available in the field of morphosyntax. Eight of our thirteen chapters (Chapters 4–11) are therefore devoted to this domain. We have selected a number of morphosyntactic topics which are currently widely debated in the literature, with particular emphasis on verb morphology and usage (Chapters 4–8), word order, clause types and clausal connections (Chapters 9–11). Lexis, on the other hand, lends itself particularly to descriptive accounts, and since there are a number of recent surveys available, such as Wise (1997), we have devoted less space to lexical issues. As regards phonology, the issues we have chosen to address in detail are those which have received particular attention from generative and post-generative phonologists, but, as will be clear in Chapters 1–3, this does not mean that they have not also been of interest to phonologists of other schools.

Notes

1. Throughout the book cross-references to Part II are made as follows: the number in bold refers to the number of the chapter and the following numbers to the appropriate section or subsection.
2. Work by Labov and others on English suggests conversely that women are innovative in their usage (e.g. Labov 1990).
3. We shall not be making comparisons between the articulations of similar sounds in French and English, details of which can be found in, *inter alia*, Price (1991). We shall also not be considering sound-spelling correspondences, for which the reader is referred to Chapter 2 of Battye and Hintze (1992) and to Léon (1978).
4. In polysyllabic words and in running speech, the following principles can be taken to indicate when sequences of adjacent consonants belong to the same branching coda or onset or whether they belong to different syllables: if the final consonant of the cluster is a liquid (see below), then both consonants belong to the onset of the syllable whose nucleus is the following vowel, as in [ta.blo] (*tableau*). If the final consonant of the sequence is not a liquid, the first consonant belongs to the coda of the syllable whose nucleus is the preceding vowel as in [paʁ.tiʁ].
5. We shall henceforth mark syllabification only when pertinent to the current topic, for example in Chapter 1 below.
6. The non-standard variants of /r/, i.e. [ʀ] and [r], are also included in brackets for reference.
7. The full alphabet is widely available, including, for example, in Laver (1994:593) and in the *Handbook of the International Phonetic Association* (1999). Labelled diagrams of the vocal tract showing the articulators involved for

each place of articulation are also widely available; see, for example, Battye and Hintze (1992:79), Price (1991:15), Tranel (1987a:19). These works also give detailed descriptions of voicing and manner of articulation.

8. They are also sometimes referred to as palatal, although they are articulated much further forward in the mouth than sounds which the IPA would classify as palatal.

9. The term 'semiconsonants' is also used, although less frequently than the other two.

10. We follow the common convention of using the symbol /r/ in **broad** transcriptions, that is, those enclosed by slashes, reserving the symbol [ʁ] for **narrow** transcriptions, that is, those enclosed by square brackets. The significance of these two types of transcription is explained in Section 3.2.1 below.

11. For example, Martinet's (1960) account reserves the term *morphème* for grammatical units (such as *-ons*, *-ez*), as opposed to lexical units (termed *lexèmes*); the term *monème* is employed as the term which covers both of these (see Section 3.2.2).

12. Note that *être* has fewer written forms than a regular *-er* verb because it only has one form for the past participle (*été*), whereas there are four for the regular *-er* verb (e.g. *chanté, chantée, chantés, chantées*).

13. As a result, the unstressed personal pronoun plays a crucial role in the marking of the person of the verb. Note that the plural marker *-s* of *ils* and *elles* typically has no phonetic realization, except when forms appear in a phonetic environment where liaison is appropriate: for example *il avait* [ilavε], *ils avaient* [ilzavε]; *il avait été* [ilavεtete], *ils avaient été* [ilzavεtete], etc.

14. **Deictic** is the adjective related to **deixis**, the term applied to linguistic elements which locate discourse in time and space, for instance adverbials such as *ici, là, maintenant*, pronouns such as *je, il, celle-ci*, and tenses.

15. Definitions of the active voice which speak of the grammatical subject as the agent (i.e. the semantic role indicating who or what is responsible for, or instigates, the action) can be problematic (Vassant 1980:143), since the active may, for example, indicate the state of the subject, as in *J'ai une migraine épouvantable*, or an action undergone by the subject: *Il a reçu un coup fatal*.

16. Note that not all passives are simple paraphrases of an active sentence. Even in (8) and (9) we may note a change in the focus of the sentence (see Chapter 8).

17. Note also that in (11), the selection restrictions which apply to the verb *voir* (i.e. the fact that the subject must be animate) are also satisfied. The sentence **la Tour Eiffel a vu mon frère* would not be acceptable.

18. The symbol * indicates that an example is ungrammatical.

19. Substitution involves the replacement of one term by another in the text; ellipsis involves the omission of an element; anaphora involves reference within the text by one linguistic element to another.

20. For examples of such surveys, see the discussion in Müller (1985:66–7).

21. For a detailed study of these processes, including their history and a long list of examples, see George (1980).

22. For a discussion of the terms, as well as *abréviation* and *abrègement* see Calvet (1980:6–7), Mortureux (1994:11) and Germain and Lapierre (1988).
23. The term 'neutralization' was first coined by Trubetzkoy. See Chapter 3 of Lass (1980) for further discussion of the concept.
24. Note that Martinet's use of terminology is different; see note 11 above and Section 3.2.2 below.
25. The exceptions to this are the limited number of cases where allophones occur in so-called **free variation**, that is, where the choice between them is determined by stylistic or sociolinguistic factors. For example, the choice between allophones of /r/ in French depends partly on the regional background of the speaker. Note that the choice of allophone does not affect the meaning of the word, that is, they are not contrastive.
26. This problem is also addressed by Martinet. For example, in the case of *nous travaillons*, he maintains that the *signifié*, 'first person plural' is represented discontinuously by /nu/ and /ɔ̃/ (Martinet 1960:101).
27. Note that there is considerable variation in the terminology and abbreviations used by different linguists and in different versions of the model, but that they are not relevant to the discussion here.
28. This is a simplified version of the rule, ignoring any auxiliary, based on Kayne (1975:115).
29. The semantic and phonological components are considered to be 'interpretative' since it is claimed that the rules of these components require syntactic information to operate on. For discussion of this, see Horrocks (1987:28–30).
30. 'D' here stands for determiner.
31. These are phoneme-like units.
32. Autosegmental phonology works by conventions rather than rules, but the difference is not pertinent in this case.
33. That is, not linked together in linear sequence.
34. See McMahon (1994, Chapter 6) for a discussion of typological approaches.
35. It is important to note that variation and change are also of central importance to Martinet, but there are certain crucial differences between his approach and that of Labovian variationists. For further details see Labov (1972).
36. For a summary of the issues and further references, see Milroy (1987).
37. Thus, for example, by the time Hansen's younger subjects are aged between 40 and 55, they may well be producing the same patterns of schwa pronunciation in conversational speech as her current 40- to 55-year-olds. In that case, the patterns observed in the 1994 study will be seen to represent stable age-grading rather than change in progress.
38. See Section 3.2.3 above for Tesnière's use of the term.

Part

II

Issues

1

Word-final consonants

1.1   Introduction

The individual consonants of French pose relatively few problems for the phonologist: with a few exceptions their phonemic status can generally be established without difficulty, and they have regularly alternating allophones, as outlined in Part I, Section 2.1.3. However, the consonants as a class do pose a major problem for phonologists when they occur word-finally. It is not difficult to find examples of word-final consonants (WFCs): the words *cerise, sept, sur, sac, arbre, table, gomme, rouge, tête* and *coude* all end phonetically in consonants, whether voiced, voiceless, fricative, occlusive, nasal or liquid. These consonants are always pronounced, forming the coda of the final syllable of the word when it is spoken in isolation or phrase-finally, and undergoing *enchaînement* to become the onset of the following syllable when immediately followed by a word beginning with a vowel (see Part I, Section 2.1.1). Some of the words listed end in clusters of up to three consonants, others in a single consonant. However, with other words it is less clear whether there is a WFC at all; for example *petit* in *le petit garçon* ([ləpətigaʁsɔ̃]) has no final consonant, despite its orthography, whereas in *le petit homme* ([ləpətitɔm]) it has one, and that final [t] forms the onset of the last syllable of the string. This variable pronunciation of WFCs before word-initial vowels is known as **liaison**, and provides a fertile field for phonological study. It is possible to trace the history of this behaviour, and to account for it historically, by appealing to universal phonetic principles; accounting for what goes on in contemporary French is a more difficult task.

After an overview of the problems WFCs pose synchronically, we shall examine in turn some of the proposed solutions and attempt to assess their adequacy. In the course of this examination it will become evident that the issues raised by WFCs in French have important implications which reach beyond the detail of phonological analyses to general theoretical and methodological questions, such as how different parts of the grammar relate to each other, and what sort of data need to be taken into account in theoretical analyses.[1]

1.2 The problem in detail

The consonants which occur word-finally in words such as those listed above pose no immediately obvious problem for synchronic phonology. Given the phonetic string:

(1)   [lasəʁizʁuʒ syʁlatabloʁɑ̃ʒ][2]

we can, without too much difficulty (setting aside for the moment the question of the status of some of the vowels in these words), posit a phonemic string:

(2)   /lasərizruʒ syrlatablorɑ̃ʒ/[3]

and can identify the words /la/, /səriz/, /ruʒ/, /syr/, /la/, /tabl/, /orɑ̃ʒ/. The consonants at the ends of the words *cerise, rouge, sur, table* and *orange* are all fixed, that is they are always pronounced. The problems arise where this is not the case, that is when the same word is pronounced sometimes with, and sometimes without, a final consonant.[4] For example, if the red cherry of (1) is a small one, we might encounter the phonetic string:

(3)   [lapətitsəʁizʁuʒ syʁlatabloʁɑ̃ʒ]

It would be dangerous, however, to conclude that the new word was /pətit/, since we know that there is a word with the same meaning and function in the string:

(4)   [ləpətigaʁsɔ̃]

The examination of further occurrences of the word *petit* will show that there are two singular surface forms: [pəti], which occurs before masculine nouns beginning with consonants and at the end of a rhythmic group, and [pətit], which occurs before masculine nouns beginning with vowels and in agreement with all feminine nouns, whatever the position of the adjective. It is possible to offer an historical explanation of the variable presence of [t], but given that speakers of a language do not have an innate knowledge of the history of their language, a synchronic account of the phonology of this word is problematic: where does the final consonant come from, and how do speakers know when to pronounce *petit* with a final [t] or without? In the case of [pətitsɐʁiz] versus [pətigaʁsɔ̃], the difference is clearly a grammatical one; in the case of [pətigaʁsɔ̃] versus [pətitɔm], the selection of one form rather than the other is phonologically determined, depending on whether the following word begins with a vowel or a consonant.

The focus of this chapter will be on the latter type of alternation, that is, so-called **liaison consonants**. Whereas all the consonants of French can occur in word-final position, liaison involves only a subset of these: [t, z, n, ʁ, p, k, v], with [t] and [z] the most commonly concerned, and [v] only occurring in the strings *neuf ans* and *neuf heures*. We shall use the term 'liaison consonants' to refer to these seven consonants where they occur variably in a given word, but refer to WFCs as 'fixed consonants' elsewhere; thus [t] in *vite* is a fixed consonant because the word is always pronounced [vit], but [t] at the end of *petit* is a liaison consonant, because the word is pronounced variably as described above.

As well as being restricted to certain consonants, liaison is restricted to certain syntactic contexts: it never occurs, for example, after a singular noun or proper noun (e.g. [ʒɑ̃atɑ̃] (*Jean attend*), never *[ʒɑ̃natɑ̃]), or after *on* and *en* in inverted structures (e.g. [vatɔ̃eseje] (*va-t-on essayer?*), never *[vatɔ̃neseje]). By contrast, the liaison consonant [z] always appears when a plural determiner is followed by a noun beginning with a vowel ([lezami], [dezɑ̃fɑ̃], never *[leami], *[deɑ̃fɑ̃]). In other contexts, the possible liaison consonant may or may not be pronounced, its occurrence being determined by speaker choice according to the formality of the situation. A list of the main contexts where liaison is impossible, 'obligatory' and optional can be found in Table 2.33 of Battye and Hintze (1992:138).

The necessity of incorporating this syntactic information into an account of the behaviour of WFCs adds a further complication to the task: speakers must be integrating both syntactic and phonological information in order to know, for example, that *les hommes* must always be pronounced [lezɔm], whereas *les chats intelligents* can be pronounced either [leʃaɛ̃teliʒɑ̃] or [leʃazɛ̃teliʒɑ̃], and *donnez-en à Jean* is never pronounced *[dɔnezɑ̃naʒɑ̃] even though *en* is pronounced [ɑ̃n] in *j'en ai pris deux*. They must, in addition, be accessing sociolinguistic information in order to decide the appropriateness of a given pronunciation to a given situation when the liaison is optional. We shall return to these issues in 1.5 and 1.6 below.

We have established, then, that liaison is a multifaceted phenomenon with complex behaviour. However, the most basic question posed at the beginning of this section remains, and is by no means easy to address: how does the linguist decide, when confronted with the data in (3) and (4), what is the underlying phonological form of the word *petit*? As will become clear, liaison cannot be taken in isolation; it is also necessary to take into account the behaviour of fixed final consonants. Moreover, because of the way the issue of WFCs interacts with other issues concerning word juncture, we shall also be touching on word-final [ə].

1.3   Orthographically based accounts of liaison

Many of the general descriptions of the phonetics of French before the
1960s (and many written since then) were normative in purpose and, explicitly
or implicitly, took as their starting point for the description of liaison the
written forms of words. For example, Armstrong's chapter on liaison begins:

> Many French words ending in a consonant letter have two pronunciations,
> one in which the final consonant letter has no sound-value, and the other
> in which it has [. . .] The pronunciation which words ending in a conso-
> nant letter have in isolation and before a word beginning with a vowel
> sound may be called the *normal* form. The pronunciation which words
> ending in a consonant letter have *in certain cases* before a word beginning
> with a vowel sound may be called the *liaison* form (Armstrong 1932:159,
> her italics).

This is by far the easiest way to describe the phenomenon, but it is not a
very satisfactory approach from a linguistic point of view, since our aim is to
account for the patterns acquired by native speakers of French, rather than
patterns painstakingly learned by foreigners, who often take the written form
as their point of departure. In the following discussion of liaison, we shall
avoid reference to spelling where possible; sound–spelling correspondences
may be found, for example, in Léon (1978:121).

Indeed, some of the complexity of the problem can be eliminated from
the start by avoiding reference to orthography. Consider the following case
of 'impossible liaison', involving the conjunction *et*:

(5)   Avant et après le repas
       [avãeapʁelʁəpa].

Et is never pronounced with a consonant at the end, nor is the noun *thé*,
which ends in the same vowel; however, whereas the former might be cited
as an example of 'impossible liaison' the latter never is, simply because
there is no written consonant following the final vowel. If the orthographic
difference between the two words is ignored, there is no reason to treat
them phonologically as ending differently, since a phonological analysis is
concerned with the functioning of the sound system, rather than rules for
learning to read: one can simply represent *et*, and other cases of 'impossible
liaison', as ending in a vowel, just as *thé* does, and thus the specification that
et does not enter into liaison is redundant. In other words, although the
observation that the orthographic final consonant of *et* is never pronounced
in liaison is useful pedagogically, it is not necessary to incorporate it into a
purely linguistic model of WFCs.

1.4 Theoretical accounts of word-final consonants

1.4.1 The phonemic perspective

The basic question posed by WFCs for a phonemic analysis is whether liaison consonants should figure in the phonemic representation of lexemes or not. The fact that the presence versus absence of [t] in *petit* does not change the identity of the word suggests that it should not. However, if the phonemic representation of the word is /pəti/, there is no way of predicting from the phonological context either that there is a prevocalic consonantal allophone (compare *joli homme*, where there never is) or that this consonant will be [t].

A possible solution – which is the way Martinet deals with other examples of morphemes with more than one form (for example verb stems) – would be to list two forms in the lexicon for *petit*, /pəti/ and /pətit/, and to do the same for all other words with liaison forms. This is treating liaison as suppletive morphology and is the solution outlined by Carton (1974:88): 'Le mot *voit* a donc deux formes orales: /vwat/ et /vwa/, cette dernière pouvant être considérée comme la variante de la première devant consonne'. It is not entirely satisfactory for two main reasons. First, it is uneconomical and increases the size of the lexicon considerably (since each lexeme with a liaison consonant then has two allomorphs). Second, it implicitly accords the word-final /t/ a significant status in this word (as does the inclusion of /t/ in the phonemic representation), which is hard to justify, since the presence of the consonant is not contrastive; rather it is merely a phonetic phenomenon which occurs in predictable phonological contexts (i.e. something akin to the non-distinctive occurrence of assimilatory voicing in [k̬]). Another alternative is to 'tag' each word in the lexicon which has liaison forms with the appropriate consonant, but this is again a solution which complicates the lexicon.

1.4.2 Generative phonology

1.4.2.1 Abstract generative phonology

The study universally acknowledged as initiating the theoretical debates around liaison in the generative tradition is Schane (1968). Schane, and others who followed in his wake, for example Dell (1973), postulated that the underlying forms of words with liaison consonants included representations of those consonants, which were then deleted when they were followed with words beginning with consonants or before a pause. While this idea was not unique to generative phonology, it was within generative phonology that it was most fully developed.

A version of Schane's 'truncation rule' is given here as (6), where '#' represents a word boundary, the curly brackets mean that either one or the other of the environments within them applies, and '‖' represents a pause:

(6) $\begin{bmatrix} +\text{cons} \\ -\text{voc} \end{bmatrix} \rightarrow \emptyset / \underline{\quad} \# \begin{Bmatrix} \| \\ [+\text{cons}] \end{Bmatrix}$

The rule states that non-liquid consonants are deleted word-finally before segments which contain the feature [+consonantal] (i.e. all consonants) or before a pause. This is apparently a very elegant solution which obviates the need to find an explanation for how speakers know that the phonetic liaison consonant of *petit* is [t], because the consonant is present in the underlying representation. Versions of the derivations of a liaison consonant followed by a vowel and by a consonant are given in (7a) and (7b) respectively[5]:

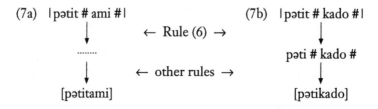

(7a) |pətit # ami #|

← Rule (6) →

[pətitami]

(7b) |pətit # kado #|

pəti # kado #

← other rules →

[pətikado]

The inclusion of /t/ in a phonemic representation of *petit* was rejected in 1.4.1 above because [t] ~ zero alternation is demonstrably not phonemic. This objection carries less weight in abstract generative phonology, since the aim is to identify a single underlying form for each morpheme; thus the root morphemes of *petit* and *petite* share the same representation (whereas in a phonemic account they need to be different). In fact, including /t/ in the underlying representation is a positive advantage, since it allows gender agreement in adjectives to be accounted for with the same rule as the one which models liaison, with a minor adjustment to make it apply across morpheme boundaries as well as word boundaries. Thus, the underlying representations of the masculine and feminine forms of *petit(e)* would be |pətit + <zero>| and |pətit + ə|, which would surface as [pəti] and [pətit] respectively (following the application of an additional rule to delete the feminine schwa).[6]

However, there remains a problem, in that rule (6) is too general: as pointed out in 1.2 above, liaison only involves a subset of consonants; moreover, some of these are only deleted in a restricted set of circumstances. For example, /r/ is in fact deleted, contrary to the prediction of rule (6), which excludes liquids, but only when preceded by /e/: *le premier chat* ([ləpʁəmjeʃa]), but *choisir le chat* ([ʃwaziʁləʃa]). This problem does not invalidate the approach of using deletion, but suggests that the rule needs to be refined. One solution would be to replace it with a series of rules for each of the series of consonants concerned, which would require one for the obstruents which are deleted (/p, t, d, s/), one for /r/ following /e/, one for /j/ following /i/ and one for /k/ and /g/ following nasal vowels. Schane (1973:825) outlines the rules and exceptions that would be necessary, and concludes that 'the picture turns out to be far from pretty', since several rules are required to express essentially the same phenomenon, some of which are phonologically unmotivated, such as the grouping of /p/, /t/, /d/ and /s/, which do not form a natural class amongst the obstruents. His conclusion is that the general truncation rule (as in (6) above) should be maintained to express the generality of the principle, but with constraints specifying the exceptional cases to which it does not apply; this could be formulated as in (8) (Schane 1973:827), which is a shorthand way of saying 'the deletion rule does not apply to /k/, /b/, /g/, /f/, /v/ or /z/':

(8)   k, b, g, f, v, z → [−deletion rule].

A further constraint is then necessary in this case to specify that the rule does apply exceptionally to /k/ and /g/ when they follow a nasal vowel, as in *un long été* [œ̃lɔ̃kete].

This solution, while maintaining the apparent generality of the deletion process, is itself far from 'pretty' once all the constraints are specified. Moreover, a further major problem remains in that rule (6) would delete the final /t/ of *net*, *huit* and *gîte* as well as that of *petit*. Since the preceding phonological context is the same in *huit* and *gîte* as in *petit*, a constraint cannot be formulated on a phonological basis, and another solution has to be found. For *net* and *huit*, the only solution is to specify these particular lexical items as [−deletion rule]; this again detracts somewhat from the simplicity promised by the original rule, but the complication is held to be minor since there are a limited number of cases.[7] The solution for consonants in words like *gîte*, *vide*, *pipe*, and *vice* is to 'protect' them with a following underlying schwa vowel, which prevents the deletion rule applying (since the following context is then a vowel rather than a word boundary followed by a consonant). Their underlying representations are therefore |ʒitə|, |vidə|, |pipə| and |visə|.

The obvious question posed by this solution is whether there is any independent justification for the presence of this vowel other than its protective role and its historical existence, and why words specified as [−deletion rule] cannot simply be assigned a protective schwa. A possible answer is that the [ə] does sometimes surface, namely before *h-aspiré*, as in *la pipe haïtienne* ([lapipəaisjɛn]) or *le camarade hargneux* ([ləkamaʁadəaʁɲø]). Yet even before *h-aspiré* its appearance is by no means regular. For cases where the [ə] does not appear in the surface form, it is necessary to posit a rule to delete it, which must always be applied after the consonant deletion rule (otherwise there will be nothing to prevent the deletion of the consonant). A possible derivation of the word *pipe*, with a 'protected' fixed final consonant is given in (9).

(9) |pipə # blø #|

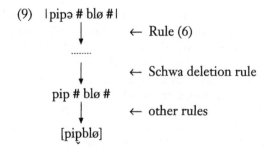

In short, when the abstract deletion account of liaison works, it provides an apparently elegant answer to the problem of accounting for how speakers know both when to pronounce liaison consonants, and which consonant to pronounce for which word. However, when the complexities of the whole picture are taken into account, the analysis turns out to be less simple than might have been hoped, necessitating either a series of apparently unrelated rules, or various constraints to delimit the application of the basic rule, as well as the expedient of a 'protective' underlying schwa and the treatment of some lexemes as exceptions.[8] We now turn to the major alternative linear generative approach.

1.4.2.2   Concrete generative phonology

While Schane and others espoused the deletion account of liaison, other linguists were exploring the logically opposite possibility, an insertion account, which can be expressed as in (10):

(10) $\emptyset \rightarrow C /\_\_ V$

A major advantage of this approach is that the problem of fixed final consonants created by the deletion account simply disappears: fixed consonants appear in the underlying representation (there is no reason for them not to), and require neither a protective schwa nor being specified as exceptions to an over-general rule.

The two linguists most closely associated with this account of liaison are Klausenburger (e.g. 1974, 1984) and Tranel (e.g. 1981). They worked on the phenomenon independently, but at the same time and within the same theoretical framework, namely the offshoot of generative phonology known as 'Natural generative phonology'. With rule (10), however, the original problem, which the deletion account seemed to have resolved, re-surfaces, namely how a speaker knows when to insert a consonant and which consonant to insert. Klausenburger at one point calls this a 'pseudo-problem' (1978:28, n.3), arguing that it is possible to appeal to morphological facts such as the alternation between the root forms of *petit* and *petite* or *petitesse* to supply that information. This, of course, presupposes that the model has a satisfactory account of where the [t] in *petitesse* comes from, and that all the forms which undergo liaison also enter into these morphological alternations involving the same consonant, which is not always the case. For example, *grand*, whose liaison consonant is [t] (cf. *grand ami*, [gʁɑ̃tami]), takes a root-final [d] when entering into inflection or derivation (cf. *grande*, [gʁɑ̃d]; *grandeur* [gʁɑ̃dœʁ]).

Tranel, by contrast, goes into the mechanism of insertion in some detail, exploiting the variable distribution of liaison in different grammatical contexts to help provide the correct consonant. He divides liaison words into several different categories: plural forms; verbs, of which there are three sub-categories; masculine singular adjectives; and 'invariable' words (e.g. prepositions). For the first two of these categories, there is in fact little or no choice of liaison consonant: the only plural linking consonant is [z], conjugated verb forms can only link with [t] or [z], and infinitival verb forms can only link with [ʁ]. Thus both the major problems – how the speaker knows when to insert a consonant and how s/he knows which consonant to insert – are answered by including reference to the syntax in the insertion rule. Examples (12a) and (12b) illustrate Tranel's formalization of insertion rules for plural verb liaison, which relate to the phrases in (11a) and (11b) respectively[9]:

(11a)   nous arriverons ensemble [nuzaʁivʁɔ̃(z)ɑ̃sɑ̃bl]
vous chantiez encore [vuʃɑ̃tje(z)ɑ̃kɔʁ]

(11b)   ils arrivent ensemble [ilzaʁiv(t)ɑ̃sɑ̃bl]
elles chantèrent encore [ɛlʃɑ̃tɛʁ(t)ɑ̃kɔʁ]

(12a)
$$\left. \begin{array}{c} X \\ \end{array} \right] V \begin{bmatrix} -\text{third person} \\ +\text{plural} \end{bmatrix} \qquad \# \qquad [+\text{syll}]$$

$$1 \qquad\qquad 2 \qquad 3 \;\Rightarrow\; 1 \; 2 \; z \; 2 \; 3$$

(12b)
$$\left. \begin{array}{c} X \\ \end{array} \right] V \begin{bmatrix} +\text{third person} \\ +\text{plural} \end{bmatrix} \qquad \# \qquad [+\text{syll}]$$

$$1 \qquad\qquad 2 \qquad 3 \;\Rightarrow\; 1 \; 2 \; t \; 2 \; 3$$

These transformational rules appear rather daunting, but they are in fact quite simple to read. 1 represents the context immediately preceding the position to be occupied by the liaison consonant, in this case a verb (X]V), which is marked by the syntax as being first- or second-person plural (in (12a)) or third person plural (in (12b)). It is followed by a word boundary (numbered 2), which is in turn followed by a vowel ([+syll], numbered 3). The rule transforms the sequence of these three elements (1-2-3) into a sequence 1-2-z/t-2-3, that is the verb, followed by a word boundary, followed by an inserted [z] or [t], followed by another word boundary, followed by the vowel.[10] The answer to the question of how the speaker knows which consonant to insert lies, then, in the syntax: if the word is a first- or second-person plural verb, the consonant will be [z], if it is third person plural, it will be [t].

This type of rule works equally well for the other verb contexts, but unfortunately once again what appears initially to be a relatively simple solution to the problem of liaison proves to be more complex when the whole range of possible contexts is examined. Masculine singular adjectives do not behave uniformly as a class with respect to which liaison consonant they take, so the consonant cannot here be identified with reference to the syntax, as with the verbs. Tranel adopts a solution suggested by Schane (1978), and proposes marking the lexical entries of adjectives which enter into liaison with the relevant liaison consonant, as in (13) (after Tranel 1981:238):

(13)	*joli*	/ʒɔli/		*long*	/lɔ̃/	(/g/)
	petit	/pəti/	(/t/)	*léger*	/leʒe/	(/r/)
	grand	/grɑ̃/	(/d/)[11]	*certain*	/sɛrtɛ̃/	(/n/)
	gros	/gro/	(/s/)			

Schane (1978) claims that this solution is merely a notational variant of the deletion account, that is, it is a different way of saying the same thing. Tranel argues, however, that there is a 'crucial difference between the insertion and deletion analyses' in that the consonants between brackets in (13) are not part of the phonological representations, but are merely 'idiosyncratic phonological markings' attached to the lexical entries indicating which liaison consonant occurs when the rule of liaison for masculine singular adjectives is applied. It is nevertheless easy to feel some sympathy with Schane's criticism since there appears to be a very fine line between the insertion and deletion accounts at this point.

A similarly unpredictable situation exists with words not involved in inflection or derivation which have liaison consonants, for example, prepositions like *après* or adverbs like *très*. Again no general insertion account is possible and it is necessary to specify which consonant occurs with each individual preposition, adverb, quantifier or pronoun. Thus once again a promising solution to the problems posed by liaison works well for a specific set of cases, but proves less satisfactory when applied to all possible liaison cases.

1.4.3   Non-linear phonology

As Durand (1993a) points out, one of the major problems with linear generative phonology is the absence of reference to the syllable and higher levels of prosodic structure. By contrast, as we saw in Part I, the syllable and links between levels of structure above and below the melodic (i.e. broadly segmental) level are central to non-linear phonological representations, and they have been extremely useful in dealing with French final consonants. In this section, we shall be using representations derived from the basic model shown in Part I, Section 3.3.4, but in order to save space and simplify the figures below as much as possible, parts of the model unnecessary to the particular argument will sometimes be omitted. Note in particular that the presence of 'OR' always implies the presence of 'σ' above, linked to O and R by association lines, as well as the presence of 'N' and optionally 'C' below R.

The crucial fact about non-linear representations so far as French final consonants is concerned is that, although consonants and vowels are normally attached to skeletal slots, they do not have to be attached at all stages. However, they are only pronounced when they are associated to a syllable via a skeletal slot.[12] Consonants which are present in the underlying representation but not associated to a skeletal slot are known as **floating consonants** or **latent consonants**. In this way we can distinguish between the fixed final [t] of *net* and the floating liaison [t] in *petit* as shown in (14a) and (14b):

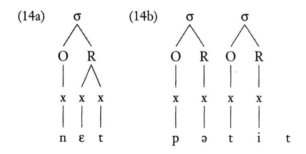

Thus, the problem of which liaison consonant *petit* takes is resolved, since the consonant is present in the underlying representation as it was in the deletion account. The associated problem of disposing of the underlying consonant in non-liaison contexts has also 'disappeared', since the consonant simply will not be pronounced unless it is licensed by being attached to the higher levels of structure.

The remaining issue to be resolved is then of course how the floating consonant 'becomes' licensed, and therefore pronounced, in liaison contexts. This is where reference to syllable structure becomes important. Different branches of non-linear phonology differ in their views of what is the minimum basic syllable structure and how it relates to the skeletal and melodic tiers. However, they all agree that a syllable must consist of at least an onset and a rime (see Part I, Section 2.1.1). Therefore, vowel-initial words like *ami* have onsets at the beginning which are 'empty', that is, not occupied by a consonant or semivowel, as in (15):

(15)

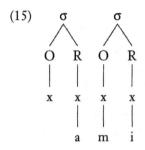

It is this empty onset which is then able to act as the trigger, and the site, for the latent liaison consonant to be linked to the prosodic structure and hence licensed and phonetically realized. This depends on a general principle which states that floating consonants will automatically associate to a following empty onset. Thus if *petit* occurs preceding *ami*, the floating [t] on the melodic tier will automatically project onto the empty X slot, yielding the pronunciation [pətitami], as shown in (16).

(16)

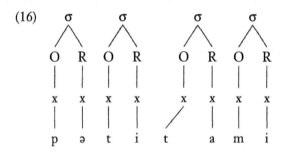

In the case of *petit chat*, however, the following onset is already filled by the first consonant of *chat* and the floating consonant is therefore unable to project onto it and is hence unlicensed and not realized phonetically, as shown in (17):

(17)

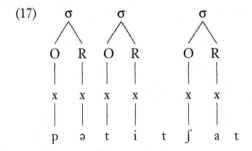

(17) also illustrates how absolute final floating consonants stay silent: a consonant at the end of a string by definition has nothing following it and so has no following onset with which to associate, leaving it without phonetic realization (cf. also (14b) above).

Another phonetic fact captured by this sort of analysis, but not reflected at all in linear generative or pre-generative accounts of liaison, is the *enchaînement* of the liaison consonant. Since *enchaînement* also applies to fixed WFCs, the general principle which motivates liaison can be extended to account for this also, by stating that the preferred syllable structure in French is CV and that any consonant, whether floating or fixed, followed by an empty onset in the same rhythmic group will automatically associate to that onset. In the case of fixed consonants, the consonant is delinked from the coda slot in exactly the same way as the delinking of /d/ from [+voice] in Figure 7 of Part I, Section 3.3.4.

Clearly the relatively simple expedient of making reference to prosodic structure circumvents some of the problems with the linear deletion and insertion accounts of liaison whilst at the same time incorporating facts about *enchaînement* for which there is no place in linear models. However, the incorporation of these facts itself entails problems for the model we have presented, which in turn raise important questions about the components of the prosodic part of the model, since the *enchaînement* of fixed consonants leaves an empty coda slot which needs to be dealt with, as illustrated in (18) for *net* versus *net atout* (for a discussion see particularly Tranel (1995)):

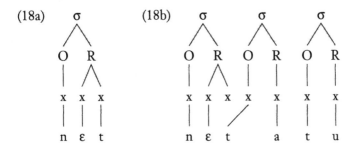

Another more central problem is posed by the example in (17) above: the floating [t] in *chat* is present because of morphological alternations between the masculine form on the one hand and feminine (*chatte*) and diminutive forms (*chaton*) on the other (/ʃa/~/ʃat/~/ʃatɔ̃/). How [t] surfaces in the feminine form in a (phonetic) coda will not concern us here but its appearance in *chaton* is by a similar mechanism as for liaison, that is, by association to the empty onset of the following syllable. The [t] of *chat* does not, however, appear in liaison contexts, which poses the problem of how to prevent it doing so and brings us uncomfortably back to the problem of the linear deletion account, namely how to differentiate between consonants which in the same phonological context behave differently. Thus, although it is generally accepted that non-linear approaches have considerable advantages over either 'abstract' consonant deletion or 'concrete' consonant insertion in accounting for the behaviour of French WFCs, there remain certain unresolved problems.

1.5   Liaison and syntax

The central issue addressed by models of liaison examined hitherto in this chapter has been the basic mechanism for modelling alternations between pronounced consonants and zero, but as stated in **1.2** above, liaison can be both 'obligatory' and 'optional'. A complete model therefore needs to be able to account for how obligatory versus optional liaison is specified, and how optional liaison is governed, that is, under what conditions a liaison consonant is, or is not, pronounced. It is clear that much depends on the syntactic relations between the words involved, for example liaison always occurs between a definite article and a following vowel-initial noun or adjective, as in [lezãfã] (*les enfants*), whereas it does not occur between a verb and a following vowel-initial preposition, as in [vuzjaleãvwatyʁ] (*vous y allez en voiture*).[13] Liaison thus provides a fertile ground for investigating the relationship between phonology and syntax, and within generative grammar there have been various alternative approaches to analysing this relationship. For example, Kaisse (1985) assumes that there is direct interaction between phonological rules and the surface syntactic structure, that is, the phonological rules related to liaison refer not only to the phonological context, but also to the syntactic surface structure in order to determine whether they apply. Selkirk (1986), on the other hand, assumes an intermediate layer of prosodic structure between the surface syntactic structure and the phonetic representation, which defines the domains within which liaison occurs. There are, however, those who would argue against even trying to model the synchronic relationship between the syntax and phonology of liaison, amongst them Morin and Kaye (1982). They argue that the influence of syntax on liaison is mainly a historical rather than a synchronic one, and that its synchronic role is therefore better modelled as far as possible in the morphology rather than by a set of general syntactic principles. This, however, leads, as pointed out by Paradis and El Fenne (1995), to a rather painstaking enumeration of liaison domains.

1.6   Variationist analyses of liaison

It is universally recognised that optional liaison is a phenomenon which is highly dependent on style. Theoretical phonological accounts of liaison incorporate this in terms of optional rules of WFC deletion or insertion, yet few give proposals for what may govern the operation of these optional rules. Selkirk (1980) unusually does incorporate stylistic variability in her model, by positing three levels of style, Style III being the most elevated. Each Style has its own separate grammar, which produces liaison contexts generated by general syntactic rules together with some additional rules known as readjustment rules. In Style I these rules generate only a limited set of liaison contexts. The grammar of Style II contains all the rules of Style I plus an additional set of readjustment rules generating additional liaison contexts, and that of Style III has a further set of rules and thus generates a further set of contexts. This model is still a very abstract one, presenting styles as discrete, albeit cumulative, grammars between which the speaker switches in the same way as s/he might switch from one language to another. As variationist studies have shown clearly, however, style-shifting is a matter of a continuum.

The nature of style-shifting is one area amongst many where variationist studies of liaison have raised questions of more general theoretical import.[14] Studies using empirical methodology are particularly revealing with regard to liaison. Many theoretical studies (and some descriptive ones) are based on introspection, on judgements elicited from native speakers or on their subjects' readings of carefully constructed sentences. Empirical studies of more natural speech have produced evidence that calls into question some of the supposed facts on which the theoretical models are based. For example, Green and Hintze (1988, 1990) showed in pilot studies of data collected in semi-formal interviews and transcribed and quantified according to strict criteria, that although some of the received wisdom is reflected in their results, such as the predominance of /z/, /t/ and /n/ as liaison consonants, much is not. For example, they found, as had Encrevé (1983, 1988), that the pronunciation of a liaison consonant does not always entail its *enchaînement* to the onset of the following vowel. Thus, one speaker pronounced *qui est intermittente* as [ki.ɛt | ʔɛ̃.tɛʁ.mi.tɑ̃t] (where '.' indicates a syllable boundary and '|' a phonetic rhythm group boundary), rather than the expected [ki.ɛ.tɛ̃.tɛʁ.mi.tɑ̃t]. This has serious implications for the non-linear analysis of liaison presented in 1.4.3 above, since the pronunciation of the liaison consonant in this account depends crucially on its projecting onto the onset slot of the following syllable.[15] There were also findings which called into question those of other variationist studies. Obligatory liaison sites were excluded from Ashby's (1981b) study of liaison in Tours speech on the grounds that they were categorical and therefore not of interest to a variationist study. However, Green and Hintze (1990) found that liaison did not always occur at supposedly obligatory sites, which suggests that their exclusion may have led Ashby to miss some potentially very interesting findings. More seriously, they argue that Ashby's results might actually have been distorted in crucial respects by the decision to exclude obligatory liaison.[16]

Other variationist studies have also called into question aspects of the models reviewed in this chapter. Amongst them are Van Ameringen and Cedergren (1981), who question one of the earliest generative attempts to formalize the relationship between liaison and syntax, Selkirk's (1980) analysis of liaison sites in terms of boundaries between syntactic constituents, where she claims that stylistic variation can be explained as variation between the syntactic contexts in which liaison occurs. They demonstrate that Selkirk's model does not reflect the occurrence of liaison in different varieties of French spoken in Montreal. For example, Selkirk's analysis predicts that all subject pronoun-plus-verb sequences should behave the same way in a given style, because the syntactic context is the same, and all the pronouns are monosyllabic. However, the Montreal data show different Sp-V as behaving differently from each other, with speakers in the lowest social group pronouncing the liaison consonant 40% of the time in *on est*, but hardly ever in *ils ont*.

De Jong (1990) reviewed both Kaisse (1985) and Selkirk (1986). Although he concluded that Selkirk's was the more satisfactory analysis of the syntactic conditioning of liaison, he had to propose what amounts to a major adjustment to her model because his empirical data from a corpus of Orléans French contradicted the traditional 'facts' concerning obligatory liaison on which Selkirk's analysis was based. His (1994) study of liaison not only raises further questions of (substantial) detail regarding models of liaison, but also leads him to question the very nature of the phenomenon, arguing that liaison is not acquired in the same way as other phonological processes, but is learned, in the same way as vocabulary is learned.[17]

Liaison has continued to be a topic of debate amongst phonological theorists, as shown in the list of Suggested Reading below, but studies such as Green and Hintze (1988, 1990) and De Jong (1990, 1994) show that there is an urgent need to review the empirical basis on which theoretical edifices are built.

Suggested Reading

Descriptive studies of liaison:
  Delattre (1947, 1955, 1956), Fouché (1959), Léon (1978), Tranel (1987a).
Discussions of deletion versus insertion:
  Klausenburger (1984, 1994), Schane (1978).
Non-linear analyses:
  Clements and Keyser (1983), Durand (1986) (Dependency Phonology), Encrevé (1988), Tranel (1993) (Moraic Phonology), Tranel (1995), Wetzels (1987).
Liaison and syntax:
  Booij and De Jong (1987), De Jong (1990), Malécot (1975), Morin and Kaye (1982), Selkirk (1974, 1980, 1986).
Empirical studies and their implications:
  Booij and De Jong (1987), De Jong (1993, 1994), Encrevé (1988), Green and Hintze (1988, 1990), Morin (1987a).

Liaison and (socio)linguistic change:
  Ashby (1981b), Delattre (1947), Green and Hintze (1990).
H-aspiré:
  Clements and Keyser (1983), Klausenburger (1994), Tranel (1981, 1987a),
  Wetzels (1987).

Notes

1. We shall not be discussing, either here or in Chapter 3 below, the problem of the so-called *h-aspiré*, which is closely bound up with both liaison and schwa, since it blocks the pronunciation of word-final prevocalic consonants and triggers pronunciation of word-final prevocalic schwa (in *les huttes* ([leyt]) and *ce homard* ([səomaʁ]) respectively). References to discussions of the problem are given in the list of Suggested Reading at the end of this chapter.
2. *La cerise rouge sur la table orange.*
3. Here and in Chapter 2, /ə/ will be treated, for convenience, as though it is a phoneme of French despite the theoretical problems discussed in Chapter 3. Similarly, nasal vowels are treated here as being phonemically /Ṽ/; the problems associated with this analysis are the subject of Chapter 2.
4. The problem considered here concerns solely final consonants which are regularly in alternation with zero in specific phonological environments, rather than the elision of, for example, the final /l/ of *table*, as in [syʁlatab] (*sur la table*), or [tabdənɥi] (*table de nuit*), which are governed more by register than by the following phonological segment.
5. In this and following derivations, a dotted line means that the preceding rule did not apply to this string; the label 'other rules' relates to other phonological processes which may or may not apply at this stage in the derivation, and to rules deleting segments like word boundary markers. The vertical lines enclosing the underlying representations indicate that these are different in nature from structuralist phonemic representations.
6. This apparent advantage is not without problems. For example, the WFCs of the feminine and liaison forms of *grand(e)* are not the same. For discussion of the problematic role of introducing unpronounced schwas to prevent consonant deletion see below in this section, and Chapter 3.6.3.
7. Note that these cases are not restricted to final /t/, cf. *cep, vis, sud.*
8. Schane was by no means the only proponent of this approach; other important studies include Dell (1973) and Selkirk (1980), to which the reader is referred, and in which the same problems occur.
9. Examples (11a) and (11b) and rules (12a) and (12b) are from Tranel (1981:224).
10. The reason why the word boundary is duplicated is not important here.

11. In fact the problem posed by the fact that *grand* takes [t] as its liaison consonant is not so intractable as suggested above, since it can be derived from an underlying /d/ by a regular devoicing rule. In the same way, the [s]~[z] alternation in *gros* > *grossesse* ([gʁosɛs]) ~ *gros enfants* ([gʁozɑ̃fɑ̃]) can be derived by a regular voicing rule.

12. See Part I, Section 3.3.4. The technical term for this is 'prosodic licensing': the segment is 'licensed' to be pronounced by being associated with the prosodic levels of structure.

13. Note that this is different from the morphosyntactic information in the insertion account, which concerned only the syntactic category of the word containing the liaison consonant itself, not the syntactic relationship between that word and the following word.

14. Others include methodological issues, such as data collection and analysis techniques, the sociolinguistic conditioning of variability, and the relationship between linguistic variation and change. The latter question, which was raised in Part I, Section 3.5, is discussed in detail with relation to schwa in Chapter 3 below.

15. The implications of this are examined in detail in Encrevé (1988). Note that his data are taken from a very particular style of discourse, that of prominent politicians in television interviews. Nevertheless, Green and Hintze's findings show that liaison without *enchaînement* is not restricted to this register.

16. For a detailed critique see Green and Hintze (1990:76–7).

17. De Jong's theoretical position is that potential for liaison is a property of lexical items, a position similar to Klausenburger (e.g. 1984), who takes the concrete insertion model one step further and sees liaison as suppletive morphology.

2

Nasal vowels

2.1 Introduction

The four French nasal vowels of the maximal system, /ɛ̃/, /œ̃/, /ɔ̃/ and /ɑ̃/, developed over several centuries from a much larger set of vowels and diphthongs which were followed by nasal consonants, as shown in Table 2.1 below. Evolution of the nasal vowels continues in Modern French, where it is generally accepted that in most varieties /œ̃/ is in the process of merging with /ɛ̃/. Whereas the phenomena of liaison and schwa examined in Chapters 1 and 3 pose common problems for generative and non-generative phonologists alike, the issues raised by the nasal vowels are very different for different theoretical paradigms. This chapter therefore falls into three distinct parts, each examining a particular set of issues concerning these vowels. The first reviews their historical development and calls into question the reliability of standard interpretations of textual evidence. The second

Table 2.1 Orthographic and phonetic representations of VN sequences and corresponding Ṽ in Old and Modern French (after Hajek (1993:150))

			Old French	Modern French
aN	[aN]	*banc*	[baŋk]	[bɑ̃]
eN	[eN]	*vent*	[vent]	[vɑ̃]
oN	[oN]	*pont*	[pont]	[pɔ̃]
iN	[iN]	*vin*	[vin]	[vɛ̃]
uN	[yN]	*un*	[yn]	[œ̃]
aiN	[ajN]	*pain*	[pajn]	[pɛ̃]
eiN	[ejN]	*plein*	[pleijn]	[plɛ̃]
oiN	[ojN]	*coin*	[kojn]	[kwɛ̃]
ieN	[ieN]	*bien*	[bien]	[bjɛ̃]
uiN	[uiN]	*juin*	[dʒyjn]	[ʒɥɛ̃]

examines structuralist questions arising from the oppositions into which these vowels can be shown to enter. We then turn to generative analyses of their synchronic patterning, and the extent to which diachronic processes and morphophonological alternations should be incorporated into such a synchronic model. The chapter concludes with a brief examination of the implications for the analyses reviewed of the patterning of nasal vowels in one non-standard variety.

2.2   The history of nasal vowels

There is much uncertainty and disagreement over the precise dating of the historical changes which led to the present system of nasal vowels in French. What is certain is that nasalization of vowels came about as a result of the assimilation of vowels preceding nasal consonants to the nasality of their following consonant; this was followed by changes in vowel quality, principally vowel lowering, and later the following nasal consonant was lost.[1]

Whilst the existence of the historical process of vowel nasalization is generally accepted as a fact, much controversy surrounds the sequence and dating of some of the subprocesses involved, which we shall examine with reference to the monophthongs only. The most common account of the French nasal vowels in standard texts on the history of French (e.g. Fouché 1958, Pope 1952) and in more recent textbooks (e.g. Laborderie 1994) holds that nasalization first affected the open vowel [a] in the tenth century and spread to the mid-high vowels, [e] and then [o], and finally, by the thirteenth century, to the high vowels [i] and [y]. According to this view, as each vowel became nasalized its quality also lowered, and thus a causal link is established in two respects between vowel quality and nasalization: open vowel quality facilitates nasalization; and nasalization in turn causes vowel lowering. The label 'traditional' is frequently assigned to this account, but dissenting voices have in fact been heard since at least the beginning of the twentieth century, arguing that all the vowels were nasalized at the same time, probably as early as the ninth century, and that the lowering took place much later, in Middle French.[2] The objections to the traditional account are of two main types: first, that the textual evidence for the proposed chronology is inconclusive, and second, that the phonetic explanation for the causal relationship between nasality and lowering vowel quality is erroneous.

2.2.1   Textual evidence

The phonetic interpretation of historical texts is a notoriously difficult task, and the difficulty is compounded in the case of the French nasal vowels by the fact that their basic orthographic representation did not change with the changes in pronunciation, remaining vowel-plus-nasal-consonant (VN).[3] Philologists therefore have to rely for their evidence on patterns of assonance in verse. Thus, if the vowel of a given VN sequence occurs in assonance with a VC sequence, the two vowels are taken to be identical in quality. In the earliest hagiographic poems (see, for example, Ayres-Bennett (1996)), dating from the ninth to the eleventh century, aN and eN sequences are found in assonance only with aN and eN respectively, and never with aC and eC; by contrast, iN and uN assonate both with iN and uN and with iC and uC. This suggests that the vowels in, for example, aN and aC are different, whereas those of iN and iC are the same, which is taken to indicate that whereas prenasal [a] had nasalized by this stage, [i] had not. The fact that aN and eN, which had earlier been kept apart, are found in assonance in the twelfth-century *Chanson de Roland* is, moreover, taken to indicate that by then the quality of [e] had lowered to become merged with [a].

This account seems very neat, but as its opponents have pointed out, the textual evidence does not show such straightforward patterns of VN/VC assonance and non-assonance as is claimed.[4] There are in fact examples of aN/aC assonance in the *Chanson de Roland*; these have been traditionally held to be mere scribal errors, but as early as 1927 Bédier maintained that they were too frequent to be written off as such, and his view has been echoed by many subsequent commentators. Moreover, Van Reenen (1985, 1987) found that in the *Chanson de Roland* there was already a statistically significant tendency for iN and uN to assonate more frequently with iN and uN than with iC and uC, which suggests that the vowels represented were beginning to differ much earlier than claimed by the traditional account.

Even if the textual distribution of these assonance pairs were more straightforward, it is by no means certain that they have been interpreted correctly. As Rochet points out, 'The fact that eN and aN do not assonate with eC and aC in the *Eulalie*, the *Léger*, and the *Alexis* only shows that eN and eC (as well as aN and aC) were felt to be different by the poet and the audience, but it does not indicate which phonetic feature was responsible for this difference' (1976:51–2). In other words, there is no reason to assume that the failure of aN and aC to assonate is due to the first vowel being nasal and the second oral; it could equally well indicate that the quality of the vowels is different. The contention of Rochet and other critics of the traditional view is that all vowels in VN sequences were nasalized by the ninth century and that nasality did not make those vowels sufficiently different from their oral counterparts to block assonance between VN and VC pairs. Their subsequent gradual divergence is due, then, to changes in quality and not to their nasalizing at different times. Furthermore, the lowering of the nasalized vowels cannot, in this view, be due to their nasalization, since if this were the case, and if all vowels were nasalized at the same time, then they would all have lowered at the same time, which traditionalists and their critics agree was not the case.

2.2.2   Phonetic explanations

Proponents of the traditional account are aware that the textual evidence is problematic, but they defend their interpretation on the grounds that it is consistent with certain supposedly universal phonetic facts, particularly that nasalization is easier to produce with low vowels: 'Low vowels nasalise more readily than high ones because it is not quite easy [*sic*] to combine the lowering of the soft palate that is required to open the nose passage with the raising of the back or front of the tongue' (Pope 1952:168). It is also claimed (e.g. Haudricourt 1947, Martinet 1970) that low nasal vowels are easier to perceive than high ones. However, there is a large body of experimental work, reviewed by *inter alios* Rochet (1976) and Hajek (1993), which shows both these claims to be false. For example, House and Stevens (1956) demonstrate that it requires more effort to produce perceptible nasality in low vowels than in high ones. Cross-linguistic comparison also calls into question the causal link between the height of the vowel and nasalization: if this is a strong effect, we would expect to see it reflected in a universal preponderance of low nasal vowels, with high nasal vowels being comparatively rare. However, there is evidence that many languages have high nasal vowels (Ruhlen 1973), and Hajek (1993) reports finding an apparent preference for nasality in high vowels in at least four languages.

Thus, both the textual and phonetic evidence adduced in favour of the traditional account of vowel nasalization in French are seen to be open to question. However, although the critiques of this account can demonstrate that it is not so well founded as its proponents claim, they do not, as they readily admit, provide positive evidence in support of the alternative nongradualist account, and there remains no definitive answer to the question of the exact course of the development of the modern nasal vowels.

2.3   Structuralist accounts: the phonemic status of nasal vowels

Although it is certain that the historical VN sequences evolved into four nasal vowel phonemes, their evolution did not cease at this stage, as mentioned above. The phonemic status of /ã/ and /ɔ̃/ is undisputed[5], but it is generally accepted that the opposition between /ɛ̃/ and /œ̃/ is being lost in favour of /ɛ̃/. While there are minimal pairs which suggest /œ̃/ has distinctive phonemic status, they tend to involve either rare words, for example /alœ̃/ (*alun*) versus /alɛ̃/ (*Alain*) and /bʁœ̃/ (*brun*) versus /bʁɛ̃/ (*brin*), or rather tortuous pairings, such as /œ̃kapabl/ (*un capable*) versus /ɛ̃kapabl/ (*incapable*), and speakers' pronunciation of these words is at best inconsistent. Armstrong noted this as long ago as 1932: 'There is a tendency for some French people to make very little difference, if any, between the pronunciation of *brun* and *brin*: it is brɛ̃ for both words' (1932:78); and Walter cites evidence which suggests that the tendency originated amongst '[le] peuple parisien' in the early nineteenth century (1976:321). Nevertheless, the vowel [œ̃] is a very tenacious one, with Price stating in 1971 that '[œ̃] has disappeared in the speech of many [but note not "all"] speakers' (1971:87). Although Valdman (1993) presents a three-vowel system as the norm, with a note on /œ̃/, Lodge and others (1997) still present the four vowels, albeit with a note that many native speakers do not distinguish /œ̃/ and /ɛ̃/.[6]

The main question for the structuralist linguist wishing to give an account of the phonemic system of French is whether to state that there are three nasal vowel phonemes or four, and the answer depends on the analytical criteria employed. It could be argued that if it is possible to differentiate between even a single minimal pair on the basis of the distinction between /œ̃/ and /ɛ̃/, then they must be posited as separate phonemes, even if the majority of speakers do not consistently make the distinction. A counter-argument to this would be that the functional load of the opposition – the number of minimal pairs and the frequency of some of the lexical items involved – is so low that a four-phoneme analysis is only justifiable if the majority of speakers do consistently distinguish between /œ̃/ and /ɛ̃/.

On the basis of the latter criterion, the fact that only twenty per cent of Martinet's northern French subjects in his survey in a Second World War prison camp reported making no distinction between *brun* and *brin* or between *alun* and *Alain* (Martinet 1945:148–9), would seem to justify positing four phonemes in an account of the French of that time.[7] Reichstein's (1960) study of Parisian schoolgirls indicated that a dramatic shift was taking place: 82% of her subjects did not differentiate between *brun* and *brin*. Walter's (1976) study of 16 Parisian adults shows nine of them pronouncing on average 70% of a list of lexemes with distinctive /œ̃/ as [œ̃], whereas the other seven, whose average age was about ten years younger, produced [œ̃] only 8% of the time.

Taken together, these studies indicate that a sharp decline has taken place in the maintenance of the distinction, a trend which appears to have continued towards the end of the century, and which indicates that it may soon be possible to state unequivocally that there are three nasal vowel phonemes in French. However, it is clear that residual /œ̃/ still exists, and this highlights a problem with a strict structuralist analysis, which insists on portraying the phonology as a stable system of phonemic oppositions and does not allow for the kind of variable situation which the evidence shows has existed for well over a hundred years.[8]

Martinet was the first structural linguist to draw attention to this problem, and to the necessity of recognising what he called 'synchronie dynamique' where 'l'attention se concentre, certes, sur un seul et même état, mais sans qu'on renonce jamais à y relever des variations et à y évaluer le caractère progressif ou récessif de chaque trait' (1975:9). But although Martinet and Walter, in particular, have produced many empirical studies describing the dynamic properties of the French vowel system, no satisfactory theoretical construct has yet been elaborated to model a dynamic system. Thus, although the variable situation can be illustrated descriptively, usually by presenting a phonemic system for each of a series of idiolects, there is no way of representing the fact that the variability itself is part of the system shared by the majority of native speakers.

2.4   Generative and post-generative accounts of the nasal vowels[9]

The major questions for generative phonologists concerning the French nasal vowels arise from the morphological alternations into which they enter; in a structuralist account these would be dealt with in a separate part of the grammar, the morphology. The complex history of the nasal vowels has led to a situation in which all the nasal vowels are regularly found in allomorphic alternation with a VN sequence, for example the root morphemes in [vẽ] (*vin*) and [vinikyltœʁ] (*viniculteur*), and in [pʁɑ̃] (*prend*) and [pʁɛn] (*prennent*). Table 2.2 gives a series of examples of such correspondences.

Table 2.2   Alternations between nasal vowels and VN sequences in conservative Standard French

	/ɛ̃/			/ɑ̃/	
1.	[divɛ̃] (*divin*)	[divin] (*divine*)	14.	[pʁɑ̃] (*prend*)	[pʁɛn] (*prennent*)
2.	[ɛ̃sɔlvabl] (*insolvable*)	[inedi] (*inédit*)	15.	[pʁɑ̃] (*prend*)	[pʁəne] (*prenez*)
			16.	[bɑ̃] (*ban*)	[baniʁ] (*bannir*)
3.	[plɛ̃] (*plein*)	[plenityd] (*plénitude*)	17.	[flɑ̃be] (*flamber*)	[flam] (*flamme*)
4.	[plɛ̃] (*plein*)	[plɛn] (*pleine*)			
5.	[vɛ̃] (*vain*)	[vɛn] (*vaine*)			
6.	[seʁtɛ̃] (*certain*)	[seʁtɛnaʒ] (*certain âge*)			
7.	[vjɛ̃] (*vient*)	[vjɛn] (*viennent*)			
8.	[swɛ̃] (*soin*)	[swaɲ] (*soigne*)			
9.	[vɛ̃] (*vain*)	[vanite] (*vanité*)			
10.	[vjɛ̃] (*vient*)	[vənɔ̃] (*venons*)			
	/œ̃/			/ɔ̃/	
11.	[bʁœ̃] (*brun*)	[bʁyn] (*brune*)	18.	[bɔ̃] (*bon*)	[bɔn] (*bonne*)
12.	[œ̃] (*un*)	[yn] (*une*)	19.	[sɔ̃] (*son*)	[sɔne] (*sonner*)
13.	[ʒœ̃] (*jeun*)	[ʒøn] (*jeûne*)	20.	[kʁɑ̃pɔ̃] (*crampon*)	[kʁɑ̃pɔne] (*cramponner*)

There are some regular patterns of alternation which stand out in Table 2.2:

- [ɔ̃] always alternates with [ɔn] (as in examples 18–20)
- [œ̃] generally alternates with [yn], with the odd rare exception (11–13).

However:

- Both [ɛ̃] and [ɑ̃] alternate with [ɛn] (4, 5, 6, 14), [aN] (8, 9, 16, 17) and [ən] (10, 15)
- [ɛ̃] also alternates with [in] (1, 2) and [en] (3).

These alternations are not predictable from the phonological context, at least not in a straightforward way; for example:

- The alternations between [ɑ̃] and [ɛn] versus [ən] in 14 and 15 have the same preceding phonological context – they both follow [ʁ]
- [ən] in 15 is followed by [e], but so is [an] in 16
- [ɛ̃] alternating with [in] in 1 versus [ɛn] in 6 occurs in both cases in the second syllable of a disyllabic word.[10]

It is thus not possible to state unambiguously the correspondences between the pairs of forms from the surface phonology alone.

The question that arises is the extent to which morphological facts should be incorporated into a phonological account, particularly where the phonetic relationship between the forms is far from transparent, or the semantic relationship arguably no longer obvious (even though both might be explicable in historical terms). The most abstract analyses go further than simply incorporating these patterns into their accounts of alternating forms, arguing that the existence of such alternations justifies the analysis of both alternating and non-alternating Ṽs as being synchronically derived from VNs, as they are diachronically. This in turn raises further questions: to what extent is it desirable to impose a uniform analysis on historically related phenomena? Can historical processes constitute evidence for the synchronic workings of a language even when the historical process of change is complete?

2.4.1   Nasal vowels in abstract generative phonology

2.4.1.1   Alternating forms

Schane (e.g. 1968), Dell (1973) and Selkirk (1972) all derive alternating nasal vowels from an underlying VN sequence, albeit with significant differences between their analyses. We shall again concentrate on Schane as exemplifying the 'abstract' approach to the problem. His argument for adopting underlying VN is one of simplicity: in the case of /ɛ̃/ (setting aside for the moment the parallel alternations with /ɑ̃/[11]), it is simpler to derive one surface Ṽ from many underlying VNs than to derive the many surface VNs from one underlying $\tilde{V}$, since in the absence of regular phonological conditioning, the latter procedure would involve tagging each lexical item to identify which VN should be derived from the underlying vowel.[12] To achieve the derivation, Schane postulates two rules, which can be expressed as (1) and (2):

(1)   V → [+nas] /___ N $\left\{ \begin{array}{c} \# \\ [+\text{cons}] \end{array} \right\}$

(2)   N → Ø / $\tilde{V}$___

(1) nasalizes any vowel which is followed by a nasal consonant and then either a word boundary or another consonant, and (2) subsequently deletes the following nasal consonant. VNs followed by a vowel do not fulfil the conditions and therefore do not undergo nasalization.[13] Examples of derivations involving example 19 from Table 2.2 are given as (3a) and (3b):

(3a) |sɔn #| (3b) |sɔne #|
         ↓   ← Rule (1) →   ↓
       sɔ̃n #   ·······
         ↓   ← Rule (2) →   ↓
       sɔ̃ #   ·······
         ↓   ← other rules →   ↓
       [sɔ̃]   [sɔne]

The many-to-one relationship between VN and [ɛ̃] and [œ̃] is dealt with by a rule adjusting the quality of the nasalized vowel to [+low]. This rule applies after rule (1) and changes the intermediate derived vowels /ĩ/ (in *divin*) and /ẽ/ (*plein*) to /ɛ̃/, and /ỹ/ (*brun*) and /ø̃/ (*jeune*) to /œ̃/. The solution does not go far enough, however, for it does not account for the different surface vowels generated from common underlying VN representations. If the underlying vowel is simply taken to be the oral vowel of the alternating surface form, the same $\tilde{V}$ will surface in 4 and 14 of Table 2.2, and in 9 and 16: applying rules (1), (2) and the quality-adjustment rule would incorrectly yield *[pʁɛ̃] for *prend* and *[vã] for *vain*.[14]

Because of this and related problems with morphological alternations involving oral vowels, Schane argues for an abstract set of underlying representations where he makes a distinction not made on the surface between tense and lax vowels.[15] Table 2.3 reproduces Schane's table of underlying representations and their corresponding derived oral and nasal vowels. Following his conventions, tense vowels are represented by upper case symbols and lax vowels with lower case. The underlying representations of the root forms for 1 and 11 in Table 2.2 would thus be |divIn| and |brUn|. The problem of *prend* is then solved by deriving *prend* from underlying |prɛn|

Table 2.3 Correspondences between underlying representations and derived oral and nasal vowels, adapted from Schane (1968:48). Capitalized vowels are [+tense], lower case are [–tense]. Numbers refer to examples in Table **2.2**

Underlying vowel	Derived oral vowel	Derived nasal vowel	Examples
I	i	ɛ̃	1, 2
E	e / ɛ	ɛ̃	3, 4, 6
a	a / ɛ	ɛ̃	5, 9
ɛ	jɛ	jɛ̃	7
e	wa	wɛ̃	8
A	a	ã	16, 17
Ɛ	ɛ	ã	14
Ɔ	ɔ	ɔ̃	18, 19, 20
U	y	œ̃	11, 12
o	ø	œ̃	13

(whereas *pleine* is derived from underlying |plɛn|). One more rule of quality adjustment is needed in order to derive the correct set of surface forms from these underlying representations, and that is one enabling central [ã] to be derived from underlying [+front] |Ɛ|.

The fact that *plein* alternates with both *plénitude* ([en]) and *pleine* ([ɛn]), is dealt with by general rules governing vowel quality in pretonic versus tonic syllables, as is the alternation of *vaine* with both *vanité* ([an]) and *vaine* ([ɛn]). However, there still remain a few unresolved issues. One is the alternation between surface [ən] and [ɛn] in *venons* ~ *viennent* (~ *vient*) and *prenons* ~ *prennent* (~ *prend*). This cannot be resolved through purely phonological means, because as well as the three-way [ən] ~ [(j)ɛn] ~ [(j)ɛ̃] alternations, where [ən] is the pretonic and [(j)ɛn] the tonic form, there are four-way alternations where both [ən] and [ɛn] are pretonic and there is also tonic [(j)ɛn]. This is the case of the root morpheme of *venir*, which is shared by *avènement* ([avɛnmã]), as well as *venir*, *vient* and *viennent*. To achieve the correct derivations in these cases, Schane has to resort to tagging the words as learned versus non-learned, and specifying different conditions for the application of pre-nasalization vowel quality-changing rules to the different classes of word.[16]

One further unresolved issue is how to prevent the application of rules (1) and (2) to word-final VN sequences which surface as [VN], as in, for example, *divine*, *prennent* and *flamme*. Again, the solution adopted is one which has already been posited to account for other related phenomena: the 'protective' feminine or verbal-suffix schwa, which is posited in the underlying representations of these forms and then deleted after the application of rules (1) and (2) when no longer needed to prevent nasalization of the vowel and deletion of the consonant.

2.4.1.2   Non-alternating forms

Having made the case for treating alternating nasal vowels as derived from underlying VN sequences, Schane goes on to extend this analysis to those nasal vowels which do not enter into any morphological alternations, as in [sɛ̃k] (*cinq*), [sãbl] (*semble*), [vãdʁ] (*vendre*). This he justifies on the grounds of the economy of the system, arguing that eliminating any [+nas] vowels from the set of underlying units means that no vowel has to be specified for [+/−nas]. If, on the other hand, it were necessary to specify the feature [+nas] for the vowels of even the restricted set of non-alternating morphemes, then all vowels would need to be specified for [+/−nas], 'which would add a considerable number of features to the lexicon' (Schane 1968:143). Since the nasalization rules are already in the grammar for independently motivated reasons (the need to relate alternating forms), applying them to these few extra morphemes adds no extra complexity to the system.

This proposal is not unproblematic, however: as shown in Table 2.3 above, surface [ã] can be derived from two different underlying vowels: |A| or |Ɛ|; and [ɛ̃] from three: |I|, |E| or |a|. In the case of alternating nasal vowels, the choice of underlying form is determined by the need also to generate the correct corresponding [VN] sequence. However, with non-alternating morphemes there is by definition no corresponding surface [VN] form and the choice of underlying form becomes an arbitrary one. It is of course possible to appeal to the historical derivation of the morphemes, as reflected in the spelling, but this begs the question of whether a model based on historical facts can justifiably be taken to represent how the modern language works synchronically.

Dell's treatment of nasal vowels is brief and comes in the context of a discussion of schwa, but it highlights another difficulty with the analysis which argues that all nasal vowels derive from underlying VN. Dell (1973:192) discusses the case of phonetically invariable adjectives like *bleu* and *marron*. The absence of a (phonetic) feminine suffix in *bleue* is explained by the fact that the root ends in a vowel and the feminine schwa which is present in the underlying representation |blø + ə| is thus deleted. However, in the case of *marron*, adding a feminine schwa to underlying |marɔn| would block rules (1) and (2) and yield *[maʁɔn], which is incorrect. Dell acknowledges that this is a problem, but his explanation is rather weak: '[l'invariabilité] de *marron* témoigne d'un comportement aberrant du point de vue syntaxique ou morphologique'. In other words, *marron* has to be tagged in the lexicon as not taking the feminine agreement morpheme when modifying a feminine noun. Looked at purely as a matter of simplicity, it may perhaps be possible to show this *faute de mieux* proposal is more 'economical' for the lexicon than having to specify all vowels for the feature [+/−nasal]; nevertheless, it remains unsatisfactory in that it is an *ad hoc* solution without any independent motivation.

The reverse problem arises for morpheme-internal vowels followed by nasal consonants in words like *samedi* ([samdi]) and *mannequin* ([mankɛ̃]), where an underlying schwa has to be postulated to prevent the incorrect derivations *[sãdi] and *[mãkɛ̃] respectively (compare *tandis* ([tãdi]) and *manquer* ([mãke])). Again, the argument can be adduced that since underlying schwa has to be postulated elsewhere for independent reasons, it represents no great extra cost to the system, but there are general counter-arguments which need to be considered too (see Chapter 3). Dell (1970, cited in Tranel 1981) justifies the underlying schwa by appealing to experimental evidence from slow speech, which showed that speakers pronounce schwa in words like *samedi* when forced to speak slowly. However, it would be very difficult to prove that they were not merely showing the influence of the orthographic *e* in cases where there is one (and Dell concedes this possibility). In an informal experiment conducted by Tranel, no speakers produced schwa in slow production of words which had [VN] sequences without a following orthographic *e*. If slow speech is the justifying criterion for positing an underlying schwa, then this means that one cannot be posited for words like *stencil* ([stɛnsil]), thus leaving another group of morphemes which have to be specially marked in the lexicon as not undergoing nasalization.

2.4.2   Nasal vowels in concrete generative phonology

2.4.2.1   Non-alternating forms

Tranel (1981) opens his assault on the abstract, underlying-VN analysis of the nasal vowels with a critique of the claim that the analysis should apply to all nasal vowels whether the surface vowels enter into morphological alternations or not. He first gives an elaborate demonstration of the difficulty of measuring simplicity or economy, which, as we have seen, is not a straightforward matter. He then goes on to counter other evidence which has been adduced to support underlying |VN| for non-alternating nasals. He demonstrates that not only are some of the arguments questionable, but the insistence on |VN| in these cases is also actually detrimental to the analysis of the overall system (1981:16–36). The validity of this critique (first presented in Tranel 1974) had in fact already been conceded by Schane (1978:77).

Tranel's simple alternative is to posit underlying nasal vowels in all non-alternating cases. As well as dealing with individual problematic cases such as *marron*, this analysis also eliminates the vexed question of how children acquiring French would know that there were underlying |VN| sequences in morphemes which they only ever hear with a nasal vowel.[17] To adopt this solution is not merely to opt for what appears to be the neatest answer to a puzzle: it is also to state that the historical process which began with the purely phonetic effect of a vowel assimilating to a following nasal consonant has led to the incorporation of nasal vowels into the inventory of underlying segments and the consequent necessitation of [+/–nas] as a distinctive feature for French vowels, whereas before it was distinctive only for consonants. In other words, nasal vowels have been lexicalized (that is, have distinctive representations in the lexicon) and the phonological inventory of French vowels has undergone a fundamental change since the time when there were no nasal vowels, but many VN sequences. This position is of course already implicit in the structuralist analysis of the nasal vowels as phonemes.

2.4.2.2   Alternating forms

Although Tranel argues for underlying nasal vowels in non-alternating cases, he demonstrates that it is not possible to posit underlying nasal vowels in all cases.[18] Instead he maintains that since non-alternating cases show that both |Ṽ| (*marron, cinq*) and |VN| (*samedi, stencil*) are necessary, there is no reason why both cannot be available in underlying representations to account for the behaviour of alternating morphemes rather than a uniform solution being imposed. He proceeds to demonstrate how different solutions are appropriate to different sets of alternations.

In fact, Tranel takes this non-uniformity to the extent of positing different underlying representations for sets of forms which are in a derivational relationship with each other, for example, nouns and verbs (e.g. [bukɛ̃] (*bouquin*) ~ [bukine] (*bouquiner*), [paʁfœ̃] (*parfum*) ~ [paʁfyme] (*parfumer*)). The root morphemes {'bouquin-'} and {'parfum-'} would each have two different underlying representations (|bukɛ̃| and |bukin|, and |parfœ̃| and |parfym|). However, the correspondences between the two sets are not ignored because there are so-called 'via' rules capturing the relationship between them. The via rules differ from derivational rules in that they simply state the relationship between two morphologically related forms, rather than providing a dynamic mechanism to derive both from a common underlying form. The via rule in this case is given here as (4) (1981:92):

$$(4) \quad \begin{bmatrix} X & \begin{bmatrix} V \\ +\text{nasal} \end{bmatrix} \end{bmatrix}_{\text{Noun}} \Rightarrow \begin{bmatrix} X & \begin{bmatrix} V \\ -\text{nasal} \end{bmatrix} n \end{bmatrix}_{\text{Verb}}$$

The rule states that where a noun contains an underlying morpheme-final nasal vowel, the corresponding verb will contain an oral vowel followed by |n|. Although via rules are not dynamic, the directionality of the relationship is necessary in (4) because it is not always possible to predict from the verb form whether the corresponding nominal root will have [Ṽ] or [VN]: taking the verb as the starting point, as in the rule given in (5) (which is the reverse of (4)), would correctly describe the relationship between *bouquiner* and *bouquin*, but not that between *téléphoner* and *(le) téléphone*, where it would incorrectly predict the pronunciation *[telefɔ̃].

$$(5) \quad \begin{bmatrix} X & \begin{bmatrix} V \\ -\text{nasal} \end{bmatrix} n \end{bmatrix}_{\text{Verb}} \Rightarrow \begin{bmatrix} X & \begin{bmatrix} V \\ +\text{nasal} \end{bmatrix} \end{bmatrix}_{\text{Noun}}$$

Equally importantly, rule (4) reflects the direction of the productive word formation process in the language: the verbs in these pairs tend to be derived from nouns and not the other way round (although of course post-verbal nouns do exist – see Chapter 13).

It can be argued that by introducing another type of rule into the system, this proposal complicates the phonology unnecessarily, but again there are more interesting consequences than just those affecting the apparent simplicity of the account. One is what it says about the nature of the links between related forms in the minds of speakers. The abstract account strongly implies that there is a real, productive link for speakers between such forms as, for example, *soin* and *soigner*, because they share the same lexical entry. However, as Tranel points out, in pairs like these, where the verb is well established, it is questionable whether such an active process takes place each time a speaker produces one of these words. By contrast, in pairs like *solution* and *solutionner*, where the verb is recognized as a neologism, speakers are aware at some level of an active process of derivation taking place. The abstract rules imply that the same process is occurring when speakers produce *soigner* as when they produce *solutionner*, whereas the concrete solution recognizes that this is not the case: (4) simply states a link between two morphemes, and would apply to *soin* ~ *soigner*, whereas *solutionner* would be actively derived from *solution* by another type of rule, albeit one identical in content to rule (4).

Having separate lexical entries is a less satisfactory solution for inflectional alternations like those in gender agreement or verbal paradigms, where there clearly does need to be a single lexical entry, since the same lexeme is involved. When these word classes are dealt with separately from others containing nasals, the correspondences between Ṽ and VN are simplified somewhat, since only a subset of the Ṽ~VN correspondences is present in each paradigm. For example, when the verbal inflections are analysed separately there are seen to be predictable alternations between [jɛ̃] and [jɛn] (e.g. *venir*), [wɛ̃] and [waɲ] (*joindre*), [ɛ̃] and [ɛɲ] (*craindre*), and [ɑ̃] and [ɛn] (*prendre*).[19] It should therefore be straightforward to formulate a rule for verbal inflections deriving the nasal vowels from |VN| like the rule in (1) above, or a rule working in the opposite direction, denasalizing an underlying |Ṽ| and inserting an [n] in much the same way as final consonants are inserted.

However, Tranel does not adopt a unique underlying representation, arguing first that the choice of underlying representation in these cases would be arbitrary, since it is possible to predict the correct nasal vowel from any of the VN combinations and *vice versa* (which was not the case for the verb → noun derivations discussed above). A second and more important argument is that the alternations cannot be made to 'work' on a purely phonological basis without the postulation of an underlying schwa, which is undesirable for the concrete approach. Without an underlying schwa, it would not be possible correctly to generate both [vjɛ̃] and [vjɛn] from a single underlying representation, since both the [jṼ] and the [jVN] sequence occur word-finally following the same consonant. Tranel thus proposes that both sets of allomorphs be listed in the lexicon, with rules distributing them in the correct grammatical context. He does not illustrate how this proposal would be implemented, but it is clear that the addition to the grammar is of a greater degree of complexity than the addition of the 'via' rule (4) above: in *venir* the [jɛ̃] and [jɛn] forms are distributed differently amongst grammatical persons in different tenses and moods, which means that the morphological marking cannot simply designate all present indicative morphs or all first-person morphs as taking [Ṽ] or [VN]. A similar, but in some respects even more complex, solution is posited for gender alternation in nouns and adjectives (for a fuller account see Tranel 1981:100–21).

There are obvious advantages to the non-uniform account of nasal vowels and VN sequences, principally that the problem of accounting for non-alternating forms with underlying VN is eliminated. Our brief discussion of the alternating forms shows that something is also to be gained by analysing separately different parts of the grammar. Note, however, that although this separation of grammatical subsystems is not something which is deemed desirable in the abstract generative model, one could equally well attempt to maintain the uniform underlying VN of the abstract analysis by formulating different rules to apply to the separate subsystems.[20] The disadvantage of taking a non-uniform account too far is that one can lose sight of the generalization that, with a few exceptions, [Ṽ] and [VN] are in complementary distribution in French in purely phonological terms. Where the concrete account differs dramatically from the abstract one is in postulating a separate level of not only derivational, but also inflectional morphology; this, as demonstrated here, adds considerable complexity to the grammar.

2.4.3   A non-linear proposal

There have been many different accounts of French nasal vowels in non-linear phonological frameworks, and it is not possible to give a detailed comparison here, since this would involve investigating details of the ways in which different analyses model the complex internal structure of segments. Instead, we shall offer as an example of this type of proposal an outline of an early autosegmental account.

Prunet (1986) proposes a solution parallel to the proposal for liaison examined in Chapter 1, that is, a 'floating nasal'. The difference between the accounts of liaison and of the nasal vowels lies in the stipulation that a floating nasal which does not have a skeletal slot to which to attach, projects onto a preceding nucleus, as illustrated in (6) for *bon*, whereas a floating liaison consonant projects onto a following onset. Because it is now attached to a vocalic node, the floating nasal surfaces as nasalization on the vowel rather than as a separate nasal consonant.

(6)

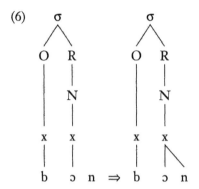

There is a striking similarity between this account and the abstract linear account in that both have an underlying nasal element independent of the vowel. There is a further similarity in how the surface nasal consonant in *bonne* is derived. Prunet states that the nasal consonant surfaces when it has an empty skeletal slot to project onto, as with liaison consonants, but whereas in the case of liaison this slot is provided in the first syllable of the following word, it is not clear in his account where it comes from in *bonne* in contexts like *elle est bonne*, where there is no following syllable. We have to assume that, as in the abstract linear account, the surfacing of [n] depends on an underlying following syllable whose nuclear vowel is a schwa which is subsequently deleted, as in (7):

(7)

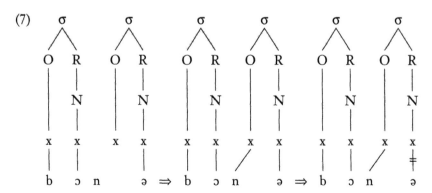

The proposal thus does not appear to have any advantages over the abstract linear one, except that the presence of higher level prosodic structures in the non-linear account allows the formalization of the fact that the surface [n] forms the coda of the syllable which precedes it (by the delinking of the [n] from O and its linking to the preceding R in coda position). In the linear account, no syllable structure is given and thus there is no apparent difference between [bɔn] in *bonne* and in *bon ami*.

2.5   Nasal vowels and liaison

In liaison situations, word-final surface nasal vowels mostly denasalize and are followed by [n], hence *certain* ~ *certain âge* (Table **2.2**, example 6). This poses a problem for the abstract linear account of nasalization outlined in **2.4.1.1** above, since applying the rules given there in cases like *certain* would yield surface nasal vowels in both the liaison and the non-liaison forms. Consequently, rule (1) of the abstract linear account, which states that a vowel is nasalized when followed by a nasal consonant and either a word boundary or another consonant, cannot stand as it is: the context in which the second vowel of the underlying |sertEn| occurs is exactly one of those specified for the application of that rule, namely a following nasal consonant followed by a word boundary, and therefore the word-final VN sequence would undergo vowel nasalization and N-deletion to yield *[œ̃sɛʁtɛ̃aʒ]. The rule needs to be modified as in (8):

$$(8) \quad V \rightarrow [+nas] /\underline{\quad} N \ (\#) \left\{ \begin{array}{l} || \\ [+cons] \end{array} \right\}$$

(8) states that vowel nasalization occurs in |VN| sequences followed by an optional word boundary[21] and either a pause or a consonant. Rule (2), which deletes a nasal consonant following a nasalized vowel, does not need to be modified, since its application is governed by its preceding context. Liaison can thus be handled with the same rules as those needed for deriving morphologically alternating forms.

Tranel (1981) takes a different approach, proposing a single form for alternating adjectives, but different rules governing the gender- and liaison-related alternations they enter into. Thus the underlying representation of *bon* is |bɔ̃|. The alternation between *bon* (*courage*) and *bonne* (*conscience*) is achieved with one morphophonological rule which simultaneously changes the vowel to [−nas] and inserts [n] at the end of the morpheme, whereas that between *bon* (*courage*) and *bon* (*après-midi*) is handled by two separate phonological rules, the first inserting [n] between *bon* and a word beginning

with a following vowel and the second denasalizing the vowel. This insertion account suffers from the same problem as the concrete account of
liaison with other consonants, namely that not all nouns and adjectives
with a final nasal vowel in the masculine singular have final [n] in their
feminine and liaison forms. Moreover, there is the extra difficulty that
where the following consonant is not a nasal, the vowel is not denasalized,
for example, [gʁãtami] (*grand ami*), [gʁãd] (*grande*), [blã ʃ] (*blanche*), [lɔ̃g]
(*longue*); consequently, the words in question have to be marked as exceptions to rules (8) and (2), and special rules applied. In addition, since,
as we have seen, there is not a one-to-one correspondence between nasal
and oral vowels, the surface vowel also has to be specified for each individual word.

There is a further complicating factor in liaison involving nasal vowels,
in that there are words which take a nasal consonant in liaison, but are
nevertheless preceded by a surface nasal vowel, for example [mɔ̃nami] (*mon
ami*), [bjɛ̃nɛme] (*bien-aimé*). These cases cause a problem for the abstract
analysis, since each word has to be marked as an exception to rule (2).
However, because they are primarily possessive pronouns and adverbials,
the concrete analysis – which, as we have seen, allows different rules to be
applied to different classes of words – can specify that rule (2) does not apply
to these particular classes, thus avoiding treating the individual words as
exceptions. In the particular non-linear approach examined above, the nasal
element can attach to both the preceding vowel and the following onset slot
in the same way as the feature [–voice] links to both [d] and [s] in Figure 7
of Part I, Section 3.3.4. This is illustrated in (9):

(9)
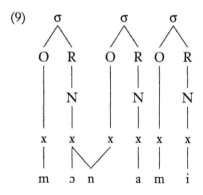

However, while (9) describes the phenomenon, it provides no motivation for
why the [n] should attach to both the preceding and following slots. For
Prunet, the patterns of association are conditioned by reference to the syntactic structure (for details see Prunet 1986:227–33); this solution could
also be applied, with minor modifications, to a linear account.

2.6   Nasal vowels in southern French

Where Standard French has nasal vowels which sometimes enter into morphological alternations with VN sequences, many speakers in southern France produce sequences of a vowel, which can be oral, nasal or partially nasalized, followed by a nasal consonant. For example, Carton and others transcribe their Provençal informant's pronunciation of *appelants* and *example* as [apəlaãŋ] and [ɛzaãmplə] respectively (1983:52), where the superscript ∞ symbol represents a pronunciation which is 'légèrement nasalisée' (1983:8). The vowel quality is somewhat more close than standard French, and the nasal consonant either assimilates to the place of articulation of any following consonant, or is velar pre-pausally.

The question posed by regional variation of this kind is whether it should be assumed that non-standard pronunciations are simply allophonic or surface variants derived from a system which is common to standard and non-standard varieties, or whether they should be analysed as a separate system.

Durand (1988) takes issue both with Detrich (1979) and others who implicitly or explicitly analyse these vowels as though the speakers had standard French underlying phoneme inventories and were producing allophonic variants, and with Tranel (1981), who assumes that Midi [VN] sequences are the product of a denasalization process which again operates on the same underlying representations as standard French. Instead Durand argues that the Midi nasal vowels are actually less problematic than the standard French ones for an abstract-style generative analysis. In the dialect on which his study is based, that of Pézenas in Languedoc, the most normal pronunciation is of an oral vowel followed by a nasal consonant, although there are variant pronunciations with partially and fully nasalized vowels. This is then the most obvious candidate for an underlying representation, with the nasality on the vowels explicable in terms of optional rules of assimilation. The difference between this dialect and standard French resides then in the absence of a nasal deletion rule like (2) above. The vexed question of protective schwa is not an issue because of course the nasal is not deleted; in any case it is present in the surface forms of feminine adjectives and there is no good reason for not postulating it in the underlying representation.

There is a further complication in the Pézenas dialect in that the nasal consonant is frequently not pronounced when it precedes a consonant cluster, hence [traspɔrte] (*transporter*), [kɔstate] (*constater*). Sometimes the vowel is nasal, but most commonly it is oral; sometimes the consonant is pronounced and sometimes it is not. As Durand points out, a concrete analysis based on Standard French and positing underlying nasal vowels in these cases would then have to explain the denasalization of the vowel. It is much simpler to describe the variable process by taking VN as the starting point and positing deletion of the nasal consonant which occurs variably before or after assimilation has taken place.

The analysis of Pézenas French is not necessarily more straightforward than that of the standard language, and there are other varieties which pose their own problems for phonological analysis. What is clear, however, is that it is not safe simply to assume that the system underlying non-standard varieties is the same as that of the standard language.

Suggested Reading

History:
> The traditional account: Fouché (1958), Pope (1952), Price (1971).
> Critiques of the traditional account: Ayres-Bennett (1996), Hajek (1993, 1997), Lote (1940–43), Matte (1984), Price (1971), Rochet (1976), Sampson (1999), van Reenen (1987).

Distinction between /œ̃/ and /ɛ̃/:
> Hansen (1998), Malécot and Lindsay (1976), Walter (1976).

Generative and non-linear analyses:
> Bouchard (1983), Carr (1994), Dell (1973), Durand (1988), Prunet (1986), Schane (1968, 1973), Scullen (1994), Selkirk (1972), Tranel (1978, 1981).

Liaison:
> Prunet (1986), Tranel (1981, Chapter IV).

Variation:
> Hansen (1998), Morin (1977), Walker (1984).

Notes

1. This process was only carried to completion where the nasal consonant following the nasalized vowel was itself followed by a consonant or a word boundary. Where the nasal consonant was followed by a vowel, the nasalized vowel was subsequently denasalized, leaving a VN sequence in the modern language.
2. For example Suchier (1906), and later Lote (1940–43).
3. For convenience we shall use italicized 'VN' to represent sequences of unspecified written vowel-plus-nasal-consonant sequences and 'VC' to represent unspecified written vowel-plus-consonant sequences, replacing 'V', 'N' and 'C' with specific letters where appropriate.
4. Although the interpretation of oN/oC assonance is somewhat complicated. See, for example, Rochet (1976:78–82) for details.
5. Although in some northern varieties of French, for example, in parts of Normandy the distinction between this pair of vowels is not consistently maintained.
6. In Canadian French, by contrast, there appears to be a phonologically stable system of four distinct phonemes, although the phonetic quality of

the Canadian French nasal vowels is different from that of European French, and they also have diphthongized allophones. For more details, see, for example, Walker (1984).

7. Although his informants may not have been accurately reporting what they actually produced in normal speech.

8. It should be noted that this problem has not been resolved, or even addressed, by generative and post-generative phonology, as is shown below by our necessary working assumption of a four-vowel system.

9. In this section, we will follow the assumption made in much of the generative literature that there are four distinctive nasal vowels in French.

10. Moreover, it will not suffice to say that different correspondences come into play with different classes of words: *vient/viennent* and *prend/prennent* are both verbal pairs, where the same stem VN sequence alternates with different nasal vowels; *vient/viennent* and *vient/venons* belong to the same verb, and yet the same nasal vowel alternates with different VN sequences.

11. We follow Schane (1968) here, in representing this vowel as |ã| and [ã], although its quality is in fact more retracted.

12. Note that in the cases of |œ̃| and |ã| it would also be necessary to indicate which was the surface nasal consonant, since [œ̃] alternates with [ym] as well as [yn] (cf. *parfum ~ parfumerie*), and [ã] with [am] as well as [Vn] (cf. *flamber ~ flamme*). In the case of *flamme*, the place of articulation could be predicted from the bilabial consonant following the nasal vowel, but no such contextual cues are available for *parfumerie*.

13. Note that although there are close parallels between this analysis and the traditional historical account of vowel nasalization, the rules do not reproduce the hypothesized historical process exactly.

14. Note, however, that in the case of *vain* there is an alternative candidate for the underlying form in the feminine *vaine* – [vɛn]. Note also that [pʁɛ̃] would in fact be the correct surface form in some non-standard varieties of French.

15. The only phonetically lax vowel in French is [ə] when it is articulated with a relative lack of muscular tension. For the other vowels, [+/−tense] is a purely formal feature invoked for the convenience of the analysis. Since this distinction has been independently motivated for the analysis of oral vowels, it is deemed not to add to the complexity of the account of the nasal vowels.

16. This is another example of a solution which was formulated to deal with oral vowel quality problems. It is a particularly messy solution because it requires entire words rather than morphemes to be identified as learned or unlearned (since the same root morpheme is concerned), which means that the classification cannot be listed in the lexicon, but must happen after the morphemes are strung together as words.

17. In the case of alternating forms they would be able to work out that |VN| is a possible underlying representation of a surface [Ṽ] because of the surface [VN] forms which alternate with it.

18. See Tranel (1981:87–90) for reasons why this is not a possible solution.

19. Tranel does not comment here on the third surface [VN] sequence, [ən], which occurs in *venir* and *prendre*.
20. Indeed the learned ~ non-learned division which Schane found necessary to account for *venir* and *avènement* (see 2.4.1.1 above) and other such pairs shows that the abstract account also had to resort to such divisions.
21. The word boundary is optional so that the rule continues to apply word-internally, as in *insolvable* (Table 2.2, example 2).

3

Schwa: a maverick vowel

3.1 Introduction: 'Qu'est-ce que le "e muet"?' (Martinet (1974a))

The vowel which we referred to in Part I as 'canonically a central vowel' (Section 2.1.4), is known *inter alia* as 'schwa', 'mute *e*', '*e* caduc', '*e* instable', '*e* féminin' and 'E'. This multiplicity of names is symptomatic of the multiple problems posed by the vowel, which concern both its phonetic and phonological identity and its unusual behaviour in various contexts in Modern French. The problems are mirrored in other languages (see, for example, Van Oostendorp 1998), but it is perhaps French which has received the most attention in this respect.

Like other oral and nasal vowels of French, schwa alternates morphologically, as in [ʒəte] (*jeter*[1]) versus [ʒɛt] (*jète*), or [pəze] (*peser*) versus [pwa] (*poids*). Unlike the other vowels, schwa cannot occur in stressed syllables; when it occurs in absolute final position, in certain regional varieties and in some stylistically or pragmatically marked contexts (see, for example, 3.8.2 below), the preceding syllable receives tonic stress and the post-tonic schwa is unstressed. Schwa is also a maverick vowel in two other major respects: its phonetic quality is much more variable than that of other vowels; and unlike other vowels, it alternates both contrastively and allophonically with zero, as in /mɔ̃tərjɔ̃/ (*monterions*) versus /mɔ̃trjɔ̃/ (*montrions*) and [ynsəmɛn] (*une semaine*) versus [lasmɛn] (*la semaine*) respectively. These aspects of the behaviour of schwa of course interact with its morphological alternations, but we shall disregard this interaction for the purposes of the present chapter, where we focus on the more unusual characteristics of the vowel.[2]

In this chapter we begin by addressing questions of terminology and the phonetic characteristics of schwa before turning to its phonological characteristics, that is, the descriptive and analytical problems posed by schwa ~ zero alternation, both as a synchronic phenomenon and in the light of ongoing changes which have been observed. In the course of the discussion, other questions of general theoretical import will inevitably be raised; these include whether reference to orthography is legitimate in an account of a phonological phenomenon; the relative importance of phonetic and distributional information in determining the underlying representation of a phonological unit, and what constitutes evidence for (and against) language change.

3.2 Terminology

Walter calls this vowel, 'une voyelle impossible à nommer' (1990:27). Of the six names cited above, five make reference to orthographic *e*, and the other, 'schwa', is unlike the designation used for any other vowel, where reference is made explicitly to phonetic qualities of frontness/backness, closure and lip-rounding. The terms which refer to orthography cover any letter *e* which (i) does not have a written accent; (ii) does not represent [e] or [ε] or another phonetic vowel when in combination with other letters (e.g. *-en-*, *-eu-*, *-eau-*); (iii) does not serve to indicate that a letter *g* or *c* is pronounced as a fricative rather than a stop (e.g. in *mangeable*). This would include *calepin*, where the *e* is almost never pronounced, and *belette*, where it always is. In the first case the term 'mute *e*' is apt, since there is an unpronounced *e*, but in the second the term is wholly inappropriate because the *e* is in fact pronounced. By contrast, '*e* caduc' or '*e* instable' is inappropriate for *calepin* because the situation is perfectly stable (except in 'spelling speech'): there is no vowel between [l] and [p]. '*E* féminin' is inappropriate to both words since strictly it only refers to word-final *e* in, for example, *bleue* or *table*. Moreover, none of these names is appropriate for cases where the vowel is represented with letters other than *e*, for example *ai* in *faisan*, *on* in *Monsieur*; these vowels share the phonetic and behavioural characteristics discussed below, and only differ in their orthography.[3]

As will become clear, because of the problematic nature of the vowel, it is convenient to use orthography as an initial point of reference. Nevertheless, although reference to orthography can be useful, it cannot form the basis of argumentation for modelling how the phonology of a language works, and for this reason we shall henceforth use the term 'schwa'.

3.3 The phonetic identity of schwa

The symbol [ə], by which schwa is designated in Modern French, has a place on the IPA vowel chart mid-way between front and back and between open and close. This position is sometimes referred to as 'neutral', since it represents perhaps the closest tongue position to when the vocal tract is at rest. In reality, the quality of this vowel can vary substantially, and in French it is most often pronounced forward of this position, with a degree of lip-rounding, giving it the quality of [ø] or [œ]. Walter (1977:50) notes that many people pronounce this vowel 'exactement de la même manière que l'un des phonèmes de la série antérieure /ø/ ou /œ/'. In data collected from Parisian informants, she found, on the basis of auditory transcriptions, that 44% of the 5,603 schwas were pronounced [œ], 33% [ø] and 24% [ə] (Walter 1976:317).

By contrast, in an experimental study, Malécot and Chollet (1977) showed that in conversational speech schwa did overlap to a large extent with [ø] in an acoustic measure of vowel quality, and that it overlapped far more with other vowels than any of them did with each other. However, there were also some cases where it did not overlap with other vowels, and the degree of overlap with [œ] proved to be no greater than with [e] or [y], suggesting that the assumption that its quality is 'like [ø] or [œ]'·may be inaccurate. Nevertheless, some general texts still state categorically that it is pronounced as one or other of these two vowels, for example Tranel (1987a).

Even when the pronunciation does not overlap with that of any of the front vowels, there is still some lip-rounding and the vowel is not the same as the first vowel in English *potato* ([pəteɪtəʊ]), which is generally more centralized and unrounded. This fact illustrates the compromises involved in using even the supposedly objective points of reference provided by the IPA: the choice of the symbol [ə], whose position on the IPA chart is not normally that of French schwa, rather than a symbol such as [ə̈][4], has more to do with reflecting the possible phonological nature and unusual distribution of the vowel than its precise phonetic quality. We shall use the symbol [ə] in discussing the phonological and distributional properties of schwa; however, as will become clear, the precise phonetic quality of schwa sometimes has a bearing on these broader issues, and alternative symbols will be used when this is under discussion.

3.4   The variable phonological behaviour of schwa

3.4.1   The data

Perhaps the most problematic characteristic of schwa from the linguist's point of view is its allophonic alternation with zero. This is a highly variable phenomenon, which, except for the regular patterns of elision found in clitics (as in *le chat* vs *l'entrée*), is difficult to describe. The alternation is partially conditioned phonetically: according to the position of schwa in the word and rhythmic group; according to the number and nature of preceding and following consonants; and according to the prosodic status of the following syllable. In addition, syntactic, pragmatic and sociolinguistic conditioning play an important role. Syntactic factors particularly affect word-final schwa: as with liaison, its pronunciation is influenced by the nature of the syntactic link with the following word. Sociolinguistic and stylistic factors affect schwa in all positions: it is pronounced more often in slower than faster speech, and in higher than lower registers, and these factors interact in complex ways, as exemplified by the different patterns of style-shifting of the corpus recorded by Hansen in 1989 (see **3.8.1** below).

Patterns of pronunciation also vary from region to region; for instance, Carton (1974:207) reports that in eastern France, 'une même personne dira *j'te vois* ou *je t'vois*, selon les circonstances' whereas in other regions *j'te vois* would be the norm. Most strikingly different are the patterns of pronunciation in southern French, where many more schwas are pronounced, as a result of the historical influence of the Occitan substrate. Schwa is also subject to a high degree of idiosyncratic variability: it is not unusual for two speakers with the same sociolinguistic characteristics such as regional origin, age and sex to produce consistently different patterns of schwa pronunciation in identical strings of words. As Dell says, then, 'Le comportement de schwa est l'un des domaines où les variations d'un locuteur à l'autre sont très fréquentes, même entre gens dont les prononciations sont très semblables' (1973:195).

3.4.2 Descriptive accounts

Towards the end of the nineteenth century, Maurice Grammont formulated the famous 'loi des trois consonnes', which tried to capture the patterns of pronunciation of schwa in a single descriptive principle: if the non-pronunciation of schwa would lead to a sequence of three or more adjacent consonants, then schwa was pronounced. Hence, *librement* is pronounced [libʁəmã], with schwa, since the non-pronunciation of schwa would lead to a sequence of three consonants, *[bʁm], whereas *seulement* is pronounced without: [sølmã]. The principle applies to sequences of words within the same rhythmic group as well as across words, thus [sãlkuto] (*sans le couteau*), with no schwa, but [avɛkləkuto] (*avec le couteau*), with a schwa preventing the sequence *[klk] occurring. However, there are many exceptions to this simple formulation. Not only are there words in French which have sequences of more than three consonants and never have schwa, such as [ɛksplikasjɔ̃] (*explication*), there are also frequently heard strings with three or more consonants where a schwa could be pronounced but is not, for example [vulpʁ̥əne] (*vous le prenez*), [dãltʁ̥ɛ̃] (*dans le train*). It is often pointed out that a more accurate general principle is formulated by reference to the number of consonants preceding a potential schwa: if there are two or more, and the potential schwa is followed by a consonant, it will generally be pronounced, hence [pʁəne] (*prenez*) rather than *[pʁne], and [vãdʁədi] (*vendredi*) rather than *[vãdʁdi].[5]

Delattre devotes a whole paper to the pronunciation of schwa in monosyllabic words in absolute initial position,[6] concluding that, 'la loi des trois consonnes [. . .] n'est plus d'aucun secours lorsqu'il s'agit de l'*e* instable de monosyllabe initial' (Delattre 1966:35). He explains the patterns of schwa occurrence in terms of the interaction of two factors. The first is 'le facteur psychologique', which concerns the supposed psychological prominence of the phrase-initial position, for which a potential schwa in initial position 'competes' with the vowel of the following syllable. Where one of these monosyllabic words is followed by a syllable with a non-schwa vowel, he predicts that this 'stable' vowel will successfully compete against the 'unstable' schwa for the phrase-initial syllable position, resulting in [ʒnɛpakɔ̃pʁi] (*je n'ai pas compris*[7], where the first syllable is [ʒnɛ] rather than [ʒə]). The second factor is 'le facteur mécanique', concerning the manner of articulation of the initial consonant: schwa is more susceptible to being pronounced in words beginning with stops, especially voiceless ones, than in those beginning with fricatives or sonorants. Where the monosyllabic word begins with a stop, the mechanical factor will outweigh the positional one, giving [təsuvjɛ̃ty] (*te souviens-tu?*) rather than [tsuvjɛ̃ty]. Where two of these monosyllabic words occur together at the beginning of a phrase, the competition for the phrase-initial syllable is between two equally 'unstable' vowels, and so the first schwa will be pronounced, unless the relative phonetic properties of the consonants favour its pronunciation in the second, that is, in effect, unless the first is a fricative or sonorant and the second a stop; thus [ʒənkɔ̃pʁãpa] (*je ne comprends pas*), but [ʒtəkɔ̃pʁã] (*je te comprends*).

Similar (but not identical) interacting effects of phonetic context are found to influence schwa pronunciation in initial, medial and final syllables of polysyllabic words. Furthermore, the pronunciation of schwa is variable across prosodic, morphological and syntactic contexts, and across registers and varieties; yet despite the evident inadequacy of descriptive accounts based purely on the segmental phonetic context, it is striking that many authors restrict their observations to this (e.g. Béchade 1992).

Amongst those who do mention the role of other linguistic factors there is a high degree of inconsistency as to what is mentioned. Thus, Delattre (1966) notes variability between lexical items: for single phrase-initial monosyllables he estimates that schwa is pronounced 1/10 of the time in *je*, *ce* and *se*, 1/4 of the time in *le*, 1/3 of the time in *ne* and *me*, half the time in *de*, and 2/3 of the time in *te* and *que*. As well as the nature of preceding consonant sequences, Tranel (1987a) lists the syntactic link between words and their position in the prosodic structure as influencing the pronunciation of word-final schwa. Thus, he claims that schwa is more likely in *(l)'énorme chagrin*, an adjective-noun sequence, than in the noun-verb sequence *(les) normes chagrinent*; and that it is more likely in *une carte verte*, where the following word is monosyllabic (and the following syllable stressed), than in *une carte vermeille*, where it is not. Valdman (1993) gives seven phonetic rules for schwa pronunciation, two of which are categorical and the rest variable. The only non-phonetic factor is mentioned after these and concerns the pragmatic prominence of the word involved: according to him, the first schwa of *demande* is more likely to be pronounced in *Ce n'est pas du tout ce que je te demande!*, where *ce que je te demande* is the most important part of the sentence from a communicative perspective, than in *Ce que je te demande, c'est de te taire!*, where *ce que je te demande* is given information, and what is new (and therefore communicatively more important) is *c'est de te taire* (1993:190). Most descriptive accounts at least mention stylistic variability, often in terms of the speech rate, but very few discuss regional variation.

It is clear, then, that attempts to formulate a simple principle to describe patterns of schwa pronunciation are bound to be inadequate, since these are governed by complex linguistic, pragmatic and sociolinguistic effects, the interaction of which has yet to be satisfactorily quantified. Until such complex quantification is carried out, it will not be possible to build an accurate descriptive model of variable schwa.

3.5   The phonemic identity of schwa

In Part I, Section 2.1.4, schwa is listed as part of the vowel system of French, but it is in fact by no means certain that it is justifiable to call it a phoneme on a par with the other vowel phonemes of the language. The question of the phonological status of schwa is inextricably bound up with questions of how to account for its behaviour.

It is possible to find minimal pairs which suggest that schwa could be a phoneme of French: for example, Dauses (1973) gives *ample rang*, /ɑ̃plərɑ̃/, versus *en pleurant*, /ɑ̃plœrɑ̃/, and *elle se le demande*, /ɛlsəldəmɑ̃d/, versus *elle seule demande*, /ɛlsœldəmɑ̃d/, which some of his adult Parisian informants differentiated systematically. There also exist many oft-cited minimal pairs where schwa contrasts with zero, for example *dehors*, /dəɔr/, versus *dors*, /dɔr/, *laisse-le entrer*, /lɛsləɑ̃tre/, versus *laisse l'entrée*, /lɛslɑ̃tre/. There are thus clearly cases where schwa contrasts significantly with /œ/ and with zero, and this would suggest it should be considered as a phoneme.

However, in the case of *dehors* and *monterions*, schwa contrasts with zero but not with /ø/ or /œ/. Given that the phonetic quality of schwa is commonly close to or identical with [œ] or [ø], it could be argued, therefore, that, at least in these cases, the phonemic contrast is between /Œ/[8] and zero, and that the vowel in question is not schwa at all. This argument is possible in the case of these two words because the schwas they contain are relatively fixed, that is, they are almost always pronounced. We shall take up further the phonemic implications of fixed schwa when we examine its changing patterns in **3.8** below.

The case of *laisse-le̞ entrer* versus *laisse l'entrée* is more complex. It is true that the presence of schwa versus zero signals a meaningful difference between these two strings of phonemes, just as in Section 3.2.1 of Part I the presence of /i/ versus /y/ was shown to signal a meaningful difference between the words *lis* and *lu*. However, the direct object pronoun *le̞* in *laisse-le̞ entrer* can also be pronounced with no phonetic schwa, as in *je l'ai vu*.[9] A common structuralist account of variable schwa is to state that it is a phoneme with two allophones, schwa and zero which are in partially free variation. This presents a conflict, in that whereas the allophonic analysis correctly implies that there is no significant contrast between schwa and zero in the [lə] versus [l] of, for example, [pʁɑ̃l(ə)ʃa] (*prends le̞ chat*), this cannot hold for the alternation between schwa and zero in *laisse-le̞ entrer* versus *laisse l'entrée*, which is significant. Moreover, the semantic distinction in the latter pair also exists between *le̞* in *laisse-le̞ chanter* and *le̞* in *laisse le̞ chat*, but here there is no phonetic difference to differentiate between the words: both are usually pronounced [lə]. This results in the anomalous situation of a minimal pair, *le̞* (object pronoun) ~ *le̞* (definite article), where the phonemic contrast differentiating the two members is /ə/ versus zero, and yet both words can be shown in other contexts to be pronounced either [lə] or [l], that is, either with schwa or zero.

The parallel problem for generative phonology is what to take as the underlying representation of schwa. Some abstract linear generative phonologists (e.g. Schane 1968) partially addressed this problem by taking as the underlying form the non-schwa vowels which alternate with schwa. Dell (1973) takes a different position, arguing for underlying schwa. For him the underlying vowel cannot be /œ/ because not only is there phonetic alternation between surface schwa and zero, which is not normally the case for /œ/, but schwa also enters into morphological alternations which do not occur with /œ/ (compare [kʁəve] ~ [kʁɛv] (*crever* ~ *crève*) with [abʁœve] ~ [abʁœv] (*abreuvez* ~ *abreuve*)). Note that although Dell and subsequent generativists discuss the phonetic quality of schwa, these arguments regarding its phonological status are entirely based on its distribution. Nevertheless, as Anderson points out following his discussion of the phonetic similarity of schwa and /œ/, 'most [linear generative phonologists] continue to write /ə/ in some forms and /œ/ in others, leaving the problem of the underlying value of /ə/ unsolved' (Anderson 1982:538).

3.6   Schwa ~ zero alternation: epenthesis versus deletion

Even if a satisfactory description had been elaborated of the effects which interact to govern the pronunciation versus non-pronunciation of schwa, this would not in itself constitute a phonological model. The central question here is not how to predict the likelihood of schwa being pronounced in a given set of (socio-)linguistic circumstances, but how to tell whether a schwa has the potential to appear at all.

This basic problem has been avoided hitherto by our explicitly and implicitly taking an orthographically based approach, stating that there is something present, usually *e*, which may be pronounced as schwa or may not be pronounced. An exclusively phonological account has to decide, in effect, whether there really is 'something' system-internal which is present at the phonemic or underlying level, and is optionally pronounced, or whether schwa is a purely phonetic element which is optionally inserted by some mechanism into the surface phonetics. The choice between these two basic starting points, which we shall refer to as deletion and epenthesis respectively, has been at the core of the debates about schwa within all major theoretical paradigms.

The question introduced in **3.4** above of how to incorporate the factors governing the variable pronunciation of schwa versus zero has been addressed in different ways by the scholars discussed below. Their accounts of the roles of these factors are at best partial, so we shall restrict ourselves here to the basic question: whatever the nature of the conditioning factors incorporated into these rules, should they model the alternation in terms of the deletion or the epenthesis of schwa?

The deletion versus epenthesis dichotomy is directly related to the phonemic status of schwa: if schwa is held to be a phoneme, then it is present in the phonemic representation of words and thus its non-pronunciation can be seen as representing the absence of something which is present at a more abstract level, even though it is expressed, as shown in **3.5** above, in terms of alternation between two allophones, schwa on the one hand and 'zero' on the other. The nature of the main question to be asked here is different, however: whereas the status of schwa as a phoneme or not rested on whether it contrasted meaningfully with other segments, the deletion versus epenthesis accounts of schwa ~ zero alternation are judged on whether they correctly predict the phonetic absence or presence of schwa.

3.6.1   Schwa ~ zero alternation as deletion

Traditional descriptions of schwa ~ zero alternation assume a deletion model by implication, although they do not do so explicitly. Thus, if anything,

Grammont and Delattre are giving a deletion account: Grammont, for example, says he calls schwa '*e*-caduc' because it is 'susceptible de tomber' (1948:115), implying that there is something present which can disappear.

Most linear generative accounts, including those of the concrete generative phonologists such as Tranel (1981), agree that initial and medial variable schwa is best dealt with by positing variable deletion of a segment which is present in the underlying representation. One problem with this approach is that the rules for deletion need to be prevented from applying to cases such as *belette* and *dehors*, where schwa is always pronounced. A possible solution would be to mark these schwas in the underlying representation as being exceptions to which a rule of deletion does not apply, but this is an *ad hoc* solution which complicates the account unnecessarily and adds no linguistic insight, since there is nothing which marks these cases as a class apart except for the fact that the schwa is not deleted. Generative and non-generative accounts alike agree that there is no good synchronic linguistic reason for treating this vowel as the same as allophonically alternating schwa. Since the quality of these 'fixed' schwas is often [ø] or [œ], it is analysed as being derived from /Œ/, a vowel to which schwa deletion does not apply. Once these fixed schwas are reanalysed as being /Œ/ and not schwa, then an optional rule of schwa deletion (or a rule stating that the phoneme /ə/ is realized as zero) can be applied to all remaining cases of schwa without affecting words like *belette*.

3.6.2   Schwa ~ zero alternation as epenthesis

The alternative to deletion is the view that schwa ~ zero alternation is best accounted for by positing the insertion of phonetic schwa into a string which contains no underlying schwa. Foremost amongst the proponents of epenthesis is Martinet, who treats fixed schwas as belonging to /Œ/, and variable schwas as epenthetic phonetic items inserted principally to make strings of consonants more easily pronounceable. In his view schwa is merely a 'lubrifiant' (1974a:216), since distributional criteria do not justify according it phonemic status. The fact that schwa can be absent in words where it is variable is taken to prove that its presence is not significant, and this fact is in turn taken as evidence in support of Martinet's analysis. The argument is somewhat weakened, however, by the fact that there are other phonemes which are variably elided in French, such as liquids in word-final consonant clusters, and yet are still present in the phonemic representation of the words in which they occur: *battre* can sometimes be pronounced [bat], but this is not taken to indicate that the phonemic representation of the word is */bat/.[10]

The place of schwa in the system is formalized by Martinet (e.g. 1972, 1974a) in terms of consonant allophony, following an idea first mooted in the early eighteenth century by Giles Vaudelin (see Cohen 1946): /l/, for example, is deemed to have two allophones, [l] and [lə]. As Tranel (1987b) points out, this formalization neatly captures the fact that schwa is unique amongst the French vowels in being unable to appear syllable-initially. It also captures the fact that the word-final schwa in words like *quatre* cannot be pronounced unless the second consonant of the preceding cluster is also pronounced: *[katə] is not a possible pronunciation of the word. Schwa is thus seen to be dependent for its pronunciation on the preceding consonant, which is accounted for in this model by the implication that it only exists as an integral part of one allophone of the consonant. A disadvantage of this approach is that it greatly increases the number of consonant allophones in the analysis. More seriously, schwa is treated in this account as a series of independent phenomena belonging to different consonant phonemes and the fact that, for example, [lə], [də], and [kə] have something in common is thus in effect lost.

The phonemic representation of words with variable schwa shows no trace of the schwa in the epenthetic account, so *petit* would be /pti/ and *le* (object pronoun) and *le* (definite article) would be /l/. This is justified on the grounds that, 'à quelques rares exceptions près, les usagers du français ne tiennent pas compte du "e muet" dans l'identification de leurs mots: ce qui est permanent dans *petite* c'est /ptit/' (Martinet and Walter 1973:23). One problem with this is that the 'rares exceptions' include common words such as *le* and *le*, which in *laisse-le entrer* and *laisse l'entrée* respectively are unambiguously distinguished for native speakers by the presence versus absence of schwa (see **3.5** above); the significant role of the presence versus absence of schwa in this case is not accounted for by treating schwa simply as a 'lubrifiant'.

A further, and more general, problem with epenthesis is accounting for how speakers know when to produce epenthetic schwa. Vachek (1933) is reported by Martinet (1974a:216) as claiming that the appearance of schwa is entirely predictable, but this is clearly not the case. Even if the complexity of the distribution indicated above is ignored and a simplistic *loi des trois consonnes* (or principle based on the permissible number of preceding consonants) is assumed to be valid, an account is needed of why there are words with sequences of more than three consonants, like *explication*, which are never pronounced with schwa. A possible explanation in this case lies in the syllable affinity of the consonants: /spl/ is an acceptable syllable onset in French (compare *splendeur*), so the only site where schwa might be inserted in *explication* is after the [k], which is a single consonant immediately preceded by a vowel (and hence would not trigger schwa insertion). There is, however, no place in structuralist or functionalist phonemic analyses for an appeal to syllable structure, so in their terms the non-appearance of schwa here is actually far from predictable.

The same is the case with pairs such as [s(ə)lav] (*se lave*), which has variable schwa, versus [slav] (*Slave*), which never has schwa between the two consonants: there is no way to predict from an underlying /slav/ sequence that there may be a schwa in *se lave* but never in *Slave*. This suggests that speakers need to know that there is a potential schwa in a given string, which means that there has to be some indication in the phonemic representation of something present. The formalization of schwa as part of a compound [Cə] allophone does not avoid this problem, since for exactly the same reasons there is no way to predict when [C] rather than [Cə] will occur.

3.6.3   The special case of word-final schwa

As described in **3.6.1**, both abstract and concrete generative accounts generally treat schwa ~ zero alternation in terms of deletion. However, the case of word-final schwa is exceptionally treated by both as inter-consonantal epenthesis. This solution is less problematic in generative phonology than in a phonemic account, since generative rules have access to information about morpheme and word boundaries, which allows the epenthesis to be restricted to CC sequences with an intermediate word boundary. Thus a schwa can be inserted, for instance, between the |t| and |b| of |kart#blø| (*carte bleue*) to give [kaʁtəblø], but not between the |r| and |t| of the first word. A phonemic account would only have access to the sequence of phonemes, and would not have a formal way of distinguishing between the two sequences.

There is, however, a major difference between concrete and abstract generative accounts of schwa word-finally. Both deal with the surface appearance of schwa at word boundaries by epenthesis, and for concrete generative phonologists (e.g. Tranel 1981), schwa never occurs word-finally in the underlying representation. However, in the abstract account (e.g. Dell 1973) there is an underlying schwa, which is deleted at a certain stage in the derivation. This is a different schwa from the one which eventually surfaces in the phonetic representation (which is subsequently inserted by epenthesis). It is important to stress that the two schwas are not the same, and they have completely unrelated functions. The epenthetic schwa is posited to account for the variable appearance of schwa in speakers' pronunciation of strings like *carte bleu*, *ours*([ə]) *blanc* etc. The deleted schwa is a completely separate segment posited purely for structural reasons, as a 'protective schwa' to block the application of certain rules such as final consonant deletion (see **1.4.2**), and nasalization (see **2.4.1.1**).[11]

In this debate, there are clearly two issues. One is the specific question of accounting for the schwa which surfaces in *carte bleu* and *ours blanc*; as already mentioned, it is agreed that this is a matter of epenthesis, which it is straightforward to model in generative phonology. The other concerns the more general question of whether it is valid to posit an abstract underlying segment at all to achieve unrelated derivational outcomes such as the non-nasalization of the vowel of *samedi* (underlying representation: |samədi|) or the non-deletion of the final [t] of *petite* (underlying representation: |pətit + ə|). Even if the validity of this abstract mechanism (which has already been discussed in Chapters 1 and 2) is accepted, it is not necessarily correct to assume that the abstract vowel is schwa. In fact, any underlying vowel would suffice as a protective block on these rules, but schwa is selected on the grounds that it can be shown to underlie the vowel which surfaces in some rare cases, such as with a following *h-aspiré*.[12] It has also been argued, in Schane (1972), that the existence in southern French of phonetic schwas corresponding to the underlying locations of protective schwa constitutes further evidence for the existence of the latter in all varieties of French. However, there is plenty of evidence to show that this correspondence is not always regular, and even if it were, as Tranel (1981) demonstrates, it can be dangerous to assume that all dialects of a language must share identical underlying representations (see also **2.6**).

3.7   Non-linear accounts of schwa ~ zero alternation

Schwa has naturally continued to be the object of attention for proponents of more recent developments in phonological theory. One non-linear analysis proposed by Anderson (1982) is to model schwa as an empty vowel slot; that is, there is a skeletal V slot present in the underlying representation of the morpheme, but it has no features attached to it, as illustrated in (1):

(1)   V
      |
      [ ]

When the consonant preceding the empty slot is syllabified with the preceding vowel, as in (2a), there is no reason for the features to be filled in, and the slot remains empty. A further principle subsequently deletes the syllable, giving the output in (2b) (for *la semaine*):

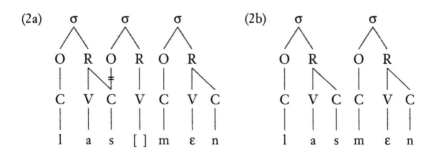

If the consonant preceding the empty vowel slot is unable to syllabify with the preceding vowel because the coda of the preceding syllable is full, as in (3a), the feature matrix is filled in as [ø] (or [œ]) and the syllable is pronounced, as in (3b) (*une semaine*):

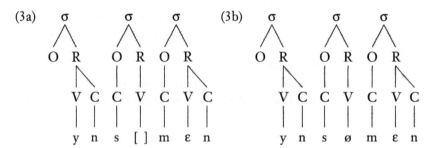

This solution has various advantages. It is in some respects an epenthetic account, but the empty skeletal V slot allows the potential schwa site to be marked in the underlying representation, thus avoiding the unwanted epenthesis which causes such a problem for the structuralist and linear generative analyses. Moreover, because there are no features linked to the skeletal slot, the problem of identifying the underlying vowel as different from [ø] or [œ], even though it surfaces most often as a front rounded vowel, is avoided, since no artificial difference has to be introduced into its feature matrix.[13] However, there are also some problems; for example, what happens in the case of initial schwas, as in [ʒpɑ̃s] (*je pense*), where there is no preceding syllable to which the consonant may attach? More fundamentally, since the basic syllable structure in French is CV[14], the behaviour of the pre-schwa consonant is aberrant in attaching to the syllable of a preceding vowel slot in the skeletal tier rather than to that of the following (albeit empty) vowel slot, and no explanation is given within this account of why it should do so.

The problem of motivating the attachment of a preceding consonant to a preceding syllable is addressed by Tranel (1987b) who posits the opposite model to Anderson's, that is, one with no skeletal slot corresponding to variable schwa, but a floating schwa, like the floating word-final consonants proposed to account for liaison (see **1.4.3**). This is schematized in (4):

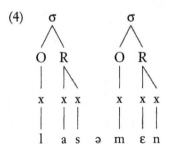

Because there is no following vocalic skeletal slot, the /s/ of *semaine* will have no reason to syllabify onto the following schwa, and will therefore automatically syllabify onto the preceding /a/ vowel, just as the /n/ at the end of *semaine* syllabifies onto the preceding /ɛ/ because it too has no following empty vowel slot to which to attach. This eliminates the problem of the apparently unexplained leftward attachment of consonants preceding a potential schwa. Since the schwa is not attached to a skeletal slot, and thus not to a syllable either, it is not pronounced. If, as in *une semaine* in (4) above, the preceding consonant is unable to syllabify with the preceding vowel, a special rule of syllable formation generates a new syllable, and a new skeletal slot to which both the /s/ and the schwa attach, giving the output in (5):

(5)

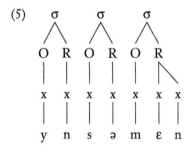

The problem of having to justify the non-pronunciation of schwa in *je pense* is also attenuated by there not being a vocalic skeletal slot to which the /ʒ/ could syllabify, but the resultant [ʒ̊p] sequence in the onset is still not explicable except in terms of an *ad hoc* rule applying late in the derivation to allow [ʒ̊] to share the onset node of the following [p] (Tranel 1987b:852).

These two different non-linear models of schwa thus each have an element of deletion and epenthesis at different levels of structure. They apparently go some way to giving an account of simple cases of variable medial schwa which avoids the problem of erroneously predicting its occurrence, but there remain problems in both models for the prediction of initial variable schwa, which still needs to be treated as a special case.

3.8   Changing patterns of schwa ~ zero alternation

All schwas have evolved from non-schwa vowels in Latin, and all are assumed at some stage regularly to have been pronounced as the mid central lax vowel represented in the IPA as [ə] and subsequently to have become more fronted and lip-rounded, although as we have already noted, their pronunciation in contemporary French is highly variable. There is some evidence that schwa is continuing to undergo change in certain contexts in both its pronunciation and its allophonic alternation with zero, but there is disagreement about the nature and direction of its evolution, particularly in word-initial position.

3.8.1   Word-initial schwa: stabilization in progress?

Walter comments that, 'ce qui apparaît actuellement, c'est une stabilisation grandissante de la voyelle de première syllabe, quel que soit le nombre des consonnes précédentes, et en particulier lorsqu'il y en a une seule [. . .]. La constatation a été faite depuis de nombreuses années' (Walter 1990:29). This runs counter to assertions by, amongst others, Malécot, who claims that schwa in all positions is undergoing 'progressively spreading elision' (1976:93), that is deletion in an increasing number of contexts. Hansen (1994) presents an empirical study of word-initial schwa which attempts to assess whether the pronunciation of schwa really is becoming fixed in these contexts by comparing two corpora of Parisian French collected in 1972–74 and 1989. She hypothesizes that if stabilization is increasing, the younger speakers in both corpora should pronounce schwa in this position more often than the older speakers, reflecting the patterns of change in progress (see Part I, Section 3.5). Her results for word-initial position are shown in Figure 3.1, and indicate the young people in both corpora pronouncing schwa in this position less frequently than older speakers, which would seem to suggest that the change is in the opposite direction.[15] However, when comparisons are made across real rather than apparent time, the picture is not so clear-cut: the direction of the effect is the same in both corpora, but the difference between the rates of schwa pronunciation in conversational

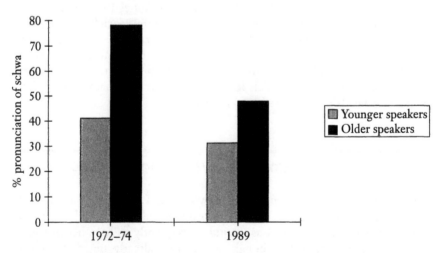

Figure 3.1   The pronunciation of word-initial schwa in Parisian speakers recorded in 1972–74 and 1989 (adapted from Hansen (1994:34–5), Figures 1 and 2)

speech by the younger speakers in the 1972–74 corpus and by those in the later corpus is not statistically significant. Had the age-grading been a reflection of change in progress, one would expect the rate of schwa pronunciation of the younger speakers in the earlier corpus to be the same as that of adults in the later corpus (since by then their generation would be 15 years older), and that of the younger speakers in the later corpus to be significantly lower. It seems, then, that non-pronunciation of schwa is a fairly stable feature of younger people's speech and that the pronunciation of schwa increases as they become older. In fact in read speech the youngest speakers in the 1989 corpus pronounce more schwa than older speakers (see Hansen 1994:36), which suggests that they are aware that pronunciation with schwa is the prestige norm and are distancing themselves from that norm in conversational speech.

The comparative findings thus do not constitute evidence against the 'stabilisation grandissante' of schwa, but neither do they constitute positive evidence for it. Hansen goes on to examine the linguistic factors governing the pronunciation of schwa in this position in her corpus to see whether they show any evidence of changing patterns, and particularly evidence of lexical diffusion. Her analysis shows that there are lexemes where schwa is never pronounced in conversational speech (e.g. *semaine*, *sera*), and others where it is always pronounced (e.g. *relation*, *mener*), and many degrees of variability in between, which is what one would expect to find when a sound change is diffusing through the lexicon (see Part I, Section 3.5). However, there is also complex interaction between this lexical conditioning and various other linguistic factors:

- The interaction between preceding and following consonants plays a role, but a more complex one than that suggested by Malécot (1976)
- A preceding /r/ highly favours pronunciation of schwa whatever the following consonant and whether the syllable represents the prefix *re-* (as in *remonter*) or not (as in *regarder*)
- Frequent words are much less likely to be pronounced with initial schwa than less frequent ones.

Robust variation of a phonological feature between lexemes is normally taken as indicative of the spread of change, and the fact that words which used to be variable are now invariably pronounced with schwa indicates that the change may indeed be in the direction of stabilization. However, the fact that more frequent words favour the non-pronunciation of schwa shows that if this is the case, the change is still not very far advanced. Thus, both the sociolinguistic and the linguistic evidence in Hansen's study are inconclusive, as she acknowledges, and only ongoing monitoring of the situation will reveal whether change is in the direction of Malécot's claimed 'progressively spreading elision' or of Walter's 'stabilisation grandissante'.

Whether or not Hansen's findings are truly indicative of change in progress, it is clear that some change has occurred which has resulted in the non-alternating pronunciation of word-initial schwa, for example in *belette*, and this has implications for the analysis of the phonological system. The justification for analysing schwa hitherto as something other than /Œ/, despite the phonetic similarity between surface schwa and [ø] or [œ], has been that schwa alternates allophonically with zero whereas /Œ/ does not, but this ceases to be a valid argument when schwa is always pronounced. The evidence given here supports the suggestion made in 3.5 above that since there are no other synchronic grounds for treating fixed schwas as the same as alternating schwas, and since although they contrast with zero (e.g. *dehors* vs. *dors*) they do not contrast with /Œ/, they should be reanalysed as /Œ/. In other words an historical change is deemed to have taken place by which the vowels concerned have passed from being phonemically schwa to being /Œ/.

Walter makes an explicit link between the stabilization of schwa and its changing pronunciation: 'A partir du moment où la voyelle traditionnellement appelée *e* "muet" se réalisait chez de plus en plus de personnes comme un de ces phonèmes [/ø/ or /œ/] à part entière [...] on pouvait s'attendre à ce qu'elle se comportât comme les phonèmes de la langue, c'est-à-dire qu'elle ne tombât pas.' (Walter 1990:34). This is too strong a claim to make on the basis of pronunciation alone, stating as it does that any schwa which is consistently pronounced as [ø] or [œ] will eventually become fixed, with the strong implication that all schwas will. Note that the justification for the reanalysis of schwa as /Œ/ is both phonetic and distributional, and that the wide range of evidence surveyed in earlier sections of this chapter shows clearly that phonetic similarity alone does not justify the analysis of two segments as phonemically the same.

3.8.2   Change in non-initial schwa

As with the word-initial schwas, there is disagreement in the literature about whether schwa in word-medial syllables is becoming more or less frequently pronounced. Fónagy (1989:238) includes *appelez* (pronounced [apəle]) without further comment in a list of examples of the increasing frequency of schwa pronunciation (most of which are word-initial), but Walter (1990) draws a sharp distinction between the stabilization of word-initial schwa, which is pronounced even when the word is not at the beginning of the rhythmic group (e.g. [deʃəmine] (*des cheminées*)), and the regular non-pronunciation of word-medial schwa (e.g. [samdi] (*samedi*)). It is reasonable to assume that the pronunciation of schwa in this context is influenced by the same variables as those we have seen to influence its pronunciation in other contexts, for example the nature of the preceding and following consonants, speech rate and register. However, since there are no quantitative data available which treat this particular context separately, it is not yet possible to know whether Fónagy's inclusion of *appelez* is indicative of a movement towards increased categorical word-internal schwa pronunciation or whether the example he cites merely indicates that there is indeed a degree of variability, which could be very small.

Word-finally in pre-pausal position schwa pronunciation is generally held to occur only in elevated declamatory styles. However, Fónagy also describes the increased frequency of pre-pausal schwa, which he calls '*e* d'appui', in the casual speech of young people. Many of his subjects were observed during television programmes or films, but some were observed in real life, for example a young travel agent who pronounced schwa at the end of 'C'est bizarr*e*' and 'Il y a un changement quand mêm*e*'. This supporting schwa is particularly common at the end of interrogatives, exclamatives, imperatives and other utterances with a marked pragmatic function, such as the expression of surprise or indignation. His examples include: 'Mais qu'est-ce qui se pass*e*?' (by a young woman in the metro), 'Bonjour[ə]' (by a telephone switchboard operator), 'Venez vit*e*!' (by a young woman in a film). However, it is highly unlikely that this trend represents a move towards the eventual stabilization of word-final schwa, since outside this particular set of pragmatic circumstances it appears far less frequently than word-initial or word-medial schwa.

Suggested Reading

Historical development:
  Fouché (1958), Morin (1978).
Descriptions of schwa:
  Delattre (1966), Léon (1978), Price (1971), Tranel (1981, 1987a).
The phonetic and phonemic identity of schwa:
  Martinet (1972), Morin (1978), Walker (1993).
Schwa ~ zero alternation:
  Delattre (1966), Grammont (1948), Malécot (1976).
Schwa in generative phonology:
  Anderson (1982), Dell (1973), Dell and Selkirk (1978), Morin (1988), Schane (1968), Tranel (1987b, 1988), Verluyten (1988).
Variation and change in patterns of schwa pronunciation:
  Durand, Slater and Wise (1988), Fónagy (1989), Hansen (1994), Lefebvre (1988), Walter (1990).

Notes

1. Throughout this chapter, we shall follow the convention of underlining in the orthographical representation the letter *e* corresponding to the token of schwa under discussion.

2. As we saw in Part I, this kind of alternation is dealt with in the morphology rather than in the phonology of a structuralist description, but generative phonology has to give an account of it as a (morpho-)phonological issue, and it therefore has implications for the underlying representation of a surface schwa. Concerning the debate surrounding how such alternations are handled, and their relation to schwa representation, see Schane (1968), Dell (1973), Morin (1988) and Tranel (1988).

3. For further brief discussions of these orthographical terms see Carton (1974:63–4), and Walter (1990:27–8).

4. 'Mid centralized [ø]'.

5. See, for example, Delattre (1966), Price (1991), Tranel (1987a), Valdman (1993).

6. Henceforth, we shall use the term 'initial schwa' to refer to schwa in initial syllables. It should be noted that schwa is always preceded by at least one consonant in the syllable, and thus never occurs in word-initial position.

7. Note that the schwa in *ne* is not counted as a potential competitor with the preceding schwa in this case, since it has been eliminated by the categorical process of elision due to the following vowel of *ai*.

8. For convenience we have used the archiphoneme symbol /Œ/ in this chapter to represent '/ø/ or /œ/', since in most cases, the alternative pronunciation to schwa could be either [ø] or [œ], and the alternative phonemic analysis either /ø/ or /œ/.

9. It could be argued that postverbal *le*, where schwa is always pronounced, is an allomorph on a par with *moi* (as opposed to preverbal *me*). In that case, it would be amenable to analysis as /Œ/ in the same way as the schwa of *dehors*. Difficulties, however, remain as illustrated by the examples below containing the masculine singular definite article.

10. The contrast between /batr/ (*battre*) and /bat/ (*(qu'il) batte*) is clearly real for speakers of French, and depends on the presence versus absence of /r/.

11. Note that protective schwas are also posited word-internally for words like *samedi* (where it serves to block nasalization), where they never occur on the surface.

12. The surface schwa in these cases is derived from the underlying vowel and is not epenthetic. For a counter-proposal of insertion before *h-aspiré*, see Tranel (1981:286–8). Note too that some accounts (e.g. Schane 1968) do indeed posit a non-schwa underlying vowel as mentioned in 3.5.

13. The model also has advantages when applied to morphological alternations between schwa and /e/. For details see Anderson (1982) and Tranel (1987b).

14. See Chapter 1 for an explanation of how this is reflected in the phenomenon of *enchaînement*.

15. Ironically, given his claim that deletion is spreading, Malécot found less deletion in his youngest group of speakers than in some of his adult speakers, but he maintains that this is because the youngest speakers have just entered adulthood and are thus emulating conservative prestige forms, calling them '"apprentices" of the "establishment"' (Malécot 1976:106). His claim is, in effect, that they are hypercorrecting. It is true that for all the speakers aged 30 and over the tendency is for more deletion the younger the speakers, but the percentage differences are extremely small, with just a 4% difference between the oldest and second-youngest groups, and they were not subjected to statistical analysis; moreover, the figures take all possible occurrences of schwa together, whatever its position in the utterance, so they need to be interpreted with caution.

4

Verb morphology: conjugation classes and the definition of regularity

4.1 Introduction

In this chapter we will focus on one of the major and most widely discussed issues in the field of verb morphology, which has preoccupied the writers both of pedagogic grammars and of linguistic analyses of Modern French: how the different verb paradigms should be grouped together into conjugation classes. As we have seen in Part I (Section 2.2), a striking characteristic of French verb morphology is the difference between the morphology of written and spoken French, and in particular the much reduced system of spoken French. Consequently, a major question in discussions of the classification of verbs is whether analysis should be based primarily, or indeed exclusively, on either written or spoken forms. In presenting and evaluating different analyses of French verbs into conjugation classes, a number of other related problems will be discussed:

- Desiderata: for what purpose and for whom are the analyses intended
- Whether the analysis should focus on infinitive endings or on stems
- Which forms should be accounted for in the analysis, and in particular whether the *passé simple*, imperfect subjunctive, infinitive and participles should be included
- The extent to which the choice of allomorph is explicable in phonological terms
- The definition of regularity and irregularity.

4.2 Preliminaries: segmentation

Since the majority of classification schemes are based on looking at either verb endings (and especially infinitive endings) or verb stems, it is important to be able to identify these. As we shall see, there is considerable disagreement between linguists regarding how best to segment forms, and variation according to whether the emphasis is placed on written or spoken forms.

4.2.1 Problems of segmentation

In Part I (3.2.2), we alluded to some of the difficulties associated with structuralist approaches to verb morphology, in which the morphemes are identified by the twin processes of commutation and distribution. Thus while the segmentation of the verb *aimer* is relatively easy, so that the stem *aim-* is identified on the basis of *aim-ons, aim-ez, aim-e, aim-é* etc., and the ending by comparison with forms such as *aim-er, mang-er, chant-er* etc., there are significant difficulties with this approach when there is variation in the stem or the verb is suppletive. What, for example, is the correct segmentation of forms such as *(il) a* and *(ils) ont*? There is, moreover, frequent disagreement between different linguists as to which forms should be segmented. For example, Dubois considers that the forms *vais* [vɛ], *va, vas* [va] and *vont* [vɔ̃] constitute three different stems and does not attempt to segment them further, whereas Gross considers that these forms contain one stem, *v-*, plus the endings *-ais, -as, -a, -ont*. Similarly, Martinet chooses not to segment *(vous) êtes*, whereas Dubois argues that the [t] of [ɛt] might be seen as analogous to that of [dit] and [fɛt] and thus should be segmented (Pinchon and Coute 1981:43). The treatment of variation in verb stems in different approaches will be discussed further below (**4.7**).

As already suggested, differences between written and spoken French may be reflected in different segmentation of verb forms in the two media. In the following examples, taken from Pinchon and Coute (1981:35), the analysis based on the orthographic form results in more segments than that based on the surface phonetic form (the number of elements does not include the subject pronoun):

(1) *tu li-s*   (2 elements)   /ty li/   (1 element)
     il jou-e   (2 elements)   /il ʒu/   (1 element)
     il lis-ai-t (3 elements)   /il liz-ɛ/ (2 elements)

The number of stems or roots can also vary between written and spoken French, although here the different phonetic stem forms might simply be explained as allophonic variants ([u]~[w]; [i]~[j]):

(2) *joue-* (1 stem)   [ʒu]~[ʒwɔ̃] (2 different stems, as in *je joue* [ʒəʒu]
                            vs *nous jouons* [nuʒwɔ̃])
     appréci- (1 stem)   [apresi]~[apresj] (2 different stems, as in *j'apprécie*
                            [ʒapresi] vs *nous apprécions* [nuzapresjɔ̃])[1]

In the following example the difficulty relates to the presence of an orthographic *-e*, which is required to ensure that the *g* of the stem is pronounced [ʒ] when followed by *-o* or *-a*:

(3) *nag-/nage-* (2 different stems)   /naʒ/ (1 stem)

Such asymmetries have led to much debate as to whether an adequate account of verb morphology should focus primarily on written or spoken morphology, or, indeed, whether they should seek to bridge the gap between the two media. In broad terms we may note a tendency away from analysis of written forms to an increased preoccupation with accounting for spoken forms (see below).

4.2.2   Stem and ending versus stem, infix and ending

There is further disagreement amongst linguists regarding whether it is preferable to make a simple twofold division into stem and ending, or whether it is possible, or indeed desirable, to segment the 'ending' further into smaller component parts. Rather than making a traditional segmentation (based here on orthographic forms) along the lines, for instance: *chant-ons, chant-ez, chant-ions, chant-iez*, which gives four different endings (*-ons, -ez, -ions, -iez*), might there be an advantage in considering that we have here two endings, *-ons* and *-ez*, preceded in the case of *chantions* and *chantiez* by an infix *-i-*? We shall consider here two examples of this kind of segmentation, one based on written forms (Price 1971), and the other on spoken forms (Pinchon and Coute 1981).

Price segments the following written forms into stem, one or two infixes, plus ending:

Table 4.1   A sample of the segmentation of written forms into stem, infix, ending (Price 1971:168–82)

	Stem	Infix(es)	Ending
chantais	*chant-*	*-ai-*	*-s*
chanterai	*chante-*	*-r-*	*-ai*
chanterais	*chante-*	*-r- + -ai-*	*-s*
chantions	*chant-*	*-i-*	*-ons*
finissons	*fini-*	*-ss-*[2]	*-ons*
finissions	*fini-*	*-ss- + -i-*	*-ons*

There appear to be a number of advantages to this approach. First, it allows easier identification of the similarities and differences between forms and thus the capturing of generalizations. Second, it leads to a significant reduction in the number of endings in the inventory. Indeed, with very few exceptions, Price manages to reduce the number of endings for the written forms of the three persons singular, for example, to one of three fundamental types:

(i)   *-e, -es, -e* used for   (a)   the present indicative of all *-er* verbs and a few others, notably *ouvrir, couvrir, offrir, souffrir*;

(b)   the present subjunctive of all verbs except *être* and *avoir*.

(ii)   *-s, -s, -t* used for   (a)   the present indicative of all verbs except regular *-er* verbs, *avoir* and *aller*[3];

(b) the *passé simple* of all verbs except *-er* verbs;
(c) the imperfect and conditional forms of all verbs.

(iii) *-ai, -as, -a* used for (a) the present indicative of *avoir*;
(b) the future tense of all verbs;
(c) the *passé simple* of *-er* verbs.

The ending for the first person singular is always therefore *-e, -ai*, or *-s* regardless of whether, for instance, the *-s* is preceded directly by the stem as in *(je) mets*, or is the ending of an imperfect or conditional form, *(je) mettais, mettrais*.

Some tenses which do not follow exactly one of these patterns may be considered as representing 'mixed sets'. For instance, the endings of the imperfect subjunctive of all verbs and of the present subjunctive of *avoir* (*-e, -es, -t*) might be construed as a mixture of types (i) and (ii), while the present indicative endings of *aller* (*-s, -s, -a*) represent a mixture of types (ii) and (iii) together with variation in the stem.[4] In the case of the other persons the simplification results in a choice between one of two forms: *-ons/-mes* for the first person plural; *-ez/-tes* for the second person plural; *-ent/-ont* for the third person plural. In this scheme the number of infixes is similarly limited to *-ss-* [s], *-i-* [i]~[j], *-ai-* and *-r-*.

There are, however, a number of difficulties with this approach. The decision to base the analysis on written forms often complicates unnecessarily the description. For instance, in Table **4.**1 two different stems *chant-* and *chante-* are identified, although they are pronounced identically. As can be seen from Table **4.**2 below, the description of stems is in general not simplified. Price simply lists, for example, the following verb forms, in which the stems are indicated with bold type:

Table 4.2 Examples of variation in verb stems (Price 1971:182)

mettre	*mets* [mε]	*mettent*	*mis*			
devoir	*doit*	*doivent*	*devons*	*dut*		
voir	*voit* [vwa]	*voyons* [vwaj-]	*verrai*	*vit*		
vouloir	*veut*	*veulent*	*voulons*	*voudrai*	*veuille*	
prendre	*prends* [prɑ̃]	*prennent*	*prenons*	*prendrai* [prɑ̃d-]	*pris*	
pouvoir	*peut*	*peuvent*	*pouvons*	*pourrons*	*puisse*	*put*

Indeed, it might be argued (but see below) that the only verbs with the same stem in all parts of the verb are those following the pattern of *finir, punir* which always have a stem ending in *-i* (*fini-, puni-*). In addition, Price ignores the problem of how to analyse the stem of the present tense of *avoir* if the endings for this are considered to be *-ai, -as, -a*, conforming to type (ii). The question is therefore left open as to whether we are dealing here with no stem or some kind of 'empty' stem. Note too how in the case of *prendre* reference has also been made to the pronunciation of the stems in order to distinguish *prends* [prã] and *prendrai* [prãd], which, if the analysis were based exclusively on written forms, would only render one stem *prend-*.

The advantages of basing the analysis on spoken forms can be seen from Pinchon and Coute's (1981) segmentation. In this system all regular verbs are composed of a series of 2, 3 or 4 elements as follows:

Table 4.3   Segmentation of spoken forms (Pinchon and Coute 1981:41)

1: base lexicale (compulsory) (variable)	2: marque 1 (optional) /r/ Ø	3: marque 2 (optional) /ɛ/ /j/ Ø	4: désinance (compulsory) /ɔ̃/ /e/ /ɛ/ /a/ Ø

Pinchon and Coute go on to argue that the distribution of these elements according to the tense and ending is fairly straightforward, as Table 4.4 illustrates:

Table 4.4   Distribution and possible combinations of the four elements throughout the conjugations (Pinchon and Coute 1981:41)

variable	éléments stables				
1	2	3	4		Séries formées
base	(ə)r	(i)j	ɔ̃	e	Cond. Prés. 4–5[5]
base	(ə)r	ɛ			Cond. Prés. 1–2–3–6
base	(ə)r		ɛ / ɔ̃	a / e	Futur 1–2–3– 4–5–6
base		(i)j	ɔ̃	e	Imp. 4–5, Subj. Prés. 4–5
base			ɛ		Imp. 1–2–3–6
base			ɔ̃	e	Ind. Prés. 4–5
base			zéro		Ind. Prés. 1– 2–3–6; Subj. Prés. 1–2–3–6

As should already be evident from the above discussion, there is considerable disagreement between linguists as to what should be considered as part of the stem, and what as an infix. Whilst Price (1971), Wagner and Pinchon (1962), and Marty (1971), for instance, consider the /s/ of /finisɔ̃/, /finise/ etc. to be an infix and the root or stem to be /fini/, Pinchon and Coute (1981) and the linguists we shall discuss in **4.5** and **4.**6 below argue that the /s/ is rather part of the stem, although they differ amongst themselves as to whether the verb has two stems, /fini/ and /finis/, or one stem, /finis/, which loses its final consonant in certain circumstances. Whilst Pinchon and Coute's *marque 1* and *marque 2* are purely inflectional markers, Marty (1971) includes stem consonants amongst his infixes (such as the /d/ of *vendre*), whilst Wagner and Pinchon (1962) place alongside the *-ss-* of verbs of the *finir* type (which they call a 'suffix'), derivational suffixes as found, for instance, in *criailler* (vs *crier*) or *rêvasser* (vs *rêver*).

It is striking that despite the very obvious difficulties of segmenting French verb forms, virtually all accounts of French verb morphology continue to attempt to segment forms into their component morphemes. A rare exception is Morin (1998) who argues for a word-based approach in his discussion of the workings of analogy in creating non-standard forms (see **4.8** below).

4.3 Classification into verb conjugation classes: desiderata

What is required of a system that classifies verbs into conjugation classes? Ideally, such a classification should comprise a relatively small number of classes, and these should capture real regularities and meaningful generalizations between different verbs. It should be relatively easy and uncontroversial to place any given verb in the system. In addition, the groupings might reflect not only the coherence of the categories, but also frequency of usage; a successful scheme might also explain how speakers and learners make conjugation 'errors' through the working of analogy.

When evaluating a classification scheme, a further consideration to take into account is its purpose, including for whom it is intended. For instance, simplicity and learnability will be primary concerns for pedagogic accounts – this is the reason given by Béchade (1992) for retaining a traditional classification – while linguistic descriptions might tolerate more complexity, if at the same time the scheme appeared more faithfully to capture meaningful generalizations and have greater explanatory value. Some accounts make the modelling of native speaker competence central; Morin (1987b:14), for example, argues that any scheme should be a 'modèle de la grammaire du sujet parlant'.

In **4.4** we will offer a critical discussion of traditional classifications; these traditional schemes will then be contrasted with Dubois's radically different analysis (4.5), and with those schemes that argue that all French verbs belong essentially to one of two classes (4.6).

4.4   Traditional classifications

Traditional classifications, such as those generally taught in schools, exhibit the following principal characteristics: they are based on infinitive endings, on the written forms, and are partly historical in nature.[6] Many textbooks use a three-fold classification of the type:

Class 1:   infinitive ending in -er (and first person singular in -e). This is by far the most numerous class, comprising some 90% of all verbs (c. 4000 verbs). It is fairly regular and is an open or productive class in the sense that new French verbs are typically assimilated into this class.

Class 2:   infinitive ending in -ir and with a lengthened stem with -ss- (or infix, see above). This class comprises a little over 300 verbs and is more homogeneous and predictable than the first. It is only minimally productive, that is, very few new verbs are assimilated into this conjugation (a notable example is *alunir* formed on the analogy of *atterrir*).

Class 3:   comprising all other verbs.[7] This is somewhat larger than class 2 (350–70 members), is a very heterogeneous grouping of verbs which are mostly frequently used[8], and is non-productive. It is generally said to have three subclasses:
   -ir verbs without the infix -(i)ss-, e.g. *servir*
   -oir verbs (c.30 members), e.g. *valoir*
   -re verbs (c.100 members), e.g. *lire*.

While there are a number of variations on this type of classification, the status of schemes based on infinitive endings is confirmed by the fact that since 1910 there has been official recognition of one such scheme. This divides verbs into two main groups, a 'living' conjugation, into which new verbs enter and which includes -er verbs and -ir verbs with the infix -(i)ss-, and a 'dead' conjugation comprising -ir, -oir, and -re verbs. To these must be added, of course, irregular and defective verbs (see below).[9]

What is perhaps more surprising is the fact that the traditional three-fold conjugation classification is adopted by a number of leading generativists, and notably Schane (1968), despite the originality of many aspects of his account of French. Schane (1968:67) maintains that the division of verbs into three principal conjugations based on infinitive endings is correct, the first 'productive' conjugation comprising -er verbs, the second -ir verbs, whether with or without -*iss*, and the third -*re* and -*oir* verbs. He justifies this division, however, on internal structural evidence, arguing that the conjugations are distinguishable by their thematic vowel, which is tense |A| in the first conjugation and |I| in the second conjugation, and in the case of the third conjugation tense |E| for -*oir* verbs and lax |e| for -*re* verbs.[10] While the motivation for Schane's classification at first appears very different from the traditional rationale, when we consider the relationship between the thematic vowel chosen by Schane and the vowel of the Latin infinitive (e.g. *aimer* < *am*a̱*re*; *sentir* < *sent*i̱*re*; *devoir* < *deb*ē̱*re*; *mettre* < *mitt*e̱*re*), the links become evident. Indeed this has motivated some to consider that Schane's morphological analysis is, in some respects, very traditional. Only in a few cases does Schane offer a different classification from that based on the infinitive endings; for example, verbs of the type *venir, mourir* are said to be not second but third conjugation verbs on the grounds that they display stem alternation which is characteristic of third conjugation verbs. They therefore have the thematic vowel |E| which is raised to /i/ in the infinitive when it is stressed.

What are the strengths and weaknesses of traditional classifications based on written infinitive endings? On the positive side, they are relatively simple compared with some of the alternative systems proposed, a fact which probably explains their central place in teaching French verb morphology both to native speakers and to foreigners. In addition, Martinet (1974b:107) notes the frequency of occurrence of infinitives in spoken French and the fact that children hear them from an early age, whether in injunctions of the type, *il faut boire*, in the compound future, *on va s'amuser*, or after verbs such as *pouvoir, savoir,* and *vouloir*.

However, a number of substantial objections have been made against these classifications. There are difficulties of a general nature associated with the threefold classification – it relies too heavily on historical and etymological considerations at the expense of synchronic reality, it underplays the closed nature of certain conjugations, and it is based on the written language and therefore does not take account of the gulf between written and spoken forms and the primacy which should be assigned to the latter by linguists.

Two other important criticisms may be levelled against it. First, it may be argued that this scheme does not reflect the complexity of verb morphology in that verbs with the same infinitive ending may nevertheless conjugate very differently. (A contrast is generally made with the situation in Latin where it is said that the infinitive ending furnished the model for a complete class of verbs; however, even here predictability of form is not complete, for example, the verbs *amare, sonare* and *stare* all belong to the same class based on the identity of the infinitive ending, yet their perfect forms, *amavi, sonui, steti*, are formed in quite different ways.) Class 3 is a particularly diverse and heterogeneous category, as indeed are its subclasses. For instance, members of the

-ir subclass (i.e. those without the infix *-(i)ss-*) may exhibit considerable variation in the way they conjugate. In other words, knowledge of the infinitive does not allow automatic generation of the other forms of the paradigm. While *venir*, for instance, has four different stems (/vjẽ/, /vən/, /vjen/, /vjẽd/) plus the 'historic' stem /vẽ/, *courir* and *ouvrir*, for example, both have only one stem; yet these two verbs also differ in that the latter uses the endings typical of an *-er* verb in the present indicative. Whereas the past participle of *courir* is *couru* and *venir, venu*, that of *mourir* is *mort* while *ouvrir* has *ouvert*. Again, while *partir* has as the first person plural of the present indicative *partons*, its derivative *répartir* has *répartissons*. The class of *-re* verbs is equally lacking in unity, both in the diversity in the number of stems of its members (compare *rendre, croire, boire*) and in the differences of endings (*vous dites/vous contredisez*). Second, basing the classification on written infinitival endings can fail to capture generalizations and can mask similarities between verb paradigms. A frequently cited example of this is provided by the pair *croire* and *voir*, which in the traditional scheme are members of different subclasses of Class 3 verbs. Yet not only are their infinitive endings phonologically identical (/krwar/, /vwar/), they also manifest a number of similarities of conjugation, e.g. *croyais/voyais; cru/vu*. More generally, in the spoken language there is in the case of many verbs a contrast between a 'short' stem which ends in a vowel and a 'long' stem which ends in a consonant (e.g. /fini/ ~ /finis/; /rã/ ~ /rãd/).

4.5 Stem-based models

These difficulties have lead linguists to consider radically different approaches to this question. One such alternative approach was first elaborated by Martinet in 1958 (reprinted as Martinet 1974b), and then developed in slightly different ways by Jean Dubois (1967:56–79), and Wagner and Pinchon (1962).[11] These schemes all differ from traditional analyses in two important respects: first, the emphasis is placed firmly on analysis of spoken and not written forms; and second, classes are based not on infinitive endings, but on the number of different stems (called *bases* by Dubois and *thèmes* by Martinet) each verb has (excluding the stems of the *passé simple* and the imperfect subjunctive), and then, as a secondary consideration in order to determine subclasses within the main groupings, on the distribution of the different stems throughout the different persons and tenses of the verb.

For example, whilst the verbs *finir* and *appuyer* both have two stems and therefore belong to the same conjugation, their stems are distributed differently. In the case of *finir*, the shorter stem (/fini/) is used for the three persons singular present indicative and the future, and the longer form (/finis/) for the three persons plural present indicative and the imperfect, whereas *appuyer* uses the shorter form (/apųi/) for the three persons singular and the third person plural present indicative and for the future, and the longer form (/apųij/) for the first and second persons plural present indicative and the imperfect. In calculating the number of stems for each verb, oppositions are discounted which are in some way determined by phonetic or phonological considerations, whether this concerns the syllable type (*nous complétons* [kɔ̃pletɔ̃]~*il complète* [kɔ̃plɛt]) or the phonetic context (*il anesthésie* [anɛstezi]~*il anesthésiait* [anɛstezjɛ]). Here, there is some variation between different linguists: Martinet considers that the verbs *jeter* and *geler* have one *thème* with vocalic alternation, whilst Dubois considers these verbs to have two different *bases*.

The stem-based schemes differ significantly amongst themselves, however, in the number of forms included in the classification. Whilst all focus on the *formes simples*, which Dubois (1967:59) terms the 'formes verbales proprement dites', there is disagreement between scholars proposing a scheme of this type as to which forms should properly be included in the description. Dubois and Martinet exclude not only the *formes composées*, but also the *passé simple* and the imperfect subjunctive, forms which are now rare in spoken French. However, Dubois goes further in also excluding the impersonal forms of the verb, namely the present and past participles, deemed to be 'adjectifs dérivés', and crucially the infinitive, viewed as a special type of substantive. In other words, what was fundamental to the definition of traditional schemes is now excluded from consideration. This is in spite of the role of the past participle and the infinitive in the formation of other tenses (*je vais faire, je suis allé*, etc.). In practice the decision to exclude the infinitive generally makes no difference to the calculation of the number of stems, since the future frequently shares the same stem with the infinitive, but we shall return below to the question of the desirability of excluding the past participle and the infinitive from the analysis.

For ease of exposition we shall concentrate on Dubois's classification in our presentation. By focusing on stems rather than on endings, Dubois arrives at seven conjugations of French verbs, ranging from the first conjugation, which has seven different stems, to the seventh conjugation, whose members have a single stem for all parts of the verb. Stems are identified by considering all the oppositions which exist between different persons and tense forms of each verb. Dubois notes that if all possible oppositions were formally marked with a different verb form, then theoretically there would be a maximum of 42 different stems for each verb, but in practice in the spoken language the maximum different number of stems is just seven and this only applies to the verb *être*, which is therefore in a class of its own. Even if the stems of the *passé simple* and imperfect subjunctive, [fy]/[fys]/[fyr], are included, the total number of stems is still only ten. The following schema of the present indicative shows Dubois's methodology; in each case oppositions are identified, for example in the first case between the stem of the first person singular and that of the second and third person singular:

(4)   {1st person sing} / {2nd and 3rd person sing}
      [sɥi]   [ɛ]
      {3rd person sing} / {3rd person pl}
      [ɛ]   [sɔ̃]
      {1st, 2nd and 3rd person sing} / {1st person pl}
      [sɥi] – [ɛ]   [sɔm]
      {1st person pl} / {2nd person pl}
      [sɔm]   [et]

This results in the identification of four distinctive stems: [sɥi], [sɔm], [sɔ̃] and [ɛ] (with [ɛt] as a variant). To these must be added the present subjunctive stem, [swa], that of the imperfect, [et], and the future stem, [s(ə)r].

The same process of identifying opposing stems and of considering their distribution is repeated for all other verbs. It should be noted that the conjugations with a larger number of stems comprise relatively few members, but that these are verbs which are frequently used and which therefore retain their variation; in particular, they usually have auxiliary or modal usages.

The second conjugation of verbs with six different stems has two members, *faire* and *aller*[12]:

(5)   *faire*: [fɛ] / [fɔ̃] / [fas] / [f(ə)ra] / [fəzɔ̃] / [fɛt]
      aller: [vɛ] / [va] / [vɔ̃] / [aj] / [ira] / [al]

The third class, verbs with five stems, comprises the verbs *avoir*, *pouvoir* and *vouloir*:

(6)   *avoir*:   [ɛ] / [a] / [ɔ̃] / [ɔra] / [av]
      pouvoir: [pø] / [pœv] / [pɥis] / [pura] / [puvɛ]
      vouloir: [vø] / [vœl] / [vœj] / [vudra] / [vulɛ]

Typical of verbs of the fourth class, which includes verbs with a relatively high frequency such as *venir*, *tenir*, *prendre*, *apprendre*, *valoir*, and *comprendre*, is the verb *savoir* with its four distinctive stems:

(7)   [sɛ] / [sav] / [so] / [saʃ]

Once the fifth conjugation is reached, members of each class become much more numerous and their frequency of occurrence more variable; here three subclasses are identified according to the different stems throughout the paradigms. For subclass 1, the first three persons present indicative (stem a) are different from the third person plural present indicative (stem b) and from the first and second persons plural present indicative, imperfect and future tenses (stem c):

(8)   *devoir*:   [dwa] / [dwav] / [dəv]
      mouvoir: [mø] / [møv] / [muv]

In the second subclass, the three persons singular present indicative are again homophonous (stem a), but the imperfect shares the stem of the third person plural present indicative (stem b), whilst the future has a different stem (stem c). For example:

(9)   *paraître*: [parɛ] / [parɛs] / [parɛtra]
      resoudre: [rezu] / [rezɔlv] / [rezudra]

Turning to the third subclass, this has stem a for the three persons singular and the third person plural of the present indicative, stem b in the imperfect and the first and second persons plural present indicative, and stem c for the future:

(10)   *voir*:   [vwa] / [vwajɛ] / [vɛra]
       envoyer: [ãvwa] / [ãvwajɛ] / [ãvɛra]

It is worth noting the similarity of patterning of these two verbs, which, in the traditional classification, would be placed in different conjugations.

The sixth conjugation, verbs with two stems, similarly has three subclasses determined according to the distribution of the stems:

(11)   (a) *finir*:   [fini] / [finisɛ] (alternation between zero/[s])
           écrire: [ekri] / [ekrivɛ] (zero/[v])
       (b) *nettoyer*: [netwa],[netwara] / [netwajɛ] (zero/[j])
           croire: [krwa],[krwara] / [krwajɛ] (zero/[j])
       (c) *partir*:   [par] / [part] (zero/[t])
           répondre: [repɔ̃] / [repɔ̃d] (zero/[d])
           pleuvoir: [plø/] / [plœv] (zero/[v])[13]

Members of the final class, verbs with one stem, are again highly variable as regards the frequency of usage of the verbs. This group corresponds largely to the traditional first conjugation, but also includes verbs such as *ouvrir* and *exclure*. Here again the novelty of Dubois's scheme is obvious: *semer* and *chanter*, traditionally members of the same conjugation, now belong to two different classes; similarly *exclure* (one stem) and *avoir* (five stems) are placed in quite distinct categories.

What are the advantages of Dubois's approach? As we have seen, it suc-
ceeds in bringing together verbs which on the basis of their infinitive ending
appear very different, but which conjugate similarly such as *remuer* and
conclure. It has been argued that the classification reflects well the frequency
of usage of verbs, as recorded, for instance, by *Le Français fondamental*
(Gougenheim and others (1956)), in which *être* was by far the most commonly occurring verb with a frequency of 14083, followed by *avoir* (11552),
faire (3174) and *aller* (1876). While the order of frequency does not strictly
follow the placing of verbs into classes – for example, *savoir* (1432) in class 4
is more frequent than *vouloir* (881) in class 3 – and it becomes less predictable as the number of members of the class increases – for instance, *arriver*
(with a frequency of 568) is in tenth position in their list of frequency of
occurrence of verbs – the scheme does broadly mirror the fact that it is the
verbs with most stems which are the most common in French, while those
with fewer stems are either less common or more variable in their frequency
of occurrence. The reason for this is clear: verbs with multiple stems, and
which therefore are theoretically more difficult to conjugate, remain in currency because their frequency of usage means that children have considerable exposure to them and therefore quickly acquire the variety of forms.[14]
The classification is also said to reflect the fact that it is the class with one
stem which is largely productive today (*télécopier*, *sécuriser*) and into which
borrowings are assimilated (*surfer*, *se shooter*), and only exceptionally the class
with two stems when there is analogical pressure (*alunir* on the analogy of
atterrir). Indeed there is evidence to suggest that speakers substitute verbs
with one stem for those with greater variation (e.g. *agoniser* instead of *agonir*,
solutionner rather than *résoudre*; see **4**.8 below).

On the negative side, the scheme appears to create some rather unnatural
classes. Pinchon (1986:166–7) cites the example of the fourth conjugation
whose members have four stems, and questions the value of bringing together in one class the verbs *venir*, *prendre* and *valoir*, since the verbs do not
have the same distribution of stems in their paradigms (see Table **4**.5).
Rather it would seem that there is greater relatedness between *prendre* and
craindre, than between, say, *prendre* and *valoir*. A second difficulty arises from
the decision to exclude the infinitive and the past participle, since both are
used in the formation of tenses which are central to the spoken language.
Indeed, without the *passé composé* and the *passé simple* the imperfect tense is
left as the sole past tense. Third, it might be considered undesirable to have
a class (the first conjugation) which has a membership of one (*être*). Fourth,
it is not always clear how Dubois segments his forms since sometimes the
forms listed are pure stems (e.g. [av], [sav]), whilst on other occasions he lists
the complete forms, notably in the case of the future forms (e.g. [ira], [ɔra]).
Finally, it might be argued that Dubois's scheme is more complex than
traditional ones, notably from a pedagogic viewpoint. Indeed, it could be

Table 4.5 Distribution of the four stems of *valoir*, *prendre* and *venir* (Pinchon 1986:166–7)[15]

ind. pr. 1–2–3	vo-	prã-	vjɛ̃-
fut.	vod-	prãd-	vjɛ̃d-
ind. pr. 4–5	val-	prən-	vən-
ind. pr. 6	val-	prɛn-	vjɛn-
impft	val- ˙	prən-	vən-
subj. 4–5	val-	prən-	vən-
subj. 1–2–3–6	vaj-	prɛn-	vjɛn-

contended that it is only possible to know a verb's class and the number of stems it possesses once the complete paradigm has been acquired.

4.6 'Two-class' models

If Dubois's scheme increases the number of conjugation classes to seven, a number of other schemes, such as those of Van den Eynde and Blanche-Benveniste (1970), Plénat (1981) and Gardes-Tamine (1988), reduce the number of main classes to two. Whilst these classifications have different theoretical underpinnings and are intended for different audiences (Plénat's approach is generative in the mould of Chomsky and Halle's *The Sound Pattern of English* (1968), Van den Eynde and Blanche-Benveniste's is essentially structuralist, and Gardes-Tamine is working within a pedagogical context), they share a desire to show that what appears to be great variation in verb paradigms can be reduced, notably if the phonological characteristics of French are taken into account.[16]

Once again we will focus principally on one example of this type of model, that of Gardes-Tamine (1988:I:55–63), which draws heavily on Van den Eynde and Blanche-Benveniste's approach (1970). These schemes share a number of common features. First, the focus is on spoken forms, but the initial division into two classes is based not on stems, but on infinitive endings. For instance, on the basis of pairs such as *saler/salir* and *porter/partir*, Gardes-Tamine argues that *-ir* and *-er* can occur in similar environments and she therefore makes a primary division into two main classes of verbs, those with an infinitive ending in /e/ and those in /r/.[17] Second, it is noted that verbs in the first class (or Class A for Van den Eynde and Blanche-Benveniste) generally do not show variation in the stem[18], whereas those in the second class (or Class B, or in Plénat's terms 'l'autre conjugaison') usually have two and sometimes more stems (e.g. /par/ ~ /part/; /sali/ ~ /salis/). Third, it is argued that there are three subclasses of Class II, each character-ized by the presence of one of three allomorphs of the infinitive morpheme °r – /war, ir, r/ – the complementary distribution of which is phonologically conditioned and entirely predictable from the phonetic characteristics of the root:

(12)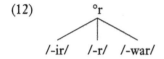

In other words, -ir, -re and -oir verbs are accounted for in one class and the main task is then simply to detail the distribution of the different allomorphs.[19]

Van den Eynde and Blanche-Benveniste and Gardes-Tamine alike there-fore express the conviction that verb morphology is much simpler than many other accounts would suggest. In general the choice of stem allomorph is determined by phonological tendencies which are largely predictable. The stems of class two verbs are generally distributed according to either phono-logical or morphological considerations. For instance, if the ending begins with a vowel (note the simple division into stem and ending here), the longer stem will occur, while if the ending begins with a consonant or there is no ending, then the shorter stem will be used:

(13) *finissant/finis*   /finis-/~/fini-/
      servant/sers   /sɛrv-/~/sɛr-/
      partant/pars   /part-/~/par-/

Loss of the final consonant of the stem may, as we have seen, also entail a change in the stem vowel as will be seen in the case of *craindre* below. As an example of a morphological condition, Gardes-Tamine cites the case of the *passé simple*; here the choice of the inflectional ending is closely related to the infinitive ending, so that if the infinitive ends in /war/ the *passé simple* will usually end in /y/ and this will be added to a severely shortened form of the stem which has typically lost the final consonant of the weak stem and the preceding vowel:

(14) *nous savons/je sus*   /sav-/ ~ /s-/ + /y/

In the case of the other members of class two, the *passé simple* generally ends in /i/ which is added to the longer stem (*il partit*). In short, there is a preference for a unique stem for each verb from which the others are derived, and priority is given to phonological conditioning.

Once these simple principles are established, the bulk of the discussion focuses on setting out the phonological conditions for the appearance of the different allomorphs in combination with other forms. For example, Gardes-Tamine devotes considerable space to examining how the choice of infinitive allomorph in Class II is largely determined by the phonological characteristics of the stem. For instance, the allomorph /-r/ may occur after all vowels, but there are restrictions on the consonants it may follow. These are the non-nasal stops, /p/ (*rompre* /rɔ̃pr/); /t/ (*battre* /batr/); /d/ (*vendre* /vãdr/); /k/ (*vaincre* /vɛ̃kr/) (and theoretically also /b/ and /g/ although in practice there are no examples of these in French), and the fricative /v/ (*vivre* /vivr/) (and in theory also /f/). When one of the other consonants occurs, the correct infinitive is formed either by selecting one of the other allomorphs or by modifying the stem in some way. In the latter case a greater degree of abstraction is allowed to enter the analysis in order to generate the correct surface forms. In other words, in order to show a patterning between the weak stem and the infinitive form, rules are introduced to allow the combination of stem and infinitive ending necessary to create the infinitive form which actually occurs. So, for example, if the (weak) stem ends in /s/ or /z/, then the addition of /r/ causes the loss of the final consonant (in order to avoid the occurrence of a consonant cluster which is not found in French (/*sr/, /*zr/))[20]:

(15)   *lire/lisons*: °liz + r → /lir/
       finir/finissons: °finis + r → /finir/

If, however, the final /s/ is preceded by one of the vowels /ɛ/ or /a/, then the final consonant becomes /t/:

(16)   *connaître/connaissons*: °kɔnɛs + r → /kɔnɛtr/

Again, if the stem ends in /nj/ (Gardes-Tamine does not use /ɲ/ in her system), then /nj/ is replaced by /d/ and the loss of the nasal consonant results in the nasalization of the stem vowel:

(17)   *craindre/craignons*: °krɛnj + r → /krɛ̃dr/

If the stem ends in /r/, /j/, or a nasal other than /nj/, then the allomorph /ir/ is selected, or, expressed differently, /i/ is used as a 'liaison' vowel in order to avoid a consonant cluster which is either phonologically impossible or rare in French:

(18) *dormir/dormons*: °dɔrm + r → /dɔrmir/
      mourir/mourons: °mur + r → /murir/
      cueillir/cueillons: °køj + r → /køjir/

If the stem ends with /ən/ then both /r/ and /ir/ occur:

(19) *prendre/prenons*: °prən + r → /prãdr/
      tenir/tenons: °tən + r → /tənir/

A weakness here is that Gardes-Tamine does not elaborate on how you know which one to use with any given verb. Van den Eynde and Blanche-Benveniste prefer simply to exclude *venir* and *tenir* from the discussion, at least temporarily, to avoid this difficulty, but have been criticized for not providing a comprehensive account.

In addition, if a final /t/ or /v/ is preceded by /r/ or a nasal vowel, then /ir/ is selected:

(20) *partir/partons*: °part + r → /partir/
      servir/servons: °sɛrv + r → /sɛrvir/
      mentir/mentons: °mãt + r → /mãtir/

Finally, if the stem ends in /l/ or /v/ and this consonant is preceded by an oral vowel other than /i/ (excluding then, for example, *vivre* discussed above) then the 'liaison vowel' is /wa/ giving /war/:

(21) *vouloir/voulons*: °vul + r → /vulwar/
      pouvoir/pouvons: °puv + r → /puvwar/

Omitting the special case of /-ən/ and the occurrence of /r/ after vowels, non-nasal stops and fricatives, she then summarizes in tabular form the complementary distribution of the allomorphs:

Table 4.6 Distribution of the allomorphs of the infinitive morpheme °r (after Gardes-Tamine 1988:I:58)

	/r/	/ir/	/war/
/s/, /z/, /nj/	+	−	−
/r/, /j/, nasals other than /nj/	−	+	−
V + /l/ or /v/ and V ≠ /i/	−	−	+

These rules allow Gardes-Tamine to account for almost all verbs, with very few exceptions. One such exception would be the verb *écrire* which we might expect to generate /*ekrivr/ on the basis of °ekriv + r; instead the consonant must be dropped to produce /ekrir/. However, other cases which might initially appear to be exceptions such as *croire* (°krwaj + r → /*krajir/) are eliminated by arguing that the stem is not /krwaj/ but /krwa/ and that the /j/ is simply a liaison (or linking) segment between a stem ending in a vowel and the vowel of the ending (*croy-ons*).

This classification has a number of positive features. While it is based on the spoken language and on stems, it is considerably simpler than Dubois's system in having only two main classes. In addition, the three classes -*ir*, -*re* and -*oir* are neatly brought under one class and the choice of one ending over another is seen to be largely explicable in phonological terms.

On the other hand, there are a number of outstanding difficulties, not least concerning questions of segmentation (as discussed in **4.2** above) and the identification of a verb's stem(s). Morin (1987b:26) criticizes Van den Eynde and Blanche-Benveniste's paper on a number of grounds: he questions, for example, their decision to make a distinction between °l in the root °vul of *vouloir* and °L in the root °muL of *moudre* on the basis that they have different infinitive endings – thereby raising important questions about the status of the abstract forms (those we have noted here with a superscript °). Furthermore he argues that the sort of phonological conditioning that they describe does not have a role in the grammar of native speakers, and that the model takes little or no account of paradigms which he considers play an important role in verb morphology (see **4.8** below).

In addition we may note that the generation of forms is not entirely predictable as we have seen in the case of verbs with a stem ending in /ən/, and that Van den Eynde and Blanche-Benveniste exclude forms from their analysis which do not easily fit this model. No clear line is drawn between those variations in the stem which can be treated as allomorphs and those where it is impossible to do so. As a result, Gardes-Tamine does not discuss, for example, the treatment of verbs with multiple stems such as *être*. Whilst Gardes-Tamine's grammar is said to be descriptive, intended for undergraduates and teachers, the pedagogic applications of the approach are not stated, and it is not entirely clear why one would wish to have such an elaborate mechanism to be able to generate the correct form of the infinitive from the weak stem in such a context.

4.7 Defining irregularity

One of the consequences of examining different types of classifications is that it highlights the need to consider what is meant by an 'irregular' verb.

The definition of regularity and irregularity is not theory neutral, but rather depends to a large extent on the type of classification of conjugations which is proposed.

In traditional schemes irregularity is defined in terms of variation in the stem; thus for Grevisse (1993:661) all Class 3 verbs are irregular since they have have a 'radical variable'. However, even within a traditional framework the concept of irregularity is not fixed. As Judge and Healey comment (1983:249), it is possible to devise ever finer categories or subclasses of verbs to account for more and more atypical paradigms. But against this must be balanced the need – especially important in a pedagogic context – to have categories which capture meaningful generalizations and which show the patterning of forms across the conjugation classes. Once a category has only one or two members it might be better to consider these verbs 'irregular' rather than endlessly proliferating categories. The difficulty lies in making a judgement as to when a category is too small to be useful.

Pinchon and Coute point out (1981:117) that in schemes such as Dubois's which are based on stems, 'irregular' verbs can no longer be defined as verbs with a variable stem.[21] They therefore choose to define an irregular verb as one which has an abnormal distribution of one or more of elements 2, 3, or 4 as set out in Table **4.4** above. Under this definition a verb like *prendre* is no longer irregular. Indeed, in their view there are only five irregular verbs, *être, avoir, aller, faire, dire*, of which the following are the irregular forms:

(22) être   /sɥi/   /ɛ/   /sɔm/   /ɛt/   /sɔ̃/
      avoir   /ɛ/   /a/   /ʒ/[22]
      aller   /vɛ/   /va/   /vɔ̃/
      faire   /fɛt/   /fɔ̃/
      dire   /dit/

Since changes in stem do not constitute irregularity, forms like *aille* and *irai* are considered regular in their analysis.

In what we have termed 'two-class' models, every effort is made to bring all verbs under one of the two classes, and therefore to minimize the number of irregular forms, by considering alternations in the form of either stems or endings as variants of a single form. Gardes-Tamine (1988:I:60) therefore considers as irregular only those verbs for which the allomorphs of the stem are not predictable, such as /saʃ-/ as the present subjunctive stem of *savoir*. This approach is very similar to that taken in generative accounts such as Schane (1968), where an important motivation is to try to demonstrate that what appears to be irregularity at the surface level can be explained by showing that the forms derive from a single underlying phonological representation and that there are phonological rules to account for the alternations in the vast majority of cases. Thus, for example, Schane (1968:68) posits one underlying representation, |dɔrm|, for both /dɔrm/ and /dɔr/, and then derives /dɔr/ from this by means of a phonological rule of final consonant truncation which deletes the final consonant when it is not followed by a vowel (which is the same rule posited to account for liaison, see Chapter 1). In other words, there is said to be an underlying regularity or homogeneity to forms which appear to be heterogeneous on the surface. Only those forms which cannot be related in this way are considered suppletive, and for them two (or more) underlying representations are specified.

As we have seen in Chapters 2 and 3, a central question for generative accounts is how abstract the underlying forms should be allowed to be, or what constraints should be placed on the underlying forms posited. An extreme position is adopted by Foley (1979) who has no place for suppletion in his scheme and therefore has to posit highly abstract underlying forms; thus he attempts to show that even verbs such as *pouvoir, faire, avoir*, and *être* are not 'theoretically irregular', but rather follow regular developments 'once the correct etyma have been established' (1979:240).[23] Most theorists would not follow him to this extent since such a position requires underlying forms that are very remote from the surface reality coupled with complex rules which appear phonologically implausible. For example, *pouvoir* is said to have the unique underlying root **pot*; Foley then claims that the infinitive *pouvoir* is derived from underlying **pot-e-se*, the present participle *pouvant* from underlying **pot-e-ant*, the present subjunctive *puisse* from underlying **pot-e-ya-t*, and the imperfect subjunctive *pusse* from underlying **pot-e-s-ya-t*, etc.

Schane (1968:67) limits his discussion rather to regular and 'irregular' verbs where the stems exhibit phonological alternation, and he is not concerned with 'irregular' verbs with suppletive stems, which for him should be noted in the lexicon (e.g. *vas/allez*). However, even in his more restrained account the choice of underlying form – which at times look suspiciously like forms which occurred very early on in the history of French, or like the orthographic form – is not without difficulty. Smith (1969) is in general sympathetic to Schane's approach but dislikes, for instance, Schane's choice of |vedere| as the underlying form for *voir* since the motivation for selecting this as the underlying form seems to be simply to create a parallel with *croire* whose underlying form is said to be |credere|, which in turn seems to be justified only because there is an (irregular) alternation between the verb and the noun *crédibilité*.[24] While it may be observed that *vedette* does exist alongside *voir*, this type of alternation may be thought to be very different from the type of regular alternation which exists in *achevez, achève, achèvement* or even *venons, viennent* or *devons, doivent*, and therefore not a suitable basis for justifying abstract underlying forms.

While there is considerable advantage then in trying to capture and explain regular variation in stems, the choice of a single phonological representation for each root (with the exception of suppletive verbs) is not straightforward.

We might note in passing that the same difficulties may be observed in Schane's argument that there is a single person marker for each person, regardless of the tense or mood of the verb. For example, in order for Schane (1968:82) to be able to maintain his assertion that |S| is the underlying form for the first person singular, he has to have a rule converting |S| to |i| in the first person singular of the future tense, the first singular vocalization rule, which operates only in the first person singular and where |S| is preceded by tense |A|.[25] It has been argued that the combination of the morphological restrictions on the rule and the unnaturalness of the process phonologically make this a highly dubious rule.

In short, generative accounts aim to show that surface irregularities may mask an underlying regularity. Schane argues that a number of apparently 'irregular' verbs may be characterized by the absence of a thematic vowel, thereby 'explaining' the concept of irregular verb. For instance, he argues that the anomalies in the conjugation of *écrire* are explained by the absence of the thematic vowel |e| (Schane 1968:112).

4.8   Variation and change

We have already noted how there is a tendency not only to place all new verbs into the regular -*er* conjugation, including borrowings such as *stariser* or *cloner*, but also that there is considerable evidence to suggest that verbs considered difficult to conjugate such as *résoudre* or *émouvoir* are replaced, particularly in speech, by more regular ones such as *solutionner* and *émotionner* (see, for example, Martinet (1974b), Sauvageot (1962)). In *français populaire* this trend is carried even further, with forms such as *concluer* for *conclure* and *romper* for *rompre* regularly attested. Sauvageot (1962:64) sums up this evolution as follows:

> La tendance à ne plus se servir que de thèmes uniques a entraîné un vaste mouvement de simplification dans la forme parlée de notre conjugaison.

Morin (1998) examines certain popular forms which occur in Quebec French, such as *ils jou*[z]*ent* and *ils continu*[s]*ent* in which a new consonant has appeared in the strong root in the plural. Typically these new forms are found when the stem ends in a vowel, thereby creating a new plural form, but sometimes a change of consonant is attested, for example, *ils écri*[z]*ent* for *ils écrivent*.

These forms raise interesting questions as to how best to approach French verb morphology. Morin argues that these consonants cannot be viewed as part of the verb stem since they do not appear in the imperfect tense (**il* *jou*[z]*ait*) as one might expect if this were the case (cf. *ils lisent/il lisait*). The alternative analysis of seeing this consonant as part of the ending [ʒu + z] – the [-z] of *ils lisent* [li + z] is therefore seen as morphologically distinct from the [z] of *vous lisez* [liz + e] – also has its weaknesses, not least because sporadically an analogical [s] or [z] is found in weak forms (e.g. *rempli*[z]*ait*, *prescri*[z]*ait*, *continu*[s]*ait*). In other words, both segmentations seem to be required in order to account for these popular forms.

Because of these difficulties of segmentation Morin rejects a morpheme-based approach and favours instead a word-based 'analyse analogique' in which analogical patterns operate directly on forms without segmenting them. For example, using the 'model' of [li]$_{[3s, prés.]}$: [liz]$_{[3p, prés]}$ the following analogical pattern can be deduced:

(23) $[X]_{[3s, prés.]} \rightarrow [Xz]_{[3p, prés]}$, *propriétés phon.* X = Y [+syll]

This is to be read as follows: from a third person singular form which ends in a vowel (X, Y are variables, so X = Y [+syll] refers to a word ending in a vowel) the third person plural is formed by adding [z]. This pattern would then allow the creation of the analogical form [preskriz] from [preskri]. Similarly on the basis of the model [lav]$_{[3p, prés.]}$: [lavɛ]$_{[3s, imparf.]}$, the following patterning for the creation of the imperfect can be seen:

(24) $[X]_{[3p, prés.]} \rightarrow [Xɛ]_{[3s, imparf.]}$

(24) therefore allows the creation of the form *il prescri*[z]*ait* from the third person plural [preskriz]. (23) behaves *as if* the [z] of [preskriz] were part of the ending, whereas (24) behaves *as if* the [z] were part of the stem.

It is stressed that analogy does not work just on the basis of one pattern, but on the basis of all possible patterns, which may reinforce each other or compete against each other. Thus (24) is not the only possible pattern for the formation of the third person plural present indicative; the following are amongst the patterns which are also available:

(25) $[X]_{[3s, prés.]} \rightarrow [X]_{[3p, prés]}$ (on the model of LAVER, CONCLURE, etc.)
$[X]_{[3s, prés.]} \rightarrow [Xs]_{[3p, prés]}$ (on the model of FOURNIR, MAUDIRE, etc.)
$[X]_{[3s, prés.]} \rightarrow [Xv]_{[3p, prés]}$ (on the model of DEVOIR, SUIVRE, etc.)
$[Xɛ]_{[3s, prés.]} \rightarrow [Xav]_{[3p, prés]}$ (on the model of SAVOIR)

Once the analogical forms have been created, they can then become lexicalized.

Morin admits himself that his model is still rather schematic. It remains to be seen whether other linguists will adopt what Anderson (1992) calls an 'a-morphous' approach to French verb morphology along the lines outlined by Morin.

Suggested Reading

General accounts:
Arrivé, Gadet and Galmiche (1986), Béchade (1992), Curat (1991), Judge and Healey (1983), Pinchon and Coute (1981), Price (1971), Riegel, Pellat and Rioul (1994).
Spoken French and variation:
Martinet (1974b), Marty (1971), Morin (1998), Sauvageot (1962).
Generative approaches:
Dell (1973), Foley (1979), Kiefer (1973), Schane (1968).
Stem-based accounts:
Dubois (1967), Martinet (1974b), Wagner and Pinchon (1962).
Two-class schemes:
Gardes-Tamine (1988), Plénat (1981, 1987b), Van den Eynde and Blanche-Benveniste (1970).

Notes

1. Throughout this and subsequent chapters we normally follow the transcription conventions of individual authors when citing or in detailed discussion of their models. These are occasionally different from our general transcription conventions; for example, some authors use the symbol [r] in phonetic transcriptions.
2. The decision as to whether the infix is considered to be *-ss-* or *-iss-* interacts with the analysis of the verb stem and whether in this case, for example, the analysis should be *fini-* + *-ss-* + *ons*, *fin-* + *-iss-* + *ons*, or indeed *fin-* + the thematic vowel *-i-* + the infix *-ss-* + *-ons*.
3. In order for this generalization to be made Price (1971:171–2) has to note the following: (i) that the *-d* at the end of the stem of most regular *-re* verbs functions as 'a purely orthographic substitute' for *-t* in the third person singular (*il rend*); (ii) in the case of *vaincre, convaincre* the *-t* is omitted after the final consonant of the stem; (iii) *-x* likewise serves as a purely orthographic substitute for *-s* in *veux, peux, vaux*.
4. Note that *être* follows type (ii) exactly, but that the endings are combined with a change of stem.
5. The persons of the verb are indicated here using the convention 1,2,3 for the three persons singular and 4,5,6 for the three persons plural.
6. The scheme of four conjugations based on the Latin patterns (*-er, -ir, -oir, -re*) is now relatively rare, but see the comments on Schane (1968) below.
7. This usually excludes *avoir* and *être*, as well as defective verbs (see note 9 below).
8. Note that of the 280 verbs listed in *Le Français élémentaire*, 196 are class 1, 10 are class 2 and 73 are class 3.

9. Most schemes have a separate category for defective verbs, that is, verbs which lack certain persons or tenses. These include impersonal verbs, used only in the third person singular (and of which the meteorological expressions constitute an important subgroup) as well as verbs only employed in certain tenses or persons (e.g. *gésir*).

10. The distinction between tense and lax vowels is discussed in Chapter 2, note 15. Note that, in theory at least, Schane's account is not based on written forms.

11. This approach is also adopted, for example, by Pinchon and Coute (1981); the different variations of it are compared in Pinchon (1986). A number of contemporary grammars, such as Riegel, Pellat and Rioul (1994:263-87) combine elements of the traditional classification with reference to the number of stems. In their approach, the written endings of the infinitive are used to generate four main classes (excluding defective verbs) and then subclasses are created according to the number of stems (considered in both their orthographic and phonetic form) in each conjugation.

12. In examples (5)–(11), the forms listed are those given by Dubois. There is something of an inconsistency in the presentation since Dubois sometimes lists just the stem (e.g [av] as in *avons, avez*, etc.) and sometimes lists the complete form which enters into oppositions with other forms (e.g. [f(ə)ra], [fəzɔ̃], [ira], [əra], etc.).

13. There are two verbs with different patterns of distribution, *mourir* and *acquérir*.

14. However, analogical pressure is evident even in the case of some frequently used verbs, such as *°vous faisez* for *vous faites*.

15. The forms given by Pinchon for the first three persons present indicative and for the future of *venir* ([vje-] and [vjed-]) are undoubtedly misprints.

16. Another variation on this approach is found in Swiggers and Van den Eynde (1987) who use an Item-and-Arrangement model (see Part I, Section 3.2.2) and an inductive approach to reduce their initial 74 classes down to two main classes.

17. Gardes-Tamine uses phonetic transcription for all her forms. This is somewhat confusing since she herself emphasizes the fact that French verb morphology is broadly governed by the phonological characteristics of the language. We have therefore modified her transcription and essentially used the conventions adopted by Van den Eynde and Blanche-Benveniste (to whom Gardes-Tamine herself refers), that is, phonemic rather than phonetic transcription for actual forms and a superscript ° before morphemes or 'formes structurelles'.

18. It is, moreover, argued that what variation there is may largely be accounted for in phonological terms, that is either because of the syllable type (/(ʒ)em/~/emɔ̃/) or because of the tendency for a glide to occur where otherwise two vowels would be adjacent (/ni/~/njɔ̃/).

19. Plénat (1987b) shows how this model can equally be used within a generative framework. At the underlying level the form of the root is constant in all tenses (except in the case of suppletive verbs), and all inflectional endings are likewise said to be the same for all verbs. In each case the root is separated

from the inflectional ending by a thematic vowel, which is again said to be the same for all members of 'l'autre conjugaison'. For further discussion of generative approaches, see 4.7 below.

20. Van den Eynde and Blanche-Benveniste have 'règles de soustraction' and 'morphophonèmes soustractifs' to deal with such cases.

21. It is perhaps rather surprising that Wagner and Pinchon (1962:223) still base their definitions of regular and irregular verbs on whether the stem (or *radical* in their terminology) varies or not; they differentiate between 'verbes irréguliers', which show variation in the stem and 'verbes essentiellement irréguliers' which are conjugated using several different stems.

22. The present subjunctive forms of *être* and *avoir* are said to be purely graphic anomalies.

23. Note that his etyma, or earlier forms, are also 'theoretical' or abstract forms. Gertner (1973) claims to offer another generative account, but his work has been severely criticized since his main preoccupation seems to be to 'predict' as many forms as possible on the basis of the smallest possible number of what are often extremely artificial rules.

24. In other words, Schane is not just seeking to account for alternatives within the verb paradigm, he is also seeking to relate the stem to other derivationally related forms.

25. There is then a subsequent rule converting |Ai| to /e/.

5

Aspect in French

5.1 Introduction: tense versus aspect

In Part I, Section 2.3.1 we defined tense as 'grammaticalized expression of location in time' (Comrie 1985:9) and aspect as a more subjective perspective on events. In this chapter, we shall examine in some detail the highly problematic concept of aspect in the French verb system, looking at various models of aspect, evaluating their strengths and weaknesses and finally examining contexts where the notion of aspect is valuable in the analysis of linguistic problems.

Most definitions, in spite of what may be serious differences in terminology or application, have in common the assertion that aspect is a more subjective view of time than tense, and that it has to do with an 'internal' perspective on time, rather than the 'external' perspective expressed by tense, which localizes an event or situation in time, or relates the localization of an event to another point in time (see Part I, Section 2.3.1). Thus Comrie differentiates tense and aspect as follows: tense, he argues, 'relates the time of the situation referred to to some other time, usually to the moment of speaking', whereas 'aspects are different ways of viewing the internal temporal constituency of a situation' (Comrie 1976:1–3). By way of illustration, he cites the opposition in French between *il lisait* and *il lut*, pointing out that the distinction between them is not one of tense, 'since in both cases we have absolute past tense' (1976:3), or in Reichenbach's (1947) terms (see Part I, Section 2.3.1), both involve the following notional time line:

$$\text{R, E} \qquad\qquad\qquad \text{S}$$

Rather, the distinction concerns how the process of reading is viewed; as delimited and complete ('perfective' aspect, marked here by the *passé simple*, henceforth PS) or without regard to its completion/in progress ('imperfective' aspect, marked here by the *imparfait*, henceforth IMP). Other linguists' accounts also emphasize the internal, subjective perspective on time:

lorsque, au lieu de la place qu'il occupe par rapport au repère temporel choisi, on considère le procès sous l'angle de son déroulement interne, on est en présence de la catégorie d'aspect (Imbs 1960:15)

l'aspect nous indique où en est le procès au point de vue de son développement (Klum 1961:118)

l'aspect caractérise l'angle de vision sous lequel une action est envisagée (Pfister 1974:403)

l'aspect est une perspective locutoriale sur l'action/l'état représenté(e) par le lexème du verbe, choisie librement par le sujet parlant (Wunderli 1989:76)

unlike tense [. . .] aspect is not a relational category, nor is it deictic; it is not concerned with relating the time of a situation to any other time point, but rather with how the speaker chooses to profile the situation (Fleischman 1990:19).

It is possible, therefore, to say at the outset that in broad terms, whereas tense is a more objective grammaticalization of time, aspect is defined as a subjective, internal perspective on time.

Why is aspect such a notoriously problematic concept in French? The major reason for this is that the notion of aspect was first applied to a different type of verb system, that is the Slavonic system, one where perfective and imperfective aspects are marked explicitly for each verb by two different forms. The morphologically regular nature of aspectual markers in such a system makes it possible to establish a reasonably clear and coherent definition of aspect. It is only relatively recently, in the early part of the twentieth century, that the notion of aspect has been applied to the French verb system, appearing in works such as Vendryes' *Le Langage* (1921), Brunot's *La Pensée et la langue* (1922) and Guillaume's *Temps et verbe* (1929). Unlike the Slavonic system, the French verb system does not have regular sets of morphological oppositions which might be said to mark aspectual contrasts such as perfectivity and imperfectivity. Moreover, this lack of regular sets of morphological oppositions makes it very difficult not only to define exactly what is meant when we talk about aspect in French, but also to find a coherent terminology for any oppositions that might be considered to be aspectual. These difficulties have led to a proliferation of approaches to aspect in French: aspect is defined by different theories in different ways, a variety of terminology is used, and theories differ as to which oppositions in the French verb system and which lexical contrasts they consider to be aspectual. For these reasons, aspect in French has been considered 'a rag-bag for real or fancied distinctions of the most disparate character' (Reid 1970:148).

5.2   Aspectual categories and distinctions

Before evaluating in more detail a number of aspectual theories, we shall outline briefly the types of opposition mentioned in the literature and the linguistic phenomena associated with aspect in French. Perhaps the most frequently-cited opposition is between imperfective and perfective aspect (see **5**.1 above). Thus for example, the IMP might be said to be imperfective and the PS perfective, or verbs such as *trouver, fermer, mourir* considered perfective (since they imply an end point) and others such as *exister, marcher, parler* imperfective. The perfective/imperfective contrast is also often invoked to explain the use of certain verbal periphrases such as *être en train de faire qqch* to stress imperfectivity (e.g. *je suis en train de chanter*), or the regional *passé surcomposé* (e.g. *je l'ai eu fait*) which, amongst other functions, stresses perfectivity (see **6**.5.2.3). A related contrast is that between *aspect global* (where the process is conceived of as a whole) and *aspect sécant* (where the process is viewed in progress and is thus partly complete and partly incomplete, with no delimiting contours); this aspectual distinction might also be invoked in relation to the PS/IMP contrast. A further related contrast is that between 'punctual' aspect (where the action or state is viewed as momentary, or without duration) and 'durative' aspect (where the action is viewed as having duration); once again, this contrast is often cited in relation to the PS/IMP opposition.

The distinction between 'incomplete' and 'complete' (*inaccompli/accompli*) is an aspectual contrast frequently invoked with respect to the simple and compound forms, for example, *il mange* versus *il a mangé*. Other aspectual terminology used in relation to French includes 'inchoative' versus 'terminative' categories; inchoative aspect implies that the process is viewed in relation to its beginning, whereas terminative aspect sees it in relation to its end point. 'Iterative' aspect refers to cases where the process is repeated regularly, whereas with 'semelfactive' aspect, the process occurs only once; adverbials such as *quelquefois, souvent, tous les jours* etc. may be used to stress iterativity, as may certain verbal suffixes such as *-ailler* (e.g. *criailler*) or prefixes such as *re-* (e.g. *reprendre, redire*). 'Progressive' aspect is cited in relation to periphrases such as *être en train de* (e.g. *je suis en train de chanter*) or '*aller* + present participle' (e.g. *la rivière va montant*), where the progressive development of the action is to the fore.

A number of problematic issues are already emerging. First, many of the aspectual concepts mentioned are similar to each other, particularly those involving notions of completion and/or end points (e.g. perfective/ imperfective, *global/sécant* etc.); similar notions are referred to by a variety of terminology. Second, and perhaps more significantly, it can be seen from the aspectual categories mentioned that a number of different linguistic phenomena are involved, including lexical oppositions, verbal periphrases and affixes, as well as morphological contrasts within the verbal system such as that between the imperfect and the *passé simple* or the use of auxiliaries (e.g. simple versus compound forms). In the following section, we shall explore some of the problematic issues arising from the different nature of these phenomena, before moving on to look at specific theories of aspect in French.

5.3   Lexical versus grammatical aspect[1]

A distinction is traditionally made between lexical and grammatical aspect. In broad terms, lexical aspect is involved when the aspectual force of the construction (such as the value of perfectivity or imperfectivity) is conveyed by a lexical item (for example, the sense of the verb in question). Thus in a construction such as:

(1)   A trois heures il a fini son repas

notwithstanding any aspectual force contained in the tense used, the semantic content of the verb *finir* contains within it notions of perfectivity and completion. In the same way, in a construction such as:

(2)   A trois heures il a commencé son repas

the semantic force of the verb *commencer* has certain implications as regards aspect, in that it marks the beginning of an action which is not viewed in relation to an end point. Grammatical aspect, on the other hand, concerns the marking of aspectual nuances by morphological means, that is, normally the use of certain verb forms. Thus, as in the example cited above by Comrie, the distinction between *il lisait* and *il lut* can be said to be aspectual, in that imperfectivity and perfectivity are opposed within absolute past time, and the opposition is marked by different morphological endings. Alternatively, the aspectual contrast between simple and compound forms would be considered a case of grammatical aspect. In practice, however, a number of problems arise. It is, for example, difficult in many cases to say with certainty to what extent the aspectual force of a given construction comes from grammatical elements, and to what extent it depends on lexical items (the verb itself or adverbials in the environment), or on the combination of the two. Moreover there is considerable debate as to whether certain aspectual markers are grammatical or lexical by nature. While oppositions such as *fit/faisait* or *fait/a fait* are clearly grammatical by nature, and oppositions such as *chercher/ trouver* clearly lexical, there are many cases which do not fall neatly into one of these two large categories, notably verbal periphrases such as *être en train de*, '*aller* + present participle' etc. as well as certain affixes and infixes.[2] As we shall see in some of the models examined in 5.4 below, the inclusion of both lexical and grammatical markers in a theoretical model can pose a number of problems (see for example Brunot (5.4.2), Reid (5.4.5), Martin (5.4.6), Wilmet (5.4.7)). Note that we shall make use of a concept akin to lexical aspect in our discussion of the passive in 8.4.2.4.

Some scholars classify lexical markers of aspect under the category *mode d'action* or *Aktionsart*, or, perhaps more usefully, under Vendler's label 'situation type'.[3] Vendler (1967:97–121) divides verb phrases into four different situation types, defined according to semantic and syntactic criteria: activities (e.g. *running, pushing a cart*), accomplishments (e.g. *running a mile, drawing a circle*), achievements (e.g. *reaching the top*) and states (e.g. *loving*). Accomplishments and achievements are 'telic', in that they have an end point, a goal; states and activities on the other hand are 'atelic' (they do not necessarily have an end point or goal). For example, Vendler classifies *running* and *running a mile* as an activity and an accomplishment respectively, the difference between them being that *running a mile* has an end point (the point where a mile has been run) whereas *running* can go on indefinitely. Similarly, one fundamental difference between accomplishments and achievements is that achievements occur at a single moment, whereas accomplishments can take place over a period of time. Although situation type and aspect are two different concepts, there are nonetheless compatibilities and incompatibilities between certain situation types and certain morphological markers of aspect. For example, in French, there is a high degree of compatibility between states (3) and activities (4) on the one hand, and morphological markers of imperfectivity such as the imperfect tense on the other:

(3) Il était intelligent

(4) Je fumais hier soir.

As Fleischman points out (1990:21), states tend to be incompatible with progressive aspect where this exists as a formal category in a language. For example in British English, it is not possible to say:

(5) *I am knowing Physics.

What are the advantages of Vendler's type of classification? There are two significant points to be made. First, Vendler's categories go beyond a classification of the verb; they are based on the whole verb phrase, or predicate. This has the advantage of taking full account of the syntactic context in which a verb is used, a context which, as we have seen, can be crucial in determining the aspectual force of a given combination of lexical items.

Second, Vendler's classification allows an analysis of the use of particular auxiliaries which can change the situation type of the verb. Fleischman (1990:22) cites the examples of *begin to*, *start to* and *go and* as auxiliaries which can shift the focus to the initial boundary of a verb, and of *stop* and *finish* as auxiliaries which can 'give an achievement profile to state, activity and accomplishment situations' (1990:22). Thus for example, the verb *study* (an activity) can be converted to an achievement if used with the auxiliary *finish*, as in (6):

> (6)   I finished studying and went out.

In short, Vendler's categorization offers a more sophisticated analysis of lexical items in context than what might otherwise be a rather loose definition of lexical aspect. It is an influential model which has been criticized, exploited and reworked by a number of scholars (for detailed accounts, see Rand 1993:33–40; Vetters 1996:87–106).

5.4   Approaches to aspect in French

5.4.1   Introduction

Given the difficulties involved in applying the notion of aspect to the French verb system, it is not surprising that there has been a proliferation of theories relating to aspect in French. In this section, we examine briefly some of the best-known theories. The choice is necessarily selective, but the idea is to include a range of types of model as well as a historical spread from earlier approaches such as Brunot (1922) and Guillaume (1929) through to more recent theories.[4] Note the extent to which these theories vary in approach, some encompassing a wide variety of aspectual markers in French, others which are more restricted. In some cases, aspectual theory is part of a much larger linguistic theory and is very much a reflection of a particular approach to language (for example, Brunot and Guillaume). Note also how various theories treat the question of grammatical versus lexical aspect. As a point of comparison, we shall examine in each case how the theory handles three specific linguistic areas which might be considered aspectual in nature: the PS/IMP distinction, the use of the literary verbal periphrasis '*aller* + present participle' and lexical oppositions such as *chercher/trouver*.

5.4.2   Brunot (1922)

Brunot's chapter in *La Pensée et la langue* entitled 'moyens d'expression des aspects' reflects very much his general approach to language in this work, in that his starting point is not the traditional parts of speech as presented in many other grammars, but rather the idea which is being expressed. As Iordan and Orr (1970:340) put it, Brunot's approach holds that 'when we talk, the idea comes first, and expression afterwards; so in grammar we must begin with the content and then pass to the form'. His approach to aspect thus begins with aspectual notions (e.g. *aspect de durée, aspect de développement, aspect d'accomplissement*) and then goes on to discuss the ways in which these might be expressed in French. Brunot's is an eclectic approach: a large number of different types of aspect are discussed for past, present and future times. The aspectual markers themselves are also very varied and include morphological markers such as verb endings, as well as verbal periphrases (e.g. *être en train de, être sur le point de*) and lexical markers such as the prefix *pour* and adverbs marking, for example, habitual actions (e.g. *d'habitude*). Table **5**.1 shows Brunot's table for the active voice. Time is divided into the three major zones (past, present and future) with subcategories, to which three major aspectual zones are added (though forms are not given for every theoretically possible category), one of which itself contains three sub-categories ('l'action est présentée comme durant, se répétant, progressant'). It should be stressed, however, that Brunot's discussion of aspect in *La Pensée et la langue* includes many more categories and aspectual markers than those appearing in the table.

Brunot's approach is clearly an early one which grapples with the notion of aspect in French. Its major strength is its inclusivity and the fact that it takes as its starting point the aspectual notion, allowing widely differing linguistic elements to be classified together where they express a common idea. The major drawbacks are a mirror image of the advantages. There is a lack of regularity and homogeneity in this eclectic classification; there is an uneven spread across the table, with some categories containing sub-categories or several possible aspectual markers and others only one category and perhaps no markers of aspect at all. The terms in some categories are not clearly defined; for example, the distinctions between *se faisant, durant* and *progressant* are not entirely clear. There is no apparent difference in the table between different registers; examples of the *passé surcomposé* for instance (see **6**.5.2.3) appear alongside highly literary expressions such as *son mal va empirant*. Constructions with quite different temporal or aspectual forces are sometimes classified together (e.g. *j'arrive* and *je viens d'arriver*; *je vais partir* and *il est sur le point de partir*). Nor is there any distinction between basic usage and discourse-pragmatic usage; the one example of the imperfect in Brunot's table does not represent a 'core' function of the imperfect (see **6**.1), but rather a case of the *imparfait narratif*, that is, an imperfect in the context of a punctual/perfective past (*une minute après, le train partait*: see **6**.4.2.2). The use of verbal periphrases and lexical items is also problematic; there is no obvious dividing line between grammatical and lexical markers and it is not clear whether there are any limits on the lexical items which

Table 5.1 Brunot's aspectual markers for the active voice

Actif

		TEMPS ABSOLUS				
		PASSÉ		PRÉSENT	FUTUR	
		ORDINAIRE	RÉCENT		PROCHAIN	ORDINAIRE
A L A D A T E D O N N É E	L'action est présentée comme se faisant	Le coup partit, deux perdrits [*sic*] tombèrent. Le train est arrivé en retard, il a attendu 20 minutes en gare de Lyon. Une minute après, le train partait.	J'arrive. Je viens d'arriver. Je ne fais que d'arriver. Il sort d'en prendre.	Il neige. Le fusil éclate. Les vitres volent en éclats. Le train part.	Je viens. Je vais partir. Je m'en vais vous dire. Il est sur le point de partir. – pour	Je partirai. Les fruits tomberont. On coupera le blé.
	L'action est présentée comme durant, se répétant, progressant	Au Moyen Age, on chercha en vain la pierre philosophale. Les anciens ont cru la terre immobile. Sa renommée alla toujours grandissant. La puissance de la France est allée croissant jusqu'au XIXe siècle.		Cette fillette grandit. On sonne la cloche en cas d'incendie. Son mal va empirant.		Les générations béniront votre nom. Vous prendrez cette potion toutes les heures. Sa majorité ira grossissant à chaque élection.
	L'action est présentée comme accomplie	Il eut vite expédié cette affaire. En un instant, il a eu expédié sa correspondance.		Le train est parti. Le malheureux a vécu (il est mort).		Je serai revenu à midi. J'aurai déjeuné pour 8 heures. J'aurai bientôt fait de le distinguer.

might be considered to be aspectual. In short, Brunot is not proposing a model as such; rather, what we find is an early attempt to describe aspectual phenomena in French.

As far as our three test cases are concerned, '*aller* + present participle' appears in all three time zones, as a marker of progressive aspect (as we would expect), but with no indication in the table of its highly literary nature. Lexical pairs do not appear in the table, but are discussed by Brunot in his chapter. The IMP, as outlined above, is not included in the categories of repetition and duration as we might have expected; the example quoted is a case of discourse-pragmatic usage (see above). Nor is the IMP discussed with reference to the aspectual function of the PS.

5.4.3 Guillaume (1929, 1964)

Guillaume's aspectual theory is radically different from the type of approach we find in Brunot. It too is part of a larger linguistic theory, one which sees language in kinetic terms, and where thought is delimited by a series of *coupes* (see Part I, Section 3.6.1). For Guillaume, aspect is of primary importance in the classification of the verb, in the sense that aspectual categories precede, as it were, temporal ones: 'c'est toujours après avoir assigné au verbe un aspect qu'on lui assigne un temps' (1964:190). To label his three aspectual categories (see below) as temporal would be to misunderstand the difference between aspect and tense, according to which aspect views time 'intérieurement à l'image verbale de langue' (that is, a fundamental part of the mental processes which precede articulation), whereas tense views time 'extérieurement à celle-ci en tant que lieu d'univers imparti au verbe, par visée de discours' (that is, more closely tied to the use of language in context) (1964:190). Tense is part of the *temps in esse* (see Part I, Section 3.6.1); it is concerned with 'temps expliqué' and is divisible into precise epochs such as past, present and future. Aspect, on the other hand, is concerned with an internal perspective, with 'temps impliqué', defined as 'celui que le verbe emporte avec soi' (1964:48).

In *Temps et verbe* (1929) and *Langage et science du langage* (1964), Guillaume elaborates his theory of aspect in French, positing three aspectual categories within the *temps in posse* (see Part I, Section 3.6.1). The notion of *tension* is fundamental to his conception of aspect. The verbal image is viewed in terms of a line between the points A and B:

$$\underset{A}{\underline{\qquad t_0 + t_1 + t_2 \qquad\qquad\qquad\qquad\qquad t_{n-2} + t_{n-1} + t_n \qquad}}_{\qquad B}$$

At t_0 for example, the verb has not yet 'spent' any of its *tension*; at the intermediary positions t_1, t_2 etc., the verb has spent some of its *tension* (this part is referred to as *détension*); and at t_n, there is only *détension*, since the *tension* is fully spent. Guillaume posits three aspects in *Temps et verbe* (1929:20):

aspect tensif ('il représente le verbe en tension'), *aspect extensif* ('il sert à renouveler la tension du verbe, au moment où elle expire et à la prolonger au-delà d'elle-même, en extension') and *aspect bi-extensif* ('il reprend en tension, au moment où elle expire, l'extension précédemment obtenue par le même moyen'). These correspond in present time to the *forme simple* (e.g. *marcher*), the *forme composée* (e.g. *avoir marché*) and the *forme surcomposée* (e.g. *avoir eu marché*) respectively (see Guillaume 1929:20–4) and are labelled *aspect immanent, aspect transcendant* and *aspect bi-transcendant* in *Langage et science du langage*. His explanation of the model in *Temps et verbe* reveals certain similarities between his view of aspect and a number of more traditional temporal and aspectual concepts such as sequence and completion (1929:21–2). This is also evident in his account in *Langage et science du langage*:

> l'aspect premier immanent (simple) retient l'esprit dans l'image verbale, non outrepassé; l'aspect second transcendant (composé) le porte en dehors d'elle, dans une subséquence aussi proche ou lointaine qu'il est besoin, et l'aspect bi-transcendant (surcomposé) dans la subséquence du subséquent déjà conçu (1964:190).

The tripartite aspectual division operates for all time zones (1964:190). Thus for example, to the *aspect tensif/immanent* (*je marchais*), correspond the *aspect extensif/transcendant* (*j'avais marché*) and the *aspect bi-extensif/bi-transcendant* (*j'avais eu marché*).

As far as our three test cases are concerned, Guillaume alludes in *Langage et science du langage* to the fact that aspectual markers in various languages encompass both grammatical and lexical elements: 'les différentiations inscrites dans le temps impliqué sont généralement rendues d'une manière semi-lexicale par des faits de vocabulaire, de dérivation, d'emploi de préverbes et d'auxiliaires' (1964:49), although specific cases such as lexical pairs or verbal periphrases are not discussed. The distinction between the imperfect and the *passé simple* is not aspectual for Guillaume. Rather, within the *temps in esse*, he posits two different *chronotypes*, that is, two different types of temporal movement (1929:52):

> le premier, ω, prélevé sur le passé, c'est-à-dire sur du temps qui a existé effectivement et *s'en va* est un *chronotype réel et décadent*. Le second, α, prélevé sur le futur, c'est-à-dire sur du temps qui n'a pas encore existé effectivement, qui *vient*, est un *chronotype virtuel et incident*.

The imperfect involves the former; the verbal image can always be divided into a section which is already complete and a section which is not (1929:53). Thus in the case of *marchait*, part of the action of walking is complete while part has not yet happened. The *passé simple* involves the chronotype α; each *passé simple* verb marks the beginning of a new event (e.g. *il marcha, il s'arrêta, il prit une décision*); it is not possible to make a division between part of the event which is complete and part which is incomplete (see Guillaume 1929:60–75 for a full explanation). Note that this analysis of the *passé simple/* imperfect distinction is a minority one, and is not necessarily followed by other Guillaumeans such as Martin (5.4.6 below).

The strength of Guillaume's approach lies primarily in the neatness and homogeneity of the model; the aspectual categories parallel exactly a neat morphological opposition between simple, compound and double compound forms. It is, furthermore, a highly influential model; we shall see traces of Guillaumean theory in Imbs, Martin and Wilmet, for example. However, aspect is only fully elaborated with respect to one particular type of distinction, one which many other theories see as primarily temporal rather than aspectual.

5.4.4   Imbs (1960)

In the introduction to his *L'Emploi des temps verbaux en français moderne*, Imbs defines both tense and aspect. Tense situates an event in time and is conceived of as a series of epochs along a time line. A division between past, present and future constitutes the *système primaire*, while a division which is relative to a 'point d'origine' constitutes a *système secondaire*. Temporal distinctions may be expressed by means of morphological markers such as verb forms but also by adverbials such as *hier, aujourd'hui, le lendemain* etc. Aspect is intimately linked to tense and may be expressed by the same set of verbal morphemes. It is however fundamentally different in nature, as Imbs's definition suggests (see **5.1** above); aspect is an internal perspective on time, where 'on considère le procès sous l'angle de son déroulement interne' (1960:15). Imbs (1960:16) acknowledges the lack of regular morphological markers of aspect in French, but cites a number of types of aspectual opposition in the French system as well as a number of possible markers:[5]

> *inaccompli/accompli* – e.g. present/*passé composé*
> durative/punctual – e.g. *imparfait/passé simple*
> imperfective/perfective – e.g. *verbe simple/verbe composé*; *battre/abattre*
> inchoative/terminative – e.g. *se mettre à/cesser de*.

He adds to these the *aspect itératif (répétition)* which he acknowledges to be different by nature to the other aspectual markers, in that it does not concern 'le processus verbal dans son déroulement' (1960:16).

It is clear from these examples and from his table of 'formes temporelles du verbe' (1960:7) that Imbs's is a broad, inclusive definition of aspect. Both lexical and grammatical elements are potential aspectual markers, including a variety of verbal periphrases such as *être sur le point de, être en train de, 'aller + infinitive'* etc. The IMP/PS opposition Imbs considers 'incontestablement une opposition d'aspect' (1960:15), in this case between the durative IMP and the punctual PS. Within durative aspect Imbs posits a progressive category in which he places the '*aller* + present participle' construction (1960:16), and lexical oppositions between pairs of verbs are also included in his account. One of the advantages of Imbs's approach is that it is broad, allowing many different linguistic elements to be classified as aspectual. On the negative side, there is no sense of an aspectual system; several different types of concept are involved, some of which are reflected in grammatical opposi-tions, others in lexical phenomena. Moreover, some of the categories are not easy to distinguish in the abstract (e.g. *inaccompli/accompli*, *duratif/ponctuel*, *imperfectif/perfectif*); they perhaps only seem clear in context because Imbs is able to provide a morphological opposition in French to illustrate each of them.

5.4.5   Reid (1970)

Reid's article is an attempt to give a systematic account of aspect in the French verb; it is not part of a larger linguistic theory as such. For Reid, aspect is a highly subjective category, assigned to a verb form only after the two more objective categories of time and stage have been assigned.[6] His analysis is unusual in making three distinctions at this level, rather than the traditional binary one between tense and aspect. Time he divides into the three sub-categories of past, present and future. The category stage consists also of three sub-categories, namely completion, actuality and imminence, corresponding to the distinction between various simple and compound forms (see Table 5.2). The more subjective category of aspect contains a binary divide between continuance and attainment, with this distinction appearing in French in past time only. Such a classification leads to the system in Table 5.2 for direct speech in contemporary French.

The distinction between the *passé simple* and the imperfect appears in Reid's system as a distinction within past time, stage of actuality, between the aspect of attainment in the case of the *passé simple* (the action, already objectively past, is viewed from an internal perspective as having been attained) and the aspect of continuance in the case of the imperfect (the action, although objectively past, is viewed from an internal perspective as in a process of continuance). Reid's aspectual markers are mostly gram-matical by nature, although he does include verbal periphrases such as *être en train de*. Lexical distinctions between pairs of verbs are discussed, only to be rejected as aspectual markers by Reid (1970:149), for whom aspect is funda-mentally grammatical. The '*aller* + present participle' construction, while not included in Reid's table, is by nature similar to other elements such as *être sur le point de*, '*aller* + infinitive' which do appear. Presumably, '*aller* + present participle' could be classified under any of the time zones as stage of actuality, aspect of continuance.

Table 5.2 Reid's classification for direct speech (Reid 1970:159)

STAGE	ASPECT	Past	TIME Present	Future
Completion	Attainment	L eut, C a eu, chanté	a chanté	aura chanté
	Continuance	avait chanté		
Actuality	Attainment	L chanta, C a chanté	chante	chantera
	Continuance	chantait		
Imminence	Attainment	(L fut, C a été, sur le point de chanter)	va chanter	(sera sur le point de chanter, devra chanter)
	Continuance	allait chanter		

(L = literary, C = colloquial)

Reid's system has considerable advantages. Unlike many other analyses, he is able both to posit a system with clear categories and to capture the subjective nature of aspect. He also distinguishes between the objectively complete (stage) and a more subjective perspective of attainment (aspect). On the negative side, the fact that Reid considers aspect to have systematic implications has some unfortunate consequences for the model he proposes. There is for instance a certain imbalance such that aspect is only marked in past time; in the present and future time zones, the forms are aspectually neutral. The distinction between time and stage also means that *va chanter* and *chantera* appear in very different categories (see Table 5.2), whereas for some speakers, these forms are not necessarily as distinct in meaning. More-over, there is an arbitrariness about which verbal periphrases are included; while '*aller* + infinitive' and *être sur le point de* are included, '*aller* + present participle' is not, nor is *être en train de*, to take two examples. Finally, the desire for a symmetrical table obliges Reid to note a rather contrived con-struction for the category of future imminence (*sera sur le point de chanter*); many other linguists simply admit that there are no formal exponents for the concept of 'future in the future' in French.

5.4.6 Martin (1971)

Martin's theory is contained within a study of tense and aspect in Middle French. His approach uses the Guillaumean concepts of *temps expliqué* and *temps impliqué* in distinguishing tense and aspect. 'Le temps expliqué permet de fixer le moment du procès' (1971:49); it concerns such concepts as the *visée* ('le lieu du procès dans le temps'), the *origine* ('le point sur l'axe des temps à partir duquel le procès est vu'), and the *référence* ('le lieu du temps à travers lequel l'esprit fixe la visée'). Aspect, on the other hand, falls within the domain of *temps impliqué*, which for Martin involves a number of types of distinction. These he divides into three main categories, with a number of sub-categories in some cases.

First he distinguishes *aspect ponctuel* from *aspect duratif*: 'le procès (action ou état) peut être caractérisé par l'étendue de temps qu'il occupe' (1971:50). Punctual aspect might be conveyed, for example, by certain types of verb such as *jaillir* or *s'élancer*, as opposed to the durative aspect conveyed by such verbs as *s'ennuyer*, or *traîner*. Within the category of durative aspect, Martin also discusses *l'aspect de la continuité* (which subdivides into *aspect linéaire* and *aspect progressif*, e.g. *marcher* vs *avancer*), *l'aspect de la discontinuité* or *aspect itératif* (e.g. *répéter*, *recharger*), and he notes that Ducháček further distinguishes *l'aspect itératif* from *l'aspect fréquentatif*, *l'aspect multiplicatif* and *l'aspect distributif* (see Martin 1971:51).

Martin's second major aspectual distinction is that between *aspect de l'accompli* and *aspect de l'inaccompli* or *aspect perfectif* and *aspect imperfectif* (1971:52). In Guillaumean terms, the former (in each case) represents 'l'aspect du procès entièrement en détension, c'est-à-dire dont il ne reste aucune partie à accomplir', (e.g. *marché* (1971:52)), whereas the latter represents 'l'aspect du procès vu entièrement (*marcher*) ou partiellement en tension (*marchant*)' (1971:53).

Third, Martin posits an aspectual distinction between *aspect inchoatif* ('l'aspect du procès qui envisage la phase initiale', e.g. *se mettre à*) and *aspect terminatif* ('qui envisage la phase terminale', e.g. *finir de*).

Having cited examples of both lexical and grammatical aspect, Martin goes on to narrow his definition of aspect, separating out aspect and *modalité d'action* (1971:54–6); he considers aspect, strictly speaking, to be concerned with grammatical elements, whereas *modalité d'action* is concerned with lexical elements: 'nous désignerons par *aspect* toute catégorie réservée à la détermination du temps impliqué, et par *modalité d'action* son expression lexicale' (1971:56). *Modalité d'action* is therefore 'le pendant exact au niveau du lexème de l'aspect grammatical' (1971:56), although grammatical aspect and *modalité d'action* clearly interact in context. Moreover, *modalité d'action* is a large and eclectic category, whereas grammatical aspect is reduced to a relatively small number of specific oppositions. As far as our three test cases are concerned, one is included as a case of grammatical aspect, one as *modalité d'action* and the other is potentially a case of *modalité d'action*. The IMP/PS distinction is for Martin a case of durative-imperfective vs punctual-perfective aspect; in asserting that it is 'incontestablement grammaticale', Martin disagrees with Guillaume's theory, in spite of the strong Guillaumean influence perceptible elsewhere in his analysis (1971:70–7). The construction '*aller* + present 'participle' is classed as a verbal periphrasis under *modalité d'action*, and although the pair *chercher/trouver* is not included explicitly, other verbs are listed as markers of *modalité d'action* (1971:77).

Martin's model is an inclusive one, which offers a clear distinction between aspect and *modalité d'action*. However, it is not particularly homogeneous or neat and categories seem at times to overlap in their definition (for example, the distinction between durative and imperfective on the one hand and punctual and perfective on the other, is not entirely clear).

5.4.7   Wilmet (1991, 1995, 1997)[7]

In general terms, Wilmet's classification of aspect in French encompasses a wide range of concepts and a variety of markers. The following tree diagram explains the major classes:

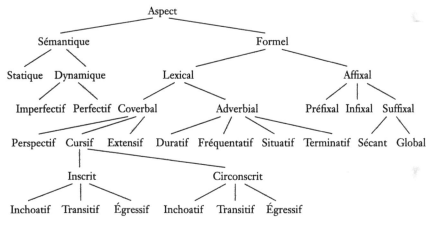

Figure 5.1   Wilmet's model of aspect (Wilmet 1997:325)

Wilmet posits a fundamental distinction between *aspect sémantique* and *aspect formel*, the former corresponding broadly to the traditional idea of lexical aspect. In explaining many of the aspectual distinctions, he makes use of the concept of a process AB, with a *terminus a quo A* and a *terminus ad quem B* (note the Guillaumean influence). Within *aspect sémantique*, Wilmet makes a broad distinction between stative verbs which 'posent simultanément dans le temps le *terminus a quo A* et le *terminus ad quem B* du procès AB' (e.g. *avoir, savoir, croire*) and dynamic verbs, which 'posent successivement dans le temps le *terminus a quo A* et le *terminus ad quem B* du procès AB' (e.g. *marcher, sortir, exploser* (1991:212)). Dynamic verbs are further subdivided into imperfective (e.g. *commencer*) and perfective categories (e.g. *écrire une lettre* (1991:212)). The sub-categories within *aspect formel* are numerous. Within *aspect affixal*, we have *aspect préfixal* (the use of prefixes such as *re-*, *a-, en-*: e.g. *sécher/ressécher, dormir/endormir*), *aspect infixal* (e.g. infixes such as *-in-, -el-*: *pleuvoir/pleuviner* etc.) and *aspect suffixal*: the last concerns morphological endings, and posits a basic binary distinction between *aspect sécant* (which 'scinde le procès AB entre le *terminus a quo A* et le *terminus ad quem B*, laissant ouvert aux extrémités l'intervalle A>B') and *aspect global* (which 'saisit le procès AB en bloc [. . .] fermant à ses extrémités l'intervalle A>B' (1991:216)). Within *aspect formel*, Wilmet has a large number of sub-categories which he considers to be lexical: these include adverbial elements and coverbal elements (e.g. verbal auxiliaries, verbal periphrases, verbs such as *commencer à, finir de* etc.) which are in turn sub-divided.

How does his theory handle our three test cases? The PS/IMP is classed clearly in the category of *aspect formel*, within the sub-categories of *aspect affixal* and *aspect suffixal*; within the latter sub-category, the PS marks *aspect global* whereas the IMP marks *aspect sécant*. The '*aller* + present participle' construction is classed under *aspect formel, lexical, coverbal, cursif, circonscrit, transitif*, i.e. the median phase of a process (from the choice of initial, median and final) which is in progress.[8] The *chercher/trouver* opposition would come under *aspect sémantique*.

The advantages of Wilmet's theory are considerable; it is in many respects the most sophisticated of the models examined here. While creating a sense of system through the tree diagram, Wilmet avoids imposing a rigid classification into which linguistic elements might fit rather uncomfortably, causing uneven spread or arbitrary selection for inclusion. Not all classes need to be subdivided into the same subgroups in order to make the model neat and symmetrical; binary, tripartite or other types of distinction can be used where appropriate. Wilmet also captures the basic lexical/grammatical distinction while at the same time allowing the more lexical elements amongst the grammatical markers (such as some auxiliaries and adverbs) to be classi-fied in a different way from the more strictly morphological markers. In starting with the widely differing types of aspectual markers in French and then grouping them into groups and subgroups, Wilmet manages to be inclusive while at the same time capturing generalities. If there is a draw-back, it is probably the complexity of this model; the classification of a given aspectual marker can be multi-layered (see, for example, the account of '*aller* + present participle' above).

5.4.8   General issues

It will be clear from the discussion thus far that the concept of aspect is highly problematic for a number of reasons. Not only are there no regular morphological markers of aspect in French, but also there is little consensus as to which oppositions or even which types of opposition are aspectual by nature, and there is no coherence in the terminology used. The advantages and disadvantages of the different analyses tend to complement each other; a rigid system, while offering apparent coherence, can cause arbitrary inclusion and exclusion as well as uneven classes; conversely, too eclectic an account is usually unable to capture generalities. It is also possible to see a progression from the earliest models such as Brunot's, through to Wilmet's model which draws on a wide range of earlier approaches.

In addition to these classificatory difficulties, the aspectual interpretation of any given construction is dependent not on one factor, such as the morphological ending or the verbal prefix, but rather on a host of contextual factors, including the situation type of the verb as well as other contextual elements such as the presence of temporal adverbials. Furthermore, a number of verb forms which might be considered aspectual markers are used differently in different registers, or *plans d'énonciation*, of French.[9] Since the *passé composé*, for example, functions in *discours* both as a past punctual and as a present perfective, whereas it functions purely as the latter in *histoire*, the opposition *fit/faisait* is exclusive to *histoire* and the opposition *a fait/faisait* cannot possibly be of the same order in both *plans d'énonciation*. In other cases, a form may be encountered much more frequently in one variety of French than another. A clear example of this is the *passé surcomposé régional* (see 6.5.2.3), one of the key functions of which is to stress aspectual perfectivity, for example:

(7) J'ai beaucoup de camarades que je peux plus voir maintenant parce que c'est trop loin m'enfin **on s'est eu écrit(s)** même avec d'autres – et puis maintenant on a tout abandonné maintenant je ne sais plus écrire (Carruthers 1994:176).

The regional *passé surcomposé* (PSC) is, however, only encountered in the spoken registers of certain regions, and is highly stigmatized in sociolinguistic terms. On the other hand, '*aller* + present participle' as a marker of durative or progressive aspect, is highly literary and effectively defunct in most varieties of French. Reid attempts to address this problem by labelling some forms 'L' (literary) and others 'C' (colloquial), but in so doing, he only really touches the surface of the problem. Moreover, for discourse-pragmatic approaches (see 5.5.4 below), contextual factors including register and medium are of crucial importance in interpreting the function of a particular tense in discourse.

5.5   Applications of the notion of aspect

5.5.1   Introduction

Given the highly problematic nature of aspect in French, what, if any, are the arguments for considering aspect to be a useful category? To what extent is a category which concerns an internal subjective perspective on time – however its sub-categories are classified – an indispensable tool when it comes to explaining certain phenomena, both synchronic and diachronic?

5.5.2   Diachronic phenomena

Chapter 6 will examine in more detail the evolution of certain past tenses and will highlight the role of aspectual factors in diachronic developments. By way of example, we shall discuss briefly one such development here, that is, the creation of the compound forms in Vulgar Latin. One of the factors considered fundamental in this development is the double function of the Latin form *fecit* as a marker of both the past punctual (essentially a temporal function) and the present perfective (essentially an aspectual function). By Vulgar Latin, the temporal function has become dominant, and the new present perfective, that is, the compound past (*habet factum*), is formed (see **6**.2.1). This new form also has temporal connotations, which in turn become dominant over time to the point where the compound past is first and foremost a temporal marker in contemporary spoken French. In this process from Vulgar Latin through to Modern French, the pattern has been for usages to be coined initially for aspectual reasons, and for the temporal connotations which are inevitably present, to come to dominate, thus causing a diachronic shift from the aspectual to the temporal. This in turn might cause new usages to be coined to fill the aspectual gaps, and so the cycle might continue. It would be impossible to explain this kind of evolution in the tense system without recourse to the notion of aspect.

5.5.3   Aspectual concepts

In spite of major differences between aspectual theories, there is a general consensus that aspectual notions are necessary in order to explain certain phenomena in French. These have been discussed in sections **5**.2–**5**.4; suffice it to say here that it is difficult to see how the function of certain forms such as the PS and the IMP, certain verbal periphrases, the use of certain auxiliaries etc. could be explained adequately without recourse to the notion of aspect, whether or not we consider that aspect in French can be systematized.

5.5.4   Aspect and discourse-pragmatics

Recently, much illuminating work has been done from a discourse-pragmatic perspective on the functions tenses can assume in particular discourse contexts. In many cases, the aspectual properties of the form in question are inextricably linked to the discourse-pragmatic effects produced. In Chapter 6, we will examine the discourse-pragmatic functions of some of the past tenses, such as the *imparfait narratif* and the use of the PS in journalism. In these examples, the aspectual properties are part of the basic meaning of the tense in question; the discourse-pragmatic functions are, as Fleischman puts it, 'motivated extensions' (1990:23) of the core temporal and aspectual functions. As a case study illustrating the application of aspectual notions in the field of discourse-pragmatics, we shall examine in more detail here Monville-Burston and Waugh's (1991) findings in relation to the French present tense (PR) in newspaper usage.

In French, the PR is, in aspectual terms, neither perfective nor imperfective, marking as it does the equivalent in English of both *I sing* and *I am singing*, the interpretation of a given example being heavily dependent on context.[10] One of the consequences of this is that a Historic Present (HPR), that is a PR used to mark past time, can mark both a perfective and an imperfective past. Monville-Burston and Waugh (1991) argue that the aspectual multivalency of the PR may be used to create discourse-pragmatic effects in journalistic discourse. The PR is felt to have both perfective connotations (where it is a HPR occurring where a PS might have appeared) and imperfective ones (where it substitutes for the IMP), although the extent to which perfectivity or imperfectivity is to the fore depends very much on context. Monville-Burston and Waugh (1991:103) cite cases such as (8), where in the shift from PS to PR 'the perfectivity of the HPR usually comes out strongly, supported by the perfectivity of the preceding PS', as opposed to cases such as (9) where the shift is from *passé composé* (PC) to PR, and where the current relevance which is characteristic of the PC combines with the imperfective properties of the PR to dull the sense of perfectivity:

(8) Il y a un tiers de siècle, lorsqu'il **fonda** son entreprise, il **choisit** sur un catalogue une couleur qui lui plaisait pour ses camions et ses engins. Nom de guerre de ce minium très orange: minorange. Aussitôt, François Bouygues **s'en empare** comme d'un talisman (Monville-Burston and Waugh 1991:103)

(9) Des sourires et de la fermeté, les Français **en ont ramassé** à la pelle. Fermeté dans le langage et sur le fond du discours. Lorsqu'il **appelle** les Français à faire 'faire bloc' autour des acquis des dernières années . . . M.Mitterrand **feint** de s'adresser à tous, mais **parle** essentiellement à la gauche (Monville-Burston and Waugh 1991:103).

They cite several cases of declarative verbs (e.g. *dire, déclarer, affirmer, prétendre* etc.), where the nuances of imperfectivity dominate, and the journalist can give an impression that the statement not only was made at a particular point in time, but that it continues to be current. In (10), the statements are current because Mitterrand is stubbornly insisting on what he has said, whereas in (11), the request represents a continuing appeal:

(10)   Février 1984, à la Haye, le chef de l'Etat **explique** à ses partenaires européens: 'que l'Europe soit capable de lancer dans l'espace une station habitée . . .' Mai 1985, à Brest, le président de la République . . . **n'hésite** pas à prophétiser: 'de mon point de vue la stratégie sera nécessairement spatiale . . .' Aujourd'hui, M. Mitterrand **réitère** sa profession de foi (Monville-Burston and Waugh 1991:107)

(11)   Dans une lettre ouverte à M. François Mitterrand, Petre Uhl . . . lui **demande** d'intervenir 'publiquement et énergiquement afin d'empêcher la condamnation honteuse de Vaclav Havel' (Monville-Burston and Waugh 1991:107).

In short, as these examples illustrate, the notion of aspect may be crucial to our understanding of certain techniques employed by writers or journalists to create effects within the text.[11] Aspect is thus an important category in the domain of stylistics and discourse analysis.

Finally, at the heart of this interplay between tense, aspect and discourse-pragmatics lies the question: to what extent do discourse-pragmatic factors influence aspectual developments which in turn, as part of the cycle described in 5.5.2, lead to a re-analysis of temporal functions and ultimately of the tense system? At what point does a marked usage of a verb form come to be found so frequently that it ceases to be marked, and thus becomes the unmarked (that is, normal) function of that form? There is strong evidence from the history of French and from other languages that pragmatic usage can indeed in certain cases lead to grammatical re-analysis.[12] Our discussion of the development of the past tenses in the next chapter will return to these questions.

Suggested Reading

Models:
   Brunot (1922), Guillaume (1929, 1964), Imbs (1960) Martin (1971), Reid (1970), Vet (1980), Wilmet (1991, 1995, 1997).
Discussions of aspect:
   Cohen (1989), Comrie (1985), Thelin (ed) (1990).
Discussions of aspect in French:
   David and Martin (eds) (1980), Lerat (1981), Posner (1972), Vet and Vetters (eds) (1994), Vetters (1996), Wunderli (1989), *Folia Linguistica* 30(1) (1986).
Imperfect and *passé simple*:
   see Chapter 6 Suggested Reading.
Aspect and discourse-pragmatics:
   Fleischman (1983, 1990, 1991), Hopper (ed) (1982), Judge (1998), Monville-Burston and Waugh (1991), Waugh (1991), Waugh and Monville-Burston (1986).

Notes

1. See also Lerat (1981) for a discussion of the problematic nature of lexical aspect in French.
2. See Posner (1972) for a discussion.
3. For a discussion of the origin of the notion of *mode d'action*, see Martin (1971:54–6).
4. Note that aspect has generally not been a central preoccupation of generative grammar. See, however, Vet (1980:47–54) for a discussion of Verkuhl's treatment of aspect in Dutch.
5. Imbs also includes a number of aspectual sub-categories such as the *résultatif* (a subcategory of *accompli*) or the *progressif* (a subcategory of *duratif*).
6. Note that this is in direct opposition to Guillaume's view that aspect precedes tense (see 5.4.3).
7. Wilmet's theories are discussed in a number of his publications, including two recent articles (1991, 1995) and his *Grammaire critique du français* (1997).
8. For a detailed discussion, see Wilmet (1997:319).
9. For a discussion of *plans d'énonciation* and definitions of *discours* and *histoire*, see Part I, Section 3.4.2, and Part II 6.3.2.
10. Note that with reference to the present, some commentators prefer to use the aspectual opposition durative/punctual rather than imperfective/perfective. We shall use the latter here, since Monville-Burston and Waugh's case study employs these terms.
11. See also Judge (1998) who discusses the aspectual multivalency of the PR in journalism as well as the alternation of the PR with other tenses in what she calls a *système multifocal*. For an analysis of the use of the HPR in literary contexts, see Fleischman (1990:285–310).
12. See for example Fleischman (1983) and Hopper (1987).

6

Past tenses: complex and changing relationships

6.1   Introduction

One of the areas of the French verb system which has attracted most attention amongst researchers is that of the past tenses. In this chapter, we investigate the relationships between the various past tenses in French, in particular that between the *passé simple* and the *passé composé*. Most major French grammars give full accounts of the various functions of each tense, of which the following is a very brief summary which will serve as a basic reference point:

The *passé simple* (PS):

- This is the classic narrative tense in French, usually marking foregrounded events in chronological sequence. Events are viewed externally and globally and have a delimited beginning and end:

    (1)   Elle se leva, mit son manteau et sortit.

Given the variety of aspectual terminology used in the literature (e.g. punctual, perfective, *global* etc.), we shall adopt one of the common labels throughout this chapter for the sake of consistency, that is, 'past punctual'. The PS is highly compatible with verbs expressing achievements or accomplishments (see Vendler's categories, 5.3), but is not incompatible with duration, where it may be used alongside an adverbial complement or might indicate the beginning or end of a process:

    (2)   La reine régna cinquante ans.

Since the event is viewed as delimited within past time, it is also viewed as cut off from the present. We note at this stage that the PS is highly restricted in terms of the contexts in which it might be found, and has been virtually eliminated from standard spoken French.[1]

The *passé composé* (PC):

- Operates aspectually as a present perfective, in that it marks completion with respect to the present, for example:

    (3) J'ai terminé ma thèse maintenant.

- Fulfils in oral French (and in certain other circumstances – see **6.3.5**) the same function as the PS in literary French: that is, it is a past punctual which situates delimited past time events on the narrative line:

    (4) Je suis allée à la piscine hier.

These are the PC's two principal functions. It also operates temporally as a marker of anteriority with respect to the present (in this case, the present is generic/habitual):

    (5) Une fois que j'ai pris mon repas du soir je regarde la télé.

The PC can also mark future time; this might be an immediate future as in (6) (the PC will often appear alongside an adverb indicating rapidity or an immediate deadline), or a case of hypothetical completion or anteriority relative to a future time as in (7):

    (6) J'ai fini dans un instant

    (7) Si je ne l'ai pas trouvé avant vendredi, je ne viendrai pas.

The *imparfait* (IMP):

- Unlike the PS which views an event or state externally as a global whole, with a delimited beginning and end, the imperfect views events from the inside, without regard to the beginning or end of the process. In aspectual terms, a variety of terminology is found (e.g. imperfective, *sécant*, durative; see Chapter 5); we shall normally use the term 'imperfective' in this chapter. Its aspectual properties make the imperfect highly compatible with verbs expressing states (8) and activities (9), and it is often used in descriptions (10), or to mark repeated actions (11):

    (8) Elle se sentait seule

    (9) Il dormait bien dans ce lit

(10)   Le soleil brillait, le ciel était bleu, il faisait beau

(11)   Tous les jours j'allais au travail à pied.

Its descriptive powers and its ability to express a continuing action mean that the IMP is frequently associated with the background in narration, where the PS is associated with the foreground. In indirect speech, the PR is usually rendered by the IMP:

(12)   Elle m'a dit qu'elle voulait prendre des vacances.

The IMP can also be used modally in conditional sentences (13), to express wishes or regrets (14), or to express attenuation or politeness (15):[2]

(13)   S'il travaillait plus, il réussirait

(14)   Si seulement il voulait le faire

(15)   Je voulais vous demander si je pouvais partir plus tôt.

The *plus-que-parfait* (PLP):

- Operates temporally as a marker of anteriority, in that it marks a time prior to a point in the past:

(16)   J'avais décidé d'aller à l'université mais je n'ai pas réussi mon bac.

- Operates aspectually as a past perfective, where completion is usually expressed in relation to an imperfect (often used in a generic or habitual sense):

(17)   Une fois que j'avais pris mon repas du soir je regardais la télé.

The PLP is also used modally (18), to express attenuation (19), and in certain types of conditional construction (20):

(18)   Si seulement tu avais gagné

(19)   J'étais venu demander votre permission

(20)   Si j'avais su, je serais parti plus tôt.

The *passé antérieur* (PA):

- Marks aspectual perfectivity and temporal anteriority in a restricted set of subordinate temporal clauses, where the main clause usually contains a PS:

    (21)   Quand il eut quitté l'université il commença à travailler.

- Marks the rapid completion of an action:

    (22)   Il eut vite pris la décision.

Like the PS (to which it is related formally through the auxiliary), the PA is highly restricted in usage, and has been effectively eliminated from spoken French.

The *passé surcomposé* (PSC):

- Like the PA, the PSC marks anteriority and perfectivity in a restricted set of subordinate temporal clauses, where the main clause normally contains a PC:

    (23)   Quand il a eu quitté l'université il a commencé à travailler.

- Like the PA, the PSC marks the rapid completion of a past action:

    (24)   Il a eu vite pris la décision.

Whereas the PA is used in the variety of French where the PS is found, the PSC is normally restricted to varieties where the PC rather than the PS marks the past punctual. As we shall see in **6.5.2.3**, it is marginalized by many normative grammars.

- There is also a regional form of PSC, which usually stresses one or more of the following features: distance in the past, aspectual perfectivity, the exceptional nature of an event, subjectivity on the part of the speaker:

    (25)   On a eu bien rigolé des fois.

A number of problematic issues arise – both diachronically and synchronically – from the complex set of relationships between the past tenses in French. In this chapter, we shall investigate the evolution of the relationship between the PS and the PC, and in particular the loss of the PS from spoken French. Although emphasis will be on the PS/PC relationship, we shall also examine some of the major issues which arise in terms of the development and analysis of the IMP, PLP, PA and PSC.

6.2   The *passé simple/passé composé* relationship: a complex history

6.2.1   The development of the compound tenses

The past tense system of Classical Latin includes an imperfect (*faciebat*), a pluperfect (*fecerat*), and a form which serves to mark both the present perfective (the semantic equivalent of 'she has done') and the past punctual ('she did'), i.e. *fecit*. One form (*fecit*) therefore performs two key functions, operating in two different temporal zones as both a present perfective and a past punctual. It thus co-occurs with both present and past temporal adverbs and with present and past forms of the subjunctive in dependent clauses. As Harris (working within a typological framework) points out (1982:47), a form such as *fecit* which marks aspectual perfectivity also implicitly marks temporal anteriority, since by definition the event is temporally in the past, even if it has present relevance. It can therefore be very difficult to separate out the aspectual and the temporal values of such a paradigm. There is evidence that the Latin grammarians saw the aspectual value as dominant in forms such as *fecit*, but that, as Harris argues, by Vulgar Latin, the temporal value had become dominant, thus following the pattern whereby temporal values tend over time to predominate over aspectual ones (1982:47).

The double function of the paradigm *fecit* is one of the reasons widely cited for the creation in Vulgar Latin of a range of new forms, that is, the compound tenses, one of the most significant developments in the evolution of the Romance verbal system. These are formed by combining the auxiliary verb *habere* (>*avoir*), with a past participle; thus the present perfective is formed by combining the present tense of the verb 'to have' with the past participle, giving compounds such as *habet factum*. Indeed, there is a formal precedent for the construction, in that Classical Latin has a passive structure where the auxiliary *habere* and the past participle are found, that is, *habet litteras scriptas* (lit. 's/he has the letters written': see Harris 1978:135). In this example, the auxiliary verb retains its full semantic value, and the past participle is adjectival in function, although in more colloquial registers there are early examples of *habere* with a past participle which are clearly not possessive, notably with cognitive verbs. Over time, the semantic value of *habere* diminishes and the structure is used with a wider variety of verbs. Moreover, the union between the auxiliary and the past participle increases, such that the structure is felt to be a compound paradigm, rather than the combination of two separate elements (Harris 1982:47). A whole series of compounds is thus formed, including a past perfective (*habebat/habuit factum*), which will oust the synthetic *fecerat*. These developments follow the pattern expected in a typological shift from an OV to VO language (see Part I, Section 3.4.1); there is an increase in analytic forms such as verbal auxiliaries and a corresponding loss of synthetic forms.

Clearly, in their original form, the compound tenses evolved for pragmatic reasons as markers of aspect; a form such as the present perfective, *habet factum*, contrasts with the past punctual *fecit*, and the ambiguity created by the double function of *fecit* is resolved. The evolution of this system from Classical Latin to Vulgar Latin can be represented as follows:

Table 6.1   Classical Latin and Vulgar Latin systems (adapted from Harris 1978:136)

	CL	VL
present perfective	fecit	habet factum
past punctual	fecit	fecit
past perfective	fecerat	habuit/habebat factum
past imperfective	faciebat	faciebat

As is the case in Classical Latin with *fecit*, the new form *habet factum*, although originally a marker of aspect, necessarily has temporal properties, and is therefore in a position to mark a past event with present relevance. We shall see that in subsequent developments, the temporal connotations of this form are to become increasingly dominant.

6.2.2   'Functional multiplicity' in the Old French period[3]

Research on the use of the past tenses in Old French has been enriched by the work of scholars who have focused on the role of textual and contextual factors (such as Blanc 1964; Sutherland 1939) and, more recently, by insights from the discourse-pragmatic tradition (see Part I, Section 3.4.2). The latter approach stresses the differences between the cultural/linguistic context in which these tenses were operating, and the context in which we are conditioned to examine their function – that of a modern literate society. The Old French examples available to us appear in manuscripts of the period, and come from a variety of genres. Most of the literary texts from the heyday of Old French are written in verse; they are epics and romances, intended not for private reading but for live public performance. They are thus fundamentally oral in character; as such, they share some features with modern oral French, but are not necessarily indicative of conversational usage, since they are carefully crafted performances rather than spontaneous informal conversation. There are fewer prose texts, most of which are translations of religious texts or legal documents (see Ayres-Bennett 1996:58–9). Later in the Old French period, during the thirteenth century, the use of prose expands considerably, with significant increases in the number of historical texts, chronicles and translations. These prose texts, unlike the earlier verse epics and romances, are intended for private, individual reading.

What are the consequences of this for the past tense system of Old French? A modern speaker reading an Old French text would be struck by the apparently arbitrary (from a contemporary perspective) use of tense, particularly as regards the forms used to mark events on the narrative line. Old French tense usage is much more flexible than in Modern French. Each tense can mark a variety of notions, with much overlap in function. Moreover, tense and aspect are used as part of the dramatic performance of verse forms, to create effects and to perform a variety of textual and expressive functions. The forms which emerge in the Old French period from the Vulgar Latin forms can be summarized as follows:[4]

Table 6.2 Vulgar Latin and Old French systems (adapted from Harris 1978:136, 143)

	VL	OF
present perfective	habet factum	a fait
past punctual	fecit	fit
past perfective	habuit/habebat factum	ot/avoit fait
imperfective	faciebat	faisoit

In practice, the PS and the PC are both used to mark past punctual events on the narrative line; the present tense (PR) is also used for this purpose. The PC is used least frequently in this context, but the PS and PR are often found alongside each other in rapid succession, a phenomenon known as tense-switching (see Foulet 1970:220–1; Ayres-Bennett 1996:54). The PC thus has two different functions. First, it is a present perfective (the purpose it originally fulfilled in Vulgar Latin); for convenience, we shall use Fleischman's term $Perf_1$ for this function (1990:45). Increasingly, it also marks a past event with present relevance ($Perf_2$), as the temporal connotations of this present perfective come to the fore. In the following section of the Oxford text of the *Chanson de Roland* (c.1100), adapted from Fleischman's annotated version (1990:46), we can see the alternation between the PS, the PR and the PC ($Perf_1$ and $Perf_2$):

(26)   Ço **dist** [PS] li reis: 'Sunez en vostre corn' AOI

Gefreid d'Anjou **ad** sun greisle **sunét** [PC $Perf_2$].
Franceis **descendent** [PR], Carles l'**ad comandét** [PC $Perf_2$];
Tuz lur amis qu'il **unt** morz **truvét** [PC $Perf_2$];
Ad un carner sempres les **unt portét** [PC $Perf_1$].
Asez i **ad** [PR] evesques e abez . . .

The King said: 'Go sound your horn.' AOI
The horn of Geoffroy of Anjou has been sounded.
The French dismount, Charles has commanded it.
All the comrades that they have found dead there
are borne off at at once to a common grave.
There are bishops and abbots in great number.
(Fleischman's translation, 1990:46; see Ayres-Bennett
1996:67 for a discussion of the meaning of AOI)

It is especially as Perf$_1$ in the earlier texts (translated by Fleischman in example (26) using the passive form of the narrative present) that the PC alternates with the PS; it continues to do so in narrative with telic verbs (verbs expressing a goal or end state), before declining in this function. As Perf$_2$, the PC declines in use in narrative texts, but remains frequent in dialogue. Fleischman (1990:48) argues that in Old French, the PC is not yet evolving to a past which has no link to the speaker's present, although Beck claims that this is indeed the case (1988:138). The exact sense of a given form with regard to present relevance will clearly depend not only on the tense used, but also on contextual factors such as co-occurring adverbs and on the situation type of the verb (see Vendler's categories in 5.3). Indeed, basing his argument on Harris (1982:47–8), Beck argues that 'the change from perfect to preterite in Old French proceeded from verbs expressing physical end states to verbs of cognitive activity and speech acts, and eventually to intransitive verbs' (1988:140).[5]

This functional multiplicity in Old French is closely linked to the oral nature of the discourse and the situation of dramatic performance. The cultural norms within which oral narratives are structured are significantly different from literary narratives in a number of ways. Amongst these, Fleischman stresses the link between on the one hand literate societies and linear patterns of time where events are recounted in the order in which they occur, and on the other hand, oral societies where oral memory and linear plot are not necessarily compatible (1990:131–5). Gesture, intonation and tense-aspect markers are used orally where written narratives might make use of complex syntactic strategies such as patterns of subordination or complex conjunctions.[6] Given this context, tense-aspect markers, in particular tense switches (e.g. PS to PR, PR to PS) are used for such purposes as foregrounding and backgrounding certain events and states, marking narrative boundaries between different sections of text, regulating the pace of narration (accelerating or slowing down the pace), and changing perspective (or narrative point of view).[7] Indeed, the same events on a narrative line can be marked by different tenses, depending on how such phenomena are manipulated for effect. Rhyme and assonance will also play a role in the choice of tense. The picture as far as past tense usage in Old French is concerned is thus one of 'functional multiplicity', with extensive overlaps throughout the system.

6.2.3   Developments in Middle French, and Early Modern analyses

As mentioned above, in the later Old French period the rise in importance and frequency of prose texts designed for private reading goes hand
in hand with certain developments in tense usage. These emerging prose
texts (historical accounts, chronicles, translations) demand a more strictly
chronological use of tense. This can be seen clearly in a chronicle such as
Geoffroy de Villehardouin's *Conqueste de Costentinoble* (early thirteenth century), or in the *Lettre de Jean Sarrasin à Nicolas Arrode* (1249), where the
tense switching evident in the orally performed texts has given way to
much more logical patterns (Ayres-Bennett 1996:82, 97). The PS for
example is used consistently in its modern function as a past punctual, while
the use of the PS to mark a recent past decreases after the thirteenth
century, being used in Middle French (approximately 1300–1500) for recent
past events only where they have no connection to the present; moreover,
in this function, the PS appears in quoted speech only (see Fleischman
1990:49).

How does French move from this stage to a point where the PS is eliminated from spoken French? In parallel with the rise of prose as a genre/
medium, and the decline of the orally performed verse forms, comes also the
invention of printing in the late fifteenth century. From a situation in the
medieval period where the distinction between oral and written forms is
much less clear, since literary manuscripts are essentially written versions of
orally performed stories, the two media increasingly start to diverge. In
other words, the shifts in tense usage need to be seen in the context of a slow
change from an oral to a literate culture. Against this background, it is
relatively easy to see that the PC with its associations with present relevance
might lend itself easily to marking a past which is associated with the speaker.
The PS on the other hand, marks a past which is disconnected from the
present, and thus also more removed from the speaker; in the burgeoning
medium of prose, it becomes increasingly the dominant marker of the past
punctual. The functions of the PS and PC are, in other words, becoming
increasingly familiar as they begin to reflect 'modern' usage.

In Early Modern French (approximately sixteenth and seventeenth centuries), the early grammarians are clearly grappling with the description of
the functions of these forms. The sense of present relevance associated with
the PC is embodied in what has become known as the 'twenty-four hour
rule', laid down by one of France's earliest grammarians, Henri Estienne, in
the sixteenth century. According to this rule, the PS is appropriate for time
which has elapsed more than twenty-four hours prior to the speaker's present,
and the PC for time within the past twenty-four hours. Estienne articulates
this rule in his *Traicté de la conformité du langage français avec le grec* (1565),
and is followed in the next century by Maupas (1607) and Oudin (1632).
There is, however, considerable debate as to whether the rule does in fact

correspond to Early Modern French usage. It certainly forms part of the linguistic code which informs writers of the period; evidence cited by Weinrich (1973) from seventeenth-century writers such as Madame de Sévigné, Corneille and Racine supports this, certain punctual adverbials such as *hier* regularly triggering a PS (see Galet 1977; Caron and Liu 1999). Significantly however, there is also evidence that the PC is used increasingly to mark past time where the period involved is more than twenty-four hours. For example, there are cases where a writer uses the PC and is then corrected: Corneille was corrected by the *Académie Française* for his use of a PC in *Le Cid* to mark an action which was outside the stipulated twenty-four hours (see Weinrich 1973:295) and in the eighteenth century, Voltaire was corrected in a letter to his editor for using a PC alongside the adverbial *hier* (Weinrich 1973:297). Racine obeyed the rule in his tragedies, but there is evidence in his private correspondence that the PC was also used to mark the past punctual. Foulet (1920:304–7) cites many examples from letters by Mme de Sévigné, Racine and Mme Racine which show the PS and PC used alongside each other as past punctuals:

(27)   J'arrivai avant-hier de Marly, et j'ai retrouvé toute la famille en bonne santé.

Indeed Caron and Liu (1999:38) argue that the PC is used in letters in the majority of cases. Thus the PS in Early Modern French is already a restricted form, serving as a past punctual in some cases, but replaced in many, especially in less formal varieties, by the PC. The gradual shift to majority use of the PC in such varieties can be seen particularly clearly in the patterns of co-occurrence with adverbials. Caron and Liu (1999) trace the use of PS and PC alongside punctual adverbials (such as *hier*, *le lendemain*, *la veille*, dates and times) in letters dating from the seventeenth to the nineteenth century; their statistics suggest a clear decline in the use of the PS (this is particularly rapid in the second half of the eighteenth century) and a corresponding rise in the use of the PC as well as interesting sociolinguistic correspondences (for example, women adopt the 'new' PC more quickly than men, and Parisians do so before the provinces).[8]

Moreover, there is some dispute in the Early Modern period about the form of the PS, with forms such as *donnit*, *dansit*, *frappit* preferred by some speakers, but resisted by many grammarians (Foulet 1920:296–301).[9] Vaugelas in his *Remarques sur la langue françoise* (1647), in debating between the use of *véquit* and *vécut*, observes that the PS is often avoided in favour of the PC, thereby suggesting that the two tenses are virtually interchangeable, and certainly that both are used:

Tant y a que la diuersité des opinions est si grande sur ce sujet, que quelques vns n'ont point pris d'autre party, que d'euiter tant qu'il se peut, ce preterit,

et de se seruir de l'autre, que les Grammairiens appellent indefini ou composé,
j'ay vescu (Vaugelas 1647:109).

In any case, this debate cannot have helped the survival of the PS against the
PC. By the eighteenth century, the grammarian Buffier (*Grammaire françoise*,
1709) points out that close attention needs to be paid to the use of the PS
and PC: the PC for example is appropriate in cases of present relevance (for
instance, where adverbs such as *cette année*, *ces jours-ci* are used, and with
immediately recent pasts such as *ce matin*, *il n'y a qu'un moment*). However,
not only is Buffier's definition not entirely logical in itself, but he also notes
that 'dans les autres occasions on se sert presque indiferemment ou du prétérit
simple ou du composé du prétérit' (quoted from Foulet 1920:307), thus making
it clear that the two are widely interchangeable in practice.

Are there other factors which might have helped to eliminate the PS or
preserve the PC in oral French? First, changes within the tense system are
part of a much broader shift from a synthetic language to an analytic one:
the rise of the analytic compound forms is part of the typological change
from an OV to a VO language and is stressed by those working in a
typological framework (e.g. Harris 1978). Second, in terms of the conjugation of the PS and PC paradigm, the compound forms follow a regular
pattern of conjugated auxiliaries followed by a past participle. The PC is
part of a whole series of such forms (PLP, PA, *futur antérieur* (FA) etc.), all
conjugated following the same principle. The PS, by contrast, is more unusual
in its conjugation within the French verb system, especially as regards the
first and second person plural; the only related form is the imperfect subjunctive which itself has weakened and is now replaced by the conditional
in many contexts. This argument should not be overstated; it is not a question of difficulty in conjugating the PS actually causing change; rather, its
formal singularity within the system, in contrast to the familiarity of the
compound forms, may have helped hasten the change once it had already
commenced. In short, a combination of factors came into play, including
analogical and morphological factors as well as broader socio-historical and
cultural ones.[10]

6.3   The *passé composé/passé simple* in Modern French: changing relationships

6.3.1   Introduction

In Modern French, discussion of the PS and PC in standard reference grammars focuses not just on the functions of the two forms in relation to each

other, but also on questions of register, medium etc.[11] The PS has effectively disappeared from the standard spoken language; it is now essentially a written tense, used mainly, although not exclusively, in literary narratives.[12] There are many written contexts where the PS is not used (such as informal letters or documents), and other written contexts where both the PS and the PC are found as past punctuals (such as newspapers). Delineating the precise functions of the PC and PS is complex and there is much variation in the extent to, and the manner in which, different media and registers make use of the two tenses. In this section, we shall examine a number of central pre-occupations in the analysis and description of the PS and PC, looking in particular at how textual and discourse-pragmatic approaches have shed light on the matter.

6.3.2   Two 'textual' models

Both Benveniste (1966) and Weinrich (1973) account for the use of the PS and PC through models which posit 'binary' textual systems. For Benveniste (1966:237–50), the divide is not between spoken and written French, but between two different *plans d'énonciation* or levels of discourse, each with its own verb system, that is, *discours* (in which the PC is normally found) and *histoire* (in which the PS is found) (see Part I, Section 3.4.2):

> dans l'énonciation historique, sont admis (en formes de 3e personne): l'aoriste, l'imparfait, le plus-que-parfait et le prospectif; sont exclus: le présent, le parfait, le futur (simple et composé); dans l'énonciation de discours, sont admis tous les temps à toutes les formes; est exclu l'aoriste (simple et composé) (1966:245).[13]

Benveniste also argues that markers of the speaker's 'here and now', such as *je, tu, nous, vous, ici, maintenant*, are excluded from *histoire* (1966:239).

The major advantage of Benveniste's model is that it captures the sense of a binary divide between a type of discourse which uses the PS and one which does not, while at the same time acknowledging that some varieties of writ-ten French (such as letters, some journalistic texts, other informal written texts) use the PC rather than the PS to mark the past punctual. *Histoire* is thus a restricted sub-category of the written language. The drawbacks of the model, however, are considerable. There is a certain circularity in the argument whereby a *plan d'énonciation* is defined according to the tenses found, and the tenses are defined in terms of the *plan d'énonciation*. There are also counter-examples; the present tense is of course found in literary narratives (even where these are not constructed entirely in the *présent historique*), as is the PC with the value of a present perfective, and the first person can indeed co-occur with the PS. There are also examples of literary or historical texts written in the PC; Bénézech (1992:184) cites a seventeenth-century example from Bossuet, and a famous twentieth-century example is Camus's *L'Etranger*. Most fundamental of all, a glance at a contemporary issue of many French newspapers would reveal that in this discourse type, the PS and PC co-occur as markers of the past punctual; we shall explore this in more detail in **6.3.3**.

Weinrich (1973) too posits a binary model, in his case based on the *monde raconté* versus the *monde commenté*. The former makes use of the PS, IMP, PA, PLP, CONDL (conditional), whereas the latter uses the PR, PC and FUT (future). Where Benveniste's distinction is between two *plans d'énonciation*, Weinrich's is between two *attitudes de locution* (speech attitudes); the *monde raconté* engages an attitude of *détente*, the *monde commenté* one of *tension*, where the reader's attention is on a high degree of alert. This binary divide does indeed correspond to tense usage in certain types of text, such as the cases Weinrich cites, that is, a literary narrative on the one hand (*monde raconté*) and a piece of dialogue on the other (*monde commenté*). However, there are major problems with this analysis. In addition to counterexamples such as newspaper texts where PS and PC co-occur, it can also be argued that the whole idea of *tension* is flawed, since the degree of attention or detachment is dependent on a host of other factors such as the content and nature of the text, as well as use of adverbs, pronouns, exclamations, question forms etc.

In short, binary models, whether spoken/written, *discours/histoire* or *monde commenté/monde raconté*, although capturing certain realities about the use of the PS as opposed to the PC, are highly problematic, since there are both definitional problems and counter-examples. In the next section we shall examine recent approaches to one such counter-example.

6.3.3   *Passé simple/passé composé* alternation

As has already been mentioned, one of the most striking counter-examples to binary systems such as Benveniste's or Weinrich's is journalistic French, where the PS and PC frequently co-occur as past punctuals within the same text. This alternation is complex, a wide range of factors coming into play. Engel (1990) explores these on the basis of a large corpus of contemporary French newspapers. Her approach is both qualitative (she gives a close analysis of specific examples) and quantitative (the findings are backed by substantial statistical work), and draws on both discourse-pragmatic and variationist approaches. She finds that usage of the PC and the PS is linked to a host of factors of a linguistic and discourse-pragmatic order, including the type of text concerned, the qualities of the article (the nature of the text and its style), grammatical person, co-occurrence of adverbial expressions, tense sequence, use with *être*, clause type and morphological/phonological factors. Engel's work highlights two important points which are not evident in traditional analyses of the PS and PC. First, the choice of PS or PC is complex, and the factors which come into play are multiple; they are temporal, aspectual, morphosyntactic, semantic, stylistic and discourse-pragmatic. Second, crucially, the majority of choices are expressed in terms of probabilities rather than obligatory rules; in journalistic French it is difficult to establish watertight rules which describe the use of the PS and the PC.

What effect might this PS/PC co-occurrence have in a journalistic text? In a large-scale study of the PS and PC in newspaper and magazine usage, Waugh and Monville-Burston (1986) explore the discourse-pragmatic function of the PS as a marker of 'detachment' and 'dimensionalization'. Both notions derive from the PS's basic temporal and aspectual functions as a marker of a past which is detached from the present and one which has delimited temporal contours. These temporal and aspectual notions are then elaborated in pragmatic terms which are connected to the original temporal and aspectual functions but which operate at a discourse or textual level. Thus detachment, for example, 'signals that a unit, detached from its context, possesses precise dimensions which define it' while dimensionalization signals 'the delimitation of a figure with clear-cut contours or dimensions' (1986:851). For example, a PS may be used to signal the formal limits of a text or part of a text – hence the sense of 'clear-cut contours' alluded to above. Waugh and Monville-Burston cite cases where the PS marks the beginning or end of a text, or both. In (28), the PC and PS refer to the same time period; the PS signals the start of the article, and subsequent events are recounted in the PC (the relevant verb forms are emboldened for clarity):

(28)   Fréderic Pottecher **fut** et reste, un peu, à la justice ce que Roger Couderc **fut** et reste au rugby. Pendant trente ans, il **a suivi** la cour avec une passion généreuse et charnelle. A la radio d'abord, à la télévision ensuite, il **a rendu compte** de tous les grands procès depuis la Libération (1986:857).

In terms of dimensionalization, the PS can throw an event into relief, even if only temporarily (29), and may co-occur with other markers of emphasis such as adverbials or the superlative:

(29)   MM Jacques et Robert Margnat, poursuivis, le premier pour un transfert de 598 000 FF, le second pour une opération portant sur 2 129 000 FF, **ont affiché** une fort grande maîtrise. Ce **fut** surtout pour dire qu'ils n'**ont** jamais **rencontré** M. Boissonnat (1986:865).

Dimensionalization can also take the form of a 'zoom lens effect', where the mental camera seems to focus in on an event:

(30)   Pour les femmes: le diplôme est un sésame pour l'emploi. Et la carrière? ... Par exemple, en 1983, 2807 candidats **se sont présentés** en première année à HEC (41% de filles), 264 **furent reçus** dont 34% de filles (1986:866).

Elsewhere, the PC may open the text, and the PS be used for the central body of information; the PC signals the first event in the narrative, which is then taken up in the PS.[14] This type of patterning is associated with an energetic style and textual tension, and is also found in literature. The PS may even be used for backgrounding a piece of information, or inserting it in a parenthetical manner (see Waugh and Monville-Burston 1986:868–70).[15]

6.3.4   The PS as story marker?

The PS is not only generally restricted to certain varieties of written French, but is also often regarded as the hallmark of a story, as the following lines from Robbe-Grillet's *Djinn* illustrate:

(31)   Voilà. Un robot rencontre une jeune dame ...
       Mon auditrice ne me laisse pas aller plus loin.
       Tu ne sais pas raconter, dit-elle.
       Une vraie histoire, c'est forcément au passé.
       – Si tu veux. Un robot, donc, a rencontré une ...
       – Mais non, pas ce passé là. Une histoire, ça doit être au passé historique.
       Ou bien personne ne sait que c'est une histoire (1981:51).

The occurrence of a PS in literary French thus usually signals that we are entering the world of storytelling. Indeed an examination of many nineteenth-century French novels would reveal a tense patterning where the PS is the narrative tense *par excellence*, and where the system corresponds closely to that of Benveniste's *histoire*. The situation is, however, more complex than this might at first suggest since, while the PS does indeed signal entry into the story world, the converse is not the case: literary stories do not obligatorily use the PS. Extensive use of the PR is one obvious exception; examples here include narratives in the historic present (which, in spite of the disapproval of the seventeenth-century grammarians, established itself in the eighteenth century), or in the PR of the twentieth-century *nouveau roman*. The latter is not necessarily linked to the past at all: it may be a more timeless present (often creating an impression of objectivity), or alternatively one which is bound up with the consciousness of the narrator (and is thus much more subjective).[16]

It might be argued that these uses of the PR for storytelling achieve their effect precisely because they subvert traditions, and that they therefore do not represent a change in the system itself. However, it is equally possible to argue that the tense patterns observed in literature, whether the systems close to Benveniste's *histoire* or tendencies found in contemporary novels, are a reflection of the fictional worlds they embody, and that both the fictional worlds and the language used to embody them are changing. Tense usage in literature thus enjoys a complex relationship with the evolution of the tense system in other types of discourse, such as spoken French or journalism.

As far as oral French is concerned, use of the PS is extremely rare, and it does not usually occur in spontaneous conversation. It is frequently noted that a PS may very occasionally be used in the regional French of the areas where it is found in the dialectal substratum, notably in the Midi, although Blanche-Benveniste's evidence (1997:53) suggests that even here it is no longer used. A PS may also occur where oral storytelling is involved. Blanche-Benveniste (1997:53) cites examples where the PS imbues a conversational narrative with a sense of solemnity, as well as cases where children use it as a 'temps intellectuel' to lend historical weight to a narrative. The PS may be used by contemporary *conteurs* as the basic narrative tense, but is not mandatory: both the PR and the PC are common.

6.3.5   The PC: a semantic hybrid?

Of all the forms in the past tense system of contemporary French, it is the PC which has the widest variety of functions, and this raises a number of problematic issues with respect to its description and classification. As we have seen, its two principal functions are those of present perfective (in all varieties of French), and past punctual (in oral French and in other varieties where the PS is not used). Contextual factors, explicit or implicit in the discourse situation, indicate which usage is intended. For instance in (3) above, we know from the 'here-now' adverbial that the PC marks the present perfective, whereas in (4), the adverbial signals the past. The PC's use as past punctual is now considered to be the basic usage, not least because it is much more frequent, is less dependent on context for its interpretation (most native speakers will cite the past punctual as its basic meaning) and is the normal reading for *avoir* verbs.[17] This supports Harris's typological argument (see **6.2.1** above) that temporal properties often come to predominate over initially dominant aspectual values. In this section, we shall examine briefly two different analyses which both attempt to capture the sense of the PC as a 'semantic hybrid' (Waugh 1987:35).

Waugh (1987) argues that in contemporary French, the basic function of the PC is already established as a marker of temporal past, but that its uses demonstrate a process of transition from its former function (where it was created to mark aspectual perfectivity) to its future function (where it may come only to represent a temporal past). She argues that this is better modelled in terms of a continuum, with the PC-preterite at one end (that is, the past punctual function), the PC-perfect at the other, and transitional uses in between. At the PC-perfect end, there is greater focus on the auxiliary and on the aftermath of the event; at the PC-preterite end, there is greater focus on the past participle and on the event itself rather than the aftermath (see Waugh (1987) for full details).

As Waugh herself acknowledges, one major difficulty with this is that there may be some indeterminacy as to which of the values predominates; context and individual perspective will be important in interpretation. Cases such as (32) with *depuis, jusqu'à* etc. have both past and present focus, as do other examples where, in spite of a past time adverbial, the sense of present relevance is strong with the PC, emphasized by a subsequent present tense (33):

(32)   Depuis le vingt juin j'ai perdu six kilos (1987:28)

(33)   Par la motion qu'il a rendue publique hier matin, le parti socialiste fait connaître sa position (1987:29).

In cases such as (34) (see Mahmoudian 1989), two interpretations are possible, depending on the context; the speaker may mean that the subject *has had* two children in her lifetime (present perfective), or alternatively that the subject *gave birth* to twins (past punctual):

(34)   Elle a eu deux bébés.

Vet's model (1992) accounts for the multiple functions of the PC by arguing that there are not two principal functions, but rather four: PC1 (the *présent résultatif*; e.g. *Pierre est parti maintenant*); PC1Q (the PC *expérientiel*; this is a type of present perfective, where Q is a quantifier such as *jamais*, e.g. *as-tu jamais été à Florence?*); PC2 (*antérieur du présent*, that is, a past punctual where the PC appears in the context of present time and where it is usually surrounded by present tenses); PC3 (a *passé narratif*; as the title suggests, this PC is situated in the context of a past time narrative and parallels the use of the PS in many literary contexts). One of the advantages of Vet's four categories is that, since they are more finely nuanced than the traditional binary divide between present perfective and past punctual, some of the problematic examples such as (32) and (33) can be categorized; (32) is a case of PC1Q in Vet's classification, while (33) is a case of PC2, since although the PC marks a past punctual, the focus of the surrounding discourse is on the present.

In short, the term 'semantic hybrid' is entirely appropriate for a multivalent form which is so highly context-sensitive and which is capable of marking present perfect, a recent past, a distant past, a past with present relevance, a past with little present relevance, anteriority, to mention just some of its temporal and aspectual functions. The question of how best to account for this remains open. As both Waugh and Vet recognize, the function of the PC cannot be accounted for adequately by a division into two main functions, and factors such as context and *mode d'action*/situation type also play a crucial role in interpretation.

Note finally that the PC's status as a semantic hybrid is also one of the key reasons cited for the development of the *venir de* construction in French, as an unambiguous marker of the recent past:

(35)   Il vient de prendre cette décision

(36)   Elle vient de partir.

The development of this analytic form parallels that of the more strongly grammaticalized compound future (*aller* + infinitive). Indeed Harris (1978:151) argues, as part of the cycle of typological change outlined in **6.2.1**, that as the PC in Modern French assumes a primarily temporal function, the compound periphrasis *venir de* comes in to act as a clear marker of a recent past.[18]

6.4   The Imperfect

6.4.1   Diachronic perspectives

As is clear from Tables **6.1** and **6.2**, the imperfect in Old French is a direct descendant of the Latin imperfect *faciebat*. In Old French, the IMP performs all the functions it performs in Modern French, but is used less frequently on the whole; Martin (1971) argues that it is never used in more than 17% of the verb forms in a text. The IMP is replaced in many contexts by a PS, which is often used to mark states/continuous actions. In this context, the PS is used with atelic verbs, especially *avoir*, *être* and modal auxiliaries. In the following example which is taken from *Aucassin et Nicolette* and discussed in Fleischman (1990:43), the PS is used where Modern French would use an imperfect:

(37)   Aucassin **fu** [PS] armés sor son ceval,
         si con vos **aves oï** et **entendu** [PC].
         Dix! con li **sist** [PS] li escus au col . . .
         Et li vallés **fu** [PS] grans et fors . . .
         et li cevaus sur quoi il **sist** [PS] rades et corans.

> Aucassin was on his horse, fully armed,
> as you now have heard.
> God! How well his shield sat on his neck . . .
> And the lad was big and strong . . .
> And the horse he was sitting on was swift and spirited.
> (Fleischman's translation, 1990:42)

In late Old French, with the rise of the medium of prose and its preference for a more strictly chronological use of tense, the use of the IMP increases in descriptions of people and objects (see Ayres-Bennett 1996:97). This increase continues through the Middle French period as the imperfect expands in all the functions with which it is associated in Modern French.

6.4.2   Developments in Modern French

6.4.2.1   Analysis of the imperfect

One characteristic of the imperfect which has traditionally been central to its definition is its imperfectivity (see Chapter 5).[19] In the last twenty years or so, a challenge to that 'aspectual analysis' has come from a number of researchers who propose an 'anaphoric analysis' of the IMP.[20] In essence, it is one which sees the IMP as marking simultaneity to a point of reference in the past R (in Reichenbachian terms, see Part I, Section 2.3.1), where R is either already established, or newly given or inferrable from the context.

In the early stages, Kamp's argument (1981) was that whereas the PS introduces an event which moves the narrative forward, the discourse event introduced by the IMP includes the most recently introduced PS events. This argument has been refined and developed by Kamp and Rohrer (1983), Vet and Molendijk (1986), Molendijk (1990, 1994, 1996); the definition of the point with which the IMP is simultaneous has been redefined in terms of a 'space-time region' (Vet and Molendijk 1986), and the problematic question of establishing the reference point R has also been discussed (Molendijk 1994). Building on all the developments of Kamp's original work, Molendijk (1994:27) is able to refine the rules according to which the IMP is seen fundamentally as a marker of 'global simultaneity' with the PS event.

A second 'strand' within the anaphoric approach has also developed, led by Berthonneau and Kleiber's work (1993) and refined and expanded in Berthonneau and Kleiber (1998) in response to points made by, amongst others, Molendijk (1996); it is further discussed in Tasmowski-De Ryck and De Mulder (1998). The controversy centres on the nature of the anaphora, Berthonneau and Kleiber arguing that the IMP is not simultaneous to a temporal point in the past, but rather that 'la relation anaphorique entre la situation antécédent du passé et la situation présentée à l'imparfait est une relation de type partie (imparfait) – tout (antécédent)' (1993:68); this type of relation is reflected in their analysis of the IMP as an *anaphore méronymique*.

The aspectual analysis has been defended by a number of scholars. Salkie (1999), for example, has argued convincingly that all the uses of the imperfect can be accounted for through an aspectual analysis of this tense, and that indeed the temporal apparatus required to explain some of the more complex examples is unnecessarily cumbersome. Moreover, given the fact that aspect often concerns questions of perspective, differences in interpretation can arise relatively easily. Molendijk would argue that constructions such as (38) involve perfectivity, since 'le fait mentionné est présenté comme étant valable pendant toute une période bien délimitée: celle qui couvre la vie entière d'Hélène' (1990:18):

(38)   Hélène était la fille du Roi de Pologne.

Salkie on the other hand would argue that the focus is not on the boundaries of the life (had the focus been on the beginning and end, the PS would have been used) but on the state of being daughter which existed during her' entire life: the perspective is imperfective. Wilmet (1996) too rejects the anaphoric analysis, giving a robust defense of the IMP as a marker of *aspect sécant*, while Bres (1997), drawing heavily on Guillaume, also supports an aspectual analysis, maintaining that anaphora is an effect produced by the basic temporal and aspectual properties of the IMP.

6.4.2.2   Discourse-pragmatic developments

In discourse-pragmatic terms, one important development has taken place over the course of the last two centuries (although earlier examples can be found; see Vetters (1996:127)), that is, the emergence of what is known as the *imparfait narratif*. In essence, this is the use of the imperfect where we would expect a past punctual – that is, a PS in a literary context, a PC in spoken French. It has also been labelled *imparfait historique* (where emphasis is on the precise date/time of the event as in (39) below) and *imparfait pittoresque* (where emphasis is on descriptive qualities as in (44) below) (see Riegel, Pellat and Rioul 1994:308). In an article which traces the emergence of this form in French literature, Muller (1966) sees its origins in contexts where a precise temporal indication (such as a date or time) is given:

(39)   A la même minute, le 13 janvier, à trois heures, pendant que je
        parlais, le premier tocsin de l'insurrection **sonnait** à Palerme (Hugo,
        cited in Muller 1966:258).

The imperfect has the effect of expanding the event, lending it breadth and depth. Its imperfective properties are superimposed on the punctual nature of the event as signalled by the adverbials. This usage increases in the middle of the nineteenth century, spreading to travel literature, memoirs etc., and is found in the work of Nerval, Chateaubriand and Sand, to name a few. It is also adopted by the novel, especially the *roman feuilleton*. Its use increases, becoming particularly frequent with the Goncourt brothers (40) and subsequent authors such as Maupassant and Daudet, the romantics and the naturalists, as well as in modern literary prose (examples 40–43 are taken from Muller (1966)):

(40)   Charles-Louis Mauperin était né en 1787 . . . il entrait au service à l'âge de seize ans. Il se signalait en Italie. Au combat de Pordenone . . . il répondait à la sommation.

More recently, the *imparfait narratif* has also penetrated journalism, where it is common in a variety of types of article (41–43):

(41)   Dès 1954, s'installait à Saigon le gouvernement Diem soutenu par les Etats-Unis

(42)   Il y a cent ans mourait X

(43)   Hier, le F.C. accueillait sur son terrain le S.C.

Its use has expanded in terms of the verbs with which it appears (the strongest effects are produced with verbs of achievement and accomplishment; see 5.3) and the contexts in which it can occur (a precise temporal indication is no longer required). Where it is used, the *imparfait narratif* can create a cinematographic effect. As Riegel, Pellat and Rioul put it, 'le fait est envisagé de l'intérieur dans son déroulement et l'imparfait efface ses limites, pourtant bien réelles' (1994:308).

Although initially a literary development, there is now evidence that the imperfect may be used in spoken French where we might expect the past punctual (that is, a PC). Labelle (1987) cites cases where the majority of the verbs at the climax of oral narratives appear in the imperfect:[21]

(44)   Une affaire de train qui s'en venait/ puis il s'en venait vite hein/ so l'autre il a mis les brakes/ mais **c'était** glissant hein/ puis les quatre roues **barraient**/ puis il s'en **allait** puis ah s-/ avoir pris le trou là, le bord là, le champ là, on aurait tombé dix pieds, quelque chose de même, tu sais/ puis on **voyait** le train/ le gars **savait** pas quoi faire là hein/ puis on **tournait**/ puis on **allait** tout croche/ en tout cas le chose il a arrivé/ il a eu juste arrêté/ puis là le train a passé, vroum.

Labelle (1987:18–19) argues that, far from occupying the background, the imperfect in these narratives has the effect of foregrounding the event by making it more intense. She considers these IMPs to be narrative in the sense that they cannot be removed without disrupting the narrative sequence, even though they do not all recount events as such. The sense of them being *imparfaits narratifs* is most clear with the verbs *barraient, s'en allait, tournait* and *allait*: the effect is one of the central events in the accident happening in slow motion.[22]

Do these usages of the IMP represent a possible change in the system? Since the effects produced by the *imparfait narratif* depend for their impact on the contrast with the expected form, it seems more likely that they will remain examples of variation for stylistic/pragmatic effect. However, as we know from the evolution of the past tenses since Vulgar Latin and Old French, and the history of the PC in particular, many grammatical developments have pragmatic origins.

One final comment on the IMP relates also to its expansion in oral French and its use where we would expect a PC functioning as a past punctual. In a detailed study of the spoken French of a speaker from a very low socio-economic status – from what they term the *sous-prolétariat* – Auvigne and Monté have found evidence of what they call 'l'emploi généralisé de l'imparfait' (1982:50), notably the use of the IMP as a past punctual. The result in this case, in contrast to the stylistic effect of the *imparfait narratif*, is to hinder comprehension, since the run of imperfects only serves to blur all sense of foreground and background, or punctual versus iterative events:

(45)   Et je faisais une comédie – j'te jure – je foutais le bordel chez ma grand'mère en attendant que ma mère elle rentrait – que mon grand'père – je voyais que ma mère elle rentrait toute seule – ah! c'était fini – je restais dans mon coin – je parlais même pas – j'ai resté vraiment bloquée.

This data must however be considered with caution. There is no widespread evidence of the phenomenon, and the speaker at the centre of Auvigne and Monté's paper is a very extreme example of the *sous-prolétariat* who has been brought up by her grandmother living in a cave, as well as in various institutions – 'enfance instable, placements rudimentaires, études entravées dès l'enfance, puis interrompues avant le diplôme, mariage précoce, maternités rapprochées' (1982:25).

6.5   Past in the past: *plus-que-parfait, passé antérieur* and *passé surcomposé*

6.5.1   Diachronic perspectives

As is evident in Tables **6**.1 and **6**.2, two compound forms develop to mark the past perfective in Vulgar Latin, one with the simple past of *habere* (*avoir* in Old French) as its auxiliary (e.g. VL *habuit factum* > OF *ot fait*) and the other with the imperfect (e.g. VL *habebat factum* > OF *avoit fait*). In the earliest French texts, the PA is more common than the PLP, paralleling the fact that the PS is more frequent than the IMP. The PLP performs the same functions as in Modern French, but the PA is used much more widely, for example:

(46)   Entre le dol del pedra e de la medre
        Vint la pulcele que il out espusede ...
            (from *La Vie de Saint Alexis*, quoted in Ayres-Bennett 1996:46).

        While the father and mother were grieving in this way,
        there came the girl that he had married.
        (Ayres-Bennett's translation, 1996:48)

In terms of semantic function, the two seem virtually interchangeable in many contexts, though if there is a contrast, it parallels that between the IMP and the PS, that is, the PA is more strongly associated with globally viewed delimited periods. Moreover, there are already indications that the PA is preferred after conjunctions marking anteriority; Foulet sees in this the beginnings of its modern restricted usage (1970:227). Use of the PLP continues to increase alongside the PA (see for example Ayres-Bennett's (1996:97) commentary on the *Lettre de Jean Sarrasin à Nicolas Arrode 1249*), to the point after the Old French period where the PLP is found more frequently than the PA. This pattern continues, paralleling the increase in use of the imperfect (the auxiliary tense of the PLP); in contrast, the use of the PA becomes increasingly restricted, in line with the decline of its auxiliary, the PS (see Ayres-Bennett 1996:97). As far as the PSC is concerned, examples in subordinate temporal clauses marking anteriority can be dated to the fourteenth century, its use paralleling the PA: whereas the PA marks anteriority to a PS, the PSC marks anteriority to a PC in the main clause. The logic is that as the PC is increasingly used rather than the PS to mark the past punctual in oral French, so too the PSC increasingly marks anteriority to the PC.

6.5.2   Developments in Modern French

6.5.2.1   The pluperfect

In addition to its traditional uses, there is evidence that the PLP is used in contemporary French to mark a past punctual which is cut off from the present. This occurs especially in the spoken medium, where the PLP replaces a PC, which, as a semantic hybrid marking a wide variety of notions, and as a form which is necessarily linked to the present through its auxiliary, is felt to be no longer capable of marking unambiguously a past punctual which is cut off from the present. This type of PLP is found in contexts where it might contrast with a PR or a future, and the past in question may indeed be very recent (47) or relatively recent (48):

(47)   Hier je vous avais parlé de Victor Hugo

(48)   Mais il faudra suivre aussi le Mexique, qui avait fait une excellente entrée l'année dernière . . . (examples from Arnavielle 1978:617).

The double layer of distance provided by the PLP cuts the event off from the present moment. This may of course take the form of temporal distance; but equally it may reflect a complete lack of present relevance, or psychological distance such as embarrassment (49), or a total change of circumstances (50):

(49)   Jamais madame, jamais nous n'avons dit ça . . . je crois, je crois que c'était le docteur de P . . . , ça me revient, je crois bien . . . il avait dit ça, mais c'était plus une boutade qu'un véritable conseil (Majumdar and Morris 1980:8).

Example (50), a journalistic use, refers to an interview with Pope John-Paul II before the papal conclave in which he was elected:

(50)   Un journaliste de la télévision italienne avait interviewé le cardinal Wojtyla avant l'ouverture du conclave et lui avait demandé quelles étaient les chances de voir un Polonais accéder au trône de Saint-Pierre. 'Il est trop tôt pour qu'il y ait un pape polonais' avait alors répondu celui qui allait devenir Jean-Paul II (Majumdar and Morris 1980:10).

Clearly in this example, the circumstances of the interview situation have completely changed at the time of writing. The use of the PLP to mark a punctual past cut off from the present appears at the moment to be a marked use of the form. It will however be interesting to watch the development of this usage in contemporary French, particularly in relation to the function of the PC.[23]

Finally, given the rarity of the PSC and the fact that the PLP can mark anteriority to the PC on the time line, might the PLP be moving into the territory of the PSC in contemporary French? The answer to this appears to be negative; surveys suggest that it is the multivalent PC which is replacing the PSC.[24]

6.5.2.2   The past anterior

If the PLP is increasing in usage, the opposite seems to be true of the PA. Not only is it restricted to a small number of subordinate temporal clauses and a type of discourse which uses the PS as its simple past marker (itself of course in decline), but there are indications that its use is by no means the norm in this context. Evidence from journalistic French suggests that it is rare in this type of discourse: in a corpus of 50 newspapers, Olsson (1971) finds only four PAs, and for both Zezula (1969:344) and Herzog (1981:20), the frequency is extremely low compared to the other past tenses.[25] Although the evidence from literary French suggests more widespread use (see Olsson 1971), the PS is frequently used where we might expect a PA in order to mark anteriority to a PS in the main clause (Olsson 1971). Indeed, Olsson concludes that the PA is a marked form, whose use varies greatly from author to author, depending on his or her 'grammaire individuelle' (1971:105).

6.5.2.3   The passé surcomposé

The *passé surcomposé* and indeed all the other double compound tenses are formed by adding the past participle (e.g. *fait*) to the compound form of the auxiliary verb (e.g. *a eu*) to give double compound forms such as *il a eu fait, il a eu pris* etc.[26] In theory, spoken French uses the PSC to mark anteriority and completion in relation to a PC, as do written varieties which use a PC as the past punctual. In practice, however, the PSC is both problematic and rare. Research suggests that a number of factors contribute to this; these include the marginalization of the form by French grammarians through the ages (especially the school grammar tradition), unease over the forms for *être* verbs (where many speakers use forms such as *elle est eu venue*) and pronominals (e.g. *je me suis eu lavé*), the multivalency of the PC which is capable of appearing in this context (e.g. *une fois que j'ai quitté l'école j'ai trouvé un emploi*), and the associations which this type of PSC has with the stigmatized regional use of the form.

In certain regional varieties of French, the PSC can be employed in any type of clause to stress one or more of a number of notions, that is, completion or aspectual perfectivity, distance in the past, the exceptional nature of an event, subjective involvement on the part of the speaker, or indeterminacy, for example:

(51)   J'ai beaucoup de camarades que je peux plus voir maintenant parce que c'est trop loin m'enfin on s'est eu écrit(s) même avec d'autres – et puis maintenant on a tout abandonné maintenant je ne sais plus écrire (Carruthers 1994:176)

(52)   Si tu veux faire quatorze mille kilomètres en vingt-et-un jours comme j'ai eu fait il faut travailler seize heures par jour (*ibid.*:181).

This usage has its roots in the dialects of the *langue d'oc* and *franco-provençal* areas. Since it is found in most of these dialects, it is widely assumed that the regional French usage is a calque on the dialect construction. Harris (1978:155) argues that this construction is a further development in the typological cycle of compound forms, another layer of compounding being introduced to stress aspectual perfectivity in the context of a weakened present perfective, that is, the PC, which now has to perform a variety of functions. However, since the regional PSC has developed in precisely the dialects where the PS has usually survived (and thus where the PC is a clear marker of the present perfective), it has been argued that the double compound construction is formed not by double compounding the auxiliary, but rather by adding the particle *eu* to the compound construction. This argument is supported by the construction commonly found with *être* verbs (i.e. *elle est eu venue* rather than *elle a été venue*) and by the pronominal forms (e.g. *je me suis eu lavé* etc.). The regional PSC is heavily condemned by French grammarians, and stigmatized by speakers as representing rural, uneducated speech. It is quite possible that the negative connotations of the regional PSC have influenced perceptions of the more standard PSC, resulting in the marginalization of both forms, albeit to different extents.

Suggested Reading

History:
  Blumenthal (1986), Harris (1978, 1982), Martin (1971), Wilmet (1976).
Modern French (general):
  Borillo, Vetters and Vuillaume (eds) (1998), Vet (1980), Vogeleer and others (eds) (1998), *Langages* 112 (1993).
Modern French PC/PS – loss of PS:
  Caron and Liu (1999), Van Vliet (1983), Vet (1992), Waugh (1987), Wilmet (1992).
Modern French PS/IMP – role of IMP:
  Berthonneau and Kleiber (1993, 1998), Bres (1997, 1998b), Ducrot (1979), Le Goffic (1995, 1986a (ed)), Molendijk (1990, 1996), Muller (1966), Salkie (1999), Wilmet (1996).
Pluperfect, past anterior, double compounds:
  Carruthers (1992, 1993, 1994), Engel (1994, 1996), Majumdar and Morris (1980), Salkie (1989), Wilmet (1973).
Tense and text/discourse-pragmatics:
  Beck (1988), Benveniste (1966), Engel (1990), Fleischman (1990), Pottier (1995), Schøsler (1985), Weinrich (1973).

Notes

1. See **6.3.4** for details of where it might still be used in oral French.
2. For a definition of modality, see Part I, Section 2.3.1. For a detailed discussion of the expression of modality in French, see Chapter 7.
3. The term 'functional multiplicity' is borrowed from Beck (1988).
4. For an account of the function of each tense, see Foulet (1970:218–32).
5. The precise timing of this development is difficult to pinpoint accurately. Moreover, the example cited by Beck is problematic, since it is a case of an intransitive verb (*venuz i est*), that is, the type of verb which, theoretically, was affected last by the change. In the following section of the *Roland*, the PC follows a series of PS forms of the same verb, *venir*:

   > Li quens Rollant est muntet el destrer.
   > Cuntre lui vient sis cumpainz Oliver.
   > **Vint** [PS] i Gerins e li proz quens Gerers,
   > E **vint** [PS] i Otes, si i **vint** [PS] Berengers
   > E **vint** [PS] i Astors e Anseïs, li veillz,
   > **Vint** [PS] i Gerart de Rossillon li fiers;
   > **Venuz i est** [PC] li riches dux Gaifiers.
   > Dist l'arcevsque . . .

6. There are clearly connections here with certain patterns found in modern oral French (for example, tense switching). See Fleischman (1990) and Bres (1998a).
7. See Fleischman (1990) for a detailed discussion of these phenomena.
8. See Caron and Liu (1999) for other correlations.
9. Walter (1995) notes that in the area *oïl de l'Ouest* (i.e. from Normandy, through eastern Brittany and south to Charentes), the dialects normally use the *-i* forms of the PS. She argues that these distinctive forms helped the PS survive in this particular area in spite of its loss elsewhere in the *langue d'oïl*.
10. See Engel (1998) for further discussion.
11. See, for example, Chevalier and others (1964:340, 347) and Riegel, Pellat and Rioul (1994:301).
12. See **6.3.4** below.
13. L'aoriste = le PS, le prospectif = le conditionnel.
14. For examples, see Waugh and Monville-Burston (1986).
15. For further work on the non-referential functions of the PS in journalism see Wiberg (1995). For an interesting account of tense alternation in the songs of Brassens, see Delbart (1996).
16. For a discussion, see Fleischman (1990:263–310).
17. See Waugh (1987:6). In the case of *être* verbs, a reading of present perfective is most common.
18. For more details on this construction, see Vetters (1989).

19. Typical presentations in reference grammars include the *Grammaire Larousse* (Chevalier and others 1964:341) and Riegel, Pellat and Rioul (1994:305).
20. Salkie (1999) refers to this as the 'relative past time analysis'.
21. Labelle's narratives are Canadian, hence the presence of Anglo-Americanisms. Pauses are marked with a forward slash (/).
22. Note that both the aspectual and the anaphoric analyses claim to account for the *imparfait narratif*; the aspectual analysis would argue that the event is viewed in terms of its duration, as being in progress (see Vetters 1996:128), while the anaphoric analysis sees the temporal adverb which often accompanies the *imparfait narratif* as the point of temporal reference in the past to which the IMP is anaphoric.
23. For an interesting account of the use of a narrative pluperfect in literature, see Soelberg (1989).
24. See Carruthers (1993) and Engel (1996).
25. Olsson's study concentrates on the use of tense after the conjunctions *quand* and *lorsque*.
26. Other *formes surcomposées* include the *plus-que-parfait surcomposé* (*avait eu fait*), *conditionnel passé surcomposé* (*aurait eu fait*), *futur antérieur surcomposé* (*aura eu fait*). The PSC is the most common; the others are extremely rare. For more details, see Carruthers (1993, 1994, 1996).

7

Mood and modality: the French subjunctive

7.1 Introduction

There has been considerable debate, but often relatively little agreement, amongst linguists regarding how best to account for usage of the subjunctive in Modern French. Although there have been numerous studies devoted to the French subjunctive since Imbs (1953), there is still considerable truth in his rather pessimistic assessment as to what faces a teacher seeking a clear explanation of its uses:

> de savant en savant il [sc. le maître] change de théorie, chacun lui fournissant *son* système du subjonctif, *sa* théorie de ses valeurs, si bien qu'au bout de sa quête il lui faut une foi solide pour ne pas sombrer dans un scepticisme radical (Imbs 1953:18).

Many linguists have contented themselves with merely listing and discussing individual examples and seeking differences of meaning – however slight – between pairs of sentences, one with a subjunctive in the subordinate clause and the other with an indicative form. Whilst some have adopted a rigid approach and attempted to categorize all usages of the subjunctive into discrete classes, others such as Martin (1983:105) have maintained that usage of the subjunctive is governed not by rigid rules but by tendencies, since one frequently encounters examples which challenge expectations or prescriptive norms.

Most recent studies make a distinction between mood and modality as outlined in Part I (Section 2.3.1), although there is less consensus in earlier works, where occasionally individual usage of metalinguistic terms is found (e.g. *le mœuf* in Damourette and Pichon [1928–40]:V:469). Traditionally a clear distinction is made between tenses and moods, but in practice these are often interlocking categories which are not always easily separated into discrete

units, as the following examples from Confais (1990:21) illustrate (see also
6.1). Whilst in the first example the imperfect clearly has a temporal value,
in (2) there is a slight modal nuance, since the action is, to some extent,
'unrealized'; in (3) and (4) the value of the imperfect is primarily modal
(hypothetical), but in (3) the temporal value is past, in (4) present:

(1)   Chaque fois que j'allais au stade, Toulouse gagnait

(2)   Quand le match a été interrompu, Toulouse gagnait

(3)   Cinq minutes de plus, et Toulouse gagnait

(4)   Si Toulouse gagnait contre Bordeaux, il prendrait la tête du
      championnat.

There has been much discussion as to whether the 'conditional' forms
(e.g. *il ferait*) should be considered as a discrete mood, or as an indicative
paradigm with the basic role of marking 'future in the past', which nevertheless lends itself readily to certain modal usages (see 7.4.5 below). Wilmet
(1970:414–15) argues that the majority of linguists consider them to be
indicative forms. Harris (1981:63), on the other hand, maintains that there is
a conditional mood in French which includes not just the *ferait* forms, but
also *fera, aura fait* and *aurait fait*; while all of these retain to a greater or
lesser extent their temporal usages, he contends that the original temporal
values are 'under threat' from the *va faire* and *allait faire* forms (see also
Ludwig 1988).

7.2   Explaining the use of the subjunctive

A number of key questions will be discussed in this section:

- Can usage of the subjunctive be accounted for in semantic terms? If so, is
  a traditional pluralist account preferable, or is it possible to 'reduce' the
  various meanings into one or two fundamental values? (7.2.1)
- What are the strengths and weaknesses of a formal, mechanical or
  structural approach? Is it possible to eliminate semantic considerations
  completely from the analysis? (7.2.2)
- What type of account is favoured by linguists who base their analysis on
  usage in specific linguistic contexts or on the description of a spoken
  corpus? (7.2.3)

7.2.1   The French subjunctive: several 'values' or a unified account?

Traditional accounts of French often classified the uses of the subjunctive according to its value in particular contexts, especially when it is embedded under certain classes of verbs (and their related nouns), such as those expressing wishes or feelings, possibility or doubt, commands or denials. Indeed, in their most extreme form these accounts occasionally spoke of there being a 'subjunctive of doubt, of wish or regret' (as summarized in Riegel, Pellat and Rioul 1994:322), confusing the 'value' of the subjunctive with the lexical content of the matrix verb (i.e. main clause verb) (cf. Imbs 1953:26). As a result, grammars contained not only a fairly long list of rules for usage, but also a considerable number of counter-examples which defied the general semantic principles. For instance, if the use of *souhaiter que, désirer que* + subjunctive was readily accounted for in this framework, that of *espérer que* + indicative was less easy to justify. Poplack (1992:242) points out that in this model the tendency is to try to subclassify the matrix verbs into ever finer semantic subclasses in the hope of identifying groups of verbs, the members of which all behave identically. Whilst this pluralist approach potentially allows the most comprehensive account of usage, it lacks explanatory value because it fails to capture meaningful generalizations. Although now largely discredited, remnants of this pluralism may be seen, for instance, in Nordahl (1969) who adopts an essentially functional approach on the grounds that 'un problème syntaxique doit être étudié syntaxiquement' (1969:10), but who nevertheless divides usages of the subjunctive into three types: the *système volitif* in which the subjunctive is virtually obligatory, the *système subjectif*, and the *système dubitatif* (of which there are ten sub-systems).

In general, however, linguists favouring a semantic account of usage have attempted to try to identify one overall value – or at most two different values – for the French subjunctive.[1] Both the *Grammaire Larousse* (Chevalier and others 1964:112) and Confais (1990) favour a dualist account which attributes two basic values to the subjunctive, that of the non-factual or possible as opposed to the probable or certain, and that of 'appréciation affective'. According to Huot (1986:84), Lerch, Regula and Tanase all distinguish between volitive contexts and those which represent a 'procès simplement envisagé' or 'un certain degré de dépendance psychologique par rapport à l'idée exprimée dans la principale'.[2] Other accounts take this search for the 'value' of the French subjunctive one step further and try to identify one fundamental value underlying all the various usages. For instance Connors (1978), having excluded all the automatic or redundant contexts from consideration, points to a unified 'potentiality' value for all usages which embraces both the meanings of volition and hypothesis.

It is striking that, if there is one overriding value to explain all usages of the subjunctive, linguists have been unable to agree as to what this is, or indeed as to whether it is appropriate to look to the domain of psychology, logic or philosophy to underpin their account. The following is a selection of some of the more important suggestions made about the meaning of the subjunctive[3]:

- The subjunctive is the mood of unreality:

  Imbs (1953:49): 'le subjonctif s'emploie chaque fois que le fait relaté n'est pas entièrement actualisé, ou que sa réalité actuelle n'est pas la visée principale du sujet parlant'

  Hanse (1960:9): 'le subjonctif énonce un fait qu'on se refuse ou hésite à placer sur le plan de la réalité'

  Grevisse (1993:1265) 'le subjonctif indique que le locuteur (ou le scripteur) ne s'engage pas sur la réalité du fait'.

  Clearly there are problems with this explanation in its simplest form since it is possible both for the subjunctive to indicate a 'real' fact (e.g. *bien qu'il soit venu, je regrette qu'il soit venu, je suis heureux qu'il soit venu*) and for the indicative to denote an action about whose reality the speaker either hesitates or refuses to comment (*je pense qu'il vient*). Alternative formulations of the same idea – for example, that the subjunctive presents an action envisaged in thought rather than actually taking place, or that the subjunctive prevents the proposition having a truth value attached to it (Tsoulas 1996:294) – do not avoid these difficulties.

- The subjunctive indicates the absence of judgement on the part of the speaker; many of the reservations expressed above are relevant to this definition:

  Damourette and Pichon ([1928–40]:V:482): 'nous considérions le subjonctif non pas du tout comme le mœuf du doute, conception trop souvent avancée, mais comme le mœuf du non-jugement'.

- The subjunctive marks possibility as opposed to probability:

  According to Guillaume (1929:32–6), the subjunctive is logically prior to the indicative since it marks possibility as opposed to probability; that is, something can be possible without being probable, but the reverse is not the case. Martin (1983:108–10) points to some problems with considering the subjunctive as a marker of possibility. A sentence which has as its main clause *il n'est pas possible que* may indicate a certainty and yet it will take a subjunctive[4]; conversely, *le fait que* takes a subjunctive yet indicates a fact. For this reason Martin, adopting a logico-semantic framework, suggests that two different notions should be invoked, that of 'possible world' and that of 'univers de croyance'. The subjunctive may then be used to indicate that the process belongs to a 'possible world' (p is possible if there exists a world in which p is true; this accounts well for examples such as *connaissez-vous un homme qui puisse le faire?*). Alternatively, the notion of 'anti-universe' may be invoked, which consists of propositions which the speaker considers false but are not necessarily so, or of worlds which are possible but which reality has eliminated. For instance, in the case of *je regrette que Pierre soit parti*, the regret presupposes that things could have been different.

• The subjunctive marks doubt:

According to Winters (1993), the prototypical meaning of the subjunctive is 'doubt'. However, at a more abstract level, the superordinate or schematic meaning is said to be 'subjectivity' (from which the three sub-groups of subjunctive usage – doubt, judgement and speech act meaning – can all be generated, and which all follow from the general notion of personal involvement in the action being commented on). The simple association of the subjunctive with the concept of doubt is problematic because it is also used in sentences when the absence of doubt is stressed: *Je ne doute pas que tu ne réussisses.*

• The subjunctive is *le mode de l'énergie psychique*:

Perhaps the best known exposition of this psychological account of the subjunctive is found in Le Bidois and Le Bidois (1935):

> Si le subjonctif, en effet, est apte à exprimer tant de modalités psychiques, ne serait-ce pas parce qu'il est [. . .] le plus mode de tous les modes, par quoi il faut entendre le plus en relation avec l'âme, le plus en harmonie avec ses modalités profondes, en d'autres termes le plus chargé de sentiment ou d'intentions? Tout notre âme paraît s'y imprimer; ses plus fortes, ses plus fines vibrations y viennent retentir (Le Bidois and Le Bidois 1935:501).

Here too is found the strongest rejection of a formal explanation for the use of the subjunctive in French:

> En somme, dans aucun des cas que l'on vient de passer en revue, le subjonctif ne paraît être une conséquence de la subordination, ni ne paraît devoir s'expliquer nécessairement vis-à-vis d'un autre verbe. Au vrai, il ne dépend que d'un état de la pensée, de laquelle il est fonction. Nul mode n'est aussi assujetti aux plus souples modalités du sentiment. De là, son aptitude à rendre les plus fines nuances psychologiques (*ibid.*:513).

An obvious drawback of this approach is the vagueness of the concept of *l'énergie psychique* and the consequent difficulty in practice of using it to differentiate subordinate clauses which have an indicative or subjunctive verb (e.g. *j'espère qu'il va venir, je souhaite qu'il vienne*).

There are a number of obvious problems associated with attempting to find one overall value for the subjunctive: there is a lack of agreement as to the fundamental value of the subjunctive, and it is relatively easy to find counter-examples to each proposition. According to Poplack (1992), some of the alternative suggestions offered (e.g. that the difference is one between assertive and non-assertive usages) are simply a case of dressing up 'semantic class' distinctions in another guise.

Perhaps the main difficulty, however, is that the majority of usages of the subjunctive do not involve a meaningful choice or positive selection of this mood as opposed to an indicative, but rather are simply required by a codified rule of grammar. This has led a number of commentators to argue that the French subjunctive is now largely an empty formal marker, devoid of semantic content, and to favour a formal or mechanical approach over a semantic account.

7.2.2   Formal or mechanical approaches

One of the earliest reactions against the semantic approach can be found in Brunot (1922). Arguing that the subjunctive is largely a *servitude grammaticale*, Brunot concludes: 'le subjonctif [...] bien souvent n'exprime plus des modalités, mais *n'est qu'une forme de subordination*' (1922:520). Conclusive proof of this is afforded for him by an example such as *je ne nie pas que* + subjunctive which, he believes, defies a semantic explanation.

A number of linguists, including Harris (1974, 1978), have followed Brunot and maintained that, since the subjunctive is largely devoid of meaning, it has become simply an additional marker of subordination in contemporary French. There are, however, two clear objections to this hypothesis in its pure form. First, the subjunctive does have a number of main clause usages; for example:

(5)   Qu'il revienne un autre jour

(6)   Moi, que je vende cette voiture! (Grevisse 1993:1265–6).

Second, there are meaningful oppositions where the choice between indicative and subjunctive is significant. These include noun clauses dependent on certain verbs such as *dire, supposer*, and *croire, penser*, etc. used in the negative:

(7)   Sonia lui a dit qu'elle aille se faire cuire un oeuf ('Sonia told her to go fly a kite') – Sonia lui a dit qu'elle va se faire cuire un oeuf ('Sonia told her that she's going to cook an egg') (Barbaud 1991:131)

(8)   Je suppose/imagine/présume qu'il est là – Supposons/imaginez/présumons qu'il soit là

(9) Sa mère ne croit pas qu'il ait volé – Sa mère ne croit pas qu'il a volé
      (see 7.3.1 below).

There are also meaningful oppositions in adverbial clauses after certain
conjunctions, notably *de sorte que*, *de manière que*, *de façon que*:

(10) J'ai écrit la lettre hier de sorte que tu la reçoive aujourd'hui – J'ai
       écrit la lettre hier de sorte que tu la reçois aujourd'hui.

Equally, the choice of mood is distinctive in certain restrictive relative clauses.
The subjunctive indicates that the speaker is by no means certain of the
existence of such a woman:

(11) Je cherche une femme qui sache parler anglais – Je cherche une
       femme qui sait parler anglais.

Harris (1978) counters the first objection by arguing that in the case of an
apparent main clause usage such as *qu'il vienne*, we are dealing with a pseudo-
subordinate clause since speakers understand this as an elliptical version of *je
veux qu'il vienne*. This position is justified by the presence of the initial *que*
which, according to Harris, is the subordinating conjunction par excellence.[5]
Note, however, that in Old French it was perfectly possible, and indeed
usual, to have main clause subjunctives without an introductory *que* (see
7.4.1 below). The introductory *que* appears to have become increasingly
necessary over time not for syntactic reasons, but because the morphological
distinctions between indicative and subjunctive forms were increasingly eroded
(cf. *il parle/qu'il parle*).[6]

While many would shy from seeing the subjunctive as a purely formal
category, several linguists, including the generativist Gross (1978:64), have
tried to avoid the semantic approach to analysing the subjunctive by adopting a functional account. Rothe (1967), for instance, borrowing the concept
of commutation from structuralist phonology and morphology (see Part I,
Section 3.2), divides usages into those where there is an opposition, those
where there is variation, and those where there is no choice (for an extended
critique of this approach see Wunderli 1976:28–51). Note, however, that he
is obliged to introduce semantic considerations when determining whether
an opposition is meaningful or not (e.g. in the analysis of the two meanings
of the verb *dire* according to whether it is followed by an indicative or by a
subjunctive verb in the dependent clause). He is, moreover, forced to admit
that there are no oppositions which are 100% automatic, and that in practice
the borderlines between his three categories are rather fluid.

Boysen (1971) similarly attempts to apply a kind of taxonomic structuralism, using Togeby's *méthode immanente*, to analyse usage of the French
subjunctive; in particular he introduces the notion of hierarchy.[7] First, there
is a syntagmatic hierarchy which comprises three levels:

(i)   *le niveau homonexe*, where the subjunctive is explained by factors **within** the same proposition (i.e. main clause usages);

(ii) *le niveau homo-hétéronexe*, where the relative positioning of the clauses is important (e.g. *qu'il fasse le travail, je le crois*);

(iii) *le niveau hétéronexe*.

Within *le niveau hétéronexe* there is a systematic hierarchy. The most important factor is whether the choice of mood is influenced by the fact that the construction is negative (*construction négative* (Cn)). Thereafter two other hierarchies come into play: a hierarchy of presupposition and a hierarchy of frequency. Looking at a range of factors – D (dérivatif), F (flexif), S (syntaxe), R (racine) – Boysen considers verb by verb what the hierarchy of presupposition is in each case.[8] For instance, for the verb *empêcher* he offers the hierarchy $Cn \leftarrow S^6 + S^7$, that is, when the construction is negative, the embedded verb is indicative if there is no subject (S^6), but subjunctive when the subject is animate (S^7); it may be indicative if the subject is inanimate (although the subjunctive is more frequent). In the case of the hierarchy of frequency Boysen considers the role played by the same features in determining whether a subjunctive is more or less likely where either the indicative or subjunctive is possible. For example, in the case of the verb *supposer* ($F^2 + S^6 + S^7 + R$), important features are the flexion (if the verb is in the imperative this triggers a subjunctive in the dependent clause), whether there is a subject present (where there is no subject present as in the case of *à supposer que, en supposant* the verb often takes the subjunctive), whether the subject is animate or not (nearly all cases of subjunctive usage not expressed by the previous rules have an inanimate subject), and the root itself (although the subjunctive is rare apart from the cases already mentioned).

The advantage of this approach is that it tries to capture the fact that a number of interlocking factors influence the choice of mood. The difficulty arises from the fact that each verb has to be considered separately resulting in a very cumbersome system which does not readily express generalizations. Once again it is questionable as to whether Boysen is able to eliminate completely the semantic from consideration, since he speaks, for instance, of usage being dependent on the semantic nuance of the verb, or whether the subject is animate or inanimate (1971:117). In short, there are problems with viewing the subjunctive simply as a *servitude grammaticale*.

7.2.3   Other approaches

Imbs (1953) attempts to find a compromise between the extremes of either the purely mechanical approach and those accounts which attempt to attribute a semantic function to the subjunctive (according to the context in which it is used) by maintaining that the subjunctive is always *un terme corrélatif*, that is, it is always found in conjunction with another element which combines with it to convey the modality (cf. Judge and Healey (1983:131) who refer to 'the harmonizing subjunctive'). In main clauses the correlative element is usually a marked intonation, whether expressive or affective, whereas in subordinate clauses it may be a combination of intonation, the general sense of the main clause, the meaning of the matrix verb or verbal noun or of a conjunction:

> Dans l'expression de cette modalité il [le subjonctif] est en *continuité de signification* avec son terme corrélatif, qui implique ou appelle la même nuance modale que lui. Mais il est aussi en *opposition* avec ce terme, parce que celui-ci dissimule la modalité sous sa valeur sémantique, alors que le subjonctif l'exprime à titre principal, en l'actualisant par un morphème grammatical spécifique [. . .] Parler d'un subjonctif de doute, c'est donc énoncer qu'un subjonctif est employé en corrélation avec un autre terme qui lui donne cette coloration sémantique particulière (Imbs 1953:48).

Imbs places the emphasis not on the **meaning** of the subjunctive, but rather on the **uses** to which it is put in conjunction with other elements. He argues that in French the modality is only fully actualized when it is also expressed by a specific verbal morpheme. The only case where there is not a combination of semantic factors and grammatical ones is where the subordinate noun clause precedes the main clause (*Que ses amis le méconnussent le remplissait d'amertume*) which, as we shall see (7.3.1), poses problems of interpretation for all commentators (Imbs 1953:37). In practice Imbs notes that the choice between indicative and subjunctive depends at times on subtle semantic nuances and is more a question of stylistics than of fixed rules (*ibid.*:45).

Other linguists have espoused a more flexible approach in accounting for the uses of the French subjunctive[9]; this is particularly true of those studies which aim to describe the complexities of usage as documented in a corpus. One of the most interesting examples of this approach is Poplack (1992), which is based on the description of a corpus of the spoken French of Ontario. Poplack claims that it is impossible to categorize uses of the subjunctive according to whether they are obligatory, optional or contrastive, since usage of the subjunctive is inherently variable. She cogently argues that a simple binary distinction such as that between assertive and non-assertive does not capture relevant generalizations for her data since there is variation in frequency of usage of the subjunctive within each category; for instance, in her class of non-factive/strongly assertive verbs she includes not only *avoir hâte*, followed by the subjunctive in every occurrence, but also *espérer* and *avoir l'espoir* where the rate of occurrence of the subjunctive falls to 21% and 0% respectively.[10] Volitive verbs are equally variable in their rate of occurrence with the subjunctive (*demander* 100%, *souhaiter* 40%, *prier* 0%).

While Poplack superficially finds three classes of matrix verbs in her data – those with which the subjunctive is categorical (*dire, demander, désirer, concevoir* with a negative, etc.), those with which it never co-occurs (*prier, se plaindre, être surpris, avoir l'espoir*, etc.) and those with which it is variable (*vouloir* 91%, *avoir peur* 64%, *penser* with a negative 13%, *empêcher* 'stop' 8%) – she notes that none of the verbs in the first two classes occurs more than three or four times in the corpus and suggests that, if they had, we would expect to find the same variability for all of these. Even a verb like *il faut* occurs followed by the present subjunctive, the present indicative and the conditional. In short, for Poplack the subjunctive is one variant of a linguistic variable, and therefore its usage is necessarily not associated with a difference of meaning.[11] It is possible to show that the choice of one or other variant is conditioned or even promoted by the existence of certain factors in the environment, but not determined by them.

In order to look more closely at the factors determining the choice of mood, Poplack examines the case of *falloir* which is followed in her corpus by the subjunctive 89% of the time and accounts for nearly two thirds of all her examples of the subjunctive (Poplack 1992:247). The factors which contribute to the choice of the subjunctive mood in noun clauses governed by *falloir* are:

- The tense of the matrix verb: while one is at least as likely to find a subjunctive in the dependent clause when the main clause verb is in the imperfect (.65)[12], the *passé composé* (.54), the present (.52), or the future (.51), the probability drops dramatically when the main clause verb is in the conditional (.10) (*ibid.*:247). Moreover, where the subjunctive is not selected there seems to be a kind of tense concordance operating (*ibid.*:253); when the whole corpus was analysed it was found that in 78% of cases an embedded conditional followed a main clause conditional, while in the case of the periphrastic future the main clause contained another periphrastic future in every occurrence. This then seems to provide further evidence for the non-semantic nature of mood usage.
- The distance between the matrix and the embedded verb: where there is no distance, the subjunctive is slightly more likely (.53), but the presence of a parenthesis between the verbs reduces the likelihood dramatically (.17).
- The morphological form and/or frequency of the embedded form: if the embedded verb is suppletive or commonly occurring it is much more likely to be in the subjunctive (.65) than if it is a regular or rare form (.29). This suggests that there are certain 'routines' which speakers adopt – ten suppletive verbs represent more than two thirds of the 1669 tokens of verbs embedded under *falloir*.

With other 'lexical heads' or matrix verbs, the first and third factors remain important and two additional factors come into play:

- The presence or absence of *que*[13]: where *que* is present the subjunctive is slightly more likely than the indicative (.52), whereas absence of the conjunction tends to trigger an indicative in the dependent clause (.39).
- The semantic class of the main clause verb: while volitive (.77) and emotive (.66) verbs in the corpus clearly favoured the subjunctive, the indicative was strongly preferred after verbs of opinion (.09). However, Poplack also finds considerable variation within the semantic classes (the rates of usage cited represent the average for the class). This would suggest that it is the lexical rather than the semantic properties which are important since one commonly find verbs which are 'basically synonymous' (semantically and syntactically; *ibid*.:255) but which behave very differently (e.g. *préférer* + subjunctive 10%, *aimer mieux* + subjunctive 2%).

7.3   Problematic cases

In this section we will consider how best to explain certain specific uses of the subjunctive. For a full description of the appropriate contexts for use of the subjunctive see Riegel, Pellat and Rioul (1994) or Grevisse (1993), and the discussion of the history of the subjunctive below (7.4.1).

7.3.1   Noun clauses

One of the most difficult usages to explain is that where the subjunctive is imposed by the positioning of the noun clause at the beginning of the sentence (*Que M soit à Hollywood ne veut rien dire*). Brunot (1922), for example, considers this usage to be quite illogical. The explanation offered for its usage depends closely on the general framework adopted. For instance, Riegel, Pellat and Rioul (1994:324) argue that preposing the subordinate clause has the effect of suspending the affirmative nature of the proposition, that is, the process is evoked without being asserted. Martin (1983:119–20), on the other hand, sees *(le fait) que* in a sentence like *(le fait) que Pierre soit rentré si vite me fait grand plaisir* as a sort of operator which, while posing the reality of what follows, at the same simultaneously evokes the anti-universe.

Another case which has generated much interest is that where the matrix verb is a verb of opinion that is either in the negative or interrogative, and where once again a choice between an indicative and subjunctive verb in the embedded clause is available. Closer examination of the data has shown that this is not a question of a simple choice but that the selection of one structure over the other depends on a number of syntactic factors. Huot (1986) has demonstrated that it is an oversimplification to say that interrogation triggers the use of the subjunctive in the matrix verb. In the case of partial interrogation, use of the subjunctive is very limited; in negative interrogatives it is only possible where there is inversion of a clitic subject and verb, and it is totally excluded for indirect questions. A blanket statement about usage in total interrogatives is equally inappropriate. She claims (1986:97) that when the interrogation is marked either by intonation or by *est-ce que*, use of the subjunctive is excluded (**Est-ce que tu crois que Jean soit un bon candidat?*), and if in the case of complex inversion the subjunctive is not impossible, it is certainly doubtful.[14] It is where the interrogation is marked by the inversion of a clitic subject that the subjunctive is permitted, especially if the verb is in the present or imperfect and the clitic is a second person (*Penses-tu que Jean soit là?*).

There are also limitations on the use of the subjunctive where the main clause verb is negated. Here use of the subjunctive interacts with the question of the scope of the negation and negative raising (see **11.2**; Prince 1976, Connors 1978). Compare the following sentences:

(12)   Je ne pense pas qu'il vient; j'en suis sûr

(13)   Je ne pense pas qu'il vienne.

In the case of (12) it is only the proposition of the main clause or the higher verb which is negated, not the proposition of the embedded clause. In (13) it is the hypothesis of the embedded clause which the speaker refuses to adopt (Connors 1978:47). Huot (1986:90) points out, however, that the difference of interpretation is only very clear in the first person.[15] Moreover, the tense of the main clause verb is important: if the main clause is in the present, imperfect or perhaps the past conditional a subjunctive is possible, otherwise a subjunctive is either impossible or at least questionable:

(14)   ??Je n'ai jamais pensé que Jean fût un bon candidat[16]

(15)   *Je ne penserai pas que Jean soit un bon candidat.

The choice of the negative particle (or *forclusif*, see **11.1.1**) is also significant since the subjunctive is only common when this is *pas*; for example:

(16)   ??Je ne pense jamais qu'il soit l'heure de partir

is highly questionable, although

(17)   Je ne pense plus que Jean soit un bon candidat

seems perfectly acceptable.

Martin (1983) also attempts to account for the choice between indicative and subjunctive in the embedded sentence after negated expressions of certainty or probability by evoking the notion of scope. His account uses the notion of logical operators showing the different scope of the negative in the two cases (where 'p' refers to 'une phrase quelconque'). He argues that the indicative is used when the negative idea bears on the sentence as a whole, as in:

(18)   Pierre n'est pas certain que Sophie reviendra
       NÉG [CERT(p)]

The subjunctive is used, however, when the negation bears on the idea of certainty itself 'et l'inverse en une idée d'inexistence probable' (Martin 1983:122):

(19)   Pierre n'est pas certain que Sophie revienne
       [NÉG (CERT)]p = INCERTITUDE (p)

In the case of a main clause expressing negated doubt or possibility, the negative may be implicit (e.g. *On s'aperçoit à peine*). On the other hand, *il est hors de doute* may be found with a subjunctive in the embedded clause: here again the concept of a hierarchy of factors may be important since the notion of *doute* seems to remain in the speaker's mind and trigger the use of the subjunctive.

A preoccupation of generativist accounts has been to try to account theoretically for what is known as the subject obviation principle. This refers to the fact that a sentence like **je veux que je vienne* in which there is identity of the subject of the subordinate clause with that of the main clause is not permitted, if the embedded verb would have to be in the subjunctive, and an infinitival construction is preferred instead. This condition, also known as the Subjunctive Disjoint Reference Effect, does not apply to indicative verbs. Tsoulas (1996), for example, seeks to account for this feature by appealing to Principles of Binding Theory (see Part I, Section 3.3.2), which specify what can be interpreted as coreferential or as disjoint. Once again, however, studies based on corpora suggest that such usages are not unattested; Poplack (1992:238) records such examples as: *J'aimerais que je comprenne* . . . ; *Mais je fallais j'y alle* [sic] *la mener puis aller la chercher.*[17]

7.3.2   Adjectival clauses

The types of adjectival clauses in which a subjunctive is possible are listed by Grevisse (1993:1591–3): with a superlative antecedent or similar construction; where the value of the subjunctive is to emphasize the absolute value of the main clause; when the relative depends on a negative or interrogative main clause or on a conditional sentence; with an indefinite antecedent; by attraction; or 'd'une manière générale, quand le locuteur ne s'engage pas sur la réalité du fait exprimé par la relative'.

Two of these usages merit further discussion. A number of different explanations have been offered for usage of the subjunctive in a relative clause with a superlative antecedent. For instance, Brunot argues that the noun has an idea of 'potentiality', while Togeby suggests it is the notion of 'appréciation subjective' which is important (see Nordahl 1970:106–7). Perhaps the best-known definition of when to use the indicative or subjunctive is given by Damourette and Pichon ([1928–40]:V:568): 'la relative au subjonctif se présentait comme spécialement attachée à l'adjectif, celle à l'indicatif comme spécialement attachée au substantif'. They argue that in the case of the sentence *Louise est la plus belle fille que j'aie vue* the quality of beauty is conceived in abstract terms; Louise is not necessarily the most beautiful woman, but 'la-plus-belle-que-j'aie vue'. When the indicative is used in the subordinate clause, *Louise est la plus belle fille que j'ai vue*, the speaker specifies a real individual, the most beautiful woman, amongst the sub-class of the women he has seen, and identifies this with Louise.

A different approach is taken by Nordahl (1970) who bases his examination on the examination of a corpus of written material published in the period 1963–68.[18] Once again, as in Poplack's study (7.2.3 above), detailed examination of attested usage leads him to be nuanced in his conclusions, and in particular to note the variability of usage. First, he demonstrates convincingly that superlatives – whether analytic (e.g. *le plus rapide*) or synthetic (e.g. *le meilleur*) in form – should not be simply grouped with other so-called 'equivalents', such as *le seul, le premier, le dernier*, since the rate of occurrence of the subjunctive is different in each case. Thus whilst the rate of occurrence of the subjunctive after a superlative is 75.2%, it falls to 57.5% after *le seul*, to 22.7% after *le premier* and to 9.7% after *le dernier*. Second, choice of the subjunctive or indicative is found not to be random, but to depend on a number of specific contextual factors; in 94.3% of cases where a superlative is followed by a relative clause with the verb in the subjunctive, at least one of the following five factors is present:

- The verb of the embedded clause is *être* used 'comme verbe plein': *C'est le monde le plus réel qui soit*. The function of the subjunctive here seems to be to suggest the unlimited field of comparison and the uniqueness of the antecedent.
- *Connaître* is the verb in the embedded clause (22 examples of the subjunctive vs 1 of the indicative).
- The temporal adverb *jamais* is present (35 vs 1).
- There is a restrictive element, whether temporal or spatial (18 vs 2).
- *Pouvoir* is used as an auxiliary verb (51 vs 13), *C'est la chose la plus sûre qu'on puisse dire*. Nordahl suggests that this factor is perhaps the least important, as the figures suggest, because the idea of potentiality is already expressed in *pouvoir*, and use of the subjunctive is therefore to some extent redundant.

On the other hand, Nordahl notes that there are contexts where the indicative is compulsory, such as the *c'est . . . qui* construction (*Ce sont les plus affreuses qui sont les plus malignes*) or when the relative 'ne détermine pas un superlatif, mais son complément' (De Boer cited by Nordahl 1970:117), as in *C'était la plus vivante des manifestations auxquelles j'ai assisté*.

The second usage of the subjunctive in an adjectival clause which has attracted attention is where there is an indefinite antecedent, since this is one of the contexts where the choice of mood is meaningful. Kampers-Manhe (1991) discusses how the choice of mood interacts with certain syntactic factors, notably the choice of the determiner and the lexical category of the verb. Use of the subjunctive is incompatible with the use of a definite article, demonstrative or possessive adjective, since these would generate a specific meaning, and the subjunctive always implies an indefinite antecedent. Thus, while *je veux une maison qui soit jolie* is perfectly acceptable, **je veux la maison qui soit jolie* is not. Usage of the subjunctive is similarly incompatible with 'non-generic' verbs; this explains why, for instance, *je veux une maison qui soit jolie* and *je cherche une maison qui ait des volets rouges* are unproblematic, but **j'ai une maison qui soit jolie* and **je vois une maison qui ait des volets rouges* are rejected by native speakers.

7.4   The vitality of the subjunctive

The question of the extent to which the subjunctive marks modality in Modern French has been brought into closer focus by some linguists who have compared contemporary usage with that in Old French and asked not only whether the subjunctive has lost ground as a meaningful category but also whether there is a growing tendency to avoid its usage altogether.

7.4.1   The history of the subjunctive

Old French inherited from Latin three principal main clause usages of the subjunctive: the jussive (e.g. *veniat*, 'let him come'); the optative (*dei te ament*, 'may the gods favour you'); and the potential, defined by Woodcock (1959:89) as an action represented 'not as an event which the speaker merely wishes to record, but as *something which he has thought of*, as being possible, likely, or even certain' (e.g. *crederes victos*, 'you might have thought them beaten'). Attenuated statements may also be used for politeness (*velim hoc facere*, 'I should like to do this') (Harris 1978:168). All these usages are well attested in Old French texts; the important point is that in Old French these main clause usages are only very rarely introduced by *que* (or *si, se*) in contrast to the situation in Modern French:

(20) Seignors barons, de vos *ait*   My lord barons, God have mercy
        Deus mercit,   on you!
      Tutes voz anmes *otreit* il pareïs,   May he grant paradise to all your
                                                          souls,
      En seintes flurs il les *facet* gesir!   And give them rest among holy
                                                          flowers!
                  (*Chanson de Roland*, Ayres-Bennett 1996:60)

(21) Dieux dist: 'Lumiere *soit* faite'.   God said, 'Let there be light'.
                  (The Old French Bible, Ayres-Bennett 1996:74)

The imperfect subjunctive may be used to express an unfulfilled wish:

(22) Melz me *venist*, amis, que morte fusse.   It would be better for me,
                                                          lord, if I were dead.
                  (*La Vie de Saint Alexis*, Ayres-Bennett 1996:46)

The majority of main clause usages in Modern French require an introduc-
tory *que*, notably the jussive and optative usages (see 7.2.2). Exceptions are
hypotheses of the type 'soit un triangle', and fixed or rare expressions such as
usage of the first person of *savoir* in the negative as an attenuated statement
(*Je ne sache*), *pouvoir* in the optative (*Puissé-arracher ces hauts faits à ton ombre*,
Béchade 1986), or other formulaic expressions (*Fasse le ciel!*).
  One of the most important usages of the imperfect subjunctive in Old
French was in both the protasis (the subordinate hypothetical clause) and the
apodosis (the 'main' clause indicating the possible consequence) of conditional
sentences:

(23) Si me *leüst*, si t'*oüsse* guardét.   If I had been allowed, I would have
                                                          looked after you.
                                                                          (*ibid.*)

The imperfect subjunctive could be used in this situation to express both a
non-past/improbable condition and a past/impossible condition. Thus, out of
context, the following example from *Alexis* could have two possible readings:

(24) Se Deu *ploüst*, sire en *doüsses* estra.   If it pleased God, you would be
                                                          lord of it/If it had pleased God,
                                                          you would have been lord of it.
                                                          (Aspland 1979:14)

It is perhaps because of this potential ambiguity that the modern structure
using an imperfect indicative in the *si* clause and a present conditional in the
'main' clause arose. Today, usage of the imperfect or pluperfect subjunctive
in such structures is considered literary and rather archaic.

Even in Latin not all subordinate clause usages were selected on the basis of meaning: note, for example, that in Classical Latin *quamvis* ('although') was followed by the subjunctive, while its synonym *quamquam* took the indicative. This tendency was somewhat extended in Vulgar Latin when it became increasingly usual for a noun clause introduced by *ut* to be followed by a subjunctive verb.

Many of the subordinate noun clause usages of Old French are familiar to us since they have continued into Modern French, for instance after verbs of desire, command, preference, prohibition, prevention or fear:

> (25) E tuit li preient que d'els *aiet* mercit.   And all pray to him to have
>   mercy on them.
>   (*La Vie de Saint Alexis*, Ayres-Bennett 1996:47)

> (26) Je veul et comant que cil de Moiremont *aient* et *prengnent* leastalage
>   et le eminage au marchié de Columbé ...
>   I wish and command that [the monks] of Morimond have and take
>   the right to a stall and the grain tax in Colombey ...
>   (*Donation testamentaire*, Ayres-Bennett 1996:89)

One of the principal differences between Old French and Modern French usage is that in Old French the subjunctive could be used after verbs of opinion or seeming to indicate that the content of the subordinate clause is either untrue or unverified:

> (27) Ço lur est vis que *tengent* Deu medisme.   It seems to them as if
>   they are holding God
>   himself.
>   (*La Vie de Saint Alexis*, Ayres-Bennett 1996:48)

In the following example from the Life of Saint Brendan the use of the subjunctive indicates that he was wrong in his thinking:

> (28) E quidoue que *fust* celét   And he thought that it was hidden
>   A lui qui fist cel estelét.   From him who made the starry skies.
>   (Aspland 1979:22)

The subjunctive is used in adjectival clauses to express purpose or a wish, after a superlative or when the relative clause depends on an interrogative or negative main clause:

> (29) N'i ad icel ne *demeint* irance.   There is not one who does not dis-
>   play anger.
>   (*Chanson de Roland*, Ayres-Bennett 1996:60)

It will be clear from the brief account above that there is much continuity of usage between Old French and modern usage; in general, however, change has been in the direction of loss of the subjunctive as a meaningful category. Bailard (1980) seeks to explain the changes precisely in terms of a loss in semantic transparency of the mood. He argues that mood is inherently mean-ingful; when changes in usage took place as a result of other syntactic changes, the meaning of the mood became opaque. This was compensated for by increasing rule simplicity. After the subjunctive had become opaque in what he calls 'the noun clause of communication' (which includes subordinate clauses dependent on verbs of saying or of opinion), mood became re-analysed in French as a mark of the assertiveness of the main clause as a whole, with the indicative marking assertion and the subjunctive lack of assertion. Here again the explanation for change is dependent on the overall framework adopted for explaining usage of the subjunctive.

7.4.2   The vitality of the subjunctive in Modern French

A number of linguists have asked whether we are witnessing the demise and eventual future loss of the subjunctive from French. As early as 1922 Brunot noted some of the changes which had occurred in the usage of the sub-junctive during the history of French; while he concluded that there was as yet no sign of the forms disappearing from usage, as he claimed had been the case in the North-East of France (where, according to him, a construction of the type *il faut que je viens* is common), he nevertheless noted that the subjunctive had suffered from the imposition of rigid rules governing its behaviour:

> En l'exigeant derrière une principale négative sans considération du sens, on en réduisait l'emploi à un fait de pure subordination grammaticale, on vidait le mode de sa valeur réelle, et on en préparait l'abandon (Brunot 1922:524).

Since then, other linguists have set out arguments in support of the vitality of the subjunctive in contemporary French. Cohen (1965:27) points out that children acquire the subjunctive long before they start school. For instance, he cites a child of two years four months saying *Veux bien toi tu fasses un gros pâté*; even less advanced children have acquired the subjunctive by the begin-ning of their fifth year. The fact that children of 20–30 months invent distinctive analogical forms for this mood, such as *il faut que papa peinde, il faut qu'il s'assoise*, is further proof of its vitality in his eyes.

The second type of evidence cited in support of the health of the subjunc-tive concerns cases where the subjunctive is being used in Modern French where traditionally one might expect an indicative. These contrary indica-tions (Grevisse 1993:1265) include the use of the subjunctive after *après que*, *suivant que, à condition que, tout . . . que, de ce que*, in clauses after verbs of feeling and *s'attendre que* (cf. Wunderli 1976). Cohen (1965:265–6) goes so far as to speak of 'un certain regain de goût pour le subjonctif éventuel'.

How are these 'gains' to be interpreted? The use of the subjunctive after *après que* – in the face of the criticisms of the French Academy (*Mise en garde*, 19 November 1964; Grevisse 1993:1637) – has clearly gained ground.[19] Canut and Ledegen (1998) discuss a number of reasons which have been offered to explain this usage. The most common suggestion is the analogy with *avant que*. According to this account, the development reflects not so much a gain in ground for the subjunctive but further evidence of the importance of formal triggers (a conjunction one element of which is *que*) at the expense of semantic considerations (whereas *avant que* introduces a clause the action of which has not yet happened at the time of the main clause action and is therefore unrealized in relation to it, *après que* introduces an action which has occurred at the time of the main clause action and is therefore a fact). What this account does not explain is why analogy worked in favour of the subjunctive after *après que* and not in favour of the indicative after *avant que*. The same difficulty occurs with the suggestion that the change occurred because of the homophony in literary usages between indicative forms in the past anterior and the pluperfect subjunctive forms in the third person singular. Canut and Ledegen, using a Guillaumean framework, prefer to see a difference of *visée* in the use of the indicative versus subjunctive after *après que*; if the intention is simply to situate the events in chronological time then the indicative is used, whereas the subjunctive emphasizes the 'écart temporel' between the two events.

7.4.3   The vitality of the subjunctive and variation

Discussion of the vitality of the subjunctive must necessarily take into account the distribution of its usage according to medium, register and geography to see whether there is any evidence to support the hypothesis that there is change in progress. Currently, sociolinguistic studies of the use of the subjunctive are still relatively few in number and more research is needed in this area.

7.4.3.1   Written and spoken French

According to Poplack (1992:258), studies on the use of the subjunctive in modern spoken French show remarkable agreement on a number of issues. First, contexts in which the subjunctive is even an option in the spoken language are extremely rare, not exceeding five or ten per half hour of speech.[20] Second, in these contexts between a third and a half of the surface forms are morphologically ambiguous. In Sand's study (1983), for instance, 86 of the 214 tokens of verbs embedded under a verb of will/desire were ambiguous. Third, of all the contexts which are supposed to trigger the subjunctive, a minimum of 40% (and in Poplack (1992) two thirds) are made up of *falloir que*[21]; moreover, in all studies this verb turns up with the subjunctive between 80 and 100 per cent of the time, so that these figures inflate the overall rate of subjunctive selection. Indeed there appears to be a relatively small number of contexts in which the subjunctive tends to occur, such as after *vouloir que, pour que*. In Sand's (1983) recording of c. 22 hours of the conversation of young people aged 10–12 and 17–18 in Caen in 1976–78, 92 of the 111 unambiguous examples of the subjunctive occurred after *falloir* and another nine after *vouloir*.[22] This suggests that there are relatively few contexts in the spoken language where the subjunctive is really vigorous and that these tend to feature another restricted set of suppletive verbs. Time and time again surveys show that in speech there are certain favoured contexts for use of the subjunctive. Where the subjunctive is not selected in these favoured contexts there is usually a reason for the choice – for example, there may be a distance between the main clause and the embedded verb. As we might expect, there is also much more optionality after verbs of feeling and negated verbs of opinion. Cohen (1965:260) therefore concludes that the subjunctive is still very much alive in spoken French, but that the patterns and distribution of forms is different from that of the written language.

7.4.3.2   SES and register

A rapid sociolinguistic survey carried out on the GARS data suggested that use of the subjunctive is not in general confined to one social grouping but shared by all, although some structures such as *le fait que* are more restricted in their distribution (Blanche-Benveniste and others 1990:197–9). Auvigne and Monté's study (1982) of the speech of a 'sous-prolétariat' woman (see **6.4.2.2**) records a very high degree of non-usage of the subjunctive even after common expressions such as *c'est mieux que, vouloir que* and *avant que*. Moreover, where the subjunctive is used, it appears to be quasi-formulaic, so for instance *pour qu'i' puisse* is used on a number of occasions even where *pour* followed by an infinitive would be possible. However, given the extreme situation of this woman and methodological problems with the survey, we should not perhaps consider her speech as representative of low SES usage.

Use of an imperfect subjunctive in speech characterizes the speaker in terms of education and family position, whether real or aspired to, or it may be used as a mark of respect, whether genuine or not, towards the addressee (Müller 1985:59). While then, if we leave aside Auvigne and Monté's data, there seems to be fairly stable patterning in the case of the present subjunctive, there is evidence of differentiation in the case of the imperfect subjunctive, since loss has spread across most, but not all, social groups.

Information about register is sparser and more anecdotal. Boysen (1971:133) cites examples from Van der Molen of the use of *falloir* with the indicative which he associates with a low register, although it is not clear whether he is simply confusing spoken and low-register usage. Bauche (1951:109, 114–15) considers *je veux qu'il vient* as frequent in *français populaire*.[23] He also points to a tendency to create analogical subjunctive forms with simplified morphology (*que j'alle, que j'aye, qu'il falle, que je save, que je peuve*, etc.).

7.4.3.3   Geographic variation

Knowledge of regional usage is similarly thin and anecdotal. For example, as regards the use of *espérer* with the subjunctive, Cohen (1965:149) admits that 'la carte reste à faire'. Studies of usage in other francophone countries are equally patchy. Cohen (1965:81) mentions in passing examples of the type *je ne veux pas que tu viens avec nous autres* as being typical of the popular French of Algeria. We have already referred in some detail to Poplack's work on the French of Ottawa-Hull. Laurier's study (1989) is based on French in Ontario where French is very much in a minority situation (c. 5% of the population, and speakers little exposed to standard French). Here he found that there was some difference in frequency of usage of the subjunctive according to whether French or English is the dominant language (French dominant 67%; bilingual 63%, English dominant 47%), but this was not as important as frequency of occurrence of a particular construction. Once again frequency is most important in perpetuating the use of the subjunctive, together with use of the subjunctive with a limited set of suppletive verbs (*aller, être*, etc.). In a recent paper Rottet (1998) notes the massive decrease in the use of the subjunctive between generations in the Cajun French community of the Terrebonne-Lafourche area, where the Cajun French dialect has been in decline at least since the 1940s. He notes in particular the preference by younger speakers for replacing finite clauses taking the subjunctive by non-finite clauses with verbs in the infinitive, and sees this as symptomatic of language decline, here probably encouraged by the influence of English.

7.4.4   The imperfect subjunctive

More attention has been devoted to discussing the causes and extent of the demise of the imperfect subjunctive – and the morphologically related pluperfect subjunctive – from usage, and especially from spoken usage. According to Barral (1980:7), the imperfect subjunctive largely disappeared from spoken French at the end of the nineteenth century. Indeed Grevisse notes that from the eighteenth century, grammarians complain about the non-observance of sequence of tense rules, examples of which date even from the previous century.[24] This has led to discussion of two major issues: what are the consequences of this loss for the French language, and in what circum-stances is it appropriate to use these forms in writing?

A series of commentators have pointed out that the subjunctive is, to use Guillaume's term, *un mode intemporel*, and that the difference between the various forms of the subjunctive is instead aspectual. For Guillaume (Barral 1980:59–60) the present and perfect subjunctive have a prospective sense, while the imperfect and pluperfect have a retrospective sense; according to Béchade (1986:63) the morphologically simple forms indicate incomplete action and the compound forms completed actions.[25] In any case, choice of the appropriate tense for subordinate clauses was traditionally governed not by considerations of time but by sequence of tense rules as codified by normative grammars. One of the best known versions of these conventions is Gide's, which permits the use of either the present or the imperfect sub-junctive after a main clause imperfect or conditional verb (Barral 1980:340):

- Je veux qu'il fasse
- Je $\begin{cases} \text{voulais} \\ \text{voudrais} \end{cases}$ qu'il fasse – ou qu'il fît

   J' $\begin{cases} \text{avais voulu} \\ \text{aurais voulu} \end{cases}$ qu'il fît.

It might be argued that, since the choice of the appropriate tense form is largely governed by fixed rules which are dictated by the tense of the main clause verb, the time of the action is not represented by the tense of the embedded clause verb. The number of forms of the subjunctive could there-fore be reduced without any great loss to the language. In other words, the establishment of the sequence of tense rules for the use of the subjunctive could be considered directly responsible for the demise of the imperfect subjunctive since they denied it any role in marking the time of the action (Barral 1980:600). According to Cohen, nearly all the losses for the imper-fect and pluperfect subjunctives are gains for the present and perfect sub-junctives, although there are some notable exceptions to this, for instance, concessives. He therefore concludes (Cohen 1965:262): 'Si on considère les choses dans l'ensemble, le bloc subjonctif a gardé sa masse'.[26]

It should, however, be noted that, despite the sequence of tense rules, certain usages of the subjunctive are governed not by temporal considerations but by modal nuances 'qui vont du possible à l'irréel' (Barral 1980:12).[27] To take an example from Dauzat, the imperfect subjunctive may be used after a main clause conditional in contrast to the present subjunctive when an idea of unreality is to be conveyed. He cites the case of *il faudrait qu'on* **appliquât** *(mais on ne le fait pas)* and *il suffirait qu'on* **applique** *(on le fera peut-être)* (*ibid.*:341); although these sentences are not strictly minimal pairs, the contrast is nevertheless striking. An imperfect subjunctive may be selected in an opta-tive construction to indicate an unrealizable wish, or at least one that is highly unlikely to be fulfilled (*Ah! qu'elle ne fût jamais née!* (Grevisse 1993:1272)), or, in a highly literary context, an unfulfillable condition: *Le sort est jeté maintenant; dussé-je crever, je ne lâcherai pas.* Even where the value of the tense is temporal, usage may not follow the sequence of tense rules. Grevisse notes that a past tense in the main clause may be followed by a present subjunctive to mark that the fact expressed is present or future in relation to the time of speaking, or reflects a general truth: *Je n'ai jamais dit qu'aucune société soit parfaite.* Similarly Dauzat contrasts *je voulais qu'il vînt hier* with *je voulais qu'il vienne aujourd'hui* (cited in Barral 1980:341). Surprisingly, an imperfect or pluperfect may be used after *avant que* despite the fact that this logically marks a posterior event: *M. [. . .] la perdit de vue avant qu'elle ne fût arrivée.*

These modal values associated with the different tenses of the subjunctive may then account for what Cohen (1965:104) describes as a 'fait étonnant', where the imperfect (and more rarely the pluperfect) subjunctive is found in an embedded clause dependent on a main clause the verb of which is in the present or future with a 'valeur éventuel':

(30)   Que voulez-vous que fît M. Picani? (Cohen 1965:105)

(31)   Il se peut que son état de grossesse, comme le croyait Bernard, ne fût pas étranger à cette humeur (Mauriac, cited by Béchade 1986:68).

Alternatively it may be used to express a continuous action in the past:

(32)   Il ne faut pas croire que sa raison fût en désordre (Grevisse 1993:1272).

Cohen (1965:269) concludes:

l'imparfait (et plus-que-parfait) du subjonctif subsistant dans l'écrit, en alternance avec le présent (et le passé composé), d'une part se prête à des jeux subtils d'expression, d'autre part participe à des emplois capricieux, comme d'une fleur qui tantôt on met à la boutonnière, et tantôt non.

More recently, linguists aiming to describe corpus-based usage (cf. Poplack and Nordahl discussed above) have tried to account systematically for the factors in the linguistic context which favour the continued use of the imperfect subjunctive in written French. Lindqvist (1979), using a corpus of 26 French novels published between 1954 and 1964 and 32 issues of *L'Express* dating from 1964, analysed the choice of tense of the subjunctive in subordinate noun clauses which depend on a main clause, the verb of which is in a past tense. His results show clearly that there is relatively little difference in the frequency of occurrence of the present (56%) and imperfect (44%) subjunctives introduced by a past tense verb (which together accounted for

92% of usages). Rather the choice of one in preference to the other appears to be conditioned by a range of other factors:

- The tense of the subordinating verb: after a past conditional (63%) or a *passé simple* (70%) the imperfect predominates, whereas after a present conditional (86%) or a perfect (91%) main clause verb, the present subjunctive is much more common.
- The person of the verb: the third person singular is more likely to be used in the imperfect subjunctive than any other person. For example, when the verb of the main clause is in the imperfect, the tense of the subordinate clause verb is as follows:

		present (%)	imperfect (%)
	1	94	6
sing	2	100	0
	3	**36**	**64**
	1	83	17
pl	2	100	0
	3	62	38

- The particular verb in the embedded clause, and notably whether this is *avoir* or *être*: for instance, after an imperfect tense in the main clause the imperfect subjunctive occurs at a rate of 65% when the lexical item is *avoir* or *être*, but only 48% for all other verbs; when the third person singular usages are removed from the statistics, the difference is even more striking (46% vs 15%). There is also variation within the class of 'other' verbs: some verbs e.g. *craindre*, *attendre* clearly favour the imperfect subjunctive (perhaps because of the mode of action of the subordinating verb).
- The type of main clause, whether affirmative or not: here the differences are relatively slight but where the main clause verb is in the imperfect, the imperfect subjunctive is selected 63% of the time following an affirmative main clause, but 72% when it is non-affirmative.
- The aspectual value of the subordinate clause: again, following an imperfect in the main clause, the imperfect is favoured 56% of the time for expressing an incomplete action, but this rises to 76% for a completed action. Often a present tense subjunctive is selected to indicate a posterior action.

Lindqvist concludes that it is an over-simplification to say that the imperfect subjunctive is disappearing from usage. Rather its use depends on a number of factors – morphological (person of the verb), syntactic (tense of the subordinating verb, construction of the main clause, function of the subordinate clause), semantic (aspectual considerations), and lexical (sense of the individual verbs).

Similar conclusions are reached by Charles Muller (1986) when he looks at the use of the imperfect subjunctive in a number of twentieth-century novels. While he notices a marked decline in the use of the subjunctive in the 1960s (a fall from 248 to 75 per 100,000 words), he nevertheless identifies the same factors influencing usage: the person of the verb, and the use of *avoir* and *être* (accounting for more than half of his examples of the imperfect subjunctive). In addition, Muller observes considerable variation between the preferred usage of individual authors: eight authors (one third of his corpus) account for more than two-thirds of his attestations, while another eight barely account for one twentieth of the occurrences. On the basis of these findings, he argues that criteria for the selection of the tense of the subjunctive are becoming increasingly amorphous and that stylistic considerations are important. There are also differences according to the genre of the work, correlating with the question of those genres in which it is appropriate to use the *passé simple* (*discours narratif*); for example, the imperfect subjunctive occurs less often in drama, which approximates perhaps most closely to spoken usage:

Table 7.1 Frequency of usage of the present and imperfect subjunctive and of the *passé simple* as a percentage of all verb forms in different genres (Muller 1986:226)

	present subjunctive (%)	imperfect subjunctive (%)	*passé simple* (%)
drama	2.8	0.2	0.2
novels	1.5	2.4	17.6
essays	2.8	1.2	6.2
press	2.7	0.6	5.2
scientific/ technical writing	2.3	0.7	4.3

7.4.5   Alternative markers of modality

Discussion of the vitality of the subjunctive has naturally led to consideration of two further issues. Can usage of the subjunctive be adequately explained without examining alternative ways of marking modality in Modern French? Are these alternatives in all cases strictly equivalent to the version with the subjunctive?

A whole range of alternative markers of modality are available in Modern French. A nuance of doubt may be indicated either by intonation or lexically (*probablement*, *peut-être*). Frequently, there is marked selection of a tense with modal value. Two forms particularly lend themselves to modal exploitation, the future and the present conditional[28], since they both refer to an event that has not yet happened and which is therefore somewhat uncertain. Martin (1983:105) gives the following example, first cited by Nordahl, as one such case: 'Il faut souhaiter que la Coupe d'Or . . . **remettra** dimanche prochain les deux mêmes équipes en présence' (*Le Figaro*, 25 August 1959). A modal reading of a tense may be produced when there is a clash between the temporal setting and the usual time value of the verb form (*ce sera Pierre; le président serait mort*). An imperfect may also be used to attenuate the directness of a statement, for instance for the sake of politeness (*je voulais vous demander*), because of the connection between the aspectual category imperfective and irrealis modality (Fleischman 1995:519; see also **6**.1). Finally, the modal auxiliaries *pouvoir, devoir, falloir, savoir* and *falloir* may serve to mark modality (*ce doit être Pierre*).

Other alternative constructions are available which circumvent the need for a marker of modality. Where there is identity of subject between the main and subordinate clause, an infinitival clause is often preferred (*je ne sais quoi faire, avant de partir, je cherche une maison où dormir*); elsewhere *voir* may be used in an auxiliary function (*je veux le voir venir*) or a nominal construction may be selected (*avant son départ, elle travaille jusqu'à la nuit tombée*). In some cases a simple substitution of indicative for subjunctive is possible (*qu'il est malade, je le sais*); as we have seen (**7**.2.3), Poplack's (1992) study suggests that there is a tendency towards tense concordance, that is, selection of the same tense for the embedded clause as the main clause.

While there is very broad semantic equivalence in most cases between the usages with the subjunctive and the alternative constructions, this is not always the case. Kampers-Manhe (1991:67) argues, for example, that use of a conditional instead of a subjunctive in an adjectival clause with an indefinite antecedent is not strictly equivalent. For instance, in *je cherche une maison qui aurait des volets verts*, the NP is interpreted as having a specific identifiable referent but whose reality is submitted to a condition or according to the say-so of a third party, whereas with a subjunctive the speaker is not sure whether such a house exists at all. Further close examination of such pairs of examples is needed as part of a continuing process of evaluating the vitality of the subjunctive in Modern French.

Suggested Reading

General studies:
   Cohen (1965), Confais (1990), Hanse (1960), Imbs (1953), Ludwig (1988),
   Martin (1983), Nordahl (1969), Rothe (1967), Tanase (1943), Van der Molen
   (1923), Wunderli (1976).
History of the subjunctive forms and Old French usage:
   Jensen (1974), Moignet (1959), Soutet (1998).

Use of particular forms of the subjunctive:
  Barral (1980), Muller (1986) (imperfect subjunctive); Havu (1996) (perfect subjunctive).
Use of the subjunctive in specific clause types:
  Boysen (1971), Canut and Ledegen (1998), Huot (1986), Kampers-Manhe (1991), Lindqvist (1979), Nordahl (1970).
Variation:
  Blanche-Benveniste and others (1990), Laurier (1989), Poplack (1992), Sand (1983).

Notes

1. Motivation for the dualist approach may in part be historical, mirroring the Greek differentiation of the optative and subjunctive moods in the distinction between subjunctives marking 'desire' and those expressing 'doubt'.
2. This account is somewhat simplified since both Lerch (1931) and Regula (1936), for example, suggest that the 'subjonctif du sujet psychologique' or of uncertainty is derived from the subjunctive expressing desire or volition.
3. A critique of some of the different approaches to the subjunctive from a pedagogic point of view is found in Mailhac (1996).
4. This is perhaps where some notion of a hierarchy of factors might be useful (see 7.2.2 below); here the negative seems to take precedence over the question of certainty.
5. Martin (1983:106–7) also points to the decisive role of *que*, arguing that with the exception of certain fixed main clause usages, once *que* is removed from a construction, the indicative is favoured over the subjunctive (*jusqu'à ce qu'il revienne/jusqu'au moment où il reviendra*). Conversely, Rothe (1967:60–1) insists that *que* is not an essential part of the use of the subjunctive since on the one hand *que* is not always present in relative clauses or with *comme si* or *si*, and on the other hand *que* is not necessarily followed by a clause with a verb in the subjunctive.
6. Other main clause usages without *que* are largely fossilized remnants of this earlier productive usage (e.g. *vive le roi! fasse le ciel! plût aux dieux!*).
7. Note that he excludes the future and conditional from his statistics contrasting the number of usages of the subjunctive versus the indicative, which means that his figures are not comparable to those in other studies.
8. D refers to one of 7 prefixes which may influence the choice of mood; F to the influence of inflectional markers of person, tense, etc. (e.g. F^2: influence de l'impératif); S to the influence of syntactic features (e.g. S^6: influence de la présence ou de l'absence d'un sujet; S^7: influence du caractère animé ou inanimé du sujet); R to the influence of the root (used to account for those examples which have not been explained when the three other factors,

D, F and S have been examined, as illustrated, for example, in the contrast between *j'entends qu'il vient* and *j'entends qu'il vienne*). The arrows indicate that one group of factors presupposes another, whilst the plus signs indicate that there is no such presupposition.

9. Börjeson (1966) suggests that multiple factors influence the choice of mood, including questions of reality, attraction of mood, opposition, relationship with other tenses, and the number of tenses of the subjunctive (e.g. the absence of a future subjunctive in French).

10. In each case she excludes from her calculation forms which are homophonous with the indicative.

11. While Poplack points to the importance of the semantic class of the main verb, the variability within each class leads her to argue that it is lexical rather than semantic properties which are significant (see below).

12. The data has been analysed according to a variable rule analysis which enables Poplack to determine which factors have a statistically significant effect on the choice of mood. The factor weights vary between 0 and 1, and figures above .5 may be interpreted as favouring the choice of the subjunctive, while figures below .5 disfavour it. Note that these factor weights are relative measures within each set. Where percentages are given, they refer to overall occurrence rates.

13. *Que* is frequently omitted in Canadian French, whether there is an indicative or a subjunctive in the subordinate clause: *Faut tu connaisses quelqu'un qui connaisse quelqu'un; Faut tu connais quelqu'un.*

14. Native speaker judgements seem to vary quite considerably over the acceptability of sentences of the type **Est-ce que tu crois que Jean soit un bon candidat?*; four of the five native speakers we questioned on this found it perfectly acceptable, although the fifth found it 'highly doubtful'.

15. Note, however, these examples from the *Grand Larousse* (1971–78:5759) cited as (9) above:

Sa mère ne croit pas qu'il a volé (elle refuse de le croire)
Sa mère ne croit pas qu'il ait volé (sa mère croit qu'il n'a pas volé).

16. However, native speakers seem generally to find the use of a present subjunctive acceptable here (*Je n'ai jamais pensé que Jean soit un bon candidat*).

17. Lalaire (1998), in a recent monograph on the French subjunctive which adopts a Government-and-Binding framework, rejects the variationist quantitative approach and uses primarily native speaker judgment of fabricated examples in his account which aims to show that syntax plays a crucial role in determining modal variation in subordinate clauses.

18. 50 books (novels, essays, etc.), 26 numbers of *Le Monde hebdomadaire* (1968) and 26 complete numbers of *Paris Match*.

19. Wunderli (1976) notes examples dating from the thirteenth to the seventeenth centuries, but observes that, perhaps under the force of normative pressure, they seem to disappear in the eighteenth and nineteenth centuries only to reappear in the twentieth century.

20. A survey carried out by GARS (the Groupe Aixois de Recherche en Syntaxe) found 452 examples of morphologically distinctive subjunctive forms in 27 hours of recordings of speech.

21. In fact in the GARS survey 35% of examples were found after the impersonal verbs such as *il faut que, c'est important que, c'est dommage que, c'est bien que, c'est déjà bon que* (Blanche-Benveniste and others 1990:197), but this percentage is still very significant.

22. Moreover in these two contexts there are very few exceptions of the type *elle veut pas qu'il lit tout haut; il faut qu'il retient l'électricité.*

23. If Bauche's findings were to be substantiated by other, more detailed, studies, this might suggest that change of usage is beginning to occur, starting in the lowest registers.

24. The imperfect subjunctive does survive in certain regions of France such as the Midi and the Wallon liégeois (Grevisse 1993:1271).

25. For discussion of examples where the perfect subjunctive has, not its usual value of marking an event anterior to that of the main clause, but that of expressing an event simultaneous to that of the main clause, see Havu (1996).

26. Some commentators suggest that it was the anomalous nature of the forms of the imperfect subjunctive which led to their demise. It is important to remember, however, that the forms of the imperfect subjunctive are not especially difficult to conjugate or ridiculous phonetically per se (cf. *fascination/fascinassions* Grevisse 1993:1271), but that once they began to fall into disuse – a loss evidently allied to the demise of the *passé simple* from spoken French – they became less familiar and hence on the one hand less easy to conjugate and on the other hand suitable for exploitation for comic purposes.

27. Brunot had already denied the importance of the sequence of tense rules (Grevisse 1993:1269), and Cohen (1965:95) admits they are less and less frequently observed.

28. The future may also be selected when there is a need unambiguously to express futurity since the subjunctive has no specific future form. According to Martin (1983:131–3) the future orientates towards certainty, whilst the conditional tends to place the process in a future full of uncertainty.

8

Pronominal verbs

8.1 Introduction

Two main issues have dominated recent discussions of French pronominal verbs. First, the position of these verbs within the system of voice in French and the question of whether it is appropriate to speak of a pronominal voice for French (see **8.**2). Second, and more importantly, how to classify the different types of usage of pronominal verbs. Much of the debate has centred on whether French possesses a number of discrete classes of pronominal verbs, or whether it is possible to seek a unified account for all their different functions (see **8.**3).

In Section **8.**4 we will go on to focus on one usage of pronominal verbs, the so-called pronominal passive construction, and consider its relationship to the periphrastic or 'true' passive formed with *être* and a past participle, the active construction with the indefinite subject pronoun *on*, and other apparently semantically 'equivalent' constructions. As in the discussion of alternatives to the subjunctive, the main issue here is whether these structures are indeed equivalents; in particular we shall discuss whether, as is often claimed, French prefers to avoid the 'true' passive, or whether there are factors which make its usage in certain contexts not only preferable but essential.

8.2 Pronominal verbs and voice

8.2.1 How many voices for French?

In Part I (Section 2.3.1) we outlined the traditional distinction between active, passive and middle voice and noted the difficulties with trying to apply this scheme to French. A number of grammarians and linguists have nevertheless adopted this traditional threefold categorization of voice for French, calling the categories active, passive and variously *voix réflexive, voix réfléchie, voix moyenne* or *voix pronominale*. It is striking that those who espouse this scheme represent a wide range of theoretical approaches, including Damourette and Pichon ([1928–40]:V:662), Jones (1996:111), Judge and Healey (1983:96), and Wilmet (1997:458).

The difficulty with this threefold scheme lies in deciding on the definition and membership of the third category, since the class of pronominal verbs in French (if defined formally by the presence of one of the personal pronouns of the series *me, te, se, nous* and *vous* in the same person as the subject, and by the use of the auxiliary *être* in the formation of compound tenses[1]) does not clearly express one voice according to traditional definitions. The term 'reflexive verb' is, moreover, misleading since the reflexive usage is only one of a number of different meanings associated with pronominal verbs. Thus, as we shall see, whilst a pronominal verb may have a reflexive (*je me lave*) or reciprocal (*ils se battent*) interpretation, certain forms seem to be the equivalent of a passive construction (*les œufs se vendent à la douzaine*), whilst in other cases it is difficult to attribute any semantic role to the reflexive pronoun which appears rather to be an intrinsic part of the lexical item (*Paul s'est évanoui*). Some linguists view the reflexive and reciprocal usages as core and place all other pronominal uses in the same class on the basis of the formal similarity of the structures. Jones (1996:111), on the other hand, reserves the term pronominal voice for those uses where the clitic does not have a straightforward reflexive or reciprocal interpretation, including Intrinsic, Middle and Neutral uses (see **8**.3.2 below).

Alongside the terms reflexive and pronominal, two other labels are used to refer to the third class, 'middle' and 'medio-passive'. The designation 'middle' is especially problematic since it has two different usages in the literature. Some linguists, including Guillaume (1943:24), favour a broad definition which Stéfanini (1962:114) notes can be used to 'définir la voix pronominale par opposition à l'active et passive, comme une synthèse des deux: le sujet d'un moyen est à la fois actif et passif'. On the other hand, many consider the so-called 'middle' or 'medio-passive' usage to be simply one of the usages of pronominal verbs (see **8**.3.2 below).

As a result of these uncertainties a number of linguists have chosen to restrict the number of voices in French to two – the active and the passive – and to view pronominal verbs as a special case of the active.[2] Gardes-Tamine (1988:II:87), for instance, prefers to speak of pronominal **forms** rather than a pronominal **voice** because of the difficulty of identifying one underlying value for all uses. Other terms used to avoid the term voice include *tournures (active et passive), tours* or *conjugaisons*. Riegel, Pellat and Rioul (1994:255) make a distinction between *verbes pronominaux* (which include those verbs which only occur in a pronominal form and those where the pronominal usage bears no semantic relation to the non-pronominal counterpart) and *constructions pronominales d'un verbe* (embracing the reflexive and pronominal passive usage).

Changing preferences in the use of terminology are reflected in official recommendations for grammatical terminology. In 1910 – in what is essentially a morphological definition – reference was to three **forms** of the verb: active, passive and pronominal. According to the *Progression grammaticale dans l'enseignement du premier degré* of 1950, the term voice was recommended for active and passive, but the third category was simply called *verbes pronominaux*. The recommendation of 22 July 1975 adopts a syntactic definition and speaks of four *tournures* (*active*, *passive*, *pronominale* and *impersonnelle*), 'le terme de *tournure* étant donné comme synonyme de *voix* pour les tournures active et passive exclusivement' (*Grand Larousse de la langue française* 1971–78:4679). This fourfold division highlights another set of problems since it implies that impersonal usages are somehow separate from active, passive and pronominal ones, whereas in practice all three of these may be used impersonally (Battye and Hintze 1992:279–80):

(1)   Il pleut [active]

(2)   Il a été abattu des arbres (par le bûcheron) [passive]

(3)   Il s'ouvre plusieurs portes quand vous êtes riche [pronominal].

Whilst all the approaches so far discussed work broadly within the traditional framework, modifying it where necessary to adapt it to French usage, both Guillaume and the generativists introduce more radical revisions.[3]

8.2.2   Guillaume

In an important paper dated 1943 Guillaume asks the question 'Existe-t-il un déponent en français?'. Deponent verbs in Latin grammar were those which had exclusively passive morphology, but which functioned as active verbs. Guillaume maintains that there are two main categories of voice which he terms *les voix analytiques* and *les voix synthétiques*. The former category includes the active voice and the passive voice since these are mutually exclusive, while the latter comprises those which are mixed in type. He then argues that Latin did not have three voices, the active, passive and deponent, as it is traditionally stated, but only two, the active and the mixed, the latter comprising examples where the same form may have either an active or passive meaning; thus forms which are traditionally considered to be passives may be used with either an active or passive meaning (*sequor* 'I follow'/*amor* 'I am loved'; *secutus sum* 'I followed'/*amatus sum* 'I was loved').

The main difference between Latin and French lies in the almost complete loss of this synthetic mixed voice in favour of a passive voice. However, the mixed type survives in French in a minor way in those active verbs which nevertheless form their compound tenses with *être*, since this is seen as the passive auxiliary: *mourir, être mort; naître, être né; entrer, être entré; sortir, être sorti*, etc. In addition, the synthetic voice has been 'reconstituted' in French in the form of the *voix réfléchie* (1943:17), since the same form may express the active (*Pierre se déplace*), the middle[4] (e.g. *Pierre s'ennuie*), or the passive (*les choses se disent*).

Stéfanini (1962) follows Guillaume in seeing the pronominal as a synthetic voice which unites active and passive. For him the different uses of the pronominal verbs may be explained by the different proportions of these two elements. Thus while *je me lave* is predominantly active, and *la maison se construit* is almost totally passive, in the case of *je m'irrite* the proportion is equal, a usage which he therefore terms 'middle' (*moyen*).

8.2.3   Generative approaches to voice

Whereas voice was traditionally conceived as a category of the verb, in early generative grammar it was a sentence category. The relationship between active and passive sentences was of great interest to generativists since pairs of active and passive sentences appeared to be semantically equivalent while showing considerable formal differences in terms of word order, agreement, etc. (Roberts 1994). This encouraged the view that they shared the same deep structure – taken to be similar to the active sentence – and that the passive was derived from the active by the 'passive' transformation. However, not all passives are simple paraphrases of an active sentence. This is notably the case when the sentence contains a negative or a quantifier (Riegel, Pellat and Rioul 1994:434–5) as in the following pairs of sentences:

(4)   Un seul étudiant n'a pas vu le film ≠ Le film n'a pas été vu par un seul étudiant

(5)   Tout le monde aime quelqu'un ≠ Quelqu'un est aimé par tout le monde.

Such examples pose problems for these early generative accounts. The question of whether the passive and active sentences are always semantically equivalent will be further discussed in Section **8.4** below.

Dubois (1967:80ff.) offers a rather different view of the passive transformation; for him, the passive transformation includes all cases where the order of the noun phrases is inverted, but their function remains unchanged. If the active is expressed as:

(6)   active = $[P_1]$ = $[(SN_1)$ + $([V] + [SN_2])]$
             (le soleil)   (jaunit les papiers)

then the passive transformation results in the order of the NPs being reversed:

(7) [P′₁] = [(SN₂)   + ([V′] +   [d] + [SN₁])]
              (Les papiers) (sont jaunis) (par) (le soleil).[5]

In practice, Dubois espouses a much broader definition of the passive than traditional or most generative accounts, since he considers that the passive transformation may invert the order of the NPs while retaining their semantic role in four different ways. He lists, alongside traditional passive sentences formed with *être* followed by a past participle:

    I   Les nuages ont caché le soleil → Le soleil est caché par les nuages

three other products of the passive transformation. First, simple inversion of the NPs of symmetrical verbs, which does not require a change of verb form or the addition of an auxiliary:

    II   Le soleil jaunit les papiers → Les papiers jaunissent au soleil.

Second, pronominal constructions:

    III   L'humidité gâte les fruits → Les fruits se gâtent à l'humidité

and third, constructions using *faire* or *laisser*:

    IV   Pierre tomba sous le choc → Le choc fit tomber Pierre.

In short, the morphological basis of the passive is abandoned in favour of a broader conception of a movement rule which preserves the function of the nouns. From a formal viewpoint the outcomes of the passive transformation are much more heterogeneous in character.

    Generative treatments of passive sentences have modified with changing models of generative grammar (see Part I, Section 3.3.2). The specific passive transformation of early generative accounts has been replaced by the more general Principle of Move-Alpha; the subject position of the underlying structure does not contain an argument, which allows the object NP to move into that position. For an example of a generative treatment of passives within a Government-Binding framework, see Baker, Johnson and Roberts (1989).

8.3   The classification of pronominal verbs

In this section we will examine the question of whether it is possible, or indeed desirable, to classify different types of pronominal verbs, or whether it is preferable to offer a unified account of their different usages.

8.3.1   Fourfold schemes

8.3.1.1   Dangeau's tradition

Many grammars, whether traditional (Grevisse 1993), Guillaumean (Stéfanini 1962) or transformational (Kayne 1975, Ruwet 1972), adopt a fourfold classification of pronominal verbs based essentially on that first elaborated in the middle of the eighteenth century by the Abbé de Dangeau (1754:200–9). According to Dangeau, two of the classes retain their active voice: the *Identiques* (Reflexives), 'les verbes qui marquent une action, dont l'objet est la personne même qui fait l'action'; and the *Réciproques*, which have a plural subject. In the case of the third class, the *Neutrisez*, 'les verbes actifs deviennent des neutres; & quoique de leur nature ils soient actifs, ils viennent par l'usage à n'avoir plus la signification active' (e.g. *fâcher quelqu'un* → *cest homme se fâche*); some, however, do not have an active counterpart (e.g. *se repentir, se souvenir*) but are said to be 'neutrisez' because of the way they are used, whilst others have a different meaning from their active counterpart (*plaire*). The fourth class, the *Passivez*, are used in the third person only: 'ce sont des verbes actifs de leur nature, qui par le moyen du pronom *se*, ont une signification [passive][6]' (*ce livre se vend chez un tel*). In this scheme, based on semantic considerations, the reflexive and reciprocal are taken as the core type.

Wilmet (1997) retains the four categories of reflexive, reciprocal, passive and neutral but employs a mixture of semantic, syntactic and pragmatic criteria to distinguish them. The passive is differentiated from the other three on the grounds that it does not permit an agentive subject, the neutral from reflexive/reciprocal on the grounds that in the latter the clitic is an object pronoun but not in the case of the neutral, and the reflexive and reciprocal are separated on pragmatic grounds, according to the context.

Subsequent fourfold schemes have tended to retain the three categories of reflexive, reciprocal and passive pronominals, and to deal with the fourth category in one of two ways. Some have preferred to replace the fourth category with 'inherently' or 'essentially' pronominal verbs, that is, verbs which do not have a non-pronominal counterpart and of which there are about sixty, including a number of slang ones. Others have chosen to re-label the fourth class; for instance, Stéfanini (1962) and Grevisse (1993:1135) refer to them as *subjectifs*.[7] This category is defined in rather vague terms by Grevisse:

> Les verbes pronominaux sont dits subjectifs lorsque le pronom complément n'a pas de fonction grammaticale précise. C'est un élément pour ainsi dire incorporé au verbe. Il indique souvent que l'être désigné par le sujet est en même temps concerné plus ou moins par l'action (Grevisse 1993:1135).

Grevisse lists different examples of this category: certain verbs of motion which include *en* (*s'en aller, s'enfuir*, etc.); those which can only be used in their pronominal form (*s'abstenir, s'arroger*); those where there is a semantic difference between the pronominal and non-pronominal uses (*douter/se douter*, *jouer/se jouer*); and those where there is no discernible difference in meaning (*achopper/s'achopper*).

8.3.1.2   Subcategorizing the pronominaux subjectifs

In view of this heterogeneity, Zribi-Hertz (1987) questions the naturalness of the category of *pronominaux subjectifs* and seeks to introduce finer, more systematic, distinctions into it. This class is, she claims, particularly problematic, partly because it is often defined negatively[8], but especially because of its heterogeneous nature. She therefore distinguishes four subclasses: verbs which are essentially pronominal (*s'évanouir, se repentir*); those which have non-pronominal counterparts with a different meaning (*jouer/se jouer*); those which have a non-pronominal counterpart which is a near synonym (*mourir/ se mourir*); and those verbs where the pronominal usage seems to serve to make a normally transitive verb intransitive[9]:

(8a)   Pierre a cassé/brisé la branche
(8b)   La branche s'est cassée/brisée.

Members of this fourth subclass of the *pronominaux subjectifs* may have a non-pronominal counterpart, but this is not regularly the case:

(9)   La branche a cassé/*La branche a brisé.

These verbs, where the subject of the intransitive usage may regularly feature as the object of the same verb used transitively, are variously termed *verbes symétriques, à renversement*, or *diathétiquement neutres* (8a/8b); the distributional equivalence between the class of subjects of these intransitive verbs and the direct objects of the same verbs used transitively may be expressed as follows:

$$(10) \quad NP_0 \quad V \quad NP_1 \quad \leftarrow \quad NP_1 \qquad (se) \; V$$

	Pierre a cassé la branche			la branche	s'est cassée
					a cassé

The usages form a discrete subclass, in which the reflexive clitic acts as an optional (*casser*) or obligatory (*briser*) marker of 'intransitivity', or rather ergativity.[10] Zribi-Hertz notes that the class of *verbes subjectifs* is often thought to contain irregular or idiosyncratic lexical phenomena; however, she argues that this fourth subclass, which she terms the *formes ergatives réflexives*, is a regular and productive category, and its members may be characterized by three distributional properties:

- They are regularly compatible with 'processive' or 'progressive' expressions or semantic contexts (see **5**.2); for example, *la branche est en train de se casser, le métal se rouille peu à peu.*
- They are regularly compatible with prepositions and complements expressing a cause, such as *sous l'effet de, à cause de, du fait de*; for example, *la branche s'est cassée sous l'effet de l'ouragan, le métal se rouille avec l'humidité.*
- When the subject of these verbs is a person, this has an involuntary or non-agentive interpretation, which is a general characteristic of ergative verbs; for instance, *Alfred s'abêtit.*

In short, they tend to express a change of state undergone involuntarily by the subject. Zribi-Hertz argues for the productivity of this subclass on the grounds that of 5400 transitive verbs in French 1700 (or a third) were accessible to the *construction réflexive ergative.*

A number of criticisms of this account are made by Attal (1988). These include doubts about the productivity of the *construction réflexive ergative* on the grounds that while *la glace fond* is acceptable, **la glace se fond* is impossible, that is, the productivity appears to have its limits. In addition, he wonders how to treat an example like *se prendre* where the sense is not the same as *prendre* used transitively; that is, although *se prendre* appears to be structurally similar to the *construction réflexive ergative,* it has a particular meaning. Third, he questions the association of the class with progressive expressions, citing *le corps s'est écrasé au fond du ravin* as an apparent counter-example. Another difficulty lies in his conviction that the limits between the passive and the *construction réflexive ergative* are often fuzzy.

Labelle (1990) attempts to meet some of these objections by trying to account systematically for why members of what she calls the class of inchoative verbs denoting changes of state appear to behave in different ways. As we have seen, while some may only be used in what appears to be an intransitive construction (*la neige fond*), others may only be used pronominally (*le vase se brise*), while a third group may be used in both constructions (*le vase casse/se casse*). Labelle argues against the claim that both the intransitive and reflexive constructions are **unaccusative** (see note 10); rather she makes a distinction between the reflexive usage which she considers to be unaccusative, and the superficially intransitive construction which she terms **unergative**, on the grounds that there are systematic syntactic and semantic differences between them. Syntactically, these two types of construction differ in that the unaccusative, unlike the unergative, takes the auxiliary *être* and not *avoir*, it can be used impersonally, and its argument may be relativized when it is embedded under *croire* (e.g. *l'homme est arrivé → l'homme que je croyais être arrivé; le couple s'est rencontré hier soir → le couple que tu crois s'être recontré hier soir* (Labelle 1990:304–6)).

As regards the semantic differences between the two constructions, Labelle follows Rothemberg (1974) in arguing that the intransitive construction is used where the entities have inherent characteristics sufficient for bringing about the process (*la neige fond, la branche casse*), while the pronominal is the only one possible for entities having inherent qualities which are insufficient for bringing about the process (*il vit le mouchoir se rougir*). Here the entity that undergoes the change is the locus of the change, but not the motor or the controller of it. This then leaves Labelle to explain those cases where both the reflexive and the superficially intransitive construction are possible. She argues that the intransitive construction focuses on the process itself, whereas the reflexive focuses on the result of the process. For instance, while *gonfler* and *se gonfler* are both possible, only *se gonfler* accepts a complement introduced with *de* meaning 'from':

(11a)   *Le ballon gonfle de gaz carbonique depuis 5 minutes
(11b)   Le ballon se gonfle de gaz carbonique depuis 5 minutes.

8.3.2   Problems with differentiating the categories

One of the major difficulties associated with attempting to classify different types of pronominal verbs is that it is far from easy to delimit the different classes. Melis (1990:18–19) notes that on the whole two strategies are employed to differentiate them. Some (Gougenheim, Sandfeld, and Goosse in his revised edition of Grevisse's *Le Bon Usage*) favour functional criteria: an opposition is made between those usages where the pronoun has a function, and those where it does not, and the latter category is then subdivided into neutral and passive usages. Others consider the productivity of the different usages. Using a generative framework, Ruwet (1972) establishes three different classes of pronominal constructions (excluding intrinsics), which are accounted for in two different ways. In the case of the reflexive/reciprocal usages (where the restrictions on the selection of the subject are the same as those on the subject of a transitive construction) and the 'middles' (where the selection restrictions are the same as those on the object of the transitive construction), Ruwet argues that these should be treated transformationally (with the transitive construction generated in the base and the pronominal derived from it by transformation), since these usages are productive. On the other hand, the class of *neutres* are capricious and show, for example, regional variation; since they display idiosyncratic behaviour in relation to the non-pronominal usages (*la branche a cassé/la branche s'est cassée*; *la branche a brisé/la branche s'est brisée*; *Marie a accouché/*Marie s'est accouchée*[11]), they should be listed in the lexicon and simply subcategorized as [+se] or [+réfléchi]. As we have seen, both Zribi-Hertz and Labelle question whether all members of the class of Neutrals are non-productive, thereby undermining the basis of this classification.

Jones (1996) begins by defining three major types of pronominal verbs in the following terms:

- **Intrinsic**: contrary to many who restrict this class to those which only appear with the reflexive clitic (*s'écrouler*), Jones also includes pronominal verbs whose meaning (e.g. *rendre/se rendre*) or syntactic properties (*pouvoir/ se pouvoir*) differ significantly from the non-pronominal construction in ways which do not conform to a general pattern.
- **Neutral**: intransitive forms of verbs which can also be used transitively (*la porte s'est ouverte/Pierre a ouvert la porte*); these verbs do not allow the participation of an agent, that is, they are neutral with respect to the way the action was brought about.
- **Middle**: while these are superficially similar to the neutral class, the middle interpretation implies the involvement of a human agent (e.g. *ce vin se boit chambré; ce journal se lit en cinq minutes*).[12]

In practice, however, Jones notes that these differences are often difficult to sustain. For instance, in both the intrinsically pronominal verbs and the neutrals the *se* acts as a marker of intransitivity, so the difference between them in terms of their relationship to non-pronominal uses of the same verb is largely a matter of degree. Similarly, *se coucher* and *s'asseoir* are often treated as intrinsically pronominal verbs because they are like *s'agenouiller*, *se prosterner* which have no non-pronominal counterpart; they could equally, however, be treated as reflexive uses. Finally, Jones notes the difficulty, commented on by a large number of linguists, that a construction may, out of context, be ambiguous, say between a middle and a neutral reading. Take the example *la porte du château enchanté s'ouvrait*. Is this 'neutral' ('was opening') or 'middle' ('could be opened')?

In view of the difficulties of using semantic criteria for differentiating the categories, other linguists have looked for syntactic features to differentiate, for instance, neutral and middle uses. Following Burzio, Wehrli (1986) notes that neuter *se*[13] can occur both in adjunct phrases (an optional or secondary element of a construction which may be removed without altering the structural identity of the rest of the construction) and in causative constructions (in French the *faire faire* construction), whereas middle *se* cannot:

(12a)   La fenêtre est tombée sans se casser [neuter]
(12b)   *La partie s'est terminée sans se gagner [middle]

(13a)   Le chef a fait se réunir l'équipe [neuter]
(13b)   *J'ai fait se nettoyer ma veste [middle].

Lyons (1982:180), however, suggests that the data are not so straightforward and that many speakers find usage of the neutral *se* in the causative construction rather odd, perhaps because the agentless reading of the verb sits uncomfortably with the causativity of the *faire* construction.

8.3.3   Alternative classifications

Given the difficulties associated with making clear-cut distinctions between the different types of pronominal usages, two different strategies have been adopted. Some linguists have continued to maintain that there are different types of pronominal verbs, but have generally argued for fewer classes of them. At the simplest level, the number of categories may be reduced to three, as in the *Grand Larousse de la langue française*, by including the reciprocals in the reflexive class along with 'successives' (e.g. *les mois se suivent*) and complex constructions including *laisser* and *faire*. Blanche-Benveniste and others (1984) also put the reflexive and reciprocal usages in one class since in each case *se* can commute both with another pronoun (*il se/me/le regarde*) and with a NP (*il regarde les oiseaux*); their two other categories comprise on the one hand the intrinsic class and those *de sens lexicalisé* since in these usages the *se* neither enters into a paradigm with other pronouns, nor can it be related to another verb construction, and on the other hand the pronominal passives, since while *se* does not enter into a paradigm with other pronouns in this usage, it can be related to other constructions (*ce livre se vend bien/ce livre est bien vendu/on vend bien ce livre*). In an alternative threefold classification, Lyons (1982) suggests that the middle and neutral are not syntactically or semantically distinct constructions and that they belong in the same class.

Many of the problems identified above remain with these threefold schemes. We will therefore now consider unified explanations.

8.3.4   Unified explanations

The arbitrariness of some of the classifications and the fuzziness of the boundaries between the different classes have led a number of linguists to try to provide a unified explanation for all the different usages of pronominal verbs. Different readings of the pronominal constructions are then context-dependent. Following Guillaume who considered 'l'unité de la voix pronominale' to reside in the use of *être* as the auxiliary, Stéfanini (1962) maintains that all pronominal usages are examples of the *voix moyenne* in which there is both an active and passive role for the subject in the process, or 'l'alliance de la tension et de la détension verbale' (thereby closely linking this analysis with the treatment of aspect in the Guillaumean system). The abstract and general nature of this approach is not without its problems. If this middle voice may express (Stéfanini 1962:700) 'un procès fondamentalement actif' and 'la passivité complète', then it is not easy to see wherein lies the unity of the middle voice or what is the specificity of the other two voices. Melis (1990:30–1) argues in addition that the account remains at the level of observed effects rather than providing an explanation for the systematic nature of the different voices.

One of the clearest expositions of a unified explanation is to be found in Burston's (1979) paper which argues against what he terms 'the fortuitous homonymy hypothesis' according to which it is a matter of chance that the semantically distinct functions of the different pronominal constructions are expressed formally in the same way. Instead Burston asserts the formal and semantic invariance of the class of pronominal verbs. For him, *se* represents one formal entity and in all occurrences it is an object pronoun. As in many traditional analyses, he takes the reflexive/reciprocal usages as fundamental and considers how other types can be accommodated to the account offered for them. The semantic unity of the class is said to lie in the fact that in all cases the subject undergoes directly or indirectly the effect of the process which it instigates, and *se* is therefore always meaningfully functional. In the case of the reflexive and reciprocal this may be represented diagrammatically as follows:

He then looks at two other usages where *se* is said to be meaningfully functional: passive *se*, and *se* used to intransitivize normally transitive verbs (*le soleil se couche*). Comparing the pronominal passive with the 'true' passive reveals systematic differences in their usage, such that Burston concludes that the passive pronominal is not a passive either in form or in meaning. He contrasts the examples:

(14)   Une fortune est facilement gaspillée

(15)   Une fortune se gaspille facilement

and argues that in (14) the past participle is predicated **in its entirety** to the subject ('is easily wasted') whereas in (15) the subject contributes positively to the phenomenon it is undergoing ('easily wastes away'). This is, in his view, a non-agentive participation of the subject; the intrinsic qualities of the subject are seen as predisposing it towards, and thus facilitating, the eventual outcome of the verbal process. Diagrammatically this usage may be represented as:

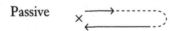

In all three usages so far discussed the subject undergoes directly or indirectly the effects of the process which it instigates; the pronominal passive is different from the other two only in that the subject is less involved in the instigation of the verb.

Turning to the so-called intransitive usages, Burston argues that these constitute another contextual variant and are simply not intransitive. In the case of *s'asseoir* or *se promener* the relationship to reflexive usages is fairly clear, as is the object function of the clitic pronoun. In the case of verbs of emotion such as *s'irriter* or *s'énerver*, the subject both manifests the sentiment and is affected by it. Diagrammatically the intransitive usage is represented:

Intransitive

Two other usages, the pleonastic one (*le pâté a moisi/s'est moisi*) and the intrinsic one, are cases where traditionally the clitic pronoun is said to be devoid of significant grammatical function. Burston argues that the occurrence of *se* is never gratuitous or meaningless, since the corresponding pronominal and non-pronominal usages are never completely interchangeable. For instance, the non-pronominal usage may be much more frequent (as is the case with *fondre*) or not interchangeable with the pronominal one in all contexts (**La glace se fond à 0°*). Two other claims are made about the pleonastic usage: the subject here is viewed as a *siège* rather than a patient with respect to the verbal process; and the primary function of the *se* in this construction is to objectify the subject, so that in fact there is a subtle difference in meaning between the pronominal and non-pronominal usages, that is, to impart a sense of perceived effect on the subject, akin to the intransitive function. Compare the following:

(16)   Elle rit de nous

(17)   Elle se rit de nous.

Burston argues that (16) is spontaneous whereas (17) conveys a mediated response in that the mockery affects the subject as well as the object towards which it is directed.

Finally, Burston turns to the intrinsic class. Here, he argues, the *se* is generally felt to contribute a subtle difference of meaning, but one which is not dissociable from the verb. It is viewed therefore as 'a kind of semantically vague, agglutinated morphological prefix' (Burston 1979:166). Often these verbs are of limited occurrence, but the lack of a non-pronominal counterpart may simply be a historical loss. It is argued that the *se* is the same object pronoun with the same essential meaning and the same range of contextual interpretations as in other uses: some may be reflexive or reciprocal in meaning (e.g. *Les soldats s'égaillèrent dans un bois pour ne pas être vus*), whilst others are pseudo-passives (e.g. *Il [Chalier] s'était épris d'un amour pour la liberté, d'une grande pitié pour les pauvres*). Burston concedes that probably a verb by verb study of these verbs is necessary.

In the case of those absolute intrinsic pronominal verbs that do not have a non-pronominal counterpart it is difficult to see exactly what the subtle difference in meaning is which the *se* contributes. Burston is forced himself to consider it a semantically vague particle, and this somewhat weakens his contention that the *se* of pronominal verbs is never gratuitous or meaningless.[14]

A number of other linguists begin by introducing various classes of pronominal verbs only to move towards a unified explanation for all these uses. For example, Melis (1990) devotes the majority of his book to setting up three major usages of pronominal verbs before offering a unified account.[15] In order to explain the multiplicity of usages, he introduces the notion of three prototypes or 'core' usages around which other usages cluster that do not necessarily share all the features of the prototype. The three salient features for Melis are [subjectif], [objectif], and [datif], although these usages are not always clearly separated, as Figure **8**.1 suggests:

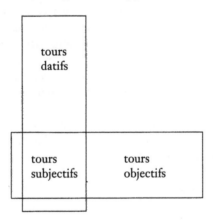

Figure 8.1   The three salient features, or 'core' usages, of pronominal verbs in French (Melis 1990:46)

Considering first the analysis of those constructions in which the reflexive pronoun functions as a dative, prototypical examples comprise four elements: subject, reflexive pronoun, verb, and direct object (e.g. *Il se lave les mains; il se permet une petite distraction*). Melis argues that these cannot be reduced to a simple variant of the non-pronominal construction and that they are not isolated or marginal usages as some grammarians would have us believe. For instance, he notes the plethora of expressions using this construction as words to express the concept of 'eating': *se mettre la ceinture; se caler les joues; s'en coller (s'en mettre) une ventrée; s'emplir (se garnir, se remplir) l'estomac, le jabot, la panse, le sac, le ventre; se taper la cloche, une gnafrée, une goinfrée, une ventrée* (1990:50). In another subtype, the *se* forms part of the verb[16] (*il s'est enfilé cinq verres en une heure*), whilst in a third subtype the reflexive pronoun may be added to a structure which can function equally well without the reflexive pronoun (*Paul s'est mangé cinq gâteaux*). This construction is not only too regular and productive to be relegated to a class of intrinsically pronominal verbs, it also has a specific function:

> Le tour sert en effet à poser le référent du sujet comme le lieu où le procès verbal prend sa source et à rapporter le résultat du procès à ce même référent considéré comme le terme ou la cible. (*ibid.*:51–2)

For instance Melis argues that the sentence:

(18)   On s'y fait de bien curieuses nuits

could be paraphrased as 'On y fait de bien curieuses nuits et les nuits faites là sont à soi'.

In the case of the second cluster of usages, the 'tours subjectifs', the reflexive pronoun is equivalent to the object pronoun and the object seems affected by the verbal process as in:

(19)   Il se soigne

which may be formalized as:

(20)   Il le V   ↔   Il se V
       Il le soigne   ↔   Il se soigne.

The formulation is intended to indicate that the 'reflexive' pronoun may be interpreted as analogous to the direct object pronoun since it has the same relation with the subject and verb and 'occupe, semble-t-il, une place dans le même paradigme syntaxique' (*ibid.*:58). The prototypical usages here are the reflexive and reciprocal ones, those where the subject is animate and has the role of agent. Other usages which group around this core include 'metonymic' usages such as *se coiffer, se peigner* where the action is done to part of the body, and movement verbs such as *se lever*[17], as well as numerous peripheral or more marginal usages. Despite the strong links these constructions have with transitive verbs, Melis denies that they can be simply assimilated to this class of verbs: rather the reflexive pronoun is 'un opérateur de clôture' (*ibid.*:82) which circumscribes the limits of application of the verb to the sphere of the subject.

The third cluster of usages, the 'tours objectifs', are those where the subject corresponds to the object and not to the subject of the transitive construction, so that the subject may not be interpreted as an agent, even if it is animate.

This class is traditionally divided into 'tours médio-passifs'[18], in which an agent is understood (e.g. *Ça ne se dit pas/on ne dit pas ça*; il les V ↔ ils se V), and the non-agentive ones, which include the intransitive usages and the *verbes à renversement* (e.g. *Le sucre se caramélise (sous l'effet de la chaleur)*).

Melis notes, as others do, that often the distinctions between these categories may be neutralized, since there are cases where two or more interpretations of the same construction are possible; for example, *Julie s'habille chez Ferré* could be seen as either a subjective or an objective construction (*ibid.*:117–18). He concludes that the explanation for pronominal constructions cannot lie in the comparison of them with non-pronominal usages, but must rather be sought in the reflexive pronoun which is the single common feature of all usages (*ibid.*:121). Working from the non-agentive objective usages which he had termed 'inaccusatifs' (unaccusatives), he argues that all other pronominal usages may similarly be considered unaccusative since they conform to the tests for this class elaborated by Labelle ((1990), see above). Two other factors support this analysis of pronominal verbs as a kind of intransitive construction: the subject of the pronominal infinitive behaves like that of an infinitive without an object in the causative construction:

(21)   Pierre a fait se raser Paul

and there may be inversion of subject and verb after an interrogative or relative, as with a verb with no object:

(22)   Je me demande comment s'est rasé Paul.

The unaccusative character of pronominal constructions is linked to the fact that the subject has certain features which are characteristic of objects. The reflexive pronoun prevents the realization of an external argument by an independent element.[19] While the pronoun is formally an accusative it does not fill the position of an argument. In short, since the subject is in some way also an object, 'le phénomène fondamental qui caractérise le tour pronominal est l'interprétation du sujet comme l'argument interne du verbe' (Melis 1990:127).[20]

We may note that Melis sees a difference between Modern French and Old French usage of pronominal verbs. He argues that whereas in Old French the clitic was attached to the subject, in Modern French it is bound to the verbal lexeme: 'le tour pronominal est caractérisé par l'association du pronom réflexif et du verbe comme lexème' (*ibid.*:139). This creates a unity which cannot be broken, a fact which helps to account for the rare cases of non-agreement which are attested and for child usages of the type *je me se-lave*. This leads Melis to deny that pronominal uses are a mixture of active and passive ones. Indeed, he questions the very existence of a category of voice. Instead he sees the category of voice as the product of the interaction of the more basic categories of valency and aspect (*ibid.*:140), concerning the selection of the argument and the difference between *accompli* and *inaccompli*. Pronominal usage is different from the active in the selection of an internal argument as subject, and from the passive in the use of non-completed aspect which allows the presentation of the process 'dans son dynamisme' (*ibid.*:143).

The value of such an approach is that it allows a unified account of all pronominal constructions. In arguing for prototypes around which more peripheral usages are grouped, Melis alleviates the difficulty of trying to draw clear demarcation lines between different usages and sees them rather as forming a sort of continuum of usages which are more or less linked.

8.4   The pronominal passive

Much of the discussion of the pronominal passive construction has focused on the extent to which this usage is interchangeable with the 'true' passive and other ways of expressing a passive idea. Are these constructions really equivalents, or is the choice of one rather than another constrained? One of the fullest treatments of this issue is to be found in Zribi-Hertz (1982) who examines a list of properties which are said to differentiate the pronominal and 'true' passive constructions, and questions the validity of these. She notes that some of the differences are presented as absolute whilst others are seen as preferences. Throughout she emphasizes the importance of context in the interpretation of the different constructions.

8.4.1   Constraints on the usage of the pronominal passive

A feature typically said to characterize the pronominal passive usage is that it does not usually permit the explicit expression of an agent in a *par NP* construction, although such a usage was possible up to the seventeenth century. This then forms an important difference both from the 'true' passive usage where the expression of the agent is possible, and from the use of the active construction with *on* which explicitly brings in a human agent, although concealing his or her identity:

(23)   On a volé ma voiture.

While this restriction in general holds true, it is possible to find counter-examples; Melis (1990:93), following Pinchon, cites the following example from Klum:

(24)   L'objet de cette étude est le français de la prose contemporaine tel qu'il s'écrit par des romanciers et écrivains d'autres catégories choisies par nous.

Moreover, when the *ne . . . que* construction is used, the expression of the agent becomes compulsory:

(25)   Ça ne se dit que par des paresseux (Melis 1990:94).

This may explain the use of the agentive phrase in the following example which might be paraphrased as 'ne peut être confiée qu'à un spécialiste agréé':

(26)   Cette réparation doit se faire par un technicien autorisé (*ibid.*).

Ruwet (1972:110) argues that some of the apparent counter-examples can be put aside since in these the *par NP* phrase expresses not the agent, but an instrumental idea, as can be seen from the fact that the sentence may be interrogated by means of the interrogative *comment*; he cites for example:

(27)   L'éducation du cœur se fait par les mères

(28)   Ce genre de liaison se rompt par le départ.

Other examples are much more difficult to explain in this way. Grevisse (1993:488) suggests that some of these may simply be relics of earlier usage:

(29)   Tous ces sacrifices se faisaient par des riches et par des pauvres (Michelet).

While the agent may not be expressed explicitly in the pronominal passive construction, there is typically an implied agent which is generally human and undetermined, although even this is not absolute (Melis 1990:92):

(30)   Un pont, ça se détruit facilement, il y suffit d'un gros orage.

Despite these counter-examples there is a strong tendency not to permit the expression of an agent with the pronominal passive, and this differentiates it on the whole from the 'true' passive. Zribi-Hertz (1982:352–3) notes, however, that impersonal passives with an intransitive VP also do not allow an agent:

(31)   Il a été mangé du poulet par plusieurs clients

(32)   *Il a été mangé ici par plusieurs clients

(33)   *Il a été dormi dans ce lit par plusieurs monarques

(34)   *Il a été parlé à ce colloque par plusieurs Américains.

A second constraint on the pronominal passive is that the construction only permits third person subjects[21] and in general favours inanimate subjects (e.g. *Jerico s'aperçoit*; *des cigares s'allumèrent*) because of the potential ambiguity with an animate subject. For example, the sentence

(35)   Le coupable se jette à l'eau

is more likely to be read as a reflexive ('throws himself') than as a passive ('is thrown'). Certain verbs such as *s'appeler* (Grevisse 1993:1140) appear to be counter-examples to this condition, although some grammarians simply do not consider these to be pronominal passive usages. Pinchon (1986:189) claims that pronominal passives with animate subjects are in fact less rare than is often claimed, citing examples such as:

(36)   Les grands peintres s'imitent difficilement

(37)   Un ami d'enfance se retrouve toujours avec plaisir.

An animate subject may also be employed if it is duplicated by *ça* as a stylistic effect (Gardes-Tamine 1988:II:88):

(38)   Les enfants, ça s'élève à la trique.

A third constraint is that usually the pronominal passive is restricted to the expression of general statements, not specific events located in time, that is, the pronominal passive is said to be non-punctual, habitual, normative or generic, as is the case in (36) and (37) above. This may explain why there is frequently an adverbial expression present:

(39)   Ces livres se vendent bien/facilement

(40)   ?Ces livres se vendent.

Once again this apparent constraint is in fact only a tendency since counter-examples are attested, notably when the verb denotes a 'processus non-concret' as in:

(41)   La question s'est discutée hier matin avec passion dans la salle de conseil

or when the structure is impersonal:

(42)   Il se boit beaucoup de vin ce soir.

This leads Zribi-Hertz to conclude that the only absolute limitation on the use of pronominal passives is the fact that it is limited to transitive verbs.

For Stéfanini (1962:126) 'le tour s'emploie toutes les fois qu'il est parfaite-ment clair'.

8.4.2 Limits on the usage of the 'true' passive

If there are limits on usage of the pronominal passive construction, equally there are restrictions on usage of one of its apparent equivalents, the 'true' passive. Comparison with English has typically led commentators to suggest that the passive is not favoured in French, although there has been some suggestion of a possible increase in frequency of usage of the construction due to the influence of English. Clearly the frequency of the construction depends to some extent on the type of text, with a higher concentration of passives occurring in scientific writing and in the *faits divers* columns of newspapers than in conversation and notably in *français populaire* (Gadet 1992:84). Krassin (1994:71–2) cites the results of a number of surveys which show that the passive is less common in speech than writing. For example, in the Orléans spoken corpus, 96.8% of the constructions are active, 1.6% passive and a mere 0.6% pronominal structures; on the other hand, Karasch's study of the written language found 74% sentences to be active, and 26% passive, of which 14% used the *être* + past participle structure (Krassin 1994:72).

Aside from these preferences according to text type, there are a number of syntactic, lexical and semantic constraints on the use of the passive.

8.4.2.1 Syntactic constraints[22]

The following are the main limitations:

- On the whole, only the direct object of an active sentence may be made the subject of a passive sentence; the exceptions, *obéir*, *désobéir* and *pardonner*, can be explained by the fact that up to the seventeenth century these verbs could be used transitively (e.g. *la plus grande beauté d'une femme était d'obéir son mari* (Malherbe, cited by Grevisse 1993:395)). Intransitive verbs then may not be employed in the passive unless they are used impersonally without an agent, notably in administrative language (*Il sera sursis à toute procédure* (Grevisse 1993:1124)).
- It is generally not possible to passivize a sentence when a possessive adjective modifies the object (*Pierre m'a prêté son livre*); this reflects a general difficulty with beginning with a possessive which is not specified until later in the sentence.
- A passive is virtually impossible if the subject of the corresponding active sentence is *je* or *tu* (**Le verre a été cassé par moi*). However, in a contrastive context or when the *ne . . . que* construction is employed, such usage is acceptable: *Le vase a été cassé par moi, et non par les enfants*; *C'est par toi que cette solution a été trouvée* (Pinchon 1986:212).

- A passive is not possible if in the active construction a preposition has been elided: *Beaucoup de gens ont voté Jaurès/*Jaurès a été voté par beaucoup de gens*.

Equally there are limits on when the agent may be expressed. *On* may not be made the agent of a passive (*Des milliers de lettres ont été reçues (*par on)*), nor can the grammatical subject of an active be made the agent if it has the semantic role of patient in the corresponding active sentence (*??Des coups de sifflet ont été reçus par/de Pierre*).

8.4.2.2   Lexical constraints

There are certain verbs which are never passivizable, such as *pouvoir, comporter*, and others which are only passivizable in certain usages, such as *avoir* which may only be used in the passive when it means 'to dupe, subjugate'. Verbs which cannot be passivized include copular verbs (*devenir, rester*), measure verbs (*coûter, valoir*) and symmetrical verbs (*épouser*); this restriction also applies to certain fixed expressions such as *perdre la mémoire, prendre l'air, prendre la fuite*, etc.

8.4.2.3   Semantic constraints

We have already noted how there is a difference in meaning between active and passive sentences with a negative or quantifier (**8.2.3** above). In addition, if the active is impossible, the passive is also unacceptable (**X,Y,Z a salé la mer / *L'eau de mer a été salée*). In general, verbs used metaphorically cannot be passivized without losing their metaphorical sense (e.g. *perdre ses parents, ramasser une pelle*), although there are some exceptions to this (e.g. *casser la croûte/promettre monts et merveilles*). In certain figurative uses a complement is obligatory (Gardes-Tamine 1988:II:85):

(43)   Mille arrière-pensées sous-tendent la conversation

(44)   La conversation est sous-tendue par mille arrière-pensées

(45)   *La conversation est sous-tendue.

8.4.2.4   Aspectual questions

The most subtle and most debated restrictions on the use of the passive relate to notions of verbal aspect. While stative/imperfective verbs can occur in the passive in a simple tense with an imperfective or continuous value (e.g. *Le bar est fréquenté par les Gitanes*), non-stative/perfective verbs are rare in these usages since the resultative reading is more usual (e.g. *Le blé est vendu* is understood as 'has been sold'/'is sold' rather than as 'is being sold');

in other words whilst the time relations between active and passive sentences seem to correspond in the case of stative/imperfective verbs (*Les Gitanes fréquentent le bar*), this is not the case for non-stative/perfective verbs (*Le blé est vendu ≃ on a vendu le blé*). The process passive therefore tends to be strongly associated with punctual aspect.

Desclés and Guentchéva (1993) suggest that there are two main approaches to this question in the literature. Some accounts argue that the 'true' passive has 'une valeur stative', unlike the pronominal passive which generally expresses a process (examples and their interpretation are taken from Desclés and Guentchéva (1993)):

(46)   Toutes les feuilles du jardin ont été ramassées (par les enfants) [ÉTAT]

(47)   Attention: les feuilles se ramassent avec une pelle [PROCESSUS].

The simple label [ÉTAT] here seems potentially misleading, since the emphasis is on the **resultant** state of the process. Other studies maintain that the periphrastic passive does not always have a stative value and that different aspectual readings are possible depending on the context, the choice of tense, and the lexical qualities of the verb (examples and their interpretation are again taken from Desclés and Guentchéva (1993)):

(48)   Regarde, toutes les feuilles du jardin sont maintenant ramassées [ÉTAT]

(49)   Regarde, on ramasse toutes les feuilles du jardin [PROCESSUS]

(50)   Tiens, tiens, les feuilles sont ramassées par les pompiers [PROCESSUS]

(51)   Les pompiers sont en train de ramasser les feuilles [PROCESSUS].

The importance of context can be seen by the fact that the addition of an adverbial (e.g. *Le blé est vendu en ce moment au-dessous de son cours normal par les Etats-Unis; Les œufs sont vendus à la douzaine*) or an agent (e.g. *Les verres sont remplis par le sommelier*) can force the process reading as opposed to one indicating a resultant state.

8.4.3   Reasons for selecting the 'true' passive

The most obvious reason for selecting the passive rather than the pronominal construction, or the active construction with *on*, is that it is the only construction which allows the complete suppression of the agent since in the others there is an implied human agent. The 'short passive', that is the form which eliminates all mention of the logical subject as in (52), may then be the only appropriate construction if the speaker does not know, or does not wish to reveal, the identity of the logical subject. Jones (1996:109) contrasts examples (52) and (53):

(52)   Ces documents ont été perdus

(53)   On a perdu ces documents.

The second construction may also be avoided because of the possible interpretation of *on* as an equivalent of *nous*, which is a common feature of informal speech. Quantitative studies show that the majority of passives do not have an agent (Riegel, Pellat and Rioul 1994:439; Pinchon 1986:213) and it is perhaps for this reason that Declés and Guentchéva (1993) consider the short passive to be the basic construction. As a result the long passive allows attention to be focused on the identity of the logical subject:

(54)   Les documents ont été perdus par le patron.

In addition there are a number of grammatical and pragmatic factors which may encourage a speaker or writer to favour the passive over the active. Dubois (1967) details a number of these including:

- A preference for the grammatical subject to be animate and the object inanimate. For example, *Un passant a été renversé par une voiture* will tend to be preferred to *Une voiture a renversé un passant*. Research by Granger (cited in Pinchon 1986:210) seems to confirm this is a factor, if not necessarily the principal one, since 79% of the passive sentences of his literary corpus have the order +Animate, –Animate, whereas only 21% use the order –Animate, +Animate.
- A preference to move from a singular noun to a plural one. Dubois cites the example of *Un propriétaire terrien a été enlevé vendredi par six hommes*. Again Granger's statistics seem to suppport this (the order singular – plural occurs in 72% of passive sentences, the reverse in 28% of them). However, the reason offered for this preference by Dubois – that it is somehow more economical – seems highly dubious.
- A preference for moving from the known to the unknown, or for topicalization: *X est un préfet actif.* ***Ses mérites*** *ont été hautement appreciés par le gouvernement.*
- Consideration of the thematic organization and cohesion of the text; passivization may then be favoured when the subject is modified by a clause and is therefore long or complex, as in *la Grande-Bretagne est composée de l'Angleterre, du pays de Galles, de l'Ecosse et de l'Irlande du Nord*. It may be selected in a relative clause in order to avoid a change of subject (*les hommes politiques qui ont été consultés hier par le chef de l'Etat se sont montrés*

très réservés) and indeed the relative clause may be reduced to a simple participial phrase (*l'accord, approuvé par les deux partis, est entré en vigueur*).

- Avoidance of ambiguity, for example where an anaphoric object has more than one possible antecedent; Riegel, Pellat and Rioul (1994:441) cite the following example: *Jean est encore à Strasbourg. (a) Pierre a déjà rejoint son [= de Jean/de Pierre] père/(b) Son [= de Jean] père a déjà été rejoint par Pierre.*
- Morphological preferences: for example, the passive permits the use of *fût/fussent* rather than other forms of the imperfect subjunctive.

For any given sentence such grammatical and pragmatic factors may well interact in complex and interesting ways to make the choice of the passive more or less likely. To cite Pinchon (1986:214):

> Tous ces facteurs interviennent dans le choix du passif, certains se cumulent, d'autres s'annulent, il semble difficile d'établir une hiérarchie entre eux. Ce qui paraît prédominer, d'après les enquêtes de S. Granger, c'est l'organisation thématique de la phrase. Si l'on considère que la phrase comporte un thème qui est donné et un rhème qui apporte un élément nouveau, et que l'ordre thème-rhème est l'ordre habituel, on constate que la phrase passive qui répond à cette organisation correspond à 98,2% des cas.

In short, while in theory the passive, pronominal passive, and active construction with *on*, are all possible ways of expressing the same idea, in practice they are frequently not interchangeable. Not only do they differ from the point of view of the expression of the agent, and the aspectual values they imply[23], other semantic connotations may also be associated with the usage of certain verbs. Wilmet (1997:461) cites the following examples in which the pronominal passive construction is not a simple equivalent of the 'true' passive but implies a notion of possibility (55) or necessity (56):

(55)   Une patate, ça s'écrase (= **peut** être écrasée)

(56)   Une femme, ça se prépare (= **doit** être préparée).

8.4.4   Other alternatives to the passive

A number of other structures are available in French as alternative means of rendering a passive idea, including certain specific pronominal structures.[24] These include the use of *faire, se faire* which retain a factitive or causative nuance (*il a fait payer ses dettes par Jean/il s'est fait piquer par un frelon*); *laisser, se laisser* which implies 'participation tolérative' (*il a laissé payer ses dettes par Jean/il s'est laissé frapper sans réagir* (Riegel, Pellat and Rioul 1994:443)); and *voir, se voir* (*Pierre a vu payer ses dettes par Jean/Le père se voit offrir un livre*). As the last example shows, the *se voir* construction allows the promotion of the indirect object of the active sentence to subject position.

Once again closer examination of these structures shows that they are not always simple equivalents of the passive. For instance, Tasmowski-De Ryck and Van Oevelen (1987) note that while the *se faire* + infinitive structure is often very similar to the passive + NP, at other times it appears to have its own value:

(57)   Il se fit conduire dans la loge de la triomphatrice.

In particular they argue that the subject of the causative pronominal construction is not a patient in the same way as the subject of a passive construction. Contrast their examples:

(58)   Il s'est lâchement fait embusquer à l'arrière

(59)   Il a été lâchement embusqué à l'arrière.

In (58) the cowardice is that of the subject, in (59) that of his ambushers. Once again it is impossible simply to equate this construction with the passive; if the context disallows any participation of the subject, then the choice of the causative pronominal construction becomes meaningless. This is why the subject of this construction is generally animate, although there are exceptions, provided the subject allows some degree of non-passivity:

(60)   Ce verbe peut donc se faire suivre d'un complément de lieu.

In other words, the subject of this construction must always be to some extent responsible for what happens to it.

Suggested Reading

General studies:
  Grevisse (1993), Jones (1996), Pinchon (1986), Stéfanini (1962), Wilmet (1997).
Definitional questions:
  Geniušienė (1987), Lyons (1982), Zribi-Hertz (1982, 1987).
Unified accounts:
  Boons, Guillet and Leclère (1976), Burston (1979), Melis (1990), Wehrli (1986).
Transformational approaches:
  Dubois (1967), Kayne (1975), Ruwet (1972).
Studies of particular constructions:
  Labelle (1990), Tasmowski-De Ryck and Van Oevelen (1987), Zribi-Hertz (1982).
Voice:
  Guillaume (1943), Pottier (1978), Vassant (1980).

Notes

1. These are subject to variation. Bauche (1951:116) considers the use of *avoir* with pronominal verbs to be a feature of *français populaire*, and a number of commentators note that in children's language and popular speech there is a tendency for the 'reflexive' pronoun always to be *se* rather than to agree with the person of the subject (*nous étions allés se baigner*; *tu s'en vas*, etc). Furthermore, Grevisse (1993:1138) notes that there is regional variation as to which verbs may be used pronominally; so, for instance in the South *je me signe* and *je me suis accompagné* are attested.
2. Blanche-Benveniste and others (1984:119) do not consider the passive to be grammaticalized in French, noting that there is not complete 'reversability' between active and passive constructions.
3. Another very different conception of the category of voice can be found in Pottier (1978), who distinguishes six classes of voice: the existential, equative, situative, descriptive, possessive, and subjective.
4. The middle is defined as follows: 'Du sujet au verbe, le rapport, en un tel cas, est celui, contradictoire et équivoque, de l'être agissant qui dans son activité même se sent agi' (Guillaume 1943:18).
5. Where P = *phrase*, V = *verbe*, SN = *syntagme nominal*, and d = *démarcatif*, a function filled here by the preposition *par*.
6. The published text reads 'active', clearly a misprint.
7. Other labels include *moyens*, *intransitifs* and *neutres*.
8. Zribi-Hertz (1987) lists some of the different attempts to define the class, including that of Grevisse who maintains that the function of the reflexive clitic is to indicate 'un intérêt particulier de ce sujet dans l'action' and Gougenheim who asserts that the subject here 'a contribué pour une part si minime soit elle à l'action subie'.
9. Another thread of argument which runs through many of the discussions is the question of whether pronominal verbs should be defined and analysed in relation to their non-pronominal counterparts, or whether it is better to view them independently.
10. A distinction is made between **intransitivity** where the single argument of the verb, the subject, is the agent, and **ergativity**, where the argument is non-agentive. In certain accounts the surface subject of **ergative** or **unaccusative** verbs is treated as an (underlying) direct object (e.g. *The vase breaks/Δ breaks the vase*).
11. Here we have a good example of regional variation since *Marie s'est accouchée* is acceptable in the *français populaire* of Belgium, for example.
12. Jones and Ruwet avoid using the label 'pronominal passive'. Although they do not state their reasons, this may be to avoid any possible confusion with the 'true' passive (see note 18 below on Melis's justification for using the expression 'tours médio-passifs').
13. The more usual term is 'neutral', but some linguists such as Wehrli favour 'neuter' *se* presumably calqued on the French term *neutre*.

14. Wehrli (1986) offers a unified explanation within a generative framework: in all uses *se* is said to absorb an argument, which may be any NP-type argument whether external (an argument of the verb located outside the VP, particularly a subject NP) or internal (an argument of the verb located within the VP, e.g. an object NP). In the case of inherent *se* and ergative *se*, the absorption is lexicalized:

	internal argument	external argument
lexicalized	inherent *se*	ergative *se*
non-lexicalized	reflexive/reciprocal	middle *se*

15. See also Boons, Guillet and Leclère (1976). Melis (1985) does not yet offer a unified account.
16. This is often a verb of movement.
17. Where the subject is inanimate (*Le vent se lève*), it is difficult to see this as an agent or put it on a par with the subject of a transitive verb. Melis (1990:77–8) argues that this is a case of neutralization between the subjective and objective usages, and increased independence from the related transitive construction.
18. Melis prefers to avoid the term 'passifs' to prevent these verbs being simply assimilated to passives.
19. This is similar to Wehrli's approach (1986), see note 14 above; the difference is that for Melis the argument is always an external argument (Melis 1990:125).
20. See Riegel, Pellat and Rioul (1994:255) who argue that the semantic common denominator lies in the fact that 'le processus verbal implique que les rôles sémantiques du sujet et du complément pronominal soient tenus par le même référent ou bien que l'un soit absorbé par l'autre avec différents effets interprétatifs'.
21. Exceptions to this restriction occur only in certain specialized contexts such as advertising. Zribi-Hertz (1982) cites the example of an advertising slogan for a suitcase which reads: 'Je me transporte facile, je vous suis indispensable'.
22. This section uses material from Wilmet (1997), Judge and Healey (1983), Grevisse (1993) and Jones (1996). See also Blanche-Benveniste and others (1984:126–7) and Pinchon (1986:203–14). For an excellent recent account of the passive in French, see Gaatone (1998).
23. Sentences whose subject is *on* may have both aspectual values.
24. Certain verbs and expressions (e.g. *subir, faire l'objet de, être la cible de, être la proie de, être la victime de*) may also establish the same links between the subject and the complement as the passive. This is also true of adjectives in *-ible/-able* and certain nouns.

9

Declarative word order:
French as an SVO language

9.1 Introduction

French is traditionally described as a subject-verb-complement (SVC) or an SVO language, since this is considered to be the unmarked order of constituents in declaratives such as:

(1) Mon frère a vu la Tour Eiffel.

However, as was noted in Part I, not all non-SVO structures are unacceptable: while certain non-SVO structures such as OVS, $SO_{N(oun)}V$ and VSO are impossible in Modern French declaratives, others are entirely grammatical, such as $SO_{P(ronoun)}V$, CVS, VOS, and $CS(C_P)V$ (see Part I, Section 2.3.2). A number of questions arise from this situation, such as:

- How SVO has emerged as the standard word order in Modern French declaratives
- To what extent it can be said that SVO is indeed the unmarked word order
- How the exceptions to SVO can be analysed (how have they arisen, are they subject to syntactic, pragmatic, semantic constraints?)
- To what extent these exceptions are fixed, or constitute instances of pragmatic or stylistic flexibility
- To what extent sociolinguistic or stylistic factors play a role
- Whether non-SVO declaratives have implications for theories of syntactic evolution in French.

9.2   Historical Analyses

9.2.1   The data[1]

In Classical Latin, the role of sentence constituents as subjects, objects etc. is indicated, not by their position in the phrase, but by a case system, whereby lexical items carry a suffix indicating whether they are nominative (usually the subject), accusative (usually direct object and used after some prepositions), genitive (usually indicating possession), dative (indirect object), or ablative (used after many prepositions); for example, *frater* (nominative), *fratrem* (accusative), *fratris* (genitive), *fratri* (dative), *fratre* (ablative). The most frequently attested word order is SOV, although there is much variation; since the nouns are case marked, a fixed word order is not necessary to distinguish the different functions such as subject, object etc., and orders other than SOV can be used to emphasize certain elements if desired. Moreover, in later texts, SOV is less dominant and there is increased use of SVO.

In Vulgar Latin, alongside the phonetic erosion of many case endings which leads to a reduction to the two-case system found in Old French (e.g. the loss of final *-m*, the loss of the distinction between *portă*, *portam* and *portā*, or *murŭm* and *murō*; see Price 1971:94), and the rise in the use of prepositions to mark functions such as the dative (e.g. *ad*) or genitive (e.g. *de*), word order becomes increasingly fixed. By the end of the Old French period, the most dominant pattern for declaratives is SVO.[2] A number of other patterns are also possible in Old French, the most frequent of which is OVS, an order which is no longer possible in Modern French (see Part I, Section 2.3.2). In one of the more detailed corpus-based analyses of word order in Old French declaratives, which takes account both of the broad patterns (e.g. CVS, SVC etc.) and of the individual representations of constituents within these (e.g. whether C represents O_N or O_P, whether S represents S_N or S_P etc.), Marchello-Nizia distinguishes the various attested word orders in terms of their frequency (1995:57–8):

- Patterns which are not attested: these are of the broad type VOS and include VO_NS_P and CVO_NS_P. VO_NS_N, a pattern which is perfectly possible in Modern French (see Part I, example (18)), is extremely rare in Old French.
- Patterns which are rare: SOV ($S_{N/P}O_NV$), VSO ($VS_{N/P}O_N$), CVOS (CVO_NS_N), OSV ($O_NS_{N/P}V$); some sub-types of these ($S_{N/P}O_NV$, $O_NS_{N/P}V$) have disappeared.
- Patterns which are relatively frequent: OV(S) (O_NVS_N, O_NVS_P) and VO (VO_N). The first of these types has disappeared in declaratives and the second is highly constrained in Modern French where expression of the subject is now compulsory.
- Patterns which are frequent: SVO ($S_{N/P}VO_N$) and CVO (CVO_N, $CVS_{N/P}O_N$).

We note the strong preference for a verb-second construction (V2), most of the frequently-attested patterns conforming to this model. Thus Old French is often referred to as a V2 language.[3] The order CVS embraces examples where a complement such as an adverb or an adjectival epithet is placed at the head of the sentence, for example linking the phrase anaphorically to the previous one:

(2)   Ad une voix crient la gent menude (*Alexis*: Ayres-Bennett 1996,47)
       With one voice the common people cry (Ayres-Bennett's translation).

Note that where this occurs, and where both an object and subject follow the verb, it is impossible for a pronominal subject to follow the object and very rare for a nominal subject to do so; the subject usually precedes the object. CVS also embraces examples where the object precedes the verb and the subject follows it, that is, an order which is impossible in Modern French:

(3)   Dis blanches mules fist amener Marsilies (*Roland*: Price 1971,259)
       Marsilies sent for ten white mules (Price's translation).

OVS is possible in Old French because the two-case system distinguishes, at least in theory (though see below), between the nominative (often the subject or a vocative) and the oblique (fulfilling a variety of functions including direct or indirect object). French has evolved from this situation to one where SVC is the dominant word order in declaratives, and where certain other orders are no longer possible; these include orders involving a combination of S and the sequence O_NV (e.g. O_NVS_N, O_NVS_P, S_NO_NV, S_PO_NV) and most of those where the postposed nominal object is separated from the verb, as well as those where the subject is not expressed in Old French but where it is now compulsory. In the next section, we shall examine a number of analyses of this evolution.[4]

9.2.2   Traditional analyses

The traditional explanation, notably in nineteenth-century accounts, is essentially phonetic. Such a theory argues that it is the phonetic erosion of suffixed endings which constitutes the primary explanation for the shift to a fixed word order; in the case of French, only the oblique case remains at the end of the Old French period, probably because it fulfils a much wider range of functions than the nominative and because relations between the singular and plural forms are constant.[5] The logic is that since case endings are no longer capable of marking the distinction between subject and object, a fixed word order becomes the means of marking case function.

There is, however, a danger of overestimating the importance of the loss of the case system, and many arguments have been advanced to counter the suggestion that it is the 'cause' of syntactic change. With reference specifically to French, these include the advanced state of decline of the case system in Old French, the fact that the nominative/oblique distinction was not generally marked for feminine nouns, the existence of many indeclinables, the many other possible methods of disambiguating subjects and objects in Old French, the levels of dialectal variation, and the fact that SVO is already much more common in Old French than OVS.[6] Moreover, evidence from other languages suggests that case systems and SVO ordering can co-exist (e.g. Slavonic languages, Finnish) and that the absence of case marking does not necessarily lead to a fixed word order (e.g. Chinese); furthermore, in Indo-European, the loss of the case system follows the fixing of SVO order.[7]

9.2.3   Typological approaches

More recently, other explanations have been sought for developments in word order, whereby the phonetic erosion involved in the loss of the case markers is seen not as the cause of syntactic change, but rather as concomitant with it.

Typological analyses (see Part I, Section 3.4.1)[8] have tended to focus on the emergence of the subject in pre-verbal position, at the head of the phrase; the argument is that in a V2 language such as Old French, it is likely that in many instances, the subject will appear in the pre-verbal slot, as the 'topicalized' element in the sentence.[9] Within a typological framework, the emergence of the subject in pre-verbal position can be seen as part of a major syntactic drift from an SOV language to an SVO language.

In terms of Greenberg's language universals (which establish relationships between certain grammatical features and the ordering of the three elements S, V and O across a wide range of languages), Latin exhibits a number of linguistic features usually found in SOV languages.[10] Similarly Modern French, an SVO language, exhibits many of the features typical of this type. Harris (1978:6) summarizes the major features in the following table:

Table 9.1   Harris's summary table of OV and VO features (Harris 1978:6)

OV	VO
[i] direct object precedes main verb	main verb precedes direct object
[ii] noun precedes suffixes and/or postpositions	prepositions precede noun
[iii] main verb precedes auxiliaries (auxiliaries are not numerous)	auxiliaries precede main verb (auxiliaries are numerous)
[iv] standard precedes comparative	comparative precedes standard
[v] adjectives, relative clauses, } precede dependent genitives } noun	adjectives, relative clauses, } follow dependent genitives } noun

Note the parallelism between OV languages and the use of a case system (i.e. suffixes) on the one hand, and VO languages and the use of prepositions on the other. In the framework of a typological shift, the syntax of Old French represents an intermediate stage in the drift from SOV to SVO, a stage of TVX (topic-verb-other constituents): that is, a V2 stage where T is realised in a number of different ways (e.g. subject, object, adverb). Since, however, the topic slot is frequently occupied by the subject of the sentence, SVC becomes grammaticalized as the normal or unmarked word order, ousting the other main Old French order, OVS, which becomes increasingly problematic due to the breakdown of the two-case system. Modern French examples of inversion after an initial adverb such as *ainsi, à peine* are thus viewed from a typological perspective as a remnant of this TVX stage (see Ayres-Bennett 1996:56):

(4)   Ainsi vivaient-ils en paix.

As a remnant of an older usage, this kind of inversion is associated strongly with the more formal varieties of the written medium and occurs with a fixed set of adverbs.

Further evidence of the typological shift towards an SVO language is afforded by interrogative structures. Harris (1978:31) contends that so strong is the desire to maintain the unmarked Subject-Verb word order for all constructions, that there is a growing tendency in Modern French not to invert the subject and verb even in interrogative structures where inversion has a grammatical function. In the case of 'total interrogation' or yes/no questions the retention of the unmarked word order may be achieved in one of three ways. First, intonation alone is usually sufficient to mark the interrogation without the need to employ a discrete syntactic structure. Second, *est-ce que*, itself a fixed inverted structure, may be used as a sentence-initial interrogative particle. Third, the particle [ti] – originating from structures such as *dort-il, est-il?* – may be used, as in the example, *On y va-t'y quand même?* The status and currency of this [ti] is, however, a matter of dispute (Désirat and Hordé 1988:152–3).[11] There are equally a number of ways in which the SVO word order may be maintained for partial interrogation. Take the case of *Où va-t-il?*:

(5)   (a)   Où est-ce qu'il va?
      (b)   Où il va?
      (c)   Il va où?
      (d)   Où qu'il va?
      (e)   Où c'est qu'il va?
      (f)   Où que c'est qu'il va?

However, while it is clear that there is a tendency to avoid inversion in Modern French interrogatives, at least in speech, the choice by speakers or writers of one interrogative structure over another is affected by a number of factors, suggesting that we are not dealing with a simple case of change. These factors may be grammatical (e.g. inversion is extremely rare with the first person singular pronoun, and is also less likely when the subject is a noun than when it is a pronoun); sociolinguistic (related to the age or sex of the speaker, or concerned with the register or medium used); pragmatic or discoursal (see Coveney 1996).[12]

There has been considerable criticism of typological models. Some of the arguments in relation specifically to the evolution of French have already been mentioned: these include the fact that Latin is already a language in transition (it does not map neatly onto the features of an SOV language), the fact that the case system is already in an advanced state of decline in Old French, and the sheer complexity of the factors involved in analysing variation and change (sociolinguistic, pragmatic etc.). More generally, there are exceptions to the broad typological patterns (see the comments above on case system and word order) and there are also questions which arise, such as why, if a language is typologically 'perfect', it continues to undergo language change. There is a temptation to attempt to explain all linguistic change in terms of the model: a change which fits the model demonstrates consistency, one which does not has to be explained by invoking pragmatic or sociolinguistic forces, or by arguing that the timing of the change is particularly early or late. Indeed, as McMahon points out (1994:148), the implied inevitability of typological change is undermined by the fact that different languages move at radically different paces (see McMahon 1994:146–60 for detailed discussion).

9.2.4   Marchello-Nizia (1995): the role of the object

A further important factor in the establishment of SVC concerns the fixing of the object position in the phrase. This is highlighted and explored in detail by Marchello-Nizia (1995:67–8), who draws on a variety of theoretical approaches, notably the typological framework, Skårup's (1975) division of the phrase into preverbal and postverbal zones, the *Approche pronominale* and Culioli's (1991, 1999) *théorie de l'énonciation* (see Part I, Sections 3.4.1, 3.6.2 and 3.4.2). She argues that a much more accurate picture of the exact timing and motivation for the emergence of SVO can be gained from an examination of developments in the position of the object through the Old French period, and specifically in the context of the shift from word stress to group stress, the development of relationships between the verb and clitic pronouns (both subject and object), and the rise of the medium of prose.

Marchello-Nizia argues that in the twelfth century, both SVO and OVS are possible and are unmarked word orders, but that SVO is dominant in constructions where the subject is expressed, and therefore where each of the elements S, V and O is present. These constructions are in fact in the minority (e.g. only 26% of declaratives in the *Chanson de Roland*), since the subject is frequently not expressed at all (74% of declaratives in the *Roland*). Nominal objects are placed in most cases after the verb (66% of the *Roland*), but are nonetheless found relatively frequently in verse texts before the verb (34% of examples in the *Roland*).

By the thirteenth century, and with the increasing development of the medium of prose, expression of the subject has increased (e.g. to 49% for the prose text *La Quête du Saint-Graal*), but is still far from mandatory. The subject is still frequently found after the verb but, as in the earlier verse texts, where the subject is expressed, the most frequent word order is SVO_N (74%). Moreover, first position in the phrase is more frequently occupied by the subject than previously (36%), the increase being largely due to an increased expression of the subject. Much more striking, argues Marchello-Nizia, is the fact that certain elements are rarely, if ever, used in initial position, notably the verb and, crucially, direct objects: whereas in the twelfth-century *Chanson de Roland* (verse), the object appears in 28% of clauses in initial position, this figure is reduced to 3% in the thirteenth-century *Quête* (prose). For Marchello-Nizia, this fixing of the object in postverbal position represents 'la vraie caractéristique de la prose française naissante' (1995:83).

From the thirteenth century onwards, as the medium of prose develops, examples of $O_N V$ become cases of marked word order, either archaisms in fixed phrases or examples where the subject or object is emphasized by its unusual position. Through Middle French (approximately 1300–1500), the order $O_N VS$ undergoes a process of complete degrammaticalization; increasingly rare, it is grammatically unacceptable by the time the Modern French period begins (seventeenth century). The position of pronominal objects is also fixed by the end of the twelfth century. The heart of Marchello-Nizia's argument is therefore that the position of both nominal and pronominal objects is fixed very early in the history of the French language (by the end of the twelfth century); orders which do not fit these patterns becoming increasingly rare and/or marked. The fixing of the subject position is, she argues, a much slower process, with postposition and pre-position possible for a long period, along with the non-expression of the subject. Moreover, the fixing of VO as the unmarked order is closely linked to the increasing strength of the bond between the different elements of the verbal group, that is, the subject and object pronouns and the verb. Crucially, it is also linked to the gradual shift from word stress to group stress; in this context, the Old French data demonstrate a transitional stage where it is still possible to use the direct object in initial marked position.[13]

9.2.5   Examples

The emergence of SVO through Old French can be seen clearly in the texts of the period. The extracts analysed in Ayres-Bennett (1996) show the evolution in Old French from the earlier patterns in verse where greater varieties of word order are found (e.g. *Alexis* [mid-eleventh-century verse], *Roland* [early-twelfth-century verse]), through increasing use of SVO (e.g. the Old French Bible [early-thirteenth-century prose], the *Lettre d'Hippocrate* [mid-thirteenth-century prose]), to texts where SVO dominates (e.g. *Lettre de Jean Sarassin à Nicolas Arrode* [mid-thirteenth-century prose]).

Through Middle French and the sixteenth century, SVO continues to increase, although inversion is still possible (if not compulsory) after initial adverbs, notably *or* (see Chartier, Calvin, and Thevet in Ayres-Bennett 1996). By the beginning of the Modern French period, SVO is clearly the preferred and unmarked word order in declaratives. The seventeenth-century preference for *netteté* means that SVO, which is emerging as the dominant word order, becomes associated by grammarians with clear, unambiguous sentence structure; the selection of texts in Ayres-Bennett (1996) from the seventeenth through to the twentieth century shows SVO firmly established as the unmarked order.

9.3   Modern French as an SVO language

9.3.1   The data: statistics and corpora

How accurate is it to speak of SVO as the unmarked word order in Modern French declaratives? If we label constituents on a strictly grammatical basis, classifying pronominal subjects as S rather than as part of the verb V (an option which might be logical if we consider the subject pronouns to behave like prefixed markers of person; see **9.3.3.2**), then the evidence suggests that SVO is the unmarked word order in Modern French declaratives, in the sense that it is statistically by far the most frequently attested order. In Moreau's survey (1987), statistics based on a corpus of oral French reveal that in declaratives where each of the elements S, V and O is present, the order SVO is found in 70% of cases.[14] This statistic is, however, rather misleading, since prototypical $S_N VO$ sentences such as example (1) above are in fact relatively rare in spoken French. Indeed, Posner goes so far as to say that 'in the spoken idiom the so-called unmarked order hardly ever occurs' (1997:354). A number of factors come into play. Lexical noun phrases (henceforth NPs – see Part I, Section 2.3) rarely appear in subject position, which is much more likely to be filled by a clitic pronoun, as in:

(6)   Il a vu la Tour Eiffel.

Jeanjean's data (1981) from a corpus of oral French confirm this, revealing that patterns for lexical and clitic subjects and objects are quite different, the subject tending in the vast majority of cases (92%) to be clitic rather than lexical, and most of the lexical subjects appearing alongside clitics (i.e. in detached constructions – see **9.3.3**), for example:

(7)   Il a vu la Tour Eiffel mon frère.

Patterns for objects are completely different: there are more lexical objects (as opposed to clitics), there are no apparent differences in behaviour for clitics and lexical objects, and very few lexical objects are coupled with clitic pronouns (e.g. in detached structures). In other words, there appears to be a special relationship between the grammatical function of subject and clitic pronouns: most subjects are clitics, and lexical subjects are usually coupled with a clitic. Lambrecht (1987) too argues that SVO is not the dominant word order in actual discourse, citing statistics from a corpus of spoken French which put the percentage of lexical subjects at 3% and the percentage of clitics at 97% of the total subjects. He argues that the preferred structure is 'clitic + verb' (with an optional complement before the clitic and optional material after it). Like Jeanjean (1981), he maintains that most subjects are pre-verbal clitics, and that most lexical nouns occur in positions other than that of pre-verbal subject. Indeed, in the rare cases where the subject S is a lexical NP, the subject is often pragmatically backgrounded in the discourse.[15]

There are, moreover, a number of exceptions to SVO patterning. In the discussion which follows we shall bear in mind various factors such as the extent to which the exception is fixed or optional, how common it is, and whether sociolinguistic, stylistic or pragmatic factors come into play. We shall then assess the implications of all of these factors for the question of whether French is an SVO language.

9.3.2   A fixed exception

One of the most obvious exceptions to SVO is the order of direct and indirect object pronouns, for instance *je te vois*, *il le lui donne*, that is, SO$_p$V. Note that this exception is fixed (no other order is grammatically acceptable in French), and is entirely independent of stylistic or sociolinguistic factors. The explanation which is generally accepted is that found in Harris (1978:21–3). Many Latin pronouns yielded two different pronouns in Old French, a stressed and unstressed form: *me > moi/me*, *te > toi/te*, *illos > eux/les*. The unstressed form occurs immediately beside the verb in the sentence, with the verb bearing the main stress of the unit, and the unstressed pronoun tightly bound to the verb. The preverbal positioning of the unstressed pronoun then conforms to a pattern observed across Romance languages, whereby 'the closer the union between the verb and the preceding elements, the greater the tendency for the pronoun object to be placed before the verb'

(Harris (1978:22), quoting Ramsden (1963:24)). We shall see below that the fixed tight bond between the pronoun (which is marked for case) and the verb is of central importance in the development of left- and right-detached structures in Modern French.

9.3.3   Detachment

9.3.3.1   The data

'Detachment' or 'dislocation' is a very different type of exception to SVO, one which poses interesting questions for theories of word order evolution. Although frequently cited as a modern development, examples may be found in Old French texts, but it is difficult to estimate from the texts how widely the structure is used in the spoken language.[16] In broad terms, detachment occurs when an element in the clause is detached and placed either at the beginning or the end, while being represented within the clause by the corresponding pronominal form. There are also cases where no pronoun is present; we shall return to these in **9.3.6**. Detachment may be to the left (left detachment or LD – see (8)) or to the right (RD – see (9)):

(8)   Les femmes je leur fais pas confiance (Blasco 1997:14)

(9)   Je la supporte pas la chaleur.

It may be simple (8, 9) or multiple (where more than one element is detached (10)):

(10)   Je la supporte pas moi la chaleur.

The most likely grammatical elements to participate in detachment are lexical nouns and stressed personal pronouns (notably *moi* as in (11)). Although encountered less frequently, other elements such as adjectives may be detached (12):

(11)   Moi j'aime pas ça

(12)   Heureuse elle l'est certainement.

Detached structures such as these can thus generate a variety of non-SVO orders, including some where the object appears in initial position, for example:

(13)   Les huîtres je les adore.

Within LD, two major sub-types exist. The more frequent sub-type has no overt indication of the function of the detached noun, but the appropriate clitic pronoun is present within the clause (14):

(14)   Les enfants je leur donne trop de bonbons.

In other words, the fact that the detached noun is an indirect object is not marked by the presence of a preposition (e.g. *aux enfants*). This construction has a characteristic intonation, with a rise throughout the detached element and a falling intonation in the verbal construction, and there is often a pause between the detached element and the rest of the phrase.

The second sub-type of LD occurs where the noun is case-marked by a preposition (15), the clitic pronoun marking case being no longer required:

(15)   Aux enfants je donne trop de bonbons.

This type of detachment is much rarer and is usually found in more formal varieties, probably for the reason that the presence of the preposition at the head of the sentence implies a level of pre-planning unlikely in spontaneous speech. In the case of RD, both the clitic pronoun and the preposition are usually present (16), and therefore normally only nouns which have a corresponding clitic pronoun can be right-detached:

(16)   Je leur donne trop de bonbons aux enfants.

There are, however, rare examples where the preposition does not appear:

(17)   Ça nous est égal nous (Ashby 1988:208).

Due to the double function marking, Blasco (1997) applies the label 'double marquage' to examples like (16), and it is for this reason that an RD element is considered to be more tightly bound in syntactic terms than an LD element to the main clause. Note, however, that in spoken French, the medium in which detachment is particularly frequent, it is not always easy to delimit the syntactic units and to draw clear lines between different types of detachment. Consider for example (18):

(18)   Elle me dit moi j'en ai marre moi je vais dire à maman et tout (Blanche-Benveniste 1988:12).

It is well established that detachment, both LD and RD, is generally found not with referents which are brand new, but rather with elements where there is a semantic link with the preceding discourse. In practice, this means that the referent may already be given in the discourse, either in the immediate sentence or in the broader discourse, or, if it is new, it is normally inferrable from the context (and thus in this sense not brand new).[17] For this reason, the referent is almost always definite. Again, the evidence suggests that RD referents are more closely tied to the discourse than LD referents. For example, since the speaker has to retain the information carried in the clitic element and the preposition in his/her mind until the referent is named, the RD element must appear immediately after the clause containing the clitic (Lambrecht 1987:234); an LD element can be further removed from the corresponding clitic. Similarly, far fewer RD elements concern new referents; most are actually present in the discourse rather than merely inferrable.

9.3.3.2   Problematic issues

Given that detachment can produce a variety of non-SVO structures, the question arises as to whether the choice is essentially pragmatically motivated, or whether one or more of the detached structures might be becoming the normal unmarked word order of contemporary French. In other words, we might ask whether, in the light of the frequency of detached structures, we are witnessing a change of word order in contemporary French. As far as LD is concerned, Harris argues (1978, 1985) that the fixing of SVO as the standard word order for declaratives left the way open for a pragmatically marked order to emerge, with the topic at the head of the phrase. According to this theory, the placing of non-subject nouns in topic position (through the use of detachment) then extended to subject NPs. Harris (1978:119) argues, however, that certain types of RD, which were originally pragmatically motivated (taking the form of a 'tail' serving as an afterthought), are indeed in the process of grammaticalization (e.g. *il dort lui*). In Modern French, the clitic subject pronoun is now obligatory and is the key marker of person in the verb; Harris (1978:119) argues that the pronoun can therefore be analysed as part of the verb, such that *il dort lui* represents a VS structure, with the detached pronoun *lui* joined prosodically and intonationally with the rest of the clause (see also Ashby 1982:32). Such an analysis, according to Harris, would fit Vennemann's model of cyclical change, with French now moving towards a V-initial structure.

This analysis of the subject pronouns is controversial; it suggests that they are essentially affixes, thereby raising problematic definitional questions about the distinction between clitics and affixes (see the discussion in Spencer and Zwicky 1998:19–20). Moreover, the argument rests on the validity of the typological approach which, as we have seen, has been widely challenged. The discussion of detachment in the following sections will explore the implications of Harris's claim.

9.3.3.3   Discourse function[18]

If detachment is essentially a pragmatic device, we would expect to find that its use clearly produces certain pragmatic effects. On the other hand, if the type *il dort lui* is becoming grammaticalized, we would expect to find substantial numbers of examples of this structure where the detached word order appears to be unmarked, and where no obvious pragmatic effects are found. Studies which deal with the pragmatic function of left detachment (e.g. Barnes 1985, Ashby 1988, Lambrecht 1981, 1994:181–4) are generally agreed that it is primarily a device which topicalizes and foregrounds the referent. Topicalization may take the form of 'topic-shifting' and the marking of contrast may also be considered a type of topic shift, for instance:

(19)   Les grandes personnes peuvent parler tant qu'elles voudront; les enfants, on les fait taire.

The following table from Ashby (1988:217) gives the distribution of functions of LD in a corpus of contemporary spoken French. Note that, between them, the pragmatic functions of topic-shift and contrast (i.e. those bound up with topicalization) constitute 77% of LDs in Ashby's corpus:

Table 9.2   Observed and relative frequencies of left-dislocated pronouns and nouns, by pragmatic function (Ashby 1988:217)

Pragmatic function	Pronouns		Nouns	
	No	%	No	%
Contrast	112	24%	79	21%
Topic shift	249	53%	279	73%
Turn taking	25	5%	0	–
Weak	84	18%	23	6%
Total	470		381	

As far as RD is concerned, Ashby's data (1988) suggest a wider range of functions than LD, although RD can also mark both topic-shift and contrast. Pragmatic functions of RD include clarification of the referent (where the referent is stated in the RD), epithet usage (where the referent is given not as the original noun or person but in the form of an epithet) and use as a filler or for turn-closing in conversation:

Table 9.3   Observed and relative frequencies of right-dislocated pronouns and nouns, by pragmatic function (Ashby 1988:217)

Pragmatic function	Pronouns		Nouns	
	No	%	No	%
Contrast	31	18	5	6
Topic shift	7	4	4	5
Filler	23	13	0	–
Clarification	8	5	23	29
Epithet	0	–	3	4
Turn closing	48	28	30	38
Weak	56	32	14	18
Total[a]	173		79	

[a] Some tokens displayed two pragmatic functions (e.g. contrast and turn closing). Such tokens were coded twice; consequently the totals given in Tables **9.2** and **9.3** are greater than the actual number of right dislocations occurring in the corpus.

Thus far, it would seem that detached structures do indeed have clear pragmatic functions, many of which concern topicalization.[19]

This said, in support of the argument that detachment is becoming grammaticalized, a substantial number (albeit a minority) of both the RD and LD examples do not appear to have a clear pragmatic function: they have a 'weak' pragmatic function to use Ashby's terminology. This is especially true for the category of right-detached pronouns, that is, precisely Harris's V-initial structure (e.g. *il mange lui*). The statistics in Ashby's tables (Tables **9.2** and **9.3** above) confirm this, weak pragmatic function accounting for 32% of RD pronouns and 18% of RD nouns, as opposed to 18% of LD pronouns and 6% of nouns. Work on the acoustic profile of RDs (Ashby 1994) also suggests that in Modern French they certainly do not display the properties of afterthoughts (this would be an argument for considering them to be pragmatically motivated) since in most cases, there is no pause between the main clause and the RD. However, it is equally not possible to argue that they are simply the equivalent of unmarked normal subjects as Harris suggests (i.e. that RD has become grammaticalized), since in a sizable minority, there is indeed a pause before the RD.

Finally, most pragmatically weak examples of LD are cases of the construction 'NP + *c'est*', and indeed Barnes argues that this structure has effectively undergone a process of grammaticalization in many cases:

> (after being offered orange juice)
> (20)   Oui un jus d'orange c'est très bien oui (Barnes 1985:53).

Barnes's evidence (1985:49) suggests that LD is virtually obligatory with lexical subjects of *être* where *c'est* is an appropriate anaphor; the neutrality and therefore flexibility of *c'est* allows it to cover a variety of antecedents.

9.3.3.4   Stylistic factors

In addition to the fact that detached structures are usually pragmatically marked, they are also in many respects stylistically marked. In a broad survey of twentieth-century grammars, Gadet (1991) finds that detachment is widely viewed as a feature of oral French, and as such is frequently associated with spontaneous, informal varieties and with expressive usage. Carroll's study (1982b) based on a corpus of Canadian French refines this notion, suggesting that the types of detached structures are similar across different levels of formality, the difference being that the more informal varieties are most likely to detach more elements (see also Ossipov (1997)). Perhaps the most satisfactory explanation of detachment as an oral phenomenon lies less in its connections with orality per se and more in the connection between the oral medium and unplanned discourse; detachment is a feature of oral unplanned discourse.[20]

Moreover, in terms of its classification in grammars, there is a lack of coherent terminology, with some grammarians including detachment under widely differing headings (*clivage, dislocation, topicalisation, focalisation, emphase, ordre des mots* etc.), others using rhetorical terms, non-technical terms or inventing new terms. There is also evidence that detachment is stigmatized in the language learning process; according to Dannequin (1977:75), French children are often corrected in a language learning situation for using such structures.

9.3.3.5   Sociolinguistic factors

If certain types of detached structure are becoming grammaticalized as the unmarked word order in French, we would expect from previous sociolinguistic research, that right dislocation (i.e. Harris's 'new' word order) would be correlated with certain speaker variables (age, gender, social group etc.) indicating a linguistic change in progress. However, Ashby's survey (1982), based on a substantial stratified corpus of spoken French from different social groups, age groups, genders etc. finds that RD occurs in only 17% of structures where there is both a subject clitic and a co-referential noun or pronoun, and that there is no correlation between RD and speaker variables. In other words, there is as yet no compelling sociolinguistic evidence to suggest that right dislocation is becoming grammaticalized.

9.3.3.6   Theoretical implications and further questions

The neatness of Harris's typological argument, although pointing up broad patterns, does not appear to correspond to the complexity of the data, which suggest that detached structures remain both pragmatically and stylistically marked. However, even if it is not possible to argue that French is moving to a V-initial language, it remains true that detached structures, which can produce a variety of non-SVO orders, are a major feature of the modern spoken language (see for example Jeanjean 1981, Lambrecht 1987, Moreau 1987). What implications might this have? How can this be accounted for theoretically?

For Lambrecht (1987), working within a theoretical approach which is concerned with pragmatic structuring (see Part I, Section 3.4.2), LD and RD structures correspond to 'topic' and 'antitopic' structures respectively. In strict grammatical terms, for Lambrecht the detached element falls outside the main clause, which conforms to the preferred structure in Modern French, that is 'clitic + verb'. Lambrecht's argument is thus that when the speaker wants to topicalize a lexical NP, detachment is a key device for so doing, since a subject NP in French is not normally topicalized (see **9**.3.1 above). In other words, detachment is a pragmatic device which topicalizes a referent whilst keeping the preferred unmarked word order of French, with a clitic subject rather than a lexical one. Ashby's statistics (1982) testify to the importance of detachment in general and the sociolinguistic evidence suggests that the notions of topic and antitopic are becoming increasingly integrated syntactically into the basic sentence structure of French, through LD and RD respectively.[21] In Ashby's survey (1982:39), 47% of sentences involve detachment, and these are more prevalent amongst the lower socio-economic groups and the younger speakers: all younger speakers use more detached structures than older ones (indeed for the younger speakers, they form the majority type of sentence), but within the older age group, the upper SES groups use the forms less frequently.

As far as pragmatic word ordering is concerned, Lambrecht concludes that the frequently cited claim, that there is a universal principle whereby topic expressions tend to be placed in initial position in the sentence, needs to be refined (1994:199–205). Citing evidence from a variety of sources including Modern French, he argues that:

> the topic-first principle can be maintained as a universal ordering tendency, as long as it is only applied to accented and lexical and pronominal topic expressions with a topic announcing function (1994:202).

RD or 'antitopic' constructions are analysed as involving an unaccented element which is already known and which is 'put on hold' in the speaker's mind. Modern French could thus be analysed as a topic-prominent language, where the topic is not just the element which the sentence is about (i.e. the more traditional definition), but rather an accented one with a topic-announcing function.

Finally, the patterns produced by detachment do not break the constraints on the position of the object outlined by Marchello-Nizia (see **9.2.4**). Even where the object is placed in initial position (as in example (13)), the order O_NV does not occur, since the subject pronoun precedes the verb and the object reappears inside the main construction in the form of a clitic pronoun which is effectively case-marked.

9.3.4   Inversion

There are a number of cases in Modern French where the subject and verb undergo inversion. A context in which inversion is normally found in the written medium is in *incises*, that is, the parenthetical expressions such as *dit-il, demanda-t-elle, pensait-il* which follow direct speech. Jones argues that inversion here signals 'that the *incise* is not part of the quotation' (1996:471) and is thus a marked order which has a discourse function in the text.[22]

Elsewhere the motivation is grammatical; in example (4) for instance, inversion is triggered by the adverb *ainsi*. However, even where inversion is grammatically motivated, it is usually optional rather than compulsory; in some cases (e.g. following *sans doute, à peine*) there is the option either of adding *que* to the adverbial expression (21b), in which case SVC ordering is used in the subordinate clause, or of inserting the adverbial in a non-initial position, again preserving the SVC ordering (21c):

(21a)   Sans doute allait-il mourir
(21b)   Sans doute qu'il allait mourir
(21c)   Il allait sans doute mourir.

Moreover, the choice of construction is not arbitrary; not all orders are possible in every case, and there may be semantic differences between the various permutations.[23] Much of the time, the motivation is expressive or stylistic. Factors such as the type of discourse (literary, journalistic etc.), the medium, and the degree of formality are all important.

Adverbials or adjectives with an anaphoric relation to the previous discourse may also be found in initial position, triggering inversion; these often indicate comparison or contrast:

(22)   Différent est le cas d'une œuvre comme le Roman de la Rose (Grevisse 1993:339).

Tel can be used in a similar way to refer to subsequent discourse:

(23)   Telle était la fatigue de son long voyage (Barrès cited in Grevisse 1993:340).

A variety of types of adverbials and adjectives can trigger inversion for expressive effect, including temporal (24) and spatial adverbs (25), and all sorts of adjectives (e.g. 26); examples are cited in Grevisse (1993:340):

(24) Déjà faut-il le désirer (Gide)

(25) Ici se cache une sève maligne (La Bruyère)

(26) Amères sont les larmes qu'on verse à vingt ans (Green).

This patterning is particularly frequent with adjectives of quantity such as *rare, nombreux, grand* etc.:

(27) Grande fut ma surprise (Moreau cited in Grevisse 1993:340)

(28) Multiples sont les discours que l'on peut soumettre à l'analyse (Allaire 1973:216).

Inversion in this context is by no means compulsory, and usually has an expressive function. Either the initial element can be highlighted by placing it unexpectedly in initial position, or, since phrasal stress falls at the end of the phrase in French, emphasis can fall on the focus:

(29) Dans cette région depuis Tchernobyl naissent beaucoup de petits handicapés (Cadiot 1992:70).

Verbs too can appear at the head of the clause, triggering inversion and throwing stress onto the subject at the end of the phrase:

(30) Restait à réaliser la deuxième partie de leur programme (Price 1971:262).

Constructions such as (31) which demonstrate a VO_NS_N pattern are a relatively new development (they were very rare in Old French), and there are certain constraints which apply. The subject has to be a noun (rather than a pronoun), and normally one which is 'programmed' by the predicate, that is, predictable from it:[24]

(31) Assistaient à la réunion cinq membres du comité (Cadiot 1992:71).

The verb and complement are the topic of the phrase (i.e. the thing which the utterance is about), while the postposed subject (which is often relatively long) is the focus, carrying the most salient part of the information.

Stylistic motivation for inversion can relate to factors such as balance within the phrase or the weighting of different parts of the phrase. In the following example, given that the speaker wishes to position the expression of place at the beginning, the inversion keeps the phrase balanced, with the verb in central position:

(32)   Sur la table se trouvait un magnétophone (Jones 1996:468).

In many cases, the length and weight of the postposed subject is of considerable importance, with longer subjects more likely to be postposed.[25]

In terms of medium and register, inversion is most frequently found in more formal written varieties of Modern French; many examples are literary, although Clifford (1973:436–8) quotes journalistic, academic, and even oral (radio) examples:

(33)   Dramatiques ont été les événements qui ont déterminé le général de Gaulle à faire jouer . . . l'article 16 (from *L'Aurore 1961*).

In her study of a substantial literary corpus, Clifford cites a number of nineteenth-century authors (Flaubert, Zola, the Goncourts, Balzac) where the sense of delay in relation to the emerging subject can be exploited, and sometimes increased, by the presence of intervening adverbs (1973:435). Inversion may also be used as a literary device, characterizing different types of narration within a text, and marking the transition either from one narration to another or between different styles (1973:430–6).

What implications do these uses of inversion have for the status of SVO as the unmarked word order in contemporary French? Note that unlike the ordering of pronouns, inversion in most of these contexts is optional. Where it is obligatory in written French, for example in *incises*, it has a discourse function in the text, and where it might be said to be grammatically motivated (i.e. after adverbs), there are ways of preserving an SVO pattern, and there are often constraints which apply. Most of the time, inversion is either pragmatic (often used for topicalization or highlighting) or stylistic (motivated by considerations such as balance within the phrase). In other words, for the most part, inversion constitutes an example of flexibility in contemporary French; it offers the possibility, within certain constraints, of varying the standard word order for effect. By nature, this suggests that such inversion is most likely to occur in varieties of planned as opposed to spontaneous discourse, and indeed most examples quoted by grammarians are literary.

Clifford also argues that inversion is on the increase in journalism and non-fictional writing, and even in the spoken medium, although the example cited from spoken French (1973:437), is, by her own admission, a case of pre-planned discourse. Use of inversion for expressive effect also suggests that the effect is produced precisely because SVO, particularly where S is a lexical NP, is pragmatically unmarked (see Lambrecht's argument, above

(9.3.1)). Note also that Marchello-Nizia's theory that it is the direct object which has become strictly fixed in Modern French is supported by evidence from inversion; the order VO_N is not violated, since O_NVS and VSO_N are not found.

9.3.5   Cleft constructions

We shall mention these constructions only briefly, since although they signal pragmatic flexibility, allowing for example the object to be placed before the main verb as in (34), they are not, strictly speaking, examples of non-SVO structures; each part of the cleft construction respects standard word order:

(34)   C'est surtout son père qu'il n'a jamais revu (Blanche-Benveniste 1996:113).

There are several different types of clefts in French, for example:

(35)   C'est le champagne que j'aime le plus (Blanche-Benveniste and others 1990:61)

(36)   Ce qui est hors de prix c'est la pierre (Blanche-Benveniste and others 1990:63)

(37)   (Il) y a Jean qui a téléphoné (Lambrecht 1988:136)

(38)   J'ai les yeux qui m'font mal (Lambrecht 1988:137).

Two clauses are present in these constructions which are attested since Old French and which, according to Posner (1997:355), were 'in common use by the sixteenth century'. For example, in (35) (a typical cleft construction) and (37) (a presentational cleft), the first clause poses the lexical NP *c'est le champagne* or *(il) y a Jean*, and the second (a relative clause) expresses the action/ state etc. in which the NP is involved, *le champagne est hors de prix, Jean a téléphoné*. Thus the lexical NP which could have appeared in the form of a lexical NP subject (e.g. *le champagne, Jean*) is said to be clefted. Examples such as (36) are often referred to as 'pseudo-clefts', since they are a mixed strategy combining detachment and clefting.[26] Like detachment, clefts can be used for a variety of pragmatic ends. For example, they can be used to highlight the focus of the phrase (see note 9), particularly where a contrast is marked:

(39)   C'est Claire qui aime le chocolat et non pas Régine (Riegel, Pellat and Rioul 1994:431)

(40)   C'est moi qui ai tout pris et pas les autres (Blanche-Benveniste and others 1990:61).

Whereas detachment concerns an NP which is already topical (we noted above that the referent is usually not brand new), presentational clefts can introduce new topics (Lambrecht 1988:155) and can also be used in what Lambrecht (1988:138) calls 'event reporting', that is, the presentation of a non-topical referent as an 'element in some unexpected or surprising piece of information'. Thus indefinite nouns, which cannot normally be used in detached structures, are ideal candidates for presentational clefts which can then introduce as a focus an element which will be a topic in the next sentence:

(41)   Il y a quelqu'un qui veut participer.

In short, clefts are not a case of non-SVO constructions, but are rather an example of pragmatic marking in French. Like detachment, clefts allow certain pragmatic effects to occur within Lambrecht's preferred clause type of 'clitic + verb' which cannot otherwise be achieved in a language where the lexical subject NP is of low topic status. As Lambrecht puts it, 'the "mixed strategy" of cleft formation allows the language to have its cake and eat it too. It represents one of the specific solutions in French to the conflict between syntax and pragmatics' (1988:143). Note, however, that Blanche-Benveniste warns against a simplistic analysis of clefts as 'merely' pragmatic constructions without taking account of a syntactic dimension; she examines some of the constraints on clefts and some of the contexts in which clefting seems to have become grammaticalized (1997:96–98), for instance, before *pour ça*:

(42)   C'est pour ça qu'il faut jamais en prendre le soir de la vitamine C.

9.3.6   Binary constructions

Binary constructions constitute an area which as yet has been only tentatively explored, but which also represents a type of structure which can break with the canonical SVO order. Deulofeu defines *constructions binaires* as 'deux éléments d'énoncé dans une relation de couple, toujours réalisée sur une chaine rompue [...] la relation n'est pas marquée par des catégories grammaticales' (1977:37), for example:

(43)   Ce métier on se déplace tous les jours (Deulofeu 1977:55)

(44)   Le même argent on peut payer un loyer (Deulofeu 1977:40).

The purest form of binary occurs where two elements occur together and are related to each other within a larger construction, but where the relationship is not marked by any grammatical form (such as an anaphoric pronoun or a preposition). Such a patterning is illustrated by Deulofeu's representation of binaries as [(a) (b)]), the two parts of the construction thus having full syntactic autonomy. Intonation patterns are crucial, often supplying the key as to how the construction is to be interpreted. For example, a rise in the first constituent followed by a fall in the second usually suggests that the second carries information about the predicate.

What are the implications of binaries for SVO ordering? It is very difficult to comment in detail since much research remains to be done on these forms which, by all accounts, are 'très relâchées' (Gadet 1989:173). Moreover, given the fact that the linear chain is broken, it is often difficult, as in examples (43) and (44), to label items as S, V and O etc. In any case, although binaries often involve non-SVO orders, and although they suggest considerable flexibility in contemporary French word order, like detachment, they do not violate the $O_N V$ constraint; nowhere do we find cases of OVS binaries, for example.

9.3.7   Other constructions

Certain examples of CSV do not fall neatly into any of the categories already discussed, although like detachment, they are characteristic of the spoken medium:

(45)   Les poireaux je déteste (Blanche-Benveniste 1996:113)

(46)   Dix-sept ans il a (*ibid.*).

There are at least two different sub-types, each with different intonation patterns (see Blanche-Benveniste 1996) as well as constraints on usage. The type represented by (45) involves two opposing intonation patterns in the two parts of the clause; if the first part involves a rise, the second will involve a fall, and vice versa. According to Sabio, the second type (e.g. (46)) 's'achève[nt] sur un ton bas extrême de nature terminale, le reste de la construction étant pourvu d'un schème intonatif plat de type parenthétique' (1992:37–8, cited in Blanche-Benveniste 1996:114). Once again, this type of construction is associated with certain pragmatic functions such as topicalization and highlighting.[27] For example, (47) and (48) involve pragmatic highlighting of the preposed complement:

(47)   La nappe je mets

(48)   Un verre de sangria par personne ils donnaient.

In common with detachment and clefting, these structures demonstrate the inextricable links between syntax and pragmatics; in these cases, intonation patterns are also crucial. Again, Marchello-Nizia's point that it is the position of the direct object which has become increasingly fixed in French is not challenged by these data: we do not find the order $O_N V$ amongst the examples.

9.4   Conclusions

Is Modern French an SVO language? If we consider the subject pronoun as S, then statistically speaking, SVO is the most frequent grammatical order. Moreover, certain grammatically motivated exceptions to SVO, notably interrogatives and inversion after adverbials, are often abandoned in the spoken medium in favour of patterns which conform to SVO. Nonetheless, the fact remains that prototypical examples of SVO involving a lexical NP are rare. There are a number of non-SVO patterns in contemporary French, involving inversion, detachment, clefting, binaries and others, some of which are statistically very frequent, notably detachment. However, these phenomena normally represent marked choices; they are usually stylistic devices or pragmatic strategies. Moreover, they often involve the interaction of syntax and other linguistic elements such as intonation. They occur in different frequencies, are often associated with particular registers, media or domains, and are often subject to linguistic constraints. Together, these possibilities suggest that there is considerable pragmatic flexibility with regard to word order although as yet, the evidence does not seem strong enough to argue, as Harris claims, that French is moving to a V-initial stage. We note finally that none of the marked orders allows for the possibility of $O_N V$ and that the order OVS, which was possible (indeed frequent) in Old French, is no longer a feature of Modern French.

Suggested Reading

History:
    Ayres-Bennett (1996), Harris (1978), Marchello-Nizia (1995), Roberts (1993).
Modern French (general):
    Harris (1985), Jones (1996), Lambrecht (1987), Moreau (1987), *Travaux de linguistique* 14/15 (1987).
Detachment:
    Ashby (1982, 1988, 1994), Barnes (1985), Blasco (1995, 1997), Combettes (1998), Fradin (1990), Lambrecht (1994), Marchello-Nizia (1998a, 1998b).
Inversion:
    Clifford (1973), Le Bidois (1952), Wall (1980).
Clefts:
    Lambrecht (1988), Rouboud (1997).
Binaries:
    Deulofeu (1977), Gadet (1989).

Notes

1. For details of the evolution of word order and the case system for nouns and adjectives, see Price (1971:93–114) and Harris (1978:18–66).
2. For discussion of word order in Old French and examples, see Foulet (1970:306–32), Price (1971:259–60), Marchello-Nizia (1995:51–6), Ayres-Bennett (1996:58–97), Posner (1997:356–7).
3. This is often attributed to a Germanic influence (originating in the fifth-century invasions), although Posner (1997:358) notes that there is some doubt as to whether the Germanic varieties were indeed V2 at the time of greatest influence.
4. For further discussion, see Marchello-Nizia (1995:61–7). For a recent generative approach drawing on X-bar syntax, see Bauer (1995); citing evidence from a wide range of languages, she argues that the fundamental shift is from the left-branching pattern of Proto-Indo-European to the right-branching pattern of Modern French. For a discussion, see John Green's review (Green 1997).
5. For a discussion, see Price (1971:96–8).
6. See Price (1971:96), Harris (1978:49), Schøsler (1984), Posner (1997:334).
7. See Bauer (1995:6–9).
8. See Harris (1978) for a typological approach to the history of French.
9. The term 'topic' is defined by different theoretical frameworks in different ways. Harris gives a basic definition; the topic is 'that element which is known in advance, or given' (1978:257). See Part I (Section 3.4.2) for Lambrecht's definition of both topic and focus within a pragmatic framework, and Lambrecht (1994) for detailed discussion.
10. Note however that Latin is widely viewed as a language in transition, that is, no longer clearly an SOV language (see for example Harris 1978:18–19).
11. Harris (1978:33) argues that so great is the desire to maintain SVO word order that [ti] is sometimes combined with *est-ce que* to avoid even the inversion of this structure (*C'est-y que l'homme voit la femme?*). This argument seems dubious given the fact that he himself states that speakers view *est-ce que* as a sentence-initial particle rather than as an inverted clause. The spelling of [ti] is also controversial; in the example above, the appearance of *t'y* may be influenced by the *y* of *on y va*.
12. For a generative analysis of the evolution of inversion in interrogative structures within a Principles and Parameters framework, see Roberts (1993).
13. It is of course the case that Marchello-Nizia's argument is based on written texts, where word order may be less free than in the spoken language.
14. Note that there are methodological problems with Moreau's analysis. In four examples (1987:61), the clitic pronoun is analysed as part of the verb V in detached structures, but as the subject S in non-detached structures. Both categories, S and V, can therefore represent different realities in different examples.

15. For a detailed discussion of high and low topic status with examples from large stretches of discourse, see Lambrecht (1987).
16. Marchello-Nizia (1998a:163) dates the earliest examples to the eleventh century and notes that they are relatively rare in Old French. For an example in context, see Ayres-Bennett (1996:93).
17. Marchello-Nizia (1998a) notes that this is also the case in the Old French examples.
18. See Marchello-Nizia (1998b) for a discussion of the evolution in the function of detached structures from Old to Modern French. She explores detachment against the background of major syntactic changes, such as the fixing of SVO order and the compulsory use of pronouns.
19. Note that 'topichood' is often considered as a continuum, with the possibility of high and low topicality and a range of degrees in between. Cadiot (1992), for example, looks at degrees of topichood in a variety of constructions (including different types of detachment), assessing the role of prosodic factors such as pauses as well as syntactic and pragmatic factors.
20. See Barnes (1985:114) and Ashby (1988:226).
21. Ossipov's statistics (1997) also support Ashby's argument.
22. See Jones (1996:471) for details on the syntactic properties of *incises*.
23. This is explored in detail for a variety of adverbs by Joly (1983).
24. See Price (1971:262) and Marchello-Nizia (1995:84).
25. This is also true for subordinate clauses. For a detailed study of the factors influencing inversion in subordinate clauses in French, see Wall (1980).
26. For details on pseudo-clefts, see Blanche-Benveniste (1997:98–100).
27. See Blanche-Benveniste (1996) for a detailed discussion.

10

Relations between clauses: subordination, coordination, parataxis

10.1 Introduction

This chapter discusses a number of problematic issues concerning the ways in which clauses are linked in discourse (see Part I, Sections 2.3.3 and 2.3.4). Two distinct linguistic levels are explored. In **10.2** and **10.3**, the focus will be on relations between clauses within the sentence; aspects of complex sentences will be discussed, such as the definition of subordination and co-ordination, and the description of certain non-standard types of subordinate clause traditionally associated with the spoken medium. In **10.4**, the focus shifts to combining clauses in larger stretches of discourse, whether texts or speech; we shall look in particular at the role of parataxis, subordination and coordination as indicators of linguistic sophistication.

10.2 Relations within the sentence: questions of definition

10.2.1 Introduction

As was discussed in Part I (Section 2.3.3), the traditional distinction between subordination and coordination hinges on the notion of dependency: whereas coordination joins elements of equal status, subordination involves a hier-archical relationship, whereby the subordinate clause is said to be dependent on the main clause. However, close examination of the treatment by gram-marians of coordination and subordination reveals what Pierrard (1987:31) calls a 'flou terminologique' and a lack of unanimity as to definitions and classification.[1] The problems inherent in providing a watertight definition of subordination are immediately visible in the *Grammaire Larousse's* section on the subject, which defines subordination in terms of dependence or lack of autonomy between two clauses, but then goes on to say 'certaines propositions, de forme subordonnée, entrent cependant dans une relation nettement coordinative' (Chevalier and others 1964:109). *Si* is cited as a classic example of the phenomenon, the two clauses in cases such as (1) enjoying relative autonomy:

(1)   S'il contenait peu d'œuvres de premier ordre, le Salon d'Automne contenait un certain nombre de tableaux intéressants (Chevalier and others 1964:109).

In some cases, it is the clause introduced by *que* which seems to operate as the main clause, with the other clause in a relation of dependence to it:

(2)   À peine le doux souffle d'un vent favorable avait rempli nos voiles que la terre de Phénicie disparut à nos yeux (*ibid.*).

This type of example, which does not fit the standard definition, has been labelled *subordination inversée*, reflecting the form of the structure, if not its function, since, as the *Grammaire Larousse* points out, 'la première proposition marque le fait qui est premier pour celui qui parle' (*ibid.*).

The notion of dependency, central to the definition of subordination, is at the heart of the problem. Syntactically, it implies that the two parts of the construction are not grammatically autonomous, but rather that one 's'appuie sur l'autre (terme primaire ou principal) qui lui sert de support' (Wagner and Pinchon 1962:20), and that there is thus a hierarchy between them. One of the strongest and most obvious types of dependency is that between the primary verb and its argument:

(3)   Je veux qu'il parte.

Elements in the subordinate clause may be controlled in referential or modal terms by elements in the main clause. In (3), the verb *vouloir* requires a subjunctive in the subordinate clause; in the relative clause in (4), the past participial and adjectival agreement is required by the noun *table*:

(4)   La table que j'ai achetée était italienne.

However, the concept of dependency is complex, and difficult to define in terms of watertight criteria. In·some cases, especially completives (see Part I, Section 2.3.3), the problems often centre on relations between the verb and elements in the subordinate clause. In the category of circumstantials (temporals, causals, etc.; see Part I, Section 2.3.3), the level or degree of dependency may vary in strength. Indeed Piot argues that there is a large degree of independence between the two clauses in the case of many circumstantials, maintaining that this criterion is central to the distinction between circumstantials and other types of subordinate clause, such as relatives and completives:

> ce trait commun aux deux processus (coordination et subordination) était généralement admis comme allant de soi pour le premier alors qu'il se révèle essentiel pour le second de ces processus, dans la mesure où il constitue un critère de différentiation sans appel entre les phrases introduites par une *conjs* [conjonction de subordination] et toutes les autres sortes de 'propositions' ou 'phrases subordonnées' de la grammaire traditionnelle (Piot 1988:13).

There has been a large amount of research in this area, including theoretical debate, as well as studies of particular types of construction, and of particular subordinators and coordinators.[2] In **10**.2.2 and **10**.2.3, we shall discuss different approaches to the issues, focusing on the definition of subordination in **10**.2.2, and on the distinctions between subordinating conjunctions, coordinating conjunctions and coordinating adverbs in **10**.2.3.

10.2.2   Defining subordination

By way of example, we shall discuss briefly two recent approaches to different aspects of the problem, both within the theoretical framework of the *Approche pronominale* (see Part I, Section 3.6.2) and both concerning the key notion of dependency.

Blanche-Benveniste's discussion (1982) is based very much around the syntactic properties of the main verb, and specifically around whether or not it is a *verbe constructeur*, in which case we are dealing with subordination. Using the theoretical framework of the *Approche pronominale*, she explores cases which look like subordinates, but which are not in fact subordinate clauses. She first examines clear examples of subordination, extracting and defining the essential syntactic properties which make them subordinates. The two key properties are:

- Proportionality between the subordinate clause and a pronoun (see Part I, Section 3.6.2):

  (5)   On sait qu'il part demain (1982:77)
  (5a) On le sait / on sait ça (*ibid.*:78)

- The capacity of the main clause verb (the *verbe constructeur*) to take complements independently of the verb in the subordinate clause (5b), to undergo negation (5c) or interrogation (5d), to take the full range of tenses and aspects (5e) and moods (5f):

(5b)   On sait très bien qu'il part demain
(5c)   On ne sait pas qu'il part demain
(5d)   Savez-vous qu'il part demain? (*ibid.*:79)
(5e)   On a su qu'il partait demain (*ibid.*:79 (adapted))
(5f)   Sachez qu'il part demain (*ibid.*:79)

Using these key criteria, Blanche-Benveniste is able to distinguish cases of subordination such as (6):

(6)   Il a trouvé que la terre était ronde (*ibid.*:90)
(6a)   Il l'a trouvé / il a trouvé ça (*ibid.*)

from cases of *fausse subordination* such as (7) which seem at first to resemble (6):

(7)   Je trouve que cette voiture est confortable (*ibid.*:90).

In (7), pronominal proportionality is problematic (7a), as is the insertion of adverbial complements (7b):

(7a)   ?Je trouve ça / ?je le trouve (*ibid.*)
(7b)   ?Je trouve sans peine que cette voiture est confortable (*ibid.*:91).[3]

As Blanche-Benveniste herself acknowledges, the precise limits of subordination can be difficult to delineate, especially in an oral corpus, and there are a number of cases where two interpretations are possible, one where the main clause verb is analysed as a *verbe constructeur* and one where it is not. In the following example, *je crois que* may be read as a *verbe constructeur* (and thus (8) would represent an example of subordination), in which case *je crois* = *je le crois tous les jours*:

(8)   L'organisme humain se renouvelle tous les jours tous les jours je crois qu'on est nouveau de par nos cellules (Blanche-Benveniste 1982:107).

Alternatively, if *je crois* is understood merely as the rough equivalent of the expression *il me semble*, the example is not one of subordination, since *croire* does not operate as a *verbe constructeur*. Indeed, Blanche-Benveniste prefers the latter interpretation where she describes the first verb as having a modalizing effect with respect to the second.[4]

The advantage of Blanche-Benveniste's approach is principally that it provides a set of syntactic criteria which distinguish between cases which look structurally and morphologically similar. The potential drawback is the existence of borderline cases (e.g. 8) or examples where acceptability judgements relating to the criteria invoked are not clear-cut: in some cases, it is debatable whether substitution by a pronoun or the presence of an adverb is acceptable or not (e.g. 7a).

Deulofeu's starting point (1986) is an investigation of problematic cases of the particle *que* conjoining two clauses, in particular structures which have traditionally posed problems for grammarians, leading to the proposal of such unsatisfactory classes as *subordination inversée* or *subordination à valeur coordonnante*. The broad tendency in contemporary French is for *que* to increase in usage in a variety of contexts; it was grammarians and writers who codified specific usages for the complex range of conjunctions in Modern French, each with precise functions, many of which were performed in Old French by the polyvalent particle *que*. Gadet (1989:163–4) identifies seven different classes of extended *que* usage in Modern French, including extended use of *que* introducing completives, in circumstantials, as a coordinator, and introducing speech (direct and indirect). As Gadet acknowledges however, many examples are open to several analyses, depending on how contextual features are read. (9) could be interpreted as a circumstantial (*puisque?*), a relative (albeit non-standard), or as a case where *que* simply operates as a coordinator (Gadet 1989:165):

(9)   Je vous mentionne juste le problème que je n'en parlerai pas ici.

It is evident from Gadet's list that these non-standard uses of *que* involve examples of both subordination and coordination and that this distinction is particularly problematic in such cases.

Working within the *Approche pronominale*, Deulofeu seeks strict syntactic criteria on which to base his definition of subordination, one which will distinguish adequately between the 'marginal' cases of *que* which fall within the category and those which do not. Deulofeu posits a tripartite distinction between:

(i)   clear cases of dependency where the subordinate clause is governed by the verb in the main clause (these are cases of subordination);
(ii)   examples where the main clause verb does not govern the subordinate clause, but where there are nevertheless 'indices de dépendance' between the two clauses (these are also cases of subordination);
(iii) examples where there is no relationship of dependency between the two clauses and which are thus not cases of subordination.

As far as the definition of subordination is concerned, the key distinction is that between (ii) and (iii), that is, between examples such as (10) and (11):

(10)   Il me le donnerait que je ne le voudrais pas (Deulofeu 1986:98).

(11)   Il faudrait partir qu'il se fait tard (*ibid.*:97).

In cases like (10), Deulofeu points to the 'indices de dépendance' which make these examples of subordination; in (10), the first part of the construction is no longer viable if the second part is removed. In other examples, there are constraints on the verb forms in the two clauses; in (12), the negative in the main clause imposes a subjunctive in the subordinate clause:

(12)   Il ne part pas que je ne le sache (*ibid.*:98).

Elsewhere, there are pairs of adverbs which are linked to each other, in that the presence of one presupposes the presence of the other (13):

(13)   Il était encore là que déjà l'autre s'en allait (*ibid.*).

Clearly the nature of the constraints imposed by the antecedent can vary according to such factors as the conjunction used, or the noun or verb or adverbs in the main clause. For Deulofeu, such examples all exhibit 'indices de dépendance'; they do not fit the traditional notion of hierarchy, and do not demonstrate the kind of unilateral dependency normally found with verbal governance, where the subordinate clause is always dependent on the main clause. Rather they demonstrate a type of 'corrélation syntaxique', or pseudo-correlation, a kind of interdependence between the two clauses (1986:99).

This kind of correlation or interdependence falls within the category of subordination for Deulofeu, and is to be distinguished from his third category, *greffes* (literally, 'grafts'), where the two clauses are completely independent of each other in morpho-syntactic, modal and sometimes prosodic terms. Even if there are semantic effects such as addition, consequence or opposition, these are not in any way a function of the particle *que* which joins the two clauses:

(14)   Il était pas là tu peux en être sûr que d'ailleurs la lumière était éteinte (*ibid.*:101)

(15)   Il a pas pu le faire que Jean lui il aurait pu (*ibid.*:102).

There may even be a falling intonation at the end of the first clause, suggesting the end of a sense group. These *greffes* fall outside the definition of subordination in even its looser sense of syntactic correlation, and Deulofeu goes as far as to say 'je serais tenté de dire que l'on peut, par le biais de *que*, greffer une construction verbale sur à peu près n'importe quoi' (1986:102).

Like Blanche-Benveniste's analysis, Deulofeu's categories have the advantage of offering a set of superficially clear syntactic criteria to define subordination. Moreover, he deals specifically with problematic examples, ones which have traditionally been treated unsatisfactorily by grammarians. However, the concept of syntactic correlation will be a relatively fluid one, with potentially much variation in the type and strength of the 'indices de dépendance'. Perhaps most importantly, as Gadet points out (1989:167), the interpretation of some structures is not at all obvious. Constructions such as (16) are susceptible to at least two readings:

(16) J'ai plein de choses à vous dire qu'on est pas contents du tout.

(16) could be analysed either as a completive, or as a case of *téléscopage* (of *j'ai plein de choses à vous dire* and *j'ai à vous dire qu'on est pas contents du tout*), or as the apparent insertion of a section of indirect speech triggered by the verb *dire* (for a full discussion see Gadet 1989:162–7).

10.2.3 Subordinating and coordinating conjunctions, and coordinating adverbs

Looking specifically at the conjunctions involved in subordination and co-ordination, Piot (1988, 1993) distinguishes between *conjonctions de subordination* and *conjonctions de coordination* in rigorously syntactic terms. Working within a transformational framework, she is concerned mainly with various types of circumstantial clauses. Subordinating conjunctions are defined in terms of four principal characteristics. The first is permutability, that is, the fact that the two clauses can be reversed:

(17)   Pierre est venu parce que nous étions là (Piot 1993:144)
(17a)   Parce que nous étions là Pierre est venu (*ibid.*).

This is not possible with coordinating conjunctions, as in (18):

(18)   Pierre est venu mais nous étions là (*ibid.*)
(18a)   *Mais nous étions là Pierre est venu (*ibid.*).

The second is the fact that where two coordinated subordinate clauses are introduced by the same conjunction, the conjunction can be replaced by *que*:[5]

(19)   Marie est partie quand nous étions là et que Jacques est arrivé (*ibid.*).

Third, a substantial number of subordinating conjunctions (which Piot labels *prépositions-conjonctions*) can be replaced by a corresponding preposition plus noun or pronoun, the conjunction serving as the underlying form (in generative terms) from which the other surface possibilities are derived by applying transformational rules. Thus in (20), the subordinating conjunction *après que* followed by a verb clause containing a finite verb can be replaced by the preposition *après* followed by the noun *arrivée*:

(20)   Jean est parti après que nous sommes arrivés (Piot 1993:146)
(20a)   Jean est reparti après notre arrivée (*ibid.*).

Finally, unlike the case of coordinating conjunctions (21), it is impossible to eliminate the subject of the subordinate clause, where it is the same as that of the main clause (21a):

(21)   Marie parle et lit (*ibid.*:149)
(21a)   *Marie chante du fait que rêve (*ibid.*).

Coordinating conjunctions, by contrast, are not normally permutable (18a), and the subject can usually be eliminated in cases of coordination (21). In addition, coordinating conjunctions join phrases of the same syntactic status; for example, two finite verbal constructions can be coordinated (22), whereas the corresponding verbal and nominal constructions cannot (22a):

(22)   Pierre est venu mais Marie part (Piot 1993:151)
(22a)   *Pierre est venu mais le départ de Marie (*ibid.*).

Piot's criteria are obviously particularly useful in the analysis of conjunctions. They also offer relatively clear-cut criteria on which to base categorical distinctions, and according to which changes of category can be observed (Piot 1993:157–8). On the negative side, there are, as Piot herself points out, counter-examples to almost all her criteria; she cites one exception to the permutability criterion (i.e. the class of consequential conjunctions; *ibid.*:144), and one to the property by which the conjunction is replaced in a coordinated construction by *que* (i.e. comparatives such as *davantage que*; *ibid.*:145). She also notes that both *or* and *car* are exceptions to the rule whereby the subject can be eliminated where coordinating conjunctions are themselves coordinated (*ibid.*:150). Moreover, the analysis of examples like (20) is clearly inextricably linked to the transformational framework within which she is working; there are, however, problematic issues which arise, since the various structures involved (e.g. 20a) cannot simply be said to be semantically equivalent.

The traditional coordinating conjunctions (*mais, ou, et, donc, or, ni, car*) are not the only markers of coordination, which can also be signalled by certain adverbs such as *puis, alors, ensuite* etc.[6] Adverbs share the properties of coordinating conjunctions in terms of lack of permutability, possible elimination of the subject in coordination, and the fact that they join elements of equal syntactic status. However coordinating conjunctions (23a), unlike adverbs (23), cannot be preceded by another coordinating conjunction:

(23)   Pierre est venu et alors Marie n'était pas là (Piot 1993:151)
(23a)   *Pierre est venu et or Marie n'était pas là (*ibid.*).

Also, unlike conjunctions, adverbs are flexible in their positioning within the second phrase:

(24)   Pierre est là, donc nous viendrons rapidement (Piot 1993:152)
(24a) Pierre est là, nous viendrons donc rapidement (*ibid.*)
(24b) Pierre est là, nous viendrons rapidement donc (*ibid.*).[7]

Note however that this criterion (one which distinguishes adverbs from both coordinating and subordinating conjunctions) raises certain semantic complexities; positioning the adverb in particular places can change the nuance of the phrase, depending on which elements the adverb is felt to 'govern' (see Piot 1993:152).

Other analyses suggest a more fluid line between subordination and co-ordination, and between coordinating conjunctions and coordinating adverbs. Hobaek-Haff (1987), working specifically on coordination, sets up a list of criteria for membership of the class of coordinator, and then codes a number of elements positively (+) or negatively (–):

Table 10.1 Criteria for coordination (Hobaek-Haff 1987:92)

1. La proposition introduite par le terme en question ne peut pas être permutée en tête de phrase
2. Le terme en question ne se place jamais au milieu d'un des éléments reliés
3. Le terme est incompatible avec *et* ou *ou*
4. Le terme peut coordonner un nombre illimité d'éléments
5. Le terme peut relier des propositions subordonnées
6. Le terme ne peut pas subir la négation, ni être modifié par un adverbe quelconque
7. La proposition introduite par le terme en question n'admet pas une mise en relief à l'aide de *c'est ... que ...*

	1	2	3	4	5	6	7
et	+	+	+	+	+	+	+
ou	+	+	+	+	+	+	+
ni	+	+	+	+	+	+	+
mais	+	+	+	–	+	+	+
car	+	+	+	–	–	+	+
or	+	+	+	–	–	+	+
donc	+	–	–	–	+	+	+
puisque	–	+	–	–	–	+	+
parce que	–	+	–	–	–	–	–
quand	–	+	–	–	–	–	–

Criteria 1, 2 and 3 are essential, and tally broadly with Piot's criteria, while 4 and 5 are not necessary, but are met by most coordinating conjunctions. The fact that some coordinating conjunctions do not meet these criteria suggests, according to Hobaek-Haff, that there is a continuum rather than a clear-cut divide between coordinators and other categories, in particular subordinators, and that there are therefore 'core' or 'optimal' coordinators. Criteria 6 and 7 suggest that there are subordinators (i.e. *puisque, parce que, quand*) which share certain properties of coordinators.[8] Hobaek-Haff's approach suggests that, although there is general agreement as to the core properties of coordinators, it is difficult to make a categorical distinction between coordinating conjunctions and coordinating adverbs on the one hand, and between coordinators and subordinators on the other.[9] It allows for a sense of core versus more marginal cases, and could be particularly useful in the analysis of elements which change category, either in diachronic or synchronic terms.[10]

Finally, in the context of a corpus-based study of subordination and orality, Koch (1995) posits a typology of integration, based on the nature of the integration of the two conjoined clauses. This takes the form of a continuum; at one end (type I), the category *parataxe asyndétique* (represented as [A][B]) includes cases where two clauses are simply juxtaposed, and thus where the integration is minimal. At the other end (type VI), Koch places cases where the second clause contains a nominalization rather than a conjugated verb (e.g. *vous notez que la désignation de Ganelon est imposée* . . . Koch (1995:19)). The more traditional distinction between coordination and subordination corresponds to the distinction between types III (*parataxe syndétique*) and IV (*subordination à verbe conjugué*) in his continuum. Koch's perspective is different from those whose approaches we have discussed thus far; his typology is devised as a means to analyse subordination in different types of oral discourse. It is thus not primarily syntactic and does not therefore set up strict syntactic criteria on which to base categorizations. What it does suggest, however, is that from the perspective of discourse analysis, there is a continuum rather than a clear dividing line between different types of integration across clauses; coordination and subordination have a place in this continuum but are part of a much broader scale which includes both stronger and weaker forms of integration.

10.3   Spoken French: a case study of the *relative du français populaire*

The notion of subordination is fraught with difficulties when applied to the spoken medium. In **10.2** we examined some of the problems relating to definitions of subordination in the oral medium raised by classes such as *fausses subordinations* and *greffes*. In this section we shall look at one specific problematic category: the so-called *relative du français populaire*.

The standard system of relative clauses in French is a complex one, consisting as it does of the double series of *qui/que* relatives and *lequel, laquelle, dont, etc.* The broad tendency in contemporary spoken French is towards an increased use of the particle *que* (which enjoyed a much wider range of functions in Old French), and away from the series involving *lequel, laquelle, dont*, etc. Gadet (1989:147–59; 1995) divides the relatives found into four major types, with a number of different sub-types (Gadet's example of each type is used by way of illustration (1989:147–8)):

- The *relative standard*

    (25)   L'homme dont je parle

    (26)   L'homme de qui je parle

    (27)   L'homme duquel je parle.

- The *relative dite 'de français populaire'* (or the *relative résomptive*) where *que* is used with a clitic, or a prepositional phrase:

    (28)   L'homme que j'en parle

    (29)   L'homme que je parle de lui

    (30)   L'homme que je parle de sa femme.

Instead of performing several syntactic functions as would standard relative clauses (i.e. marking the syntactic frontier between the two components, representing the antecedent through a *reprise* construction, and marking the function of the initial noun through the choice of relative pronoun), Gadet points out (1989:149) that the *que* in these relatives signals only the frontier between the two components, the remaining two functions being filled by the pronoun or the preposition plus noun/pronoun. Not only is there a less complex amalgam of functions performed by these relatives, they also allow standard word order to be preserved in the subordinate clause. Moreover, this type of relative brings the constructions close to circumstantials, to the point where degrees of ambiguity may be found and different analyses are possible. The following example, cited by Gadet (1989:152–3), might be interpreted as a relative (where the sense of *que* is close to *où*), or a circumstantial (where the sense is close to *quand*):

    (31)   Son jules était enfermé dans l'ascenseur qu'y avait eu un court-circuit.

These relatives are also particularly frequent with *c'est . . . que* (32) and in cases where there is an *incise* after the *que* (33):

(32)   Il était grand et costaud mais c'est un type que je l'ai toujours vu avec une bouteille de whisky dans le sac (Gadet 1989:151)

(33)   C'est des choses que quand on a bu on les oublie (Gadet 1995:151).

• The *relative défective* or *réduite*

(34)   L'homme que je parle.

These are particularly problematic, since, unlike the *relative populaire* where a pronoun or preposition is present, there is no indication at all of the type of relation involved. As Gadet points out (1989:149; 1995:152), this may make them difficult to interpret if cited out of context, since the relation signalled by the *que* can be vague. Since however they are normally used in context, the problem is rarely insurmountable. For some speakers, they are only used with locative antecedents:

(35)   Le fameux cinéma qu'on s'était donné rendez-vous vient de fermer (Gadet 1989:152)

and they are particularly common within a cleft construction:

(36)   La cinq c'est la seule qu'ils ont écrit (Gadet 1995:153).

• The *relative 'pléonastique'*

(37)   L'homme dont j'en parle

(38)   L'homme dont je parle de lui

(39)   L'homme dont je parle de sa femme.

These are indicative of hypercorrection, composed as they are of both the standard pronoun and the *reprise* construction, thus doubly marking the relation.

There are a number of problematic issues arising from these non-standard relatives. First, as Gadet points out, it is not always easy to categorize constructions into one of the above four categories. We noted in passing the case of example (31); Gadet cites a number of others (1989:151–5), including the following:

(40)   Elle avait son manteau qu'elle allait régulièrement au marché avec

(41)   Y en a encore là qu'i doit pas y avoir grand-chose après

(42)   Le gars que les flics étaient dessus/ i saignait comme un boeuf.

On the one hand, these can be interpreted as *relatives du français populaire*; on the other, they can be read as *relatives défectives* with the *avec*, *après* and *dessus* simply forming part of the main clause:

(40a)   Elle allait régulièrement au marché avec

(41a)   Doit pas y avoir grand-chose après

(42a)   Les flics étaient dessus.

Similarly, (43) could be analysed either as a relative or simply as a case of coordination (1989:153), similar to Deulofeu's *greffes* (see **10.2.2**):

(43)   J'ai téléphoné à Martine qu'elle n'était pas là.

Indeed, as Gadet indicates (1995:146), an analysis in terms of a continuum rather than a typology of discrete categories may correspond best to the data.

The various types of non-standard relative are attested in regional variet-ies of French and in most of the other Romance languages (Gadet 1995:145). In sociolinguistic terms, the *relative populaire* (of which there are examples in Old French) is attested in almost all social groups, albeit in different pro-portions (Gadet 1995:151) and there may be much variation in usage even within the speech of one individual. In stylistic terms, the *relative populaire* is associated with less formal registers, although different types of non-standard relative are stigmatized to different degrees (Gadet 1995:142). Roy, Lefebvre and Régimbald's (1982) results on the acquisition of rela-tives amongst Montreal adolescents support this; non-standard relatives are attested amongst all groups, but speakers from lower social backgrounds produce higher quantities of non-standard relatives, and the speakers from higher groups are more sensitive to the status of the non-standard forms. The *relative défective* is firmly associated with lower social groups and/or less well educated speakers while the *relative pléonastique* occurs in situations of linguistic insecurity (Gadet 1995:151). Gadet (1988:47) has also shown that many twentieth-century grammarians do not discuss the non-standard relatives at all, thus confirming and contributing to the marginalization of these forms.

Gadet (1989:157) argues that in all probability, most speakers have in their linguistic competence the full system of relatives, though not all speakers make use of all types. This is broadly in line with Roy, Lefebvre and Régimbald's evidence (1982) on the acquisition of relatives and with Deulofeu's theory (1981) that all the relatives form part of one 'super-system'. Deulofeu finds that speakers who have the non-standard forms in their linguistic competence also use the standard forms, so that:

> on peut décrire le secteur des relatives en posant un super-système dont toutes les variétés dialectales et sociales, y compris la variété standard, constituent des normes particulières de réalisation, exploitant chacune une partie des possibilités du système (1981:136).

He argues that the stigmatized non-standard relatives have acquired this status for essentially historical reasons; while the super-system has remained broadly the same since the Middle Ages, the work of grammarians, notably in the sixteenth and seventeenth centuries, which established certain types of relative as forming part of the prestige standard while relegating others to stigmatized non-standard status, has shaped the norm which has been passed on from generation to generation through the school grammar tradition.[11] In contemporary French, therefore, some speakers use the full range of relatives while others use only the standard forms.

In semantic terms, for those speakers who use more than the standard relative, the different types do not necessarily have the same meaning. We have already seen that the non-standard relatives can be ambiguous, or have different connotations, and can be analysed in different ways (see example (31)). Gadet (1989:157) further illustrates this point with a non-standard example from Giono:

(44)   La bonne soupe d'Arsule, une pleine écuellée que les bords en étaient baveux.

She argues that the standard counterpart does not convey the same nuance of two consecutive actions:

(44a)   Une pleine écuellée dont les bords étaient baveux.

Gadet further argues that a speaker may choose a particular type of non-standard relative for stylistic or discourse-pragmatic reasons; the linguistic context as well as factors relating to information structuring may play a role in the choice of construction (Gadet 1995:151–3).[12] This is an area where much research remains to be done, notably on the semantics of the different relatives, on the classification of types and sub-types, and on the syntactic constraints which affect usage.[13]

10.4   Relations within discourse: parataxis, coordination and subordination as degrees of progression in linguistic sophistication?

This Section explores the relationship between the ways in which clauses are linked within larger stretches of discourse, and the nature and type of discourse concerned. The choice of issues is again by no means exhaustive. Clausal cohesion forms only part of the overall cohesion of discourse; many other elements are involved, such as various types of anaphora, substitution and ellipsis (see Part I, Section 2.3.4). Clausal cohesion is also closely linked to argumentation in discourse (see Part I, Section 3.4.2), that is, to the strategies deployed by the speaker to convey particular points of view or perspectives[14]; the relationship between subordination, coordination and parataxis on the one hand and argumentation strategies on the other, could form the basis for a different type of section.

The progression from parataxis through coordination to subordination is often seen as a progression from the less to the more sophisticated methods of discourse structuring or textual cohesion. For example, amongst the features of spoken French, high levels of parataxis are frequently cited, along with relatively low levels of a restricted number of subordinate clauses. As Müller puts it (1985:99), 'le français parlé peut fort bien n'utiliser qu'un minimum de conjonctions de subordination parce qu'il préfère la construction parataxique'. Similarly, Riegel, Pellat and Rioul (1994:473) state 'aussi la langue orale utilise-t-elle peu la subordination (en dehors des relatives en *qui* et *que* et des complétives ou circonstancielles les plus simples) et lui préfère-t-elle les modes de construction parataxiques par coordination ou par simple juxtaposition'. This kind of progression is discussed in relation to various factors, of which we shall explore briefly three in this section. We shall address such questions as: are the traditional associations borne out by the data? What is syntactic complexity? Is syntactic complexity necessarily an indicator of sophistication, either in historical or synchronic terms? In each case, we shall see that a simple correlation is rarely found.[15]

10.4.1   Language acquisition

Children's speech is traditionally associated with syntactic simplicity. Indeed, some of the manuals on language acquisition assume and advocate a progression from parataxis through the use of coordinating adverbs and conjunctions to subordination. Lentin's classic text *Apprendre à parler à l'enfant de moins de 6 ans* (1973) is aimed at a wide variety of people connected with the language learning process (such as parents, teachers and researchers). In a discussion of the acquisition of syntactic structures at the *École Maternelle* stage (at about 4 years), Lentin (1973:84) cites four different responses to the question 'tu mets tes sandales ce matin?' by four children demonstrating different levels of syntactic sophistication:

(45)   I pleut j'mets pas mes sandales

(46)   I pleut eh ben j'mets pas mes sandales

(47)   I pleut alors j'mets pas mes sandales

(48)   Je mets pas mes sandales parce qu'i pleut.

A progression is assumed from (45) to (48), from the most basic level of 'phrases simples', through coordination ('ensuite viendront les phrases juxtaposées ou coordonnées; les énoncés s'allongeront, reflétant une suite de pensées plus compliquées') to subordination ('puis les premières complexités introduites par des subordonnants seront à leur tour utilisées' (Lentin 1973:140)). This final stage Lentin refers to as the 'niveau du récit oral' (*ibid.*:139) or the 'niveau maximal du langage' (*ibid.*:140). It represents the level of syntactic complexity which the child should be aiming to reach: 'les enfants de quatre ans qui "parlent comme des livres" emploient beaucoup de propositions subordonnées, voire même des emboîtements (enchâssements) de subordonnées [. . .] il faut vraiment essayer de faire parler individuellement chaque enfant pour l'entraîner à cette structuration' (*ibid.*:140). In terms of its timing, this process correlates broadly with evidence from English which suggests that the most basic patterns of coordination and subordination are acquired around the age of three to three and a half, with more complex patterns developing right through until puberty (Crystal 1976:44–51).

What does the available evidence tell us about syntactic complexity in children's versus adult speech? In an analysis of the use of various conjunctions amongst a group of adults and children between six and twelve years, Jeanjean finds that children (irrespective of social class or age) use the same subordinating strategies as adults, but with an even greater variety: 'tous les enfants emploient ces schémas, et souvent dans des configurations très compliquées [. . .] la diversité des conjonctions employées par les enfants est plutôt plus grande [que chez les adultes]' (1983:204). In other words, she finds in the children's speech a wide variety of complex subordinating constructions, for example:

(49)   Ah oui de temps en temps il faut le tourner pour qu'il cuise pas toujours à la même place après quand on le coupe qu'on lui ouvre le ventre le foie on le garde et le reste on le jette parce qu'après avec le foie on fait des brochettes (Jeanjean 1983:207; child aged 10).

This is analysed by Jeanjean as *P pour que P après* (((*quand P que P*), (*P et P*)) *parce que P*).

Her evidence confirms, in line with previous research, that many subordinate structures have already been acquired by children in the six-to-twelve age bracket. Given the age group she has studied, she is able to add to well-established findings about first language acquisition the further caveat that once acquired, complex subordinate structures are used by children just as often as by adults, and in a variety of complex structures which may at times show more sophisticated patterns than those found in adult speech.

10.4.2   Social groups

There are significant problems in drawing conclusions about links between social groups and use of subordination, coordination and parataxis, due to the small quantities of available data and a number of methodological problems with much of the data which exist. The traditional association in sociolinguistic terms is between on the one hand lower social groups (and possibly less well-educated speakers) and the less complex forms of cohesion between clauses (parataxis in particular), and on the other hand, higher social groups/better educated speakers and more complex forms (subordination in particular).

Evidence comes from Lindenfeld's survey (1972) of French, which draws on Bernstein's work; the latter argues (based on American-English data) that amongst the features which characterize the 'restricted code' (versus the 'elaborated code') are high levels of simple (versus complex) sentences, the use of a small number of conjunctions and low rates of subordination. Lindenfeld measures complexity in terms of levels of subordination, which she subdivides into the three categories of circumstantials, relatives and completives. She finds that there is a link between higher social groups and complexity in the more formal registers, thus reinforcing traditional associations. However, her results need to be read with considerable caution. The correlation found concerns only relatives and completives (not circumstantials); it is limited to only one social class in one context; the number of tokens is relatively small; details on the relative structures in question are limited; methodologically there are serious difficulties, since informants give data by imagining themselves in two different situations, rather than actually finding themselves in these situations.

More reliable evidence in terms of the methodology employed comes from Robach's *Étude sociolinguistique de la segmentation syntaxique du français parlé* (1974). In this project, the data come from a well-established corpus of French which has been used in a number of variationist studies (the Orléans corpus).[16] Robach selects a stratified judgement sample of 36 interviews with three different social groups, three age groups, and an even division between the two genders (1974:37). The three social groups correspond broadly to those in professional and managerial jobs (Group A), non-managerial/professional and non-manual jobs (Group B) and manual jobs (Group C) (Robach 1974:35–7). Syntactic complexity is defined in terms of degrees of dependency, in other words, in terms of levels of subordination. Again, a correlation is found between the higher social groups and higher degrees of syntactic complexity. In turn, Robach makes a connection between higher degrees of syntactic complexity and a number of other concepts which imply intellectual sophistication, that is more logical and ordered thought patterns, as well as 'la complexité du contenu' and '(la) complexité psychologique' (*ibid.*:87). In other words, in sociolinguistic terms, high levels of subordination are clearly associated with higher social groups; in intellectual terms, subordination is associated with more sophisticated thought processes.

Data which suggest very different patterns come from Auvigne and Monté (1982). However, as discussed in **6.4.2.2**, there are a number of methodological problems; their evidence is based on one person's speech, the person in question being an extreme example of the 'sous-prolétariat'. Moreover, the sessions from which data are taken involve the speaker working on her language skills, a situation which may cause a high level of self-consciousness with respect to her speech. This said, the data reveal large quantities of embedded clauses, some types more frequent than others; for example, completives containing finite verbs and relatives using *que* are very common, while more complex relatives with *dont*, *lequel* etc. are absent. Overall, levels of subordination are high in comparison to the use of both coordination and adverbs, and embedding is more common than the basic SV construction. However, the subordination is of the most simple variety, the same structures tending to be repeated constantly (e.g. the temporal conjunction *quand*), and most subordinate constructions are highly problematic for the speaker. Crucially, the high frequency of subordination is not linked to clarity or ease of comprehension: there are large quantities of errors inhibiting comprehension: 'il n'y a aucune construction qui ne fasse pas problème à un moment ou à un autre' (1982:41).

In short, for statistical and methodological reasons, conclusions are limited as regards social class and phenomena such as subordination, coordination etc. The available evidence suggests first that while the statistics often imply that there is some correlation between social class and complexity of clause structure, we should nonetheless be cautious about drawing simplistic conclusions; and second that subordination is not necessarily a mark of sophistication per se: complex syntax is by no means synonymous with clarity of expression. More remains to be done in this field to obtain a representative picture of the structures characterizing the speech of different social groups.

10.4.3   Medium/discourse type

A considerable amount of work has been done in this area, with frequent allusions to the association between parataxis/low levels of subordination and the spoken medium. Once again, positing simplistic parallels here is problematic. In the first instance, there are many counter-examples. Blanche-Benveniste (1997:58–60) cites several examples from the GARS corpus of spoken French where the degree of embedding is very high, especially where the speaker is involved in argumentation, and where explanations or justifications are a feature of the discourse. She concludes by agreeing with Halliday's comments on English that the spoken medium is often characterized by syntactic complexity rather than the reverse, as is commonly believed.

Even where parataxis is a strong feature of oral discourse, what this often suggests is not so much that spoken French is a less sophisticated form of communication, but rather that syntax in the oral medium is operating within a different linguistic dynamic from that of written French: devices other than syntax can be used to structure the discourse and convey the types of semantic links we have discussed under subordination and coordination. This is especially true for the semantic relations conveyed by many circumstantials (e.g. temporal, causal, consequential relations), where coordinating conjunctions and adverbs can often convey broadly the same notions. Intonation can also play a crucial role. In (50), a rising pattern through the first clause followed by a fall through the second could suggest a relation similar to that conveyed by the subordinator *si* or a temporal conjunction such as *quand* or *à chaque fois que*:

(50)   Elle n'aime pas la décision / elle arrête de travailler.

Elements variously referred to as *marqueurs de structuration de la conversation* (MSC) or *Gliederungssignale* also play an important role in the oral medium; these are elements such as *bon ben, et puis* etc., which are often used as a form of oral punctuation.[17] They are sometimes used alongside co-ordinators; indeed it can be difficult to discern precisely the function of the different elements in combinations such as *et puis alors, et puis ensuite*, since elements such as *puis* and *alors* can have different functions, both temporal and atemporal, depending on context. The following passage of spoken French demonstrates this kind of patterning:

Figure 10.1   Transcription of holiday anecdote (Carruthers 1996:199–200)

1	L1	Je suis passé dans un pays . . . je suis passé dans un pays et puis
2		j'allais un peu vite
3	L2	mm
4	L1	et puis euh . . . l'Italien il . . . enfin la police italienne m'a arrêté . . . et puis
5		je ne sais pas ce qui qu'il m'a raconté bon ben il y avait le le collègue
6		qui était à côté de moi là le copain . . . bon il m'a répété quoi ce qu'il
7		me disait quoi que j'allais un peu vite
8	L2	mm
9	L1	bon ben j'ai dit bon ben oui euh peut-être alors euh . . . j'étais je
10		traversais une agglomération et puis j'étais peut-être au-dessus de la
11		vitesse hein mais il y avait il y avait pas de contrôle radar rien du tout
12		m'enfin il m'a dit que j'allais vite . . . et il m'a collé un procès quoi et
13		puis
14	L2	oh là là
15	L1	oui oui et puis alors il me dit bon ben . . . vous réglez tout de suite ou
16		alors j'envoie le procès euh . . . en France
17	L2	mm
18	L1	alors bon ben je lui ai dit bon ben j'ai j'ai fait dire par le copain que
19		je le payais parce que . . . que je le réglais parce que bon ben je voulais
20		pas que ça aille en France parce que bon ben un vit un excès de
21		vitesse hein ça allait me ça allait me coûter cher alors tandis que là-
22		bas bon ben j'ai donné cinq mille lire je crois je me rappelle oui c'est
23		cinq mille lire alors c'est alors ça faisait vingt-cinq francs ça valait
24		pas le coup de
25	L2	eh ben non
26	L1	hein alors c'est
27	L2	ça y est
28	L1	oui ça s'est passé comme ça il m'a donné le papier et puis allez
29		hop . . .

The *et puis* in lines 1 and 10 for example appear to be atemporal; in lines 4 and 15 they occur where there is a relation of succession. Both *bon ben* (lines 9, 18 and 22) and *alors* (line 15) occur in a context of succession, though this relation is more explicitly marked by *alors*. In short, the elements which together create the dynamic which conveys relations such as consequence, addition etc. include distinctly oral phenomena such as intonation and *marqueurs de structuration*, as well as explicit markers such as subordinators and coordinators.

It is also worth observing at this point that in Old French, where many of the 'texts' (i.e. performed stories such as epics and romances; see **6.2.2**) are heavily influenced by orality, syntactic features of the oral medium are also in evidence in the form of high levels of parataxis and relatively low levels of subordination (for an example, see Ayres-Bennett 1996:66–7). These patterns can be seen particularly clearly in the temporal structure of many

Old French texts, where temporal and aspectual perspective is conveyed not through complex subordinate structures which make explicit the exact nature of the temporal connections, but rather through such techniques as tense switching (e.g. from the PS to the PR), gesture and intonation (see **6.2.2** and Fleischman 1990). As the medium of prose develops, and as texts begin to be written for a reading public, temporal patterns change, and higher levels of subordination are accompanied by the expectation of a more strictly chronological use of tense. The increase in subordination is thus a reflection not of an increase in sophistication per se, but of a much broader cultural shift.

Levels of subordination, coordination etc. may, moreover, be a consequence of the way in which different types of discourse (literary, newspaper, radio, conversation etc.) tend to structure information. For example, Allaire's study (1973) of subordination in radio speech suggests that there are relatively large quantities of subordination in this type of discourse, but a strong preference for limited numbers of embedded clauses; 94% of examples of subordination contain no more than three levels of embedding, and 60% have only one level. This is in part due to the interactive nature of much of the discourse; the existence of a dialogue will limit the length of time any one speaker has at their disposal for developing layers of subordination. Moreover, given the oral context, there are limitations on the number of levels of subordination which a speaker's memory can hold at any given time (1973:218). On the other hand, her data contain a very small number of particularly complex clauses with up to sixteen levels of embedding; again, she points out that the speaker is highly likely to use a variety of prosodic (and thus exclusively oral) techniques (stress, intonation, pauses, slowing down/speeding up etc.) to structure the phrases such that comprehension is facilitated (*ibid.*:216). In terms of the choice of structures, Allaire also notes the connection with the medium of radio: frequent constructions include, amongst others, relative *qui* followed by a subordinate clause which explains what has gone before, and the use of *c'est que* to introduce a clause which explains the content of the previous clause (*ibid.*:217–18). In completives, the frequency of verbs of opinion is not surprising in a mode of discourse where the expression of opinion is so central.

Koch (1995) compares subordination in spontaneous conversation and a formal lecture. In spontaneous conversation, subordination is mainly to the right and mainly of a certain type, that is, *subordination à verbe conjugué* (see **10.2** above). Drawing on previous work, Koch maintains that this is entirely in keeping with information structuring in conversation which follows a basic pattern of 'base-development-development . . .' etc., thus accommodating certain levels of subordination of a type which parallels linear patterns of thought. There is distinctly less subordination to the left which, when it occurs, does so to less complex degrees; this too reflects the fact that spontaneous conversation is unlikely to use structures which suggest high levels of pre-planning. One exception to the general trend is the relative frequency of subordinate clauses where the order of the clauses does indeed reflect the chronology of the thought processes, for instance certain temporal and hypothetical conjunctions such as *quand j'aurai fini, si ça te plaît* . . .

The formal lecture demonstrates more complex patterns of both right and left subordination, as well as higher degrees of syntactic integration. Of particular interest in the formal lecture is the relatively high level of redundancy; on the one hand, the fact that the lecture tends to be based on written notes encourages a high degree of syntactic complexity, while on the other hand, the fact that it is delivered and received in an oral medium means that repetition and anaphoric constructions sometimes have to be used by the speaker in order to 'pace' the discourse and to facilitate comprehension where high degrees of subordination are involved. There is, in other words, both a quantitative and a qualitative difference in the patterns of subordination found in the two media.

Strong evidence of the correlation between discourse type and sentence structure also comes from a recent study by Blanche-Benveniste (1995), who examines the linking structures in conversational accounts of accidents versus written journalistic *faits divers*. The two media reveal two very different ways of structuring the chronological events. Whereas the oral accounts tend to recount events in chronological order, with a series of main clauses each containing a finite verb, the journalistic *faits divers* tend to have one main verb with the other events arranged around this clause and related to it through the use of subordinate clauses or past and present participles. In the following example, belonging to secret organisations, possessing arms, wanting to overthrow the regime and being condemned to death all precede the event of hanging; the presentation on the other hand first introduces the condemnation, followed by the other events, and ending with the hanging:

(51)   Condamnés à mort par la justice militaire pour avoir adhéré à des organisations clandestines, ainsi que pour détention d'armes et d'explosifs dans le but de renverser le régime, trois islamistes ont été pendus jeudi 16 décembre, au Caire (*Le Monde* cited in Blanche-Benveniste 1995:27).

Drawing on the work of Halliday, Blanche-Benveniste argues that the particular ordering chosen can be attributed to the demands of information structuring of the medium/type of text in question: certain facts can be placed in particular positions for effect (such as emphasis) and the others structured around them using different linking clauses. One of the results of this patterning is that certain types of linking structures, in this case a number of different subordinating constructions, may be relatively frequent in one medium/type of text (e.g. in journalistic texts) and rare in others (e.g. in oral accounts), while the reverse is true for parataxis. Different levels of parataxis/coordination/ subordination thus seem to be associated once again not with simplicity versus complexity, but with different types of information structuring.

Suggested Reading

Subordination:
  Anderson and Skytte (eds) (1995), Blanche-Benveniste (1982), Chuquet and
  Roullard (eds) (1992), Deulofeu (1986), Muller (ed) (1996, 1994), Piot (1988,
  1993), *Langue française* 77 (1988), *Travaux de linguistique* 27 (1994).
Coordination:
  Antoine (1958), Hobaek-Haff (1987), Kronning (1992), Piot (1988),
  L'Information grammaticale 46 (1990).
Relatives:
  Deulofeu (1981), Gadet (1988, 1989, 1995), Gadet and Mazière (1987), Godard
  (1988a, 1988b), Nottaris (1973), Valli (1988), *Langages* 88 (1987).
Cohesion in discourse:
  Blanche-Benveniste (1995), Gülich (1970), Koch (1995), Lindenfeld (1972),
  Robach (1974), *Cahiers de linguistique française* 8 (1985).

Notes

1. See Pierrard (1994) and Melis (1994) for discussion. Pierrard (1987) discusses the heterogeneous presentation of subordination in a number of
   contemporary grammars.
2. See the Suggested Reading list at the end of the Chapter and Hobaek-
   Haff (1987, Chapter 1) for examples of such studies.
3. For a full discussion of these and other types of *fausse subordination*, see
   Blanche-Benveniste (1982). In certain types of subordinate clause, Blanche-
   Benveniste is able to extract further defining properties, notably with respect
   to the verb in the subordinate clause.
4. Blanche-Benveniste makes a connection here between such cases of *fausse
   subordination* and Guillaume's notion of *subduction*, where the full lexical
   sense of the verb is reduced or weakened, as is the case with an auxiliary verb
   such as *avoir*. For a full discussion, see Blanche-Benveniste (1982:73–6).
   Note that in English 'that' is sometimes deleted in examples similar to (8),
   prompting Thompson and Mulac (1991) to argue that 'I think' is in the
   process of grammaticalization, conveying the sense of an epistemic adverb
   such as 'maybe' in an example like the following: 'it's just your point of
   view you know what you like to do in your spare time I think' (1991:313).
5. A generative analysis might see the second *que* as present in the underlying
   structure; it is then deleted in surface structure under certain circumstances
   (see Jones 1996:383–5).
6. For studies of particular coordinators, see the bibliography in Hobaek-
   Haff (1987).
7. Note that, given these criteria, Piot offers a reanalysis of *donc* as an adverb,
   rather than as a coordinating conjunction, as is traditionally the case.

8. For an approach to coordination and subordination in English which also proposes a gradient between the two as well as a feature coding system, such that certain coordinators are considered central and others less so, see Quirk and others (1985:920–8).

9. Note that Hobaek-Haff's classification posits a different type of profile for *donc* which is traditionally classified as a coordinating conjunction alongside *et, ou, ni, mais, car* and *or*. See also note 7 and Piot's observations about *donc* (1993:149–50).

10. For example, the English *for* constitutes an element which has undergone change in terms of its classification, moving away from the subordination end of the spectrum and more towards the coordination end (Lakoff 1968). Quirk and others (1985:927) place it on the gradient between the two.

11. Gadet (1995:143) gives examples of non-standard relatives in Old French, and Blanche-Benveniste (1997:44), drawing on Brunot, quotes eighteenth-century examples. Gadet (1995:150) argues that there is no evidence to suggest that non-standard relatives have increased or are increasing in frequency in Modern French.

12. Gadet (1995:147–9) also discusses the relationship between non-standard relatives and other 'bracketing devices' used in oral French for structuring information, notably left- and right-detachment and binary constructions (see Chapter 9).

13. Blanche-Benveniste (1997:102–4) discusses some of the constraints. For a generative analysis of relative constructions, see Godard (1988a, b) who proposes, within a Government and Binding framework, analyses which are different for standard and non-standard relatives, at both a syntactic and morphological level.

14. For theoretical background on argumentation, see Anscombre and Ducrot (1983); Grize (1990).

15. A further field which would merit investigation in this respect is language death. Rottet (1998) discusses the case of a language enclave of Cajun French in the context of studies of language death across a variety of languages. He notes that younger speakers are increasingly likely to replace finite subordinate clauses which would have contained the subjunctive, with a non-finite subordinate clause where the verb is an infinitive. As Rottet points out, more research needs to be done in this area, particularly on patterns in other enclaves and on the reasons why the shift from finite to non-finite structures is taking place: to what extent is it due to the influence of the replacing language (i.e. English in this case) or to a general pattern found across languages in a situation of language death?

16. See Part I, Section 3.5 for a discussion of variationist methodology.

17. The first term is used by the researchers who publish on the structure of discourse in the journal *Cahiers de linguistique française*. The second was coined by Gülich (1970).

11

Negation

11.1 Introduction

Negation has been the source of much discussion, both in the field of general linguistics and in French linguistics.[1] An idea of negation may be conveyed in a number of ways, including using lexical means, either through the choice of an antonymous term (*accepter/refuser*, *grand/petit*), or through derivation using one of a range of prefixes (e.g. *possible/impossible*, *violence/non-violence*, *content/mécontent*). However, the majority of studies have concentrated on syntactic means of marking negation and this will also be the focus here. French differs from other Romance languages in that the standard marker of sentence negation comprises two elements, preverbal *ne* and a post-verbal negator. While the archetypal post-verbal negative particle is now *pas*, a whole range of other particles is available, including the pronouns *personne*, *rien*, and the determiner *aucun*.

In this chapter we will concentrate on a number of issues which have been extensively written on:

- The scope of negation, that is the portion of the sentence affected by negation – in particular we will look at those cases where the negative appears to be transferred from a subordinate or infinitival clause, to which it logically belongs, to the main clause verb (e.g. *I don't think he'll come/I think he won't come*), and consider how best to account for these structures in French
- Whether *ne . . . que* and expletive *ne* should be discussed within an account of negation, or whether they are fundamentally different in nature
- The loss of *ne* from negatives in spoken French, the historical context of this change, and the factors which appear to favour or disfavour its usage in the contemporary language.

Before we turn to these issues, we shall address a number of questions of definition and terminology.

11.1.1   The nature of the component elements

There has been much debate about the status, naming and definition of each of the elements making up French negative structures: the pre-verbal *ne*, post-verbal *pas* (etc.), and *de* following a negative particle. A number of linguists writing in French have adopted the terminology of Damourette and Pichon ([1928–40]:I:132–43) for the negative elements – especially the term *forclusif* – while not necessarily espousing the psychological explanation of negation which underpins their account. Damourette and Pichon base their assessment of *ne* as a *discordantiel* on the basis of what are often termed its 'expletive *ne*' uses (see **11.3.2**), for example after comparisons of inequality, after verbs of fear, prevention, etc. and after conjunctions such as *avant que*, *sans que*, since they argue that there is a *discordance* between the subordinate clause and the central fact of the sentence. So, for instance, in the example, *Son petit cousin se présentait au cercle. Il craignait qu'il **ne** fût blackboulé*, there is a conflict or *discordance* between the desire on the part of the subject of the main clause and the possibility he foresees. *Pas* and the other negative particles are termed *forclusifs* on the basis that they 's'applique[nt] aux faits que le locuteur n'envisage pas comme faisant partie de la réalité. Ces faits sont en quelque sorte **forclos**' (*ibid.*:138). It is the combination of the *discordantiel* and the *forclusif* which together makes the 'négation pleine'.

Other linguists have offered two different explanations for the status of *ne* depending on whether it precedes a finite verb or an infinitive. When *ne* is used before a finite verb it is said to have the status of an affix. A number of features of *ne* are highlighted to indicate its lack of autonomy (see, for example, Recourcé 1996:66–9). From a phonetic point of view, liaison and enclisis are obligatory (e.g. [vu.na.ve.pa], *vous n'avez pas*). Syntactically, *ne* can only appear once and cannot be repeated before a host (i.e. the element to which it is phonologically bound as a clitic or affix). In addition, it cannot apply across a coordination of hosts, that is, it must be repeated before the second of two coordinated finite verbs:

(1a)   Jean jamais ne discute ou ne conteste les décisions de Marie
(1b)   *Jean jamais ne discute ou conteste les décisions de Marie.[2]

The difficulty is that when *ne* occurs not before a finite verb but before an infinitive, its behaviour is different; its repetition with coordinated infinitives, for example, is optional. This has led Recourcé (1996) to argue that here it is not an affix, but a 'marqueur' which is directly attached to the verb phrase.

A different account is offered by Rowlett (1998) who argues that *ne* is not inherently negative in the modern language (although it was formerly), on the basis that its usage alone is very rare (see **11.3.2.3** below), it is frequently absent in spoken French and almost categorically so in Quebec (see **11**.4), and it may be used expletively (see **11**.3.2) without a negative value. In Rowlett's view, *ne* in negative sentences inherits its negative features from a negative operator in the sentence such as *pas*.

Next, what is the status of *pas* etc.? Traditional accounts place the negative particles in the discussion of adverbs. Riegel, Pellat and Rioul (1994:411) argue, however, that it is incorrect to see *pas* as an adverb since it behaves so differently from other adverbs: for instance, it can appear in noun phrases of the type, *Pas de pitié!* or *Pas le temps de faire mieux. Ni de dîner.* Instead they prefer the more neutral term 'marqueurs de négation'. There has, moreover, been considerable discussion, at least since the seventeenth century, about the difference between *pas* and *point* (see Price 1979). In Old French there were important syntactic differences in their usage: *pas* was exclusively used adverbially to negate a verb (*je ne marche pas, je ne vais pas*), whereas *point* was employed substantively, as the direct object of the verb (*je n'ai point de pain*). While *point* came to be used adverbially, notably in Middle French, the use of *pas* with partitive expressions remained rare before the seventeenth century. The well-known formula that *point* is a 'stronger' negative than *pas* was first formulated by Vaugelas (1647); however, as Price has shown, the remark was taken out of context and repeated unthinkingly by numerous grammarians, although Vaugelas made it very clear that he thought it was very difficult to give rules to distinguish *pas* and *point*. Nevertheless we still find a recent account of French syntax (Jones 1996:347) perpetuating the claim that *point* gives greater emphasis. Gaatone (1971:61) suggests a syntactic difference: usage of *point* is more limited than that of *pas* since, with the exception of *trop*, it is rarely found before an adverb of quantity and it is not found in the preposed position (**point X ne V*). Henriette Walter (1988:94) favours a sociolinguistic explanation, considering *point* to be typical both of more elevated usage and of certain rural areas (Beauce, Bretagne, and western dialects).

Rowlett (1998) examines the status of different French *forclusifs* (*pas, plus, jamais, guère, personne, rien*) which have often in the past been treated as if they function in the same way, and argues that there are important differences between them. For Rowlett, *pas* is the only one which is inherently negative. It can function both as an adverb and as a quantifier similar to *beaucoup* (see below). *Plus, jamais* and *guère* are adverbs whose distribution is different from that of *pas*, both in terms of their co-occurrence possibilities (they can readily co-occur with each other but not, at least in the standard language, with *pas*) and in the positions they occupy in relation to infinitives. *Personne* and *rien*, on the other hand, are arguments rather than adverbials.[3]

Finally, the status of *de* after the negative particle has been the subject of debate, for instance by Gaatone (1971), Gross (1977) and Muller (1997). Is it best viewed as a preposition, as a case marker, or as part of a quantifier? Consider the pair:

(2a)   Pierre achète *des* livres
(2b)   Pierre n'achète pas *de* livres.

In his transformational account, Gross (1977) cites sentences of this kind to show that the insertion of a negative in French is not straightforward. He argues that we might think of **Pierre n'achète pas des livres* as an intermediate stage, from which the surface form is generated by the deletion of the article when preceded by *pas, jamais, plus, rien*, etc.

Gaatone (1971:121–3) prefers to consider *de* here neither as a reduction of the article to its prepositional element nor as *de* without an article. Instead he asks whether *de* should be viewed rather as part of the group, *(ne) . . . pas de*, functioning in the same way as the quantifiers *peu de, beaucoup de, assez de, trop de* etc.[4]:

(3a)   Je travaille peu   (4a)   Je (ne) travaille pas
(3b)   Je suis peu travailleur   (4b)   Je (ne) suis pas travailleur
(3c)   J'ai peu de travail   (4c)   J(e) (n')ai pas de travail

Gaatone himself has reservations about this explanation for a number of reasons. First, it separates off usage of *de* with negative adverbs (*pas de, plus de, jamais de, guère de*, etc.) from other non-adverbial negatives (*rien, personne, aucun, nul, pas un*, etc.); this means that *de* has to be accounted for in two different ways, which he believes is contrary to native speaker intuitions. Second, he claims that the functioning of negatives is only similar to that of quantifiers in certain respects. Whereas the latter may fulfil any function in the sentence, the negatives are restricted to the direct object slot. Third, he maintains that *de* and a nominal direct object may appear at a distance from the negative adverb, particularly in subordinate clauses or infinitival structures (e.g. *Elle n'avait pas laissé rentrer d'homme dans sa vie; Il ne faut pas que je prenne d'alcool ce soir*), whereas it is impossible to separate the elements of quantifiers in this way. Gaatone therefore concludes that it is perhaps better to consider *de* as a true indefinite determiner, belonging to the series, *un(e), du, de la, des*, 'série dans laquelle il représenterait la quantité nulle'.[5] However, Rowlett's recent work (1998) suggests that some of Gaatone's objections may not be valid and he claims that *pas* may function both as a negative predicative adverb and as a quantifier similar to *beaucoup* (and so be generated with an indefinite nominal expression). In particular, he cites examples of 'quantifiers at a distance' as in (5) which seem to counter Gaatone's third point:

(5a)   Marie a beaucoup acheté de livres
(5b)   Le bouquiniste a beaucoup vendu de romans.

11.2 Scope

11.2.1 Scope and context

The place of the negative does not always show which segment is affected
by the negation, or its scope. On the simplest level, two different scopes
for negatives are distinguished: total or sentential negation (e.g. *Alfred
n'est pas venu*), and partial or constituent negation (e.g. *personne n'est venu*); in
the case of sentential negation, the negative bears on the predicate as a
whole while in partial negation the negation relates to a single constituent
(here *personne*). Tesnière (1959:217–8) sees this difference as a distinction
between *négation connexionnelle*, which bears on the connection between two
nuclei, and *négation nucléaire*, which bears on a nucleus:

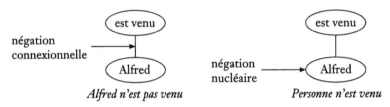

Alfred n'est pas venu   *Personne n'est venu*

Figure 11.1   Tesnière's distinction between *négation connexionnelle* and *négation
nucléaire* (Tesnière 1959:217–18)

The distinction between the two types may not, in practice, be so straightforward. Riegel, Pellat and Rioul (1994:412) point out that total negation,
while retaining its value as a sentence negator, may nevertheless affect a particular constituent. In the case of the sentence, *je n'ai pas tué avec ce couteau*,
for example, the negative bears on the instrument. Generally, if the verb is
followed by several complements, the negative bears on the last one, so in
the case of *je ne l'ai pas tué avec ce couteau pour prendre son argent* it is the motive
which is denied. However, a sentence like *Isabelle n'aime pas les glaces au
chocolat* potentially has three readings, depending on whether the negation is
taken as bearing on *aime*, on *les glaces au chocolat* (*mais elle aime bien les mousses
au chocolat*), or *au chocolat* (*mais elle aime bien les glaces à la vanille*). In practice,
intonation and the context may help to promote one of these readings.

Heldner (1981) equally argues that while negated sentences in isolation
tend to remain unspecified as to the scope of the negative *ne . . . pas*, this is
not the case for sentences in context. In her corpus of novels, plays and
newspaper articles the majority of cases of negation bear on the predicate as
a whole; it is only in about one sixth of cases that there is partial negation.
She maintains that two main factors enable the addressee of a negative
sentence to identify which part(s) of it the negative is intended to affect.

First, she assesses the role of context and in particular the role of the following affirmative clause in interpreting sentences of the type, *Je n'aime pas les femmes. J'aime les hommes* (Neg XAY, XBY), and of the type *Je ne pensais pas à la guerre, mais au temps où tu étais un petit garçon* (Neg XAY, *mais* B). Second, she argues that certain types of adverbials attract negation, independently of context, on account of their semantic structure. In the case of the sentence, *Ce matin je n'ai pas **beaucoup** mangé*, the tendency is to interpret the negative as modifying *beaucoup*, the assumption being that the speaker did eat something.

Particular problems are posed by the combination of *tout* with a negative. Gaatone (1971:59), amongst others, observes that if a sentence with *tout* is negated the resulting sentence has two possible readings. For instance, if we negate:

(6a)   Toutes les vérités sont bonnes à dire

the resulting negative sentence:

(6b)   Toutes les vérités ne sont pas bonnes à dire

has two possible interpretations:

(6c)   Aucune vérité n'est bonne à dire
(6d)   Les vérités ne sont pas toutes bonnes à dire.

In other examples the position of the negative is clearly significant:

(7)   Il ne peut pas partir / Il peut ne pas partir.

11.2.2   Negative raising?

There has been considerable discussion of sentences where, as in English, the negative appears to be transferred from the subordinate clause or infinitival complement to which it logically belongs, to the main clause verb, and of whether it is appropriate to account for these in terms of a negative 'raising' or 'transportation' rule, whereby the negative starts in the embedded or subordinate clause and is then moved or 'raised' to the main clause. This 'raising' is only applicable to certain verbs (Muller 1991:126), notably modal verbs such as *falloir, vouloir, devoir*. The sentence:

(8)   Il ne faut pas que Pierre parte

may be equivalent either to *Il faut que Pierre ne parte pas* where the negative bears on the subordinate clause verb (in which case the negative is then 'raised' to give (8)), or to *Il n'est pas obligatoire que Pierre parte*, where it is indeed the main clause verb which is negated (in which case the negative originates in the main clause).[6]

A second class of verbs to which this applies consists of those introducing a possible or probable assertion, including *penser, croire, sembler, paraître*. Muller glosses the possible interpretations of *Je ne crois/pense pas que Pierre parte* as either *Je crois/pense que Pierre ne partira pas* or *Je n'ai pas d'opinion sur le départ de Pierre*.

Third, there are verbs expressing an attitude towards a future process: *souhaiter, conseiller*. Here the equivalence is more approximate:

(9) J'ai peur d'avoir des ennuis
     – Je ne vous le souhaite pas (= Je souhaite que vous n'en ayez pas).

Some linguists have argued that these constructions are best accounted for transformationally: the negative is generated in the subordinate clause and then 'raised' to the main clause. For instance, Prince (1976) in his analysis of the relevant French constructions, suggests a process of NEG-Raising or Negative Transposition.[7] Various types of evidence are offered to support this hypothesis:

- Imperfectivity and the occurrence of time adverbials
  Negation 'imperfectivizes' a sentence. This means that while a time adverbial of the type *depuis X ans* is impossible with a positive sentence (e.g. **Fifi a oublié un mot depuis deux ans*) because it is incompatible with the 'point-action perfective', it is acceptable once the sentence is negated (*Fifi n'a pas oublié un mot depuis deux ans*). Since such time adverbials may, however, appear in a positive subordinate or embedded clause of the type, *Je n'imagine pas que Fifi ait oublié un mot depuis deux ans*, the suggestion is that the negation is originally generated in the subordinate clause (thereby allowing the time adverbial) and then subsequently raised to the main clause.
- Choice of corrective responses and tag questions
  The choice of the appropriate corrective responses – as that of the appropriate tag question[8] – is determined by whether the sentence is affirmative or negative. Compare the appropriate confirming and corrective responses to (10a), which is affirmative, with that to (11a), its negative counterpart:

(10a)	Jean vient de Rome	(11a)	Jean ne vient pas de Rome
(10b)	Mais oui	(11b)	*Mais oui
(10c)	*Mais si	(11c)	Mais si
(10d)	Mais non	(11d)	Mais non

Here again, an affirmative embedded clause dependent on a negative main clause (e.g. *Je ne suppose pas que Jean vienne de Rome*) behaves like the negative example, not the positive one; that is, the appropriate corrective response is *Mais si* and not **Mais oui.*

- Negative particles
  The absence of *ne* in the subordinate clause of an example like *Je ne crois pas que personne soit arrivé* is taken as further evidence that the negative is originally generated in the subordinate clause; *ne* is not found in the subordinate clause since the underlying structure could not contain two instances of *ne.*

- Negative polarity items
  Certain terms, known as negative polarity items, may occur only in negative sentences (e.g. *de temps, de la nuit,* or partitive *de*; for a discussion of which expressions belong to this class, see Jones 1996:354–5), yet these are possible in the subordinate clause where NEG-raising has occurred, once again suggesting that the subordinate clause is generated as negative and that the negative is raised to the main clause:

(12) Je ne crois pas qu'il ait fermé l'œil de la nuit

(13) Il ne me semble pas que Luc ait bu de vin.

Other linguists have argued, however, against a transformational explanation for these constructions. Benoît de Cornulier (1973) offers three main objections to this type of approach. First, he asserts that the argument of the behaviour of negative polarity items is not a justification for the rule since there are a number of related linguistic facts which cannot be accounted for. For example, negative polarity items are equally found after interrogatives and *si* (*Crois-tu qu'il lèverait le petit doigt pour elle?*; cf. Muller 1991:127, Jones 1996:355). Second, although in some cases there is broad equality of meaning between the so-called underlying structure with the negative in the subordinate clause and the structure with the negative 'raised' to the main clause, this is not always true. In the following pair, the presuppositions are diametrically opposite; in (14) the presupposition is that it is not God speaking, whereas in (15) the presupposition is that it is:

(14) Je ne voudrais pas être Dieu

(15) Je voudrais ne pas être Dieu.

In the following pair, it is not just the presuppositions which are different; the sentences clearly have different meanings:

(16) Je ne veux pas qu'on me voie

(17) Je veux qu'on ne me voie pas.

A third objection offered by de Cornulier is that some of the supposed underlying structures are bizarre because they contain two negatives in the same proposition. For example, supporters of a negative raising rule have to posit for the sentence *Je ne crois pas qu'il ne parlera pas* the following under-lying structure:

(18) Je crois pas que ne pas il ne parlera pas.[9]

For all these reasons de Cornulier rejects not only a transformational explanation, but all syntactic explanations for the examples discussed in this section, and he favours along with Muller a lexical explanation according to which the dual reading is the result of the lexical ambiguity of the main clause verb. It could be maintained, for example, that *devoir* is lexically ambiguous (Muller 1991:131–4), having both the sense of 'avoir le droit, pouvoir' and of 'devoir d'obligation'. A sentence like *Paul ne doit pas partir demain* may then be glossed in two ways:

(19a) Que Paul parte demain n'est pas prévu/obligatoire/nécessaire
(19b) Que Paul ne parte pas demain est obligatoire/nécessaire.[10]

11.3   *Ne … que* and expletive *ne*

Another interesting issue concerns whether two other structures should pro-perly be discussed alongside negative constructions: the *ne … que* construc-tion, which clearly has affinities with negative constructions while not having a strictly negative meaning; and structures which contain the so-called exple-tive *ne*, which should not be confused with cases where *ne* alone is used to mark negation.

11.3.1   *Ne … que*

Grammarians are often at pains to point out that the *ne … que* construction is not strictly negative, since it is semantically equivalent to 'seulement'[11], while at the same time describing it as 'la négation exceptive' or 'la négation restrictive' and discussing it in the same section or chapter as structures which are clearly negative in meaning. There is much disagreement as to whether this construction has some 'negative' value, perhaps given by some 'understood' or underlying negative construction[12], or whether it has rather the positive value of expressing otherness or alterity, or indeed whether these two positions may be reconciled. These issues have in turn raised questions about the status of both the *ne* and the *que* of this construction, in particular whether the latter is best viewed as a subordinating conjunction (Baciu 1978), a complementizer (Kayne 1975), or a preposition akin to *excepté*, *sauf*, or *hormis* (Azoulay-Vicente 1988).

Whilst pedagogic grammars continue to treat *ne ... que* alongside negative constructions, linguists such as Baciu (1978) have pointed to the features of the construction which differentiate it from other negative constructions (the examples are taken from Baciu). First, unlike other negative particles, *que* of *ne ... que* cannot generally be placed between an auxiliary verb and a past participle:

(20a)   Je n'ai lu QUE le livre
(20b)   *Je n'ai QUE lu le livre.

Je n'ai que lu is acceptable only in very specific contexts. Second, whereas the other negative particles may appear either within or at the end of a verb phrase, *que* may not appear in final position:

(21)   *Je ne marche QUE.

Third, all the other negative particles (except *personne, nulle part, aucun, nul, pas un, rien* when used in or with prepositional phrases, e.g. *Je n'aurais parlé pour rien*) closely precede the past participle or closely follow a simple verb. *Que* may only follow the verb and it does not necessarily have to follow it closely:

(22a)   Je ne lis QUE le livre
(22b)   Je ne lis le livre QUE demain.

Fourth, *pas* does not usually co-occur with another negative particle, but may combine with *ne ... que*:

(23)   Une de ces distances dans l'esprit qui ne font PAS QU'éloigner, qui séparent ... (Proust, cited by Baciu 1978:136)

(24)   Les hommes ne vivent PAS QUE de justice (cited in Riegel, Pellat and Rioul 1994:413).

Such features lead Baciu to conclude that there is nothing negative about the *ne ... que* construction[13] and to argue instead that the *que* here is the same *que* as is found in comparative constructions. The evidence for this is clearest where there is either *autre* or *autrement* in the surface structure:

(25)   Suzanne n'a d'*autre* religion QUE celle des situations nettes ...

The only difference then between this construction and other comparative structures is that whereas in the latter a comparative or *autre(ment)* is compulsory, in the case of the *ne ... que* construction it is optional.

A similar explanation is proposed by Gross (1977:88–91) within a transformational framework. For instance, he argues that the following sentences are synonymous:

(26a)   Max n'aime personne d'autre que Luc
(26b)   Max n'aime personne que Luc
(26c)   Max n'aime que Luc.

Equally, the following are said to be synonymous:

(27a)   Max n'aime rien d'autre que l'eau
(27b)   Max n'aime rien que l'eau
(27c)   Max n'aime que l'eau.

In each case Gross suggests there are two stages of deletion to reach sentence (c), a first whereby *d'autre* is deleted ((a) → (b)), and a second whereby *personne* or *rien* is deleted ((b) → (c)). He maintains that this solution avoids the problem of traditional accounts according to which *ne . . . que* is negative and (a) therefore apparently contains two negatives.

Other linguists have questioned whether it is indeed satisfactory to consider that the syntax of *ne . . . que* derives from an underlying structure which contains besides the negative a comparative element such as *autre* or *autrement*. Azoulay-Vicente (1988) makes a number of objections to the type of account offered by Gross and Baciu. Whereas the account is adequate for the above examples, it does not generate the correct surface structure when a prepositional structure is used:

(28a)   Paul ne pense à personne d'autre que Marie
(28b)   Paul ne pense à personne que Marie
(28c)   *Paul ne pense à que Marie.

Conversely, with longer or fuller prepositions, the correct surface structure is generated, but the underlying source sentences are impossible:

(29a)   *Paul ne s'asseoit près de personne d'autre que près de Marie
(29b)   *Paul ne s'asseoit près de personne que près de Marie
(29c)   Paul ne s'asseoit que près de Marie.

There are similar difficulties when the subject is postposed:

(30a)   *N'est venu personne d'autre que Paul[14]
(30b)   *N'est venu personne que Paul
(30c)   N'est venu que Paul.

For all these reasons Azoulay-Vicente considers an account which relies on the existence of an underlying *autre(ment)* as problematic. Instead, working within a Government-Binding framework, she offers the following alternative hypotheses:

- The structure underlying a *ne ... que* sentence contains a substantival negative particle of the type of *personne, rien, aucun*. This means that the *que* is not directly linked to the negative particle *ne*; rather its status is prepositional
- However, this *forclusif* or substantival negative particle is always an empty category (*catégorie vide* or CV), that is, it has no overt surface realization. The construction therefore has as its underlying structure *ne ... CV que Y*. For example, in a sentence of the type *Marie n'aime que Paul* the basic underlying structure of the *que Y* construction is said to be:

(31) $[[e_{XP2}] [[que_P] [Y_{XP3}]_{PP}]_{XP1}]$.

How does this analysis differ from those of Gross or Baciu? First, it is argued that the empty category (e) is not the result of the deletion of *personne, rien* etc. but is rather base-generated as such, that is, it is generated in the underlying structure directly. Moreover, it is not the empty category which gives the value of 'otherness' or alterity, but the *que*. Second, *que* is said to be a preposition (P) akin to *excepté, seul* or *hormis*, as a result of comparing pairs of sentences of the type:

(32a)   Marie n'aime personne (d'autre) que Paul
(32b)   Marie n'aime personne sauf Paul.

Here then the argument that the *que* of *ne ... que* is prepositional is based on a notion of semantic equivalence. In particular, it is asserted that the *que* of *ne ... que* is not a complementizer (as is the *que* of (33a)), as others have maintained; rather, restrictive *que* behaves syntactically in a number of different ways from the complementizer *que*. Note, for instance, that whereas the complementizer *que* is followed by a subordinate clause containing a finite verb (33a), restrictive *que* is followed by an infinitival construction (33d):

(33a)   Marie veut que Paul parte
(33b)   *Marie veut que (Paul) partir
(33c)   *Marie ne veut que Paul parte
(33d)   Marie ne veut que partir.[15]

The structures also behave differently when there is ellipsis of the verb of the second clause:

(34a)   Marie a voulu que Pierre boive de l'eau et que Jean boive du lait
(34b)   *Marie a voulu que Pierre boive de l'eau et que Jean du lait
(34c)   Marie a voulu que Pierre boive de l'eau et Jean du lait

(35a)   Marie n'a bu que de l'eau et Pierre n'a bu que du vin
(35b)   Marie n'a bu que de l'eau et Pierre que du vin
(35c)   *Marie n'a bu que de l'eau et Pierre du vin.[16]

Note the increased abstraction in this account, which allows an empty category to be generated in the underlying structure, a category which never has a surface realization. Whilst this solution overcomes the difficulties posed by trying to posit an underlying structure containing *autre(ment)*, the positing of an empty category only to generate the correct surface form is no longer subject to empirical confirmation.

11.3.2   Expletive *ne*

A second usage which often features in discussions of negation, but which again does not have a strictly negative meaning, is that of expletive *ne*. Note that, as in the previous case, this usage is often called *la négation explétive*, thus including the idea of negation in its designation. The principal point of discussion is what value, if any, the *ne* has in these cases, and in particular whether any negative nuance may be discerned in the structures which employ it, or whether it is completely redundant. Two main types of account of these constructions are found in the literature: those which view it as purely redundant, as is indeed implied by the term *explétif*[17]; and those which attempt to discern some relationship to negative constructions (e.g. Damourette and Pichon see it as a *discordantiel* without the *forclusif* of a full negative) or which attribute a modal value to it (Harris 1978:237; Battye and Hintze 1992:272). Wilmet (1997:509) speaks of a continuum of the uses of *ne* on a scale indicating greater or lesser degrees of negativity ranging from negative *ne* to comparative *ne* through to expletive *ne*, where its presence is theoretically optional and *pas* may be added to negate the sentence (*Pierre craint que Marie ne s'en aille/ Pierre craint que Marie ne s'en aille pas*).[18]

11.3.2.1   Usage of expletive *ne*

In listing the cases of expletive *ne*, grammars usually mention that the use of *ne* is optional, although favoured in more formal styles, and that the addition of *pas* usually entails either a change of meaning or ungrammaticality.[19] There is less agreement as to whether the *ne* has no meaning at all or whether, for instance, it is an additional marker of a non-factual state of affairs, since it typically occurs in clauses which describe hypothetical situations. The following cases are generally listed as the principal examples of this usage of *ne* which, it should be noted, only occurs in subordinate clauses introduced by *que* or by a subordinating conjunction which includes *que* (cf. Muller 1991:362–80):

- In subordinate clauses dependent on a noun or verb which expresses the idea of fear, including *craindre, crainte, peur, appréhender, redouter, trembler, risque, danger*, etc.
- After verbs of prevention such as *empêcher, éviter,* etc.
- After *prendre garde que*
- In clauses dependent on verbs of doubt or denial (*douter, nier, contester*), principally if the main clause is negative, but also occasionally when it is interrogative
- After certain subordinating conjunctions, frequently with *à moins que,* optionally after *avant que,* and fairly regularly after *sans que* when this follows a negated verb
- After *il tient à . . . que* and *il dépend de . . . que* when these are used in the negative or interrogative
- In clauses dependent on *s'en falloir*
- After *rarement* used initially
- After expressions of impatience such as *il me tarde, je suis impatient*
- In comparative constructions expressing inequality, such as those introduced by *plus, moins, autre, meilleur* or *moindre.*

Wilmet (1997:512–13), however, argues that the last case should be differentiated from the others on the grounds that it functions differently in a number of respects. First, expletive *ne* usually co-occurs with a subjunctive verb in the subordinate clause, whereas an indicative is usual in comparative constructions. Second, expletive *ne* does not have *de* in front of a nominal direct object of the verb, whereas the comparative construction does:

(36)   Je crains que Pierre n'ait bu DU vin

(37)   Pierre a bu moins de vin qu'il n'a bu DE bière.

Third, comparatives use *jamais, personne, nul, rien* whereas when the *ne* is expletive *quelqu'un, quelque chose, un jour* are employed:

(38)   Pierre craint qu'il ne vienne un jour quelqu'un (= Pierre recherche la solitude)

(39)   Pierre aime Marie plus qu'il n'a jamais aimé rien/personne.[20]

11.3.2.2   The value and currency of expletive ne

One of the best-known attempts to attribute a value to the so-called 'expletive' *ne* is offered by Damourette and Pichon. They consider *ne* to be *discordantiel*, that is to express in the subordinate clause 'une *discordance* entre cette subordonnée et le fait central de la phrase' (Damourette and Pichon [1928–40]:I:131).[21] For example, in the case of the use of *ne* after nouns and verbs expressing fear, they point to a 'discordance' between what the subject of the main clause desires and the possibility that subject envisages. Likewise, after *avant que* there is a 'discordance' between the two actions, or a temporal 'décalage' between the two processes. In this psychological explanation the presence of *ne* 'insiste sur la durée qui s'est écoulée avant l'intervention du fait nouveau; elle implique la plupart du temps que ce fait nouveau met fin à l'état du fait antérieur. C'est dire qu'elle marque la discordance entre le fait nouveau et le fait principal' (*ibid.*:135).

Others justify the use of the *ne* as a marker of modality; for instance, *ne* could be viewed as another way of indicating the uncertainty in *je crains qu'elle ne soit très malade* (Battye and Hintze 1992:272), or as a marker (comparable, say, to certain uses of the conditional) of a non-factual state of affairs (*il est plus petit que je n'avais pensé*). Grevisse (1993:1463), on the other hand, relates it to the idea of negation; thus in a sentence like *je crains qu'on ne me trompe plus* (using *plus* in the sense of 'davantage') the mind might focus on the idea of 'not being tricked', or again in the case of *avant que Louis ne parte* there is the implication that 'Louis has not left'. Grevisse concludes, however, that although some speakers feel a difference in nuance when the *ne* is present, this is not general. In addition, we might note the range of different nuances which speakers are said to feel, including an idea of doubt; emphasis on the *décalage* between two actions; the suggestion that the second action puts an end to the state expressed by the first; anteriority of the main action given as desired, etc. This is perhaps why Posner (1997:373–4), viewing these constructions with *ne* from a historical viewpoint, makes a distinction between two types of usage. With verbs of fearing and other verbs with psychologically negative resonances and after certain temporal conjunctions such as *avant que*, *ainz que* 'before', she argues that the *ne* may have implied, like the subjunctive, connotations of distancing the speaker from the truth of the proposition expressed in the subordinate clause. On the other hand, after negative verbs like *nier*, *défendre* and conjunctions such as *sans que*, or in comparisons of inequality, she argues that in Old French it seems that the negative force was more strongly felt.

There is much debate as to the currency of the use of expletive *ne* in contemporary French. Wilmet and Grevisse assert the spontaneity and vitality of the construction, as evidenced by its presence in dialects or its continued use, and indeed reinforcement, in certain contexts such as after *sans que*, despite the *Arrêté ministériel* of 26 February 1901 permitting its omission.[22] On the other hand, Muller (1991:381) suggests that its usage is artificially maintained – largely through education and the resulting increased contact with the literary language, noting that it does not appear in a corpus of children's speech.

11.3.2.3   Ne *alone to mark negation*

The above uses of expletive *ne* where the *ne* does not have a negative value should not be confused with those cases where *ne* is used without a *forclusif* in a negative sentence. In some of these, the use of *ne* on its own is compulsory (for example, with *que* meaning 'pourquoi' in either a question or an exclamation, with *ni*, in set expressions such as *à Dieu ne plaise, n'importe qui* and in proverbs (*il n'est pire eau que l'eau qui dort*), and with *savoir* or *n'avoir que faire* when they are followed by *que* plus infinitive (cf. Grevisse 1993:1448–9)). On the other hand, there is a range of other uses where *ne* is optionally present, including: after certain verbs, especially when used in simple tenses and with an infinitival complement, notably *oser, cesser, pouvoir* and *savoir* with the meaning 'to be uncertain'; sometimes with *daigner, bouger, manquer*; after hypothetical *si*, particularly when the main clause is also negative; after an interrogative pronoun or determiner in rhetorical questions, for example *qui ne le sait?*; in a subjunctive clause, whether relative or consecutive, dependent on a negative or interrogative main clause; after expressions indicating time passed introduced by *voilà, il y a (un tel temps) que, cela fait (tel temps) que, depuis que*; before *autre* followed by *que*, as in *je n'ai d'autre désir que....*

How are these constructions to be interpreted? A common solution is to point to the fact that we are dealing with a fixed list of contexts and to argue that these cases are simply relics of an earlier stage in the evolution of negation in French in which it was possible, and indeed usual, to mark negation by *ne* alone.[23]

11.4   The loss of *ne* and the marking of negation by *pas* alone

11.4.1   The historical background

In order to contextualize the discussion of the loss of *ne* from negative structures in Modern French, we will here give a brief outline of the history of negation in French (see also Posner 1997:369–72).[24]

Latin *non* in unstressed position gave Old French *ne* which during this early period sufficed alone to mark negation. From early on, however, a number of particles were used to reinforce the negative; these were originally positive in meaning and were emphatic, reinforcing the negative (e.g. *pas < passum*, 'step', *point < punctum*, 'point', *mie < mica*, 'crumb', etc.). Gradually, through repeated usage in negative contexts, these particles began to lose their emphatic value and to acquire a negative meaning themselves. By the seventeenth century grammarians were asserting that all negatives should have two parts, *ne* with *pas, point, personne, rien*, etc., and this has remained the standard usage ever since.

Today *pas* and other *forclusifs* are frequently used alone, notably in speech, to mark negation, thereby rendering the original marker of the negation, *ne*, optional. This has led some commentators to chart the history of negation in French in the following schematic way:

Table 11.1   The history of French negation (Ashby 1991:4)

1. Classical Latin:	*non*	Verb	
2. Old and Middle French:	*ne*	Verb	(*pas*, et al.)
3. Classical French:	*ne*	Verb	*pas*
4. Modern French:	(*ne*)	Verb	*pas*
5. Future French:		Verb	*pas*

There has, however, been considerable debate (see Ayres-Bennett 1994) as to the dating of this phenomenon and whether it is possible to find examples of the non-use of *ne* dating back at least to the seventeenth century. While it is indeed possible to find such examples from the classical period, the most recent research by Ashby (1997) looking at usage of comparable subjects over the period 1981–95 suggests that, even if this change has been attested for some 300 years, nevertheless it is a change which is accelerating fast, and that the rate of loss of *ne* is now rapid (see **11.4.2.6** below).

11.4.2   Factors influencing the use or non-use of *ne* in contemporary French

A great deal of research has been carried out on the frequency and status of post-verbal *pas* used alone to mark negation in Modern French, including treatment of the relative importance of different factors – whether syntactic, phonetic, lexical, semantic, stylistic or demographic – which favour the use or non-use of *ne*. Coveney (1998) has recently argued that native speakers are aware of certain constraining factors on the variable omission of *ne* and in particular of the influence of the nature of the subject of the negated verb, of the negative complement and of the presence or absence of an intensifying adverb, although not of other factors such as the type of clause or the presence or absence of an object pronoun. These findings, while interesting, are somewhat provisional since his methodology for testing informants is rather unrefined, as Coveney himself admits. Moreover, the subjects he questioned were all either language teachers or degree-level language learners who were aware of the purpose of his investigation.

11.4.2.1   Syntactic factors

Recent research on spoken corpora by Ashby (1976, 1981a, 1991, 1997[25]), Moreau (1986), Lüdicke (1982), Diller [1983], and Coveney (1996) has suggested that a number of syntactic factors influence a speaker's choice as to whether to include *ne* or not. There is general consensus that the following factors affect the rate of retention of *ne*:

- Type of clause: the *ne* is dropped more frequently in main than in subordinate clauses; conversely, its retention is particularly favoured in relative clauses, subordinate clauses where the verb is in the subjunctive and 'if . . . then' structures.
- Type of subject: the *ne* is much more likely to be dropped if the subject is pronominal rather than nominal. For example, in Diller's study *ne* was deleted in 39% of cases where the subject was a pronoun, but in only 3% of cases where the subject was a full noun phrase (including proper names). According to Ashby (1981a), the percentage of retention declines in the following order: noun subject, no surface subject (i.e. infinitival and imperative structures[26]), non-clitic pronoun subject (e.g. *cela, quelqu'un*), clitic pronoun subject.
- Type of pronoun: within the personal pronoun class there seems to be a slight preference for non-usage with singular rather than plural pronouns. Diller's survey found, for example, the following percentages of non-usage according to the choice of subject pronoun: *je* 37%; *tu/vous* (sing.) 33%; *il/elle/on* 32%; *ils/elles* 27%; *nous/vous* (plural) 21%. The rate of loss also appears to be higher when there is an impersonal subject pronoun, but this perhaps relates to the relative fixity of such expressions and the frequency of their usage (see **11.4.2.4** below).
- Type of verb: Ashby (1981a) found a tendency for *ne* to be retained with *avoir* and *être*[27] and with the modals *devoir* and *pouvoir*, but not with other verbs or *aller* as an auxiliary verb.
- Choice of the *forclusif*: while it is quite difficult to discern any clear pattern here, surveys show that *ne* is most likely to be absent when the negative particle is *pas*, and most likely to be retained with *que*.[28]

11.4.2.2   Phonetic factors

The importance of the phonetic environment for the use or absence of *ne* is frequently difficult to quantify: for instance, in a context like *on (n')a pas* it is virtually impossible to determine whether *ne* is present or not. There is, in addition, some disagreement amongst linguists about whether some contexts favour or impede its retention. On the one hand, Moreau (1986:149) concludes that there is no correlation between phonology and the frequency of *ne*, and Lüdicke (1982:44) equally denies that *ne* falls more readily in pre-consonantal than pre-vocalic position, but most other studies suggest that *ne* is favoured in intervocalic position in order to avoid vocalic hiatus (e.g. *qui a, ça a*). It is also likely that a post-pausal position favours retention, whereas a faster speech rate promotes loss of *ne*.

11.4.2.3   Semantic factors

Diller [1983] has tried to account for the variable retention rate within the pronoun subject class by considering what the pronoun stands for in the discourse. She attempts to define subjects in terms of their 'semantic weight', which includes notions of reference and specificity, and concludes that *ne* deletion is inversely proportional to the semantic weight of the subject. Alongside full NPs, which she considers have maximum semantic weight, she elaborates four categories of pronoun as follows, in decreasing order of semantic weight:

- Pronouns with a syntactic antecedent in the sentence, that is, relative pronouns, which then bear the semantic weight of their antecedent. The rate of non-occurrence of *ne* here was 4% in Diller's study, comparable to the 3% rate she found for full noun phrases.
- Pronouns with a lexical referent, that is, true personal pronouns which generally refer to a specific lexical item in the previous clause and a specific reality in the situational context; here the rate of deletion was 32%.
- Pronouns with a pragmatic reference, that is, the case of the indefinite deictics which do not have a specific referent in the previous discourse, but which correspond to some external reality and can always be replaced by a more or less adequate paraphrase (*ce*, *c'*, *ça*); with these the percentage of omission was 46%.
- Pronouns with no semantic weight, that is, 'empty' or 'dummy' pronouns such as impersonal *il* or *ce*. Non-use of *ne* rose here to 58%.

In short, Diller argues that there is a clear difference between full NPs and relative pronouns on the one hand, and other types of pronoun on the other, with the environment which is most favourable to omission being that where there is no semantic weight carried by the pronoun.

11.4.2.4   Frequently used expressions

Many commentators have pointed out that these different factors may well interact to a significant extent and therefore greatly increase the likelihood of non-use of *ne* (e.g. Sturm 1981:184). There has therefore been an attempt to look at the use of negatives in collocations of 'pre-formed sequences', or what Moreau terms 'groupes lexicaux préformés'. For example, Ashby (1981a:678) talks of certain 'formulae' where non-use of *ne* is very high, foremost among which are: *je sais pas, il faut pas* [fo pa], *c'est pas, il y a pas* (cf. Sturm 1981). It is perhaps better not to think of these as formulae, which might imply that they should be fixed and conservative, but rather as frequently used expressions.

Moreau (1986) focuses on the way four important factors – the nature of the subject, the type of verb, the verb tense, and the particular negative particle – may combine to give predetermined structures or sequences. In comparison to other structures, these have a very high rate of *ne* deletion. For instance:

Table 11.2   Rates of *ne* deletion with predetermined structures (Moreau 1986)

c'était pas	81.96%
il faut pas	80.64%
c'est pas	79.35%
je crois pas	75.00%

11.4.2.5   Stylistic factors

A key factor in the use or absence of *ne* is the formality of the setting and the register employed. This also relates to the question of subject matter. Ashby (1981a:681–2) gives clear evidence of speakers style-shifting, that is, modifying their usage according to the setting. Thus Ashby found a marked difference in the use of *ne* of three of his subjects depending on whether they were interviewed in the formal setting of the office or in an informal setting in their own home (*ne* retention was 35% in the office setting, but only 16% in the relaxed setting). In addition, Ashby found the point where the token appeared in the conversation to be significant, with retention more likely in the first half of the conversation than in the second, perhaps again as the speaker became more relaxed.

11.4.2.6   Demographic factors: region, SES, and age[29]

Clearly there is a great deal of interpersonal variation (Ashby 1997), but a number of factors in the speaker's pre-linguistic make-up seem to play a role in the likelihood of their retaining or dropping negative *ne*. Although it is sometimes difficult to compare the results based on different corpora because there is not strict comparability of methodology etc., it is evident that regional considerations are important (see Coveney 1996:64). The most striking phenomenon is the almost categorical absence of *ne* from Montreal French in comparison to metropolitan usage. Grevisse (1993:1462) adds that loss is also high in Paris and Berry in contrast to, say, Lorraine and Walloon where the average rate of retention is higher. Pohl (1968) notes that urban speakers are more likely to drop *ne* than rural ones.[30] It may also be noted that *pa* alone is the usual negator in a number of French creoles. In nearly all creoles this *pa* is placed before the finite verb alongside all tense and aspect markers, but in Réunionnais it regularly follows the first verb encountered (e.g. *muê le pa malad* ('I'm not ill'), *m i mâz pa* ('I don't eat'), Baker and Corne 1982:25) and it can also be heard post-verbally in Louisiana (Posner 1985:181–2).[31]

It appears that a speaker's SES is becoming less important in determining whether s/he will omit *ne* in negative structures. For instance, while some surveys showed SES to be influential, particularly amongst older speakers (e.g. Diller ([1983]:168) found 42% deletion in the usage of her lower class compared with 22% in her higher class; cf. Ashby 1981a:684), Coveney (1996) records relative homogeneity of rate of retention amongst his younger speakers, regardless of their social group. Désirat and Hordé (1988:155) record that as long ago as the 1950s, when the recordings were made for *Français fondamental*, non-use of *ne* was frequent, regardless of social origin, but this did not prevent speakers perceiving non-usage as not speaking well.

Of all the demographic factors, age appears to be the most significant. Two types of study have been important here. First, studies of child language acquisition indicate that use of *ne* becomes more and more reinforced as children get older through education and the acquisition of the written norms. There is strong evidence to suggest that it is a typical feature of children's language to omit negative *ne* (e.g. Nyrop 1899–1930:VI:39). Indeed Pohl (1968) believes the non-use of *ne* to be virtually categorical up to the age of three or more. Pohl examined the acquisition of negative statements by a twin boy and girl from the age of $5^{1}/_{2}$ to 12 (Pohl 1972). Since his analysis shows that it took the twins several years to acquire the *ne*, he suggests the importance of the role of schooling, parental 'correction', and the influence of the written language in establishing the 'standard' construction.

Table 11.3   Pohl's (1972) analysis of the amount of *ne* omission in children's usage

Boy:	5–6 yrs 96.8%	Girl:	5–6 yrs 72.0%	Both:	5–6 yrs 81.5%
	$6^{1}/_{2}$ yrs 95.6%		$6^{1}/_{2}$ yrs 61.0%		$6^{1}/_{2}$ yrs 75.3%
	12 yrs 63.9%		12 yrs 56.5%		12 yrs 60.6%

A second body of evidence has been provided by variationist accounts which examine the use of *ne* by speakers of different age groups with a view to finding out whether we are witnessing a change in progress or whether this is rather a case of stable variation. Since younger adult speakers are found to use *ne* less often than older adult speakers, this might be taken as evidence that usage is changing. Note, however, that whereas the overall pattern is one of decreasing non-use of *ne* as (adult) speakers get older, the figures are not straightforward: for example, Ashby (1976:134) identifies an apparent conservatism in the usage of the age group 40–49.

Table 11.4   Incidence of *ne* deletion according to age (Ashby 1976:134)

20–29	48.1%
30–39	49.2%
40–49	33.8%
50–59	39.5%
60–69	35.1%

Different explanations have been offered for the age-grading which clearly exists in the case of non-use of *ne*. For some, non-use of *ne* is a stable socio-linguistic variable, and the patterns of usage seen in Table 11.4 are therefore not indicative of change. It could be argued, for example, that pressure to conform to the prescriptive, scholastic norm which dictates that speakers use the full form at different stages of their lives is felt most strongly by middle-aged speakers and least by youth who are typically not constrained by rules, as can be seen in their use of a wide range of innovative forms (e.g. *verlan*, *franglais*).

However, Ashby's most recent research (1997) seems to give weight to the alternative hypothesis that the deletion of *ne* is now a rapidly accelerating change, even if it was until recently a stable sociolinguistic variable.[32] When the usage of *ne* of those of the ten individuals from his survey of 1976 (published as Ashby 1981a) that he was able to re-interview in 1995 was examined, it was found that most of them had not changed their rate of retention. On the other hand, when Ashby analysed comparable subjects' usage in 1976 and 1995, he found a marked decrease in usage in both his younger and older age-groups:

Table 11.5   Rate of use of *ne* (Ashby 1997)

	1976	1995
51–64	52%	19%
14–22	19%	14%

This combination of stability in the usage of the individual with instability in the usage of the community is, he maintains, symptomatic of change in progress or of 'le changement linguistique ordinaire'.

11.4.3   Other examples of the rise of *pas*

Just as in sentential negation we can trace a cycle of change from the use of *ne* on its own in Old French to mark negation, through the standard *ne . . . pas*, to contemporary spoken *pas* alone, so there is a parallel development for negating elements of a sentence, from *non* to *non pas* to contemporary *pas* (e.g. *heureux ou pas*). Use of *pas* has also flourished in certain other contexts. For example, increasingly in speech, *pas un* is favoured in preference to *aucun* or *nul*. Since *pas* on its own has lost all sense of reinforcement[33], a whole range of expressions of different frequency and formality is used in casual speech to reinforce the negative, including *pas du tout*, *pas un clou*, *pas tripette* (see Gadet 1992:79), suggesting perhaps that the cycle of change towards more than one negative marker is beginning to occur.

Suggested Reading

General works on negation:
  Gaatone (1971), Muller (1991).
History of negation:
  Ayres-Bennett (1994), Harris (1978), Posner (1985, 1997), Schwegler (1983, 1988).
Status of *ne, pas*, etc.:
  Damourette and Pichon [1928–40], Gross (1977), Jones (1996), Muller (1997), Rowlett (1998).
Negative 'raising':
  Cornulier (1973), Prince (1976).
Ne . . . que:
  Azoulay-Vicente (1988), Baciu (1978).
Loss of *ne*:
  Ashby (1976, 1981a, 1991, 1997), Ayres-Bennett (1994), Coveney (1996, 1998), Diller [1983], Lüdicke (1982), Moreau (1986), Pohl (1968, 1972, 1975), Sturm (1981).

Notes

1. There are a number of important recent studies looking at negation within a generative framework from a theoretical or comparative viewpoint; see, for example, Acquaviva (1992, 1994), Haegeman (1995), Laka (1994), Progovac (1994), Zanuttini (1997). While many of these use Romance, and indeed French, data to support their arguments, the focus of interest is primarily on general and theoretical questions. An excellent treatment of French sentence negation within a Principles-and-Parameters framework is Rowlett (1998), whose work will be referred to on a number of occasions in this chapter.

2. These examples, taken from Recourcé, are rather awkward, not least because of the positioning of *jamais*. Nevertheless, the syntactic argument appears to be valid.

3. Rowlett notes that the distribution of *rien* and *personne* is also different, the former having a distribution similar to *tout*.

4. Muller (1997), working within a generative framework, also establishes a parallel with the use of quantifiers. He argues that in *pas de N* the *de N* depends on an empty head (Je n'ai pas, [(e), de cheval]) and that the construction has the value of an indefinite quantifier.

5. Bonnard (1994) argues that *de* is not a determiner since it does not fulfil all the functions of members of that class; he prefers instead to see it simply as a 'substantiveur'.

6. Rowlett (1994) questions Muller's data and maintains that the second interpretation is not available to native speakers. Gaatone (1971:54) points out that since the 'raised' construction is more normal with *falloir, devoir, vouloir*, the other order may be exploited to create a deliberate stylistic effect. Thus, he argues, *Il faut que ce mariage ne se fasse pas* is more emphatic than *Il ne faut pas que ce mariage se fasse*.

7. Prince still uses a model which has construction-specific transformations, but the constructions could also be accounted for by a more general movement transformation.

8. These are questions which immediately follow a statement seeking confirmation. Compare *She's English, isn't she?* with *She's not English, is she?*

9. Prince maintains that in examples where NEG-raising occurs, the verb of the subordinate clause is in the subjunctive, and therefore discounts this example.

10. Muller (1991:134) suggests an alternative explanation. It could be argued that negation does not change the type of speech act: a negative imperative such as *Ne pars pas!* is still an imperative, it simply gives the opposite order. The problem with modal verbs is that while these may be used in assertions (*Luc ne doit pas sortir*), they may also convey an order. The ambiguity arises from the fact that in this case, the negative must not associate with the modal verb (*Tu ne dois pas sortir*), whilst at other times the negative does seem to apply to the modal verb to deny there is an order.

11. Baciu (1978:142) suggests the following equation:

$$\frac{\text{J'ai seulement un livre}}{\text{Je n'ai pas seulement un livre}} = \frac{\text{Je n'ai qu'un livre}}{\text{Je n'ai pas qu'un livre}}$$

12. There is also historical evidence in favour of this since *ne ... que* is a shortened form of the older construction *ne ... mais (que)*, 'not more than' (Posner 1997:371). We have already noted that Rowlett's position (1998) is diametrically opposed to this, since he argues that *ne* is never inherently negative in the modern language.

13. Damourette and Pichon ([1928–40]:I:144) call the *que* of *ne ... que* 'uniceptif' since 'ce qu'il exprime représente précisément la seule chose avec quoi le fait amplecté par *ne* ne soit point en discordance'. In this way they keep the link with related constructions which share the *discordantiel*, but differentiate it from 'la négation pleine' in which the *discordantiel* is combined with a *forclusif* not the *uniceptif*.

14. This construction appears to be less problematic for some native speakers than some of the others discussed above.

15. Note, however, that the sentences are not strictly comparable since in the fourth example the subject of the main clause and the subordinate clause is identical, whereas in the other examples the subjects of the two clauses are different.

16. Here, of course, the partitive may be playing a role in the different behaviour of the two structures. For other differences between sentences with the complementizer *que* and those with restrictive *que*, see Azoulay-Vicente (1988).

17. For example, Dubois (1967:169) describes expletive *ne* as a stylistic feature which emphasizes the difference between written and spoken French.

18. Note that expletive *ne* never occurs before an infinitive (**Je crains de ne venir*) (Riegel, Pellat and Rioul 1994:419).

19. Larrivée (1996) correctly notes that this is not always the case since *pas* may also have an expletive value, as in the sentences *Défense de ne pas poser des matériaux sur ce terrain* and *Ce n'est pas possible sans que cette réforme n'ait pas été adoptée généralement*.

20. Where *personne* is used with expletive *ne*, the sense is different. For instance, *Pierre craint qu'il ne vienne jamais personne* has the meaning 'Pierre recherche la compagnie'.

21. As in the case of the *ne . . . que* construction, this allows them to highlight the difference between these structures in which only the *discordantiel* is present, and use of *ne . . . pas* which has both a *discordantiel* and *forclusif*.

22. These guidelines are frequently ignored and may be counter-productive.

23. For a very different account see Larrivée (1995) who maintains that such usages are very much alive in written French and that they have a definite semantic coherence.

24. A typological account of French negation may be found in Harris (1978). Such an approach is strongly challenged by Schwegler (1983, 1988) who examines a number of different explanations for the changes, including pragmatic factors and what he terms the 'negative cycle'.

25. We are extremely grateful to Bill Ashby for communicating to us in typescript the results of his most recent research (Ashby 1997).

26. According to Grevisse (1993:1463) when the *ne* of the imperative falls, the object pronouns usually stay in the position they have for a negative imperative: *Vous grattez pas (=n'essayez pas) de leur trouver ci . . . de leur trouver ça* (Céline). Where, however, loss of *ne* is systematic (notably in Quebec), this entails postposition of the pronoun, giving *vas-y pas* instead of *n'y vas pas*. Note that in popular and very familiar language, deletion of both elements of the negative is occasionally heard; for example, *t'occupe* as a reduction of *(ne) t'occupe pas de ça*.

27. The fact that these verbs both have an initial vowel may be significant, see 11.4.2.2 below.

28. Grevisse (1993:1463), however, points out that in the *français populaire* of the Auvergne *que* may be used on its own with a verb as an equivalent of 'seulement', so that *j'arrive que* may be used with the meaning of 'je ne fais qu'arriver'.

29. The speaker's sex does not appear to be highly significant (Coveney 1996:85; Ashby 1997).

30. In all these cases there may be the influence of other factors (in this case, for example, phonetic considerations to do with the rate of speech).

31. Post-verbal *pa* is attested in earlier Réunionnais texts (Baker and Corne 1982:222). The variant [napa] is also found in early Mauritian texts.

32. The argument is that while examples of non-use of *ne* may be found as early as the seventeenth century (see Ayres-Bennett 1994), many of these until recent times may be explained by sociolinguistic factors.

33. Indeed, Désirat and Hordé (1988:157) argue that in spoken French *ne* could be considered simply as an emphatic particle without any negative value of its own. It is only in a few cases with a modal verb that the presence or absence of *ne* may disambiguate. For instance, the example, *On peut pas aimer ce film*, could be equivalent to *On peut ne pas aimer ce film* or *On ne peut pas aimer ce film*. In practice differences in stress patterns may be used to resolve any potential ambiguity.

12

Neologisms: internal versus external factors

12.1 Introduction

The strength of the purist tradition in France has meant that neologisms have often been seen at best as a necessary evil. Reaction to borrowings, however, has tended to be much more negative, on the grounds that by adopting material from other languages, French speakers are neglecting their 'native resources', that is, material which comes from within the French system, in favour of using external or foreign material which is likely to disrupt the balance of the system and cause problems of assimilation. Purists and *dirigistes* alike would always tend to prefer neologisms formed by derivation or composition to foreign imports or borrowings from dialects. However, given the long and varied history of word formation in French and the multiplicity of creative possibilities open to the would-be neologizer, this distinction between internal and external resources is very difficult to sustain.

To take a concrete example, the form *oléoduc* has been proposed as the preferable 'French' alternative to the English borrowing *pipeline* which is disliked not least because of the difficulties of pronouncing its second syllable. But on what grounds should *oléoduc* based on Latin *oleum* (and root of the Modern French *huile*) used in the sense of English 'oil' and formed on the analogy of, for example, *aqueduc*, be considered more French than *pipeline*? In this Chapter we will consider a range of issues which centre on the linguistic tension between internal and external resources for neologisms, including:

- The definition of borrowings and loan words
- The integration of borrowings into French
- The combination of foreign material with 'native' material to form 'hybrids' and pseudo-anglicisms
- The status of Latin and Greek material or 'learned' resources
- French attitudes towards internal and external resources for neologisms.

Throughout the chapter we shall draw on material from a variety of languages but the emphasis, especially in **12**.3 and **12**.4, will be on Anglo-American borrowings.

12.2   Definitional questions and statistics

12.2.1   What is a borrowing?

There are a number of difficulties in trying to respond to this question. First, there is the issue of how stable a foreign word is in French, that is, the extent to which it has become an integrated part of the lexical stock. Where should we draw the line between very rare or markedly stylistic uses of foreign terms and borrowings? At what point is a word so well integrated that it ceases to be a borrowing? If we were to consider as 'native' resources only those lexical items that have been in French since Vulgar Latin, the 'native' lexical stock would, of course, be seriously depleted.

Clearly many words of foreign origin borrowed into the language during the course of its history are no longer perceived as foreign by native speakers; for example, *maréchal* (< Germanic), *amour* (< Occitan), *chiffre* (< Arabic), *violon* (< Italian), *chocolat* (< Nahuatl via Spanish) are all treated as 'French' words and are now thoroughly integrated into the lexical stock. On the other hand, at this particular point in history, *baby-boomer, body-building, happening, blue chip* would all be instantly recognized as Anglo-American borrowings. The words in the above two lists represent opposite ends of a spectrum in that they differ radically in terms of the length of time they have been established in French, to the point where we might consider one group as borrowings and the other as 'French'.

Does the definition of a borrowing simply depend then on how long a particular word has been in the borrowing language? Poplack, Sankoff and Miller, whose work has focused on Canadian French, consider longstanding borrowed words as loanwords, and other borrowed terms as borrowings: whereas borrowings are integrated linguistically into the host language (phonologically, morphologically and syntactically), loanwords may be seen as more fully assimilated in that, in addition to having undergone phonological, morphological and syntactic adaptation, they 'recur relatively frequently, are widely used in the speech community, and have achieved a certain level of recognition or acceptance, if not normative approval' (Poplack, Sankoff and Miller 1988:52). The formulation of this definition suggests the difficulty of trying to 'measure' such differences. There are similar difficulties with the distinction between borrowings, 'nonce' borrowings and code-switched items: for Poplack, Sankoff and Miller, borrowings (however infrequent) are distinguished from nonce borrowings which occur only once in their corpus, and these in turn are distinguished from a single code-switched item, where, usually in the context of a bilingual community, the speaker switches for one word into the second language.

The question of when a word becomes a borrowing and when it ceases to be one is clearly highly problematic. Even where it is possible to decide that a particular form is clearly a borrowing, it is not always easy to date its arrival in the language: the first appearance of a word in French is rarely co-temporal with its adoption by the community at large, and the usage of a word in the oral medium can be considerably earlier than in written French. In addition, by no means all borrowings arrive in French on a direct route from another language. A lexical item may enter into French via an intermediary language; indeed these *mots voyageurs* can travel through two or more inter-mediary languages or through dialects before arriving in French. *Orange* for example, came into French from Arabic via Provençal, *riz* came from Hindi via Arabic, *banane* from Bantu via Portuguese.[1] Hilary Wise (1997:14) notes that the usual practice in dictionaries is to give the most recent source language, though she notes considerable inconsistencies within certain dictionaries, and a predilection for giving more detailed histories of exotic words.

12.2.2   Types of borrowing

The difficulty of defining what constitutes a borrowing is compounded by the fact that borrowing may take a number of different forms, as a glance at the following list of Anglo-Americanisms will reveal: *body-building, faisabilité, lifting, shake-hand, col-blanc, rugbyman.* Most typologies of borrowings identify broadly similar categories, many elaborating on Haugen's (1950) three prin-cipal categories of 'loan words' (usually the straight borrowing of both form and function), 'loan shifts' (which include translations of foreign terms as well as semantic borrowings), and 'loan blends' or hybrids (which mix foreign and French forms).[2]

The following are some of the more detailed categories mentioned by recent work on borrowing: **straight borrowings** (where both the sense and the form are borrowed, e.g. *walkman, leitmotif/v*), **adapted borrowings** (forms of foreign origin which are adapted, usually by taking a French suffix, e.g. *conteneur*), **pseudo-anglicisms** (words which look English but which do not correspond to an English usage, e.g. *lifting, bronzing, tennisman*), *faux-amis* or **semantic calques** (words where the foreign sense is borrowed, e.g. *développer, réaliser*), **borrowings which are learned forms** (where the bor-rowing is often thought to be a French form of learned origin, e.g. *crédible, contraceptif, unidimensionnel*), **translations** or **calques** (e.g. *liberté de la presse, liste noire, franc-maçon, science-fiction, haute-fidélité*), **compounds** or **hybrid compounds**, where one or more element is a borrowing (e.g. *baby-foot, athletic-foot, top modèle*), **abbreviated borrowings** (*pull, fast, self*).[3]

Useful as these categories are as a starting point, it will be evident through-out our discussion that clear-cut lines are not always easy to draw. It is debatable whether there is such a thing as a straight borrowing (of sense, form, pragmatic connotations, sociolinguistic associations, stylistic qualities etc.); the category of adapted borrowings can contain widely differing examples, some where the adaptation is very slight and others where it is considerable; the categories of 'pseudo' borrowings, hybrids and learned borrowings also pose complex questions of classification (see **12**.4 and **12**.5 below).

12.2.3   Statistical considerations

It is extremely difficult to estimate the number of borrowings in French for a number of reasons. In the first instance, and as we have already discussed, it is not always easy to define a lexical item as a borrowing; it is particularly difficult where the items are fleeting or not well established in the language. Second, the statistics obtained would be highly dependent on the corpus of words under investigation; the percentage of borrowings in a dictionary of French would be different from the percentage of tokens in a corpus, where certain words could be used frequently and others hardly at all. Similarly, the nature of the corpus would be crucial; a newspaper corpus might yield very different statistics from a literary text, a technical manual, a scientific report or a corpus of spoken French.

These difficulties are evident if we consider some of the statistics cited in the literature. Amongst the more recent surveys, Müller's dictionary calculations (1985:55), which count words occurring in dictionaries rather than frequency of use, estimate the percentage at approximately 6%, of which half are Anglo-American; his newspaper survey, based on an edition of *Le Monde* and *France-Soir*, puts borrowings at 3.2% (1.3% Anglo-Americanisms) and 4.6% (1% Anglo-Americanisms) respectively. Most figures are low[4], varying between 2% and 6%, but a recent survey discussed in Walter (1997a) puts the figure at nearer 13%. The discrepancy may also be related to the corpus: this is a dictionary survey, and therefore one which counts words rather than frequency of usage. It may also be a function of Walter's definitions: she speaks of *mots d'origine étrangère* rather than *emprunts*, the former embracing a much wider spectrum of vocabulary than the latter, including many long-standing borrowings which may not be counted in other surveys.

What sort of patterns emerge in a situation of diglossia? Again, the nature of the corpus is crucial. Lagueux's survey (1988), based on a corpus of French and Canadian newspapers, finds similar levels of borrowing in France and Quebec. Poplack, Sankoff and Miller's corpus (1988) of Canadian French is completely different by nature from any of the surveys mentioned above, and is particularly valuable, representing as it does full transcriptions of oral data from a community in a situation of diglossia. Here the statistics are low: Anglo-American borrowings represent under 1% of the total verbal output. The tokens of borrowings in this calculation (i.e. each occurrence of a borrowing) represent 2183 types (i.e. different words), some 3.3% of the total vocabulary. Moreover, most of the words concerned are used by one speaker only, with only 7% of the English-origin borrowings used in the community at large (Poplack, Sankoff and Miller 1988:57).

12.3   The linguistic integration of borrowings

We have seen that for some linguists the degree of linguistic integration undergone by a borrowing is, at least in part, a determining factor in defining its status – as internal or external – in the borrowing language. In this section we explore further how this integration is achieved and the limitations on full assimilation.

12.3.1   Phonological integration

12.3.1.1   The issues

It is highly unlikely that there will exist a one-to-one mapping of the sounds of the borrowed language with those of French. Where borrowing occurs, two different systems are coming into contact, some with more common ground than others. In the case of French, the foreign term is usually given a French pronunciation, that is, the nearest French phones are used. This raises a number of issues; are we talking about the nearest French phones to the foreign pronunciation of the term, or to the pronunciation generated by the spelling? Are there any examples of new phonemes, or of borrowed phones being imported into French?

In the case of Anglo-American borrowings for example, French and English share a number of similar consonants (e.g. /b/, /m/, /f/, /v/, /g/, /s/, /z/, /ʃ/) and in these instances, the French pronunciation will normally use the corresponding consonant. In other cases, there is a close correspondence, even if the sounds are not exactly the same; the French phonemes /t/ and /d/ for example are pronounced as dentals, whereas they are alveolar in English; there is less aspiration in the French consonants /p/ and /k/ than in their English counterparts. Elsewhere, there is no corresponding sound at all and another solution is found (e.g. the English /θ/, /tʃ/, /dʒ/). In practice, the series of French phones which will be used is based either on the nearest ones to the correct foreign pronunciation (*week-end* [wikɛnd], *showbusiness* [ʃobiznɛs]), or those nearest to the set of sounds in French suggested by the foreign spelling (*standard* [stɑ̃daʁ]), with a variety of possibilities in between and even the possibility of hybrid forms such as *boy-scout* [bɔjskut], where the first part reflects the former pattern and the second part the latter. Stress patterns may also be quite different from French, which does not have word stress.

Some of the earlier borrowings are the most heavily gallicized, whereas all the evidence suggests that the pronunciation of most contemporary borrowings will tend towards the foreign pronunciation of the term, a fact which perhaps partly accounts for the heightened awareness of borrowings today. The factors which determine the degree of phonetic integration will include the medium through which the borrowing enters French. A borrowing which comes into spoken French first may be pronounced as close to its original pronunciation as possible; arrival through the written medium may mean a pronunciation based on spelling. Familiarity with the borrowed language will also be a factor: the better the speaker's knowledge, the stronger the chances that the pronunciation will be closer to the original. Examples of such knowledge influencing the pronunciation of the borrowed term occur in Canadian French, where speakers' familiarity with Canadian English means that borrowings such as *camping* and *gang* are pronounced [kæmpiŋ] and [gɛ̃ŋg] (i.e. close to the North-American pronunciation), whereas the French pronounce them [kãpiŋ] and [gãg] respectively (that is, closer to the series of sounds generated by the spelling, especially with regard to the vowel in the first syllable – see Pergnier 1989:33, who, however, considers the consonant of *-ing* to be [ɲ] not [ŋ]). Frequency of use will come into play, in that a particular pronunciation may stabilize if it is commonly employed by speakers, especially if it is also promoted by the media.

In Poplack, Sankoff and Miller's survey (1988) of Canadian French, in a community where many speakers have both the North-American English and French phonological systems in their linguistic competence, the degree of integration is found to depend on the age of the word, on the extent to which it is widespread or infrequent, and on the speaker's degree of bilingual ability. Less well integrated items may use foreign phonemes such as /θ/, /ð/, /tʃ/. The older borrowings (e.g. *club, kicker* (verb), *shop, record, smart*), to which Poplack, Sankoff and Miller ascribe the status of loanword (see **12.2.1** above), are always given a French pronunciation (1988:70).

Poplack, Sankoff and Miller's results also suggest strongly that the most widespread borrowings (in terms of the quantity of speakers using them) are the most likely to be integrated phonologically into French (1988:72). Finally their results, in line with those of Haugen (1950) and Mougeon, Beniak and Valois (1985), suggest that the higher a speaker's degree of bilingualism, the less their tendency will be to integrate borrowings into French phonology. Taken together, these results suggest that 'proficient English speakers use less French phonology than monolinguals, but all speakers integrate old and widespread loanwords more than they do nonce borrowings' (Poplack, Sankoff and Miller 1988:75).

12.3.1.2   The implications

In the light of these patterns, what is the overall impact of borrowings on the French phonological system? In terms of the loss or gain of phonemes, the impact on metropolitan French is relatively slight. One important exception is the velar nasal /ŋ/, which has been acquired with the series of English borrowings ending in -ing, e.g. *footing, parking, happening* etc.[5] Two other potential imports are the English affricates /tʃ/ (as in *match*) and /dʒ/ (as in *job*), which, although occurring in some borrowings, are still very marginal to the system, and are not generally included in inventories of French phonemes.

The more significant impact is at the phonetic level, since considerable variation and instability of usage accompanies borrowing. This can be seen both at the level of the individual sounds and in the variation in the pronunciation of a given word. Retman (1978), for example, takes each of the English phonemes in turn and looks at the various possibilities for their pronunciation in French. While the transfer of some phonemes is straightforward (e.g. the English /g/ is rendered by the French sound [g] in 96% of cases, the phoneme /v/ by the fricative [v] in all cases etc.), others demonstrate considerable variation; the English /ʌ/ as in 'rush' is rendered [œ] in 34% of examples in Retman's survey (e.g. [rœʃ]), by [y] in 28% of examples (e.g. [bys]), by [ɔ] in 16% of cases (e.g. [rɔm]), by [ɔ̃] in 7% (e.g. [pɔ̃ʃ] *punch*), by [u] in 6% (e.g. [guvɛrnəmɑ̃]), and by various other sounds in a small number of cases including [ɛ̃] as in *bungalow*, [œ̃] as in *jungle*, [a] as in some pronunciations of *hold-up*, [o] as in some renderings of *self-gouvernement* < 'government', [ɑ̃] in *panca* (< *punkah*), [ø] in *puzzle*, [ɛ] by one speaker in *puncher*, and [aw] by one speaker in *cross-country*. English phonemes demonstrating high levels of variation of this nature are very numerous indeed.

At the level of the individual word, a glance at the selection of pronunciations given for some of the borrowings in Martinet and Walter's *Dictionnaire de la prononciation française dans son usage réel* reveals the levels of instability. Indeed Martinet and Walter comment on borrowings (1973:28):

> si nous nous en étions tenus aux détails des réalisations enregistrées, nous aurions été amenés, pour certains mots, à donner autant de prononciations différentes que de sujets soumis à l'enquête.

Some examples from the dictionary will illustrate the great diversity of strategies used by speakers in the pronunciation of borrowings; the figures give the number of speakers from among the seventeen informants using a given pronunciation.

(1) *Weltanschauung* (< German: 'world view'):

veltanʃawuŋg	1	'weltanʃawŋg	1	German Pronunciation 6	
veltanʃauŋ	1	veltanʃawuŋ	1	?	6
veltɑ̃nʃauŋ	1				

We can see from the transcriptions that in the five 'French' pronunciations, the areas of consonantal variation concern the final consonant (where speakers hesitate between the velar nasal [ŋ] familiar from Anglo-American borrowings, and this sound followed by the corresponding velar stop) and, albeit to a lesser extent, the initial consonant [v] and the nasal consonant [n] at the end of the second syllable. Instability in the pronunciation of the vowels appears in the final two syllables, where speakers hesitate as to which combination of the vowels [a], [u] and the semi-vowel [w] they are going to use.

(2) *ferry boat* < (English):

| feribot | 9 | fɛribɔt | 1 | English Pronunciation 5* |
| feribot | 2 | fɛrebot | 1 | |

(* = one informant gives two pronunciations, hence the total of 18 tokens)

In this example, there is no hesitation with the consonants in the 'French' pronunciations, all of which are rendered by their nearest equivalent, but there is hesitation in three of the vowels between [e] and [ɛ] for the English /e/, between [i] and [e] for the English /ɪ/, and between [o] and [ɔ] for the English diphthong /əʊ/.

12.3.2   Morphosyntactic integration

There is general agreement that most borrowings are nouns. In Walter and Walter's dictionary corpus (1991), which is drawn from the *Petit Larousse* and the *Petit Robert*, 90% of borrowings are nouns, approximately 6% are verbs, 3% adjectives, 1% adverbs, and very few are interjections (e.g. *allô, tchin-tchin*). Some of the non-noun categories come from a limited group of languages: most adverbs come from Italian, for example. A completely different type of corpus (Poplack, Sankoff and Miller 1988) reveals similar patterns: as is suggested by Figure **12**.1, which compares the percentages of different categories in native and borrowed vocabulary in a corpus of Canadian French, nouns are by far the most frequent category, with verbs, adjectives and interjections/frozen expressions constituting the other main groups:

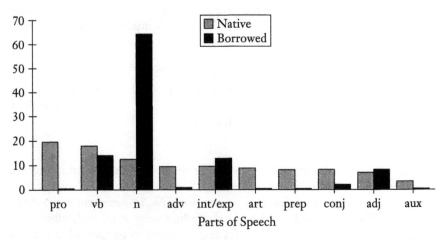

Figure 12.1 The borrowability of different parts of speech (Poplack, Sankoff and Miller (1998:63))

The frequency of nouns is attributed above all to their high semantic content and the fact that, relative to other parts of speech such as verbs, they are perceived as posing fewer problems for grammatical inflection etc.

What issues arise in the morphosyntactic integration of borrowings into French? Most nouns follow the regular French marker of plurality; most take an orthographic -*s*. Where there is a plural in the donor language which would be irregular in French, or where the word denotes a concept particular to the donor culture or is highly technical by nature, the original plural form may be kept (e.g. *lady/ladies, gentleman/gentlemen, soprano/soprani*), it may even be kept in *faux-anglicismes* such as *rugbyman/rugbymen*. This can lead to some hesitation; in the case of *soprano* for example, the *Petit Robert* entry gives 'plur. *des soprani* ou, mieux, *des sopranos*', thus allowing for the irregular foreign plural, whilst recommending the French one; the hesitation is reinforced by the fact that the French plural is not heard in the oral medium. Even where the noun is a plural form in the donor language, it is usually singular in French, and forms a plural in the usual way, for example *panini/paninis*. Compound nouns, on the other hand, tend to be invariable, for instance *baby-boom*.

Borrowed nouns are usually assigned a masculine gender. If, however, the noun has a parallel feminine form in French (*la pop-music, la dance-music, la house-music, la soul-music* etc. (cf. *la musique*), *la trash* (cf. *la poubelle*), or describes a distinctly feminine entity (*star, nurse, girl*), or has a distinctly feminine ending (e.g. *-ion, -ance, -esse, -ette*), it may be assigned a feminine gender (see Guilford 1999; Surridge 1984). Guilford (1999:71) notes, however, that the existence of a feminine noun in French where an analogy can be drawn does not necessarily mean that the borrowing will be assigned a feminine gender (e.g. *le gag* vs *une blague, une idée drôle*; *le chewing-gum* vs *la gomme à macher*). Moreover, the process of analogy can operate in different ways for apparently similar borrowings; Guilford cites the case of types of music where the link with the word *musique* is clear, and thus where the borrowing is feminine (see above), versus those which refer to a style of music, which tend to take the masculine by analogy with *style* (e.g. *le folk, le gospel, le jazz* etc.).

Roché (1992), in a study which looks at gender assignment in all types of neologism, highlights the traditional perception of the masculine as the 'unmarked' gender. He also notes a major shift in patterns for borrowings, from 36% masculine and 64% feminine in Old French to 81% masculine and 19% feminine in contemporary French, due mainly to a shift in the donor languages involved; that is, a move away from Latin in the Medieval period and other Romance languages in the Renaissance (where gender assignment was based on etymology), to Anglo-American borrowings in the last two centuries, where the unmarked masculine dominates, in some cases even where the ending might suggest the feminine gender, for example *caddie, magazine* (Roché 1992:117–18; cf. Surridge 1984).

There is also some evidence that speakers may show hesitation in the choice of gender with 'new' borrowings. This often arises because there is a choice of analogy; Guilford (1999) cites a number of such examples from the domain of popular music, including for instance *new wave* (feminine analogy with *la nouvelle vague* or *la musique*, masculine analogy with *le style*) and *noise* (masculine analogy with *bruit*, feminine analogy with *la noise*, or the feminine suffixes *-se* and *-oise*). In general, the better integrated the borrowing across the various groups in society, the more stable the gender will be. For example, Pergnier (1989:40–1) notes that the progressive social integration of *interview* has been accompanied both by increased phonological integration and by a shift from feminine (by analogy with *entrevue*) to the more usual masculine gender. Similarly, *bogue* (< English *bug*) in computer terminology is now masculine in the majority of cases, but is also attested with a feminine gender, presumably by analogy with the French *bogue* as in the outer coating of a horse chestnut, this 'French' term being a borrowing from Breton. Poplack, Sankoff and Miller's evidence confirms these broad patterns for Canadian French (1988:66–7); although it is rare to have 100% consistency in gender assignment, nonetheless it occurs relatively early in the integration of a borrowing and tends to remain consistent.

Borrowed adjectives, far fewer in number, tend to remain invariable, but there can be instability here too and an orthographic *-s* is sometimes found; since borrowings are frequently used in oral French, it is often not possible to tell whether the agreement has been made (e.g. *des parents cool, une fille snob, des mecs clean* – see Poplack, Sankoff and Miller 1988:69). Verbs, again far fewer in number than nouns, tend to fall into the *-er* category and there-fore have the advantage of regularity and ease of conjugation. As Poplack, Sankoff and Miller's evidence suggests (1988:68), the English verb serves as the root to which the suffix is added, as in the Canadian examples *afforder, checker, watcher*.

Given the fact that borrowing normally involves the transfer of nouns between languages, there is relatively small impact on French syntax. This is, however, an area of disagreement, with linguists such as Etiemble (1964) maintaining that the influence is significant, and others such as Spence (1976) and Hagège (1987) taking quite a different view. Examples frequently cited for contemporary French include an increased tendency to use English word order, both in phrases and within compounds (*air-conditionné, science-fiction*), the formation of compounds by juxtaposition (*bar-hôtel*) based on English models, increased use of the passive, adjectives used adverbially, and certain uses of the comparative and superlative.

According to Spence (1976:94ff.), these points have been greatly exagger-ated. Spence draws attention to the complexity of the situation, mentioning amongst other factors the well-attested native stylistic use of adjective-noun order in French, the existence of parallel structures in other Romance lan-guages (*norteamericano* (Spanish), *sudamericano* (Italian)), the fact that use of the passive and of adjectives as adverbs (*s'habiller jeune*) is as characteristic of French as of English (see the discussion on attitudes to borrowings in **12.6** below).

Picone (1996) argues that the increased use of noun-noun compounds in French is not motivated uniquely by English influences; he cites many other factors (1996:197), not least what he terms the 'synthetic imperative', that is, an increased tendency in the modern French lexis towards the use of terms which can express in compact synthetic form a complex amalgam of ideas. In Poplack, Sankoff and Miller's corpus, syntactic interference is minimal: only 0.05% of borrowed items show any syntactic divergence from standard French patterns, and where such divergence occurs, it concerns omission of the definite article (1988:69). Almost all borrowings involve no change of syntactic category; where this does occur, it involves the use of nouns as adjectives, and is restricted sociolinguistically to highly bilingual speakers (1988:70).

All factors considered, the morphosyntactic influence of borrowings on French appears to be low; some instability is certainly found in plurals and genders, but otherwise, on balance, the grammatical structure of French seems not to be significantly affected by the phenomenon.

12.3.3   Semantic integration

Borrowing rarely involves an entirely straightforward transfer in semantic terms of the borrowed word to the host language. Even where there is a 'straight borrowing', a word is moving from one semantic system to another. In the original language, it will often have a number of different senses, each of which may have various connotations; it will be related semantically to other words in its derivational family, its etymological family and its semantic field, and it will operate in certain sociolinguistic contexts. Once borrowed, this dynamic may change; the word may no longer have all the senses it had in the original language; it may acquire different resonances, a different set of derivational relationships (if any at all), different etymological links, different sociolinguistic contexts; and the alignment of other terms in its semantic field in the host language may be quite different from those in the original. It is also possible for subsequent semantic developments to take place once the word has entered French, since it will then find itself being used in new semantic and sociolinguistic contexts.

How does this external/internal tension manifest itself? In the case of a *faux-ami* (see **12**.2.2 above), the semantic shift is particularly clear. The verb *réaliser* for example, in addition to its original functions, is now used to mean *se rendre compte*, and is thus part of an opposition in French to which there is no parallel opposition in the donor language. Similarly, the verb *initier* has come to be used with the sense *commencer*. In the case of the noun *nurse*, the English word, which was borrowed from the French *nourrice* (1855), was subsequently reborrowed from English to French (1896) with the sense 'nourrice anglaise'; it now means 'nanny' or 'childminder', that is, its sense is close to the original *nourrice* with which it thus enters a set of semantic relationships in French, and it is related in its semantic field to *garde d'enfants*. It has a completely different meaning from its English homonym which has the sense of *infirmière*.

In some cases, the borrowing can shift sense quite substantially once it has entered the language, according to how it is used, even to the extent that it takes on the opposite sense to the original (enantiosemy). For example, the verb *flipper*, also an Anglo-American borrowing, is defined in the *Petit Robert* as 'se sentir abattu quand la drogue a fini son effet' and by extension 'être déprimé'. A further, and indeed opposite, sense given is 'être exalté'. Walter and Walter (1991:206) note the dramatic shift in its meaning from the English 'être agité, excité' through its adoption by a particular socio-linguistic and semantic domain, that is, the drugs world.

In other cases, the borrowing may represent a refinement on the French term; the word *interview*, for example, suggests a public interview, as opposed to a more private *entrevue*. In some instances of 'straight borrowing' where the borrowed and native terms are genuinely synonymous, the French term may be ousted by the borrowing; Wise (1997:70) cites the example of *espion* (thirteenth century < Italian *spione*) which ousted the Old French *espie*.

In many cases, we find a whole series of creations and borrowings. The noun *film* (1889), for example, was originally borrowed in its cinemato-graphic sense. Other related lexical items followed: the verb *filmer* (1908) was used alongside *tourner* (in one of its senses); *filmographie* (1924) was formed using *film* and the element *graphie* by analogy with *bibliographie; filmique* (1936), *filmage* (1940 – cf. *tournage*) and *filmologie* (1947) were formed by adding French (or learned) suffixes to the borrowed root; and *filmothèque* (1969 – cf. *cinémathèque*) was coined by the combination of *microfilm* and the suffix *-thèque*. *Film* can now also be used in virtually all contexts as a synonym for *pellicule* (not just when talking about the cinema), as well as in its more figurative sense as a 'very thin layer'. In other words, once the borrowing entered French with its specific function, other related forms followed by the familiar processes of lexical creation in French; internal and external forces interacted and in turn, each of the new creations entered a semantic field in French, sometimes creating apparent synonyms (e.g. *filmage/ tournage*). Other senses of the word have also been borrowed over time, such that the polysemic resonances of the term at given points in time vary considerably.

In some instances, it is possible that what started out as a technical term in a specialized domain may penetrate mainstream French vocabulary (*business, gadget, pop-music, slogan*), possibly acquiring a more general meaning in the process. Klein, Leinart and Ostyn's survey (1997) reveals that many borrow-ings in the political columns of newspapers are no longer specialist terms, but have become part of 'le français commun'. As Hagège points out (1987:81), it is difficult to predict the extent to which terms might go through this 'processus imperceptible de banalisation', since the fate of individual words varies enormously according to different sociolinguistic factors. What seems clear, however, is that those words which do enter mainstream French vocabulary are assimilated to such a very high degree in linguistic terms (i.e. phonologically, morphosyntactically etc.) that they are hardly even perceived as borrowings (e.g. *rail, tunnel*).

From the small number of examples discussed, we can see clearly that once a borrowing has entered French, the subsequent semantic complexities can be very considerable. Indeed, it is in this area that borrowing has perhaps the greatest impact on the French language. Although some patterns can be detected, the semantic integration of borrowings is, relatively speaking, highly idiosyncratic and unpredictable in comparison to their phonological and morphosyntactic integration.

12.4   'Hybrids' and pseudo-anglicisms

A number of forms, often considered to be anglicisms, exist in French which do not occur in English. In this section we will consider two major types; 'hybrid' forms which are composed of a foreign element and a native element, and pseudo-anglicisms where all the elements of the word are foreign but the form created in French does not exist in English either in the same form or with the same meaning. As Nicol Spence remarks (1976:84): 'L'anglophone est frappé par le nombre d'anglicismes – ou disons plutôt de mots d'allure anglaise – qui s'emploient dans un sens différent de celui qu'ont les mots en anglais, ou qui n'existent pas en anglais (comme *rallye-paper, shake-hand, baby-foot, baby-parc*)'. These examples once again raise the question as to whether we can clearly distinguish between borrowings and neologisms created within French, between external and internal processes.

In hybrids, a native and foreign element are combined. Sometimes these are the result of popular etymology; for example, English *poker dice* became *poker d'as* in French when speakers tried to rationalize the second element. More usually they are the result of the addition of French affixes to borrowed roots, as with *sponsoriser, squattage, speakerine* and *surbooking*. The elements *-er, -iste, -isme* and *-eur* have been used to create a series of derivatives which have no counterpart in English (e.g. *zapper, pongiste, hippisme, catcheur*). This last term derives from English *catch as catch can*, a term which has virtually disappeared from English usage.

There are a number of different types of pseudo-anglicism. These may for example be the result of ellipsis as in *le trench (coat), le basket (ball), le (news)flash, le self(-service)* (see also the discussion below on *-ing*). Another more complex example is the word *pin's*, to which an apostrophe has been added – presumably because this is considered typical of the English language; the supposed full form *pin-on badge* is clumsy in English, whose speakers simply remove the first element to give *badge*. It is much more difficult to trace the origin of other pseudo- or *faux anglicismes*, such as *le ball-trap*, *le brother-ship* or *le slip*. Here again we note the ingenuity and creativity of French speakers. One can only assume, for instance, that *brother-ship* is an extension in French of the parallel use of *sister-* in English. Another interesting type is those borrowings sometimes humourously termed 'emprunts aller-retour' (see Geckeler 1997/98), words originally borrowed from French into English and then later borrowed back into French, often with a meaning different from the original French usage. English *sport* was, for instance, borrowed from Old French *desport* meaning 'amusement, game'; similarly French *bougette* 'little bag, purse' gave *budget* in English which returned to France with the English meaning in the eighteenth century (see also the discussion of *nurse* in **12.3.3**).

The processes of derivation and composition involving 'hybrids' and pseudo-anglicisms can also be complex. We have already discussed examples where a borrowing (or an abbreviated borrowing) has formed a root, to which French affixes have been added (e.g. *filmage*, *flipper*, *basketeur*, *zesteur*, *blackos*), producing in some cases forms which are radically different both semantically and formally from the original term (e.g. *pongiste*, *offsettiste*, *standardiste*). Some compounds combining a borrowed and a native element can generate equally unusual forms (*pipi-room*). In some cases, the two elements may be Anglo-American, but the new form non-existent in English (*baby-foot*).

The case of the suffix *-ing* is interesting in this respect. Used in English either as a present participle (to denote an ongoing action), or a gerund, or a verbal noun (see Nymansson 1996), it is most often found in French as a noun marking the action and the place (*camping*), or, as discussed above, where part of the source has been removed by ellipsis, it can denote the action alone (*lifting* < 'face lift') or the place alone (*parking* < 'parking lot'), or the action and, by extension, some other feature of the action such as the clothes worn (*jogging*); *-ing* may also appear in derived forms with Anglo-American roots, thus creating words which either are not in any sense English, or which are English in form but which have an entirely different meaning in French (*footing* < 'foot' (limbs used in the action) + *-ing*, *brushing* < 'brush' (tool used) + *-ing*). A further interesting case of this is the formation within the French lexicon of a new French word using the element *-man* as in *crossman*, *tennisman*.

Might it be appropriate to argue that *-man*, or for that matter *-ing*, are now fully-integrated French suffixes? In order for this to be the case, one would need to be able to cite examples of creations in French using *-man* or *-ing* in which the root was unquestionably French. For example, the suffix *-esque* borrowed into French from Italian is now considered French because it has been added to French roots (e.g. *livresque*). It is for the moment difficult to find equally convincing examples for *-ing* or *-man*. Lafage (1998) cites some such forms in the French of Africa (in this case, Abidjan), e.g. *baisingdrome* 'pick-up joint', or *drapman* to refer to someone in difficulty, an expression which perhaps derives from the expression *être dans de beaux draps*.

While many hybrids and pseudo-anglicisms have been criticized by French purists, and are most strongly associated with the most informal varieties of the language (see George 1993:164), some see them as evidence of the creativity of the French language, and in the case of Picone (1996), as further exemplification of the power of the 'synthetic imperative'.

12.5   The status of Latin (and Greek) material

A different problem arises in the case of words of Latin origin, where there are two distinct types of words. The bulk of the lexical stock of French obviously has its roots in Latin, the words having subsequently gone through phonetic and semantic changes in the course of their evolution.[6] However, many words of Latin origin were borrowed into French at a later stage. It is this double layer of Latin which has led Walter (1997a:51) to describe French as 'une langue deux fois latine' and Wise (1997:45) to ask whether French has a 'two-tier lexis'. For example, whereas *frère/père/mère* are descended from Vulgar Latin, *fraternel, paternel* and *maternel* are Latinisms which were coined at a much later stage.

Many Latinisms came into French during the Middle Ages, the fourteenth century (notably via translation), and the Renaissance (e.g. *liberté, neutre, ostentation* (fourteenth century), *illustre* (fifteenth century), *véhicule* (sixteenth century)), at periods in history where Latin was the prestige language of scholarship in Europe. Others are more modern, even contemporary: many neologisms and borrowings in contemporary French have Latin roots. In technical and scientific domains for example, new words are often coined using learned affixes (e.g. *-ier, -ifier, hyper-, -iser, -isation, -if,* see Part I, Section 2.4.2 and Table **12.**1 below); others are learned borrowings which are adopted as the international term and easily assimilated into French, given their Latin roots (e.g. *atome, matière explosive* (French), *atom, explosive material* (English), *Atom, explosives Material* (German), *átomo, materia explosiva* (Spanish), *atomo, materia explosiva* (Italian)).

Walter's study (1997b) of information technology vocabulary exemplifies this; there are high numbers of learned international terms and, with the exception of English acronyms, the percentage of Anglo-American borrowings is otherwise very low. Moreover, in more informal varieties and in young people's speech, both of which are rich in neologisms and borrowings, learned elements are also used frequently, with prefixes such as *super-* and *hyper-* (which incidentally are virtually synonymous Latin and Greek elements) enjoying considerable vitality, and combining with French elements as well as borrowings, for example *superdoué, hyperclean.* A recent survey of neologisms in the written press also highlights the importance of learned elements, with particularly frequent use of a number of affixes such as *anti-, dé-, -iste, -ien, -phile, multi-* (Hong 1997:116). Indeed, Wise (1997:53) suggests that where there is a choice between a French and a learned affix in contemporary French, the learned one will usually be more productive. The story behind the numerous words of Latin origin in French is therefore by no means monolithic.

On the whole, French reaction is much more positive to creations based on Latin and Greek than to those borrowed or calqued on English. Indeed, for many they seem not to be considered foreign at all, perhaps due to a complex mix of internal and external considerations. First, it is frequently easier to integrate Latin material into French than certain English words, although English words of Latin origin are equally unproblematic; French is derived from Latin and has continued to draw on Latin so much that it is not felt to be alien. Second, Latin words are seen to add prestige to French and do not represent the cultural threat of Anglo-American words. Influential bodies such as the *Conseil International de la Langue Française (CILF)*, founded in 1967, have published guides to the creation of new words, which take as their premise the preference for a native over a foreign term. Interestingly, in CILF's guide to the creation of neologisms, Latin and Greek elements are treated on the same level as native French affixes, all of which are opposed to the harmful influence of a 'foreign' term:

> en matière de création de néologismes, il est vain de se reporter à un terme d'origine étrangère. C'est la définition de ce qu'on veut dénommer qu'il faut examiner pour en extraire l'aspect le plus important que l'on exprimera par une racine française, grecque ou latine. A cette racine, il est possible de combiner des éléments de composition qui permettront d'associer les connotations qu'on souhaite voir figurer dans le terme nouveau (Diki-Kidiri, Joly and Murcia 1981:12).

This preference for learned terms over foreign ones can be seen in the neologisms proposed by the official bodies charged with creating new words in contemporary French, that is, the *Commissions ministérielles de terminologie*, whose proposals are published in the *Journal officiel de néologismes* and brought together in the periodic publication of a *Dictionnaire des termes officiels* under the auspices of the *Délégation générale à la langue française*. The latest official dictionary (1994) covers domains such as *agriculture, composants électroniques, économie et finances, informatique, personnes âgées, santé, sport, techniques spatiales, tourisme* amongst others, and the following examples, from one page selected at random in the dictionary, illustrate the types of neologisms proposed. Note the dominance of 'native' processes and the strong presence of terms of learned origin:

Table 12.1 Examples of proposed neologisms (*Dictionnaire des termes officiels*: 233)

Termes étrangers ou termes impropres à éviter ou à remplacer	Termes français
critical flow depth	tirant d'eau critique
critical heat flux	densité de flux thermique critique, flux critique
critical heat flux ratio	rapport de flux thermique critique
critical velocity	vitesse critique
criticalité	criticité
criticality	criticité
cross couponing	couponnage croisé
cross currency swap	crédit croisé
cross default	défaut croisé
cross fading	fondu enchaîné
cross polarization data	donnée en polarisations croisées
cross section	section efficace
cross-servicing	soutien logistique mutuel, aide mutuelle
cross-talk	intermodulation
cruise missile	missile de croisière
crusher	manomètre à écrasement
currency linked	option de monnaies
currency swap	échange de devises dues
currentmeter	courantomètre
customer	client
customisation	adaptation à l'usager, particularisation
cut	sec, serré
cut off	point de coupure
cut off date	date butoir
cut off procedures	procédures de séparation des exercices
cybrid	cybride

12.6 Attitudes towards borrowing

Over the course of its history, attitudes towards borrowing into French have ranged from the very positive to the very negative, from the liberal to the purist, and, according to Goudaillier (1977:93), 'entre ces deux pôles', 'règne une confusion extrême, une pagaïe effroyable'. The history of these differing views is traced by Hagège (1987:17–25). Amongst the negative attitudes, he discusses Henri Estienne's passionate defence of French against the influx of Italianisms during the Renaissance, as well as the development of a defensive school of thought in the eighteenth century (led by Domergue in the *Journal de la langue française,* which campaigned actively against the influx of anglicisms) and, in the twentieth century, the proactive protective approach on the part of the French government in the form of language policy. Hagège is anxious to show that more positive reactions co-existed with the criticisms of borrowing: for some, such as Du Bellay, borrowings were seen as an enrichment of the fledgling French vernacular in the Renaissance, and in the eighteenth century, borrowings were welcomed by Fénelon when they helped improve clarity, precision and brevity, and were used freely by Rousseau and Voltaire.

What has been the response in the twentieth century to the more recent vigorous wave of Anglo-American borrowings and to the tension these have produced between internal and external processes of lexical creativity? The debate has been lively, the levels of controversy very high, and the reaction from linguists mixed. As far as negative attitudes are concerned, the focus has been both linguistic and cultural. Borrowings are seen as a threat to the French way of life, as well as to the sounds and structures of the nation's language.

It was Etiemble's *Parlez-vous franglais* (1964) which fired the first shot in the contemporary period and epitomized an aggressive opposition to the invasion of Anglo-Americanisms. For Etiemble, the *sabir atlantique* constituted by *franglais* poses major problems with spelling, morphology (in the areas of derivation, pronouns, comparative and superlative structures amongst others), syntax (adjective-noun word order, misuse of the passive), and semantics. It represents an attack on French customs, a conspiracy on the part of the US which is promoted by sections of the French media. A more recent defence of French also speaks of protecting the *patrimoine linguistique* (Gilder 1993:12), the 'langue maternelle et fraternelle, universelle et éternelle' (1993:224).

Other voices, less strident in their opposition than Etiemble's and Gilder's, have also highlighted a series of what they consider serious linguistic problems. Guiraud (1971), Goosse (1975) and Lenoble-Pinson (1991) give a flavour of such reactions: difficulties of assimilation are discussed in the areas of phonology (e.g. levels of variation, importation of new phonemes), orthography (importation of unfamiliar spellings), semantics (e.g. the difficulties arising from *faux-amis*), syntax (e.g. compounds formed by juxtapostion) and morphology (e.g. gender and plural agreements, or complexities arising from the assimilation of foreign suffixes). Defensive statements are often found, such as 'il ne s'agit pas ici de défendre le français, au nom d'un nationalisme ombrageux, contre une influence étrangère, mais de voir, le plus objectivement possible, en quoi ces mots anglais gênent la communication' (Goosse 1975:51). Alternatively, the virtues of French are extolled: 'le français se porte bien' (Lenoble-Pinson 1991:5), 'notre français est riche. Quel choix!' (1991:12), and 'il importe que le génie de la langue sache adapter, intégrer, naturaliser ou franciser l'emprunt et ne le laisse pas s'installer comme un intrus gênant, bizarre, indésirable' (1991:7).

Other linguists such as Mitterand (1963), Spence (1987), Hagège (1987), Walter (1997a) and Wise (1997) take a very different view, treating borrowings as an entirely natural phenomenon which bring a welcome enrichment to the language. Their arguments depend on the statistics concerning the small number of borrowings, their concentration in a limited number of domains (such as economics, politics, science, technology, popular culture, drugs, showbusiness/ media, advertizing and sport: see Klein, Leinart and Ostyn 1997) and a limited number of registers (mainly more informal varieties), as well as their minimal impact on the morphology, syntax and phonology of French.

Hagège sets the traditionally problematic issues in context. Even semantic complexities which can arise such as clandestine borrowings (e.g. Latinisms dating from the Middle Ages and borrowed into English from French, and subsequently from English into French), semantic calques (or *faux-amis*), and calques by translation are regarded by Hagège as natural, inevitable, and therefore acceptable processes. As regards morphosyntactic issues, he argues that compounds with structures such as *assurance maladie*, although omitting the preposition *à* or *de*, nonetheless maintain French word order (1987:46), that semantic distinctions may operate between alternative constructions such as *américain du sud* and *sud-américain* (1987:48), and that the order adjective-noun is not entirely foreign – French can make use of it for stylistic or expressive purposes (1987:51).

In the case of derivational morphology, a number of suffixes of learned origin (e.g. *-able, -age, -al, -ation, -isme, -iste* etc.) are almost identical in English and French, and Hagège argues that borrowing may even help to revivify such suffixes; in the case of distinctly English suffixes such as *-man*, these are, for a variety of reasons such as low frequency or productivity, limited in their influence (1987:32–45). In phonological terms, the only serious change to the phonological system is the addition of /ŋ/, a phoneme whose major phonetic properties as a velar nasal are familiar from other French phonemes.

In short, according to Hagège, 'l'anglais n'a pas atteint le noyau dur de la langue française' (1987:61). Mitterand also argues that the impact of borrowings needs to be 'ramenée à sa juste mesure' (1963:72), while Spence maintains that 'l'anglicisme n'est pas tellement un problème linguistique – c'est plutôt un problème d'amour-propre' (1976:102).

Finally, the number of public bodies which have been set up in the latter half of the twentieth century to monitor the French language (of which the *Délégation générale à la langue française* and the *Commissions ministérielles de terminologie* are the most important in relation to borrowings), coupled with legislation relating to the use of borrowings (i.e. the *Loi Bas Lauriol* (1975) and the *Loi Toubon* (1994)), both testify to the extent of the concern in France about linguistic borrowing.[7] As Judge puts it (1993:17) 'there has been a move towards prescriptivism and a more aggressive policy of implantation of linguistic directives'. However, it is equally evident that the impact of this legislation is by no means clear. Low fines and the relatively small number of cases brought (see Judge 1993), as well as limited knowledge amongst some professionals of the 'correct' French terms (see Gaudin 1991), suggest that the legislation may in fact be having minimal impact. Moreover, in a recent survey of attitudes to borrowings amongst young people, Guilford (1997) finds that these speakers generally have a higher degree of knowledge of the Anglo-American terms than the official French equivalent, and are much more likely to use the borrowed term.

Suggested Reading

General:
  Pergnier (ed) (1988a), (1989), Picone (1996), Walter (1997a), Walter and Walter (1991), Wise (1997), Zanola (1991).
Integration:
  Bécherel (1981b), Guilford (1997, 1999), Pergnier (1989), Poplack, Sankoff and Miller (1988), Retman (1978), Spence (1987, 1989, 1991).
Politique linguistique:
  Calvet (1996), Etiemble (1964), Gaudin (1991, 1994, 1996), Hagège (1987), Judge (1993), Wise (1997).

Notes

1. Throughout her book, *L'Aventure des mots français venus d'ailleurs* (1997), Henriette Walter gives examples of *mots voyageurs* from all over the world.
2. For examples of typologies of borrowings, see Walter and Walter (1991), Zanola (1991), Klein, Leinart and Ostyn (1997).
3. Note that one particular type of borrowing, that is, calques, is considerably more popular in Canadian than in metropolitan French. Lagueux's survey (1988), which examines various different types of calques – syntactic (*donner un call, acheter de*), one-word (*un goaleur, insécure*), semantic (*facilités*) – reveals this process to be particularly productive, presumably because of the ease with which a bilingual community can translate structures from one language to another.
4. See Mitterand (1963:68–9) and Bécherel (1981b:120) for example.
5. Note that Picone (1996:346–9) argues that while English borrowings may be the main source of the importation of this sound, there are nonetheless earlier borrowings from other languages (e.g. *gong* (1691 from Malay)), dialectal influences and onomatopoeic words (e.g. *dring*). Note too that the phonemic status of this sound in French is controversial (see Part I, Section 2.1.3).
6. See Wise (1997:45–58) for a detailed discussion.
7. On contemporary *politique linguistique*, and the recent history of governmental bodies, see Müller (1985:40–6), Hagège (1987), Judge (1993:14–23), Wise (1997:220–43).

13

'Internal' processes of word creation in French

13.1   Introduction

In Chapter 12, we discussed problematic issues arising from the interaction between internal and external factors in the creation of new words in French. In this chapter, we shall consider some of the complexities arising from the internal processes of derivation, composition etc., including:

- Definitional issues (particularly distinctions between different categories and processes)
- Questions of productivity, especially as regards variation, change and constraints on productivity
- Theoretical issues in derivational morphology
- The impact of neologisms created by internal processes on the semantic structure, the morphosyntax and the phonological structure of the language, as well as sociolinguistic and situational factors.

13.2   Definitional issues

Traditional accounts of French word formation make a distinction between on the one hand derivations created by prefixation, suffixation, or parasynthesis, and on the other hand compounds formed by the juxtaposition of two or more autonomous words (see, for example, Nyrop 1899–1930:III:5, Ewert 1933). Indeed, this was the scheme we ourselves employed in Part I, Section 2.4, when we outlined the main processes used by French speakers to create new words. In this Section, we take a closer look at this classification and consider to what extent it is appropriate or adequate for the description and analysis of Modern French neologisms.

13.2.1   Neologisms

Before examining the classifications themselves, we should perhaps comment briefly on the definition of a neologism. As is the case with borrowings, it is not easy to give a watertight definition of a 'new word'. At what point does a neologism start to be used frequently enough to be considered a viable French term and thus subsequently to be included in dictionaries? And at what point does it become so stable that it is no longer a neologism but rather is considered an established element in the lexical stock of French? The difficulties in obtaining a statistical picture of the number of neologisms are considerable, as are the problems for the lexicographer; we shall return to some of the issues in **13**.3.2.

13.2.2   Suffixes and prefixes

The distinction between suffixes and prefixes poses few difficulties. At the most basic level, suffixes and prefixes are obviously distinguished by their position in the word. We might add to this distinction the fact that suffixes generally change the grammatical class of the word, whereas prefixes do not. There are, however, two exceptions to this; these are, class-maintaining suffixes (see Part I, Section 2.4.1) and the class-changing prefix *anti-*, which can turn a noun into an adjective, for example *antitache* adjective < *tache* noun.[1] Note however that in a recent article, Corbin (2000) argues that prefixes and suffixes are not distinguished primarily by their class-changing properties; she maintains that this property is, rather, a consequence of more fundamental differences between suffixes and prefixes, such as the fact that suffixation in Indo-European languages is generally associated with the marking of case and category (for full details, see Corbin (2000)).

13.2.3   Prefixes and compounds – problematic distinctions

Much more difficult to circumscribe than the distinction between suffixes and prefixes are the distinctions between prefixes and (i) certain types of free elements such as prepositions or adverbs and (ii) elements in a particular type of compound (known as a *recomposé* – see **13**.2.5). The problems raised by (i) are discussed by Spence (1976:9–20) who alludes to the discrepancy between different inventories of prefixes such as those of Togeby (1965) (where 16 are listed) and the *Petit Larousse* where 260 elements are included, the variation in statistics depending on how prefixes are defined.

A glance at the following list of forms which feature regularly in lists of French prefixes – *dé, re, trans, in, sur, anti, hyper, super, pro, contre, avant, en* – reveals, as indeed the traditional definition of a prefix would predict, that the category includes a number of elements which cannot function autonomously; they are bound forms which can function only as prefixes. However, the list also includes learned items (*hyper, super* etc.) which are sometimes classed as elements in compounds; we shall return to these in **13**.2.5. Moreover, there are also some elements which can equally function as prepositions (*en, contre* etc.), or as adverbs (*avant*), and are therefore not, strictly speaking, bound forms. Indeed, in some cases, two related forms (often one popular and one learned) have the same origin (e.g. *pour/pro*), but only one (in this case *pro*) is a bound form and thus unproblematically classed as a prefix. What are the criteria which distinguish prefixes from free forms? Is it legitimate to classify elements such as *en, contre, avant* etc. as prefixes?

The main criterion that has been suggested for classifying all the forms listed above as prefixes is simply that of productivity (Lehmann and Martin-Berthet 1998:115–16): an element may be classed as a prefix if it is used productively to form new words. Such a definition allows a number of elements which are not bound forms to be classed as prefixes in certain contexts. Lehmann and Martin-Berthet give the example of *malvoyant* (where *mal-* is a productive prefix; compare *maladroit, malhabile* etc.) as opposed to *clairvoyant* (compound), where *clair* is an autonomous element which is not productive in the formation of new words. Similarly, the other elements classifiable as prefixes can give rise to whole series of terms. They also mention a tendency on the part of prefixes and stems (as opposed to compounds composed of two autonomous elements) towards appearing orthographically as one word rather than using hyphens. This is, however, a tendency rather than a rule, since there are many cases where so-called prefixes appear in a hyphenated form (e.g. *après-midi, arrière-plan*) or where the elements of a compound are not hyphenated (e.g. *bonhomme, télécarte*).

13.2.4   Identifying compounds

As just indicated, identifying compounds is not always entirely straightforward, since there are several orthographic possibilities, including hyphenated words (*presse-bouton*), fusion (*télécarte*), juxtaposition (*chaise longue*), and elements joined by means of prepositions such as *de* or *à*. Indeed, there is evidence from ministerial lists of official terms that this last category is particularly productive, allowing as it does the kind of precision required in technical and scientific vocabulary (see, for example, Table **12**.1), although it has also been noted that there is an increasing tendency to omit the preposition from such structures (*robe à fleurs > robe fleurs*).

Not only are there different orthographic possibilities (and indeed notorious orthographic difficulties – see Catach 1981), but there are also a very large number of different possible combinations (verb-noun, noun-noun, adjective-noun etc.). A recent typology of compounds (Mathieu-Colas 1996) proposes 25 different categories (e.g. *composés NOM + ADJECTIF, composés NOM + à + X, expansions de NOM de NOM* etc.), which can be further subcategorized, with up to 700 distinct structures. A further complicating factor is that, as with many derived forms, a number of forms which were originally created through composition are no longer necessarily recognizable as such; for example, it is not obvious synchronically that *plafond* is a compound consisting of *plat* and *fond*.

13.2.5   Recomposés

Hitherto we have defined compounds in broad terms as consisting of two or more autonomous elements which combine to form one lexical item. However, the autonomy of the two constituent parts is highly problematic in the case of one particular class of compounds, the *recomposés*. Many learned elements, such as *ultra, extra, hyper, super, micro* etc., which are very productive in a host of different domains (from highly specialized vocabulary in technical or scientific fields to informal varieties – see **13**.3), can combine with other (often non-autonomous) learned elements to create words which have been classified traditionally as a special category of compound form (e.g. *téléphone, hippodrome* etc.), known as *recomposés* (Mitterand 1963:57) or *confixations* (see Martinet 1980:135, Zwanenburg 1990:75). These are said to be compounds in that they combine two distinct and identifiable elements, but they differ from other compounds in that one or more of the elements cannot function autonomously. They are also more amenable to participating in derivational processes than are compounds (see Wise 1997:123), thus raising the question of whether the elements involved should be seen as affixes rather than elements in compounds. Indeed, such elements increasingly combine not just with other learned elements but also with French elements (*télécarte, ultrachic, hypersympa*) or even with borrowings (*hyperclean, supercool*). Where the element appears regularly and productively either before or after French words or borrowings, might there be grounds for arguing that it is functioning as an affix?

Spence (1976) starts with Robins' definition that 'morphemes may be divided into *roots* and *affixes*, the root being that part of a word structure which is left when all the affixes have been removed', and further distinguishes bound roots such as those found in the *recomposés*, from free roots. Bound roots, unlike affixes, have a semantic 'valeur de base' rather than a modifying value (as has an affix), and can be found elsewhere as roots to which affixes can be added. By way of example, Spence points to the bound root in ***thermique*** and ***thermal***, the bound root in ***statique*** and the combination of bound roots in *thermostat*, which he classes as a *recomposé*. On the other hand, Hong's recent survey (1997) of neologisms in the written press argues strongly that the vast majority of the time (90% of cases), learned elements are functioning as affixes (which are attached to bound roots) rather than in a combination of two bound roots.

Gross (1996) takes a middle position, maintaining that the *recomposés* (he labels the phenomenon *composition savante*) are, in definitional terms, 'un état intermédiaire' (1996:30) between derivation and composition; they resemble derivational processes in that the learned element is not autonomous and is attached to a bound root in much the same way as affixes, while at the same time resembling composition, since the learned elements have a clear semantic content in much the same way as free roots (as opposed to affixes). Note also that some of the so-called *recomposés* may in fact be borrowings, that is, the French version of the learned internationalized term (see **13**.3 below).

The difficulty with such elements arises in making fine distinctions between categories which look alike, and in assessing productivity. Moreover, some words may be abbreviated (e.g. *télé*, *bus*), the truncated forms starting to function autonomously in French, forming compounds with other native or learned or borrowed elements (e.g. *téléfilm*; see Lehmann and Martin-Berthet (1998:116–17)). Note also that the two elements in *mots-tiroirs* are similarly not autonomous: also known as *mots-gigognes*, *mots-centaures*, *téléscopage*, these arise where two abbreviated forms from different words are combined: *français+anglais > franglais*, *citron+orange > citrange*. Such examples contain two distinct and identifiable elements which, although they are not autonomous, are not affixes since they are not productive. Two elements may also be superposed on each other, a process known as 'haplology' (e.g. *féminin+-iser > féminiser*).

13.2.6 Compounds versus free combinations

A further difficulty with the traditional definition of a compound is that, in some cases, compounds proper may not in practice be easy to distinguish from free combinations of single elements which appear together, either as two elements juxtaposed (compounds such as *chaise longue*), or joined by means of a preposition (*pomme de terre*, *chemin de fer* etc.; Benveniste (1966:171) uses the term *synapsie* for these).

A number of criteria are regularly cited as central to the definition of a compound.[2] First, the two elements in a compound function as one referential unit; the combination of elements refers to one object, concept etc., and thus, for example, takes one article if the compound is a noun. In syntactic terms, the order of the elements is fixed and may be the reverse of standard word order (*rouge-gorge*). Moreover, there is syntactic unity in that the compound cannot be broken up by any qualifying adjectives or adverbs (**eau froide de vie* and **bébé mignon éprouvette* are not possible) or substituted by other elements (*mariage blanc > *mariage vert*). Martinet (1985:36–7), who labels derived and compound forms made up of two or more elements as **synthèmes** (as opposed to *monèmes* – see Part I, Section 3.2.2) explains this by arguing that the compound behaves like a single word (or *monème*), operating syntactically like other words in its class; furthermore, any modifying or modalizing element applies to the whole compound and cannot apply to one element only.

However, a restricted number of terms can have syntactic substitutes; Lehmann and Martin-Berthet cite the examples of *feu rouge/feu vert*, *machine à laver/machine à coudre* etc. There are even cases where adjectives or adverbs can be introduced into the syntagm, for example *être de (très) mauvaise humeur*. Spence (1976:27) argues that in 'adjective + noun' or 'noun + adjective' combinations, the distinction between compounds and free combinations is virtually impossible to maintain, with even the grammatical agreements operating in some compounds in the same way as for combinations of autonomous elements, for example *petit-enfant/petits-enfants*. Furthermore Spence (1976), drawing on Bally's work, points to one problematic category of adjectives which cannot take certain types of modifying or modalizing element in normal circumstances, that is, *adjectifs de relation*. Spence's example of *solaire* is a case of precisely such an adjective; although it occurs often in certain well-attested combinations such as *cadran solaire, chaleur solaire, système solaire, énergie solaire*, it can also occur in constructions which are one-off usages such as *explosion solaire, nuit solaire*. Spence's argument is that the criteria outlined above would force us into an incorrect categorization of such combinations as compounds, since **chaleur plus solaire* is not possible. Other similar cases cited by Spence include *cercle polaire, droit civil, bombe atomique*.

In semantic terms, compounds are said to show unity of meaning, and the meaning of the combination constituting the compound is not necessarily the sum of the meanings of the component parts; in synchronic terms, the *pomme* in *pomme de terre* does not have its contemporary sense of 'apple' (the sense is the former one of 'fruit'), and the meaning of the compound thus does not correspond to the sum of the constituent parts. Semantic unity, is, however a problematic concept; many simple nouns (as opposed to compounds) do not demonstrate semantic unity, since two or more meanings may be commonly attributed to them in the dictionary. Moreover, a sense of continuum is discernible in the semantic properties of compounds; the compound may be more or less transparent or opaque. At one end of the spectrum are opaque examples such as *pomme de terre*: these are often longstanding borrowings where the contemporary sense has moved further and further from the original, or cases of metaphorical usage (*grosse tête, liste rouge*). However, in other cases, the semantic link with the individual elements is more transparent; we can see the origins of *sourd-muet* (someone who is both deaf and dumb) or *ouvre-boîte*, and, albeit less transparently, we can analyse the semantic elements in *mauvaise herbe*. In an early analysis, Wagner makes the point that very often in compounds such as these, although the two elements are identifiable as such in formal terms, there is a sense in which they may be 'degrammaticalized' in the compound, divested of grammatical markers such as agreements and free to recombine as base elements with other words or bases in the language:

> la composition a pour effet d'extraire en quelque sorte ces éléments de l'espèce à laquelle ils appartenaient originairement, de les dégrammaticaliser en les privant des marques qui les caractérisent en emploi libre, et d'insérer l'ensemble de l'unité nouvelle dans une espèce (1968:69).

Wagner would argue that while some compounds produce a structure which is also possible in a free combination (e.g. *mauvaise herbe*), others do not (*remue-ménage*, *casse-tête*), and even where they do, there is often a new relationship between them in the compound, one which cannot be explained through recourse to their free combination in discourse (e.g. *belle-mère, fille-mère, prix choc*).[3] According to Wagner, there is a two-stage process in the creation of such compounds, the first stage involving degrammaticalization and the second recombination; this may produce compounds which would not be possible in free combinations.[4] In the light of the complexities arising in the traditional definition of compounds, Catach (1981:16–17) argues that it is more appropriate to speak of a tendency to unity, rather than clear semantic or syntactic unity as such.

In a recent study of *expressions figées*, Gross (1996) also explores the criteria which distinguish between free combinations of elements and those which constitute compounds. The degree of *figement* of a given combination of autonomous elements is assessed against a number of factors (1996:9–23) including the following:

(i)   semantic opacity (the extent to which the new combination has a different sense from the combined sense of the elements);

(ii) transformational properties (the more tightly bound the elements are – that is, the more like a compound – the less able the combination is to undergo transformational processes such as passivization, nominalization etc.);

(iii) the capacity of individual elements to be modified grammatically (in general, compounds cannot be modified (e.g. **Marie est à cette mode*) and cannot form a predication (**ce fait est divers* vs *ce fait est évident*));

(iv) whether the *figement* applies to the whole phrase or to part of it;

(v)   the strength of the *figement* (for example, the elements in *fait historique* are less tightly bound than those in *fait divers*; both **un fait très historique* and **un fait très divers* are unacceptable, but *ce fait est historique* and *un fait d'histoire* are possible whereas **ce fait est divers* is not);

(vi) insertion of synonyms (this is generally impossible in fixed expressions, e.g. *un court circuit* vs **un bref circuit*);

(vii) insertion (fixed expressions do not permit insertion of elements such as adjectives, adverbs etc.).[5]

Through a detailed exploration of different types of compound in relation to these factors, Gross demonstrates that clear-cut distinctions are difficult to make. An exploration of the criteria reveals that it is often more appropriate to speak of degrees of *figement* and of a continuum, rather than a clear divide between compounds and free phrases.[6]

As Wise points out (1997:122), given the difficulties in trying to establish a watertight set of criteria in complex areas within the lexis, we frequently have to resort to the rather loose criterion of frequency of usage, whereby a compound is recognized as such by the fact that it occurs frequently in discourse. This would, for example, exclude literary creations on grounds of infrequent usage. In short, the distinctions between compounds and other categories are difficult to draw up; moreover, the criteria involved correspond to opposite ends of a continuum rather than clear binary distinctions.

13.2.7   Compounds and phrases

The lexicalization of phrases (e.g. *le qu'en-dira-t-on*, *le va-et-vient*) also raises interesting definitional questions. Such phrases are traditionally distinguished from free combinations of elements by much the same criteria as compounds, that is, criteria which concern the semantic and morpho-syntactic unity of the phrase.[7] The difficulty arises in trying to distinguish phrases from certain varieties of compounds (e.g. *pomme de terre*, *chemin de fer* etc.). Mitterand (1963:62) argues that phrases are more flexible extensions of the base word than compounds, the base frequently being relatively free to combine with elements from other lexical items; he cites the example of the phrase *restriction mentale*, where, he argues, both *restriction* and *mentale* are free to combine with other elements. In other words, phrases are less tightly bound as groups of words than compounds, which operate as one lexical unit.

These distinctions are, however, difficult to sustain. In many compounds, which by definition contain autonomous elements, the component parts are free to combine with other elements to form new lexical items, such as *machine à laver*, *machine à coudre* etc. Spence (1976) cites the example of *nature*, as in *thé nature*, *café nature*. There seem to be three possible analyses for these structures: as completely free combinations of autonomous elements (since *nature* is free to combine with other elements to form similar phrases such as *bœuf nature*, *omelette nature*); as a lexicalized phrase (since the phrase seems to have become fixed in usage); or as a compound (similar to *café-crème*).

Even where there is liaison between the elements, which would suggest a strong bond, we cannot tell whether we are dealing with a compound or a lexicalized phrase (e.g. *pot-au-feu*, *pied-à-terre*). Wagner (1968:79) contrasts the two-stage process whereby compounds are formed (see above) with the one-stage process used for phrases; unlike compounds, the structure in lexicalized phrases is one which is always possible in free combinations, the problem with this analysis being that not all compounds are formed by a two-stage process.

At times, as with compounds, linguists have been forced to fall back on the rather unsatisfactory criterion of frequency of usage; Benveniste (1966) speaks of acceptance by the linguistic community in his comments on 'noun + preposition + noun' structures, a rather loose criterion which is difficult to define and subject to variation in different sociolinguistic groups or contexts. What is clear is that there is undoubtedly a continuum rather than a binary distinction at stake; at one end of the continuum are free combinations of elements, at the other well-established opaque compounds, with a range of forms in between demonstrating greater or lesser degrees of opacity and transparency, or of syntactic and semantic unity.

13.3   Productivity

13.3.1   Variation

The productivity of particular processes of lexical creation is highly dependent on the level of formality of the discourse, on sociolinguistic factors and
on domain. Research on neologisms in the less formal varieties – variously
labelled *français populaire*, *français branché*, *argot* or 'alternative French' (see
Part I, Section 1.2.2) – suggests certain recurring patterns in word formation
which are very similar to those found in young people's speech: the same
processes are used as in standard French, but with greater innovation, in
different proportions, and with much greater flexibility.[8]

Within derivation, a small number of suffixes are used more frequently
than in standard French (e.g. *-o* (*clodo*, *avaro*), *-os* (*rapidos*, *craignos*), *-oche* (*cinoche*,
téloche)) and types of suffixation not normally found in standard vocabulary
are attested. These include for example gratuitous suffixation, where the suffix
is redundant in semantic terms (e.g. *duraille*, *merdouille*, *ringardos*, *seulabre* –
a process described by Mandelbaum-Reiner (1991:106) as a 'signal textuel
d'argot'), and resuffixation, where one suffix is replaced by another (e.g.
amerloque, *stupéfax*). Composition also includes types which are not normally
found in standard French such as *gros qui tache*, as well as combinations of
learned and colloquial elements (*hypersympa*), or learned elements and borrowings (*supercool*), or composition and metaphor (*boîte à ragoût* 'stomach',
viande froide (*cadavre*)).

Innovative processes which are hallmarks of slang and young people's
speech include **verlan** (where the elements in the word are reversed e.g.
chicha (*haschisch*), *narco* (*connard*), *rebier* (*bière*)); **javanais** (where *av* or *ag* is
introduced into the word e.g. *gavosse* (*gosse*)); **largonji** and **loucherbem** (where
the initial consonant is substitued by an 'l' and an optional suffix added e.g.
lerche (*cher*), *lutainpem* (*putain*)).[9] Repetition of whole words or part of words
is also common, as is repetition involving vowel change (*être limite-limite*, *être
copain-copain*, *deudeuche*, *concon*, *foufou*, *chuchoter*, *cric-crac* – see Schapira 1988).
Lexical items can change grammatical class with more freedom than in
standard French (*un culot monstre*, *c'est rien con*, *côté travail*, *je positive* (< *positif*),
il assure, *se viander* 'to have an accident' < *viande*).

Finally, there is more extensive use of figurative processes such as metaphor, metonymy and synecdoche, which may describe, for example, parts of
the body (*pattes*, *bâtons*), people (*légume*, *poireau*, *un cuir* 'person who wears a
leather jacket'), objects (*neige* 'cocaine', *feu* 'revolver'), and feelings or states
(*avoir les boules*, *se dégonfler*, *claquer du bec*, *être câblé*, *être jeté*). Both hyperbole
(*dément*, *balaise* 'excellent') and euphemism or litotes (*c'est pas triste*, *c'est pas
évident*, *pas gai-gai*) are widespread and there are also more frequent cases of
extension of meaning (*craindre* > *ça craint*).

Perhaps the most striking example of variation according to domain in contemporary French is technical vocabulary, whether scientific, technological, economic, medical, musical, sporting or otherwise. Indeed various studies of subsequent editions of the *Petit Larousse* reveal the high proportion of neologisms constituted by technical vocabulary (see Noreiko 1993:172). The establishment of native French terms, usually by the government *Commissions de terminologie* (see Chapter 12), means that the French language is developing a host of new terms in specialist fields. The processes used in technical French are essentially the same as those found in standard French, some being particularly productive or demonstrating particular patterns. Müller cites as characteristic of technical French the following list of processes (1985:191–202) and a glance at the terms listed on any page of the *Dictionnaire des termes officiels* (see Table 12.1) will confirm Müller's observations:

- Extensive use of a specific group of learned affixes, thus allowing for the creation of internationalized learned forms (see the discussion in 12.5).
- Extensive use of compounds, notably in the form of a base or generic term (e.g. *système, machine*) followed by a qualifier or qualifiers, thus enabling the formation of whole series of related technical terms. Müller cites the most frequent combinations as the following: noun + adjective(s) (*contrôle opérationnel* 'operational control', *sonde nucléique* 'nucleic probe', *pétrolier-vraquier-minéralier* 'oil bulk ore'), compound syntagms (where the possibility exists of adding several terms to the base usually by means of prepositions such as *à* or *de*) which allow for a high degree of specificity (*sangle de sauvetage* 'rescue strap', *rapport de flux thermique critique* 'departure from nucleate boiling ratio', *crédit à taux révisible* 'rollover credit'), and the use of learned compounds (i.e. *recomposés*) using Latin and Greek elements. The last category allows a high degree of precision for whole series of terms, while guaranteeing maximum semantic transparency and international communicative efficiency (*hydrorésistant* 'water resistant', *optoélectronique* 'optronics', *extraterritorial* 'off shore').
- Extensive use of abbreviations, which allow a succinct form to yield maximum information. Examples include ellipsis (*micro* for *micro-ordinateur*), apocope (*synthé* for *synthétiseur*), acronyms (*Agétac* 'GATT', *ADN* 'DNA').
- High levels of unmotivated vocabulary, that is, words which are not formally transparent (e.g. *humus, smog*).
- High numbers of borrowings, a product of the international nature of technical vocabulary (see Chapter 12 above).

13.3.2   Language change

While it is a well established fact that derivation is by far the most productive of the word-formation processes in contemporary French, not all derivational processes are equally productive: there is considerable variation and change in this area. Statistics from a variety of surveys suggest that amongst the most productive nominal suffixes in contemporary French are *-(a)tion* and its sub-types *-isation*, and *-ification*, and *-eur* for instruments (*absorbeur*), *-euse* for machines (*décapeuse*), *-age* for a technical procedure (*stripage*), *-iste* for an agent (*perchiste*). On the other hand, *-aste*, and *-oir/e* are relatively unproductive. Amongst adjectives, *-ique* and *-el* are particularly productive in contemporary French.

Moreover, just as the lexis itself is subject to relatively rapid renewal, so too is there a turnover in the inventory of suffixes; although the overall number remains approximately the same, suffixes may increase or decrease in frequency or their semantic function may change. The suffixes *-on*, *-ison* and *-aison* are no longer very productive in the area of crafts with which they were originally associated (since there has been a decline in these areas of activity), although *-on* is now productive in scientific/technical fields (*proton*, *nylon*), notably in the form *-tron* (Désirat and Hordé 1988:167–8). In addition, Modern French prefers the learned form of *-aison*, that is, *-ation*. There has also been a notable shift in productivity of the learned suffixes *-iste* and *-isme*; Wise (1997:161–2) observes that, although dormant for several centuries, they have been gaining ground in French since the eighteenth century (e.g. *structuraliste*, *bilinguisme* etc.) and are now frequently used to mark movements, phenomena or ideologies.

Similarly, some prefixes are more productive than others. In Old French, *mé-* and *re-/ré-* enjoyed similar levels of productivity, whereas in Modern French, *re-/ré-* is by far the most productive verbal prefix (*réintégrer*, *reprendre*) and *mé-* is relatively unproductive. In a survey of the processes used in young people's speech in two different corpora dating from 1987 and 1994, Sourdot (1997) demonstrates the rapid rate of change in the patterns found; in this short time span, there are perceptible changes in the types of affix attested and in the use of abbreviation, for example.

13.3.3   Linguistic constraints

Finally, the productivity of particular affixes is highly constrained by linguistic factors. In other words, quite apart from the different distribution of processes and affixes in different domains and the turnover in the inventory to which we referred in **13.3.2** above, there are linguistic reasons why not all affixes are equally possible in all contexts. Aitchison cites three 'rules of thumb' for the productivity of suffixes: frequent usage increases general productivity, the appropriateness of the match of a suffix with the sound structure of the root word is another factor, as is the extent to which the base word may be kept intact (there is a preference for suffixes which allow the base to remain as close to its original form as possible, notably in terms of its sound structure and stress patterns (1987:158–9)). To take some examples in French, we shall mention just a few of the patterns discussed by Bécherel (1981a) in an examination of the suffixes involved in the formation of abstract nouns denoting qualities (such as *-ance, -eur, -esse, -erie, -ise, -ité, -itude*).[10]

In morphophonological terms, certain types of stem combine with certain suffixes: the endings *-al* and *-el* combine regularly with *-ité* to give *-alité* (e.g. *général > généralité, ponctuel > ponctualité*); the endings *-and* and *-ard* tend to take *-ise* (*gourmandise*). In semantic terms, *-esse* usually marks positive, noble qualities, often of a moral nature (*noblesse, politesse, finesse*), and can mark the more abstract of two nouns formed from the same stem (*largeur, largesse*); *-erie* often signals a negative value (*bigoterie, saloperie*) and the sense of the resultant act or state of affairs. There are, however, exceptions to the patterns; *-esse* for instance can mark the opposite of positive, noble qualities (*tristesse, bassesse*).

As these examples suggest, the exact nature of the constraints which operate on a given procedure need to be elaborated in detail for each case, and within a theoretical framework. Indeed it is precisely these theoretical issues which theories of word formation attempt to address (see **13.4**).

13.4   Neologisms and linguistic theory

What are the rules which generate words in French? Why do they generate certain words and not others? Why are some forms apparently impossible in the French language (e.g. **conservateurisme, *agitationnique*), and others entirely acceptable (e.g. **castrateurisme, *agitationnel*), even if not attested? In the light of the irregularities and the constraints on productivity discussed in **13.3.3** above, the questions posed include:

*   For a given derivation, which combinations of elements (e.g. base + affix) are possible?
*   What are the semantic, grammatical, or morphophonological properties of the elements which can or cannot combine?
*   What are the exceptions to the rules, and how can these be accommodated theoretically?

As we have seen in Part I, Section 3.3.5, word formation theory was, as Wise puts it (1997:118), 'the poor relation' in early developments in twentieth-century linguistic theory. Moreover, in the case of French, it is also well-known that work on the lexis has predominantly taken the form of a very rich lexicographical tradition. As Corbin explains, 'le petit nombre des morphologues et le peu d'intérêt que suscite cette discipline contrastent à la fois avec une riche activité lexicographique et un goût très prononcé pour l'esthétisme et le dilettantisme lexicaux' (1987:2). Taken together, these factors mean that in comparison to other areas of the language and in contrast to the lexical tradition in France, theoretical models of word formation have not received as much attention.

In Part I, Section 3.3.5, we summarized the early generative approach to derivational morphology, its influence on Guilbert's work, the reasons why it was abandoned in the wake of Chomsky's *Remarks on Nominalization*, and the direction of subsequent developments by linguists such as Aronoff. In recent years one particular generative model has come to the fore in France in the work of Corbin and the CNRS SILEX team based in the University of Lille III; the key work is Corbin's *Morphologie dérivationnelle et structuration du lexique* (1987) and much of the team's work is published in the review *Lexique*.[11] Like Halle (1973) and Aronoff (1976), Corbin assigns a separate layer to derivational morphology and the basic assumption is that all speakers have in their linguistic competence a set of Word Formation Rules (WFRs or RCMs (*règles de construction de mots*)) which are applied to morphemes to form words; in other words, 'le savoir lexical des locuteurs est régi par une grammaire dérivationnelle' (1987:35).

Corbin's is an associative model, where not only the form but the sense of the word is accounted for by the RCMs; she develops mechanisms for dealing with the many problematic cases where the sense appears not to be straightforwardly predictable. Thus, for example, in the analysis of *pommade* (which no longer has any obvious connection with the sense of *pomme*), Corbin draws on the category *catachrèse* (which accounts for cases where the meaning of a word changes as it passes from a class of objects A to a class of objects B, which shares with A all its characteristics except the fundamental one) and the analysis in Figure **13.1** is given (1991a:42):

pomme $_N \rightarrow$ $_{suf.ade}$ *pommade* $_N$ (SP: 'préparation dont l'ingrédient saillant est r(*pomme* $_N$)') $\supset$ $_{cat}$ {*pommade* $_N$} $_{cat}$ (SP: 'Préparation semblable à r(*pommade* $_N$) mais dont l'ingrédient saillant n'est plus r(*pomme* $_N$)'; SA: 'Cosmétique composé d'une base grasse et d'une ou plusieurs substances parfumées [. . .]' (*TLF*, A.), 'Préparation médicamenteuse de consistance molle [. . .]' (B.))

N   : nom
$\rightarrow$: marque l'application d'une opération dérivationnelle
suf   : suffixation
$\supset$: marque l'application d'une opération sémantique
cat   : catachrèse
SP   : sense prédictible
SA   : sens attesté
(r   : in this case, r = sense of *pomme*)

Figure 13.1 Corbin's analysis of *pommade* (1991a:42)

After the regular derivational process of suffixation with *-ade* carrying a predictable sense (giving 'a preparation with *pomme* as the basic ingredient'), the semantic rule involving *catachrèse* is applied, which generates the *sens attesté* (in this case, 'a preparation similar to the predictable sense of *pommade*, but whose basic ingredient is not in fact "apple"').

In other words, what might otherwise appear as semantic irregularities are often predictable in Corbin's model through a different kind of regularity which the rules are capable of capturing. Similarly, in formal terms, many apparent irregularities can be captured as regularities; to give one example cited by Corbin, the regularity by which the allomorph *flor-* appears rather than *fleur* preceding the suffix *-al*, corresponds to a rule of allomorphy whereby the vowel [œ] alternates with [o] in certain lexical contexts such as *chœur* > *choral*, and can thus be expressed as part of the derivation, as in Figure 13.2:

$[[\text{fleur}]_{N<+PV>}(\text{al})_{af<PV+>}]_A$

fleur $_N \rightarrow_{\text{suf.al}} +$ *fleural* $_A \Rightarrow _{\text{AllPV}}$ *floral* $_A$

$\Rightarrow$	: marque l'application d'une opération formelle postérieure aux règles de construction des mots
$\rightarrow$	: marque l'application d'une opération dérivationnelle
$_{<+PV>}$	: trait diacritique indiquant que le morphème qui en est porteur subit une postériorisation vocalique dans un contexte approprié
$_{<PV+>}$	: trait diacritique indiquant que le morphème qui en est porteur provoque une postériorisation vocalique dans un contexte approprié
af	: affixe
AllPV	: allomorphie consistant en une postériorisation vocalique
A	: adjectif

Figure 13.2 Corbin's derivation of *floral* (1991a:41)

Note that this vowel alternation is appropriately expressed as part of the morphology rather than the phonology, since there is no general phonological rule whereby stressed [œ] alternates with [o]. Corbin's model is 'stratified', since there is a hierarchy in the regularities running from the most regular to the irregular, rather than the more common binary divide usually found between regular and irregular. Note also that Corbin's model is less 'abstract' in this respect than, say, Schane's, where alternating forms such as *flor-* and *fleur-* are derived from the same underlying abstract form (1968:20ff.).

The major advantage of this approach is the capturing of regularity and the capacity of the model to deal with different degrees of regularities, leaving only the genuinely idiosyncratic unaccounted for by the rules. The disadvantage is the mirror image of this: the sheer complexity of the necessary rules may be considered to stretch the notion of regularity to its limit.

Corbin represents her model diagrammatically as follows:

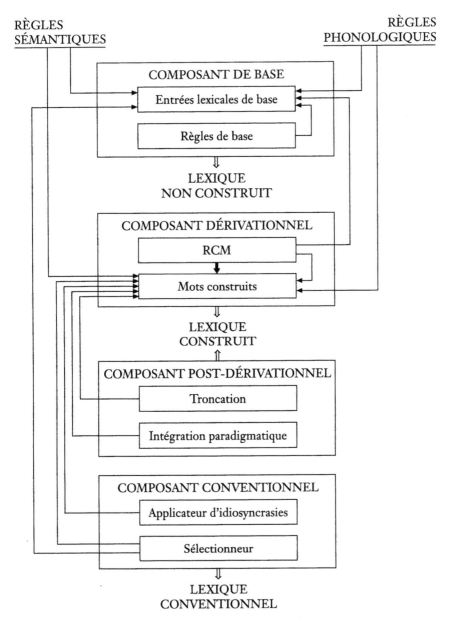

Figure 13.3   Corbin's model of derivation (1991b:19)

The *composant de base* contains

(i)   all the morphemes with their properties (bases and affixes) as well as complex words such as *royaume* which are not constructed by derivation in contemporary French, and other words created through a change in category (metaphor, lexicalization of phrases etc.);
(ii) the basic rules which account for the structure of these words. The semantic rules which feed into the base component could explain polysemy etc. while the phonological rules would contain information about allomorphic variation (see Corbin 1991b:20).

The output of the *composant de base* is the *lexique non construit*, to which the RCMs are applied to give derived forms. Post-derivational processes are also applied, such as that which truncates the form *communist(er)*$_V$ (< *communiste*$_A$) to give *communis(er)*$_V$. Finally, the *composant conventionnel* caters for the relationship with the attested lexis of the language, notably with information on idiosyncrasies which cannot be expressed in the form of regular rules, and a *sélectionneur* which reduces the list of all possible words (both those in the base component and those generated by application of the RCMs) to those which are actually attested. Corbin's model thus has the advantage of predicting the well-formedness of all and only the possible words of French, whether or not they are actually attested.

13.5   The impact of internal lexical creation on French

In Chapter 12 we discussed in some detail the impact of external elements on the French language, and in particular, the complexities which arise (phonological, morphosyntactic, semantic) as internal and external factors interact when words of foreign origin are imported. Indeed, as we discussed, these complexities are often interpreted as problems and constitute one of the main reasons why borrowings are criticized in certain quarters.

The implication behind such criticisms is that neologisms created through internal processes are much more easily assimilated. Although this is broadly true, there are nonetheless a number of complexities which arise; creating new words through native processes is not just a matter of applying a set of regular rules to produce a set of transparent forms. Sometimes sociolinguistic factors play a role; one only has to consider the controversy and disagreement which have surrounded the proposals brought forward by the *Commission de féminisation des noms de métier* (1984), in order to see how the apparently simple application of certain internal processes can be fraught with socio-political difficulties (see the discussion in Houdebine-Gravaud 1998, Yaguello 1998). In this Section, we shall discuss a selection of these complexities, assessing to what extent 'native' neologisms have an impact on the semantic, morphosyntactic and phonological structure of French.

13.5.1   Semantic complexities

Certain semantic patterns and regularities may be observed in the function of different suffixes. For example, the nominal suffixes *-ant*, *-eur*, *-ateur*, *-ante*, *-euse*, *-atrice* usually mark agents of various sorts; *-oir*, *-erie* signal the place where an action takes place; *-ité*, *-ance*, *-isme*, *-esse*, *-tude* suggest states and qualities; *-ette*, *-ine*, *-otte*, *-ille*, *-cule* mark diminutives. The most common verbal suffix is *-er*, which often appears in a fuller form such as *-ier* indicating a modifying process, or *-oyer* suggesting constant repetition (*rougeoyer*), while *-ir* often marks the sense of entering into a state (*blanchir*, *durcir*).

However, although certain broad patterns such as these may be detected, the semantic relationships between suffixes and their functions are complex; there is certainly no one-to-one correspondence.[12] Some suffixes, for example, are semantically weak in that their principal function is syntactic rather than semantic, that is, their main purpose is to change the grammatical category of the word rather than to convey a particular semantic nuance (Thiele 1987 uses the term *catégorème* for these, as opposed to suffixes which carry a distinct meaning, labelled *modificateurs*). This is often the case, for example, with *-tion*, *-eur*, *-ité*, whose principal function in many instances is simply to convert an adjective or a verb into the corresponding noun (*motiver* > *motivation*).

Some suffixes seem to be broadly synonymous, suggesting that in such cases, the speaker may have a choice of form. However, like synonymy in general, these cases are rare; Lehmann and Martin-Berthet (1998:134) cite the case of *venté*, *venteux*, both defined in the *Petit Robert* as marking 'où il y a du vent', both labelled 'rare' and both exemplified with the phrase 'une plaine ventée/venteuse'. The two different suffixes can be explained etymologically: *venteux* stems from the Latin *ventosus*, whereas *venté* is from the past participle of the verb *venter*.

Elsewhere the sense of two suffixes might be broadly similar, but only one will be found in a given context in French; for instance, both *-ation* and *-age* can refer to processes, but only one of the two is productive with the verb *dépurer* (i.e. only *dépuration* is attested as opposed to **dépurage*), while only *-age* is productive with the verb *déraper*, giving us *dérapage* but not **dérapation*. In these cases, the choice of suffix will probably be dictated by phonological or morphological factors (see **13.3.3**).

In other cases, two suffixes with broadly similar functions may both be possible, each having a different, more specialized sense (e.g. *rythmique* = 'qui est soumis à un rythme régulier' vs *rythmé* = 'qui a un rythme'). Broad synonymy is particularly prevalent in informal varieties; this is not surprising given the high levels of lexical creativity. There may be several alternatives in these registers to the standard French term, while one term can have several meanings; *ballon* for example is found in *avoir le ballon* (to be pregnant), *faire ballon* (to be left out when something is being distributed), and is used to mean 'prison'.

As with many suffixes, there are semantic patterns in the functions of prefixes: thus, for example, *re-* usually signals repetition of some sort and may be doubled up (*reremettre*), *de-/des-/dé-* suggests removal or taking away. However, frequent use has led to some prefixes – including the most productive *re-* – losing their semantic force; for example, there is no longer any perceptible difference between *emplir* and *remplir*.

Polysemy is also evident amongst affixes; one form can have different functions. In some cases, the functions are quite distinct; the prefix *dé-* can signal 'undoing/taking away' (*défaire*), or alternatively it can mark increased intensity (*démontrer*). In other cases, there tends to be one broad function which can sub-divide into two or more more specialized functions (see Lehmann and Martin-Berthet (1998:136)); thus, for example, the diminutive suffix *-ette* forms a diminutive noun from a noun (e.g. *maisonnette*) as well as deriving small instruments from verbs (e.g. *éprouvette*). Similarly, *-eur* in its broad function as the marker of an agent encompasses a number of different notions, including someone who does a particular action (*bricoleur*), someone who plays a particular sport (*footballeur*), someone who drives a particular vehicle (*camionneur*). Such semantic specialization stemming from one broad function can lead to the creation of homonyms where the suffix functions in two different ways: e.g. *-erie* (whose broad function signals a place housing a collection of certain objects or people as in *gendarmerie*) can be used both for the collective noun (in this case the police force) and for marking a place (i.e. the police station).

In short, while there are broad patterns in the meaning and function of affixes, there is certainly no one-to-one correspondence between form and function. A host of semantic complexities arise in the application of internal processes in the creation of new words.

13.5.2   Morphosyntactic complexities: compounds and abbreviations

By and large, words created through derivational processes obey standard rules as regards plurals, and most suffixes are regularly assigned a particular gender. Interesting issues arise however in the case of abbreviations (especially acronyms) and compounds. As far as abbreviated adjectives are concerned, plurals are invariable. However, some nouns take the standard *-s* (*stups* < *stupéfiants*) while others can be invariable (*les math* < *mathématiques*). There is, in other words, considerable variation in this area. Most abbreviations are nouns, and most are masculine, even if in rare cases this may result in a change of gender (*ratatouille* f. > *rata* m.). Note that uncertainty as to the correct orthography can also occur with abbreviation; George (1980:35) cites the following attested spellings for the abbreviated form of *après-midi*: *après-m'*, *après-m*, *aprèm*, *aprèm'*, *aprème*. There are also discrepancies between *-o* and *-ot* in the spelling of the suffix [o] which is often added to abbreviated forms.

As far as acronyms are concerned, most are masculine nouns which take the standard French plural, though there are some which, although originally nominal constructions, can function as invariable adjectives (*UDF, RPR*). In some cases, once the acronym has been coined, it is possible for it to behave relatively autonomously such that the speaker is no longer aware of its source (e.g. *radar, laser*). If the acronym is used frequently in French, derivatives may be formed using French suffixes or prefixes, an indication perhaps of the extent to which an acronym has been integrated into the language (e.g. *capésien, sidaïque, cégétiste, IBMeur*).

As for compounds, the rules determining the formation of plural forms are extremely complex, with nouns and adjectives for example declining in some circumstances but not in others (e.g. *francs-maçons* vs *grand(s)-tantes* – for a discussion, see Mitterand (1963:56)). Moreover, there is variation in a number of cases; both *grand-tantes/grand-mères* and *grands-tantes/grands-mères* are acceptable; *après-midi(s)* is found with and without the (*s*); it can therefore be difficult for native speakers to know whether to use an orthographic *-s* or not. Elsewhere different registers demonstrate variation, with *bonshommes* found in more formal registers and *bonhommes* in less formal. In short, considerable variation is possible here too.

13.5.3   Phonological complexities

One type of neologism which raises issues for the sound system of French is the creation of acronyms. Unlike most other examples of linguistic innovation, acronyms are usually created in the written medium (often in the press); subsequently they may be used in both written and oral French. As far as pronunciation is concerned, there are two possibilities: either the acronym is pronounced as a series of letters (this is the most common method and is the case for most of the three-letter acronyms such as RPR, CEE, CGT etc.) or the letters are joined to form a word (e.g. CAPES, SIDA, ENA). The longer the acronym, the greater chance the latter solution will be adopted, provided the series of sounds is perceived to be French, and it is with this type of acronym that derivatives are likely to be formed. In such circumstances, the acronym starts behaving like a French word in terms of its pronunciation.

Calvet (1980:41–60), however, notes a number of features which make the phonological behaviour of acronyms stand out from French pronunciation in general. First, he notes the breakdown of certain phonological oppositions such as /ø ~ œ/, /a ~ ɑ/, /e ~ ɛ/; although all these sounds may appear, they are contextual variants in acronyms, rather than phonemes. This is not surprising, since these are all relatively unstable oppositions in the French system. Other phonemes may be absent or extremely rare in acronyms; these are sounds such as /ʒ/, /ø/, /j/ and /w/ which would require particular combinations of letters to occur together, combinations which seem to be rare in acronyms.

On the other hand, certain letters can be juxtaposed in acronyms which do not normally occur together in French words, such as *fn* as in FNAC. In addition, levels of hiatus are higher than usual (e.g. IUT [iyt]). In short, the phonological system is reduced and the relative frequencies of the various phonemes are different from their usual distribution in speech.

Suggested Reading

General:
Ball (1990), Guilbert (1975), Lehmann and Martin-Berthet (1998), Mitterand (1963), Wise (1997), *Langue française* 96 (1992).
Definitional issues/processes:
Gross (1988, 1990, 1996), Mathieu-Colas (1996), Spence (1976), Wagner (1968).
Neologisms and register/medium/domain:
Borrell (1986), Calvet (1994), François-Geiger (1991), George (1993), Méla (1997), Sourdot (1991, 1997), Verdelhan-Bourgade (1991), Walter (1984, 1997b).
Neologisms and linguistic theory:
Corbin (1987, 1991a, 1991b), Gross (1988, 1990, 1996), Guilbert (1975), Plénat (1997), Temple (1996), Thiele (1987).

Notes

1. It is also possible to remove suffixes, as is the case with deverbal nouns (*transplant* < *transplanter*), a process known as back-formation or *dérivation régressive*. It operates essentially by analogy: a stem is assumed (hence the possibility of removing the affix) where in fact it did not previously exist.
2. See for example Mitterand (1963:48–51), Wise (1997:121–2), Lehmann and Martin-Berthet (1998:170–5).
3. These are labelled *exocentriques* by Martinet (1980:32) and are distinguished from the more straightforward expansions which are labelled *endocentriques*.
4. See also the discussion in Catach (1981:33–4).
5. Two other factors taken into consideration include *défigement* (the capacity of the phrase to be deconstructed and rebuilt with other elements, sometimes to comic effect, e.g. *silence, on assassine*) and etymology (whether the construction may be traced to a clear etymological origin).
6. See Gross (1988, 1990) and especially (1996) for detailed discussion of the criteria in relation to different types of combinations.
7. For an early formulation, see Nyrop (1899–1930:III:272). See also Mitterand (1963:61–2), Picoche and Marchello-Nizia (1989:336–7).

8. See the following books/articles/chapters for discussion and examples of word-formation in informal varieties of French: Ball (1990), Gadet (1992), George (1993), Verdelhan-Bourgade (1991), Walter (1991), (Wise 1997). For a discussion of innovation in young people's speech, see Walter (1984). Many of the examples cited are taken from this material.

9. For more details and examples, see Walter (1984:76–7), Müller (1985:219), George (1993:163–4), Calvet (1994:54–70). Méla (1988) gives full details of the rules and permutations possible in *verlan*.

10. This discussion is based on Bécherel's study (1981a). For other case studies of particular problems, see Adouani (1993), Anscombre and Leeman (1994), Bogacki (1983), Dugas (1992), Van Willigen (1983). For a case study involving compound forms, see Schapira (1982).

11. For a recent major publication, see Temple (1996). For an outline of a number of projects within the SILEX team, see *Lexique* 10.

12. For more discussion of the issues, see Wise (1997:110–12) and Lehmann and Martin-Berthet (1998:34–7).

References

Acquaviva, P. (1992). 'The Representation of Negative "Quantifiers"', *Rivista di linguistica* 4:319–81.

Acquaviva, P. (1994). 'The Representation of Operator Variable Dependencies in Sentential Negation', *Studia Linguistica* 94:91–132.

Adouani, A. (1993). 'Productivité du procédé de formation des substantifs déverbaux', *Le Français moderne* 62(1):37–47.

Aitchison, J. (1987). *Words in the Mind: An Introduction to the Mental Lexicon*, Oxford: Blackwell.

Allaire, S. (1973). *La Subordination dans le français parlé devant les micros de la radiodiffusion*, Paris: Klincksieck.

Andersen, H.L. and G. Skytte (eds) (1995). *La Subordination dans les langues romanes: actes du colloque international, Copenhague*, Copenhagen: Munksgaard International Publishers.

Anderson, S.R. (1982). 'The Analysis of French *schwa*: Or How to Get Something for Nothing', *Language* 58:535–71.

Anderson, S.R. (1985). *Phonology in the Twentieth Century: Theories of Rules and Theories of Representations*, Chicago: University of Chicago Press.

Anderson, S.R. (1992). *A-morphous Morphology*, Cambridge: Cambridge University Press.

Anscombre, J.-C. and O. Ducrot (1983). *L'Argumentation dans la langue*, Liège: Mardaga.

Anscombre, J.-C. and D. Leeman (1994). 'La Dérivation des adjectifs en *-ble*: morphologie ou sémantique?', *Langue française* 103:32–44.

Antoine, G. (1958). *La Coordination en français*, 2 vols, Paris: Editions d'Artrey. Reprinted (1996), Fleury-sur-Orne: Minard.

Armstrong, L.E. (1932). *The Phonetics of French*, London: Bell.

Arnavielle, T. (1978). 'Remarques sur l'emploi du plus-que-parfait de l'indicatif en français moderne', in *Mélanges de philologie romane offerts à Charles Camproux*, Montpellier: CEO, pp.615–21.

Aronoff, M. (1976). *Word Formation in Generative Grammar*, Cambridge, MA: MIT Press.

Arrivé, M., F. Gadet and M. Galmiche (1986). *La Grammaire d'aujourd'hui: guide alphabétique de linguistique française*, Paris: Flammarion.

Ashby, W.J. (1976). 'The Loss of the Negative Morpheme, *ne*, in Parisian French', *Lingua* 39:119–37.

Ashby, W.J. (1981a). 'The Loss of the Negative Particle *ne* in French: A Syntactic Change in Progress', *Language* 57:674–87.

Ashby, W.J. (1981b). 'French Liaison as a Sociolinguistic Phenomenon', in Cressey, W.W. and D.J. Napoli (eds). *Linguistic Symposium on Romance Languages*, Washington DC: Georgetown University Press, pp.46–57.

Ashby, W.J. (1982). 'The Drift of French Syntax', *Lingua* 57:29–46.

Ashby, W.J. (1988). 'The Syntax, Pragmatics, and Sociolinguistics of Left- and Right-Dislocations in French', *Lingua* 75:203–29.

Ashby, W.J. (1991). 'When Does Variation Indicate Linguistic Change in Progress?', *Journal of French Language Studies* 1:1–19.

Ashby, W.J. (1992). 'The Variable Use of *on* versus *tu/vous* for Indefinite Reference in Spoken French', *Journal of French Language Studies* 2:135–57.

Ashby, W.J. (1994). 'An Acoustic Profile of Right Dislocation in French', *Journal of French Language Studies* 4(2):127–46.

Ashby, W.J. (1997). 'Corpus et sociolinguistique: la chute de *ne* en français parlé tourangeau', manuscript.

Aspland, C.A.W. (1979). *A Medieval French Reader*, Oxford: Clarendon Press.

Attal, P. (1988). 'Verbes pronominaux dans les *Mémoires* du Cardinal de Retz', *L'Information grammaticale* 37:17–24.

Auvigne, M.-A. and M. Monté (1982). 'Recherches sur la syntaxe en milieu sous-prolétaire', *Langage et Société* 19:23–63.

Ayres-Bennett, W. (1994). 'Negative Evidence: Or Another Look at the Non-Use of Negative *ne* in Seventeenth-Century French', *French Studies* 48:63–85.

Ayres-Bennett, W. (1996). *A History of the French Language through Texts*, London: Routledge.

Azoulay-Vicente, A. (1988). 'La syntaxe de *ne . . . que*', *Lingvisticae investigationes* 12(2):205–33.

Baciu, I. (1978). 'La Négation restrictive', *Le Français moderne* 46(2):135–42.

Bailard, J. (1980). 'The Subjunctive in Latin and French Noun Clauses: The Role of Semantic Opacity in Syntactic Change', in Nuessel, F.H. Jr. (ed.). *Contemporary Studies in Romance Languages*, Bloomington: Indiana University Linguistics Club, pp.1–15.

Baker, P. and C. Corne (1982). *Isle de France Creole: Affinities and Origins*, [Ann Arbor]: Karoma.

Baker, M., K. Johnson and I. Roberts (1989). 'Passive Arguments Raised', *Linguistic Inquiry* 20:219–51.

Ball, R. (1990). 'Lexical Innovation in Present-Day French: "le français parlé"', *French Cultural Studies* 1:21–35.

Barbaud, P. (1991). 'Subjunctive and ECP', in Wanner, D. and D.A. Kibbee (eds). *New Analyses in Romance Linguistics: Selected Papers from the 18th Linguistic Symposium on Romance Languages, Urbana-Champaign, 7–9 April 1988*, Amsterdam-Philadelphia: Benjamins, pp.125–41.

Barnes, B. (1985). *The Pragmatics of Left Detachment in Spoken Standard French*, Amsterdam: Benjamins.

Barnicaud, G. and others (1967). 'Le Problème de la négation dans diverses grammaires françaises', *Langages* 7:56–73.

Barral, M. (1980). *L'Imparfait du subjonctif: étude sur l'emploi et la concordance des temps au subjonctif*, Paris: Picard.

Battye, A. and M.-A. Hintze (1992). *The French Language Today*, London: Routledge.

Bauche, H. (1951). *Le Langage populaire: grammaire, syntaxe et dictionnaire du français tel qu'on le parle dans le peuple de Paris, avec tous les termes d'argot usuel*, new revised edn, Paris: Payot.

Bauer, B.L.M. (1995). *The Emergence and Development of SVO Patterns in Latin and French*, Oxford: Oxford University Press.

Bäuerle, R., U. Egli and A. Von Stechow (eds) (1970). *Semantics from Different Points of View*, Berlin: Springer.

Béchade, H.-D. (1986). *Syntaxe du français moderne et contemporain*, Paris: PUF.

Béchade, H.-D. (1992). *Phonétique et morphologie du français moderne et contemporain*, Paris: PUF.

Bécherel, D. (1981a). 'Différentiation morpho-sémantique des suffixes nominalisateurs de l'adjectif', *Cahiers de lexicologie* 38:45–59.

Bécherel, D. (1981b). 'A propos des solutions de remplacements des anglicismes', *La Linguistique* 17(2):119–31.

Beck, J. (1988). 'On Functional Multiplicity of Tense-Aspect Forms in Old French Narrative', *Romance Philology* 42(2):129–43.

Bédier, J. (ed.) (1927). *La Chanson de Roland*, Paris: Piazza.

Bénézech, J.-L. (1992). 'Benveniste et le verbe français ou "histoire" et "discours"', *Modèles linguistiques* 14(2):181–208.

Benveniste, E. (1966). *Problèmes de linguistique générale*, vol 1, Paris: Gallimard.

Berthonneau, A.-M. and G. Kleiber (1993). 'Pour une nouvelle approche de l'imparfait: l'imparfait, un temps méronymique', *Langages* 27:55–73.

Berthonneau, A.-M. and G. Kleiber (1998). 'Imparfait, anaphore et inférences', in Borillo, Vetters and Vuillaume (eds), pp.35–65.

Blanc, M.H.A. (1964). 'Time and Tense in Old French Narrative', *Archivum Linguisticum* 16(2):96–124.

Blanc, M.H.A. and P. Biggs (1971). 'L'Enquête sociolinguistique sur le français parlé à Orléans', *Le Français dans le monde* 85:16–25.

Blanche-Benveniste, C. (1982). 'Examen de la notion de subordination', *Recherches sur le français parlé* 4:71–115.

Blanche-Benveniste, C. (1988). 'Les Régulations syntaxiques des productions de français parlé', *Linx* 18:7–20.

Blanche-Benveniste, C. (1995). 'De la rareté de certains phénomènes syntaxiques en français parlé', *Journal of French Language Studies* 5:17–29.

Blanche-Benveniste, C. (1996). 'Trois remarques sur l'ordre des mots dans la langue parlée', *Langue française* 111:109–24.

Blanche-Benveniste, C. (1997). *Approches de la langue parlée*, Paris: Ophrys.

Blanche-Benveniste, C. and others (1984). *Pronom et syntaxe: l'approche pronominale et son application à la langue française*, Paris: SELAF.

Blanche-Benveniste, C. and others (1990). *Le Français parlé: études grammaticales*, Paris: Editions du CNRS.

Blasco, M. (1995). 'Dislocation et thématisation en français parlé', *Recherches sur le français parlé* 13:45–65.

Blasco, M. (1997). 'Pour une approche syntaxique des dislocations', *Journal of French Language Studies* 7:1–21.

Blumenthal, P. (1986). *Vergangenheitstempora, Textstrukturierung und Zeitverständnis in der französischen Sprachgeschichte*, Stuttgart: Steiner.

Bogacki, C. (1983). 'Représentations sémantiques et suffixes d'adjectif', *Lingvisticae investigationes* 7(1):1–9.

Bonnard, H. (1994). 'L'Assiette négative en français', *Le Français moderne* 62:1–10.

Booij, G. (1983/4). 'French C/Ø Alternations, Extrasyllabicity and Lexical Phonology', *The Linguistic Review* 3:181–207.

Booij, G. and D. De Jong (1987). 'The Domain of Liaison: Theories and Data', *Linguistics* 25:1005–25.

Boons, J.-P., A. Guillet and C. Leclère (1976). *La Structure des phrases simples en français: constructions intransitives*, Geneva: Droz.

Borillo, A., C. Vetters and M. Vuillaume (eds) (1998). *Variations sur la référence verbale*, Amsterdam-Atlanta: Rodopi.

Börjeson, L. (1966). 'La Fréquence du subjonctif dans les subordonnées complétives introduites par "que" étudiée dans des textes français contemporain', *Studia neophilologica* 38:3–64.

Borrell, A. (1986). 'Le Vocabulaire "jeune", le parler "branché"', *Cahiers de lexicologie* 48:69–88.

Bossé-Andrieu, J. and P. Cardinal (1988). 'Les Emprunts à l'anglais dans la presse écrite québécoise', in Pergnier (ed.), pp.79–89.

Bouchard, D. (1983). 'Nasal Vowels in French without Underlying Nasal Vowels and without a Rule of Nasalization', *Cahiers linguistiques d'Ottawa* 11:29–57.

Boyer, H. (1985). 'L'Economie des temps narratifs dans le discours narratif', *Le Français moderne* 53:78–89.

Boyer, H. (1997). 'Le Statut de la suffixation en -*os*', *Langue française* 114:35–40.

Boysen, G. (1971). *Subjonctif et hiérarchie: étude sur l'emploi du subjonctif dans les propositions complétives objets de verbes en français moderne*, Odense: Odense University Press.

Bres, J. (1997). 'Habiter le temps: le couple imparfait/passé simple en français', *Langages* 127:77–95.

Bres, J. (1998a). 'De l'alternance temporelle passé composé/présent en récit conversationnel', in Borillo, Vetters and Vuillaume (eds), pp.125–36.

Bres, J. (1998b). 'Fluence du temps impliqué et orientation: l'imparfait et le passé simple revisités', in Vogeleer and others (eds), pp.157–70.

Brunot, F. (1922). *La Pensée et la langue: méthode, principes et plan d'une théorie nouvelle du langage appliquée au français*, Paris: Masson.

Buffier, C. (1709). *Grammaire françoise sur un plan nouveau*, Paris: Nicolas le Clerc, M. Brunet, Leconte and Montalant.

Burston, J.L. (1979). 'The Pronominal Verb Construction in French: An Argument against the Fortuitous Homonymy Hypothesis', *Lingua* 48:147–76.

Bybee, J. and S. Fleischman (eds) (1995). *Modality in Grammar and Discourse*, Amsterdam-Philadelphia: Benjamins.

Cadiot, P. (1992). 'Matching Syntax and Pragmatics: A Typology of Topic and Topic-related Constructions in Spoken French', *Linguistics* 30(1):57–88.

Calvet, L.-J. (1980). *Les Sigles*, Paris: PUF.

Calvet, L.-J. (1994). *L'Argot*, Paris: PUF.

Calvet, L.-J. (1996). *Les Politiques linguistiques*, Paris: PUF.

Canut, C. and G. Ledegen (1998). '*Après que* ... ou la fluctuation des modes en français parlé', *Langage et société* 85:25–53.

Caron, P. and Y.-C. Liu (1999). 'Nouvelles données sur la concurrence du passé simple et du passé composé dans la littérature épistolaire', *L'Information grammaticale* 82:38–50.

Carr, P. (1994). 'Fixed and Floating Consonants, Nasalization and /e/ Adjustment in Standard French: A Government Phonology Approach', in Lyche, C. (ed.). *French Generative Phonology: Retrospective and Perspectives*, Salford: Association for French Language Studies in association with the European Studies Research Institute, University of Salford, pp.73–94.

Carroll, S. (ed.) (1982a). *La Syntaxe comparée du français standard et populaire: approches formelles et fonctionnelles*, vol 2, Québec: Office de la langue française.

Carroll, S. (1982b). 'Les Dislocations ne sont pas si populaires que ça', in Carroll (ed.), pp.211–46.

Carruthers, J. (1992). 'Une étude sociolinguistique des formes surcomposées en français moderne', *Actas do XIX Congreso Internacional de Lingüística e Filoloxía Románicas* 3:145–62.

Carruthers, J. (1993). 'Passé composé, passé surcomposé: marqueurs de l'antériorité en français parlé', *Actes du XXe congrès international de linguistique et philologie romanes* 1:111–22.

Carruthers, J. (1994). 'The *passé surcomposé régional*: Towards a Definition of its Function in Contemporary Spoken French', *Journal of French Language Studies* 4:171–90.

Carruthers, J. (1996). 'The *passé surcomposé général*: On the Relationship between a Rare Tense and Discourse Organization', *Romance Philology* 50(2):183–200.

Cartier, A. (1977). 'Connaissance et usage d'anglicismes par des Français de Paris', *La Linguistique* 13(2):55–84.

Carton, F. (1974). *Introduction à la phonétique du français*, Paris: Bordas.

Carton, F. and others (1983). *Les Accents des Français*, Paris: Hachette.

Casagrande, J. (1984). *The Sound System of French*, Washington DC: Georgetown University Press.

Catach, N. (1981). *Orthographe et lexicographie*, Paris: Nathan.

Chevalier, J.-C. and others (1964). *Grammaire Larousse du français contemporain*, Paris: Larousse.

Chiss, J.-L., J. Filliolet and D. Maingueneau (1993). *Linguistique française: notions fondamentales, phonétique, lexique*, Paris: Hachette.

Chomsky, N. (1957). *Syntactic Structures*, The Hague: Mouton.

Chomsky, N. (1965). *Aspects of the Theory of Syntax*, Cambridge, MA: MIT Press.

Chomsky, N. (1970). 'Remarks on Nominalization', in Jacobs, R.A. and P.S. Rosenbaum (eds). *Readings in English Transformational Grammar*, Waltham, MA: Ginn.

Chomsky, N. and M. Halle (1968). *The Sound Pattern of English*, New York: Harper and Row.

Chuquet, J. and D. Roullard (eds) (1992). *Subordination*, Rennes: Presses Universitaires de Rennes.

Clements, G.N. and J. Keyser (1983). *CV Phonology: A Generative Theory of the Syllable*, Cambridge, MA: MIT Press.

Clifford, P. (1973). *Inversion of the Subject in French Narrative Prose from 1500 to the Present Day*, Oxford: Blackwell.

Cohen, M. (1946). *Le Français en 1700 d'après le témoignage de Giles Vaudelin*, Paris: Bibliothèque de l'Ecole des Hautes Etudes.

Cohen, M. (1965). *Le Subjonctif en français contemporain*, Paris: Société d'Edition d'Enseignement Supérieur.

Cohen, M. (1989). *L'Aspect verbal*, Paris: PUF.

Combettes, B. (1998). *Les Constructions détachées en français*, Paris: Ophrys.

Comrie, B. (1976). *Aspect*, Cambridge: Cambridge University Press.

Comrie, B. (1985). *Tense*, Cambridge: Cambridge University Press.

Confais, J.-P. (1990). *Temps, mode, aspect. Les Approches des morphèmes verbaux et leurs problèmes à l'exemple du français et de l'allemand*, Toulouse: Presses Universitaires du Mirail.

Connors, K. (1978). 'The Meaning of the French Subjunctive', *Linguistics* 211:45–56.

Corbin, D. (1987). *Morphologie dérivationnelle et structuration du lexique*, Tübingen: Niemeyer.

Corbin, D. (1991a). 'La Morphologie lexicale: bilan et perspectives', *Travaux de linguistique* 23:33–65.

Corbin, D. (1991b). 'La Formation des mots: structures et interprétations', *Lexique* 10:7–30.

Corbin, D. (2000). 'Préfixes et suffixes: du sens aux catégories', manuscript.

Cornulier, B. de (1973). 'Sur une règle de déplacement de négation', *Le Français moderne* 51:43–57.

Coveney, A. (1996). *Variability in Spoken French: A Sociolinguistic Study of Interrogation and Negation*, Exeter: Elm Bank.

Coveney, A. (1998). 'Awareness of Linguistic Constraints on Variable *ne* Omission', *Journal of French Language Studies* 8:159–87.

Crystal, D. (1976). *Child Language, Learning and Linguistics*, London: Arnold.

Crystal, D. (1992). *An Encyclopaedic Dictionary of Language and Languages*, Oxford: Blackwell.

Culioli, A. (1991). *Pour une linguistique de l'énonciation: opérations et représentations*, Vol I, Gap: Ophrys.

Culioli, A. (1999). *Pour une linguistique de l'énonciation: opérations et représentations*, Vols II, III, Gap-Paris: Ophrys.

Curat, H. (1991). *Morphologie verbale et référence temporelle en français moderne: essai de sémantique grammaticale*, Geneva: Droz.

Damourette, J. and E. Pichon [1928–40]. *Des mots à la pensée: essai de grammaire de la langue française 1911–1940*, 7 vols, Paris: Collection des linguistes contemporains.

Dangeau, L'Abbé de (1754). *Opuscules sur la langue françoise: par divers Académiciens*, Paris: Brunet.

Dannequin, C. (1977). *Les Enfants baillonnés*, Paris: Nathan.

Dauses, A. (1973). *Etudes sur l'e instable dans le français familier*, Tübingen: Niemeyer.

David, D. and R. Martin (eds) (1980). *La Notion d'aspect*, Metz: Université de Metz.

Debrock, M. and P. Mertens (1993). *Phonétique générale et française*, Louvain: Presses universitaires de Louvain.

De Jong, D. (1990). 'The Syntax-Phonology Interface and French Liaison', *Linguistics* 28:57–88.

De Jong, D. (1993). 'Sociophonological Aspects of Montreal French Liaison', in Ashby, W.J. and others (eds). *Linguistic Perspectives on the Romance Languages*, Amsterdam: Benjamins, pp.125–37.

De Jong, D. (1994). 'La Sociophonologie de la liaison orléanaise', in Lyche, C. (ed.). *French Generative Phonology: Retrospective and Perspectives*, Salford: Association for French Language Studies in association with the European Studies Research Institute, University of Salford, pp.95–130.

Delabre, M. (1995). '*Dont* en français contemporain: norme, grammaire et théorie linguistique', *L'Information grammaticale* 64:3–8.

Delattre, P. (1947). 'La Liaison en français, tendances et classification', *The French Review* 21:148–57.

Delattre, P. (1949). 'Le Jeu de l'*e* instable de monosyllabe initial en français', *The French Review* 22/23:455–9/43–7.

Delattre, P. (1955). 'Les Facteurs de la liaison facultative en français', *The French Review* 29:42–9.

Delattre, P. (1956). 'La Fréquence des liaisons facultatives en français,' *The French Review* 30:48–54.

Delattre, P. (1966). *Studies in French and Comparative Phonetics*, The Hague: Mouton.

Delbart, A.-R. (1996). 'Ainsi que des bossus tous deux nous rigolâmes: le passé simple dans les chansons de G. Brassens', *Revue de linguistique romane* 60:485–512.

Dell, F. (1970). *Les Règles phonologiques tardives et la morphologie dérivationnelle du français*, Ph.D. dissertation, Massachusetts Institute of Technology.

Dell, F. (1973). *Les Règles et les sons: introduction à la phonologie générative*, Paris: Hermann.

Dell, F. and E.O. Selkirk (1978). 'On a Morphologically Governed Vowel Alternation in French', in Keyser, S.J. (ed.). *Recent Transformational Studies in European Languages*, Cambridge, MA: MIT Press, pp.1–51.

De Mulder, W., L. Tasmowski-De Ryck and C. Vetters (eds) (1996). *Anaphores temporelles et (in-)cohérence*, Amsterdam-Atlanta: Rodopi.

Desclés, J.P. and Z. Guentchéva (1993). 'Le Passif dans le système des voix du français', *Langages* 109:73–102.

Désirat, C. and T. Hordé (1988). *La Langue française au XXe siècle* (originally published 1976), 2nd edn, Paris: Bordas.

Detrich, E.D. (1979). 'Nasal Consonant Epenthesis in "Southern" French', in Hollien, H. and P. Hollien (eds). *Current Issues in the Phonetic Sciences*, Amsterdam: Benjamins, pp.521–9.

Deulofeu, J. (1977). 'La Syntaxe et les constructions binaires', *Recherches sur le français parlé* 1:30–62.

Deulofeu, J. (1981). 'Perspective linguistique et sociolinguistique dans l'étude des relatives en français', *Recherches sur le français parlé* 3:135–93.

Deulofeu, J. (1986). 'Syntaxe de "que" en français parlé et le problème de la subordination', *Recherches sur le français parlé* 8:79–104.

Dictionnaire des termes officiels de la langue française, published by the *Délégation générale à la langue française*, January 1994 edition.

Di Sciullo, A.-M. and E. Williams (1987). *On the Definition of Word*, Cambridge, MA: MIT Press.

Diki-Kidiri, M., H. Joly and C. Murcia (1981). *Guide de la néologie*, Paris: CILF.

Diller, A.-M. [1983]. 'Subject NP Structure and Variable Constraints: The Case of *ne* Deletion', in Fasold, R.W. (ed.). *Variation in the Form and Use of Language*, Washington, DC: Georgetown University Press, pp.167–74.

Drozdale, E. (1988). 'L'Anglicisation du français dans la presse', in Pergnier (ed.), pp.137–45.

Dubois, J. (1965). *Grammaire structurale du français*, Vol I: *Nom et pronom*, Paris: Larousse.

Dubois, J. (1967). Grammaire structurale du français, Vol II: *Le Verbe*, Paris: Larousse.

Dubois, J. and R. Lagane (1989). *Nouvelle Grammaire du français*, Paris: Larousse.

Ducrot, O. (1979). 'L'Imparfait en français', *Linguistische Berichte* 60:1–23.

Ducrot, O. (1984). *Le Dire et le dit*, Paris: Minuit.

Ducrot, O. and others (1980). *Les Mots du discours*. Paris: Minuit.

Dugas, A. (1992). 'Le Préfixe *auto-*', *Langue française* 96:20–9.

Durand, J. (1986). 'French Liaison, Floating Segments and Other Matters in a Dependency Framework', in Durand, J. (ed.). *Dependency and Non-Linear Phonology*, London: Croom Helm, pp.161–206.

Durand, J. (1988). 'An Exploration of Nasality Phenomena in Midi French: Dependency Phonology and Underspecification', in Slater, C., J. Durand and M. Bate (eds). *French Sound Patterns: Changing Perspectives*, Colchester: Association of French Language Studies and Department of Language and Linguistics, University of Essex, pp.30–70.

Durand, J. (1993a). 'La Phonologie multidimensionnelle moderne et la description du français', *Journal of French Language Studies* 3:197–229.

Durand, J. (1993b). 'Sociolinguistic Variation and the Linguist', in Sanders (ed.), pp.257–85.

Durand, J. and C. Lyche (1994). 'Phonologie multidimensionnelle et phonologie du français: quelques tendances', in Lyche, C. (ed.). *French Generative Phonology: Retrospective and Perspectives*, Salford: Association for French Language Studies in association with the European Studies Research Institute, University of Salford, pp.3–32.

Durand, J., C. Slater and H. Wise (1988). 'Observations on *schwa* in Southern French', in Slater, C., J. Durand and M. Bate (eds). *French Sound Patterns: Changing Perspectives*, Colchester: Association of French Language Studies and Department of Language and Linguistics, University of Essex, pp.71–103.

Encrevé, P. (1983). 'La Liaison sans enchaînement', *Actes de la recherche en sciences sociales* 46:39–66.

Encrevé, P. (1988). *La Liaison avec et sans enchaînement: phonologie tridimensionnelle et usages du français*, Paris: Seuil.

Engel, D.M. (1990). *Tense and Text: A Study of French Past Tenses*, London: Routledge.

Engel, D.M. (1994). 'Plus-que-parfait: Past Anterior or Past Punctual?', *Linguisticae investigationes* 18(2):223–42.

Engel, D.M. (1996). 'Le Passé du passé', *Word* 47:41–62.

Engel, D.M. (1998). 'Combler le vide: le passé simple est-il important dans le système verbal?', in Borillo, Vetters and Vuillaume (eds), pp.91–107.

Estienne, H. (1565). *Traicté de la conformité du langage françois avec le grec*, Paris: H. Estienne.

Etiemble, R. (1964). *Parlez-vous franglais?*, Paris: Gallimard.

Ewert, A. (1933). *The French Language*, Cambridge: Cambridge University Press.

Fleischman, S. (1983). 'From Pragmatics to Grammar: Diachronic Reflections on Complex Pasts and Futures in Romance', *Lingua* 60:183–214.

Fleischman, S. (1990). *Tense and Narrativity: From Medieval Performance to Modern Fiction*, London: Routledge.

Fleischman, S. (1991). 'Verb Tense and Point of View in Narrative', in Fleischman and Waugh (eds), pp.26–54.

Fleischman, S. (1995). 'Imperfective and Irrealis', in Bybee and Fleischman (eds), pp.519–51.

Fleischman, S. and L. Waugh (eds) (1991). *Discourse Pragmatics and the Verb*, London: Routledge.

Foley, J. (1979). *Theoretical Morphology of the French Verb*, Amsterdam: Benjamins.

Fónagy, I. (1989). 'Le Français change de visage?', *Revue Romane* 24:225–54.

Fouché, P. (1958). *Phonétique historique du français*, Paris: Klincksieck.

Fouché, P. (1959). *Traité de prononciation française*, Paris: Klincksieck.

Foulet, L. (1920). 'La Disparition du prétérit', *Romania* 46:270–313.

Foulet, L. (1970). *Petite Syntaxe de l'ancien français*, 3rd edn, Paris: Champion.

Fradin, B. (1990). 'Approche des constructions à détachement: inventaire', *Revue romane* 25(1):3–34.

François, D. (1974). *Français parlé: analyse des unités phoniques et significatives d'un corpus recueilli dans la région parisienne*, 2 vols, Paris: SELAF.

François-Geiger, D. (1991). 'Panorama des argots contemporains', *Langue française* 90:5–9.

Fuchs, C. and P. Le Goffic (1992). *Les Linguistiques contemporaines: repères théoriques*, Paris: Hachette.

Gaatone, D. (1971). *Etude descriptive du système de la négation en français contemporain*, Geneva: Droz.

Gaatone, D. (1998). *Le Passif en Fançais*, Louvain-la-Neuve: Duculot.

Gadet, F. (1988). 'La Relative non-standard saisie par les grammaires', *Linx* 18:37–50.

Gadet, F. (1989). *Le Français ordinaire*, Paris: Colin.

Gadet, F. (1991). 'Simple, le français populaire?', *Linx* 25:63–78.

Gadet, F. (1992). *Le Français populaire*, Paris: PUF.

Gadet, F. (1995). 'Les Relatives non-standard en français parlé: le système et l'usage', in Andersen and Skytte (eds), pp.141–62.

Gadet, F. and F. Mazière (1987). 'L'Extraordinaire Souplesse du strument "que"', *Le Français moderne* 55:204–15.

Galet, Y. (1974). 'Illustration de la théorie des niveaux d'énonciation', *Langue française* 21:26–42.

Galet, Y. (1977). *Les Corrélations verbo-adverbiales, fonction du passé simple et du passé composé, et la théorie des niveaux d'énonciation dans la phrase française du XVIIe siècle*, Paris: Champion.

Gardes-Tamine, J. (1986). 'Le Verbe, pronominaux et unipersonnels', *L'Information grammaticale* 30:41–4.

Gardes-Tamine, J. (1988). *La Grammaire*, 2 vols, Paris: Colin.

Gauchat, L. (1905). 'L'Unité phonétique dans le patois d'une commune', in *Aus romanischen Sprachen und Literaturen: Festschrift Heinrich Morf*, Halle: Niemeyer, pp.175–232.

Gaudin, F. (1991). 'Enquête sur l'impact des arrêtés terminologiques auprès des magistrats', *La Banque des mots* 42:59–66.

Gaudin, F. (1994). 'Comparaison des politiques française, belge et québécoise en matière linguistique', *La Banque des mots* 48:77–87.

Gaudin, F. (1996). 'Droit aux mots, droit au savoir: approche glottopolitique de la loi Toubon', *Cahiers de lexicologie* 69(2):43–61.

Geckeler, H. (1997/98). 'Les Emprunts aller-retour français-anglais-français', *Travaux de linguistique et philologie* 35/36:211–21.

Geniušienė, E. (1987). *The Typology of Reflexives*, Berlin: Mouton de Gruyter.

George, K. (1980). 'L'Apocope et l'aphérèse en français familier, populaire et argotique', *Le Français moderne* 48(1):16–37.

George, K. (1993). 'Alternative French', in Sanders (ed.), pp.155–70.

Germain, C. and A. Lapierre (1988). 'Le Sigle: définition, caractéristique et emploi', *Cahiers de lexicologie* 53:55–74.

Gertner, M.H. (1973). *The Morphology of the Modern French Verb*, The Hague-Paris: Mouton.

Gilder, A. (1993). *Et si l'on parlait français?*, Paris: Le Cherche Midi.

Gilliéron, J.J. and E. Edmont (1902–10). *Atlas linguistique de la France*, Paris: Champion.

Godard, D. (1988a). *La Syntaxe des relatives en français*, Paris: CNRS.

Godard, D. (1988b). 'Français standard et non-standard: les relatives', *Linx* 18:51–88.

Goosse, A. (1975). *La Néologie française aujourd'hui*, Paris: CILF.

Goudaillier, J.-P. (1977). 'A nouveau les puristes contre la langue', *La Linguistique* 13(2):85–98.

Gougenheim, G. (1935). *Eléments de phonologie française*, Paris: Les Belles Lettres.

Gougenheim, G. and others (1956). *L'Elaboration du français fondamental*, Paris: Didier.

Grammont, M. (1894). 'La loi des trois consonnes', *Mémoires de la Société Linguistique de Paris* 8:53–90.

Grammont, M. (1948). *La Prononciation française*, Paris: Delagrave.

Grand Larousse de la langue française en sept volumes (1971–78), Paris: Larousse.

Green, J.N. (1997). Review of Bauer (1995) in *Journal of French Language Studies* 7:211–12.

Green, J.N. and M.-A. Hintze (1988). 'A Reconsideration of *liaison* and *enchaînement*', in Slater, C., J. Durand and M. Bate (eds). *French Sound Patterns: Changing Perspectives*, Colchester: Association for French Language Studies and Department of Language and Linguistics, University of Essex, pp.136–68.

Green, J.N. and M.-A. Hintze (1990). 'Variation and Change in French Linking Phenomena', in Green, J.N. and W. Ayres-Bennett (eds). *Variation and Change in French: Essays Presented to Rebecca Posner on the Occasion of her Sixtieth Birthday*, London: Routledge, pp.61–88.

Greenberg, J.H. (ed.) (1966). *Universals of Language*, Cambridge MA: MIT Press.

Grevisse, M. (1993). *Le Bon Usage: grammaire française refondue par André Goosse*, 13th edn, Paris-Louvain-la-Neuve: Duculot.

Grize, J.-B. (1990). *Logique et langage*, Paris: Ophrys.

Gross, G. (1988). 'Degré de figement des noms composés', *Langages* 90:57–72.

Gross, G. (1990). 'Définition des noms composés dans un lexique-grammaire', *Langue française* 87:84–90.

Gross, G. (1996). *Les Expressions figées en français*, Paris: Ophrys.

Gross, M. (1977). *Grammaire transformationnelle du français: syntaxe du nom*, Paris: Larousse.

Gross, M. (1978). 'Correspondance entre forme et sens à propos du subjonctif', *Langue française* 39:49–65.

Guilbert, L. (1975). *La Créativité lexicale*, Paris: Larousse.

Guilford, J. (1997). 'Les Attitudes des jeunes Français à propos des emprunts à l'anglais', *La Linguistique* 33(2):117–35.

Guilford, J. (1999). 'L'Attribution du genre aux emprunts à l'anglais', *La Linguistique* 35(1):65–85.

Guillaume, G. (1929). *Temps et verbe*, Paris: Champion.

Guillaume, G. (1943). 'Existe-t-il un déponent en français?', *Le Français moderne* 11:9–30.

Guillaume, G. (1964). *Langage et science du langage*, Paris: Nizet.

Guiraud, P. (1971). *Les Mots étrangers*, Paris: PUF.

Gülich, E. (1970). *Makrosyntax der Gliederungssignale im gesprochenen Französisch*, Munich: Fink.

Haegeman, L. (1994). *Introduction to Government and Binding Theory*, Oxford: Blackwell.

Haegeman, L. (1995). *The Syntax of Negation*, Cambridge: Cambridge University Press.

Hagège, C. (1987). *Le Français et les siècles*, Paris: Jacob.

Hagège, C. (1996). *Le Français: histoire d'un combat*, Paris: Hagège.

Hajek, J. (1993). 'Old French Nasalization and Universals of Sound Change', *Journal of French Language Studies* 3:145–64.

Hajek, J. (1997). *Universals of Sound Change in Nasalization*, Oxford: Blackwell.

Halle, M. (1973). 'Prolegomena to a Theory of Word Formation', *Linguistic Inquiry* 4:3–16.

Halliday, M.A.K. (1985a). *An Introduction to Functional Grammar*, London: Arnold.

Halliday, M.A.K. (1985b). *Spoken and Written Language*, Victoria: Deakin University.

Halliday, M.A.K. and R. Hasan (1976). *Cohesion in English*, London: Longman.

Hanse, J. (1960). *La Valeur modale du subjonctif*, Brussels: Palais des Académies.

Hansen, A.B. (1994). 'Etude du E caduc: stabilisation en cours et variations lexicales', *Journal of French Language Studies* 4:25–54.

Hansen, A.B. (1998). *Les Voyelles nasales du français parisien moderne: aspects linguistiques, sociolinguistiques et perceptuels des changements en cours*, Copenhagen: Museum Tusculanum Press, University of Copenhagen.

Harris, M.B. (1974). 'The Subjunctive Mood as a Changing Category in Romance', in *Historical Linguistics II: Theory and Description in Phonology (Proceedings of the First International Conference on Historical Linguistics, Edinburgh, 2–7 September 1973)*, Amsterdam-Oxford: North-Holland Publishing Company, pp.169–88.

Harris, M.B. (1978). *The Evolution of French Syntax: A Comparative Approach*, London: Longman.

Harris, M.B. (1981). 'On the Conditional as a Mood in French', *Folia Linguistica Historica* 2(1):55–69.

Harris, M.B. (1982). 'The *Past Simple* and the *Present Perfect* in Romance' in Vincent, N. and M.B. Harris (eds). *Studies in the Romance Verb: Essays Offered to Joe Cremona on the Occasion of his Sixtieth Birthday*, London: Croom Helm, pp.41–70.

Harris, M.B. (1985). 'Word Order in Contemporary French: A Functional View', *Working Papers in Functional Grammar* 1:1–16.

Harris, Z.S. (1957). 'Co-occurrence and transformation in linguistic structure', *Language* 33:283–340.

Haudricourt, A.G. (1947). '*En/an* en français', *Word* 3:39–47.

Haugen, E. (1950). 'The Analysis of Linguistic Borrowing', *Language* 26:210–31.

Havu, E. (1996). *De l'emploi du subjonctif passé*, Helsinki: Suomalainen Tiedeakatemia.

Heldner, C. (1981). *La Portée de la négation: un examen de quelques facteurs sémantiques et textuels pertinents à sa détermination dans des énoncés authentiques*, Stockholm: Institut d'Etudes Romanes.

Herzog, C. (1981). *Le Passé simple dans les journaux du XXe siècle*, Berne: Francke.

Hobaek-Haff, M. (1987). *Coordonnants et éléments coordonnés*, Paris-Oslo: Didier-Solum.

Hockett, C.F. (1942). 'A System of Descriptive Phonology', *Language* 18:3–21.

Hockett, C.F. (1954). 'Two Models of Grammatical Description', *Word* 10:210–34.

Hockett, C.F. (1958). *A Course in Modern Linguistics*, New York: Macmillan.

Hong, C.-H. (1997). 'Tendances de la néologie par dérivation et par formation au moyen d'éléments gréco-latins', *La Linguistique* 33(2):107–16.

Hopper, P.J. (ed.) (1982). *Tense-Aspect: Between Semantics and Pragmatics*, Amsterdam: Benjamins.

Hopper, P.J. (1987). 'Emergent Grammar', *Berkeley Linguistics Society* 13:139–57.

Horrocks, G. (1987). *Generative Grammar*, Harlow: Longman.

Houdebine-Gravaud, A.-M. (1998). 'Insécurité linguistique, imaginaire linguistique et féminisation des noms de métiers', in Singy (ed.), pp.155–76.

House, A.S. and K.N. Stevens (1956). 'Analog Studies of the Nasalization of Vowels', *Journal of Speech and Hearing Disorders* 21:218–32.

Huot, H. (1986). 'Le Subjonctif dans les complétives: subjectivité et modalisation', in Ronat, M. and D. Couquaux, *La Grammaire modulaire*, Paris: Minuit, pp.81–111.

Imbs, P. (1953). *Le Subjonctif en français moderne: essai de grammaire descriptive*, Strasbourg: Faculté des lettres de l'Université de Strasbourg.

Imbs, P. (1960). *L'Emploi des temps verbaux en français moderne*, Paris: Klincksieck.

International Phonetic Association. (1999). *Handbook of the International Phonetic Association*, Cambridge: Cambridge University Press.

Iordan, I. and J. Orr (1970). *An Introduction to Romance Linguistics: Its Schools and Scholars*, revised with a supplement by R. Posner, Oxford: Blackwell.

Jackendoff, R. (1972). *Semantic Interpretation in Generative Grammar*, Cambridge, MA: MIT Press.

Jakobson, R., G. Fant and M. Halle (1952). *Preliminaries to Speech Analysis: The Distinctive Features and their Correlates*, Cambridge, MA: MIT Press.

Jeanjean, C. (1981). 'L'Organisation des formes sujets en français de conversation: étude quantitative et grammaticale de deux corpus', *Recherches sur le français parlé* 3:99–134.

Jeanjean, C. (1983). 'A propos de l'utilisation des conjonctions chez les enfants', *Recherches sur le français parlé* 5:191–209.

Jensen, F. (1974). *The Syntax of the Old French Subjunctive*, The Hague-Paris: Mouton.

Joly, A. (1983). 'Ambiguïté et paraphrase: à propos de certaines types d'inversion en français', *Modèles linguistiques* 5(2):137–73.

Jones, D. (1950). *The Phoneme: Its Nature and Use*, Cambridge: Heffer.

Jones, M.A. (1996). *Foundations of French Syntax*, Cambridge: Cambridge University Press.

Joos, M. (ed.) (1966). *Readings in Linguistics*, Chicago: University of Chicago Press.

Judge, A. (1993). 'French: A Planned Language?', in Sanders (ed.), pp.7–26.

Judge, A. (1998). 'Choix entre le présent narratif et le système multifocal dans le contexte du récit écrit', in Vogeleer and others (eds), pp.215–35.

Judge, A. and F.G. Healey (1983). *A Reference Grammar of Modern French*, London: Arnold.

Kaisse, E. (1985). *Connected Speech: The Interaction of Syntax and Phonology*, Orlando, FL: Academic Press.

Kamp, H. (1981). 'Evénements, représentations discursives et référence temporelle', *Langages* 64:39–64.

Kamp, H. and Rohrer, C. (1983). 'Tense in Texts', in Bäuerle, R., C. Schwarze and A. von Stechow (eds). *Meaning, Use, and Interpretation of Language*, Berlin: De Gruyter, pp.250–69.

Kampers-Manhe, B. (1991). *L'Opposition subjonctif/indicatif dans les relatives*, Amsterdam-Atlanta: Rodopi.

Kayne, R.S. (1975). *French Syntax: The Transformational Cycle*, Cambridge, MA: MIT Press.

Kerbrat-Orecchioni, C. (1980). *L'Enonciation. De la subjectivité dans la langue*, Paris: Colin.

Kiefer, F. (1973). *Generative Morphologie des Neufranzösischen*, Tübingen: Niemeyer.

Klausenburger, J. (1974). 'Rule Inversion, Opacity, Conspiracies: French Liaison and Elision', *Lingua* 34:167–79.

Klausenburger, J. (1978). 'French Linking Phenomena: A Natural Generative Analysis', *Language* 54:21–40.

Klausenburger, J. (1984). *French Liaison and Linguistic Theory*, Stuttgart: Steiner.

Klausenburger, J. (1994). 'How Abstract Is/Was French Phonology? A Twenty-Five Year Retrospective', in Lyche, C. (ed.). *French Generative Phonology: Retrospective and Perspectives*, Salford: Association for French Language Studies in association with the European Studies Research Institute, University of Salford, pp.151–65.

Klein, J.-R., N. Leinart and S. Ostyn (1997). 'L'Anglicisme et la presse: enquête et analyse à travers quatre quotidiens français et belges', *Revue de linguistique romane* 61:337–60.

Klum, A. (1961). *Verbe et adverbe*, Uppsala: Almquist and Wiksell.

Koch, P. (1995). 'Subordination, intégration syntaxique et "oralité"', in Andersen and Skytte (eds), pp.13–42.

Krassin, G. (1994). *Neuere Entwicklungen in der französischen Grammatik und Grammatikforschung*, Tübingen: Niemeyer.

Labelle, M. (1987). 'L'Utilisation des temps du passé dans les narrations françaises: le passé composé, l'imparfait et le présent historique', *Revue romane* 22(1):3–29.

Labelle, M. (1990). 'Unaccusatives and Pseudo-Unaccusatives in French', *Proceedings of NELS* 20:303–17.

Laborderie, N. (1994). *Précis de phonétique historique*, Paris: Nathan.

Labov, W. (1972). *Sociolinguistic Patterns*, Pennsylvania: University of Pennsylvania Press.

Labov, W. (1990). 'The Intersection of Sex and Social Class in the Course of Linguistic Change', *Language Variation and Change* 2:205–54.

Labov, W. (1994). *Principles of Linguistic Change*, Vol I: *Internal Factors*, Oxford: Blackwell.

Lafage, S. (1998). 'Hybridation et "français des rues" à Abidjan', in Queffelec, A. (ed.), *Alternances codiques et français parlé en Afrique*, Aix-en-Provence: Université de Provence, pp.278–91.

Lagueux, P.-A. (1988). 'La Part des emprunts à l'anglais dans la création néologique en France et au Québec', in Pergnier (ed.), pp.91–111.

Laka, I. (1994). *On Syntax of Negation*, New York-London: Garland.

Lakoff, R. (1968). *Abstract Syntax and Latin Complementation*, Cambridge, MA: MIT Press.

Lalaire, L. (1998). *La Variation modale dans les subordonnées à temps fini du français moderne: approche syntaxique*, Berne: Lang.

Lambert, F. (1991). 'Observations sur la coordination par *et* en français', *Cahiers de grammaire* 16:73–102.

Lambrecht, K. (1981). *Topic, Antitopic and Verb Agreement in Non-Standard French*, Amsterdam: Benjamins.

Lambrecht, K. (1987). 'On the Status of SVO Sentences in French Discourse', in Tomlin, R.S. (ed.). *Coherence and Grounding in Discourse: Typological Studies in Language*, Amsterdam: Benjamins, vol II, pp.217–61.

Lambrecht, K. (1988). 'Presentational Cleft Constructions in Spoken French', in Haiman, J. and S.A. Thompson (eds). *Clause-Combining in Grammar and Discourse*, Amsterdam: Benjamins, pp.135–79.

Lambrecht, K. (1994). *Information Structure and Sentence Form: Topic, Focus, and the Mental Representation of Discourse Referents*, Cambridge-New York: Cambridge University Press.

Larrivée, P. (1995). '*Ne*, négation de propositions virtuelles', *Revue romane* 30(1):27–40.

Larrivée, P. (1996). '*Pas* explétif', *Revue romane* 31(1):19–28.

Lass, R. (1980). *Phonology: An Introduction to Basic Concepts*, Cambridge: Cambridge University Press.

Laurier, M. (1989). 'Le Subjonctif dans le parler franco-ontarien: un mode en voie de disparition?', in Mougeon, R. and E. Beniak (eds). *Le Français canadien parlé hors Québec: aperçu sociolinguistique*, Quebec: Presses de l'Université Laval, pp.105–26.

Laver, J. (1994). *Principles of Phonetics*, Cambridge: Cambridge University Press.

Le Bidois, G. and R. Le Bidois (1935–38). *Syntaxe du français moderne*, 2 vols, Paris: Picard.

Le Bidois, R. (1952). *L'Inversion du sujet dans la prose contemporaine (1900–1950)*, Paris: d'Artrey.

Lefebvre, A. (1988). 'La Prononciation du "e-muet" dans la région lilloise est-elle un marqueur social?', in Slater, C., J. Durand and M. Bate (eds). *French Sound Patterns: Changing Perspectives*, Colchester: Association for French Language Studies and Department of Language and Linguistics, University of Essex, pp.209–22.

Le Goffic, P. (ed.) (1986a). *Points de vue sur l'imparfait*, Caen: Centre de publications de l'Université de Caen.

Le Goffic, P. (1986b). 'Que l'imparfait n'est pas un temps du passé', in Le Goffic (ed.), pp.55–69.

Le Goffic, P. (1992). '"Que" en français: essai de vue d'ensemble', in Chuquet and Roullard (eds), pp.43–71.

Le Goffic, P. (1995). 'La Double Incomplétude de l'imparfait', *Modèles linguistiques* 16(1):133–48.

Lehmann, A. and F. Martin-Berthet (1998). *Introduction à la lexicologie: sémantique et morphologie*, Paris: Dunod.

Lehmann, W.P. (1973). 'A Structural Principle of Language and its Implications', *Language* 49:47–66.

Lenoble-Pinson, M. (1991). *Anglicismes et substituts français*, Louvain-la-Neuve: Duculot.

Lentin, L. (1973). *Apprendre à parler à l'enfant de moins de 6 ans*. Paris: ESF.

Léon, P.R. (1978). *Prononciation du français standard*, Paris: Didier.

Léon, P.R., H. Schogt and E. Burstynsky (eds) (1977). *La Phonologie*, Vol I: *Les Ecoles et les théories*, Paris: Klincksieck.

Lerat, P. (1981). 'L'Aspect dans le lexique français contemporain', *Cahiers de lexicologie* 39:48–54.

Lerch, E. (1931). *Hauptprobleme der französischen Sprache*, Vol II: *Der französische Konjunctiv*, Berlin: Braunschweig.

Lindenfeld, J. (1972). 'The Social Conditioning of Syntactic Variation in French', in Fishman, J.A. (ed.). *Advances in the Sociology of Language 2*, The Hague: Mouton, pp.77–90.

Lindqvist, C. (1979). *L'Emploi temporel dans la complétive au subjonctif introduite par un temps du passé en français contemporain*, Uppsala: Acta Universitas Upsaliensis.

Lodge, R.A. and others (1997). *Exploring the French Language*, London: Arnold.

Lote, G. (1940–43). 'La Nasalisation des voyelles françaises', *Annales de la Faculté des lettres d'Aix* 23:145–70.

Ludwig, R. (1988). *Modalität und Modus im gesprochenen Französisch*, Tübingen: Narr.

Lüdicke, A. (1982). 'Zum Ausfall der Verneinungspartikel *ne* im gesprochenen Französisch', *Zeitschrift für romanische Philologie* 98:43–58.

Lyons, C. (1982). 'Pronominal Voice in French', in Vincent, N. and M.B. Harris (eds). *Studies in the Romance Verb: Essays offered to Joe Cremona on the Occasion of his Sixtieth Birthday*, London: Croom Helm, pp.161–84.

Mahmoudian, M. (1989). 'Unité et diversité de la signification', *La Linguistique* 25(1):115–32.

Mailhac, J.-P. (1996). 'Le Subjonctif: quel type de présentation adopter?', in Engel, D. and F. Myles (eds). *Teaching Grammar: Perspectives in Higher Education*, London: AFLS and CILT, pp.137–65.

Majumdar, M.-J. and A.M. Morris (1980). 'The French Pluperfect Tense as a Punctual Past', *Archivum linguisticum* 11(1):1–12.

Malécot, A. (1975). 'French Liaison as a Function of Grammatical, Phonetic and Paralinguistic Variables', *Phonetica* 32:161–79.

Malécot, A. (1976). 'The Effect of Linguistic and Paralinguistic Variables on the Elision of the French Mute *e*', *Phonetica* 33:93–112.

Malécot, A. and P. Lindsay (1976). 'The Neutralization of /ɛ̃/ ~ /œ̃/ in French', *Phonetica* 33:45–61.

Malécot, A. and G. Chollet (1977). 'The Acoustic Status of Mute *e* in French', *Phonetica* 34:19–30.

Malkiel, Y. (1967). 'Each Word Has a History of its Own', *Glossa* 1:137–49.

Mandelbaum-Reiner, F. (1991). 'Suffixation gratuite et signalétique textuelle d'argot', *Langue française* 90:106–12.

Marchello-Nizia, C. (1995). *L'Evolution du français: ordre des mots, démonstratifs, accent tonique*, Paris: Colin.

Marchello-Nizia, C. (1998a). 'Dislocations en ancien français: thématisation ou rhématisation?', *Cahiers de praxématique* 30:161–78.

Marchello-Nizia, C. (1998b). 'Dislocations en diachronie: archéologie d'un phénomène du "français oral"', in Bilger, M., K. Van den Eynde and F. Gadet (eds). *Analyse linguistique et approches de l'oral. Recueil d'études offert en hommage à Claire Blanche-Benveniste*, Leuven: Peeters, pp.327–37.

Mareschal, G. (1988). 'Contribution à l'étude comparée de l'anglicisation en Europe francophone et au Québec', in Pergnier (ed.), pp.67–77.

Martin, R. (1970). 'La Transformation impersonnelle', *Revue de linguistique romane* 34:377–94.

Martin, R. (1971). *Temps et aspect: essai sur l'emploi des temps narratifs en moyen français*, Paris: Klincksieck.

Martin, R. (1983). *Pour une logique du sens*, Paris: PUF.

Martinet, A. (1933). 'Remarques sur le système phonologique du français', *Bulletin de la Société de linguistique* 34:191–202.

Martinet, A. (1945). *La Prononciation du français contemporain*, Paris: Droz.

Martinet, A. (1960). *Eléments de linguistique générale*, Paris: Colin.

Martinet, A. (1968). *La Synchronie dynamique*, 2nd edn, Paris: PUF.

Martinet, A. (1970). *Economie des changements phonétiques*, 3rd edn, Berne: Franck.

Martinet, A. (1972). 'La Nature phonologique d'*e* caduc', in Valdman, A. (ed.). *Papers in Linguistics and Phonetics to the Memory of Pierre Delattre*, The Hague: Mouton, pp.393–9.

Martinet, A. (1974a). *Le Français sans fard*, 2nd edn, Paris: PUF.

Martinet, A. (1974b). 'De l'économie des formes du verbe en français parlé', in Martinet (ed.), pp.91–120.

Martinet, A. (1975). *Evolution des langues et reconstruction*, Paris: PUF.

Martinet, A. (1980). *Eléments de linguistique générale*, new revised edn, Paris: Colin.

Martinet, A. (1981). 'Le Parfait en français: accompli ou préterit?', in Geckeler, H. and others, *Logos Semantikos: Studia Linguistica in honorem Eugenio Coseriu*, IV, Berlin-New York-Madrid: De Gruyter and Gredo, pp.429–33.

Martinet, A. (1985). *Syntaxe générale*, Paris: Colin.

Martinet, A. and H. Walter (1973). *Dictionnaire de la prononciation française dans son usage réel*, Geneva: Droz.

Marty, F. (1971). 'Les Formes du verbe en français parlé', in Rigault, A. (ed.). *La Grammaire du français parlé*, Paris: Hachette, pp.105–17.

Mathieu-Colas, M. (1988). 'Variations graphiques des mots composés dans le Petit Larousse et le Petit Robert', *Lingvisticae investigationes* 12(2):235–80.

Mathieu-Colas, M. (1996). 'Essai de typologie des noms composés français', *Cahiers de lexicologie* 69(2):71–125.

Matte, O. (1984). 'Réexamen de la doctrine traditionnelle sur les voyelles nasales', *Romance Philology* 38:15–31.

Matthews, P.H. (1972). *Inflectional Morphology: a Theoretical Study based on Aspects of Latin Verb Conjugation*, Cambridge: Cambridge University Press.

Matthews, P.H. (1991). *Morphology*, 2nd edn, Cambridge: Cambridge University Press.

Maupas, Ch. (1607). *Grammaire françoise*, Blois: P. Cottereau.

McMahon, A.M.S. (1994). *Understanding Language Change*, Cambridge: Cambridge University Press.

Méla, V. (1988). 'Parler verlan: règles et usages', *Langage et société* 45:47–72.

Méla, V. (1997). 'Verlan 2000', *Langue française* 114:16–34.

Melis, L. (1985). 'Les Tours pronominaux du français', in Melis, L. and others, *Les Constructions de la phrase française: invitation à la réflexion sur le passif, le pronominal, l'impersonnel, le causatif*, Ghent: Communication and Cognition.

Melis, L. (1990). *La Voie pronominale: la systématique des tours pronominaux en français moderne*, Paris-Louvain-la-Neuve: Duculot.

Melis, L. (1994). 'La Typologie des subordonnées circonstancielles et les comparatives', *Travaux de linguistique* 27:97–111.

Milroy, L. (1987). *Observing and Analysing Natural Language*, Oxford: Blackwell.

Mitterand, H. (1963). *Les Mots français*, Paris: PUF.

Moignet, G. (1959). *Essai sur le mode subjonctif en latin postclassique et en ancien français*, [Paris]: PUF.

Molendijk, A. (1990). *Le Passé simple et l'imparfait: une approche reichenbachienne*, Amsterdam: Rodopi.

Molendijk, A. (1994). 'Tense Use and Temporal Interpretation', in Vet and Vetters (eds), pp.21–47.

Molendijk, A. (1996). 'Anaphore et imparfait: la référence globale à des situations présupposées ou impliquées', in De Mulder, Tasmowski-De Ryck and Vetters (eds), pp.109–23.

Monville-Burston, M. and L. Waugh (1991). 'Multivalency: The French Historical Present in Journalistic Discourse' in Fleischman and Waugh (eds), pp.86–119.

Moreau, M.-L. (1986). 'Les Séquences préformées: entre les combinaisons libres et les idiomatismes: le cas de négation avec ou sans *ne*', *Le Français moderne* 53:137–60.

Moreau, M.-L. (1987). 'L'Ordre des constituants dans la production orale entre familiers', *Travaux de linguistique* 14/15:47–65.

Morin, Y.-C. (1977). 'Nasalization and Diphthongization in Marais Vendéen French', in Hagwara, M.P. (ed.). *Studies in Romance Linguistics*, Rowley, MA: Newbury House, pp.125–44.

Morin, Y.-C. (1978). 'The Status of Mute "e"', *Studies in French Linguistics* 1:79–160.

Morin, Y.-C. (1987a). 'French Data and Phonological Theory', *Linguistics* 25:815–43.

Morin, Y.-C. (1987b). 'Remarques sur l'organisation de la flexion des verbes français', *I.T.L. Review of Applied Linguistics*, 77/78:13–91.

Morin, Y.-C. (1988). 'De l'ajustement du *schwa* en syllabe fermée dans la phonologie du français', in Verluyten (ed.), pp.133–89.

Morin, Y.-C. (1998). 'La Flexion du verbe français à l'oral: morphématique ou analogie?', in Bilger, M., K. van den Eynde and F. Gadet (eds), *Analyse linguistique en approches de l'oral: recueil d'études offert en hommage à Claire Blanche-Benveniste*, Leuven-Paris: Peeters, pp.69–78.

Morin, Y.-C. and J. Kaye (1982). 'The Syntactic Bases for French Liaison', *Journal of Linguistics* 18:291–330.

Mortureux, M.-F. (1994). 'Siglaison-acronymie et néologie lexicale', *Linx* 30:11–32.

Mougeon, R., E. Beniak and D. Valois (1985). *Variation in the Phonological Integration of Loanwords in a Bilingual Speech Community*, Toronto: Centre for Franco-Ontarian Studies.

Müller, B. (1985). *Le Français d'aujourd'hui*, Paris: Klincksieck.

Muller, Charles (1966). 'Pour une étude diachronique de l'imparfait narratif', in *Mélanges de grammaire française offerts à M. Maurice Grevisse*, Gembloux: Duculot, pp.252–69.

Muller, Charles (1986). 'Données quantitatives en morpho-syntaxe: l'imparfait du subjonctif dans quelques romans contemporains', *Le Français moderne* 54: 220–30.

Muller, Claude (1991). *La Négation en français: syntaxe, sémantique et éléments de comparaison avec les autres langues romanes*, Geneva: Droz.

Muller, Claude (ed.) (1996). *Dépendance et intégration syntaxique: subordination, coordination, connexion*, Amsterdam: Benjamins.

Muller, Claude (1997). '*De* partitif et la négation', in Forget, D. and others (eds). *Negation and Polarity: Syntax and Semantics: Selected Papers from the Colloquium Negation: Syntax and Semantics, 11–13 May 1995, Ottawa*, Amsterdam-Philadelphia: Benjamins, 251–70.

Nordahl, H. (1969). *Les Systèmes du subjonctif corrélatif: étude sur l'emploi des modes dans la subordonnée complétive en français moderne*, Bergen-Oslo: Universitetsforlaget.

Nordahl, H. (1970). 'Le mode le plus fascinant qui soit', *Revue romane* 5:106–19.

Noreiko, S. (1993). 'New Words for New Technologies', in Sanders (ed.), pp.171–84.

Nottaris, A.A. (1973). *Syntaxe de la proposition relative en français contemporain*, Berne: Institut für Sprachwissenschaft.

Nymansson, K. (1996). 'Analyse grammaticale des formes en -*ing*', *Cahiers de lexicologie* 68(1):63–77.

Nyrop, K. (1899–1930). *Grammaire historique de la langue française*, 6 vols, Copenhagen: Gyldendalske Boghandel-Nordisk Forlag.

Offord, M. (1989). 'La Valeur sémantique de mots à terminaison en -*o* en français', *Cahiers de lexicologie* 55:39–52.

Olsson, L. (1971). *Etude sur l'emploi des temps dans les propositions introduites par 'quand' et 'lorsque' et dans les propositions qui les complètent en français contemporain*, Uppsala: Almqvist and Wiksell.

Ossipov, H. (1997). 'A Tale of two Corpora of French Dislocations', *Word* 48(2):195–205.

Oudin, A. (1632). *Grammaire françoise rapportée au langage du temps*, Paris: P. Billaine.

Ouhalla, J. (1994). *Introducing Transformational Grammar: From Rules to Principles and Parameters*, London: Arnold.

Paradis, C. and F. El Fenne (1986). 'L'Alternance C/Ø des verbes français: une analyse par contraintes et stratégies de réparation', *Revue québécoise de linguistique théorique et appliquée* 21:107–40.

Paradis, C. and F. El Fenne (1995). 'French Verbal Inflection Revisited: Constraints, Repairs and Floating Consonants', *Lingua* 95:169–204.

Pergnier, M. (ed.) (1988a). *Le Français en contact avec l'anglais*, Paris: Didier.

Pergnier, M. (1988b). 'A propos des emprunts du français à l'anglais', in Pergnier (ed.), pp.113–17.

Pergnier, M. (1989). *Les Anglicismes: danger ou enrichissement pour la langue française*, Paris: PUF.

Pfister, M. (1974). 'Imparfait, passé simple, passé composé', *Revue de linguistique romane* 38:400–17.

Picoche, J. (1977). *Précis de lexicologie française*, Paris: Nathan.

Picoche, J. and C. Marchello-Nizia (1989). *Histoire de la langue française*, Paris: Nathan.

Picone, M. (1996). *Anglicisms, Neologisms and Dynamic French*, Amsterdam: Benjamins.

Pierrard, M. (1987). 'Subordination et subordonnées: réflexions sur la typologie des subordonnées dans les grammaires du français moderne', *L'Information grammaticale* 35:31–7.

Pierrard, M. (1994). 'Subordination, dépendance et hiérarchie: la subordination propositionnelle et ses paramètres d'évaluation', *Travaux de linguistique* 27:13–28.

Pinchon, J. (1986). *Morphosyntaxe du français: étude de cas*, Paris: Hachette.

Pinchon, J. and B. Coute (1981). *Le Système verbal du français: description et applications pédagogiques*, Paris: Nathan.

Piot, M. (1988). 'Coordination-subordination: une définition générale', *Langue française* 77:5–18.

Piot, M. (1993). 'Les Connecteurs du français', *Lingvisticae Investigationes* 17(1):141–60.

Plénat, M. (1981). 'L'"autre conjugaison", ou: De la régularité des verbes irréguliers', *Cahiers de grammaire* 3.

Plénat, M. (1987a). 'On the Structure of Rime in Standard French', *Linguistics* 25:867–87.

Plénat, M. (1987b). 'Morphologie du passé simple et du participe passé des verbes de l'"autre" conjugaison', *I.T.L. Review of Applied Linguistics*, 77/78:93–150.

Plénat, M. (1997). 'Analyse morpho-phonologique d'un corpus d'adjectifs dérivés en -esque', *Journal of French Language Studies* 7(2):163–79.

Pohl, J. (1968). '*Ne* dans le français parlé contemporain: les modalités de son abandon', in Quilis, A. (ed.). *Actas do XI Congreso Internacional de Lingüística y filología románicas*, vol 3, Madrid: n.p., pp.1343–58.

Pohl, J. (1972). '*Ne* et les enfants', in *L'Homme et le signifiant*, Paris: Nathan; Brussels: Labor, pp.107–11.

Pohl, J. (1975). 'L'Omission de *ne* dans le français contemporain', *Le Français dans le monde* 111:17–23.

Pooley, T. (1994). 'Word-Final Consonant Devoicing in a Variety of Working-Class French: A Case of Language Contact?', *Journal of French Language Studies* 4(2):215–33.

Pope, M. (1952). *From Latin to Modern French with Especial Consideration of Anglo-Norman Phonology and Morphology*, Manchester: Manchester University Press.

Poplack, S. (1989). 'The Care and Handling of a Megacorpus: The Ottawa-Hull French Project', in Fasold, R. and D. Schiffrin (eds). *Language Change and Variation*, Amsterdam: Benjamins, pp.411–51.

Poplack, S. (1992). 'The Inherent Variability of the French Subjunctive', in Laeufer, C. and T.A. Morgan (eds). *Theoretical Analyses in Romance Linguistics: Selected Papers from the Nineteenth Linguistic Symposium on Romance Languages (LSRL XIX), 21–23 April 1989, Ohio State University*, Amsterdam-Philadelphia: Benjamins, pp.235–63.

Poplack, S. and D. Walker (1986). 'Going through /L/ in Canadian French', in Sankoff, D. (ed.). *Diversity and Diachrony*, Amsterdam: Benjamins, pp.173–97.

Poplack, S., D. Sankoff and C. Miller (1988). 'The Social Correlates and Linguistic Processes of Lexical Borrowing and Assimilation', *Linguistics* 26(1):47–104.

Poplack, S. and D. Turpin (1999). 'Does the *FUTUR* have a future in (Canadian) French?', *Probus* 11:133–64.

Posner, R. (1972). 'Aspects of Aspect and Tense in French', *Romance Philology* 26:94–111.

Posner, R. (1985). 'Post-Verbal Negation in Non-Standard French: A Historical and Comparative View', *Romance Philology* 39:170–97.

Posner, R. (1997). *Linguistic Change in French*, Oxford: Clarendon Press.

Pottier, B. (1978). 'Les Voix du français: sémantique et syntaxe', *Cahiers de lexicologie* 33:3–39.

Pottier, B. (1995). 'Le Temps du monde, le temps de l'énonciation et le temps de l'événement', *Modèles linguistiques* 16(1):9–26.

Price, G. (1971). *The French Language: Present and Past*, London: Arnold.

Price, G. (1979). '"Point nie bien plus fortement que pas": Vaugelas que veut-il dire?', in Höfler, M., H. Vernay and L. Wolf (eds). *Festschrift Kurt Baldinger zum 60. Geburtstag 17. November 1979*, vol 1, Tübingen: Niemeyer, pp.245–54.

Price, G. (1991). *An Introduction to French Pronunciation*, Oxford: Blackwell.

Prince, E. (1976). 'The Syntax and Semantics of NEG-Raising, with Evidence from French', *Language* 52:404–26.

Progovac, L. (1994). *Negative and Positive Polarity: A Binding Approach*, Cambridge: Cambridge University Press.

Prunet, J.-F. (1986). 'Liaison and Nasalization in French', in Neidle, C. and R. Nuñez-Cedeño (eds). *Studies in Romance Languages*, Dordrecht: Foris, pp.225–35.

Quirk, R. and others (1985). *A Comprehensive Grammar of the English Language*, London-New York: Longman.

Ramsden, H. (1963). *Weak-Pronoun Position in the Early Romance Languages*, Manchester: Manchester University Press.

Rand, S.R. (1993). *The French 'imparfait' and 'passé simple' in Discourse*, Arlington: University of Texas.

Recourcé, G. (1996). 'Une double analyse de la particule *ne* en français', *Langages* 122:62–78.

Regula, M. (1936). 'La Fonction du subjonctif dans le français moderne', *Revue de linguistique romane* 12:289–350.

Reichenbach, H. (1947). *Elements of Symbolic Logic*, London: Collier-Macmillan. Reprinted (1966), New York: Free Press.

Reichstein, R. (1960). 'Etudes des variations sociales et géographiques des faits linguistiques', *Word* 16:55–99.

Reid, T.B.W. (1970). 'Verbal Aspect in Modern French' in Combe, T.G.S. and P. Rickard (eds). *The French Language: Studies Presented to L.C. Harmer*, London: Harrap, pp.146–71.

Retman, R. (1978). 'L'Adaptation phonétique des emprunts à l'anglais en français', *La Linguistique* 14(1):111–24.

Riegel, M., J.C. Pellat and R. Rioul (1994). *Grammaire méthodique du français*, Paris: PUF.

Rizzi, L. (1982). *Issues in Italian Syntax*, Dordrecht: Foris.

Robach, I.-B. (1974). *Etude sociolinguistique de la segmentation syntaxique du français parlé*, Lund: Södergård.

Robbe-Grillet, A. (1981). *Djinn*, Paris: Minuit.

Roberts, I. (1993). *Verbs and Diachronic Syntax: A Comparative History of English and French*, Boston-London-Dordrecht: Kluwer.

Roberts, I. (1994). 'Passive', in Asher, R.E. (ed.), *The Encyclopedia of Language and Linguistics*, Oxford: Pergamon.

Roberts, I. (1997). *Comparative Syntax*, London: Arnold.

Roché, M. (1992). 'Le Masculin est-il plus productif que le féminin?', *Langue française* 96:113–24.

Rochet, B.L. (1976). *The Formation and Evolution of the French Nasal Vowels*, Tübingen: Niemeyer.

Rothe, W. (1967). *Strukturen des Konjunktivs im Französischen*, Tübingen: Niemeyer.

Rothemberg, M. (1974). *Les Verbes à la fois transitifs et intransitifs en français contemporain*, The Hague-Paris: Mouton.

Rottet, K.J. (1998). 'Clause Subordination Structures in Language Decline', *Journal of French Language Studies* 8(1):63–95.

Rouboud, M.-N. (1997). 'Les Enoncés pseudo-clivés en: le plus/le moins', *Journal of French Language Studies* 7(2):181–93.

Roulet, E. (1995). 'Etude des plans d'organisation syntaxique, hiérarchique et référentiel du dialogue: autonomie et interrelations modulaires', *Cahiers de linguistique française* 17:123–40.

Rowlett, P. (1994). Review of Muller (1991), *Journal of French Language Studies* 4(1):120–22.

Rowlett, P. (1998). *Sentential Negation in French*, New York-Oxford: Oxford University Press.

Roy, M.-M., C. Lefebvre and A. Régimbald (1982). 'Acquisition de la norme et de la structure linguistique des relatives chez deux groupes d'adolescents montréalais', in Carroll (ed.), pp.231–66.

Ruhlen, M. (1973). 'Nasal Vowels', *Working Papers in Language Universals* 12:1–36.

Ruhlen, M. (1979). 'On the Origin and Evolution of the French Nasal Vowels', *Romance Philology* 32:321–35.

Ruwet, N. (1972). *Théorie syntaxique et syntaxe du français*, Paris: Seuil.

Sabio, F. (1992). 'Les Compléments antéposés en français parlé: analyse de deux types syntaxiques et prosodiques', *Recherches sur le français parlé* 11:31–56.

Salkie, R. (1989). 'Perfect and Pluperfect: What Is the Relationship?', *Journal of Linguistics* 25:1–34.

Salkie, R. (1999). 'Does French have a relative past tense?', manuscript.

Sampson, R. (1999). *Nasal Vowel Evolution in Romance*, Oxford: Oxford University Press.

Sampson, R. (1999). 'Does French Have a Relative Past Tense?', manuscript.

Sand, J.U. (1983). 'Le Subjonctif en français oral', in Spore, J. and others (eds). *Actes du VIIIe congrès des romanistes scandinaves, 17–21 August 1981, Odense*, Odense: Odense University Press, pp.303–13.

Sanders, C. (ed.) (1993). *French Today: Language in its Social Context*, Cambridge: Cambridge University Press.

Sankoff, D. (1982). 'Sociolinguistic Method and Linguistic Theory', in Cohen, L.J. and others (eds). *Logic, Method, Philosophy of Science*, vol VI, Amsterdam: North Holland; Warsaw: Polish Scientific, pp.677–89.

Sankoff, D. (1988). 'Variable Rules', in Ammon, U., N. Dittmar and K.J. Mattheier (eds). *Sociolinguistics: An International Handbook of the Science of Language and Society*, vol II, Berlin: de Gruyter, pp.984–97.

Sankoff, D. and D. Vincent (1977). 'L'Emploi productif de *ne* dans le français parlé à Montréal', *Le Français moderne* 45:243–56.

Sankoff, D. and P. Thibault (1980). 'The Alternation between the Auxiliaries *avoir* and *être* in Montréal French', in Sankoff, G. (ed.). *The Social Life of Language*, Pennsylvania: University of Pennsylvania Press, pp.311–45.

Saussure, F. de (1916). *Cours de linguistique générale*, Paris: Payot.

Sauvageot, A. (1962). *Français écrit, français parlé*, Paris: Larousse.

Scalise, S. (1984). *Generative Morphology*, Dordrecht: Foris.

Schane, S.A. (1968). *French Phonology and Morphology*, Cambridge, MA: MIT Press.

Schane, S.A. (1972). 'The Hierarchy for the Deletion of French "e-muet"', *Linguistics* 82:63–9.

Schane, S.A. (1973). 'The Treatment of Phonological Exceptions: The Evidence from French', in Kachru, B.J. and others (eds). *Issues in Linguistics: Papers in Honour of Henry and Renée Kahane*, Chicago: Illinois University Press, pp.822–35.

Schane, S.A. (1978). 'Deletion Versus Epenthesis: A Pseudo-Controversy', *Studies in French Linguistics* 1/2:71–8.

Schapira, C. (1982). 'Les Noms composés verbe + objet direct', *Travaux de linguistique et de littérature* 20(1):271–82.

Schapira, C. (1988). 'Le Redoublement expressif dans la création lexicale', *Cahiers de lexicologie* 52:51–63.

Schøsler, L. (1984). *La Déclinaison bicasuelle de l'ancien français*, Odense: Odense University Press.

Schøsler, L. (1985). 'L'Emploi des temps du passé en ancien français: études sur quelques textes manuscrits', *Razo* 5:107–19.

Schwegler, A. (1983). 'Predicate Negation and Word-Order Change: A Problem of Multiple Causation', *Lingua* 61:297–334.

Schwegler, A. (1988). 'Word-Order Changes in Predicate Negation Strategies in Romance Languages', *Diachronica* 5:21–58.

Scullen, M.E. (1994). 'L'"Extramétricité" des voyelles initiales', in Lyche, C. (ed.). *French Generative Phonology: Retrospective and Perspectives*, Salford: Association for French Language Studies in association with the European Studies Research Institute, University of Salford, pp.259–75.

Selkirk, E.O. (1972). *The Phrase Phonology of English and French*, PhD dissertation, Massachusetts Institute of Technology.

Selkirk, E.O. (1974). 'French Liaison and the X Bar Notation', *Linguistic Inquiry* 5:573–90.

Selkirk, E.O. (1980). *The Phrase Phonology of English and French*, New York: Garland.

Selkirk, E.O. (1982). *The Syntax of Words*, Cambridge, MA: MIT Press.

Selkirk, E.O. (1986). *Phonology and Syntax: The Relation between Sound and Structure*, Cambridge, MA: MIT Press.

Singy, P. (ed.) (1998). *Les Femmes et la langue: l'insécurité linguistique en question*, Lausanne-Paris: Delachaux and Niestlé.

Skårup, P. (1975). *Les Premières zones de la proposition en ancien français*, Copenhagen: Akademisk Forlag.

Smith, N.V. (1969). Review of Schane (1968), *Language* 45:398–407.

Soelberg, N. (1989). 'Pour une poétique du plus-que-parfait – à propos des nouvelles de Christine Arnothy', *Revue romane* 24(2):272–94.

Sommerstein, A.H. (1977). *Modern Phonology*, Baltimore: University Park Press.

Sourdot, M. (1991). 'Argot, jargon, jargot', *Langue française* 90:13–27.

Sourdot, M. (1997). 'La Dynamique du français des jeunes: sept ans de mouvement à travers deux enquêtes (1987–94)', *Langue française* 114:56–81.

Soutet, O. (1998). 'La Morphologie du subjonctif français: essai de synthèse historique', *Modèles linguistiques* 19(1):7–16.

Spence, N.C.W. (1976). *Le Français contemporain*, Munich: Fink.

Spence, N.C.W. (1987). 'Faux-amis and faux-anglicismes: Problems of Classification and Definition', *Forum for Modern Language Studies* 23(2):169–83.

Spence, N.C.W. (1989). 'Qu'est-ce qu'un anglicisme?', *Revue de linguistique romane* 53:323–34.

Spence, N.C.W. (1991). 'Le Français en -ing', *Le Français moderne* 59:188–213.

Spencer, A. (1991). *Morphological Theory: An Introduction to Word Structure in Generative Grammar*, Oxford: Blackwell.

Spencer, A. and A.M. Zwicky (eds) (1998). *The Handbook of Morphology*, Oxford: Blackwell.

Stéfanini, J. (1962). *La Voix pronominale en ancien et en moyen français*, Aix-en-Provence: Publications des annales de la Faculté des lettres.

Straka, G. (1952). 'Quelques observations phonétiques sur le langage des femmes', *Orbis* 1:335–57.

Sturm, J. (1981). *Morpho-syntaktische Untersuchungen zur 'phrase négative' im gesprochenen Französisch: Die Negation mit und ohne* ne, Frankfurt am Main-Bern: Lang.

Suchier, H. (1906). *Les Voyelles toniques du vieux français*, Paris: Champion.

Surridge, M. (1984). 'Le Genre grammatical des emprunts anglais en français: la perspective diachronique', *Canadian Journal of Linguistics* 29(1):58–72.

Sutherland, D.R. (1939). 'On the Use of Tenses in Old and Middle French', in *Studies in French Language and Medieval Literature Presented to M.K. Pope*, Manchester: Manchester University Press.

Swiggers, P. and K. van den Eynde (1987). 'La Morphologie du verbe français', *I.T.L. Review of Applied Linguistics* 77/78:151–251.

Tanase, E. (1943). *Essai sur la valeur et les emplois du subjonctif en français*, Montpellier: Rouvière.

Tasmowski-De Ryck, L. and W. De Mulder (1998). 'L'Imparfait est-il un temps méronomique?', in Vogeleer and others (eds), pp.171–89.

Tasmowski-De Ryck, L. and H. Van Oevelen (1987). 'Le Causitif pronominal', *Revue romane* 22(1):40–58.

Temple, M. (1996). *Pour une sémantique des mots construits*, Paris: Presses universitaires du Septentrion.

Temple, R.A.M. (1998). *Aspects of Sociophonetic Variability in French Consonants*, PhD dissertation, University of Wales.

Tesnière, L. (1959). *Eléments de syntaxe structurale*, Paris: Klincksieck.

Thelin, N.B. (ed.) (1990). *Verbal Aspect in Discourse: Contributions to the Semantics of Time and Temporal Perspective in Slavic and Non-Slavic Languages*, Amsterdam-Philadelphia: Benjamins.

Thiele, J. (1987). *La Formation des mots en français moderne*, trans. by A. Clas, Montréal: Presses de l'Université.

Thompson, S.A. and A. Mulac (1991). 'A Quantitative Perspective on the Grammaticization of Epistemic Parentheticals in English', in Traugott, E. and B. Heine (eds). *Approaches to Grammaticalization*, vol II, Amsterdam-Philadelphia: Benjamins, pp.313–29.

Togeby, K. (1965). *Structure immanente de la langue française*, Paris: Larousse.

Tranel, B. (1974). *The Phonology of Nasal Nowels in Modern French*, Ph.D. dissertation, University of California at San Diego.

Tranel, B. (1978). 'The Status of Nasal Vowels in Modern French', *Studies in French Linguistics* 1/2:27–70.

Tranel, B. (1981). *Concreteness in Generative Phonology: Evidence from French*, Berkeley, CA-London: University of California Press.

Tranel, B. (1987a). *The Sounds of French*, Cambridge: Cambridge University Press.

Tranel, B. (1987b). 'French *schwa* and Non-Linear Phonology', *Linguistics* 25:845–66.

Tranel, B. (1988). 'À propos de l'ajustement de E en français', in Verluyten (ed.), pp.89–131.

Tranel, B. (1990). 'On Suppletion and French Liaison', *Probus* 2:167–206.

Tranel, B. (1993). 'Moraic Theory and French Liaison', in Ashby, W.J. and others (eds). *Linguistic Perspectives on the Romance Languages*, Amsterdam: Benjamins. pp.97–112.

Tranel, B. (1995). 'French Final Consonants and Non-Linear Phonology', *Lingua* 95:131–67.

Trask, R.L. (1993). *A Dictionary of Grammatical Terms in Linguistics*, London: Routledge.

Trask, R.L. (1996). *A Dictionary of Phonetics and Phonology*, London: Routledge.

Trubetskoy, N.S. (1939). *Grundzüge der Phonologie*, Göttingen: Vandenhoeck & Ruprecht.

Trubetskoy, N.S. (1949). *Principes de phonologie*, trans. by J. Cantineau, Paris: Klincksieck.

Tsoulas, G. (1996). 'The Nature of the Subjunctive and the Formal Grammar of Obviation', in Zagona, K. (ed.). *Grammatical Theory and Romance Languages: Selected Papers from the 25th Linguistic Symposium on Romance Languages (LSRL XXV), 2–4 March 1995, Seattle*, Amsterdam-Philadelphia: Benjamins, pp.293–306.

Vachek, J. (1933). 'Über die phonologische Interpretation der Diphthonge', *Studies in English* 4:87–170.

Valdman, A. (1993). *Bien entendu! Introduction à la prononciation du français*, Englewood Cliffs, NJ: Prentice Hall.

Valli, A. (1988). 'A propos de changements dans le système du relatif: état de la question en moyen français', *Recherches sur le français parlé* 8:119–36.

Van Ameringen, A. and H.J. Cedergren (1981). 'Observations sur la liaison en français de Montréal', in Sankoff, D. and H.J. Cedergren (eds). *Variation Omnibus*, Edmonton, Alberta: Linguistic Research, pp.141–9.

Van den Eynde, K. and C. Blanche-Benveniste (1970). 'Essai d'analyse de la morphologie du verbe français: présentation d'hypothèses de travail', *Orbis* 19:404–29.

Van der Molen, W. (1923). *Le Subjonctif: sa valeur psychologique et son emploi dans la langue parlée*, Zalt-Bommel: N.V. de Garde & Co's Drukkerij.

Van Oostendorp, M. (1998). '*Schwa* in Phonological Theory', *Glot International* 3:3–8.

Van Reenen, P. (1985). 'La Fiabilité des données linguistiques (à propos de la formation des voyelles nasales en ancien français)', in Moll, A. (ed.). *Actas del XVI Congrés internacional de lingüistica e filologia romàniques*, vol II, Palma de Mallorca: Moll, pp.37–51.

Van Reenen, P. (1987) 'La Formation des voyelles nasales en ancien français d'après le témoignage des assonances', in Kampers-Manhe, B. and C. Vet (eds). *Etudes de linguistique française offertes à Robert de Dardel par ses amis et collègues*, Amsterdam: Rodopi, pp.127–41.

Van Vliet, E. (1983). 'The Disappearance of the French *passé simple*: A Morphological and Sociolinguistic Study', *Word* 34(2):89–113.

Van Willigen, M. (1983). 'Remarques sur la dérivation des adverbes en -ment en français moderne', *Cahiers de lexicologie* 42:63–71.

Vassant, A. (1980). 'Lexique, sémantique et grammaire dans la voix verbale en français', *Travaux de linguistique et de littérature* 18(1):143–63.

Vaugelas, C.F. de (1647). *Remarques sur la langue françoise*, Paris: La Veuve Jean Camusat and Pierre le Petit.

Vendler, Z. (1967). *Linguistics in Philosophy*, Ithaca, NY: Cornell University Press.

Vendryes, J. (1921). *Le Langage*, Paris: La Renaissance du livre.

Vennemann, T. (1974). 'Topics, Subjects and Word Order: from SXV to SVX via TVX', in Anderson, J. and C. Jones (eds). *Historical Linguistics*, vol 1, Amsterdam: North Holland, pp.339–76.

Vennemann, T. (1975). 'An Explanation of Drift', in Li, C.N. (ed.), *Word Order and Word Order Change*, Austin: University of Texas Press, pp.269–305.

Verdelhan-Bourgade, M. (1991). 'Procédés sémantiques et lexicaux en français branché', *Langue française* 90:65–79.

Verluyten, S.P. (ed.) (1988). *La Phonologie du schwa français*, Amsterdam: John Benjamins.

Vet, C. (1980). *Temps, aspects et adverbes de temps en français contemporain: essai de sémantique formelle*, Geneva: Droz.

Vet, C. (1992). 'Le Passé composé: contextes d'emploi et interprétation', *Cahiers de praxématique* 19:37–59.

Vet, C. and A. Molendijk (1986). 'The Discourse Functions of the Past Tenses of French', in Lo Cascio, V. and C. Vet (eds). *Temporal Structure in Sentence and Discourse*, Dordrecht: Foris, pp.133–59.

Vet, C. and C. Vetters (eds) (1994). *Tense and Aspect in Discourse*, Berlin-New York: Mouton de Gruyter.

Vetters, C. (1989). 'Grammaticalité au passé récent', *Lingvisticae investigationes* 13(2):369–86.

Vetters, C. (1993). *Le Temps, de la phrase au texte*, Lille: Presses universitaires de Lille.

Vetters, C. (1996). *Temps, aspect et narration*, Amsterdam-Atlanta: Rodopi.

Vogeleer, S. and others (eds) (1998). *Temps et discours*, Louvain-la-Neuve: Peeters.

Wagner, R.-L. (1968). 'Réflexions à propos des mots construits', *Bulletin de la société de linguistique de Paris* 63:65–82.

Wagner, R.-L. and J. Pinchon (1962). *Grammaire du français classique et moderne*, Paris: Hachette.

Walker, D.C. (1984). *The Pronunciation of Canadian French*, Ottawa: University of Ottawa Press.

Walker, D.C. (1993). 'Schwa and /œ/ in French', *Canadian Journal of Linguistics/ Revue Canadienne de linguistique* 38:43–64.

Wall, K. (1980). *L'Inversion dans la subordonnée en français contemporain*, Uppsala: Acta Universitatis Upsaliensis.

Walter, H. (1976). *La Dynamique des phonèmes dans le lexique du français contemporain*, Paris: France Expansion.

Walter, H. (1977). *La Phonologie du français*, Paris: PUF.

Walter, H. (1984). 'L'Innovation lexicale chez les jeunes Parisiens', *La Linguistique* 20(2):69–84.

Walter, H. (1988). *Le Français dans tous les sens*, Paris: Laffont.

Walter, H. (1990). 'Une voyelle qui ne veut pas mourir', in Green, J.N. and W. Ayres-Bennett (eds). *Variation and Change in French: Essays Presented to Rebecca Posner on the Occasion of her Sixtieth Birthday*, London: Routledge, pp.27–36.

Walter, H. (1991). 'Où commencent les innovations lexicales?', *Langue française* 90:53–64.

Walter, H. (1995). 'Une distinction temporelle sauvée par sa forme: le passé simple en gallo', in *Dialectologie et littérature du domaine d'oil occidental: actes du colloque de Blois, Seillac (1993)*, Dijon: Association bourguignonne de dialectologie et d'onomastique, pp.373–86.

Walter, H. (1997a). *L'Aventure des mots français venus d'ailleurs*, Paris: Laffont.

Walter, H. (1997b). 'Le Lexique des très jeunes', *Langue française* 114:41–55.

Walter, H. (1997c). 'Le Lexique de l'informatique et l'emprise de l'anglais', *La Linguistique* 33(2):45–59.

Walter, H. and G. Walter (1991). *Dictionnaire des mots d'origine étrangère*, Paris: Larousse.

Wang, W.S.-Y. (ed.) (1977). *The Lexicon in Phonological Change*, The Hague: Mouton.

Waugh, L.R. (1987). 'Marking Time with the *passé composé*: Toward a Theory of the Perfect', *Lingvisticae investigationes* 11(1):1–47.

Waugh, L.R. (1991). 'Tense-Aspect and Hierarchy of Meanings: Pragmatic, Textual, Modal, Discourse, Expressive, Referential', in Waugh, L.R. and S. Rudy (1991). *New Vistas in Grammar: Invariance and Variation*, Amsterdam and Philadelphia: Benjamins, pp. 241–59.

Waugh, L.R. and M. Monville-Burston (1986). 'Aspect and Discourse Function: The French Simple Past in Newspaper Usage', *Language* 62:848–77.

Wehrli, E. (1986). 'On Some Properties of French Clitic *se*', in Borer, H. (ed.). *The Syntax of Pronominal Clitics*, Orlando: Academic Press, pp.263–83.

Weinrich, H. (1973). *Le Temps*, Paris: Seuil.

Wetzels, L. (1987). 'The Timing of Latent Consonants in Modern French', in Neidle, C. and R.A. Nuñez-Cedeño (eds). *Studies in Romance Languages*, Dordrecht: Foris, pp.283–317.

Wiberg, L.-E. (1995). *Le Passé simple: son emploi dans le discours journalistique*, Stockholm: Almqvist and Wiksell.

Williams, E. (1981). 'On the Notions "Lexically Related" and "Head of a Word"', *Linguistic Inquiry* 12:245–74.

Williams, G. (1999). *French Discourse Analysis: The Method of Poststructuralism*, London-New York: Routledge.

Wilmet, M. (1970). *Le Système de l'indicatif en moyen français: étude des "tiroirs" de l'indicatif dans les farces, sotties, et moralités françaises des XVe et XVIe siècles*, Geneva: Droz.

Wilmet, M. (1973). 'Antériorité et postériorité: réflexions sur le passé antérieur', *Revue de linguistique romane* 37:274–91.

Wilmet, M. (1976). *Etudes de morpho-syntaxe verbale*, Paris: Klincksieck.

Wilmet, M. (1991). 'L'Aspect en français: essai de synthèse', *Journal of French Language Studies* 1(2):209–22.

Wilmet, M. (1992). 'Le Passé composé: histoire d'une forme', *Cahiers de praxématique* 19:13–36.

Wilmet, M. (1995). 'L'Articulation *mode-temps-aspect* dans le système du verbe français', *Modèles linguistiques* 16(1):99–110.

Wilmet, M. (1996). 'L'Imparfait: le temps des anaphores?', in De Mulder, Tasmowski-De Ryck and Vetters (eds), pp.199–215.

Wilmet, M. (1997). *Grammaire critique du français*, Louvain-la-Neuve: Duculot-Hachette.

Winters, M.E. (1993). 'On the Semantic Structure of the French Subjunctive', in Ashby, W.J. and others (eds). *Linguistic Perspectives on the Romance Languages: Selected Papers from the 21st Linguistic Symposium on Romance Languages (LSRL XXI), 21–24 February 1991, Santa Barbara, CA*, Amsterdam-Philadelphia: Benjamins, pp.271–9.

Wise, H. (1997). *The Vocabulary of Modern French: Origins, Structure and Function*, London-New York: Routledge.

Woodcock, E.C. (1959). *A New Latin Syntax*, London: Methuen.

Wunderli, P. (1976). *Modus und Tempus: Beiträge zur synchronischen und diachronischen Morphosyntax der romanischen Sprachen*, Tübingen: Narr.

Wunderli, P. (1989). 'Le Statut précaire de l'aspect verbal en français', *Travaux de linguistique* 18:73–94.

Yaguello, M. (1998). 'Y a-t-il un français politiquement correct?', in Singy (ed.), pp.177–94.

Zanola, M.-T. (1991). *L'Emprunt lexical anglais dans le français contemporain: analyse d'un corpus de presse (1982–1989)*, Brescia: La Scuola.

Zanuttini, R. (1997) *Negation and Clausal Structure: A Comparative Study of Romance Languages*, New York-Oxford: Oxford University Press.

Zezula, J. (1969). 'Le Passé simple dans la langue de la presse française d'aujourd'hui', *Beiträge zur romanischen Philologie* 69(2):336–45.

Zink, G. (1986). *Phonétique historique du français*, Paris: PUF.

Zribi-Hertz, A. (1982). 'La Construction "*se*-moyen" du français et son statut dans le triangle: passif – moyen – réfléchi', *Lingvisticae investigationes* 6(2):345–401.

Zribi-Hertz, A. (1987). 'La Réflexivité ergative en français moderne', *Le Français moderne* 55:23–54.

Zwanenburg, D. (1990). 'Französisch: Wortbildungslehre', in Holtus, G., M. Metzeltin and C. Schmitt (eds). *Lexikon der romanischen Linguistik*, vol 5, Tübingen: Niemeyer, pp.72–7.

Index of concepts

abbreviation – *see* lexis

acronym – *see* lexis, abbreviation

active – *see* verb, voice

adapted borrowing – *see* lexis, borrowing

adjective/adjective phrase, 16, 60–1, 64, 67, 68, 86, 90, 92–3, 94, 264–5

adjectif de relation, 348

adverb/abverbial, 19, 68, 93, 242, 252, 264–5, 280–2, 299, 300, 302, 303

agent, 18, 38, 230, 235–6, 237–8, 240, 241, 242, 243, 244, 246n10, 247n17

agreement – *see* gender

allomorph/allomorphy – *see* morphology

allophone – *see* phonology

analogy, 123, 130, 139, 141n14, 174, 210, 212, 331–2

analytic vs synthetic – *see* typology/ typological shift

anaphora, 22, 55n19, 182–3, 264, 287

aphoeresis – *see* lexis, abbreviation

apocope – *see* lexis, abbreviation

Approche pronominale, 27, 51–2, 275–9

approximant – *see* consonant

archiphoneme – *see* phonology

argumentation, 47, 287, 296n14

aspect – *see* verb

assimilation

  in consonants, 10–11, 39–40, 42

  in vowels, 78, 87, 94

  of voicing, 10–11, 39–40, 42

association line – *see* phonology, non-linear phonology

assonance, 79, 95n4

autosegmental phonology – *see* phonology

auxiliary – *see* verb

binary construction – *see* word order

borrowing – *see* lexis

bound morph – *see* morphology, morph

branching coda/onset – *see* syllable

calque – *see* lexis, borrowing

Canadian French – *see* variation, geography/region

case, 38, 45–6, 249–52, 253, 271n1

causative construction, 230–1, 236, 244–5

change, 22, 45–6, 48, 49, 53, 56n35, 76n14, 77–80, 80–2, 87–8, 98, 111–15, 138–9, 160, 168–74, 181–2, 185–6, 206–9, 212–13, 215–16, 249–55, 271n1,n4, 286, 312–13, 317–18, 319, 331–2, 333–5, 335–6, 352–3

  change in progress, 49, 56n37, 112–14, 317–18

  language death, 296n15

  lexical diffusion, 49, 113

  phonetic erosion, 249, 250, 251

  synchronie dynamique, 81

  (*see also* analogy; typology/typological shift)

chronotype – *see* Guillaumean school of linguistics
circumstantial clause – *see* subordination
cleft construction – *see* word order
clitic – *see* pronoun
coda – *see* syllable
cohesion – *see* textual cohesion
commutation, 30, 33, 119, 198
competence – *see* generative grammar
complement, 19
  position of, 248–72
complementary distribution, 29, 90, 132, 134
completive clause – *see* subordination
composition/compound – *see* lexis
conditional – *see* verb
conjugation classes – *see* morphology, verb
consonant, 8–9, 10–11, 12, 13, 39, 41, 42, 54n4
  approximant, 11
  assimilation of – *see* assimilation
  enchaînement, 9, 59, 71, 73, 76n15
  floating – *see* consonant, *liaison*
  fricative, 10, 11, 99, 102
  latent – *see* consonant, *liaison*
  liaison, 9, 41, 55n13, 59–76, 77, 91, 101, 110
    and floating/latent consonants, 69–71, 91, 110
    and nasal vowels, 92–3
    and orthography, 59, 62
    and syntax, 61, 68, 72, 73–4, 76n13
    and variation, 61, 72–4, 76n14,n15
    as deletion/truncation, 63–6, 66, 68, 69, 71, 72, 92
    as insertion, 66–8, 71, 72, 76n13, 92–3
    'impossible', 61, 62
    'obligatory', 61, 72, 73
    optional, 61, 72
  liquid, 11, 54n4, 64
  nasal, 11, 78–9, 82–90, 91–3, 94, 95n1,n3, 96n10,n12,n17, 97n19
  obstruent, 10–11, 39, 65
  sonorant, 102
  stop, 10, 99, 102

trill, 11
voicing of, 10–11, 39–40, 42, 76n11
word-final, 42, 59–76 (*see also* consonant, *liaison*)
constituency grammar, 32, 33
coordination, 20–1, 22, 33, 273–96, 298
  definition of, 21, 273–82
corpus-based studies, 49, 51, 73–4, 112–14, 170–3, 176–8, 188–9, 200–2, 204, 205, 210–11, 214–16, 240, 253–4, 255, 260–4, 266–7, 282, 283–6, 288–9, 289–94, 326, 328, 329–33, 334, 352, 353
coupe – *see* Guillaumean school of linguistics
cranberry morpheme – *see* morphology, morpheme
creole, 6, 316–17

deep structure – *see* generative grammar
deixis, 17, 22, 46, 55n14, 175–6
dependence, 21, 32, 52, 273–9
dependency grammar, 32–3
derivation – *see* lexis
derivational morphology – *see* morphology
detachment – *see* word order
determiner, 16, 30, 31, 34, 50, 300
diachrony vs synchrony – *see* Structuralism, European
diglossia, 25, 326, 328
discontinuous morph – *see* morphology, morph
discours – *see* *énonciation*
discourse-pragmatics, 47, 159, 169
  discourse analysis, 46
  discourse-pragmatic usage, 149, 160–2, 169–71, 176–8, 183–5
discourse type – *see* variation
dislocation – *see* word order
distinctive features – *see* phonology
distributionalism, 32, 33
domain – *see* variation

e-caduc, e-instable, e-muet, e-féminin – *see* vowel, schwa ellipsis, 55n19 (*see also* lexis, non-affixal derivation)

enantiosemy – *see* lexis

enchaînement – *see* consonant

ending – *see* segmentation

énonciateur – *see* énonciation

énonciation
    discours, 46, 159, 175–6
    énonciateur, 46
    histoire, 46, 159, 175–6, 178
    theories of, 46–7

epenthesis – *see* vowel, schwa~zero alternation

euphemism – *see* lexis, semantic change

expletive *ne* – *see* ne explétif

faux-ami – *see* lexis, borrowing

feature matrix – *see* phonology, distinctive features

field – *see* variation

focus, 47, 55n16, 265, 267, 271n9

forclusif – *see* negation

formes surcomposées – *see* verb, tenses

free morph – *see* morphology, morph

free variation – *see* phonology, allophone

French, history of (*see also* change)
    Early Modern, 172–4, 255, 286, 339–40
    evidence for, 78–9
    Middle French, 78, 172, 182, 254–5, 299
    Old French, 37, 77, 78, 79, 169–71, 181–2, 186, 190n5, 206–9, 236, 249–55, 256, 257, 267, 271n2, 272nn16–18, 285, 296n11, 299, 312–13, 318, 331, 334

fricative – *see* consonant

Functionalism, 28–9, 39

future tense – *see* verb, tenses

gender, 31, 331–2, 358
    agreement, 31, 60–1, 64, 86, 89, 90, 92–3

generative grammar, 27, 31, 33–45, 124–5, 204, 224–5, 229, 319n1, 320n4
    competence, 34
    deep structure, 33, 35, 36, 37, 38

Government-Binding theory, 34, 37–9, 204, 225, 296n13, 308

head, 36, 44

lexicon, 35, 36, 38, 44, 86, 87, 88, 90, 96n16
    morphology in, 35–6, 42–5 (*see also* morphology)

Move-α, 37, 38, 225

performance, 34, 48

phonology in, 35–6, 42–3, 56n29 (*see also* phonology)

phrase-structure rule, 34–5, 36

Principles and Parameters, 34, 36, 37–9, 271n12, 319n1

Projection Principle, 36, 38

semantic component, 35–6, 42, 56n29

semantic interpretation, 37

standard theory, 33–6, 37

surface structure, 35, 36, 37, 38

syntax in, 34–9

trace, 37

Universal Grammar, 36, 38

X-bar theory, 34, 36–7, 38, 271n4

(*see also* transformation)

geography/region – *see* variation

glide – *see* semivowel/glide

Gliederungssignale – *see* textual cohesion

governance – *see* subordination

Government-Binding theory – *see* generative grammar

grammaticalization/ degrammaticalization, 260–2, 268, 295n4, 312, 348

greffe – *see* word order

Guillaumean school of linguistics, 27, 50, 151–3, 155–7, 183, 195–6, 210, 213, 223–4, 226
    chronotype, 152
    coupe, 50, 151
    subduction, 295n4
    temps in esse/temps in fieri/temps in posse, 50, 151, 152
    tension, 151–2, 156

h-aspiré, 65, 75n1, 109, 116n12

head – *see* generative grammar

histoire – *see* énonciation

historic present – *see* verb, tenses
homonymy – *see* lexis
hyperbole – *see* lexis, semantic change
hypotaxis, 22

imparfait pittoresque/narratif/historique –
    see verb, tenses
imperfect tense – *see* verb, tenses
incise – *see* word order
infinitive – *see* verb
infix – *see* segmentation
inflectional morphology – *see*
    morphology
interrogation, 20, 48, 202–3, 236,
    252–3, 304
intonation – *see* prosodic features
inversion – *see* word order
irregular vs regular verb – *see* verb
Item-and-Arrangement model – *see*
    morphology
Item-and-Process model – *see*
    morphology

javanais – *see* lexis
journalism – *see* variation, field/domain/
    discourse-type

language death – *see* change
langue – *see* Structuralism, European
largonji – *see* lexis
learned form – *see* lexis, borrowing
lexeme, 14, 63, 81, 89, 113
lexical diffusion – *see* change
lexicalist morphology – *see* morphology
lexis, 22–6, 48, 53, 54, 323–63
    abbreviation, 24, 56n22, 347, 352,
        360–2
        acronym, 24, 352, 361–2
        aphoeresis, 24
        apocope, 24, 352
        sigles, 24
    borrowing, 25–6, 48, 138, 323–42,
        352
        abbreviated, 325
        adapted, 325–6
        attitudes towards, 338–42
        calque, 325, 342n3
        definition of, 324–6

faux-ami, 325, 333, 341
learned form, 325, 337–9, 352
loan blend, 325
loan shift, 325
loanword, 323–5, 328
    morphosyntactic integration of,
        330–3, 340–1
    mot voyageur, 325, 342n1
    nonce borrowing, 324, 328
    phonological integration of,
        327–30, 340–1
    pseudo-/*faux-anglicisme*, 325, 331,
        335–7
    semantic calque, 325, 341
    semantic integration of, 333–5,
        340–1
composition/compound, 13, 23–4,
    43–4, 325, 344–50, 352, 360–1
    endocentrique, 362n3
    exocentrique, 362n3
    hybrid compound, 325, 331,
        335–7, 346
derivation, 8, 13, 23, 43–4, 297,
    354–8
    hybrid, 335–7
    prefix/ation, 8, 23, 40, 344–5,
        351–4, 360
    suffix/ation, 8, 15, 23, 44, 85, 325,
        336–7, 344, 351–4, 359–60,
        362n1
enantiosemy, 334
haplology, 347
javanais, 351
largonji, 351
lexicalization of phrases, 24, 350, 358
loucherbem, 351
mot-tiroir, 347
neologism, 5, 7, 22–6, 89, 138,
    323–63
    definition of, 344
non-affixal derivation, 23
    change of grammatical class, 23,
        351, 358
    ellipsis, 23, 352
parasynthetic formation, 23
polysemy, 358, 360
recomposé, 24, 344, 346–7
semantic change, 24–5

euphemism, 351
  hyperbole, 351
  litotes, 351
  metaphor, 25, 348, 351, 358
  metonymy, 25, 351
  synecdoche, 25, 351
synonymy, 334, 359
technical, 5–6, 337, 345, 352
verlan, 5, 351, 363n9
liaison – *see* consonant
liquid – *see* consonant
litotes – *see* lexis, semantic change
loan blend – *see* lexis, borrowing
loan shift – *see* lexis, borrowing
loanword – *see* lexis, borrowing
loi des trois consonnes – *see* vowel,
  schwa~zero alternation
loucherbem – *see* lexis

melodic tier – *see* phonology, non-linear
  phonology
metaphor – *see* lexis, semantic change
metonymy – *see* lexis, semantic change
middle – *see* verb, voice
minimal pair – *see* phonology
monème, 30, 55n11, 347
mood and modality – *see* verb
morph – *see* morphology
morpheme – *see* morphology
morphology, 8, 13–16, 27, 30–2, 40–1,
  42–5, 82–92, 98, 118–42
  allomorph/allomorphy, 30–1, 40,
    42–3, 44, 63, 82–5, 88–90, 118,
    132–5, 136, 356, 358
  derivational, 13, 43–5, 67, 82–5,
    88–9, 335–9, 343–63
  inflectional, 13, 31–2, 43, 44–5, 67,
    82–5, 89–90, 92–3
  generative morphology, 40–1, 42–5,
    64, 82–5, 88–90, 116n2, 124–5,
    131, 136–8, 141n19, 142n23,
    355–8
  Item-and-Arrangement model, 30–1
  Item-and-Process model, 31
  lexicalist, 43–4
  morph, 13–15, 30, 45
    bound, 14
    discontinuous, 15, 30

free, 14
    portmanteau, 15, 30
    zero, 30–1
  morpheme, 13–14, 15, 30–2, 40, 43,
    44, 63, 64, 82, 85, 86, 87, 88,
    89, 92, 96n16, 109, 123, 358
    cranberry, 30
    identification of, 30–1
  morphological markers of aspect – *see*
    verb, aspect
  readjustment rules, 43
  structuralist morphology, 30–2, 119,
    131
  Truncation Rules, 44
  verb, 4, 14–16, 31–2, 89–90, 118–42,
    144, 146, 149, 153–4, 158
    conjugation classes, 118, 123–36
    stem-based models, 126–31, 136
    traditional schemes, 124–6, 136
    'two-class' models, 131–5, 136
    written vs spoken, 4, 15–16, 118,
      119–20, 120–3, 125–6, 131, 135
  Word-and-Paradigm model, 31–2,
    44–5, 123, 139
  Word Formation Rules, 44, 354–8
  (*see also* paradigm; segmentation;
    stem; suppletion; verb, infinitive)
mot voyageur – *see* lexis, borrowing
mute e – *see* vowel, schwa

nasal – *see* consonant; vowel
ne – *see* negation
ne explétif, 297, 299, 305, 309–11, 312,
  321n17,n18,n20
negation, 4, 15, 46, 48, 50, 203–4, 241,
  297–322
  acquisition of, 317
  history of, 312–13
  marked by ne alone, 312
  négation connexionnelle, 301
  négation nucléaire, 301
  negative particle or *forclusif*, 203, 297,
    298, 299, 306, 308, 312–13, 314,
    316
  negative polarity items, 304
  negative raising, 203, 297, 302–5,
    320n6,n9
  non-use of *ne*, 4, 48, 49, 297, 312–18

pas vs *point*, 299
  scope of, 203–4, 297, 301–5
  status of *de* after a negative particle,
    298, 299–300, 320n5
  status of *ne*, 298–9
  status of *pas*, etc., 298, 299
  total vs partial, 301
  (*see also* ne . . . *que*)
norm – *see* variation
neologism – *see* lexis
ne . . . *que*, 238, 240, 297, 305–9,
  320n12,n13
  status of the elements of, 305–6, 308
neutralization – *see* phonology
nonce borrowing – *see* lexis,
  borrowing
noun phrase, definition of, 16
nucleus – *see* syllable

object
  direct object, 16, 19–20, 51
  indirect object, 16, 19, 51, 52
  nature of, 255–6
  position of, 248–72
obstruent – *see* consonant
on – *see* pronoun
onset – *see* syllable

paradigm, 14, 44–5, 135, 136, 168
parasynthetic formation – *see* lexis
parataxis, 4, 22, 282, 287–94
parole – *see* Structuralism, European
participle – *see* verb
passé composé – *see* verb, tenses
passé simple – *see* verb, tenses
passive – *see* verb, voice
performance – *see* generative grammar
phoneme – *see* phonology
phonetics, 8–13
phonology, 3–4, 7, 8, 27, 28–9, 39–42,
  48, 53, 54, 59–117
  allophone, 29, 40, 56n25, 63, 94,
    104, 105, 106–7, 108, 119
    free variation, 48, 56n25, 104
  archiphoneme, 29, 116n8
  autosegmental phonology, 41–2,
    56n32, 90–2 (*see also* phonology,
    non-linear)

distinctive features, 39–40
  feature matrix, 40, 41, 42
generative phonology, 39–41, 42–3,
  54, 63–8, 71, 77, 82–90, 104,
  106, 108–9, 110, 116n2, 136–8
  abstract generative phonology,
    63–6, 71, 83–7, 89, 90, 91–2,
    92–3, 94, 97n20, 104, 108–9
  concrete generative phonology,
    66–8, 71, 87–90, 93, 94, 106,
    108–9
  economy/simplicity in, 40–1, 65,
    66, 83–4, 86, 87, 89, 94
  morpheme boundary in, 64, 108
  word boundary in, 64, 65, 67–8,
    84, 92, 108
minimal pair, 28–9, 80, 81, 103–4
neutralization, 29, 56n23
non-linear phonology, 41–2, 68–71,
  73, 90–2, 93, 109–11
  association line, 41, 42
  floating/latent autosegment, 41, 91
    (*see also* consonant, *liaison*)
  melodic tier, 41, 68, 69
  skeletal slot, 69, 91, 109–11
  skeletal tier, 41, 69, 110
  spreading, 42
phoneme, 14, 24, 28–9, 30, 39, 40,
  41, 42, 80–2, 88, 94, 103–4, 105,
  106, 107, 108, 328
structuralist phonology, 28–9, 63, 78,
  80–2, 88, 103–4, 105, 106–8, 110
phrase-structure rule – *see* generative
  grammar
pidgin, 6
pluperfect – *see* verb, tenses
polyphony, 47
polysemy – *see* lexis
portmanteau morph – *see* morphology,
  morph
pragmatics – *see* discourse-pragmatics
predicate, 16, 32, 33, 43, 147, 301
prefix/ation – *see* lexis, derivation
present – *see* verb, tenses
Principles and Parameters – *see*
  generative grammar
Projection principle – *see* generative
  grammar

pronominal verb – *see* verb
pronoun, 7, 16, 22, 51–2, 119, 314–15
   clitic pronoun, 7, 16, 255–64, 314
   disjunctive, 256–7
   on, 5, 7, 16, 221, 237, 241, 242–3,
     244, 247n23
   position of, 248–72
   relative, 16, 21
prosodic features, 9, 42, 293
   intonation, 171, 216, 252, 258, 259,
     269, 270, 278, 291–3, 301
   rhythmic group, 9, 60, 71, 101, 114
   stress, 9, 14, 254, 327
pseudo-anglicism – *see* lexis, borrowing

quantifier, 16, 224, 241, 299, 300, 320n4
que – *see* subordination

recomposé – *see* lexis
reflexive – *see* verb, pronominal
region – *see* variation
register – *see* variation
relative clause – *see* subordination
rhythmic group – *see* prosodic features
rime – *see* syllable
root, 14, 30, 64, 66–7, 82, 84, 85, 86,
   88, 119, 335, 336, 346–7

schwa – *see* vowel
segmentation, 14–15, 30, 31, 33, 45,
   118–23, 135, 139
   stem & ending vs stem, infix &
     ending, 120–3, 140n2
semantic calque – *see* lexis, borrowing
semantic change – *see* lexis
semantic component, semantic
     interpretation – *see* generative
     grammar
semivowel/glide, 13, 39
sex – *see* variation
signifiant ~ signifié – *see* Structuralism,
   European
skeletal slot, skeletal tier – *see*
     phonology, non-linear
     phonology
socio-economic status – *see* variation
spreading – *see* phonology, non-linear
     phonology

standard – *see* variation
stem, 14, 15, 23, 30, 31, 118, 119,
   120–3, 126–31, 131–5, 136,
   138–9, 140n2,n3, 141n11,
   142n21, 345, 362n1
   strong, 14
   variation in/allomorphy, 119,
     126–31, 131–5, 136, 137
   weak, 14, 133, 135, 139
stop – *see* consonant
stress – *see* prosodic features
Structuralism, 13, 28–33, 40, 42, 48
   European, 28, 30
     langue, 28, 50
     parole, 28, 48
     signifiant ~ signifié, 28
     synchrony vs diachrony, 28
     syntagmatic vs paradigmatic
       relationships, 28
   American, 28, 30–1, 33
   (*see also* morphology; phonology;
     syntax)
style-shifting – *see* variation
subduction – *see* Guillaumean school of
     linguistics
subject, 16, 19–20, 32, 33, 35, 37, 47,
   52, 55n15, 314, 315, 316
   nature of, 253, 255–6, 314, 315, 316
   position of, 248–72
   pro-drop parameter, 37
subjunctive – *see* verb
subordination, 5, 20–1, 33, 52, 171,
   197–8, 200, 208–9, 272n25,
   273–96, 314
   circumstantial clause, 21, 274–5,
     279–81, 283
   completive clause, 21, 202–4, 274,
     275, 279
   definition of, 273–82
   governance, 52, 277–9, 281
   inversée, 274
   presentation of in grammars, 273–4
   que, extended use of 277, 278, 283
   relative clause, 21, 198, 204–6, 243,
     275, 282–6, 296n11,n12, 314
     acquisition of, 286
   (*see also* dependence)
suffix/ation – *see* lexis, derivation

suppletion, 15, 31, 43, 63, 76n17, 119,
    137
surface structure – *see* generative grammar
syllable, 8–9, 12, 13, 24, 54n4, 69–71,
    91, 92, 107, 110–11
  branching coda/onset, 9, 54n4
  closed, 9, 12
  coda, 8, 13, 54n4, 59, 69–71, 92
    empty, 71
  nucleus, 8, 13, 54n4, 69, 91
  onset, 8, 13, 54n4, 59, 69–71, 73, 92,
    107
    empty, 69–70, 71
  open, 9, 12
  post-tonic, 98
  pretonic, 9, 85
  rime, 8, 9, 69, 70, 92
  syllabification, 54n4,n5
  tonic, 9, 85, 98
synchronie dynamique – *see* change
synchrony vs diachrony – *see*
    Structuralism, European
synecdoche – *see* lexis, semantic change
synonymy – *see* lexis
syntax, 5, 7, 16–22, 27, 32–3, 34–9,
    143–322
  generative syntax, 34–9
  structuralist syntax, 32–3
  (*see also* agent; anaphora; *Approche
    pronominale*; case; causative
    construction; coordination;
    dependence; gender, agreement;
    generative grammar; Guillaumean
    school of linguistics; interrogation;
    negation; object; pronoun;
    Structuralism; subject;
    subordination; textual cohesion;
    transformation; typology;
    valency; verb; word order)
synthème, 347
synthetic (vs analytic) – *see* typology

temps in esse/temps in fieri/temps in posse
    – *see* Guillaumean school of
    linguistics
tense, tenses – *see* verb
tension – *see* Guillaumean school of
    linguistics

textual cohesion, 22, 243, 287–94
  acquisition of, 287–9
  Gliederungssignale, 291–2
topic/topicalization, 20, 47, 243, 251,
    260–4, 265–9, 271n9, 272n15,n19
trace – *see* generative grammar
transformation, 33, 34–5, 36, 37, 43,
    224–5, 229, 279–80, 300, 303–5,
    307, 320n7, 349
  NEG-Raising, 303–5
  Passive, 224–5
truncation – *see* consonant, *liaison*
Truncation Rules – *see* morphology
typology/typological shift, 45–6, 168–9,
    174, 179, 181, 189, 251–3, 259,
    262–4, 270, 321n24
  analytic vs synthetic, 168, 174
  syntactic drift, 45–6, 251–3

Universal Grammar – *see* generative
    grammar

valency, 32, 52, 237
variable, variable rule, variant – *see*
    variationist analysis
variation, 3–7, 48–9, 53, 56n35, 72–4,
    80–2, 138–9, 210–12, 253
  age, 6–7, 48, 49, 56n37, 112–13, 115,
    117n15, 246n1, 253, 262, 263,
    287–9, 316, 317–18, 337, 351,
    353
  field/domain/discourse type, 5–6,
    76n15, 169–76, 178–9, 183–5,
    188, 216, 240, 247n21, 264, 266,
    291–4, 299, 337, 341, 351–2, 353
  journalism, 5, 161–2, 175, 176–8,
    184, 188, 240, 264, 266, 294,
    326, 338
  geography/region, 6, 94–5, 95n5,
    101, 103, 109, 159, 167, 173,
    179, 188–9, 190n6, 210, 212,
    220n24, 229, 246n1,n11, 285,
    296n15, 299, 311, 316, 321n28,
    337
  Canadian French, 6, 7, 48, 74,
    95n6, 138, 212, 219n13, 262,
    285, 299, 316, 324, 326, 328,
    330, 332, 333

norm, 3–4, 5, 113
register, 4–5, 49, 72–3, 101, 102,
    113, 115, 138, 149, 173, 175–6,
    178, 210, 211, 212, 252–3, 253,
    258, 262, 264, 266, 269, 270,
    285, 291–4, 299, 311, 316, 337,
    341, 351, 361
  français populaire, 49, 138, 212, 240,
    246n1, 282–6, 321n28, 351
sex, 6–7, 48, 173, 253, 262, 322n29
socio-economic status, 6–7, 48, 49,
    185, 211, 262, 263, 285, 289–90,
    316, 317, 351
standard, 3, 7, 10
style-shifting, 73, 101, 316
written/spoken, 3, 4, 15–16, 53,
    118, 119–20, 138, 164–5, 167,
    169–72, 175–6, 178–9, 184–5,
    188, 210–11, 212–13, 214–16,
    240, 253, 258, 262, 264, 266,
    270, 271n13, 276, 282–6, 287,
    291–4, 297, 299, 311, 321n23,
    322n33, 325, 326, 328, 338
variationist analysis, 48–9, 176–7,
    200–2, 214–15, 219n17, 253,
    260–3, 289–90, 317–18
variable, 48–9
variable rule, 48
variant, 48
verb, 17–19, 118–247
  Aktionsart – *see* verb, *mode/modalité
    d'action*
  aspect (vs tense), 18, 143–63, 168,
    215, 217, 237, 241–2
  accompli, 145, 153, 156, 237
  and adverbials, 145, 146, 149, 153,
    157, 158, 303
  attainment, 154–5
  continuance, 154–5
  durative, 145, 153, 154, 156, 157,
    163n10, 165
  global, 145, 158, 164
  *immanent-transcendant-bi-
    transcendant* – *see* Guillaumean
    school of linguistics, *tension*
  imperfective, 143–6, 147, 153, 156,
    157, 161–2, 163n10, 165, 182–5,
    241–2, 303

inaccompli, 145, 153, 156, 237
inchoative, 145, 153, 156, 157, 228
iterative, 145, 153, 156
lexical vs grammatical, 146–8, 149,
    152, 153, 154, 156, 157, 158
morphological markers of, 143–63
past punctual, 160, 164–91
perfective, 143–6, 149, 153, 156,
    157, 161–2, 163n10, 165, 167,
    182–5, 188, 241–2, 303
present perfective, 160, 164–91
progressive, 145, 147, 149, 154
punctual, 145, 149, 153, 154, 156,
    163n10, 164, 242
sécant, 145, 158, 165
semelfactive, 145
tensif/extensif/bi-extensif – *see*
    Guillaumean school of
    linguistics, *tension*
terminative, 145, 153, 156, 157
using affixes 145–6, 147, 149, 152,
    157–8
auxiliary, 46, 146, 148, 152, 158, 222,
    314
compound forms
  development of, 160, 168–9
  vs simple forms, 145, 153, 213
conditional, 121, 193, 207, 215,
    216–17
defective, 141n9
deponent, 223
infinitive, 21, 50, 118, 124–6, 127,
    130, 131–2, 133, 135, 137, 217
impersonal, 220n21, 223
irregular vs regular, 118, 135–8,
    142n21
modal, 217, 314, 322n33
mode/modalité d'action, 147, 156–7,
    163n3, 181
morphology – *see* morphology, verb
mood and modality, 18, 46, 166,
    192–220, 276, 311 (*see also* verb,
    subjunctive)
participle, 23, 50, 118, 127, 130, 137,
    180
periphrasis, 7, 145, 146, 147, 149,
    152, 153, 154, 155, 156–7, 158,
    181

pronominal, 19, 50, 188, 221–47
  and voice, 221–5
  classification of, 221, 225–37
  construction/forme ergative réflexive,
    227–8, 246n10
  inherently/essentially/intrinsically,
    222, 226, 227, 229–30, 231,
    233–4, 235, 247n14
  intransitive usage, 227, 228–9, 230,
    232, 233, 236, 246n10
  middle usage, 222, 229–31, 247n14
  neutral usage, 222, 226, 229–31,
    246n13
  pleonastic usage, 233
  pronominal passive, 221, 222, 226,
    229, 231, 232–3, 236, 237–40,
    242, 244, 246n12
  reciprocal usage, 222, 226, 229,
    231, 232, 235, 247n14
  reflexive usage, 222, 226, 228, 229,
    231, 232, 235, 239, 247n14
  subjectifs, 226–9
  successive, 231
  unaccusative usage, 228, 236,
    246n10
  unergative usage, 228
  unified explanations of, 231–7
situation type, 147–8, 171, 181
  telic, 147, 171
stage, 154–5
subjunctive, 18, 50, 174, 192–220,
    310, 311, 320n9
  acquisition of, 209
  adjectival clause usages, 198,
    204–6, 208, 217
  adverbial clause usages, 198
  alternatives to, 216–17
  as *servitude grammaticale*, 197–9, 209
  as *terme corrélatif*, 192–200
  corpus-based studies, 200–2, 204,
    205–6, 210–11, 214–16
  definitions of, 192, 193–202
  formal/mechanical accounts of,
    197–9
  history of, 206–9
  in conditional sentences, 207
  main clause usages, 197, 198, 199,
    206–7, 218n6

noun clause usages, 197–8, 200–2,
    202–4, 208, 214–15
  perfect subjunctive, 213, 220n25
  pluperfect subjunctive, 213, 214
  present subjunctive, 120, 121, 128,
    136, 137, 211, 213, 214, 215,
    219n16
  imperfect subjunctive, 118, 121,
    126, 127, 137, 174, 207, 211,
    212–16, 220n24,n26
  semantic accounts of, 194–7, 198
  Subjunctive Disjoint Reference
    Effect, 204
  variation in usage of, 210–12
  vitality of, 206–17
tense
  and adverbials, 164, 171, 172–4
  definition of, 17, 143–4, 192–3
  tense and time, 17–18, 143–4
    absolute time, 17
    relative time, 18
  tense switching, 170–1, 172
tenses
  formes surcomposées, 6, 145, 149,
    152, 159, 167, 185–9
  future, 7, 121, 127, 128, 129, 155,
    216–17, 220n28
  historic present, 17, 161–2, 175,
    178–9
  imperfect, 16, 121, 128, 129, 130,
    138–9, 143–6, 149, 151, 152–3,
    153–4, 154, 156, 158, 160, 161,
    164–91, 193, 217
  *imparfait pittoresque/narratif/
    historique*, 160, 183–5
  passé composé, 17, 46, 53, 130, 145,
    153, 159, 164–91, 215
  passé simple, 46, 53, 118, 121, 126,
    127, 130, 132–3, 143–6, 152–3,
    153–4, 154, 156, 158, 160, 161,
    164–91, 215, 216, 220n26
  past anterior, 166–7, 185–9
  pluperfect, 17, 166, 185–9
  present, 15, 17, 120–1, 127–8, 129,
    138–9, 153, 161–2, 170–1, 175,
    178–9
tension – *see* Guillaumean school of
    linguistics

verbes symétriques, à renversement, 227, 236

voice, 18–19, 221–5, 236–7, 246n3
active, 18, 55n15, 221, 222, 223–4, 226, 237, 240, 246n2
medio-passive, 222
middle, 18, 220, 222, 224, 231, 246n4
passive, 5, 18–19, 55n16, 221, 222, 223–4, 224–5, 232, 237, 238, 240–5, 246n2, 247n24
voix pronominale, 222, 223, 231
voix réflexive/réfléchie, 222, 224

verlan – *see* lexis
vocabulary – *see* lexis
voice – *see* verb
vowel, 8, 11–12, 39, 41
assimilation – *see* assimilation
classification, 11–12
diphthong, 77, 95n6
lowering, 78, 79
nasal, 12, 77–97
and orthography, 78–9
denasalization, 89, 92–3, 94, 95n1
in morphological alternations, 78, 82–92
phonemic status of, 80–2, 88
nasalization, 78–80, 83–7, 91, 92
schwa, 12, 48, 49, 56n37, 64, 75n1, 77, 86, 87, 98–117
and orthography, 99, 105, 116n3
as empty V slot, 109–11
feminine, 64, 85, 86, 99
fixed, 104, 106, 112, 114
floating, 110–11
in morphological alternations, 98, 104, 116n2,n13
names for, 98, 99
phonemic status of, 103–4, 105–8, 114
phonetic quality of, 98, 99–100, 103–4, 114
protective, 65–6, 85, 86–7, 90, 91, 108–9, 116n11
schwa~zero alternation, 98, 100–15
and floating schwa, 110–11
as deletion, 105–6, 108–9, 111

as epenthesis, 105, 106–8, 108–9, 110, 111
in monosyllables, 102
lexical conditioning, 102, 113
loi des trois consonnes, 101–2
phonetic conditioning, 100–1, 101–2, 107, 114–15
pragmatic conditioning, 101, 103, 115
sociolinguistic conditioning, 101, 103, 112–15
stylistic conditioning, 101, 103, 115
syntactic conditioning, 101, 102–3
word-finally, 98, 99, 102–3, 107, 108–9, 115
word-initially, 102, 106, 110–11, 112–14, 115, 116n6
word-medially, 102, 106, 111, 114–15
tense vs lax, 84–5, 96n15

word, 9, 14, 44–5
definitions of, 14
phonetic identity of, 9
Word-and-Paradigm model – *see* morphology
Word Formation Rules – *see* morphology
word order, 19–20, 45–6, 54, 248–72
binary construction, 268–9
borrowing, 332
cleft construction, 267–8, 272n26
with relatives, 284
detachment, 48, 257–64, 272n18
acoustic properties of, 261
acquisition of, 262
dislocation, 52, 257
greffe, 278
incise, 264, 272n22, 284
inversion, 37, 252–3, 264–7
pragmatic considerations, 260–70
written/spoken French – *see* variation

X-bar theory – *see* generative grammar

zero morph – *see* morphology, morph

Index of names

Académie Française, 173, 210
Aitchison, J., 353–4
Allaire, S., 293
Anderson, S., 44–5, 104, 109–10, 139
Anscombre, J.-C., 47
Armstrong, L., 62, 80–1
Aronoff, M., 43–4, 355
Ashby, W., 7, 48, 49, 73, 260–1, 262, 263, 313–14, 315, 316, 317–18, 322n29
Attal, P., 228
Auvigne, M.-A., 185, 211, 290
Ayres-Bennett, W., 186, 252, 254–5, 313, 322n32
Azoulay-Vicente, A., 305, 307–9, 321n16

Baciu, I., 306, 307, 308, 320n11
Bailard, J., 209
Baker, P., 317, 322n31
Barnes, B., 260, 261–2
Barral, M., 212–14
Battye, A., 309, 311
Bauche, H., 212, 220n23, 246n1
Bauer, B., 271n4
Béchade, H.-D., 123, 213
Bécherel, D., 354
Beck, J., 171, 190n2
Bénézech, J.-L., 176
Beniak, E., 328
Benveniste, E., 46–7, 175–6, 179, 347, 350
Berthonneau, A.-M., 182

Blanc, M., 169
Blanche-Benveniste, C., 51–2, 131–2, 134, 135, 142n20, 179, 231, 246n2, 268, 269, 275–7, 291, 294, 296n11,n13
Blasco, M., 258
Bloomfield, L., 28, 33
Bonnard, H., 320n5
Börjeson, L., 219n9
Boysen, G., 198–9
Bres, J., 183
Brunot, F., 144, 148–51, 197, 202, 209, 220n27
Buffier, C., 174
Burston, J., 232–4
Bybee, J., 18

Cadiot, P., 272n19
Calvet, L.-J., 361–2
Canut, C., 210
Caron, P., 173
Carroll, S., 262
Carruthers, J., 191n26, 292
Carton, F., 63, 101
Catach, N., 345, 349
Cedergren, H., 73
Chevalier, J.-C., 194, 273–4
Chollet, G., 100
Chomsky, N., 33, 33–5, 38, 39, 43, 355
Clifford, P., 266
Cohen, M., 209, 211, 212, 213, 214, 220n27

Comrie, B., 17, 143
Confais, J.-P., 193, 194
Connors, K., 194
Corbin, D., 45, 344, 354–8
Corne, C., 317, 322n31
Cornulier, B. de, 304–5
Coute, B., 119, 122–3, 136, 141n11
Coveney, A., 48, 253, 313, 316, 322n29
Crystal, D., 288
Culioli, A., 47, 253
Curat, H., 15

Damourette, J., 192, 195, 205, 222,
    298, 309, 310–11, 320n13
Dangeau, L'abbé de, 226
Dannequin, C., 262
Dauses, A., 103
Dauzat, A., 214
De Jong, D., 74
Delattre, P., 102, 106
Delbart, A.-R., 190n15
Dell, F., 63, 83, 86–7, 101, 104, 108
De Mulder, W., 182
Desclés, J., 242, 243
Désirat, C., 317, 322n33
Deulofeu, J., 268–9, 277–9, 286
Diller, A.-M., 313–15, 317
Di Scullio, A.-M., 44
Dubois, J., 21, 33, 119, 123–4, 126–31,
    135, 136, 141n12, 224–5, 243–4,
    321n17
Ducrot, O., 47
Durand, J., 68, 94

Encrevé, P., 73, 76n15
Engel, D., 176–7
Estienne, H., 172
Etiemble, R., 332, 340

Fleischman, S., 18, 47, 144, 147–8, 161,
    171, 182
Foley, J., 137
Fónagy, I., 114–15
Foulet, L., 173, 186

Gaatone, D., 299, 300, 302, 320n6
Gadet, F., 262, 269, 277, 279, 283–6,
    296n11,n12

Gardes-Tamine, J., 131–5, 136, 141n17,
    222, 241
GARS (Groupe Aixois de Recherche en
    Syntaxe), 51, 211, 220n20, n21, 291
Gaudin, F., 342
George, K., 55n21, 337, 360
Gertner, M., 142n23
Gide, A., 213
Gilder, A., 340
Gilliéron, J., 49
Godard, D., 296n13
Goosse, A., 229, 340
Goudailler, J.-P., 339
Gougenheim, G., 229, 246n8
Grammont, M., 101, 106
Granger, S., 243, 244
Green, J., 73, 74, 76n15
Greenberg, J., 45, 251
Grevisse, M., 136, 195, 212, 214,
    226–7, 229, 238, 246n1,n8, 311, 316,
    321n26,n28
Gross, M., 33, 119, 198, 300, 307, 308,
    346–7, 349, 362n6
Guentchéva, Z., 242, 243
Guilbert, L., 43, 355
Guilford, J., 331, 342
Guillaume, G., 27, 50, 144, 151–3,
    155–6, 163n6, 183, 195, 210, 213,
    222, 223–4, 231, 246n4
Guiraud, P., 340
Gülich, E., 296n17

Hagège, C., 332, 334–5, 339–41
Hajek, J., 77, 80
Halle, M., 39, 43–4, 355
Halliday, M., 22, 47, 291, 294
Hanse, J., 195
Hansen, A., 48, 49, 56n37, 101, 112–14
Harris, M., 46, 168–9, 171, 174, 179,
    181, 189, 193, 197–8, 251–2, 256–7,
    259, 262, 270, 271n9,n11, 309,
    321n24
Harris, Z., 28, 33
Hasan, R., 22
Haugen, E., 325, 328
Havu, E., 220n25
Healey, F., 136, 200, 222
Heldner, C., 301–2

Herzog, C., 188
Hintze, M.-A., 73, 74, 76n15, 309, 311
Hobaek-Haff, M., 281–2
Hockett, C., 30, 31
Hong, C.-H., 346
Hordé, T., 317, 322n33
Houdebine-Gravaud, A.-M., 358
Huot, H., 203

Imbs, P., 144, 153–4, 192, 195, 199–200

Jackendoff, R., 47
Jakobson, R., 39
Jeanjean, C., 256, 288–9
Jones, M., 222, 230, 243, 246n12, 264, 299
Judge, A., 136, 163n11, 200, 222

Kaisse, E., 72, 74
Kamp, H., 182
Kampers-Manhe, B., 206, 217
Karasch, A., 240
Kaye, J., 72
Kayne, R., 36, 56n28, 305
Kerbrat-Orecchioni, C., 47
Klausenburger, J., 66–7, 76n17
Kleiber, G., 182
Klein, J.-R., 334
Klum, A., 144
Koch, P., 282, 193–4
Krassin, G., 240

Labelle, M., 185–6, 228–9, 236
Labov, W., 48, 49, 54n2, 56n35
Lafage, S., 336–7
Lagane, R., 21
Lagueux, P.-A., 326, 342n3
Lalaire, L., 219n17
Lambrecht, K., 47, 256, 259, 260, 263, 268, 271n9, 272n15
Larrivée, P., 321n19,n23
Laurier, M., 212
Le Bidois, G., 196
Le Bidois, R., 196
Ledegen, G., 210
Lefebvre, C., 286

Lehmann, W., 45, 345, 347, 359–60
Leinart, N., 334
Lenoble-Pinson, M., 340
Lentin, L., 287–8
Léon, P., 62
Lerch, E., 194, 218n2
Lindenfeld, J., 289
Lindqvist, C., 214–15
Liu, Y.-C., 173
Lüdike, A., 313, 314
Lyons, C., 230–1

McMahon, A., 253
Malécot, A., 100, 112, 113, 117n15
Mandelbaum-Reiner, F., 351
Marchello-Nizia, C., 249, 253–4, 267, 269, 272n16,n17,n18
Martin, R., 50, 155–7, 181, 192, 195–6, 202, 203–4, 218n5, 220n28
Martin-Berthet, F., 345, 347, 359–60
Martinet, A., 1, 28–9, 30, 55n11, 56n26, 63, 80, 81–2, 98, 106–8, 119, 125, 126–7, 329–30, 346, 347, 362n3
Marty, F., 123
Mathieu-Colas, M., 345
Matthews, P., 13, 44
Maupas, Ch., 172
Melis, L., 229, 231–2, 234–7, 237–8, 247n17,n18
Miller, C., 48, 324, 326, 330–1, 332, 333
Mitterand, H., 340–1, 346, 350, 361
Molendijk, A., 182–3
Monté, M., 185, 211, 290
Monville-Burston, M., 47, 161–2, 163n10, 177–8
Moreau, M.-L., 255, 271n14, 313, 314, 315, 316
Morin, Y.-C., 72, 123, 135, 138–9
Mougeon, R., 328
Müller, B., 5, 287, 326, 352
Muller, C., 299, 302–3, 305, 311, 320n4,n6,n10
Muller, Ch., 183–4, 216

Neogrammarians, 49
Nordahl, H., 194, 205–6, 214
Nyrop, K., 317

Olsson, L., 188
Ostyn, S., 334
Oudin, A., 172

Pellat, J., 141n11, 184, 202, 222,
    247n20, 287, 299, 301
Pergnier, M., 328, 332
Pfister, M., 144
Pichon, E., 192, 195, 205, 222, 298,
    309, 310–11, 320n13
Picone, M., 333, 337, 342n5
Pierrard, M., 273, 295n1
Pinchon, J., 119, 122–3, 126, 130–1,
    136, 141n11, 142n21, 239, 244, 274
Piot, M., 274–5, 279–81, 295n7
Plénat, M., 131, 141n19
Pohl, J., 316, 317
Pooley, T., 48, 49
Pope, M., 80
Poplack, S., 7, 48, 194, 197, 200–2,
    204, 210, 212, 214, 217, 219n11, 324,
    326, 330–1, 332, 333
Posner, R., 23, 255, 267, 271n3, 311,
    317, 320n12
Pottier, B., 246n3
Price, G., 81, 120–2, 123, 140n3, 299
Prince, E., 303–4, 320n9
Prunet, J.-F., 91–2, 93

Recourcé, G., 298, 319n2
Régimbald, A., 286
Regula, M., 194, 218n2
Reichenbach, H., 17, 143
Reichstein, R., 81
Reid, T., 144, 154–5
Retman, R., 329
Riegel, M., 141n11, 184, 202, 222,
    247n20, 287, 299, 301
Rioul, R., 141n11, 184, 202, 222,
    247n20, 287, 299, 301
Robach, I.-B., 289–90
Roberts, I., 271n12
Roché, M., 331
Rochet, B, 79, 95n4
Rohrer, C., 182
Rothe, W., 198, 218n5
Rottet, K., 212, 296n15
Roulet, E., 47

Rowlett, P., 298–9, 300, 319n1,
    320n3,n6
Roy, M.-M., 286
Ruwet, N., 36, 229, 238, 246n12

Sabio, F., 269
Salkie, R., 183
Sand, J., 210–11
Sandfeld, Kr., 229
Sankoff, D., 48, 324, 326, 330–1, 332,
    333
Saussure, F. de, 28
Sauvageot, A., 138
Schane, S., 43, 63–6, 68, 83–5, 96n11,
    97n20, 104, 109, 116n12, 124–5,
    136–8, 141n10, 142n24, 356
Schapira, C., 351
Schwegler, A., 321n24
Selkirk, E., 44, 72–3, 73–4, 83
Skårup, P., 253
Smith, N., 137
Sourdot, M., 353
Spence, N., 332, 335, 340–1, 344, 346,
    347–8, 350
Stéfanini, J., 50, 222, 224, 226, 231, 240
Sturm, J., 315
Sutherland, D., 169
Swiggers, P., 141n16

Tanase, E., 194
Tasmowski-De Ryck, L., 182, 245
Temple, R., 29
Tesnière, L., 32–3, 301
Thibault, P., 49
Thiele, J., 359
Togeby, K., 198
Tranel, B., 66–8, 71, 87–90, 92–3, 94,
    96n18, 97n19, 100, 102–3, 106, 107,
    108, 109, 110–11
Trubetzkoy, N., 56n23
Tsoulas, G., 195, 204
Turpin, D., 7

Valdman, A., 81, 103
Valois, D., 328
Van Ameringen, A., 73
Van den Eynde, K., 131–2, 134,
    142n20

Van der Molen, W., 212
Van Oevelen, H., 245
Van Reenen, P., 79
Vaudelin, G., 106
Vaugelas, C. Favre de, 173–4, 299
Vendler, Z., 147–8, 171
Vendryes, J., 144
Vennemann, T., 45
Vet, C., 180–1, 182

Wagner, R.-L., 123, 126, 142n21, 274, 348–9, 350
Walker, D., 7
Wall, K., 272n25
Walter, G., 25–6, 330, 334
Walter, H., 1, 7, 25–6, 81, 99, 100, 107, 112, 113, 114, 190n9, 299, 326, 329–30, 334, 337, 340–1, 342n1

Waugh, L., 47, 161–2, 163n10, 177–8, 179–80
Wehrli, E., 230, 247n14
Weinrich, H., 173, 175–6
Wiberg, L.-E., 190n15
Williams, E., 44
Wilmet, M., 50, 157–8, 163n7, 183, 193, 222, 226, 244, 309, 310, 311
Winters, M., 196
Wise, H., 23, 54, 325, 334, 337, 338, 340–1, 346, 353, 354
Wunderli, P., 144, 219n19

Yaguello, M., 358

Zezula, J., 188
Zribi-Hertz, A., 227–8, 229, 237, 238, 239, 246n8, 247n21

Lightning Source UK Ltd.
Milton Keynes UK
UKHW021822051120
372694UK00016B/330